Christianity and Constitutionalism

Christianity and Constitutionalism

Edited by

NICHOLAS ARONEY
AND
IAN LEIGH

OXFORD
UNIVERSITY PRESS

OXFORD
UNIVERSITY PRESS

Oxford University Press is a department of the University of Oxford. It furthers the University's objective of excellence in research, scholarship, and education by publishing worldwide. Oxford is a registered trade mark of Oxford University Press in the UK and certain other countries.

Published in the United States of America by Oxford University Press
198 Madison Avenue, New York, NY 10016, United States of America.

Library of Congress Control Number: 2022933698

ISBN 978-0-19-758726-3 (pbk.)
ISBN 978-0-19-758725-6 (hbk.)

DOI: 10.1093/oso/9780197587256.001.0001

Contents

PART II: CHRISTIAN PERSPECTIVES ON CONSTITUTIONALISM

PART III: CHRISTIAN THEOLOGY AND CONSTITUTIONALISM

Acknowledgments

We wish to record our thanks to a number of people. Professor John Witte Jr. of the Center for the Study of Law and Religion, Emory University, was unwavering in his support and encouragement at every stage of the project. Generous support was provided for an initial workshop held at Durham University in November 2018 by the Vasser Woolley Foundation, Inc., Atlanta, Georgia, and by our respective law schools. Nicholas Aroney acknowledges with thanks the generosity of the Institute of Advanced Studies, Durham University, for a visiting fellowship in 2018. Ian Leigh gratefully acknowledges the support of the British Academy and the Wolfson Foundation during his period as a British Academy Wolfson Research Professor. Martin Churchill, Daniel Plumbe and Anna Stirling provided valuable research assistance.

Contributors

Nicholas Aroney is Professor of Constitutional Law at the University of Queensland School of Law and an Affiliated Faculty Member of the Center for the Study of Law and Religion at Emory University School of Law.

Iain T. Benson is a Professor of Law at the University of Notre Dame Australia, Sydney Law School and Extraordinary Professor, University of the Free State, Bloemfontein.

Carlos Bernal is a former Judge of the Constitutional Court of Colombia and a Professor of Law at the University of Dayton School of Law.

Dorothea H. Bertschmann is a Tutorial Fellow of the College of the Resurrection, Mirfield, and an Honorary Fellow in the Department of Theology and Religion at Durham University.

Jonathan Burnside is a Professor of Biblical Law at the University of Bristol Law School.

Jonathan Chaplin is a member of the Centre for Faith in Public Life at Wesley House, Cambridge, and of the Divinity Faculty, University of Cambridge.

Richard Ekins is Professor of Law and Constitutional Government in the University of Oxford.

Douglas Farrow is a Professor of Theology and Ethics, McGill University.

Joel Harrison is a Senior Lecturer at Sydney Law School, University of Sydney.

R. H. Helmholz is the Ruth Wyatt Rosenson Distinguished Service Professor of Law at the University of Chicago Law School.

Mary M. Keys is an Associate Professor in the Department of Political Studies at the University of Notre Dame.

Ian Leigh is an Emeritus Professor of Law at Durham University.

Peter J. Leithart is a President of the Theopolis Institute for Biblical, Liturgical, and Cultural Studies in Birmingham, Alabama.

Joan Lockwood O'Donovan is an Honorary Reader at the University of St. Andrews School of Divinity.

David McIlroy is a Barrister at Forum Chambers; a Visiting Professor, Centre for Commercial Law Studies, Queen Mary University of London; and a Visiting Professor, University of Notre Dame (USA) in England.

John Milbank is an Emeritus Professor at the University of Nottingham Department of Theology and Religious Studies.

Colleen E. Mitchell is a Postdoctoral Research Fellow, Princeton University.

Julian Rivers is a Professor of Jurisprudence at the University of Bristol Law School.

Tracey Rowland holds the John Paul II Chair of Theology at the University of Notre Dame Australia.

Li-ann Thio is Provost Chair Professor of Law at the National University of Singapore Faculty of Law.

David VanDrunen is Robert B. Strimple Professor of Systematic Theology and Christian Ethics at Westminster Seminary, California.

John Witte Jr. is Robert W. Woodruff Professor of Law, Alonzo L. McDonald Distinguished Professor, and Director of the Center for the Study of Law and Religion at Emory University School of Law.

1

Introduction

Christianity and Constitutionalism

Nicholas Aroney and Ian Leigh

This book explores the contribution of Christianity to constitutional law and constitutionalism viewed from the perspectives of history, law, and theology. The historical chapters recount the relationship between the Christian faith and fundamental ideas about law, justice, government, and constitutionalism by focusing on particular eras and the contributions of specific figures at particular times in history. There are chapters on the Old and New Testaments, the patristic era, early Christendom, the High Middle Ages, the Reformation, and modernity. Key people considered in these chapters include the biblical figures of Moses, Jesus, Paul, and John, as well as later historical figures such as Constantine, Augustine, Thomas Aquinas, Martin Luther, John Calvin, Thomas Cranmer, and Roger Williams, reflecting several of the particular theological traditions that have developed within Christianity over time. The legal chapters focus on several of the central and most important doctrines and principles of constitutional law, evaluating them from a range of Christian perspectives. Key topics include sovereignty, the rule of law, democracy, the separation of powers, human rights, conscience, and federalism. The theological chapters then focus on particular Christian doctrines, exploring their constructive and sometimes critical implications for constitutional law and constitutionalism. There are chapters on revelation, the Trinity, Christology, political authority, natural law, subsidiarity, and eschatology.

This introductory chapter first reflects on the emergence and intellectual origins of the key controversies in constitutionalism, from its classical antecedents to the present day. This helps to ground the varying perspectives that the historical, legal, and theological contributions bring to bear on the relationship between Christianity and constitutionalism, which are summarized in the remainder of the chapter.

Nicholas Aroney and Ian Leigh, *Introduction* in *Christianity and Constitutionalism*. Edited by: Nicholas Aroney and Ian Leigh, Oxford University Press. © Oxford University Press 2022. DOI: 10.1093/oso/9780197587256.003.0001

Constitutions, Constitutional Law, and Constitutionalism

Classical Typologies

The term "constitution" can be used to designate either a *description* of the institutions and powers of government that exist within a particular political community or a *prescription* of what those institutions and powers ought to be and how they should operate.[1] However, distinguishing sharply between descriptive and prescriptive approaches to understanding constitutions and constitutionalism is not as straightforward as this might seem to suggest. Aristotle adopted an apparently descriptive approach when he distinguished several kinds of *politeia* ("constitution," "regime") based on whether a political community is ruled by one, few, or many persons. But also intrinsic to his analysis was an assessment of whether rulers govern in their own interests or for the common good. The result was six fundamental types of constitution: *monarchy*, *aristocracy*, and *polity* when powers of governance are exercised for the common good, and *tyranny*, *oligarchy*, and *democracy* when they are exercised in the interests of those who govern. Aristotle's analysis was thus descriptive insofar as it offered a method of classification of constitutions. But it also offered a moral evaluation of those systems on the basis of the purposes for which governmental power is exercised.[2]

A further dimension to our understanding of constitutions and constitutionalism arises when questions of law and legality, and especially the rule of law, are brought into consideration. Aristotle raised this issue when he asked whether it would be better to be governed by a good ruler or by good laws.[3] The advantage of governance by wise and virtuous rulers is that they are able to govern in a manner that is responsive to specific circumstances and changing conditions. The advantage of government by good laws is that this makes it difficult for bad rulers to govern in their own self-interest. Aristotle seems to have considered that the absolutely ideal form of government is monarchical rule by a wise and virtuous individual. However, he recognized that

[1] Robert Schütze, "Constitutionalism(s)" in Robert Schütze and Roger Masterman (eds), *The Cambridge Companion to Comparative Constitutional Law* (Cambridge University Press 2019) 40.
[2] Aristotle, *Politics*, especially Bks III and IV.
[3] Aristotle, *Politics*, III.15, 1286a8–9.

for many political communities the best constitution might realistically involve a mixture of oligarchy and democracy tempered by the rule of law.[4]

What does the rule of law mean in this context? At a minimum, it could mean (as Aristotle seems principally to have intended) that governance occurs through the promulgation of general rules. But it might also mean that the identity of those who rule and the powers they exercise are themselves defined and controlled by law. Here the Roman law concept of *iurisdictio* is relevant.[5] In its broadest sense, *iurisdictio* referred to the authority to administer justice. In Roman law, a general power of jurisdiction was conferred on all higher magistrates (*magistratus maiores*), whereas magistrates of lower rank (*magistratus minores*) had only limited jurisdiction. In a territorial sense, *iurisdictio* also referred to the judicial district over which magistrates were authorized to exercise judicial power. The term therefore came to be used to designate the administration of provinces under governors within the Roman Empire. Conceived in this way, the authority to govern was capable of being legally defined. The rule of law might not only mean governance through law but also governance under law.

Within a Roman imperial context, the idea of particular and limited jurisdiction applied to subordinate officials such as magistrates and governors. Although the emperor was formally bound by *ius publica* (public law), this had diminishing practical effect, especially as more and more offices and powers were consolidated in the emperor's hands.[6] Roman law came to be replete with references to the virtually unlimited power of the emperor, derived in theory from the people but increasingly absolute in practice.[7] The rule of law could not apply to the emperor unless he was understood to be exercising a kind of delegated authority pursuant to a law to which he himself was subject. Greek and Roman thought had imagined a kind of law that might possibly play this role, such as when Aristotle distinguished between the particular laws adopted by each political community and the general laws recognized by all people in accordance with nature, and when Cicero proposed that "true law" is that which is in accord with nature, and that this

[4] For nuanced discussion, see Steve Wexler and Andrew Irvine, "Aristotle on the Rule of Law" (2006) 23(1) *Polis: The Journal for Ancient Greek Political Thought* 116; George Duke, *Aristotle and Law: The Politics of Nomos* (Cambridge University Press 2020).

[5] Adolf Berger, *Encyclopedic Dictionary of Roman Law* (American Philosophical Society 1991) 493–494, 523.

[6] Werner Eck, "The Emperor, the Law and Imperial Administration" in Paul J du Plessis, Clifford Ando, and Kaius Tuori (eds), *The Oxford Handbook of Roman Law and Society* (Oxford University Press 2016) 98.

[7] E.g., Justinian, *Digest*, I.2.2 (11–12), I.3.31, and I.4.1; *Institutes*, I.2.6.

"one eternal and unchangeable law" is "valid for all nations and all times."[8] However, it was St. Paul who expressly applied this to all political authority as a matter of principle, when he said that rulers are "servants of God" responsible to administer divine justice.[9] St. Peter similarly taught that while Christians ought to be submissive to kings, governors, and other rulers, their ultimate allegiance must be to obey God rather than men.[10] This gave rise to charges that the early Christians were "acting against the decrees of Caesar, saying there is another king, Jesus."[11] The Caesars had increasingly asserted the prerogatives of deity, proclaiming themselves to be gods.[12] Under the influence of Christian teaching, however, later Roman emperors "abandoned their claim to be true divinity on earth and recognized instead in God the origin of their power."[13] From as early as the eighth century, kings and emperors were expected at their coronations to swear oaths that they would, among other things, execute justice and mercy in their judgments, and later, that they would govern in accordance with the established customs and laws of the realm.[14]

Two observations of St. Augustine (354–430) would prove influential. In his treatise on the *Freedom of the Will*, he observed that "an unjust law would seem to be no law at all," while in the *Confessions* he concluded that the "greater authority" of the divine and natural law is to be obeyed in priority to the "lesser authority" of human laws.[15] Citing this latter passage in his systematizing commentary on canon law written in the early twelfth century, Gratian drew the inference that legal customs and ordinances are to be held "null and void" if they are contrary to natural law.[16] Building on these ideas, St. Thomas Aquinas (1225–1274) defined law as an ordinance of reason for the common good, made and promulgated by him who has care of the community.[17] He proposed that four principal categories of law be recognized: the

[8] Aristotle, *Rhetoric*, 1373b; Cicero, *De re Publica*, III.22.

[9] Romans 13:1–7. See Oliver O'Donovan, *The Desire of the Nations: Rediscovering the Roots of Political Theology* (Cambridge University Press 1996) 146–151.

[10] I Peter 2:13–15; Acts 5:29.

[11] Acts 17:7.

[12] I Thessalonians 2:4. See Bruce Winter, *Divine Honours for the Caesars: The First Christians' Responses* (Eerdmans 2015).

[13] Walter Ullmann, *Principles of Government and Politics in the Middle Ages* (2nd edn, Routledge 1966) 27.

[14] WJ Loftie, *The Coronation Book of Edward VII* (Cassell 1902) 108–109. See, generally, Leopold G Legg, *English Coronation Records* (Archibald Constable 1901).

[15] Augustine, *De libero arbitrio*, I.5.11; *Confessions*, III.8 (15).

[16] Gratian, *Concordia discordantium canonum*, Dist 8, Pt 2.

[17] Thomas Aquinas, *Summa theologiae*, I-II, 90.

eternal law by which God governs the entire cosmos; the *divine* law, which is those aspects of the eternal law revealed in the Bible; the *natural* law, which is those aspects of the eternal law known by natural reason; and *human* laws, which are specific determinations of law applying the general principles of law to the conditions and circumstances of a particular time and place.[18] Like Augustine and Gratian, Aquinas considered that a human law which contains anything contrary to natural law has no binding force, that even a sound judgment issued without proper authority lacks justice, and that it is therefore expedient that the system of government should be organized and the powers of rulers tempered so as to avoid or prevent tyranny.[19]

Jurisdiction, Authority, and the Rule of Law

Aquinas also recognized a distinction between the authority of the civil government and the authority of the church, the former being responsible to make laws for the common good in temporal affairs, the latter responsible to make laws for the common good of the faithful in spiritual matters.[20] This reflected a defining feature of medieval society, grounded in the teaching of Jesus Christ distinguishing between the things that belong to Caesar and the things that belong to God, and St. Paul's teaching that Christians are citizens of an alternative *politeuma* and ambassadors of the kingdom of heaven.[21] Building on these ideas, in his masterwork *De civitate Dei*, St. Augustine proposed that there are two cities: the earthly city characterized by love of self, and the heavenly city characterized by love of God.[22] Pope Gelasius I (492–496) taught that whereas the role of kings and the role of priests had once been combined (such as when the Roman emperors bore the title *pontifex*

[18] Thomas Aquinas, *Summa theologiae*, I-II, 90–97.

[19] Thomas Aquinas, *Summa theologiae*, I-II, 95.2; II-II, 60.5–6; *De regno*, I.7.10 [51]; *Sententia libri Politicorum*, II.7.4 [245]. For more detail, see John Finnis, *Aquinas: Moral, Political, and Legal Theory* (Oxford University Press 1998) 258–266; Nicholas Aroney, "Subsidiarity, Federalism and the Best Constitution: Thomas Aquinas on City, Province and Empire" (2007) 26 Law and Philosophy 161, 203–209.

[20] Thomas Aquinas, *Summa theologiae*, II-II, 147.3. See also Gratian, *Concordia discordantium canonum*, Dist 10.

[21] Matthew 22:15–22; Philippians 3:19–20; II Corinthians 5:20; Ephesians 6:2. In the striking language of Gregory of Nyssa (ca. 335–395), all human beings—both rich and poor alike—share in a "dignity of royalty" and a "dignity of rule" due to their creation in the image of God: Gregory of Nyssa, *On the Making of Man*, IV.1; XXI.4. See Nicholas Aroney, "The Rise and Fall of Human Dignity" (2021) 46 *Brigham Young University Law Review* 101, 106–107.

[22] Augustine, *De civitate Dei*, XIV.28.

maximus), after Christ the two roles were separated on account of "human weakness," each operating in "its sphere of operation."[23] Consequently there were "two swords" by which the world is ruled: the consecrated authority of the priests and the royal power.[24] Especially after the investiture contest of the eleventh and twelfth centuries, the Roman concept of jurisdiction was used by civil lawyers and canon lawyers to identify the particular matters that fell within the authority of church and state.[25] In the striking words of Étienne de Tournai (1128–1203):

> In the same city under the same king there are two people. With two people there are two types of life. With two types of life there are two forms of government. From the two forms of government arise two jurisdictions, the city and the church. The king of the city is Christ. There are two peoples and two orders in the church, clerics and laypeople. There are two types of life, the spiritual life and the life of the flesh. There are two types of government, priestly authority and princely power. There are two jurisdictions, divine and human justice, rights, and equity. If each is rendered its due, all things will be harmonious.[26]

According to Brian Tierney, it was this insistence on jurisdictional boundaries between popes and emperors, bishops and kings, priests and princes that largely explains the emergence of what we today know as constitutional government.[27] In *Law and Revolution*, Harold Berman has shown how the Western legal tradition came to be characterized by a plurality of jurisdictions and legal systems—not only ecclesiastical and imperial, but also royal, urban, feudal, manorial, and mercantile. Berman argued that "this plurality of jurisdictions and legal systems" made "the supremacy of law both

[23] Gelasius l, *The Bond of Anathema*, reproduced in Oliver O'Donovan and Joan Lockwood O'Donovan, *From Irenaeus to Grotius: A Sourcebook in Christian Political Thought, 100–1625* (Eerdmans 1999) 178.

[24] Gelasius l, *Letter to Emperor Anastasius*, in ibid, 179. On the unfolding distinction between "two cities" and "two swords," see O'Donovan, above n 9, 193–211.

[25] Harold J Berman, *Law and Revolution: The Formation of the Western Legal Tradition* (Harvard University Press 1983) 221–224; Martin Loughlin, *Foundations of Public Law* (Oxford University Press 2010) 19–21.

[26] Stephen of Tournai, *Summa* on Gratian's *Decretum*, cited in Kenneth Pennington, "Stephen of Tournai (Étienne de Tournai) (1128–1203)" in Olivier Descamps and Rafael Domingo (eds), *Great Christian Jurists in French History* (Cambridge University Press 2019) 35, 45. See, similarly, Henry de Bracton, *De Legibus et Consuetudinibus Angliae [On the Laws and Customs of England]* (SE Thorne tr, Harvard University Press [ca 1235–1260] 1968–1977) II, 304.

[27] Brian Tierney, *Religion, Law and the Growth of Constitutional Thought* (Cambridge University Press 1982) 8–13.

necessary and possible."[28] The result was a kind of "complex space" in which a diversity of intermediate corporations and associations—religious, scholarly, commercial, and professional—operated within an overarching framework of law, qualifying the power claims of secular rulers and helping to keep them within constitutional bounds.[29]

Political authority was accordingly understood as a responsibility to administer justice according to law.[30] John of Salisbury (ca. 1110–1180) expressed a widely shared ideal when he said that the king should rule by law, according to justice, and with the counsel of the wise.[31] Although the authority exercised by medieval kings was extensive, it was nonetheless considered to be subject to God and the law. As Henry of Bracton (ca. 1210–ca. 1268) put it, "the law makes the king," and there is no king where "will" rules rather than "law."[32] Similarly, when Sir John Fortescue insisted in 1469 that English kings possess *dominium politicum et regale* ("political and regal lordship") rather than *dominium regale*, he meant that they could only rule through laws to which the lords and commons had assented in Parliament.[33] Otto von Gierke thus observed:

> The properly medieval . . . theory declared that every act of the Sovereign that broke the bounds drawn by natural law was formally null and void. As null and void therefore every judge . . . was to treat, not only every executive act, but every unlawful statute, even though it were published by Pope or Emperor. Furthermore, the unlawful order or unlawful act was null and void for the individual subjects of the State. It was just for this cause that their duty of obedience was conceived as a conditional duty, and that the right of actively resisting tyrannical measures was conceded to them.[34]

[28] Berman, above n 25, 10.

[29] John Milbank, "On Complex Space" in *The Word Made Strange: Theology, Language, Culture* (Blackwell 1997) 268; John Milbank, *Beyond Secular Order: The Representation of Being and the Representation of the People* (Wiley Blackwell 2013) 159.

[30] O'Donovan, above n 9, 233.

[31] John of Salisbury, *Policraticus* [1159] (Cary Nederman, ed, Cambridge University Press 1991) Bk IV, ch 6, 41–46. This work was written while John of Salisbury was secretary to Theobald, Archbishop of Canterbury.

[32] Bracton, above n 26, II, 33. On the complex Trinitarian and Christological theological context of Bracton's jurisprudence, see Ernst H Kantorowicz, *The King's Two Bodies: A Study in Mediaeval Political Theology* (Princeton University Press 1957) 143–192.

[33] Sir John Fortescue, *De Laudibus Legum Angliae [In Praise of the Laws of England]* (ca 1469). See Frederic William Maitland, *The Constitutional History of England* (Cambridge University Press 1908) 61, 198–199.

[34] Otto von Gierke, *Political Theories of the Middle Age* (Oxford University Press 1901) 84.

Bracton's statement was cited by Chief Justice Edward Coke in the case of *Prohibitions del Roy* (1607) to support the proposition that an English king cannot personally act as a judge but must allow the ordinary courts to fulfill that function in accordance with the law of the land.[35] In *Dr. Bonham's Case* (1610),[36] Coke went further when he claimed that there had been many cases in which the common law had "controlled" Acts of Parliament and sometimes "judged them to be void," particularly when it was found that they were "against Common right and reason, or repugnant, or impossible to be performed." Most scholars have argued that Coke did not mean that the courts would regard unreasonable statutes as simply void, but rather that they would be interpreted in accordance with reason.[37] However, some scholars, especially in the United States, have understood him to have been suggesting that unreasonable statutes would be declared entirely void and inoperative by the courts.[38] Sir William Blackstone (1723–1780), another English jurist who exercised significant influence in the United States, said:

> The law of nature, being coeval with mankind, and dictated by God himself, is of course superior in obligation to any other. It is binding over all the globe in all countries, and at all times; no human laws are of any validity, if contrary to this: and such of them as are valid derive all their force, and all their authority, mediately or immediately, from this original.[39]

By the nineteenth century, the rule of law had come to mean that the powers of government can only be exercised according to pre-existing law and that all persons, no matter what their rank and status, are subject to the same set of legal rules and principles. As Albert Venn Dicey put it, "The rule of law is contrasted with every system of government based on the exercise by persons in authority of wide, arbitrary, or discretionary powers of constraint," for it involves the principle that "every official, from the Prime Minister down to a

[35] *Prohibitions del Roy* (1607) 12 Co Rep 63; 77 ER 1342.

[36] *Thomas Bonham v College of Physicians* (1610) 8 Co Rep 107; 77 ER 638.

[37] Jeffrey Goldsworthy, *The Sovereignty of Parliament: History and Philosophy* (Clarendon Press 1999) 34, 109–124. See also JGA Pocock, *The Ancient Constitution and the Feudal Law* (Cambridge University Press 1957) ch 11.

[38] Edward S Corwin, "The Establishment of Judicial Review" (1910) 9(2) Michigan Law Review102 and 283; Edward S Corwin, "The 'Higher Law' Background of American Constitutional Law" (1928) 42 Harvard Law Review 149 and 365. See also Geoffrey de Q Walker, *The Rule of Law: Foundation of Constitutional Democracy* (Melbourne University Press 1988) 114–115.

[39] William Blackstone, *Commentaries on the Laws of England* (Clarendon Press 1765–1769) introduction, II, 41.

constable or a collector of taxes, is under the same responsibility for every act done without legal justification as any other citizen."[40]

Constitutional Deliberation and Design

The modern notion of adopting a written constitution that defines the institutions and powers of government can be traced to certain revolutionary political events in seventeenth-century England,[41] and to the constitutional ideas that developed around that time. Between 1647 and 1649, a series of manifestos were prepared, under the title of *An Agreement of the People*, by participants in Cromwell's New Model Army,[42] one of which read as follows:

> We the free People of England, to whom God hath given hearts, means and opportunity to effect the same, do with submission to his wisdom, in his name, and desiring the equity thereof may be to his praise and glory; Agree to ascertain our Government, to abolish all arbitrary Power, and to set bounds and limits both to our Supreme, and all Subordinate Authority, and remove all known Grievances.[43]

While these agreements never became law, an *Instrument of Government* (1653) was adopted as the written constitution of England during the rule of Oliver Cromwell, following the deposition and execution of Charles I in 1649. Around the same time, English colonists in North America had established political communities in which ideas of independent self-government were developing. Viewed from the perspective of British law, the constitutional foundations of these settlements derived from the authority of the Crown, but the practice of many of the colonies was to self-constitute themselves as a body politic through a solemn pact or covenant. One of the most famous was

[40] AV Dicey, *Introduction to the Study of the Law of the Constitution* (5th edn, Macmillan 1897) 33, 180, 185.

[41] Particularly during the period of the English Civil War (1642–1651), Commonwealth or Interregnum (1649–1660), Stuart Restoration (1660–1688), and Glorious Revolution (1688–89). For an alternative view, which focuses on the American and French Revolutions, see Dieter Grimm, *Constitutionalism: Past, Present, and Future* (Oxford University Press 2016) ch 2.

[42] See ASP Woodhouse (ed), *Puritanism and Liberty: Being the Army Debates (1647–9)* (Dent 1938); David Wootton (ed), *Divine Right and Democracy: An Anthology of Political Writing in Stuart England* (Penguin 1986).

[43] John Lilburne, William Walwyn, Thomas Prince, and Richard Overton, *An Agreement of the Free People of England* (1649).

the Mayflower Compact of 1620, subscribed by the first inhabitants of the colony established at Plymouth in what is now the state of Massachusetts. It declared the formation of the colony in the following terms:

> In the name of God, Amen. We, whose names are underwritten, the loyal subjects of our dread Sovereign Lord King James, by the Grace of God, of Great Britain, France, and Ireland, King, defender of the Faith, etc.
>
> Having undertaken, for the Glory of God, and advancements of the Christian faith and honor of our King and Country, a voyage to plant the first colony in the Northern parts of Virginia, do by these presents, solemnly and mutually, in the presence of God, and one another, covenant and combine ourselves together into a civil body politic.[44]

Another example was the original constitution of the state of Connecticut, which was based on a federating covenant between the people of three separate towns. The *Fundamental Orders of Connecticut* declared as follows:

> We the Inhabitants and Residents of Windsor, Hartford and Wethersfield . . . do . . . associate and conjoin ourselves to be as one Public State or Commonwealth; and do for ourselves and our successors and such as shall be adjoined to us at any time hereafter, enter into Combination and Confederation together.[45]

Drawing inspiration from these kinds of documents, the highly influential English philosopher and publicist John Locke (1632–1704) gave elegant expression in his *Second Treatise of Government* (1689) to the underlying idea of a "social contract" by which the people constitute themselves into a political society and a "contract of government" by which they establish a government that is accountable to them. But the basic idea of a founding covenant was much older than Locke. Johannes Althusius (ca. 1563–1638), a German jurist and early theorist of a kind of "social federalism,"[46] had more than half a century earlier offered an account of society in which all groups—families

[44] This compact and numerous others are collected in Donald Lutz, *Colonial Origins of the American Constitution: A Documentary History* (Liberty Fund 1998). See also Stephen L Schechter, Richard B Bernstein, and Donald S Lutz (eds), *Roots of the Republic: American Founding Documents Interpreted* (Madison House 1990).

[45] Fundamental Orders of Connecticut (1639).

[46] Thomas O Hueglin, *Early Modern Concepts for a Late Modern World: Althusius on Community and Federalism* (Wilfrid Laurier University Press 1999).

and villages, towns and cities, guilds and religious associations, provinces and commonwealths—are formed and joined together by a series of federative compacts and agreements.[47]

The institution of judicial review is today one of the primary mechanisms by which constitutional limitations on the powers of government are practically enforced. It can be exercised in relation to executive action and legislative enactments, and it can be exercised by specialist constitutional courts or generally by all courts of competent jurisdiction.[48] It can also be implemented in relatively "weak" or "strong" forms, particularly in relation to the protection of human rights.[49] In all of these forms judicial review has a complex and controversial relationship with another important contemporary constitutional doctrine: the separation of powers. Writing in 1748, the French political thinker Baron de Montesquieu (1689–1755) famously claimed in his *The Spirit of Laws* that liberty is most effectively protected where legislative, executive, and judicial powers of government are distributed among three distinct and separate institutions.[50] Writing about two decades later, Sir William Blackstone similarly observed in his highly influential *Commentaries on the Laws of England* that the English constitution established a "balance" between the Crown and the two houses of the Parliament so that each performed a "mutual check" upon the other.[51] Influenced by these ideas, one of the leading architects of the United States Constitution, James Madison, advocated the separation of powers in the following terms:

> It may be a reflection on human nature, that such devices should be necessary to control the abuses of government. But what is government itself, but the greatest of all reflections on human nature? If men were angels, no government would be necessary. If angels were to govern men, neither external nor internal controls on government would be necessary. In framing a government which is to be administered by men over men, the great difficulty

[47] Johannes Althusius, *Politica: An Abridged Translation [Politica methodice digesta atque exemplis sacris & profanes illustrata]* (Frederick Carney tr, Liberty Fund 1995, 3rd edn 1614).

[48] Alan R Brewer-Carías, *Judicial Review in Comparative Law* (Cambridge University Press 1989).

[49] Stephen Gardbaum, *The New Commonwealth Model of Constitutionalism: Theory and Practice* (Cambridge University Press 2013).

[50] Charles de Secondat Montesquieu, *The Spirit of Laws [L'esprit des lois]* (Hafner 1949) XI.6. See also John Locke, *Two Treatises of Government* (Cambridge University Press 1960 [1689]) Bk II, ch 12, distinguishing between the legislative, executive, and federative power of the commonwealth.

[51] Blackstone, above n 39, vol 1, 149–151. Blackstone was the first Vinerian Professor of English Law at Oxford University from 1758 to 1766.

> lies in this: you must first enable the government to control the governed; and in the next place oblige it to control itself.[52]

Madison's colleague Alexander Hamilton argued that the judiciary would be the "least dangerous" of the three branches of government because it would have "neither force nor will, but merely judgment," but he also maintained that the courts would have the weighty responsibility to "declare all acts contrary to the manifest tenor of the Constitution void."[53]

Hamilton's reasoning was repeated about fifteen years later by Chief Justice John Marshall in the first United States Supreme Court decision to exercise the power of judicial review. The argument was that judicial review is the result of an application of two principles: first, that it is the particular function of courts to determine and apply the law, and second, that the Constitution is a superior or paramount law binding on the executive, the legislature, and the courts alike.[54] Judicial review is controversial, however, from the point of view of democratic theory, principally because it empowers unelected judges to overrule laws enacted by democratically accountable legislatures.[55] One line of argument is that judicial review is democratically legitimate because it is the people themselves who establish the Constitution and authorize the courts to enforce it.[56] A second argument is that judicial review is necessary to protect the rights of minorities from interference by oppressive majorities.[57] Opponents of judicial review respond that constitutional language is often vague and that judges inevitably impose their own moral and political views when interpreting and applying constitutional restrictions on power.[58] Others argue that judicial review should be limited to ensuring that the democratic system is operating fairly.[59] Controversies about constitutionalism

[52] James Madison, *The Federalist No 51* (1788), in Clinton Rossiter (ed), *The Federalist Papers* (New American Library 1961).

[53] Alexander Hamilton, *The Federalist No 78* (1788), in ibid.

[54] *Marbury v Madison*, 5 US (1 Cranch) 137 (1803), 176–180.

[55] Alexander M Bickel, *The Least Dangerous Branch: The Supreme Court at the Bar of Politics* (Bobbs-Merrill 1962).

[56] Bruce Ackerman, *We the People: Foundations* (Belknap Press 1991); Bruce Ackerman, *We the People: Transformations* (Belknap Press 1998).

[57] TRS Allan, *Law, Liberty, and Justice: The Legal Foundations of British Constitutionalism* (Clarendon Press 1993).

[58] Jeremy Waldron, *Law and Disagreement* (Oxford University Press 1999); Jeremy Waldron, "The Core of the Case against Judicial Review" (2006) 115(6) Yale Law Journal 1346.

[59] John Hart Ely, *Democracy and Distrust: A Theory of Judicial Review* (Harvard University Press 1980).

and constitutional law thus often turn into debates over legal language and its interpretation.[60]

Plan of the Book

From this brief sketch it is clear that the notion of constitutionalism is contested, to say the least. This book has been designed to illuminate the influence of Christian thinking on these various controversies: whether constitutions should be understood in normative terms (based on reason and the promotion of the common good) or merely as guides to the normal methods for the exercise of political power;[61] the place of questions of legitimacy, authority, and consent concerning the division of power; and the contestable nature of rights and of judicial review. And underlying all these issues is the deeper question about whether modern constitutional law can adequately be understood or properly assessed in purely secular, nonreligious terms.[62]

The collection is divided into three parts. Part I is historical and is therefore primarily oriented to the past. It asks: how did constitutionalism come to be, and what was Christianity's contribution to that development? The chapters of this part address these questions by focusing on particular historical periods and the contributions of particular individuals. Part II is legal and is accordingly oriented mostly to the present. It asks: how is constitutionalism today understood, and what contribution can Christianity make to that understanding? The chapters in this part address particular legal and constitutional ideas and doctrines. Part III is theological and is therefore oriented to the future. It asks: what might constitutionalism become, and what contribution might Christianity make to that development? The chapters in this part focus on the contribution of particular theological doctrines to our understanding of constitutionalism.

This organization of the book is deliberately trinitarian. It is intended to create a stimulating set of contrasts and tensions between the disciplinary

[60] Antonin Scalia, *A Matter of Interpretation: Federal Courts and the Law* (Princeton University Press 1997), with commentaries by Gordon Wood, Laurence Tribe, Mary Ann Glendon, and Ronald Dworkin.

[61] One leading twentieth-century British public lawyer, J. A. G. Griffith, coined the pithy expression that the constitution is "what happens." JAG Griffith, "The Political Constitution" (1979) 42 Modern Law Review 1–21.

[62] Loughlin, above n 23, 50, 84.

perspectives of history, law, and theology in their intersection with constitutionalism. Each of these disciplines has its own characteristic way of addressing the field, and each of our authors adopts a definition of constitutionalism considered suitable to the particular subject matter of his or her chapter. Several authors adopt "negative" definitions, which treat constitutionalism as being centrally concerned with limiting the exercise of the coercive powers of government.[63] Others entertain somewhat more "positive" definitions, which understand constitutionalism to be concerned with enabling ruling institutions to govern in a manner that contributes substantially to the common good.[64]

The chapters of Parts I, II, and III are unavoidably selective and the range of topics addressed by the book cannot claim to be comprehensive. In Part I, it was necessary to make choices about which times, places, and authors would be the focus of attention. We regret a bias to Western constitutional history and Anglophone scholarship that we found difficult to avoid. The chapters in Part II focus on several of the most prominent doctrines in contemporary constitutional law. Naturally, some particular legal topics are not addressed and alternative constructions of the doctrinal terrain are possible. Part III similarly emphasizes some of the most important teachings of Christian theology, but chapters on other theological topics could have been included if space permitted. We sought to ensure that as many denominational perspectives were represented as could be accommodated within the constraints of a single volume. Our hope is that the book will stimulate more studies of the kind contained herein, addressing an ever-widening range of historical, legal, theological, and other aspects of the relationship between Christianity and constitutionalism.

Historical Chapters

The historical chapters span nearly three thousand years from the story of the people of Israel recorded in the Old Testament to the early modern period. They offer several correctives to the narrative that liberal constitutionalism has built up about its origins (and which tends to focus predominantly

[63] See, e.g., Charles Howard McIlwain, *Constitutionalism: Ancient and Modern* (rev edn, Cornell University Press 1947); Maurice JC Vile, *Constitutionalism and the Separation of Powers* (Clarendon Press 1967).

[64] See, e.g., NW Barber, *The Principles of Constitutionalism* (Oxford University Press 2018).

on the seventeenth century onward). Not least of these is that constitutional thinking is shown to predate Aristotle (who lived from 384 to 322 BC). The book of Deuteronomy, for example, which Josephus described as Israel's constitution (using the Greek term *politeia*),[65] was written many centuries earlier.

In the opening chapter of the collection, "Torah and Constitutionalism," Jonathan Burnside explores some of the key constitutional ideas associated with biblical law, concentrating on how they are applied in the Hebrew Bible and discussing their relationship to the New Testament. Drawing on the work of Daniel Elazar,[66] Burnside argues that the constitution of Israel is best understood in terms of the covenant through which the descendants of Abraham, Isaac, and Jacob were constituted as the people of God and called to be "a kingdom of priests and a holy nation" (Exod. 19:5–6). Noting the covenantal form of the book of Deuteronomy as a whole, Burnside particularly draws attention to the delineation of the functions and powers of the judges, the king, the priests, and the prophets as four distinct loci of authority in biblical Israel (Deut. 16–18). The judges were listed first, suggesting the primary role they were to play in administering justice by giving judgment in particular cases. The king's authority was likewise affirmed but also limited, particularly by his responsibility to adhere to the divinely revealed law. Similarly, one of the central duties of the priests was to teach the revealed law to the people. And the prophets were responsible to declare the will and judgment of God—independently of, and, if necessary, as a corrective to the exercise of authority by judges, kings, priests, and, indeed, other prophets. Burnside points out that this reflected the proposition that no human authority could be sovereign in any absolute sense, a proposition he argues is carried through in the New Testament teaching about the Lordship of Jesus Christ, with similar implications for constitutionalism.

Dorothea Bertschmann opens her chapter on the New Testament ("But *our* Constitution is in Heaven: New Testament Sketches on the People of God between Divine Law and Earthly Rulers") by noting the use of the term *politeuma* to designate both the heavenly "citizenship" or "homeland" of Christian believers and the "political constitution" of the Jewish people. The implication is that New Testament teaching is concerned, among other

[65] Josephus, *Antiquities*, Bk 4. "[Moses] gave them the laws and the constitution of government" (at 194).

[66] Daniel J Elazar, *The Covenant Tradition in Politics* (Transaction Publishers 1995–1999) 4 vols.

things, with the *politeuma* or "way of life" of the Christian community in this world. Such a way of life is constitutional in the sense that it involves recognition of a divine sovereignty that is not expressed in the exercise of arbitrary or unlimited power, but in a binding rule that established the people of God as a community "under authority." Bertschmann argues that the early Christians' allegiance to God in Christ impacted their relationship to earthly powers in at least three dimensions. First, it is reflected in the deft statement of Christ that there should be rendered unto Caesar the things that are Caesar's and to God the things that are God's (Matt. 22:15–22). Second, there is the admonition of the apostle Paul that every person should, as a matter of conscience, submit to the governing authorities, considering them to be servants of God, responsible to punish evil and reward good (Rom. 13:1–7). Third, it culminates in a comprehensive and devastating critique of political authority when it transgresses its limits—by shedding innocent blood, demanding god-like worship, and making claim to absolute power (Rev. 13:4; 18:24). Like everyone, the emperor stands in the shadow of God's immanent kingdom.

This last theme is taken up by Peter Leithart in his chapter on Constantine, the first avowedly Christian emperor of Rome ("Constantine and Constitutionalism"). Leithart argues, perhaps counterintuitively, that developments within the late Roman Empire, and the reign of Constantine in particular, were crucial to the emergence of constitutionalism. The key contribution, he proposes, was Constantine's recognition of the church as an independent legal entity, free to exist without harassment and without functioning as an arm of the state. As noted earlier in this introduction, the Western legal tradition developed out of reforms to the law and legal organization of the church in the eleventh and twelfth centuries. Leithart points out that none of this would have occurred if the independence of the church had not already been recognized. Following the teaching of rhetorician and apologist Lactantius (240–320), Constantine implemented a policy of toleration toward all religions, but tilted in favor of Christianity. Leithart argues that the constitutional significance of Christianity was to undermine the idea that the emperor could be a semidivine mediator between heaven and earth. Although imperial apologists like Eusebius of Caesarea attributed sacral significance to Constantine's rule, Leithart points out that the institution of the church offered an alternative community to that of the ancient empire, relativizing its claims to absolute authority and laying the foundations for the later development of constitutional government.

Corresponding themes are developed by Mary Keys and Colleen Mitchell in their chapter on St. Augustine, Bishop of Hippo ("Augustine's Constitutionalism: Citizenship, Common Good, and Consent"). They argue that although in his masterwork *De civitate Dei* (*The City of God*) Augustine sometimes seems to express a detachment and even indifference to temporal political institutions, he also indicates the outlines of a just political-legal order consisting of three essential elements: broad citizenship, the common good, and popular consent. For Augustine, a people is an assembled multitude of rational creatures bound together by a common agreement as to the objects of their love.[67] As Keys and Mitchell point out, the people are defined not by reference to their commitment to justice, but rather by reference to what they love. While this involves the use of a descriptive standard for what constitutes a political community, it gives rise to a normative evaluation: the better the objects of love, the better the people; the worse the objects, the worse the people. This enables Augustine to be highly critical of the lust for rule and domination that characterized the Roman Empire while also warning against attributing to political governance a capacity to produce true and lasting justice. For Augustine, the most efficacious way to improve the constitutions of this world is to invite people into the City of God, because the virtues that come from divine grace enable persons of all conditions to serve the good of others in a fellowship of equality in which all are united in love.[68]

It has often been argued that this duality of church and state contributed significantly to the development of constitutional government. As Harold Berman pointed out, because none of the coexisting ecclesiastical and secular legal systems that constituted the Western legal tradition claimed to be "all-inclusive or omnicompetent, each had to develop constitutional standards for locating and limiting sovereignty, for allocating governmental powers within such sovereignty, and for determining the basic rights and duties of members."[69] In his chapter ("Canon Law Constitutionalism?"), Richard Helmholz tests this proposition by focusing on the law of the medieval church, the canon law. He begins by noting one very significant obstacle to such a thesis, namely the humanly unlimited legislative and judicial authority (*plentitudo potestatis*) that was ascribed to the pope—within the

67 Augustine, *De civitate Dei*, 19.24.
68 Augustine, *De civitate Dei*, 2.19, 74; quoting Psalm 148.
69 Berman, above n 25, 225.

church, and also beyond it. If this is so, in what way could the canon law have contributed to the development of constitutional government? Helmholz's argument is threefold. First, he notes the existence within the canon law of a multitude of laws and principles, several of which contradicted or qualified the scope and meaning of texts that seemed to support the proposition that papal power was free from legal constraints. For example, there were canon law texts stating that the pope cannot establish rules that violate the Ten Commandments, the Gospels, or the decrees of the first four general councils of the church, and there were others that said that prelates should not exercise their powers without first consulting with those affected by them. A pope could also be deposed for heresy and could not dictate his successor. Second, Helmholz points out that commentators on the canon law added important juridical limitations that had a real effect on the exercise of papal power. This frequently led to beneficial interpretations of papal decisions so that their practical effect would be in accordance with underlying principles of justice and goodness. Third, he observes that the popes were in fact constrained by law—natural law, divine law, and to a substantial extent the law established by existing papal decisions. These elements of canon law amounted, he argues, to important half-steps toward constitutionalism.[70]

John Witte's chapter ("The Protestant Reformation of Constitutionalism") begins by drawing attention to Martin Luther's posting of the Ninety-Five Theses on the church door in Wittenberg in 1517 and his burning of the medieval canon law books at the city gates three years later. The contrast with the subject matter of Richard Helmholz's chapter seems very stark. As Witte argues, the early reformers were largely united in teaching that salvation comes through faith in the Gospel, not works of law, and that the church is a community of saints, not a corporation of law. These teachings helped to transform early modern Western constitutionalism in several ways. Especially in its Lutheran form, the reformation worked a significant transfer of power and property to the state. Instead of Pope Gelasius's famous "two swords" doctrine, Luther advocated a "two kingdoms" theory under which the clergy were responsible to administer the Gospel and the magistrate was responsible to administer the law. Lutheran theologians taught that the civil magistrate was responsible to implement the two tables of the Ten Commandments, and Lutheran jurists systematically expounded the law in these terms. Anabaptists went even further in the separation they

[70] See, similarly, Aquinas, *Contra impugnantes Dei cultum et religionem*, II.3.

advocated between what they often regarded as the redeemed realm of religious faith and the fallen realm of politics. The resulting "wall of separation" between church and state proposed by Menno Simons and Roger Williams was taken over by Thomas Jefferson and informed the framing of the US Constitution, although whether this also required a separation of religion and politics remains a matter of dispute. This is partly due to the influence of Calvinist theology, which charted a middle course between the Lutheran tendency to subordinate the church to the state and the Anabaptist tendency to withdraw the church from the affairs of this world. The Calvinists insisted upon an institutional separation of church and state, authorizing the state to punish crime, remedy civil wrongs, and collect taxes, and the church to determine the content of its own doctrine, liturgy, and religious practice. However, they did not advocate a neutral state that is indifferent to competing concepts of spiritual and moral good. Calvinists were in the forefront of arguments defending the rights of lower magistrates to resist tyranny on behalf of their oppressed peoples and to hold rulers to account on the basis of their oath-bound commitments to rule in accordance with the laws of God and nature. These claims developed into fully fledged arguments in favor of written constitutions that would help to preserve liberty, maintain justice, and bridle power.

In a similar vein, Joan Lockwood O'Donovan ("Understanding Law and Constitutionalism in Modernity: The Critical Contribution of English Reformation Public Theology") examines the contribution of the English Reformation to the development of modern constitutionalism in a manner that draws attention to its critical stance toward elements of both medieval Christianity and secularist modernity. At the core of the modern liberal contractarian tradition of natural rights, she argues, is an anthropology that understands human beings to be naturally self-owning individuals driven by compelling desires to preserve their lives, augment their property, and establish governments to better secure them in their natural rights. However, O'Donovan points out that this conception of the liberal state is giving way to a reality of technical and legalistic forms of domination facilitated through the twin engines of market-driven rationality and state bureaucratic control. The result is an increasing juridification of political life, particularly through the establishment of comprehensive rights charters to which all other public goods are either subordinated or assimilated. While she recognizes the value of attempts to corral natural rights jurisprudence within Catholic and Protestant theological frameworks, O'Donovan proposes a more thoroughgoing critique of the very concept of natural rights. Drawing on the resources of the political theology of the Anglican reformation, she calls for a more Christ-centered and evangelical approach.

Legal Chapters

The chapters in Part II offer a series of Christian perspectives on familiar constitutional concepts: the rule of law, sovereignty, democracy, the separation of powers, judicial review, liberty, rights, freedom of conscience, and federalism. While virtually all constitutions give effect in some way to all of these ideas, there are tensions between several of them: a conception of sovereignty as unitary and indivisible would seem to contradict the separation of powers and federalism; particular conceptions of majoritarian democracy would seem to be in tension with constitutionally enshrined rights and freedoms enforced by an unelected judiciary. The design of the book is to place these concepts deliberately in juxtaposition with each other, in a manner that opens up the field of constitutionalism to critical theological and philosophical investigation.

In his chapter on sovereignty ("Dual, Plural, and One"), Joel Harrison examines how the Christian tradition challenges the modern concept of sovereignty as involving an unlimited and indivisible power that provides the very basis for the existence of law and gives priority to the will of recognized authority. This Christian theological challenge is reflected in three dimensions: in the parallel authority of priest and king, or church and civil authority; in the cultivation of multiple sites of authority, at local, regional, and international levels; and in the coordinating, encouraging, and cultivating role of "monarchical" rule. Rather than sovereign rule, the Christian tradition has emphasized the intertwining of duality, plurality, and unity. Importantly, each of these components is understood as pursuing a shared horizon, a tradition, and a discerning of right. Harrison argues that rather than seeking to limit sovereignty by judicial protection of the rule of law and "contestable views on individual rights," Christian constitutionalism arguably poses a more radical challenge—by addressing "the relative positioning of mutually implicated authorities and groups, each exercising their authority in order to pursue a shared orientation to the good." In the face of this perspective sovereignty is not so much limited as "dissolved in the face of a higher goal or purpose."

In her chapter entitled "Higher Law/Rule of Law: The Sacred Roots and Secular Shoots of the Supreme Law," Li-ann Thio argues that the concept of the rule of law, so central to contemporary constitutional thought, requires a concept of "higher law" in order to be sustainable. Her argument consists of three essential parts. First, she shows how the idea of higher law manifests itself repeatedly within constitutional discourse. Higher law appears to be an unavoidable concept in constitutional law. Second, she proposes what a distinctively Christian conception of higher law and the rule of law might look like, and she discusses the implications this idea might have on current conceptions of constitutional law. Third, she advances a critique of contemporary constitutionalism arguing that humanistic viewpoints have a tendency to undermine the rule of law rather than support it. Thio concludes by proposing that a Christian approach to constitutionalism challenges the hegemony of the dominant conception in which the rule of law is conflated with liberalism. She offers an alternative view in which the virtues of the rule of law are balanced against its limitations, and idealizing conceptions of constitutionalism are moderated by an objective realism about human nature.

In his chapter on democracy ("Self-Government and the Kingdom of Heaven"), Richard Ekins seeks to explain how, why, and to what extent self-government should be sought by those who seek first the kingdom of heaven. He draws on the Christian tradition's idea of kingship according to law, in which the king represents the people and is subject to God and reason. From this he elaborates on what it means to be governed and to govern. Consent of the governed, he argues, is not the foundation of justified authority, but rather is a social fact that indicates who it is the people are willing to support and accord authority. Rulers, on the other hand, have good reason to share authority and to create representative assemblies, whether under parliamentary or presidential systems. The promise of such representative institutions—to enable joint action despite disagreement—is only likely to be realized, Ekins contends, when a people recognizes itself as sharing a common good to which elites and masses alike are jointly committed. Despite the need to guard against injustice (to which all forms of government are prone), self-government is so important that a free people should be slow to introduce or subject itself to positive legal limitations on its power to rule itself, whether those limitations arise from human rights law or supranational institutions.

In his account of the separation of powers ("The Biblical Foundations of the Separation of Powers and the Catalytic Judicial Role"), Carlos Bernal argues that the Bible offers both a conceptual justification and a critical reframing of the doctrine. In particular, he draws on the Old Testament for a conception of the separation of powers according to which judges should be empowered with a catalytic role. Bernal argues that, according to the scriptures, prophets play a catalytic role of incentivizing political authorities to behave in a virtuous manner in protecting the rights and interests of the people. In a modern constitutional democracy under the separation of powers, he contends, this role should be rejuvenated, with the judiciary best positioned to perform the function. Drawing on examples from South African, Indian, and Colombian constitutional jurisprudence, he illustrates how the judiciary can do so in a way that prompts the other branches to act according to their mission but does not supplant them.

In his exploration of Christian approaches to constitutional rights ("Christian Constitutional Rights?"), Julian Rivers identifies three areas of critical interaction. First, there is a longstanding foundational debate about the value of the concept of constitutional rights, which he examines, focusing particularly on Blackstone and Burke. Second, there is a debate about the content of constitutional rights. Here Rivers critiques Samuel Moyn's thesis about the regressive influence of Christianity on twentieth-century human rights. Finally, there is a debate about the construction or interpretation of constitutional rights. In view of the breadth and flexibility of modern constitutional rights doctrine, this third area is increasingly the site of political and ideological conflicts, where both Catholicism and Protestantism have distinctive emphases and concerns. Even here, however, simple either-or narratives of Christian and anti-Christian conceptions of rights should be avoided. At each of these levels the picture is complex, so that the constitutional rights project cannot be characterized, in his argument, as either distinctively Christian or anti-Christian.

Unsurprisingly, religious liberty has been of considerable importance to Christian constitutionalists. In his chapter on "Freedom of Conscience: Assessing the Christian Contribution," Ian Leigh addresses the relationship between religious liberty and freedom of conscience, seeking to re-evaluate the Christian contribution in light of current controversial conscience claims. He identifies two significant trends. The first and dominant one is for Christian writers to treat conscience as a matter of moral belief. This approach conceives freedom of religion in "Protestant" terms (i.e., as belief centered and genuinely personally held in order to be of any value) so that the right of freedom of conscience has a high degree of convergence with it. Although this approach has its origins in early Christian thought, for the purpose of the discussion Leigh focuses on the impact of seventeenth-century Christian writers on the foundations of liberal constitutionalism. The second approach, particularly associated with Thomism and natural law thinking, and reflected in modern Catholic legal thought, stresses that conscience is a form of objective moral knowledge. Both strands contrast with modern liberal approaches (themselves an offshoot of the first strand), which, in philosophical terms, regard conscience as a question of moral integrity expressive of individual autonomy and, from a legal perspective, treat it as subjective, unconfined, and unquestionable. In contrast, older Christian writers are agreed that conscience is a matter of conviction and duty. This tradition also addresses the fallibility and limits of conscience in ways highly pertinent to current controversies over conscientious objection by officials, medical professionals, and others.

Nicholas Aroney ("Federalism: A Legal, Political, and Religious Archaeology") closes Part II with a chapter that traces the relationship between federalism and Christianity, especially Reformed Christianity, through the intermingling legal, political, and religious streams of its historical development. Federations, he argues, are the institutional expression of legal, political, and religious ideas and practices that predate the modern sovereign state. Medieval Christendom was the context that laid the foundation for federalism as we know it today. Thomas Aquinas adapted the Aristotelian account of the *polis* to the complex institutional and social architecture of his day. His account reflected the duality of church and empire, and the incremental growth of other mercantile, scholarly, charitable, and religious authority structures and jurisdictions. Building on this foundation, the Calvinist Johannes Althusius (1557–1638) placed associations at the center of his political thought. These ranged from the private to the public: from family to colleges, cities, regions, and the commonwealth. Each, however, was covenantal in form. Although contemporary federations display a wide range and variety, what continues to unite them is the religious idea of the covenant (*b'rit, foedus*, *bund*). Contemporary federalism, he concludes, can only be understood when this comingling of the contributions of legal, political, and religious ideas and practices is understood.

Theological Chapters

Part III concludes the volume by exploring the implications of particular Christian theological doctrines for the field of constitutionalism as a whole. The chapters build on the two previous parts, presupposing an understanding of the historical influence of Christianity and the content of modern constitutional law. Together they scrutinize and challenge contemporary constitutional ideas in the light of Christian theology. Again, the choice of theological doctrines and the confessional perspectives from which each chapter author evaluates these constitutional ideas is deliberately diverse.

In his chapter ("Revelation: Scripture and Covenant"), David VanDrunen explores the significance of divine revelation for constitutionalism. In Christian theology, revelation is of two kinds: the general manifestation of God through the created order and the special revelation of God principally in Scripture and in the person of Jesus Christ. VanDrunen proposes that this has immediate constitutional implications: the Christian teaching that there is a self-revealing God to whom all are accountable means that even the most powerful ruler is accountable to God. The Bible begins with an account of God as the creator and ruler of all things, and the creation of human beings in the divine image responsible to rule the creation as God's royal representatives on earth. It then recounts the fall into sin and the accompanying exercise of unconstrained power by unscrupulous rulers. Both revealed truths about human nature, VanDrunen argues, suggest the need for constitutional constraints on governing power. Crucial to the divine revelation, he further proposes, are the covenants by which God defines what might be called the constitutional structure of his relationship with human beings. Of the several covenants revealed in the Bible, VanDrunen maintains that the covenant with Noah described in Genesis 9 is of special significance for constitutionalism because it describes the terms of God's relationship with all human beings, and not only with the Hebrew people or the Christian church in particular. It is also of importance because it authorizes the administration of justice by human beings precisely because they are made in the divine image, and circumscribes the exercise of such power by requiring that the punishment must fit the crime (Gen. 9:6). VanDrunen argues that such an interpretation of the biblical revelation is consistent with a modestly liberal constitutional order that is common to all peoples irrespective of their particular national or religious identities.

David McIlroy argues, similarly to VanDrunen, that the constitutional implications of Trinitarian theology should be understood in terms of the history of the triune God's dealings with humanity ("Against Leviathan: The Implications of Trinitarian Theology for Constitutionalism"). He points out that God the Father is revealed in Scripture as an all-powerful ruler who nonetheless governs the creation in a manner that is consistent with his goodness and in accordance with his covenantal promises. Human rule should accordingly be conducted in conformity with the standards of justice established by divine and natural law. McIlroy further notes that although Jesus Christ, as the eternal Son of God, was invested with all the prerogatives of divinity, he was prepared to be united to human flesh, live as a sojourner, associate with the destitute, and die a criminal's death. This suggests that all human authority should be exercised with similar humility and care for the dignity of the human beings for whom Christ demonstrated such love. Because Christ alone is King of kings and Lord of lords, no merely human ruler can rightly claim or exercise absolute power or authority. Moreover, the Holy Spirit is the agent through whom human beings freely turn to God the Father and are transformed into the likeness of the Son of God. McIlroy argues that this too places a limitation on human government: it cannot regenerate, sanctify, or perfect human beings; it can only impose external limits on their behavior through the administration of human law and justice. McIlroy proposes that human government should therefore be constitutionally limited and dispersed, not least in order to enable other human institutions—familial, social, and religious—to make their unique contributions to the good of the human community.

In his chapter on justice ("Constitutional Design and the Purpose of the Political Community"), Jonathan Chaplin proposes an account of constitutionalism and constitutional justice that draws on contemporary Reformed Protestant political theology. He proposes that justice be understood in terms of the various modes in which it is manifested, in terms of the types of legal relation that it regulates, and in terms of the concrete content of justice in each of these modes and types of legal relation. Following and developing Paul Tillich's thought in this field,[71] Chaplin suggests that justice can be variously manifested in conceptual *attribution* to persons and things in accordance with their true natures, in positive *distribution* of goods among persons in accordance

[71] Paul Tillich, *Love, Power, and Justice: Ontological Analyses and Ethical Applications* (Oxford University Press 1954).

with what is appropriate, in negative *retribution* in order to rectify injustice, and in active *contribution* by each person to the good of others. Adopting Herman Dooyeweerd's analysis,[72] Chaplin further proposes that legal relations between persons be understood in terms of a threefold distinction between rights, duties, and competences. Justice, understood in these terms, is an irreducible dimension of a moral order constituted by God's original creation, providential governance, and eschatological redemption of the universe and all it contains. Within this framework, constitutional law exists to realize constitutional justice, which is the establishment of relations of justice among the individual members and institutional components of a given political community. These relations of constitutional justice include attributions of appropriate status (e.g., citizenship), distributions of appropriate rights (e.g., voting), duties to make appropriate contributions to the common good (e.g., taxes), and competences to order appropriate retribution to rectify constitutional wrongs (e.g., judicial review). Building on Nicholas Wolterstorff's exegesis of Romans 13,[73] Chaplin maintains that the responsibility of constitutional government is limited to protecting persons from injustice, but that this includes not only the protection of citizens' rights but also the coordination of human activities toward the common good. Constitutions thus exist to facilitate the realization of public justice by simultaneously establishing, empowering, and restraining governing institutions.

Tracey Rowland focuses more specifically on the implications of Christology for constitutionalism ("Christology and Constitutionalism"). In a series of councils culminating in the Council of Chalcedon in 451, the Church concluded that the divine and human natures of Christ are united in the person of Jesus Christ "without confusion, change, division or separation." In doing so, the Church expressed its faith in the uniqueness of Christ as the only mediator between God and humanity while nonetheless upholding the importance of the distinction between the divine and human natures. Rowland argues that this confession laid the foundations of what we know as constitutionalism because it "de-divinized" all other human rule and authority. The role of the state was no longer understood in terms of comprehensive salvation, but rather in terms of the administration of limited, earthly justice. The totalitarian materialisms of the twentieth century, she argues,

[72] Herman Dooyeweerd, *A Christian Theory of Social Institutions* (John Witte Jr ed, Magnus Verbrugge tr, Paideia Press 1986).

[73] Nicholas Wolterstorff, *The Mighty and the Almighty: An Essay in Political Theology* (Cambridge University Press 2012).

denied the divinity of Christ, and therefore placed the entire weight of human well-being on the machinery of the state. Conversely, clerical theocracies deny the distinction between the divine and the human, absorbing the state into the spiritual order. Applying the same method of analysis to contemporary liberalism, Rowland further argues that it makes the opposite error of not only distinguishing between the spiritual and the temporal in institutional terms but also requiring a complete eradication of spiritual judgment from all spheres of public life. The result is not liberty, however, but rather "an explosion of legal and moral rules, an endless procession of legalization and moralization."[74] Rowland proposes that this is because the modern state cannot help but offer itself as a kind of alternative savior in the place of Christ.

In his chapter, "Natural Law and Natural Right Revisited," John Milbank scrutinizes the proposition that natural law and natural rights can properly be understood apart from an appreciation of the theological and metaphysical origins of natural law in classical and medieval thought and the emergence of a modern concept of natural right on the basis of a very different set of theological and metaphysical assumptions. He argues that the key difference is between a conception of natural law and natural right grounded in an objective cosmic right order and a conception subjectively founded in the will or capacity of the individual. The latter, he proposes, results in a bifurcation between two possibilities: a spontaneous order that mysteriously emerges from the chaos of individual choices or a politically mediated coordination of human action by state power. Despite attempts to explain and justify these in secular terms, a mutated theology still hovers in the background, preventing the official and dominant secular theories from falling into a nihilism that denies both law and right.

Iain Benson, in his chapter entitled "Subsidiarity: Origins and Contemporary Aspects," discusses the relevance of the principle of subsidiarity for constitutional law. He argues that the principle enables smaller communities (families, associations, localities) to make their own unique and essential contributions to the common good without being subsumed within the larger powers surrounding them. The larger entities, and especially the state, should provide the smaller communities with aid or support without controlling them or taking over their essential functions. Benson notes that the principle has many varied applications relevant to constitutional law,

[74] Citing Slavoj Žižek, "Liberalism and Its Discontents," *ABC Religion and Ethics*, 26 October 2012.

such as devolution and federalism. However, he points out that in Roman Catholic social teaching, the structural principle of subsidiarity must always be understood in connection with its sister concept, the moral or ethical principle of solidarity. Individuals are always persons in relationship with others. Subsidiarity is, therefore, an important antidote to both individualism and statism. The principle involves a kind of social pluralism in which individuals are embedded in networks of small and local associations that provide them with the support necessary to enable them to flourish as human beings in community with others. This implies important constitutional limitations on the purposes and powers of the state, against contemporary tendencies of state agencies to expand and deepen their regulatory and directive control over the institutions and communities of civil society.

In the concluding chapter of this book ("The Greater Operation of Liberty"), Douglas Farrow explores four key implications of Christian eschatology for constitutionalism: its capacity to orient law to human liberty, its capacity to order liberty within a divine economy of grace, its capacity to restrain both lawlessness and the overreach of law, and its capacity to direct aspirations for human justice to their proper ground in God. Freedom, Farrow points out, is ultimately a defining characteristic of God. It is not, therefore, merely the absence of restraint, oppression, or necessity; nor is it a capacity to sin or not sin, for in God there can be no such restraints and no such capacities. Rather, it is a capacity to preserve justice in the soul, an ability to share in the liberality of God, and therefore ultimately a share in God himself. Because the natural and divine law points the way to human flourishing and happiness, it does not merely restrain, or liberate from restraints; rather, it helps to perfect those who are subject to it, enabling them to secure the true liberty of the children of God. Such a vision is contrary, however, to the eschatology of its modern secularist counterpart, which according to its own myth of progress seeks to establish human perfection in this present world. In Christian teaching, the resurrection and ascension of Jesus Christ means that in human affairs all governing power is accountable to a higher authority and all law is to be measured by a higher standard of justice. It also means that only in the risen Christ are priestly and kingly functions appropriately combined, with the implication that in this present time there must remain a division of powers and a distinction between church and state, so as to avoid the extremes of both absolute theocracy and absolute autonomy. Constitutionalism, Farrow argues, is an attempt to project and protect an ordered liberty by subjecting lower law to higher law. It therefore presupposes a hierarchy of jurisdiction and an ultimate source of what is right and just. But beyond these, it also presupposes a teleology and an eschatology. When Christian teleology and eschatology are rejected, however, constitutional law becomes oriented to mere wish fulfillment.

Farrow's final remarks offer a fitting conclusion to the volume. One of the paradoxes of contemporary constitutionalism is that, while almost every independent nation-state in the world today has a written constitution,[75] the average constitution lasts only nineteen years,[76] and many countries have what scholars have called "sham," "façade," or "nominal" constitutions, which neither constrain state power nor accurately describe the practical operation of the government.[77] Like human rights,[78] it is possible that we can entertain utopian hopes for a kind of constitutionalism that seeks to harness "the power of narrative, symbol, ritual and myth" in order to reshape not only political reality but also social life and human nature.[79] Jean-Jacques Rousseau began his *Du contrat social* with the promise that he would reason with "men as they are and laws as they can be,"[80] but his scheme was utterly utopian and "unwittingly set the stage for the totalitarian states of the twentieth century."[81] Several recent titles have explored the way in which constitutions can function as a kind of civil religion within a society and have analyzed them in terms of theological categories such as faith, redemption, scripture, and tradition.[82] This reflects something of a "theological turn" in constitutional

[75] The notable exceptions and borderline cases that prove the rule include Canada, Israel, New Zealand, Saudi Arabia, and the United Kingdom.

[76] Zachary Elkins, Tom Ginsburg, and James Melton, *The Endurance of National Constitutions* (Cambridge University Press 2009) 2.

[77] David S Law and Mila Versteeg, "Sham Constitutions" (2013) 101 California Law Review 863. See also Giovanni Sartori, "Constitutionalism: A Preliminary Discussion" (1962) 56 American Political Science Review 853; Karl Loewenstein, "Constitutions and Constitutional Law in the West and in the East" (1969) 30(3) Indian Journal of Political Science 203.

[78] Samuel Moyn, *The Last Utopia: Human Rights in History* (Belknap Press 2010).

[79] Martin Loughlin, "The Constitutional Imagination" (2015) 78(1) Modern Law Review 1, 3.

[80] Jean-Jacques Rousseau, *The Social Contract and the First and Second Discourses* (Yale University Press 2002) 155.

[81] Susan Dunn, "Introduction: Rousseau's Political Triptych" in Susan Dunn (ed), *Jean-Jacques Rousseau: The Social Contract and the First and Second Discourses* (Yale University Press 2002) 1.

[82] Thomas Grey, "The Constitution as Scripture" (1984) 37(1) Stanford Law Review 1; H Jefferson Powell, *The Moral Tradition of American Constitutionalism: A Theological Interpretation* (Duke University Press 1993); Robert N Bellah, "Civil Religion in America" (2005) 134(4) Daedalus 40; Sanford Levinson, *Constitutional Faith* (Princeton University Press 2011); Jack M Balkin, *Constitutional Redemption* (Harvard University Press 2011). See also Joseph Weiler, *Un'Europa cristiana* (Rizzoli 2003).

scholarship, not altogether out of place perhaps in the postmodern climate of our age. In this context it may be beneficial to observe that Christianity offers not only a constructive contribution to the development of constitutions and constitutionalism but also a salutary warning against constitutional perfectionism and the pride of reason.[83]

[83] Steven D Smith, *The Constitution and the Pride of Reason* (Oxford University Press 1998).

PART I

THE HISTORICAL INFLUENCE OF CHRISTIANITY

2

Old Testament

Torah and Constitutionalism

Jonathan Burnside[1]

Introduction

This chapter explores some of the key constitutional ideas associated with biblical law: how they are applied across the Hebrew Bible and their relationship to the New Testament.

It should be said at once that what we find in the Bible is a long way from constitutions in the modern, European, sense. The modern constitution is tied to the rise of the nation-state, which itself consists, in broadly Weberian terms, of a people, a territory, and a government that possesses a monopoly of legitimate force. Modern constitutions are conventionally said to have substantive and formal elements. Substantively, they are concerned with the content of rules that determine both the exercise of government power and the basic legal status of the individual while, formally, they are also concerned with rules (or "higher law") that are seen as fundamental, or prior, to day-to-day legal life. Both strands are combined in eighteenth-century constitutionalism, along with a concern for codification. Obviously, there was no eighteenth-century-style constitution operating in biblical Israel. The tribes of Israel (either pre- or post-Conquest) do not constitute a state, even in the broad sense of a people exercising sovereign authority over themselves in a defined territory. There is no territory to speak of pre-Conquest, and Israel's borders are not particularly stable until the Davidic monarchy. Even then,

[1] Part 4 of this chapter has its origin in discussions at a conference, "Towards a Relational Constitution," held in St. Catharine's College Cambridge in July 2010. I am grateful to Jonathan Chaplin, Julian Rivers, and Michael Schluter, CBE, for their responses to an earlier draft. Biblical quotations are drawn from the English Standard Version (ESV) translation of the Holy Bible.

Jonathan Burnside, *Old Testament: Torah and Constitutionalism* in *Christianity and Constitutionalism*.
Edited by: Nicholas Aroney and Ian Leigh, Oxford University Press. © Oxford University Press 2022.
DOI: 10.1093/oso/9780197587256.003.0002

the most that can be said about this political arrangement, from a modern perspective, is that it is a quasi-state.[2]

However, this does not mean the *Torah* is irrelevant to constitutional thought. Constitutions, like law, predate modernity. Just as it is possible for law to exist without a state, so it is possible for a constitution to exist without a state. We can thus conceive of constitutions that are not statist or even tied to any territory or territorial element. So although Israel's *Torah* is not a constitution in a modern statist or territorial sense, it does contain substantive regulations that determine the exercise of government power and formal regulations that concern the fundamental legal status of persons. The presence of these substantive and formal elements means that we can speak of something recognizably constitutional in biblical law that may even be regarded as a "quasi-constitution" from a modern perspective. In turn, this means we can also speak of the "*Torah* and constitutionalism" because constitutionalism concerns the idea that there are values associated with good constitutional design. It is constitutionalism that provides the bridge between the biblical texts and modern constitutional thinking. This is because the *Torah* conveys profound political insights that have shaped later constitutional thought.

Recognizing the relationship between the *Torah* and constitutionalism is important given the way in which the major, and distinctive, contribution of Hebraic thought has been airbrushed out of the picture in recent centuries. A sad consequence of this is that Jewish thought has, at times, even been presented as opposed to supposedly "Christian" ideas about the constitution. A historical survey would be a chapter in itself but one example will here suffice: during the passage of the Jew Bill in England, the slogan used during the election campaign of 1754, in Lancashire, was "No Jews; Christianity and the Constitution."[3] I am thus glad to have this opportunity, in a volume expressly titled *Christianity and Constitutionalism*, to outline briefly how the *Torah* informs our assumptions regarding constitutionalism and has continuity with New Testament perspectives. We cannot speak of Christianity and

2 For this reason, although I draw widely upon Daniel Elazar's works in this chapter, I try to avoid reading into the biblical texts modern constitutional concepts and terms that seem to me insensitive to what we know, from our limited archaeological data, about ancient Israel's cultural experience. For example, Elazar repeatedly uses the terms "federal" and "confederal" to cover different periods of premonarchical Israel, although, in my view, terms such as "federal" and "confederal" are only meaningful when talking about a state.

3 David S Katz, *The Jews in the History of England 1485–1850* (Oxford University Press 1997) 246, n 18, citing contemporary editions of the *London Evening Post*.

constitutionalism without appreciating what the *Torah* teaches on the subject, starting with the importance of covenant to constitutional thought.

Covenant as a Constitutional Idea

A covenant can be defined as "a morally informed agreement or pact based upon voluntary consent and mutual oaths or promises, witnessed by the relevant higher authority, between peoples or parties having independent though not necessarily equal status, that provides for joint action . . . under conditions of mutual respect."[4] Covenant is thus "a seminal political idea"[5] because it enables people to "freely create communities and polities, peoples and publics, and civil society itself," thereby "establishing . . . enduring partnerships."[6] A covenant differs from a contract, first, in that a covenant is public in character, whereas a contract is essentially private. Second, the parties to a covenant are expected to behave toward each other in ways that go beyond the mere letter of the agreement, whereas the point of a contract is to limit the parties' obligations. Put otherwise, it is the foundation of an amicable relationship, rather than an adversarial settlement (although we do find it used also in the latter context, e.g., between Jacob and Esau). Even when contracts are used for public purposes (as with Rousseau's "social contract"), they do not involve the same degree of moral obligation as do covenants.[7] This difference between covenantal and social contract thinking is important in view of the influence of the latter on modern constitutionalism.

Israel's constitution is repeatedly grounded in covenant. It is at Sinai, in the course of a covenantal ceremony, that Moses reads the *sefer haberit* ("book of the covenant") to the people, to which they respond: "All that the LORD has spoken we will do, and we will be obedient" (Exod. 24:7). Covenant and constitution also go together in the book of Deuteronomy. Here, a generation on from Sinai, Israel's constitution is formally adapted in a covenant ceremony to settled life in the promised land (Deut. 29:10–13 [MT 29:9–12]). Covenant and constitution also belong at the end of the book of Joshua. Here, Joshua makes a covenant (*berit*) with the people (Josh. 24:25), which, along

[4] Daniel J Elazar, *Covenant and Civil Society* (Routledge 2018/1998) 8.
[5] Daniel J Elazar, *Dealing with Fundamental Regime Change*, <http://www.jcpa.org/dje/articles2/regimechange.htm> accessed 24 March 2018.
[6] Daniel J. Elazar, "The Political Theory of Covenant" (1980) 10 Publius 3, 6.
[7] Elazar, *Covenant and Civil Society*, 8–9.

with certain "statutes and rules" (*hoq v'mishpat*), forms part of a larger constitutional text (Josh. 24:26), which effectively becomes the people's (written) constitution or, as it is called, "the Book of the Law of God" (*sefer Torat Elohim*; Josh. 24:26).

Covenants are thus an inherently relational idea, being focused on relationships to such a degree that they can be said to be "the constitutionalization of a relationship."[8] In Israel's case, what is "constitutionalized" is the people's holiness, reflected in her calling to be "a kingdom of priests and a holy nation" (Exod. 19:5–6). Consistent with the relational character of the covenant, the covenantal ideal seeks to balance freedom and obligation.[9] This is reflected in the biblical texts. Whereas typical Mesopotamian and West Semitic covenants turn previously independent entities into vassals, God's covenants with Israel, by contrast, call into existence a new creation to live in freedom. Consequently, whereas vassal-suzerain treaties are formed in the Ancient Near East (ANE) between a greater king and a lesser king, at Sinai and Moab every Israelite shares in the status—and the responsibilities—of the subordinate king of the suzerainty treaty.[10] Accordingly, the covenants at both Sinai and Moab are democratic documents addressed, not to an elite, but to all those who constitute Israel. The whole people assumed responsibility for following the *Torah* (e.g., Exod. 24:3).[11] At the same time, God relates to each individual Israelite. Every single commandment of the Decalogue, for example, "can be fulfilled, or transgressed, by an individual."[12] For these and other reasons, Berman suggests that "[the] elevation of the individual in the eyes of God may well represent the most profound political teaching, and most lasting political legacy, of the Hebrew Bible."[13]

This concern for freedom is partly why covenant, as an idea, has had a major influence on the political history of human liberty. Elazar's four-volume treatment of the covenant tradition in politics traces the development of covenant traditions in the West. Covenantal peoples, and a covenantal way of life led, inter alia, to "reformed Protestantism with its federal theology, federalism as a political principle and arrangement, the

[8] Daniel J. Elazar, *Covenant and Polity in Biblical Israel* Vol 1 (Routledge, 1998) 24.

[9] Harvey Shulman, "The Bible and Political Thought: Daniel J. Elazar's Contribution to the Jewish Political Tradition," (1992) 41 Judaism, 18, 28.

[10] Joshua A Berman, *Created Equal* (Oxford University Press 2008) 40–44.

[11] Ze'ev Weisman, "The Place of the People in the Making of Law and Judgement" in David P Wright et al (eds), *Pomegranates and Golden Bells* (Eisenbrauns 1995) 407.

[12] Berman, *Created Equal*, 41.

[13] Joshua A Berman, "God's Alliance with Man" (2006) 25 Azure 104.

modern corporation [and] civil societies based upon interlocking voluntary associations."[14] Elazar points out how national covenants were used to found many of the original colonies in British North America,[15] as they had been central to Swiss,[16] Dutch,[17] Scots,[18] and English Puritan[19] societies before that. Covenantal thinking became "the common mode of political conceptualization and expression during the American Revolution,"[20] where it was reflected in numerous constitutional documents, including the Declaration of Independence.

Covenants are thus capable of major heavy lifting, in constitutional terms. They address the moral foundations of the political system (how people in a given polity should live and what their vision of justice should be), its frame of government, and even its socioeconomic basis.[21] Their appeal to transcendent authority and concern for relationships mean they are also well placed to determine questions of legitimacy (i.e., by what right a particular authority holds power and whether this is justified). Tellingly, recovenanting ceremonies were used on several occasions when the normal relationship between ruler and ruled broke down in biblical Israel, resulting in threats to the legitimacy of the House of David.[22]

Despite all this, there is a difference between a covenant and a constitution. The Sinai covenant is not, in itself, Israel's constitution; instead, it is a necessary first step to prepare Israel to receive a constitution. This is provided by the *Torah* as a whole and, most especially, by Deuteronomy (see next section). Moreover, the fact that a constitution is grounded in a covenant does not thereby make every covenant a constitution, although a specific covenant may well form the basis of a later constitution. For that reason, there is a difference between constitutionalism and what may be called "covenantalism," viz. the perceived value of grounding political arrangements in the form of a covenant. Covenantalism, then, is one of the values of biblical constitutionalism because of the importance placed on covenant faithfulness. It

[14] Elazar, "Political Theory," 5.
[15] Elazar, *Covenant and Civil Society*, 15.
[16] Ibid, 177–194.
[17] Daniel J Elazar, *Covenant and Commonwealth* (Routledge 2017) 209–228.
[18] Ibid, 269–307.
[19] Ibid, 231–267.
[20] Elazar, "Political Theory," 4.
[21] Elazar, *Covenant & Polity*, 30.
[22] Crises included Jehoash's accession (2 Chron. 23:2–3), Hezekiah's purification of the Temple (2 Chron. 29:10), and Josiah's reform (2 Kgs. 23:3); Elazar, *Regime Change*.

is a precept of constitutionalism because it is a particular way of relating to power, one that is characterized by amity, respect, relationship, and liberty.

The Deuteronomic Constitution

Within the DNA of the covenant tradition, one strand stands out. This is Deuteronomy, to which we now turn. Although Deuteronomy is not a constitution in the modern sense, we can see it as a quasi-constitution, from a modern perspective. Substantively, Deuteronomy deals with a variety of topics concerning the regulation of power. It is also concerned with the prior status of persons by setting out, formally, the fundamental way in which God relates to his people. Within that material, we can also identify more general values that comprise what we can call constitutionalism. This is further supported by the fact that this is how Deuteronomy is seen by key figures in later constitutional thought.

As far back as Roman times, Josephus described Deuteronomy as Israel's divinely authorized and comprehensive "constitution,"[23] using the Greek term *politeia*, with its overtones of statecraft.[24] This makes Deuteronomy, along with the Constitution of Athens, "one of the oldest such documents available to students of government and politics."[25] During the Diaspora, Deuteronomy formed the basis of rabbinic and medieval Jewish political thought regarding the ideal Jewish state. Both the rabbinic patriarchate in Israel during the second century AD and the exilarchate in Babylon were organized in the spirit of Deuteronomy, as were self-governing Jewish communities in Europe between the eleventh and fourteenth centuries AD.[26] With the founding of the State of Israel in 1948, Deuteronomy became a resource once again among some religious Jewish thinkers for "a proper Jewish state," thereby creating new literature based on Deuteronomy as a political constitution.[27] Deuteronomy had comparable influence in the hands of Christian theologians, political philosophers, and social reformers who regularly

[23] *Antiquities*, Book 4. "[Moses] gave them the laws and the constitution of government" (at 194).

[24] S Dean McBride Jr, "Polity of the Covenant People" in John T Strong and Steven S Tuell (eds), *Constituting the Community* (Eisenbrauns 2005) 17.

[25] Elazar, *Covenant & Polity*, 194.

[26] Daniel J. Elazar, "Deuteronomy as Israel's Ancient Constitution: Some Preliminary Reflections" (1982) 4 Jewish Political Studies Review, 3. See also Daniel J Elazar and Stuart A Cohen, *The Jewish Polity* (Indiana University Press 1985) 121–134, 137–145, 160–177.

[27] Elazar, *Covenant & Polity*, 196.

turned to this text as a biblical source for political ideas (see "Biblical constitutionalism as wisdom," below). For example, John of Salisbury's twelfth-century *Policraticus* has an extended section on Deuteronomy 17:14–20, every word of which is described as "thunder in the ears of the prince if he is wise."[28] Deuteronomy has thus been "a living tradition" in constitutional thought going back as far as three thousand years. Given the constraints of this chapter, however, we can only consider a few verses. We will concentrate on Deuteronomy 16:18–18:22 because its relationship to subsequent ideas concerning "separation of powers" attests to the enduring power of the Deuteronomic constitution.

Deuteronomy 16:18–18:22 sets out the balance of power between four different sources of authority in biblical Israel, namely judges (16:18–17:13), the king (17:14–20), priests (18:1–13), and prophets (18:14–22). It underlines the fact that the Israelite polity was to be one of "separated but shared powers," so structured that "power never could be concentrated in a single human authority."[29] This makes perfect sense in light of Israel's own experience of slavery under a totalitarian pharaoh. It is just one outworking of the radical constitutional change celebrated by Moses and the Israelites in the triumphal Song of the Sea (*Shirat HaYam*), immediately following the Exodus (Exod. 15). This proclaims that God has dethroned the kings and peoples of Philistia, Moab, Edom, and Canaan, just as God dethroned the king of Egypt. It means that, since God has overthrown these political leaders, no human ruler can be king or exercise political authority in Israel in the same way again.[30] Unsurprisingly, we find some form of separation of powers functioning prior to Deuteronomy, in which Israel's judges are, to a degree, independent of the hereditary priesthood (Exod. 18:21–26). This concern to keep power in check is but one aspect of what has been called, in a different context, "the manifesto of the monotheistic revolution"[31] and which is designed to keep Israel in the freedom God has won for her.

[28] John of Salisbury (ed), *Policraticus* (Cary J Nederman tr, Cambridge University Press 1990) 36.

[29] Elazar, *Covenant & Polity*, 205.

[30] Shawn Zelig Astor, "Historical Issues Connected to Sinai," Unpublished paper delivered at conference "What Does '*Torah* from Heaven' Mean?" Herzl Institute, 18–22 June 2017.

[31] Avigdor Shinan and Yair Zakovitch, *From Gods to God* (Jewish Publication Society 2012) 1.

The Judges (Deut. 16:18–20; 17:8–13)

The final form of Deuteronomy 16:18–18:22 presents the local judges (*shoftim*) and civil officers (*shotrim*) as first in the order of authorities. This may seem a little surprising, given the relatively lowly status of their equivalents in modern societies. However, it may reflect the reality that "while the constitution of Israel is comprehensive, the role of government is limited."[32] This means that, in biblical Israel, local government is "the most important arena of governance and . . . self-government."[33] Within this, the extended family forms the primary building block. In that sense, local judges are "more important than kings"[34] because they are the bedrock of government. We note in passing that this, in itself, challenges the modern trend toward government centralization, as well as government interference with the family as an independent political unit. Deuteronomy probably imagines here the "elders" (*zekenim*), or council of adult males, meeting at the so-called city gate (e.g., Deut. 21:18–21, 22:13–21, 25:5–10; Josh, 20:2–4; Ruth 4:1–12; and Prov. 31:23). Whereas Canaanite permanent settlements were politically independent, forming what is thought to be a series of independent Canaanite city-states, the reference in Deuteronomy 16:18 to judicial appointments being made "according to your tribes" indicates that the Israelite equivalent was subordinated to tribal government.[35]

The deliberate positioning of the *shoftim* and *shotrim* at the head of the list may be not only practical but also philosophical. The judges are commanded to "judge the people with righteous judgment" (Deut. 16:18), but the command "Justice, and only justice, you shall follow, that you may live and inherit the land that the LORD your God is giving you" (Deut. 16:20) is addressed in the singular to every individual Israelite and not only to the judges as individuals.[36] Everyone is tasked with the proper administration of justice.[37] This is reflected in the use of self-executing rules that are formulated in such a way as to reduce the need for third-party adjudication.[38] And because none can evade responsibility, everyone is answerable for the actions of their judges.

[32] Elazar, *Covenant & Polity*, 209.
[33] Ibid.
[34] Ibid, 207.
[35] Ibid.
[36] JG McConville, *God and Earthly Power* (T&T Clark 2008) 86.
[37] Berman, *Created Equal*, 69–70.
[38] Characterized by Jackson as "wisdom-laws": Bernard S Jackson, *Wisdom-Laws* (Oxford University Press 2006) 29.

I suggest the *shoftim* are placed first because they are the most visible representation of this personal responsibility, which is, in fact, underlined in the laws that follow concerning witnesses (Deut. 17:4–7).

Placing the requirement to seek justice at the start of a section on the organization of government makes the link explicit between the constitution of that government and justice. Because all Israelites are commanded to seek justice, it follows that all the biblical laws concerned with justice are deeply constitutive of the Hebrew polity. This includes laws dealing with land and the economy, matters that we might not, at first glance, associate with constitutionalism. Land ownership and distribution can be said to provide foundations for biblical constitutionalism because they form the basis for Israel's economic and political organization. Accordingly, chapters 13–22 of Joshua, which deal with the division of the land among the tribes, and which form nearly half the book, can be read as "a constitutional act of the highest order."[39] This is not how such texts are normally read, but it is how Deuteronomy suggests they should be read. Deut. 16:18ff reminds us that the Deuteronomic constitution is intensely practical and should be approached as a series of case studies in what it means to do justice in a particular society. In that sense, what matters is not the constitution per se but whether justice and righteousness are done.[40] The constitution is only a means to an end. After all, if the nations were dispossessed from the land due to their "abominations" (Deut. 18:12), it is not surprising that Israel's continuing possession of the land is contingent on her doing justice (Deut. 16:20). This raises the question of to what extent modern constitutionalism is related to questions of access, social mobility, and social justice.[41] Biblical constitutionalism is also concerned not only with justice for those who are presently alive but also with previous generations and those who are yet unborn. In this way, it challenges modern constitutionalism to recognize intergenerational justice in a radical way.

A final reason for putting the *shoftim* first may also be narrative. Judges were established, even prior to Israel's own existence as a nation (Exod. 18:21–22, 25–26; Deut. 1:15–17). By comparison, kingship—if and when it

[39] Elazar, "Joshua," 127.

[40] Weinfeld has shown that the hendiadys "justice and righteousness" (*mishpat v'tsedeqah*) in the Hebrew Bible refers to establishing conditions of social justice and equity. It is thus closely associated with ideas of mercy and loving-kindness (*hesed*): Moshe Weinfeld, *Social Justice in Ancient Israel and in the Ancient Near East* (Magnes Press 1995).

[41] For Elazar, the willingness of ancient constitutionalism to engage with "the way of life of the polity as a whole" is a major point of departure with modern constitutionalism: Deuteronomy.

would arise—was an innovation, by Israelite standards. Putting the judges at the head of the list reflects their venerability and, I suggest, Moses's own order of priorities (on Jethro's advice; Exod. 18:17–23). If this reading is on the right lines, there may be a further, implied, critique of monarchy: it was not part of the original desert regime.

At any rate, the judiciary is radically independent. The task of judging is delegated to individuals who are chosen by ordinary people (Deut. 16:18–19).[42] Already Deuteronomy goes some way toward fulfilling the hallmarks of Montesquieu's enlightened constitution, by having an independent judiciary drawn from the ranks of the common people.[43] Deuteronomy 17:6–7 reinforces this by giving similar priority to the witnesses who give testimony and who execute judgment.

The King (Deut. 17:14–20)

It has been observed that in Deuteronomy the office of the king is conceptualized "in a way that rejects all prevailing models of monarchic power within both ancient Israel and the broader Near East."[44] This is especially remarkable given the many ways in which Israel otherwise conformed to ANE royal ideology.[45] In classic covenantal style, Deuteronomy 17:15 prohibits a foreigner from becoming king. Instead, the king must be a "brother" Israelite,

[42] Though the criteria remain the same, i.e., the judges' reputation for wisdom (Deut. 16:18–19).

[43] Berman, *Created Equal*, 80. I recognize, however, that Deuteronomy differs from Montesquieu, not least in regard to separation of powers. For example, the judicial responsibilities of the Levitical priesthood potentially overlapped with the judicial role of the king. This is an example of a blurring of separation of powers, which, to modern eyes, is later clarified in the postbiblical tradition. Zimmermann argues that Montesquieu's doctrine of separation of powers was informed by Christian reflections upon power and human nature: Augusto Zimmermann, "God, Locke and Montesquieu: Some Thoughts Concerning the Religious Foundations of Modern Constitutionalism" (2010) 1 Western Australian Jurist 1. More is needed to demonstrate that the biblical ideas had specifically influenced modern constitutionalism. Indeed, we might query whether there is a separation of powers in the Bible in the strong sense intended by Montesquieu. We may note that in written constitutions, such as those of Australia and the United States, the three powers are stated explicitly and positively, while the separation of powers is a negative implication. It is possible that the same occurs in Deuteronomy. If so, it strengthens the link between it and modern constitutionalism. Even so, Deuteronomy presents the three powers in a somewhat different way, with Deuteronomy 16–18 separating two sets of what we today would call "civil" authorities (i.e., judges and kings) and "religious" authorities (i.e., priests and prophets). Although it is beyond the scope of this brief chapter to trace this out, these divisions have implications for Montesquieu's limited separation of the civil institutions of executive, legislature, and judiciary as well as for Madison's and Jefferson's separation of church and state.

[44] Bernard Levinson, "The Reconceptualization of Kingship in Deuteronomy and the Deuteronomistic History's Transformation of *Torah*" (2001) 51 Vetus Testamentum 511.

[45] Levinson, "Reconceptualization," 512–518.

someone "under the covenant."[46] Moreover, this brotherly king is limited in three main ways, in terms of "weapons, women and wealth."[47]

First, he cannot acquire "many horses for himself" (Deut. 17:16). This prevents the king from developing an elite military class in the form of a royal chariot force.[48] Like the insistence on brotherhood, this prohibition speaks volumes about Deuteronomy's concern to preserve Exodus-style egalitarianism. This is further underlined by the prohibition immediately following, that the king shall not "cause the people to return to Egypt in order to acquire many horses, since the LORD has said to you, 'You shall never return that way again' " (Deut. 17:16). The fear is that the king will reverse what God has done for Israel in the Exodus and become a new pharaoh. A decentralized form of defense acts as a check on the king's power and keeps him reliant upon YHWH for success in battle. Second, the king cannot "acquire many wives for himself, lest his heart turn away" (Deut. 17:17). Although this is often taken as a prohibition against taking foreign wives to make foreign alliances, with the added risk of idolatry, the text in fact limits multiple marriages generally with all women, not just those with foreign women. Not only does this prevent royal sexual misadventures, but also it blocks attempts to consolidate power by marrying into powerful social networks.[49] Finally, the king cannot "acquire for himself excessive silver and gold" (Deut. 17:17). This restricts "the king's control of the economic surplus . . . [and] his rights to taxation, trade, rents, fees, plunder and confiscation."[50] All three prohibitions limit "the king's abilities to use typical exclusionary power strategies" and prevent him from "assert[ing] military, political and economic independence."[51]

Tellingly, the king has only one positive duty, which is to "write for himself in a book a copy of this law" and "read in it all the days of his life that he may learn to fear the LORD his God by keeping all the words of this law and these statutes, and doing them" (Deut. 17:18–19). The Hebrew of Deuteronomy 17:18 is ambiguous regarding the role of the priests; the king may either be writing "in the presence of the Levitical priests" (per NAS translation) or writing "out of that [copy] which is before the priests the Levites" (per KJV

[46] Gerbrandt, *Kingship*, 109. "Brotherhood" is, of course, a major theme throughout the laws of Deuteronomy (e.g., Deut. 15:11, 19:18, 23:7 [23:8]).

[47] Christopher JH Wright, *Deuteronomy* (Paternoster 1996) 209.

[48] Berman, *Created Equal*, 62.

[49] Ibid, 61.

[50] Patricia Dutcher-Walls, "The Circumscription of the King: Deuteronomy 17:16–17 in Its Ancient Social Context" (2002) 121 Journal of Biblical Literature 601, 609.

[51] Ibid, 609, 615.

and JPS translations). But either way, he is to spend his time, as Levinson puts it, in the company of "the very . . . scroll that delimits his powers."[52] Such a king would truly be like a brother since the same requirement is made of the ordinary Israelite (e.g., Deut. 6:2, 10:12, 31:12).[53] The king serves the law as a legally constituted and legally constrained monarch,[54] a model citizen and servant of the people. Israelite kings were prohibited from, and never developed into, human-divine mediators between God and the people, as was the case in the neighboring empires of Egypt, Babylon, and later Rome. The king was also prohibited from trespassing upon the unique responsibilities of priests and Levites, illustrated by the condemnation of Saul's presumptuous making of the burnt offering at Gilgal when Samuel was delayed (1 Sam. 13:8–14). Similarly, a significant punishment was applied when King Uzziah usurped the role of the priests in the temple by burning incense on the altar (2 Chron. 26:16–21).

None of this should come as any surprise in the light of the Sinai covenant. Since, as we have seen, all Israelites have priestly-royal status, the role of an Israelite king is relativized from the start. If every Israelite is a vassal king in regard to God—the Great King—there can be no absolute monarch in Israel's constitution. The king's position is further relativized by being introduced after the local judges and civil officials who, be it noted, are appointed by the people and not the king.[55]

The wisdom of the Deuteronomic laws is amply illustrated by the history of its kings. Even David had (at least) eight wives, as well as concubines (which made his succession difficult), while Solomon accumulated chariots, women, and wealth.[56] Without the latter, Solomon might not have engaged in such excesses as "building temples to Kemosh, Moloch and other gods in Jerusalem."[57] The forced labor imposed by Solomon on Israel recalls that imposed by Pharaoh on Israel in Egypt.[58] This critique from within the canon suggests that Deuteronomy 17:14–20 was intended to have practical effect.

[52] Levinson, "Reconceptualization," 522.

[53] Berman, *Created Equal*, 63. "The king is . . . set apart as *an exemplar* of *Torah*-piety for all the people": Jamie A Grant, *The King as Exemplar* (Society of Biblical Literature 2004) 208, emphasis original.

[54] Elazar, *Covenant & Polity*, 199, refers to him as a "constitutional monarch."

[55] Norbert Lohfink, "Distribution of the Functions of Power" in Duane L Christensen (ed), *A Song of Power and the Power of Song* (Eisenbrauns 1993) 347.

[56] Yoram Hazony, "The Biblical Case For Limited Government," (2012) 10 First Things; https://www.firstthings.com/article/2012/10/the-biblical-case-for-limited-government; accessed 15 March 2022.

[57] Ibid.

[58] Ibid, 45.

Contrary to scholars who view these laws as utopian,[59] there are indications that the Deuteronomic vision was taken seriously. Joshua inscribes a copy of Moses's teaching on stones as part of the covenant renewal ceremony at Shechem (Josh. 8:32). This suggests that it is not only the king who was to write out the *Torah* but also Israel's republican leaders.[60] Likewise, instead of absorbing chariots and horses acquired as part of his Conquest victories into his army, Joshua hamstrings the horses and burns the chariots (Josh. 11:6, 9).[61] Nor does Joshua at any time assume to himself any of the prerogatives of monarchy. His primary role is that of military leader marshalling the armies of Israel. Following Joshua's lead, there was no monarchy in Israel for a long time and, when it finally did emerge, it remained weak, especially compared with other ANE monarchies. Even in "paganized Northern Israel, the monarch had no power . . . to impose his will by force upon his subjects,"[62] as indicated by the story of King Ahab and Naboth (1 Kgs. 21). The fact that Jezebel—a Phoenician princess accustomed to absolute forms of monarchical power—is sufficiently constrained by the political culture that she must pretend Naboth's judicial murder is in accordance with the *Torah* suggests the Deuteronomic laws had some practical impact.

Priests and Levites (Deut. 18:1–8)

Priests were another bastion of power in the ancient world. Their appearance at this point is possibly suggested by the role of the Levitical priests in Deuteronomy 17:18[63] in providing the king with (apparently) an original copy of the Deuteronomic scroll. The priests' role, like that of the king, is radically circumscribed compared with other cultic officials in the ANE. In Mesopotamian cities the temple "typically . . . controlled vast economic resources."[64] By contrast, in biblical Israel, priests were denied land ownership (e.g., Deut. 18:1-2).

59 E.g., Lohfink, "Distribution," 346. Levinson, "Reconceptualization," 512, flatly denies its practical effect ("This utopian delimitation of royal power never passed from constitutional vision into historical implementation").

60 Elazar, "Joshua," 116.

61 Ibid, 121.

62 Nahum M Sarna, "Naboth's Vineyard Revisited (1 Kings 21)" in Mordechai Cogan (ed), *Tehillah le-Moshe* (Eisenbrauns 1997) 119.

63 Lohfink, "Distribution," 336, 341.

64 Berman, *Created Equal*, 94.

Despite having an extensive brief in cultic and judicial affairs (e.g., Deut. 17:8–13), the Levitical priesthood, who served alongside the hereditary Aaronide priesthood, were also denied any earthly "portion or inheritance" (Deut. 12:12). Instead, they must live off tithes and gifts received from the people (Deut. 12:18–19). Indeed, their condition is one of such dependency that they are even bracketed with the underprivileged as being entitled to tithes (Deut. 14:28–29). Of course, the priests do have considerable status as guardians of the constitution, since their job is to teach the *Torah* to the people (Lev. 10:11; although 2 Chron. 17:7–8 suggests "certain Levites" seemingly outrank the priests in the teaching commission sent out by King Jehoshaphat). But whether primary authority is given to either priests or Levites, the point is that here too authority is constrained because the *Torah* is a public text that is widely promulgated at every level of Israelite society (e.g., Deut. 31:10–13). Anything taught by priests, or Levites, could be measured against the text itself—a further check on power.

The Prophets (Deut. 18:9–22)

The final powerbase addressed is the prophets. They probably follow the priests in the list because their ability to declare the will and judgment of God is beyond the priests' control.[65] However, their independent ability to function as a source of constraint should not be taken to imply that they either should or did outrank the priests. Different groups fulfill different functions within the constitution and, because they are different, each wields power and authority in different ways. Both priests and prophets are cross-cutting ways of exercising power (cf. the exercise of power by distinct groups in the modern state). Along with judges and the king, the net effect is to create a dispersal of power and a system of checks and balances.

Prophets held a potentially very powerful position, possessing charismatic authority to deliver "extra-constitutional knowledge of the divine will."[66] Although they do not themselves seek to rule, they can be "king-makers and critics."[67] When God promises David and his heirs permanent dominion, the fact that this is communicated via Nathan the prophet "lends it constitutional credibility."[68] Yet when, as later, David's murder of Uriah the Hittite tends

[65] Lohfink, "Distribution," 342, 351.
[66] McBride, "Polity," 31.
[67] Elazar, *Regime Change.*
[68] Ibid.

toward monarchical absolutism (2 Sam. 11:14–17), Nathan plays the reverse role and acts as "a constitutional check"[69] upon the king (2 Sam. 12:11–14). A similar role is played by the prophet Elijah in regard to Ahab (1 Kgs. 21:17–24). Yet although prophets are supposed to be a constitutional counterbalance, false prophets and sycophantic members of the royal court abounded (e.g., 1 Kgs. 22:10–12). Consequently prophets too were constrained and held accountable through public tests that challenged and evaluated the veracity of their prophetic words (Deut. 18:14–22). As a later prophet would proclaim: "To the Law and to the Testimony: if they speak not according to this word, it is because there is no light in them" (Isa. 8:20; KJV).

Torah, Constitutionalism, and Wisdom

The Deuteronomic constitution is consistent with a range of constitutional regimes. This is seen in narrative accounts of constitutional change and reforms in biblical Israel. Accordingly, this section considers the relationship between biblical constitutionalism and wisdom. At the same time, the history also reveals God's judgment on Israel's covenant unfaithfulness. In that sense it also bears witness to other ideas about the constitution in biblical law, including, critically, the centrality of divine sovereignty.

Biblical Constitutionalism as Wisdom

There is a close connection between biblical constitutionalism and wisdom. Deuteronomy 4:5–8 expects the nations to say, in response to Israel's observance of the *Torah* as a whole, " 'Surely this great nation [i.e., Israel] is a wise and understanding people.' . . . And what great nation is there, that has statutes and rules so righteous as all this law that I [Moses] set before you today?" Deuteronomy 4:5–8 only makes sense on the basis that God cares about the well-being of the nations[70] and their laws. According to rabbinic commentary, the *Torah* was given in the wilderness so that all nations could accept it as their own:

[69] Shulman, "Political Thought," 25.

[70] Thomas Kruger, "Law and Wisdom According to Deut. 4:5–8" in Bernd Schipper and D Andrew Teeter (eds), *Wisdom and Torah* (EJ Brill 2013), 35–54.

> Why was the *Torah* not given in the land of Israel? So as not to give the nations of the world the chance to say that they only reject the *Torah* because it was not offered to them on their land. . . . Three things are associated with the giving of the *Torah* [at Sinai]: Desert, fire, and water. We learn that just as these are available freely to all mankind, so too is the *Torah* a gift to all mankind (*Mechilta* 20:2).[71]

Certainly, the political wisdom of the *Torah* has had profound influence, in practice, among the nations. It laid the foundations for constitutional arrangements as diverse from each other as modern republicanism[72] and constitutional monarchy,[73] and thus constitutional government[74] and Western constitutional thought generally.[75] As Hazony points out, "So much of the Bible's political teaching has by now been absorbed into our own—the right of resistance and revolution, for example, or the concept of a limited government—that one is tempted to forget how radical these ideas originally were."[76] During the Protestant Reformation, the founders of the new Swiss, Huguenot, Rhineland, Dutch, Puritan, and Scottish commonwealths all rested their polities on Deuteronomic foundations.[77] This culminated in the American Revolutionary polemical literature between 1765 and 1805 in which Deuteronomy was quoted more frequently than the citations of all European political philosophers combined.[78]

Nor should we, in our own time, ignore the specificity of constitutional arrangements in biblical Israel. These include (1) a kind of separation of powers; (2) a "covenant" between ethnic or other groups as the basis for the constitution rather than the rights of the individual; (3) a focus on citizen obligations rather than rights; (4) a head of state that is under, and not above, the law; (5) restraints on capital and land markets to protect family and community relationships; and (6) the importance of collocated extended families for the provision of welfare. Just as these matters were included in Israel's national covenant to direct national life for generations to come, so

[71] I owe this reference to Yoram Hazony, *The Philosophy of Hebrew Scripture* (Cambridge University Press 2012) 347, n 73.

[72] Shulman, "Political Thought," 25. Eric Nelson, *The Hebrew Republic: Jewish Sources and the Transformation of European Political Thought* (Harvard University Press 2010).

[73] Levinson, "Reconceptualization," 532.

[74] Hazony, "Biblical Case," 44.

[75] Levinson, "Reconceptualization," 532.

[76] Hazony, "Biblical Case," 46.

[77] Elazar, *Deuteronomy*.

[78] Ibid.

too contemporary constitutional thinking is intended to direct public life for generations to come. Biblically influenced constitutionalism should therefore take account of what biblical law teaches on the areas of finance, avoidance of national debt, criminal justice, administration of welfare and health care, and a host of other areas and consider whether and, if so, how these ideas should shape constitutional thinking today.[79]

Compatibility with Diverse Constitutional Regimes

Understanding biblical constitutionalism as wisdom means it is consistent with a range of constitutional regimes. In fact, Israel's own history shows that the Deuteronomic constitution was compatible with a gallimaufry of constitutional regimes. This can be briefly sketched, as follows.

The first change of regime is the transition from the nomadic tribal gathering headed by Moses (and described in Exodus—Deuteronomy) to a government of settled tribes under Moses's appointed successor Joshua. Together with the high priest, and supported by a vigorous tribal leadership, they are responsible for interpreting the *Torah* and the constitution. The decline described in the book of Judges leads to further change in which power returns to tribal elders, supported by regional "judges" (*shoftim*) as well as local priests, Levites, and the occasional prophet. Over time, this degenerates into a much looser political arrangement that is "operationally hardly more than a league at times."[80] Perhaps inevitably, the next stage is a period of anarchy in which "everyone did what was right in his own eyes" (e.g., Judg. 21:25). From an Israelite perspective, the subsequent introduction of monarchy was necessary, politically, since this internal weakness made it impossible to withstand external threats from the Philistines.[81]

The first two books of Samuel show the constitutional consequences of this changing political climate, starting with the fall of the house of Eli and the hereditary priesthood (1 Sam. 1–4). Further change comes with the rise of a prophet-led regime. Here, the prophet Samuel seems to combine the authority of multiple powerbases. Separation of powers here is blurred; not

[79] For which see, generally, Jonathan Burnside, *God, Justice and Society* (Oxford University Press 2011) passim, and Schluter and Ashcroft (eds), *Jubilee Manifesto*.

[80] Daniel J Elazar, *The Book of Judges: The Israelite Tribal Federation and Its Discontents*, <http://www.jcpa.org/dje/articles/judges.htm> accessed 26 March 2018.

[81] Ibid.

only is Samuel superior to the chosen king, Saul, but also he has links to the priesthood at Shiloh. Perhaps because of this, Samuel's regime also fails. The reasons are not entirely clear but, certainly, we are left in no doubt that a regime of dynastic prophets, in the form of Samuel's sons, is no better than the regime of dynastic priests with which the book opened (1 Sam. 8:1–5).

This gives way to even greater constitutional change (1 Sam. 8:5, 19–20). Israel's request to have a king "like all the nations" is meant polemically,[82] since the nations are pejoratively contrasted with Israel (e.g., Deut. 18:9). But, as Gerbrandt points out, although Israel's request was an act of rebellion against God, it does not automatically mean that kingship itself is wrong.[83] Biblical Israel had other political institutions and systems of governance in common with other nations, including a sacrificial system, priests, and prophets. All were radically changed to reflect God's requirements.[84] This being so, kingship was not, in principle, different from any other political institution that might be adapted, as appropriate, to biblical Israel. The only question is: how would it be changed? Deuteronomy 17:15ff provides part of the answer, as we saw in "The King (Deut. 17:14–20)." God's choice of the king provides another (e.g., 1 Sam. 9:17).[85] Although kingship seems to be the second-best alternative in contrast to the spirited citizenry led by Joshua, its introduction nevertheless shows that covenantal ideals were adapted by necessity.

Soon after, in 2 Samuel, we arrive at the classic Israelite monarch in the form of King David. David seems to observe some separation of powers, reaffirming priests and prophets as distinctive powerbases, even though this will leave him open to challenge later (e.g., 2 Sam. 12). At the same time, both are subordinated to the monarchy and are brought within the royal court (2 Sam. 7, 9:15–18). Likewise, although David heads a monarchy that gives considerable power to tribal institutions, there is a marked thrust toward centralization in the form of a royal bureaucracy and standing army. This leads to various tribal revolts (e.g., 2 Sam. 15–19, 20). Nor can we forget the revolutionary constitutional change of building a temple that identified the

[82] Gerald Eddie Gerbrandt, *Kingship According to the Deuteronomistic History* (Scholars Press 1986) 109.

[83] Ibid, 109.

[84] Ibid, 110. See Levinson, "Reconceptualization," for an account of Israel's participation in ANE royal ideology.

[85] Gebrandt, "Kingship," 110. Divine choice is especially salient in Deuteronomy (witness repeated references to "the place that the LORD your God will choose"; e.g., Deut. 12:11).

dwelling of Israel's God as being in a fixed place, as opposed to a portable tent (2 Sam. 7).

Following the corruption of the republic in 1 and 2 Samuel, 1 and 2 Kings shows the fall of its successor, the monarchy. Israel's rebellion against the House of David (1 Kgs. 12) ensures this will now play out as the fortunes of a split kingdom—Israel and Judah—instead of a political union. This constitutional change is a further sign of decline. The failure of the monarchy is seen, first, in the northern, nondynastic, kingdom of Israel and, second, in the southern, dynastic, kingdom of Judah. When (what is left of) Judah returns from exile, Israel transitions again from a monarchy to a nomocracy under Ezra and Nehemiah (e.g., Neh. 8:1–8)[86] and from there the story continues, with further developments, throughout Jewish history.

The point of this brief summary is to emphasize that this variety of political regimes is possible only because no single one is mandated by the Deuteronomic constitution. Subsequent generations were faced with applying its provisions to constitutional affairs right across the spectrum from republic to monarchy, from loose to tight forms of federation and in periods when, variously, priests, prophets, and kings held the upper hand. It also means that the actual experience of applying the Deuteronomic constitution will, at times, have seemed more hierarchical or more egalitarian than at others.[87] The point is that "the biblical political tradition allows for a range of regimes, so long as the covenantal principles are not violated."[88] Choices can and must be made. Nevertheless, there are constraints. This brings us to the next section.

Centrality of Divine Sovereignty

Although God's covenant with Israel at Mount Sinai does not mandate a particular political regime, it does, critically, insist upon certain kinds

[86] Elazar and Cohen, *Jewish Polity*, 95–103. To what extent, and for how long, the Ezra/Nehemiah settlement remained in force is doubted by biblical historians, and the history from there until the Maccabees is poorly documented.

[87] This, in turn, may depend on whether divine justice is thought to operate "under delegated authority from God in some semi-autonomous manner" (which Jackson calls a "dualistic" model) or whether it should be understood as "an integral part of a single system of divine justice" (termed a "monistic" model). Jackson thinks the latter better suits the biblical texts: BS Jackson, "Human Law and Divine Justice" (2010) 9 Jewish Studies: An Internet Journal 223, <http://www.biu.ac.il/JS/JSIJ/9-2010/Jackson.pdf> accessed 30 July 2018.

[88] Shulman, "Political Thought," 29.

of relationships.[89] This means that, notwithstanding the variety noted in "Compatibility with diverse constitutional regimes" some political regimes will be off-limits to Israel if their effect is to compromise the people's relationship with God and one other, such as syncretistic alliances. As Berman puts it: "God is the sovereign, Israel the subordinate. To revere another god is not just to accept a falsehood; it means violating a relationship."[90] What is true of Israel is true of the history of covenantal alliances in general; although a wide range of political options are possible, not all are suitable vessels for carrying the covenantal relationship. The covenant might not impose any particular political regime, but the constitution is still anchored to it (as we saw in "Covenant as a constitutional idea"). Israel can experiment with different constitutional forms, but she is still tied to the covenantal "finger of God" (Exod. 31:18; Deut. 9:10).

It is here that the covenant (originally, at Sinai) becomes decisive: what ultimately matters is whether God's sovereignty is upheld or not. This is not to imply that divine sovereignty should be maintained in a positivistic sense, or purely for its own sake, so to speak. From a biblical perspective, there is no gap between affirming divine sovereignty and saying that what matters is whether justice and righteousness between and among human beings are done. That, of course, can only happen if God's sovereignty is upheld. Divine sovereignty and national obedience produce a society in which justice and righteousness are done—and is the only way in which they will be done.

All idolatry produces injustice, as we have seen in the book of Judges. Israel's decline in covenant faithfulness leads to the downfall of the republic and makes constitutional reform necessary.[91] The recurring phrase "there was no king in Israel. Everyone did what was right in his own eyes" (e.g., at Judg. 21:25) first appears in a story about syncretism (Judg. 17:6). Kingship was also necessary, spiritually, since Israel's syncretism meant she was not much different from the other peoples, who also had kings.[92] In this sense, the introduction of a king can be seen as divine punishment upon Israel.

This is the very view expressed in the proximate texts of 1 Samuel 8 and 12, where the king is portrayed by the prophets as someone who will undermine the people's freedom. Data from Alalakh (in the northern Levant) and Ugarit, ranging from the eighteenth to thirteenth century BC, indicate

[89] Ibid, 179.
[90] Berman, "God's Alliance," 79.
[91] Elazar, "Joshua," 103.
[92] Elazar, *Judges*.

that Samuel's denunciation of kingship, as recorded in 1 Samuel 8:9–17, is "an authentic description of . . . Canaanite society as it existed"[93] before and during Samuel's time. Samuel warns the people "not to impose upon themselves a Canaanite institution alien to their way of life."[94] This, then, is Israel's tragedy: "a people unable to live as they should as a free people under covenant are inexorably driven to lose their freedom."[95] Ultimately, this culminates in exile as mandated by the lengthy curses of the Deuteronomic covenant (Deut. 28:63–68). Indeed, the giving of the Deuteronomic constitution is accompanied by Moses's prophecy of Israel's complete loss of political independence (Deut. 31:24–29).

The Gospel and Constitutionalism

The relationship between the Gospel and constitutionalism is complex. As this question will be addressed in subsequent chapters, it is considered only briefly here, with reference to whether, and how, the New Testament affirms or changes the Hebrew Bible in this respect.

In broad terms, what joins the Hebrew Bible and the New Testament is the narrative nature of books like Deuteronomy, which not only look back a generation but prophetically declare what will happen to Israel, and the world, in the far future. By anticipating the "prophet-like-Moses" (Deut. 18:15), Deuteronomy shows it is keenly aware of a larger narrative that has constitutional implications. From the perspective of the New Testament, this is explicitly fulfilled when the one greater than Moses appears, from among his brothers, namely Jesus Christ, who opens up the eschatological future (Acts 3:22). Israel's liberation, and subsequent constitution, thus points forward to the deliverance of all political systems to Christ. In the life, death, and resurrection of Jesus, the challenge of relating Deuteronomy to contemporary constitutions is both clarified and deepened.

Thus, Romans 13, for example, is clear that government is a servant and that servanthood is teleological. Government is understood as the servant of public, or common, good. Accordingly, and contrary to some contemporary accounts of constitutionalism, there is a core duty to establish justice in the

[93] I Mendelsohn, "Samuel's Denunciation of Kingship in the Light of the Akkadian Documents from Ugarit" (1956) 143 Bulletin of the American Schools of Oriental Research 17, 18.

[94] Ibid, 22.

[95] Elazar, *Judges*.

public realm[96] and there is no distinction between "public" and "private." In this respect, the Gospels show continuity with the Deuteronomic model of the servant king, who is a model citizen and appointed for a purpose. These ideas are affirmed and given new energy in the Gospel. The New Testament's proclamation of Jesus as Lord intensifies the relativization of all earthly political authorities. It also intensifies humbled government:[97] all authorities are now humble servants of the Lord and of the people they govern. Rulers are accountable to God but also to other human beings. It is hard to exaggerate the significance of this "de-divinization" of temporal power,[98] which radically underlies developing understandings of constitutional order as they developed within Christian Europe.

The Gospel also deepens and radicalizes the prophetic tradition of the Hebrew Bible. The gift of prophecy is widely dispersed in the church (e.g., Acts 2:17–18; 1 Cor. 12:10), increasing its potential to provide political challenge. This intensifies the Hebraic tradition of speaking truth to power, as well as its concerns for accountability and transparency, together with the legitimacy of criticism and political opposition. Combined with the idea of the state as a servant of public good, there is now a need to consult with "the public" on their judgments of that good. In this way, the New Testament provides a democratizing thrust. Christians can and must shape whatever constitution they live under despite (or rather, because of) their lack of territorial political community.[99] But there are clearly limits to popular sovereignty. For example, Jesus's statement at his trial that all political authority is delegated from God (Matt. 26:64; John 19:11) undermines Enlightenment doctrine, which sees constitutional authority as proceeding from the wills or rights of individuals.

At the same time, the New Testament brings significant changes to how the Hebrew Bible understands constitutionalism. This is because the proclamation of Jesus as Lord thus has cosmic and political dimensions. If Jesus is Lord, then Caesar (and the government) is not. All constitutional thinking is consequently provisional and must be subject to review. Political power is

[96] See generally Oliver O'Donovan, *The Ways of Judgment* (Eerdmans 2005) 4–12.

[97] Oliver O'Donovan, *The Desire of the Nations: Rediscovering the Roots of Political Theology* (Cambridge University Press 1996) 223.

[98] Eric Voegelin, *The New Science of Politics* (University of Chicago Press 1987).

[99] From a legal perspective, jurisdiction is classically asserted over territory, people, and certain subject matters. Where Christianity asserts jurisdiction (e.g., in canon law), this has tended to be based either on persons or on subject matter and not on territory. Although territorial claims have occasionally been made by those claiming to be Christians—and continue to be made (e.g., the Vatican State)—this is not warranted on the basis of the biblical texts.

no longer the final horizon of authority, the ultimate source of identity, or the guarantor of peace. No matter how well an earthly polity organizes itself constitutionally, it can never, finally, disclose how people should live together. From the perspective of the New Testament, then, no ethnic or national narrative can rival the ending in Revelation where all nations, tribes, and tongues are gathered around the throne of the Lamb in the new Jerusalem. The church is transnational ("neither Jew nor Greek"; Gal. 3:28) and is not tied to any particular nationality or ethnicity or government. Instead, it is a new community, fully ruled in every relationship by God as revealed in Jesus. This affects how Christians seek to understand and apply the constitutional wisdom of the *Torah*. Living in the New Testament period, there are no longer any nations covenanted with God, and the New Testament "people of God" are no longer tied to any territorial political community. At the same time, the emphasis on brotherhood in Deuteronomy—intensified by the absence of ethnic barriers and inclusivity of the New Testament—raises the question of how radically egalitarian a constitutionalism informed by the *Torah* and Gospel is prepared to be.

Another major change concerns the exercise of power in the Messianic age. Whereas some Jewish political thought has expected there to be a separation of powers in the Messianic age ("even the *Mashiach* [Messiah] is not to be trusted alone with all the powers"[100]), the New Testament explicitly presents Jesus as fulfilling, embodying, and exercising kingly, priestly, and prophetic roles. He is not only the King who is greater than David (Matt. 22:41–46); he is also the Great High Priest who offers the sacrifice of himself (Heb. 9:11–28) but also the prophet greater than Moses and Elijah (Matt. 17:3) and John the Baptist (John 5:36). The New Testament's account of Jesus's life, ministry, and resurrection is intended to demonstrate that Jesus is to be trusted—supremely—with the exercise of power. However, this is not a template for tyrannical rule, for the Gospels demonstrate a profound continuity with the Deuteronomic model of the servant king and the many critiques of authoritarianism in the Hebrew Bible.

Drawing these strands together, the key question from a Christian perspective becomes: how should the fulfillment of *Torah*-inspired constitutional thinking in the Gospel of Jesus Christ shape modern constitutionalism? This presents difficult issues for constitutionalism, which subsequent chapters will explore. If Jesus is Lord, how should political constitutions stand

[100] Elazar, "Covenant as the Basis," 39.

vis-à-vis the church (and religious communities generally)? And if, as the New Testament believes, the ultimate community is now the church of Jesus Christ, to what extent should constitutionalism recognize this? Can we imagine, today, forms of constitutionalism that are explicitly theistic or even explicitly Christian? One way of answering this might be to note that, in the Hebrew Bible, God does not directly rule the people of Israel but relies instead on a person who is chosen by the people or appointed by him. On that basis, the Lordship of YHWH in the Hebrew Bible could be said to be mirrored by the Lordship of Christ over all nations in the New Testament. But this raises the question of to what extent the same ambiguity can be said to apply in the modern state.

To this we must add the further complication that the New Testament does not address political order directly. Jesus stresses the importance of all human beings living by the revealed word of God (Matt. 4:4) and seems to assume that whatever is needed for Christians to be salt and light in society has already been revealed (Matt. 5:11–20). Where a political order is laid out specifically, it is in the *Torah* and, especially, in Deuteronomy. Yet Deuteronomy is, of course, distinctive from contemporary constitutions. Israel is governed by God, through mediators, and God has far greater capacity than earthly governments to marshal and motivate an earthly polity. This level of penetration places some limits on how Deuteronomy's wisdom might map onto contemporary political constitutions. A final difficulty is that the Sinai and Moab covenants constitute a people, whereas in the Lockean liberal tradition there are two compacts, the first of which constitutes the people or the polity and the second of which constitutes the government. Finally, God's constitution of Israel was sufficient for all Israelite life (or, at least, sufficient to enable the wisdom necessary for all Israelite life), unlike contemporary constitutions. At the same time, Deuteronomy still assumes that Israel's constitution is a practical display of wisdom that other nations will admire and ought to emulate. And since the *Torah* in the Gospel of Matthew expressly takes into account the "hardness" of the human heart (Matt. 19:8), it may still be said to provide an indication of what it may be possible to achieve in such a context.

Conclusion

The *Torah* is a great gift from God to Israel that teaches about a life worth living—and a constitution worth having. The biblical history of Israel, among many other things, conveys profound political insights that have shaped political philosophy. Although its complexity belies neat summary, an account of constitutionalism in the Hebrew Bible would emphasize the sovereignty of God, covenantal politics, limited government, separation of powers, federalism, and civic virtue. Although the relationship between the *Torah* and the Gospel is complex, the New Testament is in long-range continuity with the constitutional catalysts of biblical law. Whichever way the texts of the Hebrew Bible texts are interpreted in the light of the New Testament, they should not ignore the specifics of how constitutional thought is disclosed in the scriptures of the Old and New Testaments. Despite differences in culture, history, and technology, there are abiding norms of political order, rooted in the *Torah*, that the Gospel implicitly affirms and emphasizes. Certainly, as subsequent chapters in this book will show, the *Torah* offers much more than has been appreciated in modern times in potentially guiding nations in thinking about constitutionalism. Its power is real because it operates at an ideational and moral level, for the only way a constitution can really affect people is by shaping how they think. The confluence of the *Torah* and the Gospel thus generates a uniquely powerful kind of constitutionalism, one that has shaped Western civilization down to its roots and can do so again.

3

New Testament

"But *our* Constitution is in Heaven": New Testament Sketches on the People of God between Divine Law and Earthly Rulers

Dorothea H. Bertschmann

Introduction

Toward the end of his letter to the church in Philippi, written in the late fifties or early sixties from a Roman prison, Paul makes the following statement: "But *our* πολίτευμα is in heaven, and it is from there that we are expecting a Saviour, the Lord Jesus Christ. He will transform the body of our humble bodies in conformity to the body of his glory by the power that also enables him to make all things subject to himself" (Phil. 3:19–20). The term πολίτευμα has sometimes been translated as "homeland" or "citizenship," evoking a distant country, a place where the Philippian believers are fully at home and enjoy the rights of citizens. But the term πολίτευμα has also more active, dynamic, and political connotations. It can signify political actions, political actors, and the political "constitution" under which such actions take place.[1] Josephus, for example, uses the term πολίτευμα more or less synonymously with πολιτεία in his *Adversus Apionem*, where both words stand for the characteristic "way of life" of the Jews.[2] Similarly to Josephus, Paul sees the heavenly πολίτευμα as the binding pattern for the Christ believers, shaping them into a distinctive community in the midst of other civic and political communities. Paul is anxious to keep his converts on track as a people who take their cue from heavenly realities, not earthly ones,

[1] PC Boettger, "Die eschatologische Existenz der Christen: Erwägungen zu Philipper 3.20" (1969) 60 Zeitschrift für Neutestamentliche Wissenschaft, ZNW 244–263, 250. πολίτευμα corresponds to *res publica* and *civitas* in Latin.

[2] See JMG Barclay, "Matching Theory and Praxis: Josephus's Constitutional Ideal and Paul's Strategy in Corinth" in T Engberg-Pedersen (ed), *Paul beyond the Judaism/Hellenism Divide* (Westminster John Knox 2001) 139–163 and 292–294, n 6, p 292.

Dorothea H. Bertschmann, *New Testament: "But our Constitution is in Heaven": New Testament Sketches on the People of God between Divine Law and Earthly Rulers* in *Christianity and Constitutionalism*. Edited by: Nicholas Aroney and Ian Leigh, Oxford University Press. © Oxford University Press 2022. DOI: 10.1093/oso/9780197587256.003.0003

so that they might live in a manner that clearly contrasts them with the selfish and greedy "enemies of the cross" (3:18).[3] Earlier in the letter, in 1:27 Paul admonishes the believers to walk worthily of the Gospel of Christ. The word chosen there, πολιτεύεσθαι, has political connotations in the same broad sense of πολίτευμα, as living as a distinctive people under a binding constitution or set of laws.[4] In Hellenistic Judaism the term is often used "when conduct relative to some law of life—political, moral, social or religious—is signified."[5] Here again Paul calls on his fellow believers to live out the implications of the heavenly constitution—namely, "the Gospel of Christ." These two verses with their "political language" frame the middle part of the letter and its main argument, at whose heart lies the famous Christ hymn (Phil. 2:5–11), which speaks of ultimate authority and divine worship and is thus fundamentally political too. It is widely agreed that the hymn spells out the "heavenly constitution" to which the Philippian believers are held accountable: a constitution founded on the principle of humility, which leads to harmony and a sacrificial love that always considers the needs of others. All this is perfectly embodied in Christ, who is worshipped as the Lord of all at the end of the hymn.[6]

These impressions from an early Christian document put the spotlight on two important figures of thought that the early Christian movement inherited from its Jewish nurturing soil. The first is the principle of ultimate and exclusive allegiance to the one God, who is the author and ruler of all. This basic tenet is greatly transformed in the Christological reflections of the earliest church, but without blunting the sharp edge of ultimate loyalty. The

[3] Paul uses spatial categories like "heaven" to talk about realized eschatology: the reality that is already consummated for Christ but yet to be fulfilled for the believers. See AT Lincoln, *Paradise Now and Not Yet: Studies in the Role of the Heavenly Dimension in Paul's Thought with Special Reference to His Eschatology* (Cambridge University Press 1981).

[4] In this chapter, which offers observations on selected New Testament texts, as read in their original historical and literary context, I will operate with a working definition of constitution, which focuses on "patterns of social life" rather than "forms of government" (Barclay, "Matching Theory and Praxis," 141). I will, however, show that reflections by the earliest Christians on the patterns of their social life inevitably led to reflections about political rule, loyalty, and accountability, though it took centuries of normative systematic Christian thought to develop the notion of constitutionalism as "rule of law" or constitutions as "a body of fundamental principles or established precedents according to which a state or other organization is acknowledged to be governed" (Oxford Dictionary).

[5] Cf. EC Miller, "Πολιτεύεσθε in Philippians 1.27: Some Philological and Thematic Observations" (1982) 15 Journal for the Study of the New Testament JSNT 86–96. Miller points out that Paul could have used other terms to express the Christian's manner of life ("walk") but probably deliberately chose the more politically charged term.

[6] The hymn recalls very strong monotheistic language from Isaiah 45 but does not hesitate to assign to Jesus "the name above all names" (Phil. 2:9), claiming that this does not infringe upon God's prerogatives but is "to the glory of God the Father" (Phil. 2:11b).

second is the notion that God's sovereignty is not expressed in limitless and arbitrary freedom but in some binding rule, in a kind of constitution, so to speak, which establishes and shapes the people of God as a distinctive "community under authority."[7] Both figures of thought are intertwined in early Christian teaching, since divine authority is expressed and acknowledged in the practice of the divine constitution, just as the divine constitution is given its rationale and purpose in the community's allegiance to divine authority in the framework of the covenant.[8] The two tenets render the church political in a broad sense and have the potential to impact the kind of political rule characteristically exercised by kings and governors.

As far as the people of Israel were concerned, the notion of being ruled by God and beholden to the divine constitution was expressed in many different configurations depending on the political situation in which they found themselves.[9] The requirement of exclusive allegiance to God can accommodate obedience to non-Jewish temporal rulers, as long as they do not interfere with the central connection between the people and their divine constitution. When such interference takes place, however, there is embittered resistance and the willingness to "die for the laws" either on the battlefield or as a martyr.[10]

It is in the context of persecution that a longing for God's direct rule is sometimes expressed, pre-eminently through the mediation of a messianic figure.[11] Earthly rulers are in these circumstances perceived to be direct competitors of the one true God, making it impossible for God's people to live under the divine constitution.[12] On the other hand, there are also ongoing attempts (even after the disaster of the Jewish war 70 CE) to present the

[7] The term is borrowed from Oliver O'Donovan, *The Desire of the Nations: Rediscovering the Roots of Political Theology* (Cambridge University Press 1996) 123 (the church is a "community under the authority of the risen Christ"). For Israel, see ibid, ch 2: "The Revelation of God's Kingship."

[8] See Burnside, chapter 2 above, in particular the section titled "Covenant as a Constitutional Idea."

[9] See Burnside's excellent overview of the principled openness of the covenant toward a range of "constitutions" in the sense of "forms of government" (section titled "The Range of Constitutional Regimes and Reforms in Biblical Israel"). To Burnside's examples I would like to add the important experience of exile and diaspora, where the concept of living in a covenant under a distinctive constitution continued to exist, and indeed thrive, even under conditions of political powerlessness.

[10] See 2 Macc. 7:37, where one of the martyrs cries out: "I, like my brothers, give up body and life for the laws of our ancestors." The foreign king crosses a line by demanding of his subjects to forego circumcision and eat unkosher food, therefore effectively renouncing their constitution. (See also 1 Macc. 1:41–64.) In the book of Daniel, which likely reflects the same period, the issue of worship for the emperor is dealt with at length, e.g., in Daniel chs 3 and 6.

[11] While there is the abiding hope for a Davidic Messiah, according to the Nathan promise in 2 Samuel 7, we also encounter the figure of the more mysterious "Son of Man" in Daniel 7:13–14.

[12] See Josephus, *The Jewish War*, II, 117–119. The revolutionaries refuse to accept any other master than God.

Jewish community as constituted into a more de-politicized "way of living" that can coexist with a variety of civic constitutions.[13]

In the following brief sketches I will ask how this double impulse of divine authority and divine constitution—and the Christological reshaping thereof—leaves a mark on three New Testament texts that deal directly with temporal rulers. My principal question will be this: how does the Christians' allegiance to ultimate authority of God in Christ and to the distinctive constitution established by him impact on their relationships with earthly power?[14]

Matthew 22:15–22: "Give unto Caesar . . . ": Reframing

Like all the Gospels, Matthew's account of Jesus the Christ/Messiah resonates with political vocabulary and crackles with political implications. Jesus begins his ministry by announcing the kingdom of heaven.[15] This kingdom, though in its fullness still to be hoped and prayed for, is yet being inaugurated by the words and deeds of Jesus. Matthew emphasizes Jesus's activity as a teacher, casting him as a new Moses, who authoritatively affirms and reissues the law as the divine constitution.[16] The Sermon on the Mount radicalizes the ethics of the Decalogue and popular practices of piety, making right attitudes as indispensable as right actions. But although the law is solemnly affirmed in ever greater detail (5:17), the sermon shows no interest in the careful casuistry of the Torah or its interest in temple worship and sacrifice. Instead, the focus is on practicing radical trust in the heavenly father and radical generosity toward others.

Though Jesus is not explicitly the king in this kingdom, he is introduced from the beginning as God's anointed, the Messiah, who symbolically restitutes the tribes of Israel (in the choosing of the Twelve) and who rallies the masses around him.[17]

[13] The most prominent example is again Josephus. See Barclay, "Matching Theory and Praxis," 141: "Josephus utilizes the tradition for a broader depiction of the structural characteristics of the Jewish 'way of life.'"

[14] The term "secular" is anachronistic for the deeply religious societies of the ancient world.

[15] See Matthew 4:17: "Repent, for the Kingdom of Heaven has come near." Matthew prefers βασιλεία τῶν οὐρανῶν to βασιλεία τοῦ θεοῦ.

[16] Matthew orders the teaching of Jesus in five long, thematic speeches, reflecting the five books of Moses. Like Moses, the infant Jesus has to be rescued from an evil king and sojourns in Egypt (Matt. 2:13–23). Like Moses, Jesus issues the law for the (new) people of God from a mountain (5:1).

[17] Matthew introduces Jesus as Christ and son of David (1:1) and repeats the Messianic title in 1:16 and 1:18. There is also a Davidic allusion in 1:20. On the Twelve see EP Sanders, *Jesus and Judaism* (SCM 1985) 98–106.

All this has enormous potential to put Jesus in conflict with the ruling authorities of his day. However, Jesus's kingdom, while empowering the disenfranchised, does not seem to hold out any concrete political promise of an independent Jewish state or an overthrowing of Roman occupation. The latter is briefly and soberly mentioned at times but said to be overcome by radical nonviolent "resistance" and startling goodness.[18] This does not turn Jesus into an apolitical Messiah, who is only concerned with spiritual matters, but can be read as the deeply subversive launch of an alternative political vision.[19] Still, Davies and Allison are right to state that "if one thing is clear, it is that Jesus was not a political Messiah, that he did not seek to promote a political revolution against Rome. His aim was neither non-political nor directly political."[20] The one conflict, which simmers from the beginning and which explodes with a vengeance, is the conflict between Jesus and other Jewish leaders—not Jesus and Rome.[21] Read against the backdrop of this ever darkening conflict, even the Roman governors and soldiers who finally enter the scene as Jesus's judges and executioners are cast in a relatively mild, though certainly not positive, light.[22] The struggle for proper allegiance to God (and his anointed one) and for proper obedience to God's constitution (as reissued by the Messiah) is therefore very much along the lines of an inner-Jewish struggle between prophets and people/ruler.[23]

The incident about the imperial tax has to be read within this overall Matthean plot. It is the first dispute of four in which Jesus engages after his entry into Jerusalem, mostly debating Pharisees and in one case Sadducees.[24]

[18] Consider the walking of the second mile (Matt. 5:41) and the love of enemies (5:44).

[19] For a subversive reading see, e.g., JH Yoder, *The Politics of Jesus: Vicit Agnus Noster* (2nd edn, Eerdmans 1994), who offers an interpretation, mainly of the Gospel of Luke, as promoting a revolutionary alternative vision of politics, which is bound to challenge the rulers of this world. For an anti-imperial reading on the Gospel of Matthew see also the work of Warren Carter, e.g., "Matthew's Gospel: An Anti-Imperial/Imperial Reading" (2007) 34(6) Currents in Theology and Mission 424–434.

[20] WD Davies and DC Allison, *The Gospel According to St Matthew* (T&T Clark 1991) vol II, 596.

[21] Jesus is friendly to the Roman centurion and he promises his assistance before the centurion has even made his case (Matt. 8:5–10). The example of the believing Gentile is then immediately used to blacken unbelieving Israel (8:11–13).

[22] As in Mark's Gospel, Pontius Pilate is reluctant to condemn Jesus (27:14), he makes an offer to release Barabbas (27:15–23), and he releases the body to Josephus to be buried (27:58). Unique to Matthew are the features of Pilate's wife warning him (27:19), Pilate's gesture of handwashing (27:24), and the terrible curse uttered by the Jewish people on themselves (27:25), as well as the episode of the guards at the tomb (27:22–66, 28:11–15), which all serve to strengthen the indictment of the Jewish leaders and people.

[23] See Burnside, chapter 2 above, section titled "The Deuteronomic Constitution. The Prophets."

[24] "Taken together, the four passages continue the negative characterization of Jesus' opponents, the Jerusalem leaders, a characterization that has been to the fore since 21.23." Davies and Allison, *Gospel According to St Matthew*, 211.

The question about whether it is lawful to pay taxes to the Roman emperor is both delicate and dangerous.[25] An answer in the negative would give Jesus's Herodian interlocutors the welcome opportunity to have him tried for rebellion.[26] Support for the tax could well cost Jesus a lot of sympathy. Matthew emphasizes that Jesus sees through the πονερία of the questioners.[27] Jesus's response is brief and indignant. He first embarrasses the bystanders by unmasking them as people who already carry around the imperial money needed for paying taxes, even on the temple precincts: "show me the coin," "whose likeness and inscription is this?" (v. 19–20).[28] Given that it belongs to Caesar, they might as well return it to where it came from.[29] Such a reply, though shrewd and disarming in the immediate context, might be said to be not much of a contribution to the thorny issue of taxation, which weighed heavily on many subjects of the empire.[30] Jesus limits his response to the precise question, abstracting it from its wider and weighty framework of reference. He makes no general statement about Roman power and its wide-ranging and deeply penetrating demands, such as conscription to the military and worship of the emperor.

The second part of Jesus's answer carries the main weight: "render to God the things that are God's" (v. 21). This is not added as a mitigating clause but draws attention to the real issue, from which the tax trap seeks to detract. God has not been given his due. God's constitution, old and new, has not

[25] For details about imperial taxation in Judaea at the period in question cf. E Schürer, *The History of the Jewish People in the Age of Jesus Christ* (T&T Clark 1973, rev ed 2014) vol I, 399–427.

[26] Refusing the imperial tax, as had happened under Judas the Galilean in 6 CE, is the signal for a riot (see Josephus, *The Jewish War,* II, 118; Josephus, *Jewish Antiquities,* 18.4).

[27] This is a rare but strong blanket term, replacing Mark's ὑπόκρισις (Mark 12:15).

[28] The Markan parallel mentions a δηνάριον (Mark 12:15). The "picture" and "inscription" are usually identified as what was found on the widely circulating "Tiberius denar": a picture of the emperor on the one side with the inscription "Tiberius Caesar Divi Augusti Filius Augustus" and a picture of a goddess on the other side with the inscription "Pontifex Maximus." See H St J Hart, "The Coin of 'Render unto Caesar . . . ' (A Note on Some Aspects of Mark 12:13–17; Matt. 22:15–22; Luke 20:20–26)" in E Bammel and CFD Moule (eds), *Jesus and the Politics of His Day* (Cambridge University Press 1984) 241–248. Matthew has changed the denarius into νόμισμα τοῦ κηνσοῦ, which means the "legal tender" for paying taxes, the "tax money." The point is not so much that bringing "pagan money" to the temple precincts would violate the Jewish law but rather that "by using a coin that is invested with political and religious symbols of the power of the Roman emperor they have long since acknowledged his claim to power." U Luz, *Matthew 21–28* (James E. Crouch tr, Hermeneia, Fortress 2005) 66.

[29] ἀποδίδωμι can be translated as "giving back" (cf. the Latin *reddere*), though this is not a grammatical necessity. Luz, *Matthew 21–28,* 66, n 42.

[30] See Tacitus's *Annals,* 2.42, for the year 17 CE: "Other problems had arisen in Syria and Judaea, where the provincials were finding their financial burdens oppressive and petitioning for a reduction of direct taxation."

been acknowledged by the leaders of Israel.[31] But loyalty to God certainly outweighs loyalty to political rulers.[32] This does not mean that the second injunction annuls the first one.[33] It is more correct to say that the imperial activity of tax collecting is not particularly relevant in the overall plot of God's dawning kingdom. The tax demands can be simply paid off, while the main energy is on the formation of the Gospel people, which conforms to the radical demands of the kingdom. The real issue of loyalty is whether the leaders and people of Israel are able and willing to acknowledge God's final anointed one and to obey the "better righteousness" (5:20) expressed in his constitution.

Before the magnitude and urgency of divine demands, the expectations of imperial Rome are reframed and relativized. They are not the major issue in the struggle for Israel's soul, as a Judean revolutionary would hold, but something that can be heeded with a certain nonchalance in the shadow of God's kingdom dawning.[34] The emperor himself is not addressed or construed as either a friendly or hostile player in this eschatological drama but is seen as overshadowed—although not immediately replaced—by the coming kingdom.

Still, taken by itself, Jesus's shrewd answer sets up an enormous tension. For a monotheistic and covenant-oriented Jew, the things belonging to God are all-encompassing.[35] Jesus's answer leaves open what, if anything, belongs to Caesar apart from the tax coin and how this might go together with a fundamental and all-embracing loyalty to God.

Later canonical readings found Matthew 22:15–22 to be a crucial locus classicus of the New Testament's teaching on politics. The fact that exactly the same formula ("give unto . . . what belongs to . . .") is used for such vastly different authorities—Caesar and God—focused much of the interpretive efforts into defining and delineating the spheres of spiritual and temporal

[31] Davies and Allison point out the connection of the passage with the Parable of the Wicked Tenants in Matthew 21:33–46, where the tenants refuse to give the landlord his due and where the vineyard is given to a people "that produces the fruits of the kingdom" (v.43). Davies and Allison, *Matthew*, vol III, 211.

[32] Davies and Allison aptly write that "while obedience to God can, as in the current instance, co-exist with doing what the state requires, obligation to the former obviously overshadows obligation to the latter." Davies and Allison, *Matthew*, vol III, 217.

[33] This has been suggested by SGF Brandon, *Jesus and the Zealots: A Study of the Political Factor in Primitive Christianity* (Manchester University Press 1967) 345ff.

[34] The colorful legend of Matthew 17:24–27 (the coin for the temple tax is found in a fish's mouth) might commend a similar attitude of nonchalant collaboration, which is completely uncoerced, because "the sons are free" (Matt. 17:26) but freely rendered so as to avoid offense (v. 27).

[35] Since Tertullian (*De Idololatria* 15.3s), the thought of human beings as bearers of the divine image was used to interpret the pericope about taxes. Men and women as image bearers of God owe themselves to God.

spheres of God and Caesar, respectively. The sense that Caesar is indeed *owed* something was particularly strengthened by Reformation interpretations of the passage, which sought to combat the "worldly" claims of ecclesial authorities on the one hand and Anabaptist opting out of the exercise of temporal power on the other.[36] There is a certain danger that, by isolating the formula from its narrative context, the spiritual and political spheres may be too neatly separated from each other, or that obedience to the state is construed, without qualification, as a subcategory of obedience to God. Here it should be recalled that another New Testament voice simply states that "One has to obey God more than humans" (Acts 5:29), leaving space for both cooperation with and resistance to the powers that be.

Romans 13:1–7: "Let every soul be submitted": Harmony

Romans 13:1–7 is one of the few passages in the New Testament and the only passage in the Pauline corpus where the relationship of the Christian church with the "state" is explicitly addressed. Small wonder, then, that this passage has been vastly influential—together with Matthew 22:15–22—as another locus classicus for political ethics in the New Testament.[37] His various experiences of abuse and suffering at the hands of state officials notwithstanding, Paul paints a very optimistic picture of political power as commissioned and upheld by God to punish evil and reward good (v. 1–4).[38] While there is a normative element in this brief account of temporal power, this sits uneasily with the opening blanket statement that *all* political authority is from God.[39]

The theological premise of God-given authority is unremarkable and quite conventional within Hellenistic Judaism.[40] The related topos of holding

[36] For a summary and analysis of the varied *History of Interpretation* of the pericope see Luz, *Matthew 21–28*, 63–64.

[37] For an excellent overview of the immense *Wirkungsgeschichte*, see U Wilckens, *Der Brief an die Römer: Römer 12–16* (Benzinger 1982) 43–66.

[38] Acts in particular seeks to demonstrate in an impressive narrative way Paul's unwavering optimism and trust in the basic justice of the system, mistreatments by individual officials notwithstanding. His unbroken optimism in the basic justice of the system is illustrated by his (successful) complaint about his treatment in Roman Philippi (Acts 16:37) and his appeal to the emperor (Acts 25:21)

[39] Paul calls the state a διαταγή, an ordinance, direction, or arrangement from God (13:2), and affirms that "there is no power—ἐξουσία—except from God" (13:1).

[40] Some examples for Jewish notions of the God-given authority of rulers are 2 Sam. 12:8; Jer. 27:5; Dan. 2:21; Prov. 8: 15–16; Wis. 6.1–3; Josephus, *The Jewish War*, 2.140; 1 En. 46.5; and *The Letter of Aristeas*, 224.

the authorities to account is certainly implied, but not foregrounded, by Paul.[41] Instead, the theological basis serves to support his call for a seemingly unconditional and unqualified submission to the governing authorities. On the one hand, this seems naïve. On the other hand, Paul does not seem to be advocating excessive or unbounded gestures of allegiance and loyalty to imperial Rome. His admonition aims at the willing payment of taxes and revenues as well as of other dues, such as honor and respect (v. 6–7).[42] Moreover, Paul addresses his converts in the rare third-person imperative ("let every soul be subject," v. 1): he expects the believers to submit to the state power like everybody else and to render the same signs of respect and support—no more and no less. This sober tone is all the more astonishing since the brief passage sits in the middle of two sections, which are written in a much more fiery apocalyptic vein: Paul admonishes the Roman believers to renew their thinking in clear nonconformity with the "world" (12:1–2) and to show a markedly different ethical behavior by "putting on the Lord Jesus Christ," since the "night is far gone and the day is near" (13:12).[43] The terminology is apocalyptic, counseling distance and difference from this passing world and its ways.

How, then, does the identity of the believers as the renewed people of a new creation go together with the rulers of the old world? It is certainly telling that the state powers are called the servants of God, but never the servants of Christ.[44] Perhaps this is because they are not agents in God's final eschatological drama of salvation and cannot therefore be enlisted on behalf of the church's mission. But nor should they be resisted for that matter. Paul once again highlights the distinctive "constitution," which shapes the Christian church, though he does not use the term πολίτευμα in this context. The "Christian way of living" is marked by spiritual discernment, mutual service, love, and sobriety. This "constitutional ethos" can be brought into meaningful interaction with people outside the Christian church.

[41] This is different in *The Letter to Aristeas*, for example, where the fact of divinely given authority is used to admonish the rulers (*Letter to Aristeas*, 187–291). It might well be that Paul's train of thought is not going in this direction, because he talks to the Roman believers only.

[42] The specific focus on taxes might point to a concrete historical situation, where there was some restlessness surrounding taxes and revenues as described by Suetonius, *The Lives of the Twelve Caesars* 10.44 (*The Life of Nero)* and Tacitus, *Annals*, 13.50–51. Some church members might have felt attracted by protests and gestures of withholding taxes.

[43] Interpolation theories have rightly been abandoned. The passage is connected by numerous repetitions of key vocabulary, e.g., κακός and ἀγαθός (12:2, 9, 17, 21) or ἐκδικέω, ὀργή (12:19), which is repeated in 13:3, 4, 5. Verse 7 is closely connected with v. 8 by the catchword ὀφειλή / ὀφείλω.

[44] While it is true that for Paul there is obviously no abstract "deity" but always God as the "father of the Lord Jesus Christ," Paul makes no attempt whatsoever to connect or correlate the rulers with Christ's lordship in this passage.

Between the two apocalyptic statements of 12:1–2 and 13:12–14 we have passages that consider the relationship of the believers with the outside world and therefore offer bridges between what is distinctively Christian behavior and what is everybody's duty—as sketched out in 13:1–7. From 12:9 onward we have an extension of love even to the enemies of the Christian believers and a strong instruction to forego vengeance (12:19). While this seems to set up a contrast between the Christian constitution and the activities of the governing authorities (13:4), the second "bridging passage" (13:8–10) creates an interesting point of common ground.[45] Paul starts by saying that Christians ought to owe nothing to anybody, except to love one another. Love is the central term in the Christian constitution, which, unlike taxes, revenues, and gestures of respect, cannot simply be "ticked off." Love is the permanent challenge and task of the Christ believers, which demands their full attention and care. It is thus possible that the love command corresponds structurally to Matthew's "Give to God what belongs to God," just as Paul's "Pay to all what is due to them" (Romans 13:7) corresponds to "Give to the emperor what is the emperor's."

So far, then, we have very similar theological instincts as in Matthew: The state and its demands, which are mostly tangible as tax collections, are given an approving nod. The authorities of imperial Rome are taken for granted and neither resisted nor graced with particular salvific hopes. The eschatological music simply plays elsewhere while the political authorities are on the verge of becoming a *quantité negligeable*. The most important political project at the threshold of the new age is the formation of the church as a distinctive people of God, pledging ultimate loyalty to God's Messiah and being formed and shaped by his new constitution.

However, Paul goes one step further than Matthew by affirming the abiding usefulness of temporal rule in God's greater economy. He does so in a mode of reassurance for the Roman believers, whose social and religious identity is quite precarious at times.[46] True, their Lord and Savior is not the

[45] The juxtaposition of the Christians, who forego revenge (12:19), and the state, which executes vengeance (13:4), is an important element in pacifist interpretations of Romans 13:1–7. See L Schottroff, "'Give to Caesar What Belongs to Caesar and to God What Belongs to God': A Theological Response of the Early Christian Church to its Social and Political Environment" in G Reimer and WM Swartely (eds and tr), *Love of Enemy and Nonretaliation in the New Testament* (Westminster John Knox 1992) 223–57. It is weakened by the fact that Paul mentions the vengeful punishments of the state in an altogether approving tone. He might even see them as proleptic of God's final vindication-revenge, which is promised to the believers in 12:19b.

[46] In particular the situation of the recently expelled and returned Jewish Christians might have been more than fragile. See N Elliott, "Rom. 13:1-7 in the Context of Imperial Propaganda"

Roman emperor. And granted, the demands of their constitution, mutual love in Christ, play out on a higher level than the principles of punishment and reward of the earthly πολιτεία. However, there is nevertheless considerable overlap between these two constitutions. The activities of the imperial authorities, even the pagan governors and functionaries, are working for "what is good" (Romans 13:4, εἰς τὸ ἀγαθόν). Paul does not qualify this statement, which is rather surprising, given his rhetoric in Romans 3:12 that "there is no-one, who does good."[47] The context makes it clear that "good" and "bad" relate to activities that are punishable by the government. The way in which the state is said to be "for your good" (v. 4) is in its activities to render judgment and prevent the horrors of complete lawlessness.[48] Even the Christian community with its eschatological focus still needs this space and gratefully acknowledges it. Paul makes no effort to hold the state accountable to some higher Christian good, but he reassures the believers that the state's activities will always be for "your good" too (v. 4), because the believers will do nothing bad to their neighbors (13:10) and therefore have no reason to fear the authorities' sword (v. 3). Paul is therefore convinced that the infinitely higher good of the Christian constitution effortlessly fulfills and embraces the less demanding good of civic decency, just as "the one who loves has fulfilled the (Jewish) law" (13:8). Because of this overlap and basic agreement, Christians need neither fear nor resist the state and are free to contribute toward an enterprise, which will be beneficial for them too.[49]

Paul's central achievements in this brief passage are twofold. First, he clearly distinguishes the activities of the state and the eschatological reality in which the church participates. The state is not an eschatological agent, and it

in RA Horsley (ed), *Paul and Empire: Religion and Power in Roman Imperial Society* (Trinity Press International 1997) 184–204, 191.

[47] Merklein rightly notes that "Eine inhaltliche Qualifizierung des ἀγαθόν oder Kriterien dafür werden nicht genannt." H Merklein, "Sinn und Zweck von Röm 13, 1–7: Zur semantischen und pragmatischen Struktur eines umstrittenen Texts" (1989) 261 Neues Testament und Ethik 238–270, 247.

[48] Oliver O'Donovan sees Paul as stripping temporal authority of two of its traditional functions, namely bringing about salvation and preserving tradition, and reduces its role *post Christum* to that of rendering judgment: "There remains simply the *rump* of political authority, which cannot be dispensed with yet, the exercise of judgment." See O'Donovan, *Desire*, 151. While the focus in Romans 13:1–7 is no doubt on judgment, I do not think that Paul has such a taxonomy in mind or conceives in fact of a different role for the state *post Christum*. For a further discussion of O'Donovan's interpretation of Romans 13 see D Bertschmann, *Bowing before Christ—Nodding to the State? Reading Paul Politically with Oliver O 'Donovan and John Howard Yoder* (T&T Clark 2014) esp 32–40 and 168–170.

[49] For a fuller exposition of this proposal cf. DH Bertschmann, "The Good, the Bad and the State: Romans 13:1–7 and the Dynamics of Love" (2014) 60 New Testament Studies 232–249.

is neither friend nor foe. Put differently, the church's present and coming Lord does not need the rulers of this world and is not threatened by them. Second, Paul manages to point out an overlap between the two "constitutions." Even pagan imperial governors can capture and embody the "goodness" of a law-ordered space, which deserves the believers' support and commands their respect and whole-hearted submission. More importantly, the believers' constitution of love, which commits no evil, brings them into harmony with the goals the state pursues, though theirs is a vastly different rule of life. However, these convictions will be sorely tested in times when imperial Rome would turn against Christians qua Christians, despite their law-abiding existence.

On this note we turn to the contribution of Revelation.

Revelation 17: "Babylon, mother of whores": Conflict

While the relationship with imperial Rome was not given much attention by the Matthean Jesus and was discussed in a reassuring tone by Paul, the seer John offers a comprehensive and devastating critique of empire in his visions.[50] In Revelation we encounter a situation where Christians have been killed at the hands of the authorities, though the context and extent of the persecution is unclear.[51] The collection of visions is directed in a circular letter to seven churches in Asia Minor (1:4). The point of contention is emperor worship, as the vision of the two beasts in chapter 13 makes clear.[52] The earthly ruler—who can be accommodated, relativized, and given a limited right by the people under God's constitution—has crossed a line by demanding god-like worship. This is far more than tension between two constitutions. The very issue of ultimate allegiance has come to the foreground and loyalty to the one God is under attack. Revelation responds to this attack by offering

[50] "John was not just anti-Roman; he was anti-empire." SJ Friesen, *Imperial Cults and the Apocalypse of John. Reading Revelation in the Ruins* (Oxford University Press 2001) 208

[51] The historical setting might be the aftermath of Nero's persecution in the sixties or the persecution under Domitian in the nineties. Other situations discussed are the rule of Vespasian and Titus after the Jewish war at the end of the first century or even the beginning of the second under Trajan and the persecution described by Pliny the Younger. For a brief discussion of various historical scenarios cf. JM Court, *Revelation* (Sheffield Academic Press 1994) 94–108.

[52] "They worshipped the beast, saying 'Who is like the beast, and who can fight against it?'" (13:4b; cf. 13:8 and 13:12). Bauckham suggests to see the beast from the sea, which was near mortally wounded but recovered, as "imperial Rome," which was in crisis after Nero's horrible rule and suicide. The beast from the earth stands for the protagonists of imperial worship, the propaganda machine of Rome. R Bauckham, *The Theology of the Book of Revelation* (Cambridge University Press 1993) 37.

an "alternative symbolic universe" seen from a heavenly perspective, which "open[s] the world to divine transcendence."[53]

In this universe the ongoing worship of God and the lamb is key.[54] God alone, who is creator of all, can claim absolute allegiance, not by naked power but by true authority. Like the far-flung Roman Empire, God's empire is multinational—it consists of people from "every tribe and language and people and nation" (Rev. 5:9) who have been bought by the lamb's blood in a costly, self-sacrificial act, which contrasts with the bloody conquests of Rome. The lamb, which thus exercises power through its sacrificial death, is the corecipient of worship.[55] The flipside of these heavenly worship scenes is a denunciation of an empire that has become demonic by claiming absolute power and honor. It is not human rule per se that is being decried, as the promise to the "saints" that "they shall rule on earth" (Rev. 5:10) makes clear. Rather, unrestrained political power, which absolutizes itself to the point of posing as divine, makes "Babylon" the target of God's fury and wrath. The shedding of blood of God's faithful servants is an important theme in its own right (Rev. 6:9–11) but also glaringly reveals the wider issue of an idolatrous use of political power.

In good apocalyptic fashion (see Daniel 7), Roman hegemony is depicted as a beast that emerges from the sea (chap. 13) and that rules in tandem with the beast from the earth, possibly representing the local elites, who readily cooperate with Roman power.[56] Thus, in chapter 17 the city of Rome is itself depicted as a whore: riding on a scarlet beast, she is "the great city, that rules over the kings of the earth" (17:18)—indicating, it seems, the city magistrates and client kings of Asia Minor.[57] While her downfall is predicted and mourned at great length by her former "clients" (chap. 18), at first glance the issue of "allegiance" seems to be discussed in fairly isolated and implicit fashion. Unlike the Maccabean martyrs, the believers in Revelation do not

[53] Bauckham, *Revelation,* 8.

[54] The heavenly worship is at first glance a parody of imperial worship ("Die Paraphernalia des Kaiserkultes sind deutlich sichtbar," HG Gradl, "Kaisertum und Kaiserkult: Ein Vergleich zwischen Philo's *Legatio ad Gaium* und der Offenbarung des Johannes" (2010) 56(1) New Testament Studies 116–138), except that for John imperial worship is the horribly perverted parody of the only truthful worship in heaven.

[55] For a chart that shows the progression in worship cf. Friesen, *Imperial Cults,* 199.

[56] Friesen, *Imperial Cults,* 202.

[57] A lot of the riddle presented in chapter 17 is very difficult to solve and cannot be worked out in a satisfactory way (e.g., the identity of the seven kings "of whom five have fallen, one is living, and the other has not yet come" [17:10]). However, the "seven heads" that are "seven mountains on which the woman is seated" would certainly point a first-century reader to Rome, "the city built upon seven hills." RH Mounce, *The Book of Revelation* (New International Commentary of the New Testament Eerdmans 1997) 316.

die for their ancestral laws, but rather for the "testimony of Jesus" (19:10). It is thus harder to perceive an alternative "divine constitution" on the part of the Christian believers. Good works are commended and vices and crimes decried (see the list of people banned from the heavenly Jerusalem in 21:8), but there is little description beyond this of a distinctive "way of life" in conformity to the Messiah.

However, as Bauckham points out, the self-absolutizing of political power, which is implied by the demand of divine worship and the refusal thereof, implies something like different shapes of constitutions.[58] Thus, the believers are characterized as those who not only "hold the testimony of Jesus" but also "keep the commandments of God" (12:17 and 14:12).[59] Apart from steadfastness in a trial, "holding on to the testimony of Jesus" means to refuse categorically any complicity in the demonic and inhuman system of the empire.[60]

The long funeral dirge in chapter 18 makes clear that Rome is not merely denounced for demanding worship, but also for its shameless luxurious lifestyle and oppressive economic system.[61] It will be judged not just for the shedding of the martyrs' blood, but for the blood "of all who have been slaughtered on earth" (18:24).[62] In good prophetic fashion the seer John connects idolatry with the breakdown of social justice, or, put differently, loyalty to the one God with the flourishing of the human community. In that sense the Christian martyrs can be seen as the canary in the pit, which is both particularly badly affected and prophetically alert to the abuse of political power.

With divine and earthly rule being pitted against each other in the sharpest possible contrast, there is little room left to reflect on the potential overlap of

[58] "It is a serious mistake to suppose that Revelation opposes the Roman Empire solely because of its persecution of Christians. Rather Revelation advances a thoroughgoing prophetic critique of the system of Roman power. It is a critique which makes Revelation the most powerful piece of political resistance literature from the period of the early Empire." Bauckham, *Revelation*, 38.

[59] Indeed, the name of Jesus might recall the mission and character of the earthly person, who is otherwise not mentioned. Perhaps it also means espousing the nonviolent ways of the lamb that was slain. Various authors point out that the lamb's kingdom "had been won not by inflicting suffering but by enduring suffering" (Friesen, *Imperial Cults*, 201), therefore completely subverting common standards of victory and omnipotence (cf. also JH Yoder, "The War of the Lamb" in his *Politics of Jesus*). However, given the violent campaign of the lamb and the torments inflicted on its enemies in chapters 16 and 19, I have some doubts about this view.

[60] The believers' response to the demonic "constitution" of the beast consists almost exclusively in resistance and endurance (e.g., 1:9, 2:2, 2:19).

[61] "The woman was dressed in purple and scarlet, and was glittering with gold, precious stones and pearls" (17:4).

[62] *Pace* Cullmann who is convinced that the persecution of Christians was a tragedy that could have been easily avoided if only the Roman state had not insisted on *a* cultic gesture of loyalty. O Cullmann, *The State in the New Testament* (SCM 1957) 53–55.

God's "constitution" and the activities of political rulers.[63] In the present time an inner and possibly outward exodus is asked of the Christian city dwellers, as they are called to endure and conquer in the apocalyptic power struggle ahead of them.

Conclusions

How does the confession of ultimate loyalty to ultimate authority and the sense of being shaped and held accountable by a divine constitution influence early Christian interaction with temporal power?

Starting with Matthew, we have seen a highly political vision of a newly constituted people of God gathered around a messianic leader who preaches an imminent kingdom of heaven. Nevertheless, we do not find a call for revolution against those who hold political power in a more narrow sense.[64] Roman power is not directly challenged and the personnel of imperial Rome are often treated with less hostility than Jesus's Jewish opponents. It is the latter conflict that takes center stage and escalates throughout the Gospel. In Matthew it is the new constitution of the Messiah Jesus that is the "better righteousness" exceeding and contrasting with the one of the scribes and Pharisees (Matt. 5:20). As part of this evolving conflict, Jesus is questioned about his attitude to the imperial tax. While affirming the concrete demands of taxes paid to the emperor, Jesus reframes the initial question in a larger vision of eschatological obedience, which puts the whole emphasis upon giving to God what is God's. The tax question is seen as deflecting from the matter of obedience to God and his Messiah, but the Matthean Jesus swiftly leads his opponents back to this, the only meaningful territory. The emperor is not given much attention at all; he may simply claim his money back. Like everybody else he stands in the shadow of God's imminent kingdom. It is this kingdom and its all-encompassing demands that is to claim Israel for a whole-hearted obedience. The emperor is neither friend nor foe in this drama of loyalty, which is not rendered fully to God by his people. In its

[63] Once again, it is important to see, though, that human rule is not demonized per se. The faithful martyrs shall share in God's rule; cf. the promise given to the church in Thyatira: "To everyone who conquers and continues to do my works to the end, I will give authority over the nations; to rule them with an iron rod" (3:26). The saints from every tribe and language will be "a kingdom and priests serving our God, and they will reign on earth" (5:10).

[64] This does not exclude "subversion" at the very deepest level of deconstructing ideas of rule or at the level of embodying an alternative vision of rule and community (see, e.g., Yoder, *Politics of Jesus*).

original context, therefore, the passage takes its reader's attention off the emperor and firmly focuses it on God, leaving it open what the demands of God might be and how they might go together with the emperor's in cases going beyond taxation. This underdefined openness, as well as the parallel structure of the demands, will be fertile ground for later generations to coordinate God's and the ruler's demands more precisely.

Paul has very similar instincts to Matthew at first glance. His grand narrative about God's Christ—who calls a new people out of Jews and Gentiles and who are to live according to the essence of the law, summed up as love in conformity with the Messiah who gave himself for humanity—is never directly connected with temporal rule. Paul shows a certain nonchalant indifference toward the rulers of this world, who simply are not eschatological agents for him. Like the Matthean Jesus, he counsels payment of taxes and other dues. Like Matthew, he has more important things on his mind, such as the shaping of God's people according to their new "constitution" of self-giving, forgiving love. Unlike Matthew, he attempts to link the activities of political rulers with the Christian "constitution" and to positively show a measure of overlap and harmony. The way of life the church is called to embody and express encompasses and fulfills with ease the minimum demands of civic decency, read as the principle of "nonharming," just as the Christian constitution fulfills the demands of the Jewish law. Believers can therefore be confident that the activities of state power will only ever affect them positively.

In Revelation the situation has changed. Christians have come to the attention of the Roman Empire qua Christians and have suffered at its hands. The demand of emperor worship is an impossible one for the believers in Asia Minor. Their only response can be to resist passively, to suffer, to endure, and to pray for vindication. What has been bracketed out by Matthew and Paul—the relationship between Christ and earthly "royal" figures—becomes the dominant issue now. The emperor and Christ are seen in a direct confrontation about blasphemous and true worship. The absolutizing of political power is decried as demonic. Though the critique is richer and broader than a mere ban of emperor worship, the notion of a distinctive Christian constitution fades in Revelation. In particular, the principle of love is hardly visible anymore. All energy is focused on the razor-edge issue of ultimate loyalty and worship.

And yet, paradoxically, the notion of the emperor as "Anti-Christ" might have paved the way to perceive him as "vice-Christ" after the Constantinian turn. After all, if an earthly ruler can be an evil eschatological agent, he might be directly enlisted for bringing in the kingdom of God too.

Every New Testament voice—Matthew's provocative nonchalance, Paul's low-key optimism, and Revelation's hostile critique—will need careful reconsideration and development once the church gains the support of the rulers of this world qua church and not just as individual believers.

4

Antiquity

Constantine and Constitutionalism

Peter J. Leithart

Histories of constitutionalism commonly ignore the late Roman Empire, including the period of the empire's Christianization. Charles Howard McIlwain, for example, discusses the influence of Justinian's *Institutes* on the development of Western political institutions, arguing that the Roman concept of the *populus* as the source of law came to fruition in medieval political organization more than in Renaissance absolutism. He recognizes that medieval Christendom played a significant role in the development of constitutional government, but his attention to the Christian empire is brief and superficial.[1] In a more recent survey of constitutionalism "from ancient Athens to today," Scott Gordon refers to Constantine only once, in a reference to the spurious Donation of Constantine, and his narrative moves rapidly from a discussion of Roman government to the concept of "countervailence" in the Middle Ages.[2]

The reasons for this neglect are fairly obvious. Constitutionalism focuses on limiting state power. For Thomas Paine (1737–1809), the distinction between constitution and government is fundamental.[3] Constitutions are antecedent to governments. They define the authority of governments and, importantly, the limits of that authority. Any exercise of power beyond the limits of the constitution is an exercise in power without right. When there is no prior constitution, then there is no *legal* recourse against the abuses of government. Without a constitution, "the will of the government has no

[1] Charles Howard McIlwain, *Constitutionalism: Ancient and Modern* (Cornell University Press 1947) 44–58.

[2] Scott Gordon, *Controlling the State: Constitutionalism from Ancient Athens to Today* (Harvard University Press 2002). The reference to the Donation occurs on p 150.

[3] See Thomas Paine, *Common Sense and Other Writings* (Barnes & Noble 2005) 322.

Peter J. Leithart, *Antiquity: Constantine and Constitutionalism* in *Christianity and Constitutionalism*.
Edited by: Nicholas Aroney and Ian Leigh, Oxford University Press.
DOI: 10.1093/oso/9780197587256.003.0004

check upon it, and that state is in fact a despotism."[4] Or, the only check on a government's abuse of power is the sheer extralegal force of the opposition.

Imperial Rome had a constitution of sorts, unwritten and evolving, more similar to the British than the American constitutional tradition. Yet in the late empire, the word of the emperor was to be obeyed as law.[5] Diocletian (244–311) reorganized the empire, diminishing the role of the Senate and adopting the title *Dominus*, which replaced *Princeps*. Since there were no checks on the emperor's will besides the potential force of a rival, the late Roman Empire was, on Paine's definition, a despotism. It appears that this period makes no contribution to Western constitutionalism. The late empire rather represents the governmental form that constitutionalism *overcomes*.

I argue here that, contrary to expectation, the late empire and the reign of Constantine in particular are crucial to the development of constitutional systems. Without Constantine (ca. 272–337, reigned 306–337), the Western tradition would not be a tradition of *Christian* political reflection. That much is obvious. What is not obvious is that Constantine's conversion was crucial to the development of Western constitutional principles. Harold Berman famously pointed to the Gregorian Revolution and canon law as foundation stones for the Western legal tradition.[6] To develop its own system of law, the church first needed to have liberty to survive without harassment, and without functioning as an arm of state authority. By the time of Gregory VII (pope from 1073 to 1085), of course, the Roman empire was long gone, and the church's independence had been secured by virtue of historical accident. Centuries before, Constantine laid the foundation beneath the medieval substructure by granting legal recognition to the Christian church. Important as they were, medieval institutions depended on the achievements of the Christian empire.[7]

Constantine's main contribution to constitutionalism was to recognize the Christian church as a legal entity. In the first part of this chapter, I outline Lactantius's theological argument for religious liberty and Constantine's

[4] McIlwain, *Constitutionalism*, 9.

[5] This is the opinion of Justinian's *Institutes*, quoting from Ulpian. Quoted in McIlwain, *Constitutionalism*, 44.

[6] Harold Berman, *Law and Revolution: The Formation of the Western Legal Tradition* (Harvard University Press 1983).

[7] Exploring the Christian roots of Western political order is no mere academic concern but a live issue in contemporary politics. Cf. Pope Benedict XVI's pleas for Europeans to take note of their Christian roots, not merely for historical reasons and not merely to protect the church's rights, but to preserve the common moral culture of Europe. John F Thornton and Susan B Varenne (eds), *The Essential Pope Benedict XVI: His Central Writings and Speeches* (HarperOne 2008) 328–329.

implementation of the Lactantian settlement. Lactantius (240–320), a rhetorician and a convert to Christianity, served as an advisor to Constantine and tutored the emperor's son, Crispus. Whatever Constantine may have expected, legalizing the church was not merely recognition of another religious organization. As a purely sociological phenomenon, the church was unique in the ancient world, and, of course, the church claimed to be much more than a purely sociological phenomenon. She claimed to be the bearer of the meaning of human history, a holy and separate people that was a sign of a perfected community of the future. In recognizing the church, Constantine inaugurated a "migration of the holy," a shift of the locus of sanctity from the prince to the church.[8] Legalization of the church was a blow to the belief in "sacral kingship" that was common in ancient politics right up to the imperium of Diocletian. Practically, after Constantine, Christian emperors recognized the church's leaders as spokesmen of God, to whom they were accountable. The fifth-century Gelasian theory of "two powers" or "two swords" was a Christianized form of the "separation of powers" as the church provided a "check and balance," a real counterweight to imperial authority.

The Church and the Limits of State Authority

Conservative political thinkers often describe religious liberty as the "first freedom."[9] The most basic constitutional limit on government is the prohibition of government regulation of belief. Constantine's key contribution to the history of constitutionalism was to secure this first freedom. Importantly, however, this was not merely a recognition of freedom of belief. Constantine legally recognized religious practice, specifically *Christian* practice.

The emperor's church-state settlement reflects the thinking of the rhetor Lactantius.[10] Most of the apologists who defended the church in the early centuries advocated freedom of religion. For some, its use was tactical;

[8] The phrase "migration of the holy" is taken from William T Cavanaugh, *Migrations of the Holy: God, State, and the Political Meaning of the Church* (Eerdmans 2011). Cavanaugh's book describes the modern migration of sanctity from the church to the nation-state. Cavanaugh in turn borrows the phrase from John Bossy, *Christianity in the West 1400–1700* (Oxford University Press 1985).

[9] Michael McConnell, "Why Is Religious Freedom the 'First Freedom'?" (2000) 21 Cardozo Law Review 1243.

[10] The following pages are taken, with revisions, from my *Defending Constantine: The Twilight of an Empire and the Dawn of Christendom* (IVP 2010).

freedom was the rhetoric of an oppressed minority. Lactantius, however, developed a *theological* argument for religious freedom.

Lactantius's basic plea was for freedom of conscience. "Religion is the one field in which freedom has pitched her tent," he wrote, "for religion is, first and foremost, a matter of free will, and no man can be forced under compulsion to adore what he has no will to adore." At best, coercion will force people to make a "hypocritical show" of devotion, but force cannot make a man or woman willing to worship. "If, then, anyone, out of fear of the tools of torture or vanquished by the torture itself, finally assents to the accursed pagan sacrifice, he never acts of his own free will, as compulsion was involved." This is obvious from the fact that "as soon as opportunity offers and he recovers his freedom, he comes back to his God and begs with tears for forgiveness, doing penance for that which he did, not of his own free will, which he did not possess, but under the compulsion to which he submitted, and the Church will not withhold its forgiveness." To the persecutors, he asked, "What good can you do, then, if you defile the body but cannot break the will?"[11]

Lactantius's *Divine Institutes* was in part a response to Porphyry's treatise against Christians and his treatise on *Philosophy from Oracles*. Porphyry believed that many roads led to the truth and bliss, including the way of Jesus. Yet this did not lead Porphyry to endorse a policy of toleration or religious freedom. Christians worshiped a *man*—a good man, to be sure, but only a man. Porphyry did not think the Roman Empire could tolerate man-worshiping Christians indefinitely. Christianity's humanism offended the gods and needed to be stopped. Porphyry advocated "threatening the use of force against those who worshiped a human being" but at the same time "suggested that Christianity, by forsaking its worship of Jesus, might be made compatible with traditional worship and philosophy."[12] Christians should conform to Roman practice, by offering the prescribed sacrifices. They can believe whatever they like, so long as they do what the empire and its gods demand.

In responding to Porphyry, Lactantius argued for a fuller concept of religious freedom. It was not enough to allow religious belief. Rome should also protect the liberty of religious practice.

[11] Lactantius, *Divine Institutes*, 49. Quoted in Andrew Alfoldi, *The Conversion of Constantine and Pagan Rome* (H Mattingly tr, OUP 1969) 53; cf. Harold Drake, *Constantine and the Bishops: The Politics of Intolerance* (Johns Hopkins 2000) 211.

[12] Elizabeth Digeser, *The Making of a Christian Empire: Lactantius and Rome* (Cornell University Press 2000) 108.

Lactantius cleverly drew on earlier strands of Roman political theology. Cicero had claimed that God should be approached chastely and with piety, and Lactantius took this to mean that a true God does not want force used in religion, since a forced religion cannot be chaste and pious. Force pollutes rather than purifies religion: "if you wish to defend religion by bloodshed, and by tortures, and by guilt, it will no longer be defended, but will be polluted and profaned."[13]

Lactantius also deployed traditional Roman ideals of freedom. As in the "Edict of Milan" promulgated by Constantine and Licinius, the keynote of Lactantius's argument was *libertas*. *Libertas* pitches her tent in the area of religion, and religion expresses itself in *voluntaria* rather than in *necessitas*. *Libertas* had a long history in Roman political theology.[14] Caesar and Octavian both posed as liberators of Rome, saviors who restored the glorious Roman past. Constantine's imperial propaganda rang the same note. The triumphal arch completed in 315 granted him the title *liberator urbis*; other inscriptions in the capital acclaimed him *restitutor libertatis publicae*; and coins called him *Restitutor Romae* and *Recuperatori urbis suae*. Much the same was implied by the designation of Constantine as *princeps*, for the prince was the expected "suppressor of tyranny and the surety for freedom."[15] Though drawing on the imperial ideology of the past, Lactantius redefined tyranny as religious compulsion. Porphyry was a propagandist of tyranny, and Lactantius branded Diocletian, Maxentius, Licinius, and the rest as enemies of *libertas*, as sub-Roman tyrants.

Perhaps inspired by Lactantius, Constantine forged a religious policy that seamlessly wove Christian and Roman themes together and set the ideological foundations for a Christian, yet tolerant, Roman Empire. The theory was expressed in the inscription on the statue of Constantine in Rome. He holds the sign of Christ, and the inscription reads: "in this sign of salvation I have restored to Rome, her senate, and her people, their ancient liberty and glory, delivering them from the lawless yoke of the tyrant."[16] The inscription could have adorned a statue of Octavian, who also claimed to fight for the *libertas*

[13] Lactantius, *Divine Institutes*, 5.20; see Digeser, *Making of a Christian Empire*, 57–60.

[14] CH Wirszubski, *Libertas as a Political Idea at Rome during the Late Republic and Early Principate* (CUP 1950).

[15] Alfoldi, *Conversion of Constantine and Pagan Rome*, 64.

[16] Alfoldi (*Conversion of Constantine and Pagan Rome*, 83) makes the case for this policy very effectively and concisely. He reconstructs the Latin as "Hoc salutary signo . . . senatui populoque Romano et urbi Romae iugo tyrannicae dominationis ereptae pristinam libertatem splendoremque reddidi."

of the *SPQR* and who claimed to bring "salvation" for the people. But the Christian symbol changed everything: Rome's *libertas* was now secure only *in hoc signo*—in *this* sign. And that meant that *libertas* was extended to the once-maligned Christian church.

As a Lactantian Christian emperor, Constantine tolerated paganism. That was the policy established in 313, and it was reiterated, more elaborately, after he defeated Licinius and assumed the sole imperium in 324. His "Edict to the Eastern Provinces," issued in 324, was an unusually didactic decree.[17] Constantine attacked the irrationality of polytheism and defended monotheism. He recalled his father's kindness to the church with fondness and recounted the arrogance and stupidity of the persecuting emperors, "unsound in mind" and "more zealous of cruel than gentle measures." They turned a period of peace and prosperity into a virtual civil war and proved themselves more savage than the barbarians, among whom Christians found refuge. Like Lactantius, he rejoiced that the persecutors "have experienced a miserable end, and are consigned to unceasing punishment in the depths of the lower world." He insulted the Pythian oracle as "impious" and "delusive" and described Christianity as a "holy" religion.

Having exposed the error, the savagery, the political evils of paganism, just when the reader is ready for the hammer to fall, Constantine revealed the legal thrust of the edict. Insisting that his desire was "for the common good of the world and the advantage of all mankind, that your people should enjoy a life of peace and undisturbed concord," he declared that "anyone who delight[s] in error, be made welcome to the same degree of peace and tranquility which they have who believe." He did not want them to remain in their ignorance and error, but instead hoped that "this restoration of equal privileges to all will prevail to lead them into the straight path." No one was to molest anyone else's religion: "let every one do as his soul desires." It was true that it is only possible to live a life of "holiness and purity" if one relies on the "holy laws" of "men of sound judgment." But Constantine was willing to permit "those who will hold themselves aloof from us" to keep their "temples of lies."

Constantine gave a Lactantian rationale for the policy: "The battle for deathlessness requires willing recruits. Coercion is of no avail." There is a vast difference between pursuing immortality "voluntarily" and compelling

[17] Eusebius gives the edict in full in *Life of Constantine*, 2.48–60. This is taken from the edition of Averil Cameron and Stuart G Hall (Clarendon Press 1999).

"others to do so from the fear of punishment." As it came to a close, the edict modulated from imperial pronouncement to prayer: "we"—he meant "we Christians"—"have the glorious edifice of your truth, which you have given us as our native home. We pray, however, that they too may receive the same blessing, and thus experience that heartfelt joy which unity of sentiment inspires."[18] Though framed as an official imperial document, from "Victor Constantinus, Maximus Augustus, to the people of the Eastern provinces," it was more sermon than law. Constantine was less a theocrat imposing Christianity than Billy Graham issuing an altar call.

For most pagans, Constantine's conversion was a "bearable evil," and Constantine continued to have pagan philosophers in his court for years after his conversion.[19] Pagans continued to serve in his administration and army, and he gave pagans high positions. A pagan helped him gather materials from around the East to adorn his great "Christian" city of Constantinople. His policies toward the army were particularly significant. Diocletian, Galerius, and Licinius had expelled Christians from the army because their presence offended the gods and might lead to defeat. Theodosius II later adapted this principle when he reversed, or revived, Diocletian's policy and restricted the army to Christians. Wearing a helmet emblazoned with the first letters of "Christ" (chi-rho) and bearing his shield painted with a cross, Constantine kept pagan troops and led them in a monotheistic prayer that he knew would not violate their consciences.[20]

It was a remarkable balancing act. Elizabeth Digeser offers terminology and categories that help make sense of Constantine's policies. She distinguishes forbearance from toleration, and tolerance from "concord," and explains Constantine's policy as a progression from tolerance to concord. Forbearance is a pragmatic policy, a necessary restraint, not guided by moral or political principle. Forbearance might change to persecution if the political conditions change. Rome persecuted the church sporadically between the first-century reign of Nero and the fourth-century imperium

[18] His concluding remarks suggest that Constantine issued the decree in part to cool hot-headed Christians who might want to take advantage of their political clout to shut down all pagan shrines immediately, or who might even believe that paganism had suddenly died. Instead of attacking pagans, Christians should be mixing with and evangelizing them. "Once more," he added, "let none use that to the detriment of another which he may himself have received on conviction of its truth; but let every one, if it be possible, apply what he has understood and known to the benefit of his neighbor; if otherwise, let him relinquish the attempt."

[19] Drake, *Constantine and the Bishops*, 247–249. Drake quotes the phrase "bearable evil" from Friedhelm Winkelmann.

[20] H Dorries, *Constantine the Great* (Harper and Row 1960) 37–39.

of Diocletian, but the periods of Roman acceptance of Christianity were periods of forbearance. Rome never acknowledged the church's legal right to exist. Toleration is "disapproval or disagreement coupled with an unwillingness to take action against those viewed with disfavor in the interest of some moral or political principle."[21] This principle could arise, as for Lactantius, from a theory concerning the nature of religion or, alternatively, from a theory about human nature, or about the limits of state power. By this definition, toleration does not involve an idea of the equality of all viewpoints but the opposite. Toleration assumes *disapproval* of certain religious expressions but refrains for principled reasons from using state power to suppress the disapproved religion.

Beyond toleration, Digeser introduces the category of "concord," which has the following two characteristics: "(1) its attitude of forbearance is dictated by some moral, political, or even religious principle and (2) it expects that by treating its dissenters with forbearance it is creating conditions under which they will ultimately change their behavior to conform to what the state accepts."[22] These three categories of religious policy build on one another: toleration assumes forbearance but is principled; concord assumes toleration, but in addition to basing forbearance on principle, it expects that the forbearance will have the ultimate outcome of unity if not complete uniformity.[23]

Digeser concludes that Constantine remained Lactantian but gradually moved from a policy of toleration to one of concord, especially after his defeat of Licinius in 324. "Constantine's newly disparaging attitude toward some elements of traditional cult," she argues, "marked a move away from a policy of religious liberty—in which traditional cult was not criticized—toward a policy of concord, in which forbearance toward the temple cults was intended as a means of achieving ultimate religious unity."[24]

Drawing from Lactantius, Constantine forged a policy of religious freedom, tilted in favor of Christianity. But what did he make free when he made the church free? What sort of entity did the emperor admit into Roman political life?

[21] Digeser, *Making of a Christian Empire*, 110.
[22] Digeser, *Making of a Christian Empire*, 110.
[23] For more on *concordia*, particularly in the thought of St. Augustine, see chapter 5 by Mary Keys and Colleen Mitchell below.
[24] Digeser, *Making of a Christian Empire*, 125.

The Metapolitics of Christendom

Constantine's liberation of the church and his policy of concord were imperial self-limitations. They were not embedded in a settled constitutional system that imposed *legal* restraints on the emperor's will. His will was still law, and a later emperor might flout Constantine's precedent and adopt a different policy (as Julian the Apostate [330–363] did for a time). Yet, in liberating the church, Constantine set up the preconditions for the development of institutionalized, legal constraints on the exercise of power. Without setting out to reconfigure the structures of Roman politics, the church did exactly that, and this political restructuring flowed out of convictions and practices that were fundamental to Christianity. To see how this is so, we have to examine how the "metapolitics" inherent in Christianity undermined the assumptions and institutions of antique political order.

Francis Oakley has recently argued that sacral kingship was the chief ancient form of political order, and one that had remarkable staying power far into the medieval and modern world. Sacral kingship is typically rooted in a royal cosmology that views God or the chief god as the king of the universe. The human king is an earthly figure of that heavenly, cosmic reign. In Hellenistic times, this archaic conception of kingship was given philosophical support. According to this conception, the world is governed by a logos, the "reason of the universe" analogous to ruling reason in a human being, and the king incarnates or somehow channels this logos. He does not merely *represent* the heavenly divine king; he is the agent through whom the heavenly divine king achieves justice and peace and fruitfulness on the earth. In short, "the king was conceived as 'a dynamic and personal revelation of deity,' a 'living law' (*nomos empsychos*; *lex animata*), 'himself the state, its constitution and its link with the world order.' "[25]

Hellenistic kingship triumphed in the Roman world. Republican Rome was an experiment in limited, mixed, constitutional government but, Oakley argues, never entirely shed its religious underpinnings. When kingship revived in the empire, it took on the trappings of the Hellenistic transformation of Oriental kingship, reaching a peak in the third century AD.[26] Between 235 and 285, Roman imperial government was "transformed into an absolute monarchy of quasi-oriental type," marked by the shift from *princeps* to

[25] Francis Oakley, *Kingship: The Politics of Enchantment* (Wiley-Blackwell 2006) 47–48.
[26] Ibid, 48.

dominus as the title of the emperor. Under this Hellenized Roman concept, the "will of the emperor, himself supreme judge and court of last appeal . . . was now, in effect, the dominant source of law."[27] Diocletian, Constantine's predecessor, brought Roman sacral kingship to its fullest expression.[28] On this basis, nothing like a constitution in Paine's sense can function. There is no check on the king's authority, no appeal beyond his decree.

Meanwhile, the Abrahamic religions developed a political outlook that could arrest the development of sacral kingship and a relocation of the sacred. Oakley points to the biblical doctrine of creation, which severed the continuum between God and the creation that had been used to support the king's sacral status. In pagan systems, the king was no mere man but a divine being, a manifestation of the god. In scripture, kings were all-too-human mixtures of virtues and vices, flawed heroes at best.[29] But sacral kingship proved hard to kill. When Constantine became the first Christian emperor, his apologists transposed the Hellenistic concept into a new key. Drawing on the Hellenic-Jewish synthesis of Philo of Alexandria, Eusebius of Caesarea described Constantine in terms that resembled the Hellenistic conception. The logos was now identified with Jesus, but Eusebius suggested that the emperor could, by close association with the incarnate logos, become a channel of divine power. Always there was the reservation that the emperor was not divine. Yet notions of sacral kingship persisted into the Christian empire and Byzantium. In Byzantium, the church was incorporated into the imperial system, which was supposed to reflect a harmony of spiritual and political authority.

It is true that some Christian intellectuals adapted sacral kingship to the new Christian empire. By focusing on cosmo-political *ideas*, however, Oakley misses the crucial contribution that this age made to the development of Western constitutionalism. The gospel inserted itself into the Roman world not merely as a confession or proclamation, but as a communion with institutional form. Without becoming directly political, Christianity exerted a decisive political role.[30] Christian convictions about Jesus, his death, the church, the Eucharist, and the future established a "metapolitical" framework that nurtured new possibilities for Western political life.

27 Ibid, 69.

28 Digeser, *Making of a Christian Empire*, 28.

29 Oakley, *Kingship*, 54.

30 The next several pages are a revision of a section of my *Between Babel and Beast: America and Empires in Biblical Perspective* (Wipf & Stock 2012).

Sheldon Wolin has argued that by the early part of the Roman Empire, political thought had become exhausted. Aristotle's systematic treatment of politics was applicable within the bounded space of the Greek *polis*, but the Roman imperial system had stretched the categories of Aristotelian political thought to the breaking point. Hellenistic and Roman theorists attempted to give cosmological grounding to political order, and by doing so raised politics into the realm of metaphysics. It did not work: "The reconstruction of political thought . . . was a process that began in paradox and ended in irony." Christianity appeared in this exhausted intellectual world, and "it fell to Christianity to revivify political thought."[31]

Christianity did not *aim* to revive antique political thought and life. On the contrary, the early Christians were almost apolitical, and many of the leaders of the early church boasted of the church's freedom from polluting involvement in politics. Yet,

> Christianity succeeded where the Hellenistic and late classical philosophies had failed, because it put forward a new and powerful ideal of community which called men to a life of meaningful participation. Although the nature of this community contrasted sharply with classical ideals, although its ultimate purpose lay beyond historical time and space, it contained, nevertheless, ideals of solidarity and membership that were to leave a lasting imprint, and not always for good, on the Western tradition of political thought.[32]

The church revived political thought because she was a *church*, a quasi-political yet apolitical community, soon as international as the empire itself yet lacking an earthly homeland, an army, or a visible emperor. The church was an unprecedented social and political form and burst the bonds of prior political categories.

According to Wolin, the sheer existence of the church and notions of church memberships revolutionized the "idea of political obligation." Classical political thought had insisted that human beings reached happiness, the good life, the telos of human existence, in political life. This conviction was so strong that perverse regimes or unjust laws could raise doubts

[31] Sheldon Wolin, *Politics and Vision: Continuity and Innovation in Western Political Thought* (expanded ed, Princeton University Press 2016) 86.
[32] Ibid., 87.

"about membership in political society per se." Stoics claimed "allegiance to a universal society of rational beings" but never imagined "a genuine alternative to the political order."[33]

Christians, however, "could entertain meaningful doubts about political obligation and membership" without having to face "a hard choice between membership in a political society and membership in no society at all." A Christian could choose "because already he belonged to a society that surpassed any existing one in the things that mattered most." For the first time, "the politically uncommitted [previously restricted to the odd Cynic or Stoic] had been gathered into a determinate society of their own." For the first time, political disengagement "went hand in hand with the rediscovery of community, albeit one pitched to a transcendent key."[34] Christians were not faced with the Socratic choice between compromise or exile. It was not for nothing that Roman emperors and their subordinates came to regard Christians with suspicion. Peaceable as they were, they were a subversive force in ancient political life. Christian communities also tended to ignore social divisions. Slaves could participate in the political community of the church in ways that they never could in the classical *polis* or the Roman Empire.

The Christian sense of the church as the political community to which they owed loyalty was reinforced by a fresh reading of history, which grew from typological interpretations of scripture. What emerged as the mainstream mode of reading linked Israel with the *church*, as promise and fulfillment or as distinctive stages of the single history of the kingdom of God or both together. On this reading, the fulfillment of God's Abrahamic promise through Jesus forms a kingdom as odd in its constitution as exilic Israel, a polity-within-worldly-polities that was wholly unlike every other polity. Kings like Constantine might be typified by David and Solomon in an attenuated sense, but strictly speaking, the antitype of David is Jesus or Jesus-with-his-body, who are made kings and priests in him. Before emperors can be construed as David-like, they must become subjects of the imperium *Dei*. Fundamentally, there is no sacral king but Jesus.

Christian history telling displaced sacral kings and their kingdoms from the center of history. A wandering Aramean is the man who bears the destiny of the nations—not any pharaoh or Babylonian king. Pharaohs and other

[33] Ibid, 92.
[34] Ibid.

kings play bit parts to kings of the Davidic dynasty, whose heroism is a heroism of devotion to Yahweh, God of Israel.

Christian liturgical practice was as subversive of sacral kingship as Christian teaching. Ancient order had been built around rites of sacrifice. Crudely put, Roman sacrifice was a contract with the gods: Rome kept the gods happy through sacrifice so that the gods would keep Rome happy. The church broke the sacrificial social contract.[35] Roman emperors (including Constantine) were not merely imperators but priests, holding the post of *pontifex maximus*. At great state and religious festivals, the sacred emperor played the role of chief sacrificer.

The church introduced an alternative sacrificial center and so rearranged the topography of holiness in practice as well as in theory. At the center of the new Christian community was a new ritual, the quasi-sacrifice of the Eucharist. Through participation in the Eucharist, the members of the church were formed into a more-than-human community, a human society constituted by its common participation in the living God-man, Jesus Christ. Christian belief in "a mystical body cohering around a godhead" was unprecedented in Western political thought, and by this concept "Christianity helped father the idea of a community as a non-rational, non-utilitarian body bound by a meta-rational faith, infused by a mysterious spirit taken into the members; a spirit that not only linked each participant with the center of Christ, but radiated holy ties knitting each member to his fellows."[36] Each Christian who shared in the sacrificial feast of the Eucharist was a saint (Gr. *hagios*), a holy one, sacred by the indwelling of the Holy Spirit.

By this concept, "the Christian community was not so much an association as a fusion of spirits, a pneumatic being." Eucharist was seen as the sacramental embodiment of the fulfilled project of divine imperium that began with Abraham. The community gathered at the Eucharistic meal "crossed all ethnic borders" and achieved a "unity that was not abstract, nor was it made by coercion or force," yet constituted a depth of "political allegiance" that had never before been achieved. In the Eucharist the church ritually enacted "a transcendent vision that not even the most expansive understanding of 'empire' could have competed with."[37] As David McIlroy says elsewhere in this volume, the Spirit witnesses to the Fatherhood of God and the kingship of

[35] I borrow the notion of a sacrificial Roman "social contract" from Ryan Lief Hansen, *Silence and Praise: Rhetorical Cosmology and Political Theology in the Book of Revelation* (Fortress 2014) 8.

[36] Wolin, *Politics and Vision*, 119.

[37] Ibid.

Jesus, the "firstborn from the dead, and ruler of the kings of the earth" (Rev. 1:4).[38] Binding the holy ones at the table, the Spirit testifies to the reality of the church as subjects of a new kingdom.

Even before Constantine, Christians had been laying a novel sacrificial groundwork for God's imperium. "Jesus is Lord," said the early Christians in opposition to Roman claims that Caesar was Lord, and their verbal witness was backed up with the enacted witness of martyrdom. The sacrificial deaths of the martyrs, intended by the Romans as a sacrificial prophylactic for and renewal of the *pax Romana*, instead exposed the naked power of Rome in all its pathetic weakness: "The martyr [like Jesus] denies the state power, while yielding to its violence. . . . This is not a kind of quietism in the face of the state, but a faith imbued with an idea of resistance from the very beginning." In this sense, "resistance to the state is built into the fundamental tenets of Christianity."[39] Even after Rome reconciled to Christianity, "the threat of martyrdom is always a dangerous power that the religious can wield against the state. It is the means by which the religious claim an indefeasible power: if defeat means martyrdom, then the state's victory is always precarious."[40] In her regular Eucharistic celebrations, the church refreshed her collective memory not only of Jesus's sacrificial death but also of the sacrificial deaths of those who suffered as Jesus did. In refreshing her collective memory, the church also refreshed her collective determination to resist rulers or politics that claimed authority that belonged to her Lord. The faithful resistance of martyrs opened or exposed fissures in the foundations of Rome. Rome had either to tolerate Christians and acknowledge the competitive imperium of the church or kill peaceable believers and risk exposure as fearful bullies. From Nero to Diocletian, Rome's emperors more or less followed the latter course, and the blood of saints rose to haunt them. Constantine wisely chose the former, but by incorporating a community of martyrs into Roman order, Constantine (perhaps unwittingly) institutionalized resistance to imperial whim.

In Western Christendom and Byzantium, "political order" in the narrow sense was re-embedded by the metapolitical reality of the church. At the heart of Constantine's achievement was the empire's recognition of the church as an independent polity or order of its own; the civil order's (often-grudging) acceptance of the quasi-civic order of the church in its midst; the

[38] See chapter 17 below by McIlroy.
[39] Paul Kahn, *Putting Liberalism in Its Place* (Princeton University Press 2008) 81–84.
[40] Ibid, 51.

acknowledgment of the Eucharist as the sacrificial center of a polity, a sacrificial center *not* controlled by the state; and civil government's embrace of the church's end—the kingdom of God—as its own end. Constitutional government in the West took shape within the metapolitics of Christological and ecclesial typology, a political ecclesiology, Eucharistic practice that nourished the spirit of martyrdom, and eschatology.[41]

Conclusion: Check and Balance

Pope Gelasius articulated the classic formula of the two powers of priest and king in the fifth century, nearly two centuries after Constantine's conversion and his liberation of the church. The Gelasian model lies at the root of Western concepts of "separation of powers," and the Gelasian model is rooted in turn in the achievement of Constantine.

By giving legal recognition to the church, Constantine created a rival that could serve as a check on the pretentions of political power. As noted earlier, Eusebius merged the radical politics of the church with traditions of sacral kingship, and Byzantine *symphonia* attempted to harmonize emperor and bishop. Even in the Byzantine East, however, the church never ceded her independence.[42] For their part, Western clergy overtly claimed the right to correct and check the abuses of imperial power. Ambrose's famed, and successful, confrontation of the emperor Theodosius provided an example of clerical authority for bishops and popes throughout the Middle Ages.

Importantly, the check on imperial and later royal power was not merely theoretical. It had institutional weight because of the church's status as an independent quasi-polity existing alongside the more conventional polities of the medieval West. Even on the grounds of Christianized sacral kingship, the church's sanctions had weight because the king's status depended upon

[41] On the significance of eschatology see in this volume Douglas Farrow, "The Greater Operation of Liberty."

[42] According to George Demacopoulos and Aristotle Papanikolaou, "Even after Constantine, Christians maintained a pre-Constantinian critical distance between church and state. One way to interpret the well-known model of symphonia, enshrined in Justinian's Sixth Novella, is to see the 'established' Church, even with all of its growing privileges, as distinct from the state. From the fourth century up until the fall of Constantinople, there are numerous examples, including writings of patristic thinkers, monastic protestations, and emperor-bishop squabbles, that testify to the continuation of a pre-Constantinian Christian consciousness as a community distinct from the political." They assert that "one would be hard-pressed to find a moment in Christian history where this Christian consciousness is ever eviscerated." "Editorial Introduction," *Christianity, Democracy, and the Shadow of Constantine* (Fordham University Press 2016).

participation in sacraments and sacramentals—the sacramental of royal anointing and the sacrament of the Mass. If a ruler were cut off from the Mass, his kingdom might come under the interdict, or the pope might release his subjects from their obligation to obey.

Again, here we see continuity between the resistance of the martyr church and the institutionalized counterweight of the post-Constantinian church. The martyr church was not a separatist organization that kept its distance from contact with pagans.[43] *Before* Constantine, the clash between church and empire was intense precisely because the church claimed that the world belonged to Jesus.[44] The church did not begin outside and move inward during the early fourth century. It was on the inside of the Greco-Roman world from the beginning. The clash between martyr and provincial governor is fundamentally the *same clash* as that between Ambrose and Theodosius. Before rulers began listening to episcopal rebukes, they were confronted with humble witnesses who exposed the limits of their power every time they sang Psalms in the midst of the flames.

Persecuting emperors did not know it, but the flames they kindled for martyrs consumed their own sacral pretentions and remade Roman, and Western, politics forever.

[43] G. W. Bowersock contrasts the stance of Christians and Jews toward the Greco-Roman world: "It was precisely the Christians' vigorous participation in the civic life and intellectual traditions of the Graeco-Roman world that grounded their martyrdoms in the life of the great cities. The Jews, by contrast, had conspicuously chosen a different path by remaining altogether separate in their conduct of life, except, of course, on those public occasions when the Christian martyrs united them with the polytheists in giving expression to a community hostility. But we find no Jewish rabbis teaching the people of Smyrna or Pergamum or Carthage, as Polycarp, Papylus, and Cyprian did." *Martyrdom and Rome* (CUP 1995) 56.

[44] Here I differ somewhat from the position outlined in Dorothea Bertschmann's chapter in this volume. Admittedly, the picture is complex. On the one hand, the fundamental Christian claim was that "Jesus is *kurios*," which carries the obvious corollary that Caesar is *not*. Jesus is the king of Psalm 2, heir of the nations (Acts 4:25–27). And Jesus shares his inheritance with his people: Paul wrote that Abraham was the "heir of the world" (Rom. 4:13), a promise given to Abraham's seed, the church, which constituted the "children" and "heirs" of Abraham (Gal. 3:7, 29). This is the root of what Pierre Manent has described as the "theocratic" tendency of Christianity (*An Intellectual History of Liberalism* [Rebecca Balinski tr, Princeton University Press 1995] 4–6). At the same time, the church adopted a detached, seemingly apolitical stance toward the world. As Manent puts it, with some exaggeration, "'This world,' 'Caesar's world,' did not interest [the church]" (ibid, 4). The latter stance is more obvious in patristic literature than the first. Patristic writers tend to transpose Paul's "world" into an eschatological inheritance—eternal life, the world to come, the kingdom of God. Even so, the "theocratic" language of Christ's kingship is pervasive in patristic writing, precisely because it is pervasive in the Bible.

5

Patristic Era

Augustine's Constitutionalism: Citizenship, Common Good, and Consent

Mary M. Keys and Colleen E. Mitchell

A chapter on the constitutional thought of Augustine of Hippo (354–430 AD) may seem somewhat odd from the outset.[1] Augustine is, after all, often described as indifferent to or at least little interested in forms of government, arrangements of offices, and legal codes, the stuff of regimes or constitutional orders in this world, so long as the public power wielded by these institutions does not compel persons to perform unjust or impious deeds.[2] Augustine is

[1] Some scholarly work on Augustine on constitutionalism and law does, however, exist. See, e.g., Graham Walker, *Moral Foundations of Constitutional Thought* (Princeton University Press 1990) esp 3–8, 63–64, 71–75, 164–165; Richard O Brooks and James Bernard Murphy, *Augustine and Modern Law* (Ashgate Publishing 2011); Anton-Hermann Chroust, "The Philosophy of Law of St. Augustine" (1944) 53(2) Philosophical Review, 195–202; Anton-Hermann Chroust, "The Fundamental Ideas in St. Augustine's Philosophy of Law" (1973) 18 American Journal of Jurisprudence, 57–79; Richard J Dougherty, "Law" in Karla Pollmann, Willemien Otten, Hildegund Müeller, et al (eds), *The Oxford Guide to the Historical Reception of Augustine* (Oxford University Press 2013) vol 3, 1281–1283; Mary M Keys, "Religion, Empire, and Law among Nations in *The City of God*: From the Salamanca School to Augustine, and Back Again" in Martti Koskenniemi, Mónica García-Salmones Rovira, and Paolo Amorosa (eds), *International Law and Religion: Historical and Contemporary Perspectives* (Oxford University Press, 2017) 64–86; John A McGuckin, *The Ascent of Christian Law: Patristic and Byzantine Formulations of a New Civilization* (St Vladimir's Seminary Press, 2012) 127–157.

[2] For more on Augustine's downplaying of institutions and regime change, see Gerard O'Daly, *Augustine's* City of God: *A Reader's Guide* (Clarendon Press 1999) 205, 268; Michael J Hollerich, "John Milbank, Augustine, and the "Secular" in Mark Vessey, Karla Pollmann, and Allan D Fitzgerald (eds), *History, Apocalypse, and the Secular Imagination: New Essays on Augustine's* City of God (Philosophy Documentation Center 1999) 313; Paul Weithman, "Augustine's Political Philosophy" in Eleonore Stump and Norman Kretzmann (eds), *The Cambridge Companion to Augustine* (Cambridge University Press 2001) 235; Vernon J Bourke, "*The City of God* and History" in Dorothy F Donnelly (ed), *The City of God: A Collection of Critical Essays* (New York: Peter Lang, 1995) 296, 299. Augustine's thought has not been characterized as particularly systematic. See Norman H Baynes, *Byzantine Studies and Other Essays* (Athlone Press, 1995) 304; Herbert Deane, *The Social and Political Ideas of Saint Augustine* (Columbia University Press 1963) viii; John Figgis, *The Political Aspects of St. Augustine's "City of God"* (Longmans, Green, and Co, 1921) 7; RA Markus, *Saeculum: History and Society in the Theology of St. Augustine* (Cambridge University Press 1970) 73; Weithman, "Augustine's Political Philosophy," 235. Nevertheless, his work remains widely influential. For treatments of Augustine's political thought, as well as of political Augustinianism, see Figgis, *The Political Aspects of St. Augustine's "City of God"*; Markus, *Saeculum*; Deane, *The Social and Political Ideas of Saint Augustine*; Reinhold Niebuhr, "Augustine's Political Realism" in Dorothy F Donnelly

Mary M. Keys and Colleen E. Mitchell, *Patristic Era: Augustine's Constitutionalism: Citizenship, Common Good, and Consent* in *Christianity and Constitutionalism*. Edited by: Nicholas Aroney and Ian Leigh, Oxford University Press.
 DOI: 10.1093/oso/9780197587256.003.0005

not a liberal democrat by any means, and he does not think that earthly polities can be perfectly just. Nevertheless, he does not consider all political communities equally unjust; they are better if united by better loves and pursuits, worse if animated by less worthy ones (see *City of God* [hereafter, *CG*] 19.24, 960).[3] Augustine's writings point to concrete ways in which earthly political communities can try to imitate, though always incompletely, the perfect justice and peace of the heavenly city.

A citizen of Rome, Augustine lived in a juridical culture and was himself involved in the law once he became bishop of Hippo. Francesco Lardone shows that Augustine knew Roman law well and could use legal terms precisely when arguing in favor of or against certain Roman laws.[4] When in this chapter we speak of Augustine's "constitutionalism," we use the term in a sense broadly corresponding to the classical concept of regime: to the Greek *politeia* and *politeuma* and to the Latin *civitas* and *res publica*.[5] In this usage Augustine writes as heir to a long and dynamic tradition of Roman law and arrangements of offices. The Romans lacked a formal written constitution as readers would understand constitutions today; they also never had one lawgiver, as the Athenians did. Their institutions "were the result of a long process of experimentation, but they were not immutable. On the contrary, those institutions were constantly modified to adapt them to the changing circumstances of Rome's internal and foreign politics."[6]

(ed), *The City of God: A Collection of Critical Essays* (Peter Lang 1995); Jean Bethke Elshtain, *Augustine and the Limits of Politics* (University of Notre Dame Press 1995); Robert Dodaro, *Christ and the Just Society in the Thought of Augustine* (Cambridge University Press 2004); Michael JS Bruno, *Political Augustinianism: Modern Interpretations of Augustine's Political Thought* (Project Muse 2014); Eric Gregory, *Politics and the Order of Love: An Augustinian Ethic of Democratic Citizenship* (University of Chicago Press 2008); Weithman, "Augustine's Political Philosophy"; John von Heyking, *Augustine and Politics and Longing in the World* (University of Missouri Press 2001); John Doody, Kevin L Hughes, and Kim Paffenroth (eds), *Augustine and Politics* (Lexington Books 2005).

[3] All quotations from *The City of God* are taken from the translation by RW Dyson, unless otherwise noted, in consultation with the Latin text of *Corpus Augustinianum Gissense*. Augustine, *The City of God against the Pagans* (RW Dyson ed and tr, Cambridge University Press 1998). Augustine, *Opera Omnia* CAG: *Corpus Augustinianum Gissense* (Cornelius Mayer ed, electronic edn, InteLex Corporation 2000). Citations are given by book and chapter numbers, followed by the page number from Dyson's edition (e.g., *CG* 5.17, 217, for Book 5, ch 17, p 217).

[4] Francesco Lardone, "Roman Law in the Works of St Augustine" (1933) 21 Georgetown Law Journal 435.

[5] On these terms and concepts see the helpful commentary in the chapter 3 above, by Bertschmann.

[6] Francisco Pina Polo and Manuel Cabal, "SPQR: Institutions and Popular Participation in the Roman Republic" in Paul J du Plessis, Clifford Ando, and Kaius Tuori (eds), *The Oxford Handbook of Roman Law and Society* (Oxford University Press 2016) 85–86. For more discussion of Roman constitutionalism, see Dario Mantovani and Thomas Roberts, "More Than Codes: Roman Ways of Organising and Giving Access to Legal Information" in Paul J du Plessis, Clifford Ando, and Kaius Tuori (eds), *The Oxford Handbook of Roman Law and Society* (Oxford University Press 2016) esp

This chapter argues that Augustine's masterwork *De civitate Dei* (*The City of God*) identifies and upholds certain attributes of what we would term a just constitutional polity: nonnegotiable traits of a decent political-legal order as understood by this influential author of the patristic era. The features of Augustine's constitutionalism include wide access to citizenship; laws, institutions, and social mores conducing to the common good and endeavoring to provide all citizens with equitable shares of public goods; and a basis for these two provisos and others in the consent of the people and their governors rather than in external coercion.

This chapter's first section explicates the passage perhaps most cited to show that Augustine is unconcerned with regimes or constitutions, namely the opening of chapter 17 of *City of God* book 5, and concludes that this passage does not indicate civic disinterest on the part of its author. On the contrary, *CG* 5.17 outlines key characteristics of a good political-legal order as Augustine understands it.[7] The ensuing sections of this chapter elaborate three essential aspects of Augustine's constitutionalism, all of which are highlighted in *CG* 5.17: broad and perhaps universal extension of *citizen-status*, laws and institutions conducing to the *common good* and sharing of public welfare, and a basis of these provisions and others in the *consent* of the people to be governed by them. The analysis situates Augustine's thought in the contexts of Roman law and custom defining and governing citizen status, earlier patristic-era writing, and Augustine's emphasis on Christian citizenship. The chapter concludes by considering Augustine's comments on citizenship in political societies in relationship to his call in *The City of God* to citizenship in the heavenly city.

30–31; Charles Howard McIlwain, *Constitutionalism: Ancient and Modern* (2nd edn, Cornell University Press 1947) esp 23–26, 41–66.

[7] Due to the limited scope of this chapter, we limit our discussion to the practical political observations Augustine makes in *CG* 5.17. It should be noted, however, that Augustine has previously identified five bad laws/policies in *CG* 3.21–25: (1) the Voconian Law, of which he says, "I do not know of any law that could be said or thought to be more unjust" (*CG* 3.21, 130); (2) the Treaty of Numantia, which Augustine writes is "marred by such terrible disgrace" (ibid.); (3) the Edict of Mithridates, which he laments as a "pitiful thing" (*CG* 3.22, 131); (4) the agrarian laws of the Gracchi, which were "utterly ruinous" (*CG* 3.24, 132); and (5) the Senate's decision to build a temple of Concord on the spot where citizens had been killed, which Augustine calls "absurd" (*CG* 3.25, 134).

"What difference does it make under what rule a man lives . . . ": *The City of God* 5.17

In book 5 of *The City of God*, Augustine completes his initial argument against those who blame Christianity for the ongoing political and military decline of Rome's Western Empire, and specifically for the sack of Rome by Alaric and the Visigoths in 410 AD. The case he aims to make in the first five books of his twenty-two-book opus is that the cult of Rome's ancient divinities did not procure happiness for Rome's people and political community even in this earthly life. Augustine's fifth book seeks to discover whether Rome's traditional pagan gods can reasonably be credited for its imperial expansion and glorious history. In the midst of this exploration, opening chapter 17 of book 5, Augustine pens one of the most famous or infamous passages of the masterwork of his later years: "As far as this mortal life is concerned, which is spent and finished in a few days, what difference does it make under what rule a man lives who is soon to die, provided only that those who rule him do not compel him to do what is impious and wicked?" (*CG* 5.17, 217).

Many commentators see this statement as evidence of disinterest on the part of Augustine concerning questions of political regimes or constitutions—an effort on the part of the bishop of Hippo to downplay the import of Rome's decline and impending fall, and of politics and legal orders in this world more generally. Herbert Deane, for example, quotes this passage to argue that "the institutions of social, economic and political life have no real positive value. . . . We should not worry too much about the fact that we may be in bondage to evil rulers, or to evil masters if we are slaves, for both king and subject, master and slave, are on this earth for only a brief period, and the only really important concern is man's eternal salvation."[8] Similarly, R. A. Markus suggests that this passage denotes a "detachment" that "here amounts almost to indifference to secular institutions."[9] However, when these opening remarks of *CG* 5.17 are read together with the rest of the chapter and in the context of Augustine's broader argument in *The City of God*, this interpretation appears overstated and in important respects misleading.

The first difficulty in understanding Augustine's meaning in this passage may be one of translation. Augustine rhetorically asks what difference it

[8] Deane, *Political and Social Ideas of St. Augustine*, 152.
[9] Markus, *Saeculum*, 70.

makes under *whose* rule (*sub cuius imperio*), not under "what [sort of] rule" a person lives. There is thus no specific reference to the question of regime or constitution in Augustine's remark. His query seems rather to downplay the importance of which city or nation rules, so long as the rulers (*illi qui imperant*, literally "those who command") in that political order do not compel the ruled to perform evil actions.[10] Whether a person living in North Africa in Augustine's era is governed by Carthaginians, Egyptians, Romans, or Assyrians, for example, does not matter much in its own right, ceteris paribus. To the Romans it mattered indeed that they ruled others, because they sought to be the most glorious conquerors and imperial governors of the world. Yet Augustine rejects worldly glory as a worthy end for human life and action, and this critique surrounds his commentary in *CG* 5.17 (see *CG* 5.12–16 and 19–20). Augustine's argument here thus minimizes the value of ruling over others or the dishonor of being ruled by others.

One might reasonably reply that the question concerning who—which city, country, or empire—rules necessarily involves the question of what sort of institutions, offices, and laws that polity acknowledges, for such a question determines, at least in principle, which human beings take part in government, and with what authority, power, and jurisdiction. Augustine himself indicates to the reader that he is aware of this connection between a ruling polity and its regime or constitution, as the rest of book 5, chapter 17 indicates. When his work is read in full, there are at least three respects in which what we may broadly term the "constitution" (qua regime, form of government, and fundamental written or customary law) of a political society has implications that matter greatly for the people subject to its government. These are (1) the constitution's conferral (or refusal to confer) *citizenship* on the people; (2) provisions made (or not made) by law and custom for the *common good*, including the distribution or sharing of public goods and services among all citizens, especially the poor; and (3) the basis for public institutions and laws in the *consent* (or coercion) of the governed. The sections that follow will elaborate each of these aspects of what we may term Augustine's constitutionalism, as laid out in book 5, chapter 17, and

[10] Augustine goes on to highlight just two chapters later the significant positive impact on public welfare that good and practically wise persons in positions of authority can have: "when those who are gifted with true godliness and live good lives also know the art of governing peoples, nothing could be more fortunate for human affairs than that, by the mercy of God, they have the power to do so" (*CG* 5.19, 225).

with reference to diverse passages in *The City of God* and other writings of Augustine.

Conferral of Citizenship: "that most gracious and humane step"

Immediately after questioning, at the beginning of *CG* 5.17, the extent to which it matters under whose rule a mortal lives out his or her brief lifespan, Augustine poses another rhetorical question that clarifies the thrust of his initial query; he asks whether Roman governance was injurious to the cities and nations brought into its empire, excepting the obvious harm that war's "great slaughter" had wrought in their conquest (*CG* 5.17, 217). In a remark foreshadowing Martin Luther King Jr.'s "Letter from a Birmingham Jail," Augustine notes that "the Romans themselves did not live exempt from the laws which they imposed on others" (ibid.).[11] This equal subjection to the laws points toward equal civic status and participation generally. Yet, Rome's great pride long resisted establishing what Augustine later in *The City of God* terms a broad "fellowship of equality" and a corresponding "just peace" (*CG* 19.12, 936). To live under the same legal regime as the peoples added to their domain and yet retain their superior status in the empire, Rome and its citizens needed and indeed often sought bellicose engagement and victory. The glory-loving Romans, on Augustine's account, did *not* wish to appear to be "on a merely equal footing (*una . . . eademque condicio*) with the other nations" and so harmed their own people, as well as foreign communities, by waging war (*CG* 5.17, 217; cf. 3.14, 109–113).

Augustine's analysis indicates another respect in which the conquered or otherwise annexed peoples were harmed by Rome's governance: by being refused citizenship, except in fortunate circumstances permitting its

[11] King observes that an example of injustice in law is found in "a code that a majority inflicts on a minority that is not binding on itself. . . . This is difference made legal. On the other hand, a just law is a code that a majority compels a minority to follow that it is willing to follow itself. That is sameness made legal. Let me give another explanation. An unjust law is a code inflicted upon a minority which that minority had no part in enacting or creating because they did not have the unhampered right to vote." Martin Luther King Jr., "Letter from a Birmingham City Jail (1963)" in James Melvin Washington (ed), *A Testament of Hope: The Essential Writings and Speeches of Martin Luther King, Jr* (Harper Collins Publishers 1991) 294). Although Augustine is speaking in *CG* 5.17 of conquerors/conquered rather than majority/minority dynamics, there is a similar assumption that, ceteris paribus, the willingness of a politically ascendant group to follow the same laws it expects other groups to obey is a positive sign. See also King's citation of Augustine in this influential open letter (ibid, 293).

acquisition by some individuals or local communities.[12] Augustine writes that Rome's dominion would not have been particularly harmful, and its conquered peoples would in fact have been treated as equals to their conquerors in one empire, "especially . . . if that *most gracious and humane step*[13] had been taken at once which was taken later: namely, *the admission of all who belonged to the empire to the fellowship of the city, so that they became Roman citizens*"[14] (*CG* 5.17, 217; emphasis added).

The "most gracious and humane step" to which Augustine refers is the *Constitutio Antoniniana,* also known as the Edict of Caracalla. The emperor Marcus Aurelius Antoninus, popularly known by his agnomen "Caracalla" on account of the Gallic hooded tunic that he wore, issued this edict in 212 AD, declaring all free male residents of the empire, from Scotland to Syria, to be full Roman citizens.[15] Additionally, all free women were afforded the same rights as Roman women, thereby gaining an attenuated form of citizenship. As a result of this edict, approximately three hundred million people became Roman citizens. Mary Beard writes that it is "one of the biggest single grants of citizenship—if not *the* biggest—in the history of the world."[16] A. N. Sherwin-White observes that with the *Constitutio Antoniniana* "the world that had long been regarded as the *Orbis Romanus*, first in the sense that it was subject to Rome, then in the sense that it was subject to Roman government and Roman laws, *now became such in a real sense, even from the aspect of constitutional law*, because its inhabitants were all, with the most modest exceptions, *Roman citizens*."[17]

[12] On the Roman republic and empire's distinctions among citizens (*cives*), Latins (*Latini*), and foreigners/foreign subjects (*peregrini*); their relevance to legal status and institutions; and modes of acquisition of citizenship, see Andrew Lewis, "Slavery, Family, and Status" in David Johnston (ed), *The Cambridge Companion to Roman Law* (Cambridge University Press 2015) 151–174.

[13] Augustine's phrasing mirrors his praise of the Christian emperor Theodosius I at the end of book 5 for the "humanity and grace" he showed in protecting and sharing power with the boy-emperor Valentinian (*CG* 5.26, 233). Augustus's broad grant of citizenship and Theodosius's actions toward Valentinian alike indicate that humanity and graciousness for Augustine require acknowledgment of civic equality with one's fellow human beings. Compare Romulus's murder of his brother Remus, "in order that one of them should wield the entire mastery" (*CG* 15.5, 640; cf. *CG* 3.6, 98–99, and *CG* 3.13, 109).

[14] *[P]raesertim si mox fieret, quod postea gratissime atque humanissime factum est, ut omnes ad Romanum imperium pertinentes societatem acciperent civitatis et Romani cives essent.*

[15] Mary Beard, *SPQR: A History of Ancient Rome* (Liveright Publishing Corporation 2015) 527.

[16] Ibid.

[17] AN Sherwin-White, *The Roman Citizenship* (2nd edn, Clarendon Press 1973) 279–280, emphasis added; see also 280–287, 380–393. See also FM Heichelheim, "The Text of the '*Constitutio Antoniniana*' and the Three Other Decrees of the Emperor Caracalla Contained in Papyrus Gissensis 40" (1941) 26 Journal of Egyptian Archaeology 12.

Prior to 212, citizenship was extended to individuals, groups, and even entire cities through reforms, social wars, and the discretion of generals and emperors. Citizenship—the right to declare "I am a Roman citizen"—*civis romanus sum*[18]—was greatly desired because it promised certain legal protections, such as the right to a public trial and to appeal before the people (*ius provocationis*), and exemption from demeaning forms of punishment including public whipping and crucifixion. Moreover, only full Roman citizens had the right to vote (*ius suffragiorum*) and the right to stand for civic or public office (*ius honorum*). Those with "Latin Rights," a limited form of citizenship (*civitas sine suffragatio*) granted to members of the Latin League,[19] could legally trade (*ius comercii*), migrate (*ius migrationis*), and under some circumstances contract a marriage recognized by Roman law (*ius conubii*),[20] but they were not allowed to vote or hold office.[21] Women and children too had a limited form of citizenship; they could not vote or hold office and were considered subordinate to the *paterfamilias*, the male head of the household.[22] Male citizens, as well, were often subordinate to others in Roman private law. As Andrew Lewis observes, "Subordination was a permanent feature of Roman social and legal life. . . . Male citizens over the age of puberty . . . were in principle able to participate as citizens in public life, but in private life they remained subordinate to their fathers and other male ascendants."[23] Throughout their history, the Romans did at times grant certain rights, privileges, and even full citizenship to some immigrants and

[18] See Cicero's *In Verrem* 2.5.147, 2.5.162, and 2.5.168, for his connection of this expression with protection and assistance to those who utter it, although one could not always count on these benefits, as when unjust rulers at home or abroad refused to honor them. The apostle Paul employed exactly this phrase to "[claim] the privileged status of a Roman citizen by birth, when he was arrested in Jerusalem" (Egbert Koops, "Second-Rate Citizens: Junian Latins and the *Constitutio Antoniniana*" (2012) 19(2) Maastricht Journal of European and Comparative Law 225; see Acts 22:23–29). Augustine references Paul's declaration of Roman citizenship in his commentary on the Lord's Sermon on the Mount: "The Lord's Sermon the Mount" in Boniface Ramsey (ed) Michael G Campbell (tr), *New Testament I and II*, vol 41, *The Works of Saint Augustine* (4th edn, InteLex Corp. 2014) 1.19.58, 56.

[19] On the "Latin League", see Tim Cornell, "The City-States in Latium" in Mogens Herman Hansen (ed), *A Comparative Study of Thirty City-State Cultures: An Investigation Conducted by the Copenhagen Polis Centre* (Kongelige Danske Videnskabernes Selskab 2000) 209.

[20] See Sherwin-White, *Roman Citizenship*, 33, 109, 110.

[21] For more on the status of *civitas sine suffragatio*, see Sherwin-White, *Roman Citizenship*, 38–58, 109–116; Lucia Cecchet, "Greek and Roman Citizenship: State of Research and Open Questions" in Lucia Cecchet and Anna Busetto (eds), *Citizens in the Graeco-Roman World: Aspects of Citizenship from the Archaic Period to AD 212* (Brill 2017) 10.

[22] For more on the status of children in the Roman world, see Bruce W Frier and Thomas AJ McGinn (eds), *A Casebook on Roman Family Law* (Oxford University Press 2004) 18–20, 193–320; Beryl Rawson, *Children and Childhood in Roman Italy* (Oxford University Press 2003) esp 134–145; Christian Laes, *Children in the Roman Empire: Outsiders Within* (Cambridge University Press 2011).

[23] See Andrew Lewis, "Slavery, Family, and Status," 151.

populations of conquered territories. Freedmen often gained Roman citizenship with their release from slavery, and their children were automatically recognized as citizens.[24]

Why does Augustine accord pride of place to broad access to citizenship in what we might broadly term his constitutional thought?[25] We have seen part of his reasoning already: sharing fully in citizenship places a person on an "equal footing" with others in the "fellowship of the city" (*CG* 5.17, 217), at least *de iure*, acknowledging a person's rightful participation in a political-legal "fellowship of equality" (cf. *CG* 19.12, 936). Even with the *Constitutio Antoniniana*, however, Rome never granted equal access to full citizenship, as women and slaves were excluded. Rome's restriction of full citizenship privileges, particularly the right to vote, to free males is of course not uncommon in the ancient world; in book 18 of *The City of God*, Augustine discusses Varro's explanation of the mythical reasons that Athenian women were not allowed to vote, noting without comment or irony that long ago, the women of Athens were full citizens "tak[ing] part in deliberations on matters of public concern" (*CG* 18.9, 831–832).[26] In political societies in this world, citizenship is important as it confers certain rights and privileges, but citizenship is restricted to only certain persons. In the City of God, by contrast, access to citizenship has the potential to be universal. The barriers of sex, age,

[24] See Andrew Lewis, "Slavery, Family, and Status," 151–165; Jane F Gardner, *Being a Roman Citizen* (Routledge 1993) 7–51.

[25] Augustine uses some form of the word *civis* (citizen) over a hundred times in *The City of God*. *Civitas*, which can mean citizenship or, more often, the city or political community as the united task or common work of the citizens, occurs in this work over four hundred times. Hannah Arendt claimed that "Augustine seems to have been the last to know at least what it once meant to be a citizen" (Hannah Arendt, *The Human Condition* (2nd edn, University of Chicago Press 1998) 14). By this, she meant that Augustine was the last major figure in the history of political thought who could appreciate the full political meaning of the *vita activa* before the disappearance of the ancient city-state (ibid.). For a study of Augustine's thought on the *vita activa* and *vita contemplativa*, see Colleen E Mitchell and Mary M Keys, "Love's Labor Leisured: Augustine on Charity, Contemplation, and Politics" in Giorgio Faro (ed), *Pensando il lavoro: Contributi a carattere prevalentemente filosofico* (EDUSC 2018) vol II, 315–332. For discussion of this quote from Arendt and of Augustine and citizenship more broadly, see Rowan Williams, *On Augustine* (Bloomsbury 2016) 107–129. For other discussions of citizenship in Augustine's thought, see Paul C Burns, "Augustine's Use of Varro's *Antiquitates Rerum Divinarum* in His *De Civitate Dei*" (2001) 32(1) Augustinian Studies 37–64; James Dougherty, "The Sacred City and the City of God" (1979) 10 Augustinian Studies 81–90; Philip Rousseau, "Language, Morality and Cult: Augustine and Varro" in P Rousseau and M Papoutsakis (eds), *Transformations of Late Antiquity: Essays for Peter Brown* (Ashgate 2009) 159–175.

[26] Similarly, Augustine stresses in *On Order* (*De Ordine*) that there were "philosopher-women in ancient times" when he invites his mother Monica into a philosophic dialogue underway with friends. Augustine notes that he very much appreciates Monica's love of wisdom or philosophy. He stresses also the presence of craftsmen among the philosophers. These "shone with such light of the mind and wisdom that, even given the chance of bartering their social status with that of the nobility they wouldn't take it": in Silvano Barruso (trans), *On Order* (St Augustine's Press 2007) 1.2.11.31, 43.

and status that limit citizenship in the earthly city are removed; citizenship in the heavenly city is determined by faith in the true God and his bestowal of grace.[27] The broad conferral of citizenship rights by Rome's *Constitutio Antoniniana* may be said to prefigure the far broader conferral of citizenship in the heavenly city, just as Augustine explicitly indicates that Romulus's offer of asylum and citizenship to criminals "in a certain sense" foreshadows "the remission of sins which gathers together the citizens of the eternal country" (*CG* 5.17, 218).

The Common Good: "what had once belonged to a few would belong to all"

Augustine gives us another window into the meaning and value of *civitas* qua citizenship, immediately after praising Marcus Aurelius Antoninus's conferral in 212 AD of citizenship to the empire's people. Augustine explains that through this measure, which, he opines, should have been taken centuries sooner, "that which had once belonged to a few would belong to all"[28] (*CG* 5.17, 217). What had been a private good, or a "public" good enjoyed by only a small subset of the empire's populace, would now become common to all or, more precisely, most of the people.[29] Citizenship status ordinarily has, or ought to have, concrete, particular institutional implications that facilitate citizens' sharing in common goods. As a consequence of the granting of

[27] When Augustine was writing *The City of God*, of course, gaining access to formal citizenship was not a problem so much as was understanding in what Roman *Christian* citizenship consisted. Christians were seen as a threat to Roman religion and its entire social and political order. See Matthias Riedl, "Truth versus Utility: The Debate on Civil Religion in the Roman Empire of the Third and Fourth Centuries" in R Weed and J von Heyking (eds) *Civil Religion in Political Thought: Its Perennial and Enduring Relevance in North America* (Catholic University of America Press 2010) 57–58). For more discussion of the early Church fathers and their approach toward law, citizenship, and the relationship between Christianity and Rome, see Caroline Humfress, "Patristic Sources" in David Johnston (ed), *The Cambridge Companion to Roman Law*, Cambridge Companions to the Ancient World (Cambridge University Press 2015) 97–118; John Witte Jr and Frank S Alexander (eds), *Christianity and Law: An Introduction* (Cambridge University Press 2008); McGuckin, *Ascent of Christian Law*; Ken Parry, *The Wiley Blackwell Companion to Patristics* (Wiley Blackwell 2015); Hugo Rahner, *Church and State in Early Christianity* (Ignatius Press 1992); JHWG Liebeschuetz, *Ambrose of Milan: Political Letters and Speeches* (Liverpool University Press 2005) esp 27–48. For discussion of the use of the Patristics for contemporary Catholic social thought, see Brian Matz, *Patristics and Catholic Social Thought: Hermeneutical Models for a Dialogue* (University of Notre Dame Press 2014).

[28] *ac sic esset omnium, quod erat ante paucorum.*

[29] For more on Augustine and the common good, see George J Lavere, "The Problem of the Common Good in Saint Augustine's *Civitas Terrena*" (1983) 14 Augustinian Studies 1; Joanna V Scott, "Augustine's Razor: Public vs. Private Interests in *The City of God*" in Dorothy F Donnelly (ed), *The City of God: A Collection of Critical Essays* (Peter Lang 1995).

citizenship to all free inhabitants of the empire, for instance, what we would term social welfare provision from public resources is more equitably extended to those denizens of the empire who lacked ownership of land for their sustenance (ibid.).[30]

Augustine greatly prefers the sharing of goods among many to the hoarding of goods by the few. He encourages the Romans to have a more equitable approach to the distribution of goods among their own citizenry and with their neighbors. In book 4 of *The City of God,* Augustine asks the oft-quoted question: "Justice removed, then, what are kingdoms but great bands of robbers?" Augustine continues by comparing the petty theft of a pirate to the mass pillaging Alexander the Great conducts with his great fleet; for that fleet, Alexander is deemed an "emperor," and for his small pirate ship, the pirate is labeled a "robber" (*CG* 4.4, 147–148). Augustine's criticism here is not that all earthly political communities should be understood reductively as robber bands, but that the accumulation of goods and riches for the benefit of a few and to the detriment of the many is unjust, particularly when procured by force. Rome's imperial practices of subjugating its neighboring peoples who had done Rome no harm "out of the mere desire to rule" was in fact "great robbery" (*CG* 4.6, 150). The impetus for such thievery is *libido dominandi*—the lust for domination that inspired the Romans to expand their empire.

Earthly polities can improve by eschewing such practices and encouraging greater equality through the creation of a common fund that provides for those in need (*CG* 5.18, 222–223). Such a common fund is necessary for this world, in which some human beings will always be poor and the wealthy few may strive to deprive the many for their private gain (*CG* 5.16; see Mk 14:7). But it will no longer be needed in the fulfillment of the City of God, which has no use for a public treasury, as "the treasury of truth will be the common property of all" (*CG* 5.16, 216). A perfectly just distribution of earthly goods, that is, a distribution in which each person receives his or her due, is not possible in political societies in this world. But it is possible to distribute earthly

[30] *[t]antum quod plebs illa, quae suos agros non haberet, de publico viveret.* Christos N. Tsironis notes the continuity between the Greek church fathers and Augustine on the significance of the common good as a civic and ethical standard, and its link with citizenship and just legal order: Christos N Tsironis, "The Common Good: Historical Roots in the Greek Patristic Texts" in Mathias Nebel and Thierry Collaud (eds), *Searching for the Common Good: Philosophical, Theological and Economic Approaches* (Nomos Verlag 2018) 168–169, n 63, quoting Hubertus R Drobner and Albert Viciano (eds), *Gregory of Nyssa, Homilies on the Beatitudes: An English Version with Commentary and Supporting Studies* (Brill 2000) 60.

goods more justly, as when laws, customs, and institutions are structured so that the rich few do not freely exploit the many poor.

For Augustine, good and just rulers in the regimes of this world are self-disciplined and moderate. They act with the "gentleness of mercy and the generosity of benevolence," particularly as a compensation for "whatever severe measures they may be forced to decree." Just rulers should take it upon themselves to "restrai[n]" their own "self-indulgence" and to "govern wicked desires more than any people whatsoever" (*CG* 5.24, 232). Those wielding public power are most able to harm others, seeking private advantage over common goods through their immoderation; conversely, temperate rulers can serve as an example to the people. If citizens moderate their desires, as Christianity encourages them to do, they become more capable of treating their neighbors and fellow citizens with justice and charity rather than with the desire to extort and dominate.

Concordia over Conquest: "it would be better . . . to make this provision by the free consent of the people"

Augustine's *City of God* 5.17 reveals one additional aspect of what can be understood as his constitutional thought: his emphasis on the agreement or consent (*concordia*)[31] of the governed for the efficacy of law as well as for the common good. Augustine refers to popular consent at least twice in this chapter. The first occurrence indicates the import of the consent of the governed for law's acceptance and smooth administration. Augustine notes that, while the imposition of Roman law generally did not in itself constitute a harm to the conquered peoples of the empire, this was especially the case after those peoples were granted access to full Roman citizenship. Augustine observes: "This [the imposition of Roman laws] would indeed have *been accomplished more successfully had it been done by agreement*" than by force of

[31] *Concordia*, which literally means "with one heart," can be translated as "agreement, union, harmony, concord" (DP Simpson, *Cassell's Latin Dictionary* [MacMillan Publishing Company 1968] 128). *Concordia* is related to but not exactly synonymous with the Greek term ὁμόνοια, which literally means "oneness of mind." The one focuses on unity of mind, the other on unity of heart (see Kostas Kalimtzis, *Aristotle on Political Enmity and Disease: An Inquiry into Stasis* [State University of New York Press 2000] 25–26, 59–60). However, there is still a close relation between the terms, as the Latin *cor* can also be translated as "mind," "judgment," and "understanding" (Charlton T Lewis and Charles Short, *A Latin Dictionary; Founded on Andrews' Edition of Freund's Latin Dictionary* [Trustees of Tufts University 1879] 468).

arms; but, "in that case, there would have been no glory of conquest"[32] (*CG* 5.17, 217; emphasis added).

Augustine's emphasis on consent—on concord, or agreement of wills, among people as to the institutions that govern them—goes beyond the expediency suggested by its first mention in *CG* 5.17. Reflecting on the imperial provision of public support for the common people, Augustine later writes that "it would be better for good administrators to make this provision by the free consent of the people than by extorting it from the conquered"[33] (ibid.). Augustine thus distinguishes between political and legal acts that arise out of mutual agreement and those that result from force. This suggests that grounding civic institutions on the agreement of the people is better, more just, and more desirable per se than basing them on compulsion. Whereas the Romans sought glory in triumph and conquest, Augustine thinks that the extension of earthly rule and law is both more successful and better, conducing more to the public good, if offered freely to a free people and accepted by the agreement of the governed.

Although Augustine is in favor of rule based on common agreement, it would be a mistake to read him as having the same understanding of consent (*concordia*) as modern social contract theorists. While Augustine does share the idea that consent requires agreement rather than force, his understanding of the idea is arguably richer than that implied by mere legitimacy through majority rule, noncoercion, or tacit consent. Augustine is not the first Roman thinker to use the term "*concordia*" in an explicitly political way; the Roman emperors promised *pax et concordia* as part of the Roman imperial ideology.[34] Roman political thinkers, like Cicero and Sallust, used *concordia* to describe the way in which an ideal government should function.[35]

[32] *Quod si concorditer fieret, id ipsum fieret meliore successu; sed nulla esset gloria triumphantium.*

[33] *[Q]ui pastus eius per bonos administratores rei publicae gratius a concordibus praestatur quam victis extortqueretur.*

[34] See John Alexander Lobur, *Consensus Concordia and the Formation of Roman Imperial Ideology* (Routledge 2008) 55–56; see also Henry C Boren, "Cicero's *Concordia* in Historical Perspective" in Mary Francis Gyles and Eugene Wood Davis (eds), *Studies in Memory of Wallace Everett Caldwell Professor of History at the University of North Carolina by His Friends and Students* (University of North Carolina Press 1964) 51–62.

[35] Cicero, *De Re Publica* 2.69, in James EG Zetzel (ed), *On the Commonwealth and On the Laws* (Cambridge University Press 2008) 56–57. Augustine discusses this passage in *CG* 2.21 and suggests that after Scipio states the importance of justice for a republic, his interlocutor Philus asked that the issue of justice be discussed at greater length. This passage is lost. For more discussion, see Geoff Kennedy, "Cicero, Roman Republicanism and the Contested Meaning of *Libertas*" (2013) 62 Political Studies 494–496; Kalimitzis, *Aristotle on Political Enmity and Disease*, 60–61. For more on Augustine and Cicero, see also Veronica Roberts, "Augustine's Ciceronian Response to the Ciceronian Patriot" (2016) 45(2) Perspectives on Political Science 113–124. Sallust too uses the term "*concordia*" to describe the ordering of the Roman government in his *Bellum Catilinae* 6.2 (in JC Rolfe [tr], John T

Augustine appears to have been revisiting and redefining these Roman understandings of *concordia* to construct his own.

For instance, Augustine replaces Cicero's definition of the commonwealth and of a people such that a people and their commonwealth is defined by what it loves. In books 2 and 19 of *The City of God*, Augustine expresses his doubts that Rome was ever a real commonwealth according to Cicero's definition of the term. In *De Re Publica*, Cicero's Scipio defines a "commonwealth" (*res publica*) as the "property of a people (*rem populi*)" (*CG* 2.21, 78; quoting *De Re Publica* 1.39a). A "people," Scipio goes on to explain, is "not every assembly of a multitude, but . . . an assembly united in fellowship by *common agreement* (*consensus*) as to what is right and by a community of interest" (ibid.; emphasis added).[36] Augustine argues that Rome was never a commonwealth under this definition because "true justice was never present in it" (*CG* 2.21, 80). Without true justice "there can be no right" (*CG* 19.21, 950), and without agreement about what is truly right the Romans were never a true "people" according to Scipio's definition; they formed "only a multitude of some kind, not worthy of the name of a people" (*CG* 19.21, 951).

Rather than deny that the Romans constituted a people, Augustine modifies Scipio's definition: "Let us say that a 'people' is an assembled multitude of rational creatures bound together by a *common agreement* (*concordi*) as to the *objects of their love*" (*CG* 19.24, 960; emphasis added).[37] Augustine's new emphasis is not on agreement about what is per se or in the highest degree *right*, but more simply on agreement concerning what the people *loves*. While some scholars have seen in this shift a move away from an ethical or normative standard for politics, Augustine seems rather to be crafting a broader, descriptive standard for what constitutes a political community, a standard that nonetheless gives rise to normative evaluation of its concrete fulfillment in any particular polity. The better the objects of love, he says, "the better the

Ramsey [revised], *Sallust: The War with Catiline, The War with Jugurtha*, Loeb Classical Library [Harvard University Press 2013] 28). Augustine quotes this Sallust passage in Letter 138.10 where he casts doubt that concord could exist among the Romans when their gods were always in discord with one another. For more discussion of Sallust's view of *concordia*, see Donald C Earl, *The Political Thought of Sallust* (Cambridge University Press 1961) 31–32; Daniel J Kapust, *Republicanism, Rhetoric, and Roman Political Thought: Sallust, Livy, and Tacitus* (Cambridge University Press 2011) 42, 45–46, 48–50. On *concordia* as a kind of policy of toleration under Constantine, see the chapter by Peter Leithart in this volume.

[36] *coetum iuris consensus et utilitatis communione sociatum esse determinat.*

[37] *Populus est coetus multitudinis rationalis rerum quas diligit concordi communione sociatus.*

people; and the worse the objects, the worse the people" (*CG* 19.24, 960).[38] The Romans, for instance, err in loving, for they immoderately love both Romulus, their prideful founder and false god, and the polity he founded and they inherited, which is necessarily temporal (see *CG* 22.6). By contrast, true Christians who love God before themselves have Christ as their foundation (see *CG* 22.6). Theirs is the better choice for Augustine, as they have chosen that which is truthful and everlasting. Moreover, Christ's example, teaching, and grace help people to recognize and struggle against the pride that stokes *libido dominandi*, damaging the concord of the political community.

Conclusion

We have argued that Augustine is not indifferent to earthly politics, and that he offers concrete ways in which they can be improved in what we have broadly termed his approach to constitutionalism. Augustine approves of the expansion of Roman citizenship through the *Constitutio Antoniniana*, for the sake of greater security, welfare, and dignity of the people living under the empire. He further emphasizes policies that promote the common good and the equitable distribution of goods, particularly to the poor, and endorses rule of law rooted in popular agreement or consent. While Augustine indicates important ways in which earthly politics and law can be improved, his deepest hope—for himself, his readers, and all people—is the attainment of citizenship in the heavenly Jerusalem. Indeed, he suggests that the most efficacious path to improve constitutions in this world is to invite people into the City of God, since with the virtues divine grace grants and develops, persons of all conditions have the ability to serve the good of others in a fellowship of equality and to love common goods more than private ones (see inter

[38] For more discussion of Augustine and love, see Anders Nygren, *Agape and Eros* (Philip S Watson tr, SPCK 1953) 449–562; James J O'Donnell, "Preface to the Vintage Spiritual Classics Edition" in John F Thornton and Susan B Varenne (eds), *Late Have I Loved Thee: Selected Writings of Saint Augustine on Love* (Vintage Books 2006) xvii–xxvi; William S Babcock, "*Cupiditas* and *Caritas*: The Early Augustine on Love and Human Fulfillment" in Richard John Neuhaus (ed), *Augustine Today* (William B Eerdmans Publishing Company 1993) 1–34; Ernest L Fortin, "Augustine and the Hermeneutics of Love: Some Preliminary Considerations" in Richard John Neuhaus (ed), *Augustine Today* (William B. Eerdmans Publishing Company 1993) 35–59; Oliver O'Donovan, *The Problem of Self-Love in St. Augustine* (Yale University Press 1980); Tarcisius J van Bavel, "The Double Face of Love in Augustine" (1986) 17(1) Augustinian Studies 169–181; William R Stevenson, *Christian Love and Just War: Moral Paradox and Political Life in St. Augustine and His Modern Interpreters* (Mercer University Press 1987) 77–100, esp 77–78, 80; Martha C Nussbaum, *Upheavals of Thought: The Intelligence of Emotions* (Cambridge University Press 2001) 527–556.

alia *CG* 2.19 and 28).[39] Augustine's *City of God* may well be read as intended to educate its readers, assisting them in journeying from mere love of their political communities and constitutions toward love of the heavenly city, a greater love that helps its citizens to humanize their earthly polities.

In the heavenly city women have equal citizenship, as Augustine indicates often in *The City of God*. Perhaps his most moving exemplar of a citizen of the heavenly city is his mother Monica, as described in *The Confessions*. In her journey together with her son Augustine, readers may grasp how Augustine considers heavenly citizenship to benefit also justice and mercy in this world and so improve political life here at least somewhat. Monica was born into a Christian home in the Roman province of Africa. Although she is chiefly characterized as a citizen of the heavenly City of God, she lived as a free woman with attenuated Roman citizenship rights, and for much of her life also retained some ties to the earthly city, the society of those who love themselves more than God. Augustine thus describes Monica as "lingering on the outskirts of Babylon" when she urged Augustine to delay marriage in order not to harm his prospects for education and advancement (*Confessions* 2.3.6–8, 28)[40] and later resisted Augustine's plans to "change countries," leaving his native Africa and moving to Rome (*Confessions* 5.8.14–15, 83). Nonetheless, her citizenship in the heavenly city helped her to cultivate prudence, justice, and forgiveness, and both to suffer and to mitigate when possible, for herself and for other women, the injustices that Rome's constitutional inequality of the sexes allowed and even encouraged. As Monica grew in her understanding of Christianity later in Milan, with Ambrose's guidance, she broke from some customs of her homeland that risked leading others to vice. Augustine notes that Ambrose for his part "loved [Monica] . . . for she was fervent in spirit and ever doing good," especially to the poor (*Confessions* 6.2.2, 97). Monica's death at Ostia marks the culmination of her journey to heavenly citizenship and *res publica*, with her willingness that her body be buried anywhere, even far from her homeland, so long as she is remembered at the altar of God wherever her sons might dwell (*Confessions* 9.11.27).

[39] "If 'the kings of the earth and all nations, princes and all the judges of the earth, young men and maidens, old men and children,' people of every age and each sex; if those to whom John the Baptist spoke, even the tax gatherers and the soldiers: if all these together were to hear and embrace the Christian precepts of justice and moral virtue, then would the commonwealth adorn its lands with happiness in the present life and ascend to the summit of life eternal" (*CG* 2.19, 74; quoting Psalm 148).

[40] Augustine, *Confessions* (Michael P Foley ed, FJ Sheed tr, 2nd edn, Hackett 2006).

Monica's example vividly illustrates the correct orientation a Christian ought to have toward political life. Augustine indicates through Monica that, paradoxically, such transcendence of one's political constitution in favor of a fully universal and just one, only to be attained perfectly in the age to come, liberates the citizen in this life to work patiently and bravely for justice and mercy in and through their imperfect earthly constitutions. Only the true love of God, such as Monica embraced and on which she founded her life with increasing fidelity, can ground a real *res publica*, a fully common good, and wholly free consent and concord. Concern for one's imperfect *patria* and its regime or constitution, Augustine indicates, thus points toward even deeper care and desire for citizenship in the heavenly city of God (see *CG* 2.29, 19.17, and 22.30).[41]

[41] See also Augustine's Letter 91 to Nectarius. The authors wish to dedicate this chapter to Michael P Zuckert on the occasion of his retirement from the University of Notre Dame.

6

Middle Ages

Canon Law Constitutionalism?

R. H. Helmholz

The subject of this chapter requires a definition of terms. That was the approach taken by the medieval jurists, and for this topic it remains useful today.[1] "Canon law" seems relatively easy, at least in historical perspective. It was the law of the medieval church contained in the *Corpus iuris canonici*. This basic source of ecclesiastical law was composed of Gratian's *Decretum*, compiled in the mid-twelfth century, and also the Gregorian Decretals (1234) and the *Liber sextus* (1298), the two great collections of papal decretals edited in the thirteenth, together with smaller supplementary collections added later in the Middle Ages. Along with the law found in these texts went a huge body of glosses and other juristic commentary interpreting their meaning, commentary that should not be neglected in any presentation of the meaning of the texts themselves.

The canon law found in these books governed a part of the lives of all Latin Christians, or almost the whole population of medieval Europe. Not only was it put to use in ecclesiastical courts of every land, but also, together with Roman law, the law of the church influenced political thought in pre-Enlightenment Europe. Dealing with the rights and powers of the clergy, in particular, it covered some of the same substantive ground as did the civil law, reaching related but not identical conclusions about the proper conduct of government. Hence, its contents have a legitimate claim on the attention of students of both political theory and legal history.

This much seems straightforward. But what exactly is meant by "constitutionalism"? A review of the scholarly literature on the subject does not

[1] The effort at definition that follows is not identical to that found in Jonathan Chaplin's chapter in this volume, but it appears to be at least compatible with his discussion of "Constitutional Implications" in its third section.

R. H. Helmholz, *Middle Ages: Canon Law Constitutionalism?* in *Christianity and Constitutionalism*.
Edited by: Nicholas Aroney and Ian Leigh, Oxford University Press. © Oxford University Press 2022.
DOI: 10.1093/oso/9780197587256.003.0006

provide a definition that has won universal agreement. It appears to be a contested term. Indeed, some of what has been written about the subject is complex enough to be confusing. It suggests that the term's meaning has long been uncertain.[2] The starting point used by an apparent majority of historians of the subject does, however, provide a start. It ascribes two basic components to the term.[3]

The first is the recognition of the existence of a superior law, one that binds all governmental actors. In the exercise of their authority, legislators, judges, and administrators must themselves be governed by rules that are accessible and beyond their immediate control. Even within their own undoubted sphere of competence, those who govern do not possess unbridled power; they must instead act within the bounds of established principles. So, for example, lawgivers should have the power to establish civil and criminal laws according to their best judgment, but the exercise of that power must conform to a set of standards that are independent of their own personal interests or desires. Today that function is normally served by a written constitution, one that can be changed only with difficulty and that binds all those who exercise the power to govern. In the Middle Ages, the same purpose was served by natural and divine law.

The second is the existence of a division of power and responsibility within the government itself. Constitutionalism requires that not all power be placed in the hands of the same person or the same group of persons. Today, this requirement is normally expressed by drawing a distinction between the legislative, judicial, and executive functions of government. Accordingly, the lawgiver has the power to establish civil and criminal laws, but the judgment of individual cases arising under those laws rests in the hands of the judiciary, not the lawgiver. This tripartite nature of this system is not, however, a necessary part of constitutional government. There may be only two separate institutions, and one of them may even hold the greater share of power. Even designedly authoritarian regimes may leave room for institutions that check the exercise of despotic

[2] E.g., Ulrike Müsig, "Juridification by Constitution: National Sovereignty in Eighteenth and Nineteenth Century Europe" in *Reconsidering Constitutional Formation I: National Sovereignty* (Springer 2016) 1–157.

[3] See MJC Vile, *Constitutionalism and the Separation of Powers* (2nd edn, Liberty Fund 1998) 1–22; Gerhard Casper, *Constitutionalism* (University of Chicago Press 1987) 16–18; Brian Tierney, "Medieval Canon Law and Western Constitutionalism," (1966) 52 Catholic Historical Rev. 1–17, reprinted in Brian Tierney, *Church Law and Constitutional Thought in the Middle Ages* (Variorum 1975); Günter Frankenberg, "Comparative Constitutional Law," in Mauro Bussani and Ugo Mattei (eds), *Cambridge Companion to Comparative Law* (Cambridge University Press 2012) 171–190.

power.[4] However, the tripartite form does provide a particularly sensible way in which constitutionalism can be achieved. The essential factor in all situations nevertheless remains the existence of some limitation on one person's governmental power. As Harold Laski once put it, "A state in which sovereignty is unified is morally inadequate and administratively inefficient."[5]

Although these two halves of the concept of constitutionalism are usually stated separately, they have long been connected in legal and political thought. Rightly so: they have been partners. The goal served by both has always been the same—prevention of arbitrary and oppressive rule. Putting power into different hands and limiting the reach of those hands by subjecting them to external standards of right and wrong work together to serve the goal of constitutionalism. As one of the justices of the US Supreme Court put the point recently, "A ruler must be subject to the law in exercising his power and may not govern by will alone."[6]

Absolutism in the Canon Law

This chapter's purpose is to discuss the question of whether the canon law, as it reached its maturity during the twelfth to fourteenth centuries and as it was understood and applied throughout Latin Christendom, contributed to the establishment of constitutionalism so defined.[7] A first look at the subject is not encouraging. Searching for constitutionalism in the law of the medieval church runs immediately into a large obstacle—with some reason the canon law has been commonly understood to have vested all power in all relevant

[4] Tom Ginsburg, "Administrative Law and the Judicial Control of Agents in Authoritarian Regimes," in Tom Ginsburg and Tamir Moustafa (eds), *Rule by Law: The Politics of Courts in Authoritarian Regimes* (Cambridge University Press 2008) 58–72.

[5] Harold Laski, *The Foundations of Sovereignty and Other Essays* (1921, Allen & Unwin repr 2003) vi; see also Denis Galligan and Mila Versteeg, "Theoretical Perspectives on the Social and Political Foundations of Constitutions," in Tom Ginsburg *Social and Political Foundations of Constitutions* (Cambridge University Press 2013) 3–48, at 6–8.

[6] Thomas, J. concurring in *Department of Transportation v Association of American Railroads*, 135 S Ct 1225, 1242 (2015).

[7] The following references to the texts of the canon law are used in this chapter:

Dist. 1 c. 1	Decretum Gratiani, Distinctio 1, can. 1
C. 1 q. 1 c. 1	------------, Causa 1, quaestio 1, can. 1
X 1.1.1	Decretales Gregorii IX, Lib. 1, tit. 1, cap. 1
Sext 1.1.1	Liber Sextus, Lib. 1, tit. 1, cap. 1
Clem. 1.1.1	Constitutiones Clementinae, Book 1, tit. 1, cap. 1
Extrav. 1.1.1	Extravagantes (of Pope John XXII and Communes), Lib. 1, tit. 1. cap. 1
gl. ord.	glossa ordinaria (standard commentary on texts of the Corpus iuris canonici)

categories of constitutionalism in the papacy. Its object, it is said, was to establish "a universal, ultimate pontifical authority over the emperor and all other secular powers."[8] The Church's law may have played a useful role in keeping the power of medieval kings within bounds, as Joel Harrison's chapter in this volume demonstrates, but it appears that the only checks on papal sovereignty within the church itself were those the Roman pontiffs elected to respect. Not only did they act as legislators, exercising a power to create new laws and annul old laws, but also they were the final judges of disputes that arose under those same laws. From papal decisions, there was no earthly possibility of appeal. And although long distances and primitive methods of travel prevented the medieval popes from reaching personally into every corner of Europe to administer the law they themselves had created, their legates and judges-delegate could and did carry the exercise of papal power to the far corners of Latin Christendom.[9] Papal letters containing decisions and orders to local bishops and clerics were available to make what was called the plenitude of papal power as effective in fact as it was in theory. And as for subjecting papal decisions to control from without, the medieval canon law, borrowing from Roman law precedents, proclaimed that the pope was *legibus solutus*, freed from the law's restraints.[10] The reason? He had all laws *in scrinio pectoris sui*.[11] That left little room for constitutional principles. The famous *Dictatus papae* of Pope Gregory VII stated this in apparently unambiguous terms.[12]

A considerable body of scholarly literature dealing with this subject has come into existence during the past fifty years. Most, although not all, of it has stressed the existence of what appear to have been virtually unlimited papal powers under the canon law. At least for a time, the most celebrated of English writers on this subject was an Austrian immigrant, Walter Ullmann. His "descending theme" of government, by which all earthly power was regarded as having descended from God to the popes as the successors to St. Peter, held the field, or at least the attention, of the scholarly world.[13] This

[8] DS Chambers, *Popes, Cardinals and War* (IB Tauris 2006) 8.

[9] See Robert C Figueira, "Papal Reserved Powers and the Limitations on Legatine Authority," in James Ross Sweeney and Stanley Chodorow (eds), *Popes, Teachers, and Canon Law in the Middle Ages* (Cornell University Press 1989) 191–211, where the extensive powers reserved for papal decision under the canon law, 112 in number, are listed at 206–208.

[10] Taken from reference to the emperor in Dig. 1.3.31.

[11] Sext 1.2.1.

[12] Its text is conveniently translated in Brian Tierney, *The Crisis of Church & State 1050–1300* (Prentice-Hall 1964) 49–50.

[13] See, e.g., Walter Ullmann, *Medieval Papalism: The Political Theories of the Medieval Canonists* (Methuen 1949); John Watt, *The Theory of Papal Monarchy in the Thirteenth Century* (Fordham

theme also had important consequences outside the sphere of the church's own governance. It had secular consequences. The powers of emperors or kings in government of their own realms were roughly analogous to those of the popes in the spiritual sphere of life, but whenever there was a conflict between the two, they were subject to correction by the Roman pontiffs. Effectively, the pope was *Dominus mundi*, lord of the world.

The schematic character of Ullmann's presentation of the canon law has passed out of fashion today, but his association of *plentitudo potestatis* with the papacy as the central feature of the canon law itself has not disappeared from the modern understanding of the church's law.[14] Other scholars have concluded that the age that witnessed the formulation of the canon law in the Gregorian Decretals (1234) also witnessed attempts to establish "a complete statement of papal authority over the world."[15] The rule of the Roman pontiffs over the bishops throughout Europe was complete, and it was sometimes extended to the control over lay rulers by the popes themselves. It was thus a monarchy that could be superior to that of European kings, even of the Roman emperor. It has been suggested that establishment of the church's independence was a step toward constitutional separation of powers in the secular sphere.[16] There is some truth in this, but the consensus view among historians of canon law discounts its relevance for governance of the church. It only worked one way, as far as the formal canon law was concerned. If a king asked the clergy to excommunicate an enemy, for example, this "could not be more than a request." But if the pope requested that the king proceed against heretics or despoilers of church property, "this was an order."[17] A dividing line between temporal and spiritual jurisdictions was retained in the

University Press 1965); Stanley Chodorow, *Christian Political Theory and Church Politics in the Mid-Twelfth Century* (University of California Press 1972); Colin Morris, *The Papal Monarchy: The Western Church from 1050–1250* (Oxford University Press 1989); IS Robinson, *The Papacy 1073–1198: Continuity and Innovation* (Cambridge University Press 1990) 295–321; Joseph Canning, *Ideas of Power in the Late Middle Ages, 1296–1417* (Cambridge University Press 2011); Keith Sisson, "Popes over Princes: Hierocratic Theory," in K Sisson and Atria Larson (eds), *Companion to the Medieval Papacy* (Brill 2016) 121–132.

[14] Both the doubts and the progression of scholarship on this subject are well described in Keith Sisson, *Papal Hierocratic Theory in the High Middle Ages: From Roman Primacy to Universal Papal Monarchy* (VDM 2009) 10–20.

[15] Morris, *Papal Monarchy*, 568. See also Michael Wilks, *The Problem of Sovereignty in the Later Middle Ages: The Papal Monarchy with Augustinus Triumphus and the Publicists* (Cambridge University Press 1963) 29–59 and 254–287.

[16] See Antonio Padoa-Schioppa, *Studi sul diritto canonico medievale* (CISAM 2017) 31–45.

[17] Watt, *Theory of Papal Monarchy*, 126–127.

church's law, but the number of exceptions to it, cases where the line could be crossed by God's special representatives, multiplied within it.[18]

Of course, medieval kings did not always accept this as applicable law, and the medieval canonists did not always suppose that these principles actually prevailed in the world. As they saw it, their task was to explore and explain the meaning of the texts in the *Corpus iuris canonici*. It was no necessary part of that task to describe what normally occurred in the lives of ordinary men and women.[19] The canonists themselves would not have supposed that the principles historians have discerned within the concept of papal monarchy were obediently followed in practice, any more than an English common lawyer in 1700 would have supposed that the Statute of Frauds had eliminated frauds from the world.[20] But in both cases, it seems, they would have supposed that the relevant law was that stated in canons and decretals found in the *Corpus iuris canonici*. Some of the texts found there proclaimed the powers of the papacy in unambiguous terms. Their existence appears to have excluded the possibility that the canon law could have contributed to the growth of constitutionalism in any meaningful way except by demonstrating that the powers of secular rulers were not absolute. Otherwise, the canon law could only have suggested to kings that they might aspire to imitate and displace the popes within the secular sphere.[21]

Constitutional Elements within the Canon Law

It is not the aim of this chapter to overthrow these accounts of the canon law's import. The medieval church was not a constitutional democracy. The canon law did support the foundations of papal governance within the church. It did also sometimes extend the reach of papal powers into unchartered areas of secular and political life. The chapter's aim is simply to present a more nuanced picture of the canon law than the one just outlined, focusing

[18] See Tierney, *Crisis of Church & State*, 153–155, translating Innocent IV, *Commentaria super libros quinque Decretalium* at X 2.2.10, nos 2–4 (Venice 1570, repr 2008): "Licet in multo distincta sint officia et regimina mundi, tamen quandocunque necesse est ad papam recurrendum est."

[19] They did occasionally do so, noting that the decretals prevailed "de iure, licet non de facto." See Thomas Morrissey, "Natural Rights, Natural Law and the Canonist: Franciscus Zabarella, 1360–1417" in Kenneth Pennington, Stanley Chodorow, and Keith Kendall (eds), *Proceedings of the Tenth International Congress of Medieval Canon Law* (Biblioteca Apostolica Vaticana 2001) 741.

[20] 29 Car. II, c. 3 (1677).

[21] Bart Wauters and Marco de Benito, *The History of Law in Europe: An Introduction* (Edward Elgar 2017) 67–68.

principally on the governance of the church itself. Its argument consists of three propositions.

First, the *Corpus iuris canonici* itself contained a multitude of laws and principles. Some of them contradicted, or at any rate lessened, the scope of texts that were used to state and support papal power and papal freedom from legal constraints. Second, commentators on the canon law added important limitations to those texts that magnified the scope of papal authority. The *communis opinio* of the jurists was always a force to be reckoned with. In assessing the canon law as a whole, the limitations they developed should be given some weight against those that supported authoritarian theories of church government. Third, the popes were regarded and in fact regarded themselves as constrained by the law—natural law, divine law, and (usually) the law established by existing papal decisions. In practice as well as in theory, these sources of law served as a check on the exercise of hierocratic papal rule.

It is the contention of this chapter that, taken together, these aspects of the canon law should not be ignored by historians concerned with the canon law's place in the development of European law. They amounted to half steps toward constitutionalism. Those steps are to be found in the texts of the canon law itself, in the interpretations of the medieval jurists who shaped the common understanding of the texts, and in the role played by natural and divine law in the development of canonistic thought.[22]

The Complexity of the Canonical Texts

The first of these three features is visible in the great variety of ideas contained in the canon law itself. Like the texts found within the *Corpus iuris civilis*, the canons of the medieval canon law contained many different juristic principles, and not all of them pointed in the same direction. It is only by careful selection that one can isolate a single principle as a summary of all canonical thought. To pick only one theme from them ignores the complexity and the divergent principles found in the canonical texts. One of the most famous papal decretals refused to exercise a worldly power, citing biblical passages that discouraged confusion between the spiritual and secular spheres of

[22] See Charles Reid Jr, "The Canonistic Contribution to the Western Rights Tradition: An Historical Inquiry" (1991) 33 Boston College Law Review 37–92; Wim Decock, "Collective Legal Pluralism" (2017) 26 Rechtsgeschichte 103–126, at 103.

human life (X 4.17.13). This refusal was, it is true, a voluntary renunciation of power on the part of Pope Innocent III, but it was also an oft-repeated theme of the canons, one that should not be lost from sight.[23] The two spheres of life were separate. Nor should the statement of the existence of human freedom in the choice to accept or to reject the Christian faith be ignored (X 5.6.9), although it should certainly be balanced against the rule that once accepted in baptism, the responsibilities of a Christian could not lawfully be renounced.

Some modern scholars have concluded that this made the *Corpus iuris canonici,* like the *Corpus iuris civilis,* something like a "general storehouse" of legal ideas, open to be drawn upon by men with quite different goals than those shared with authors of the texts. The texts were open to varied interpretations and sometimes even to uses quite different from those their authors intended. Perhaps it is not wise to go quite that far in asserting the ambiguity of the law as a whole, but it certainly is true that the number of texts that contained statements authorizing a large scope of papal power were matched by others that placed limits on the exercise of that same power. Popes, one canon held, could not establish rules that violated either the precepts of the Ten Commandments, the Gospels, or the decrees of the first four general councils of the church (C. 25 q. 1 c. 6). Other canons recognized that a local custom, if reasonable and not contrary to the teaching of the Christian Gospel, could prevail in litigation even though it might seem to contradict the law found in a papal decretal (X 1.4.11). Papal rights and possessions could be lost by prescription, the civilian equivalent of adverse possession, though the period required before its completion was long (C. 16 q. 3 c. 17). In these specific respects, the popes were not above the law.

The necessity (or at least the advisability) for all prelates to take counsel with men of wisdom who would be touched by a decree before acting on it was also a recurrent subject found within the canon law itself (X 3.10.4).[24] This text was not an isolated example. Pope Innocent III recognized the importance of its underlying principle in matters affecting the construction and government of local churches (X 5.32.2). Commentators also called for as wide a process of consultation with those affected as was possible and

[23] This theme is well developed in John C Moore, *Pope Innocent III (1160/61–1216): To Root Up and to Plant* (Brill 2003).

[24] See also DL d'Avray, *Papacy, Monarchy and Marriage, 860–1600* (Cambridge University Press 2015) 61, observing that "the pope needed to legitimate his decisions in the eyes of the clerical elite on whose willing or grudging support his own authority depended."

sensible.[25] Decretals like these also had an effect in practice, just as modern administrative law has been shaped in diverse ways by the requirement of prior consultation with those who will be affected by an agency's decrees. No ruler should act without consultation.

Of course, it is true that the pope's authority was final in deciding cases appealed to the Roman court. The canons stated this, but they also stated that papal interpretations of the scriptures were to be regarded as of lesser authority than the opinions of the fathers of the church (D. 20 c. 1). If a pope's words and actions were heretical, he was also subject to deposition and punishment (D. 40 c. 6). What amounted to heretical views was a matter for discussion; some thought it extended to actions that subverted the right order of ecclesiastical governance. Others seem not to have gone that far. However, it was also stated that in specific ways, a particular pope's powers were themselves limited by the rules his predecessors and church councils had established.[26] What had been decided in earlier days was not to be reversed without strong reason. Although the Roman pontiff was described as holding unquestionable authority in the church, for example, he did not have the power to choose his successor (X 1.6.6), and his power to overturn the established decrees of his predecessors was limited.[27]

Recognition of the existence of these seemingly discordant authorities within the law of the church itself is an important factor in evaluating some of the actual conflicts that occurred in the later Middle Ages. The contest over the meaning and requirements of apostolic poverty within the Franciscan order[28] and, similarly, the storms unleashed by the Conciliar Movement now serve as long-remembered examples.[29] The powers ascribed to the papacy were involved in both. Opponents in these contests inevitably brought authorities from within the canon law into play. The essential point relevant to constitutionalism within the church is that both sides in these disputes

[25] Innocent IV (Sinibaldus Fliscus) (d. 1254), *Commentaria in V libros Decretalium* at X 5.32.2, no. 2 (Venice 1570): "Illi debent vocare alios qui commode possunt vocari." See Kenneth Pennington, *Pope and Bishops: The Papal Monarchy in the Twelfth and Thirteenth Centuries* (University of Pennsylvania Press 1984) 192–194.

[26] See, e.g., James Moynihan, *Papal Immunity and Liability in the Writings of the Medieval Canonists* (Gregorian University Press 1961) 46–110.

[27] See Brian Tierney, *Origins of Papal Infallibility 1150–1350* (Brill 1972) 186–196.

[28] Patrick Nold, *Pope John XXII and His Franciscan Cardinal: Bertrand de la Tour and the Apostolic Poverty Controversy* (Clarendon Press 2003); Arthur Stephen McGrade, *The Political Thought of William of Ockham* (Cambridge University Press 1974).

[29] See Brian Tierney, *Foundations of the Conciliar Theory: The Contribution of the Medieval Canonists from Gratian to the Great Schism* (Brill 1998); Alexander Russell, *Conciliarism and Heresy in Fifteenth-Century England* (Cambridge University Press 2017) 122–126.

marshalled support from within existing canon law. Those who urged acceptance of the conciliar position and those who resisted it drew upon the same legal texts. Their understanding of the purpose of those texts differed, but they shared the reference point found in the canonical texts.[30] Did this common reliance on a common source book that could be read in different ways amount to a step toward constitutional balance in the law of the church? Perhaps. But it was only a half step. The main thing it led to in fact was argument, distinction, and disagreement. However, in a larger sense it also made a connection with constitutionalism. The texts that set limitations of the exercise of power could be invoked, and sometimes were invoked, to temper the reach of a papal decision. Famous moments in church history show that. It is a mistake to forget them, paying attention only to the winners and losing sight of those laws and decretals that described papal powers in words susceptible of stating constitutional principles. As David McIlroy's chapter argues convincingly, the Trinitarian approach to law and government itself had the effect of pushing all Christians in the direction of thinking in terms of the establishment of dispersed authority. His conclusion draws strength from some of the texts found in the *Corpus iuris canonici*.

The Attitudes of the Canonists

The second half step toward the recognition of constitutionalism in the medieval canon law was the existence of a tendency among the canonists—and it was no more than that—to read narrowly the texts upon which statements of the plenitude of papal power were based.[31] For instance, the famous papal decretal of Innocent III, *Novit ille* (X 2.1.13), could be read as a proclamation of the subjection of all secular powers to the will of the Roman pontiffs. Innocent instructed the French clergy to accept his intervention to correct King Philip's sinful behavior, which, he said, had led Philip into an unhappy war with the English kings. The decree appears to magnify papal power. However, this decretal could also be understood in a minimalist sense. Canonists suggested that it might be regarded as asserting no more than that

[30] Arthur McGrade, *The Political Thought of William of Ockham* (Cambridge University Press 1974) 218–220.

[31] Lotte Kéry, "Dekretalenrecht zwischen Zentrale und Peripherie" in Jochen Johnrendt and Harald Müller (eds), *Römisches Zentrum und kirchliche Peripherie* (Gruyter 2008) 19–45, at 40–43.

all men were subject to the church's penitential discipline for their sins.[32] The humblest priest could exercise that jurisdiction. If the decretal was read that way, it was simply as a statement of a universally recognized principle among medieval Christians. All men were subject to correction in the penitential forum. True, a full-bodied reading of this decretal could open a wedge for regular ecclesiastical intervention in temporal matters, but for the clergy to have exercised the possibility regularly would have been contrary to the *communis opinio* among commentators on the law of the church. Similarly treated were the texts that said that the Roman pontiff could do no wrong, because he was presumed to have all law in his bosom. The canonists treated this as a legal presumption. It was, therefore, one that could be rebutted.[33] Like the oft-stated principle that the king could do no wrong in English law, this rule could actually serve to restrain the exercise of papal power. It could be assumed that he must have intended to do right.

As a practical matter, the subject was raised most often and most directly within the church itself by the principle that the pope had power over the entire church. The working assumption canonists brought to the task of interpreting papal decrees was that the pope could be assumed to have wished to act justly in the exercise of his powers.[34] In their hands, this assumption sometimes had the effect of adding unexpressed conditions to documents that exercised papal prerogative rights. One of the best examples of the effect of this assumption is the interpretation given to a 1265 decree of Clement IV that was added to the *Liber sextus* (Sext 3.4.2). According to its text, "The full disposition of churches, prebends, dignities, and other benefices pertains to the Roman pontiff." It followed and expanded upon a decretal from Pope Alexander III to the bishop of London that appeared in the Gregorian Decretals (X 3.5.6). The earlier decretal had limited the reach of one papal grant of an ecclesiastical benefice by stating that it had been granted under certain limiting assumptions. In interpreting exercises of the papal prerogative powers so fully claimed in the 1265 decree, medieval canonists took advantage of the earlier decretal to add several tacit conditions to all papal provisions. They treated them as unexpressed conditions that

[32] See gl. ord. ad X 2.1.13, v. *iudicare de feodo*: "Directe scilicet, sed tantum ratione peccati et inducendo ad poenitentiam."

[33] Gl. ord. ad D. 40 c. 1, v. *quis enim*: "Sed non dicitur hic quod sancti sunt sed quod sancti praesumuntur donec contrarium constat," continuing that the same presumption should exist "in quolibet sacerdote," although the presumption would be of lesser strength.

[34] Jacobus Menochius (d. 1607), *De praesumptionibus, coniecturis, signis et indiciis*, Lib. II, praes. 86, nos. 2–6 (Venice 1587).

were also embraced within the later decree. This assumption had the effect of limiting the effectiveness of what might otherwise have been a direct papal order. Thus, it might be assumed that the grant of a benefice had been made conditionally upon the existence of a vacancy in the church in which it had been granted; if so, it also followed that the grantee had not been given power to oust an incumbent even though it had not been made expressly subject to that condition. The grant also assumed that the grantee himself possessed valid holy orders, that he had the ability and desire to fulfill the duties involved, that he intended to be resident in the benefice, and that he had no other adequate source of income or need for the revenue flowing from it.[35] The limitations need not have been stated expressly for them to be operative. They were "read into it" because of the earlier decretal.

The canon law so understood had results in practice. One of the most famous relevant incidents in English history—Bishop Robert Grosseteste's refusal to obey a papal order in 1253—is one of them. The monastic chronicler, Matthew Paris, told the story.[36] The pope involved was Innocent IV and his mandate was to provide a benefice in the church of Lincoln for his nephew, Frederick of Lavagna. The mandate had been freighted with *non obstante* clauses, apparently directing the recipients to admit the nephew without quibbling over his merits, and yet Grosseteste would not execute it. In his judgment, the nephew was unsuitable to hold the benefice. According to some later portrayals of the incident, this action was either a sign of English resentment against foreigners holding English benefices or an example of the victory of a courageous bishop who put spiritual principle over the letter of the law.[37] It may equally be seen, however, as an example of one bishop's following the common interpretation of a text of the church's law as it was understood by contemporary canonists. In his judgment, the *non obstante* clauses were not sufficient to overcome the presumption that the pope had intended that the good of the church should prevail. It was simply a question of implementing the true intent of the papal grant. There were many other

[35] See gl. ord. ad X 1.3.17, v. *Si dignus extiterit*: "conditio ista sine omni expressione subintelligitur," citing X 1.6.8, which dealt with episcopal elections but was used here in support of the broader application of the same underlying principle.

[36] Matthew of Paris, in HR Luard (ed), *Chronica majora* (Rolls Series 1872–1883) v, 393.

[37] See WA Pantin, "Grosseteste's Relations with the Papacy and the Crown" in DA Callus (ed), *Robert Grosseteste: Scholar and Bishop* (Oxford University Press 1955) 178–215, at 194–195.

similar incidents,[38] and at least in one view they were actually examples of what might be called proto-constitutionalism in action.

There is another aspect too. It is also noteworthy how often the medieval popes acted through or with others. Even had they wished to do so, they could not have done everything that was asked of them, and in practice this meant that popes normally shared power with others. This proved true in matters great and small. The assembled cardinals and the presence of large numbers of bishops and abbots at the several papal councils that were called into existence during this period provide examples of shared power in great matters.[39] True, these assemblies were called together and led by the Roman pontiff, but the men through whom papal power was exercised were not ciphers. They had interests and minds of their own. The regular delegation of papal powers of dispensation to bishops throughout the Western church in marriage cases, in the creation of notaries public, and in the admission of clerics to offices and benefices were also examples of dispersal of power in smaller, but still important, matters.[40] Delegation involved the exercise of independent judgment. Once one looks at mundane details and away from some of the statements of political theory contained in the decretals, the medieval church's government looks more balanced than it does when observed only from the perspective of the exercise of political power.

Recognition of a Higher Law and Its Practical Effects

The third half step toward constitutionalism found within the classical canon law was the recognition of superior laws, powers beyond the power of governors to amend or repeal. Like the Roman law's Digest and Institutes, the canon law began with the proposition that there were several different kinds of law. The law contained in the *Corpus iuris canonici* was, therefore, more than a set of commands enacted by the legislator. In common with all legal systems, the canon law was understood to consist of four parts: natural law,

[38] See Brian Tierney, "Limits to Obedience in the Thirteenth Century: The Case of Robert Grosseteste" in Charles Curran (ed), *Contraception: Authority and Dissent* (Herder & Herder 1969) 76–100; Pennington, *Pope and Bishops*, 115–153, esp at 132 where Grosseteste's example is noted.

[39] IS Robinson, *The Papacy 1073–1198: Continuity and Innovation* (Cambridge 1990) 33–170; Joseph Lecler, "Pars Corporis Papae: le Sacré Collège dans l'ecclésiologie médiévale" in *L'homme devant Dieu: Mélanges offerts au Père Henri de Lubac* (Aubier 1963) ii, 183–198.

[40] See the many examples in Mary Cheney, *Roger, Bishop of Worcester, 1164–1179* (Clarendon Press 1980) 166–212.

divine law, the law of nations, and positive law.[41] The first consisted of the general principles God had put in the hearts of all human beings; it was shared even by some animals. The second consisted of the specific commands God had given, first to the Jewish people and later to all followers of Christ. The third, the ancestor of modern international law, was made up of laws and standards adopted by all civilized peoples. The fourth consisted of the specific laws adopted by individual nations and peoples.

Ideally, these four sources of law worked together in harmony, albeit at different levels of generality and with somewhat different results. The law of nature held that all men possessed a right to protect their persons and their possessions from attack, for example. The law of nations amended this slightly by assigning part of the task of protection to a system of public courts. In the interests of peace in society, all men had ceded a part of the natural law's right to the government. This being so, the civil law filled in the details of how that system functioned, establishing courts and systems of written or customary law to make the natural law's right a reality. The divine law enlarged the scope of the resulting prohibition against theft and bodily attack to include a command not to covet the property of one's neighbors.

The relevance of this long-accepted understanding of law's basic character to the subject of constitutionalism in the canon law is this. In the exercise of the extensive powers that the canons conceded to them, the popes were required to follow at least the first and the second of these kinds of law.[42] They set bounds to the papal plenitude of power. Encroachments on divine or natural law were ultra vires. As Peter Leithart's chapter in this volume shows, the subject has a long history.[43] The principle of forbearance was built into the law. Li-ann Thio's chapter also provides examples that demonstrate its long-lived ability to generate practical results.

Certainly it did so when viewed in historical perspective. Constraints in theory had practical consequences. Under the canon law, popes might, for instance, issue dispensations to permit the marriage of men and women related by consanguinity or affinity, but only if the degrees of relationship between them were beyond those prescribed by natural law and those prohibitions in

[41] See D. 1 cc. 1, 7.

[42] David Smolin and Kar Yong Lim, "Living as Christians under Civil Law" in Robert Cochran Jr and David VanDrunen (eds), *Law and the Bible: Justice, Mercy and Legal Institutions* (InterVarsity Press 2013) 208–238, at 227: "Natural Law is thus a central concept for all who seek to hold oppressive rulers to account."

[43] See also Bruce Frohnen and Charles Reid Jr, "Diversity in Western Constitutionalism" (1997–1998) 29 McGeorge Law Review 27–68.

the Book of Leviticus that had not been meant to bind only the Israelites. The popes were also limited to an extent by the decisions of their predecessors. At the very least, the term "*legibus solutus*" that was used to describe the powers of emperors and popes did not create in them an unlimited power to follow their own unfettered desires. To do so would make them ministers of the devil, not ministers of justice.[44] That would be to contravene divine law. The canonical texts proclaimed that what was done with the authority of the pope was done "by the authority of God." So stated the glossa ordinaria to the Gregorian Decretals, but the gloss added, "This is true if what he has done is for a just cause."[45] This limitation was ascribed both to the force of natural law and divine command.

The relevant question, of course, is whether these limitations—stated and understood by all medieval canonists—actually had any significant consequence in the growth of constitutional thought. The canonists certainly paid lip service to them. They did so repeatedly. Of that there cannot be much doubt. Hostiensis, for example, in describing the wide power to establish law that inhered in the papal office, went on to qualify that power. The popes could not subvert principles established by the apostles, the prophets, and the holy church fathers. Neither could they make laws that "subverted the Church's status or contradicted the Christian faith."[46] The fifteenth century's most celebrated canonist, known as Panormitanus, similarly set limits to the obedience owed to the decrees of the Roman pontiffs. Commenting on a decree of Pope Innocent III placed in the Gregorian Decretals, he noted that "if the pope orders a layman not subject to him in temporal matters, to hand over something to another, [the layman] need not obey him, unless the order is based upon a legitimate cause."[47] The canonists almost always qualified their expression of the great powers of the Roman pontiffs with a qualifying phrase like that—popes could act to suspend an existing law or to take specific actions only if they acted *ex iusta causa*, for a just cause. Of course, qualifications like this sometimes left open questions. What exactly was required to prove that a papal order contradicted the divine law that

[44] Ian Christopher Levy, "Liberty of Conscience and Freedom of Religion in the Medieval Canonists and Theologians" in Timothy Ahah and Allen Hertzke (eds), *Christianity and Freedom*, vol I: *Historical Perspectives* (Cambridge University Press 2016) 149–175, 166–169.

[45] Gl. ord. ad X 1.7.2, v. *divina*.

[46] Henricus de Segusio (d. 1271), *Summa aurea*, Lib. I, tit. *De constitutionibus*, no. 3. See also Atria Larson, "Popes and the Canon Law" in Keith Sisson and Atria Larson (eds), *Companion to the Medieval Papacy: Growth of an Ideology and Institution* (Brill 2016) 135–157, at 149–151.

[47] Nicholaus de Tudeschis (d. c. 1445), *Commentaria super Decretalium Libros* at X 1.2.7, no. 16. (Venice 1615).

was accepted as at the heart of Christianity? What exactly constituted a just cause? Did such open-ended qualifications impose any real limitations on the exercise of papal power? Only if they did, it may be said, can one fully justify the contention that the medieval canon law made serious contributions to this aspect of the development of constitutionalism. If we cannot conclude that they always did, we must say only that the canon law may have provided some principles or general ideas that would prove useful in that development.

There is evidence to support both sides of that question. The documents by which the popes acted were careful in providing justifications according to this understanding of the requirements of natural and divine law. A young man who had taken deacon's orders was allowed to become a knight instead through the exercise of the papal dispensing power, but the document that authorized the step stated that he had only taken orders because of the reverence and fear he had of his parents, who had compelled him to accept ordination. He was also freed from some (but not all) of the religious obligations that went with holy orders, but this was permitted "because all of them had been introduced by purely human law" and because the young man had taken holy orders at the orders of his father and mother.[48] In other words, the document itself spelled out the just cause.

Similar limitations worked their way into the canon law itself. It was, for example, the reason commonly given for prohibiting the baptism of the children of Jewish parents against the wishes of the parents. The law of nature established the existence of special ties between parent and child. Even most animals observed a duty founded on those ties. They cared for their young. Parents thus owed support and care to their children; children owed respect and a measure of obedience to their parents.[49] It followed that even though the canonists recognized baptism as a great good, perhaps the greatest good, its bestowal against the wishes of Jewish parents was not strong enough to overcome the obligations that existed under the law of nature.[50] Similarly in the law of marriage and divorce, the papal power of dispensation to permit marriages of men and women related to each other within the prohibited

[48] Gregory Sayre (d. 1602), *Decisiones casuum conscientiae*, Lib. I, tit. 23, dec. 1 (Venice 1627): "praesertim cum haec omnia iure humano solum inducta esse constent."

[49] I have described the medieval jurists' approach to this subject at greater length in *Natural Law in Court* (Harvard University Press 2015) 18–21.

[50] See Thomas Aquinas, *Summa theologiae*, iii, 68 a.10; Ian Christopher Levy, "Liberty of Conscience and Freedom of Religion in the medieval Canonists" in Ahah and Hertzke (eds), *Christianity and Freedom*, 148–175, at 154–155; Steven Rowan, "Ulrich Zasius and the Baptism of Jewish Children" (1975) 6 Sixteenth Century Journal 3–25.

degrees of affinity and consanguinity, as defined by the Fourth Lateran Council of 1215, was limited to the outer degrees. If they were related within the first or second degrees, which were thought to be subject to prohibition by the law of nature as well as by the positive law of the church, no papal power of dispensation was available to them. This was the accepted doctrine of the day, and the popes themselves were apparently bound by it.[51]

It is also worth considering the power of ministers in the Roman court as a practical check on papal absolutism. Perhaps this does not rise to the level of a constitutional principle, but it is a fact that once they are set in place, institutions often prove difficult to dislodge. They limit the power even of the governors who established them. The cardinals in Rome, though chosen by the popes, sometimes successfully resisted papal efforts to change or reform the system they knew.[52] The creation of the *Rota Romana* as a court of appeal from the far corners of the Latin church provides another example of the practical limitations of papal powers, perhaps an even better one. Its auditors would not have assumed they were anything but representatives of the papacy, but that did not mean they did not make up their own minds about what the canon law required. That was the task assigned to them and they exercised it without placing the establishment of papal powers above the object of doing justice to the litigants who came before them.[53] The court in which that task was carried out has proved durable over the centuries. In fact, it still exists. What looks like bureaucratic inertia, when coupled with a recognition of the existence of enduring principles of justice, actually turns out to contribute indirectly to the advance of constitutionalism.[54]

Conclusion

What, then, is the conclusion from the evidence presented about the contribution of the medieval canon law to the concept and history of

[51] See d'Avray, *Papacy, Monarchy and Marriage*.

[52] Examples are found in Jane Sayers, "Papal Administration in England" in Brian Tierney and Peter Linehan (eds), *Authority and Power* (Cambridge University Press 1980) 117–121, and Brian Ferme, "Lyndwood and the Canon Law: The Papal *Plenitudo Potestatis* and the College of Cardinals" in Norman Doe, Mark Hill, and Robert Ombres (eds), *English Canon Law: Essays in Honour of Bishop Eric Kemp* (University of Wales Press 1998) 13–22.

[53] Angelo Santangelo Cordani, *La Giurisprudenza della Rota Romana nel Secolo XIV* (Giuffrè 2001) 372–389.

[54] The failure of the "court packing plan" hatched by American president Franklin Delano Roosevelt during the 1930s provides a modern example.

constitutionalism? This chapter has used the metaphor of half steps to describe it.[55] The most that can honestly be said in conclusion is that the medieval canon law contained many of the ingredients that proved important in the gradual development of Western constitutionalism as defined at the start of this chapter. Of course, that is not the equivalent of reaching the modern understanding of what the term means. But it is something. As Jonathan Burnside's chapter on the history of ancient Israel reminds us, most movements toward constitutionalism have proceeded by fits and starts. Halfway measures in both directions have long been part of our history—a profitable part. The medieval canon law explored in this chapter fits within the same broad pattern to which he calls our attention.

With all the reservations that have caused historians to treat the medieval church as the home of despotism, the evidence explored briefly in this chapter tells a different story. The church's canons, the commentaries devoted to discovering their meaning, and the common recognition of a higher law were all parts of the system of law adopted by the church. When they were added to the balance, they made a difference. It is an error to treat the canon law as an outright grant of unlimited power to a single individual. The half steps outlined in this chapter support the argument that, in some measure, the law of the medieval church did contain elements of the two basic requirements for constitutionalism that were discussed at the start of this chapter.

[55] Recent scholarship provides some support for this conclusion (though not the metaphor) among European scholars. See, e.g., Padoa-Schioppa, *Studi*, 277–295.

7

Reformation

The Protestant Reformation of Constitutionalism

John Witte Jr.

The Protestant Reformation erupted with Martin Luther's posting of the Ninety-Five Theses on the church door in Wittenberg in 1517 and his burning of the medieval canon law books at the city gates three years later. The Reformation soon split into four main branches, with ample regional and denominational variation within each branch. *Lutheranism* spread throughout the northern Holy Roman Empire, Prussia, and Scandinavia, consolidated by Luther's catechisms and the Augsburg Confession (1530), and by local Bible translations modeled on Luther's German Bible. *Anabaptists* fanned out in small communities throughout Europe, Russia, and eventually North America, most of them devoted to the founding religious principles of the Schleitheim Confession (1527) and the ideals of the New Testament. *Anglicanism* was established in England by King Henry VIII and Parliament in the 1530s and, once consolidated by the Book of Common Prayer (1559/1662) and later the King James Bible (1611), spread throughout the vast British Empire in North America, Africa, the Middle East, the Indian subcontinent, and Australasia. *Calvinist* communities, modeled on John Calvin's Geneva and anchored by the Calvin's writings and the Genevan Academy, spread into portions of Switzerland, France, Germany, Hungary, the Netherlands, Scotland, England, and North America. In Europe, this checkerboard of Protestant communities, living uneasily alongside each other and their Catholic neighbors, was protected for a time by such constitutional documents as the Peace of Augsburg (1555), the Edict of Nantes (1598), the Peace of Westphalia (1648), and the Toleration Act (1689), but religious persecution and religious warfare were tragically regular events until well into the eighteenth century.[1]

[1] See Thomas Albert Howard and Mark A. Noll (eds), *Protestantism after 500 Years* (Oxford University Press 2016); Udo Di Fabio and Johannes Schilling (eds), *Die Weltwirkung der*

John Witte Jr., *Reformation: The Protestant Reformation of Constitutionalism* in *Christianity and Constitutionalism*.
Edited by: Nicholas Aroney and Ian Leigh, Oxford University Press. © Oxford University Press 2022.
DOI: 10.1093/oso/9780197587256.003.0007

Although the Protestant Reformation built on several late medieval reform efforts, it also offered several distinct theological teachings that had direct legal implications. Early Protestant Reformers were largely united in teaching that salvation came through faith in the Gospel, not by works of the law. Each individual was to stand directly before God, to seek God's gracious forgiveness of sin, and to conduct life in accordance with the Bible and Christian conscience. To the Reformers, the medieval canon law administrated by the clergy obstructed the individual's direct relationship with God and obscured simple biblical norms for right living. Early Protestants further taught that the church was at heart a community of saints, not a corporation of law. Its cardinal signs and callings were to preach the Word, to administer the sacraments, to catechize the young, and to care for the needy. The medieval clergy's expansive legal rule in Christendom, in the Reformers' view, obstructed the divine mission of the church and usurped the role of the state as God's vice regent and legal ruler in the earthly kingdom. Protestants recognized that the church needed internal rules to govern its polity, teaching, and discipline. Church officials and councils needed to oppose legal injustice and combat political tyranny. But for most early Protestants, law was primarily the province of the state, not the church—of the magistrate, not the pastor.

These new Protestant teachings helped to transform early modern Western constitutionalism. The Protestant Reformation permanently broke the international rule of the medieval Catholic Church and canon law, splintering Western Christendom into competing nations and regions, each with its own religious and political rulers. The Protestant Reformation triggered a massive shift of power and property from the church to the state. State rulers now assumed jurisdiction over numerous subjects, persons, and social institutions previously governed by the Catholic Church and its canon law. And the Protestant Reformation catalyzed a wide range of new legal and political theories and laws, not least on constitutionalism.

But the wide variety of early modern Protestant confessions also yielded a similarly wide variety of constitutional norms and practices. Absolutist monarchists in Denmark, England, and Prussia were as fervently Protestant as democratic revolutionaries in Scotland, the Netherlands, England, and America. Strict Anglican or Lutheran religious establishments were as deeply

Reformation: Wie der Protestantismus unsere Welt verändert hat (CH Beck 2017); John Witte Jr and Amy S Wheeler (eds), *The Protestant Reformation of the Church and the World* (Westminster John Knox Press 2018).

rooted in Reformation teachings as novel Anabaptist or Calvinist theories of religious freedom. Some early modern Protestant groups were intense religious pietists and political quietists, while others worked relentlessly to develop written constitutions, enumerated bills of rights, clear separations of powers, and federalist structures of government. Some Protestants turned cheeks in expression of Christian love and martyrdom; others swung swords in pursuit of just wars and democratic revolutions.

This chapter illustrates a few of these diverse Protestant contributions to Western constitutionalism. I focus on early modern Lutherans, Anabaptists, and Calvinists on both sides of the Atlantic. Readers can learn about the medieval antecedents and parallel Anglican expressions of these views in the marvelous chapters in this volume by R. H. Helmholz and Joan Lockwood O'Donovan. More extensive discussions of the development of human rights, natural law, covenant, and federalism—within and well beyond the Protestant world—appear in the excellent chapters by John Milbank, Julian Rivers, David VanDrunen, and Nicholas Aroney.

Lutheran Constitutionalism

The Forms and Functions of the State

The Lutheran Reformation of Germany and Scandinavia gave the local Christian magistrate ample new political power over civil and spiritual affairs.[2] Luther replaced the medieval "two swords" teaching with a new "two kingdoms" theory. The *invisible* church of the heavenly kingdom, he argued, was a perfect community of saints, in which all stood equal in dignity before God, all enjoyed perfect Christian liberty, and all governed their affairs in accordance with the Gospel. The *visible* church of this earthly kingdom, however, embraced saints and sinners alike. Its members still stood directly before God and still enjoyed liberty of conscience, including the liberty to leave the visible church itself. But unlike the invisible church, the visible church

[2] For illustrative writings, see Hermann W Beyer, *Luther und das Recht* (repr edn, Salzwasser-Verlag Gmbh 2013); JM Porter (ed), *Luther—Selected Political Writings* (Fortress Press 1974). For overviews, see Martin Heckel, *Martin Luthers Reformation und das Recht* (Mohr Siebeck 2016); Virpi Mäkinen (ed), *Lutheran Reformation and the Law* (Brill 2006); Mathias Schmoeckel, *Das Recht der Reformation* (Mohr Siebeck 2014); WDJ Cargill Thompson, *The Political Thought of Martin Luther* (Philip Broadhead ed, Barnes and Noble 1984); John Witte Jr, *Law and Protestantism: The Legal Teachings of the Lutheran Reformation* (Cambridge University Press 2002).

needed both the Gospel and human law to govern its members' relationships with God and with fellow believers. The clergy must administer the Gospel. The magistrate must administer the law.

Luther was more concerned with the function than with the form of the state. On the one hand, he believed that the magistrate was God's vice regent in the earthly kingdom, called to enforce God's Word and law, to reflect God's majesty and authority, to render God's justice and judgment on earthly affairs. The state was, in this sense, a "divine office," a "holy estate," a "Godly calling" within the earthly kingdom, Luther wrote. "Law and earthly government are a great gift of God to mankind," indeed "an image, shadow, and figure of the dominion of Christ." But that divine political mandate included exercising God's judgment and wrath against human sinfulness. "Princes and magistrates are the bows and arrows of God," Luther wrote, equipped to hunt down God's enemies near and far, using military power and criminal punishment when needed. Indeed, the hand of the Christian magistrate, judge, or soldier "that wields the sword and slays is not man's hand, but God's."[3]

On the other hand, Luther regarded the magistrate as the loving "father of the community," called to care for his political subjects as if they were his children, with his political subjects honoring and obeying him as the Bible commanded. Like a devout father, the magistrate was to keep the peace and to protect his subjects from danger and damage to their persons, properties, and reputations. He was to deter his subjects from abusing themselves through drunkenness, wastrel living, prostitution, gambling, and other vices. He was to nurture and sustain his subjects through the community chest, the public almshouse, and the state-run hospital. He was to educate them through the public school, library, and lectern. He was to see to their spiritual needs by supporting the ministry of the locally established church and encouraging their attendance and participation through the laws of Sabbath observance, tithing, and holy days. He was to see to their material needs by reforming inheritance and property laws to ensure more even distribution of parents' property among their children. And the magistrate was to set a moral example of virtue, piety, love, and charity in his own home and private life for his faithful subjects to emulate and to respect.[4]

[3] *D. Martin Luthers Werke: Kritische Gesamtausgabe* (H. Böhlaus Nachfolger 1883) 30/2:554 (hereafter WA); Jaroslav Pelikan et al (eds), *Luther's Works* (Muhlenberg Press 1955–1968) 2:139; 13:44; 17:171; 44:92; 45:85; 46:96, 237 (hereafter LW).

[4] WA 30/1:155.

These twin metaphors of the Christian magistrate—as the lofty vice regent of God and as the loving father of the community—described the basics of Lutheran political theory for the next four centuries. For Luther, political authority was divine in origin but earthly in operation. It expressed God's harsh judgment against sin but also God's tender mercy for sinners. It communicated the law of God but also the lore of the local community. It depended upon the church for prophetic direction but it took over from the church all jurisdiction—governance of marriage, education, poor relief, and other earthly subjects traditionally governed by the Catholic Church's canon law. Either metaphor standing alone could be a recipe for abusive tyranny or officious paternalism—both of which sometimes occurred in Lutheran lands in later centuries. But both metaphors together provided Luther and his followers with the core ingredients of a robust Christian republicanism and budding Christian welfare state.

State Jurisdiction and Legislation

Building on Luther's views, Lutheran jurists defined more clearly the subject matter jurisdiction of the state and the ambit of the new state legislation that was to replace the medieval canon law and the medieval church courts. A decisive early contribution came from Luther's Wittenberg colleague and successor, Philip Melanchthon (1509–1560). He described the Christian magistrate as "a voice of the Ten Commandments" within the earthly kingdom. "When you think about *Obrigkeit*, about princes or lords, picture in your mind a man holding in one hand the tables of the Ten Commandments and holding in the other a sword," he wrote provocatively.[5]

Melanchthon took this image directly into his account of the positive law, which he organized using the two tables of the Decalogue. The First Table of the Decalogue, Melanchthon wrote, undergirded state laws governing spiritual morality, the relationship between persons and God. The Second Table undergirded state laws governing civil morality, the relationships between persons.

As custodians of the First Table of the Decalogue, magistrates must not only pass laws against idolatry, blasphemy, and violations of the

[5] *Melanchthons Werke*, in G. Bretschneider (ed), *Corpus Reformatorum* (H. Böhlau 1864) 22:615 (hereafter CR).

Sabbath—offenses that the First Table prohibits on its face—but also "establish pure doctrine" and right liturgy, "prohibit all wrong doctrine," "punish the obstinate," and root out the heathen and the heterodox. Melanchthon came to this position reluctantly in the 1530s and 1540s, knowing that he was departing from Luther's early call for universal "freedom of a Christian."[6] But Melanchthon lamented the perennial outbreaks of violent antinomianism and spiritual radicalism in Reformation Germany by those who took too literally Luther's teachings of free grace. To allow such blasphemy and chaos to continue without firm rejoinder, Melanchthon believed, was ultimately to betray God and the political office that enforced God's law in earthly life. Magistrates must "maintain external discipline according to *all* the commandments," he concluded, and thus must "prohibit, abolish, and punish these depravities" and "compel them to accept the Holy Gospel."[7]

This was the theoretical basis for the welter of new state laws establishing religion in Lutheran lands. These laws were set out in the hundreds of elaborate church ordinances promulgated in the sixteenth and seventeenth centuries. These church ordinances both reflected and directed the resystematization of dogma; the truncation of the sacraments; the reforms of liturgy, devotional life, and the religious calendar; the vernacularization of the Bible, liturgy, and preaching; the expansion of catechesis and religious instruction in schools and universities; the revamping of corporate worship, congregational music, religious symbolism, church art, and architecture; the radical reforms of ecclesiastical discipline and local church administration; and the new practices of tithing, baptism, confirmation, weddings, burial, diaconal care, sanctuary, and much more.

All these aspects of spiritual life had been at the heart of the spiritual jurisdiction of the medieval church and its canon law. They were now subject to the Protestant state's religious establishment laws. Particularly after the Peace of Augsburg (1555) and the Peace of Westphalia (1648) confirmed the constitutional principle that each civil ruler was free to establish the religion of his own local polity (*cuius regio eius religio*), religious establishment laws became increasingly detailed, ornate, and routinized.[8] Vestiges of these laws remain in place in Lutheran lands today, although strong new policies of

[6] LW 31:327–377.

[7] CR 22:617–618; *Melanchthon on Christian Doctrine: Loci Communes 1555*, (Clyde L. Manschrek ed and tr, Oxford University Press 1965) 324–336.

[8] In Sidney Z Ehler and John B Morrall (eds), *Church and State through the Centuries: A Collection of Historic Documents with Commentaries* (Newman Press 1954) 164–173, 189–193.

religious disestablishment are now afoot in Scandinavia and several German states.

While the First Table of the Decalogue helped define the state's spiritual jurisdiction, the Second Table supported the state's civil jurisdiction, the positive laws governing relations between persons. Melanchthon and other Lutheran writers, such as Johann Oldendorp (ca. 1486–1567), Martin Chemnitz (1522–1586), and Nicolaus Hemming (1513–1600), set out a whole series of state laws under each commandment. On the basis of the commandment "Honor thy father and mother," they argued, magistrates were obligated to prohibit and punish disobedience, disrespect, or disdain of authorities such as parents, political rulers, teachers, employers, masters, and others. Magistrates were also to build the positive laws of authority—constitutional law, administrative law, master-servant laws, and more. The commandment "Thou shalt not kill" undergirded laws against unlawful killing, violence, assault, battery, and other offenses against the bodies of one's neighbors. "Thou shalt not commit adultery" and "Thou shalt not covet thy neighbor's wife or maidservant" were the foundations of laws against sex crimes—adultery, fornication, sexual indulgence, prostitution, pornography, obscenity, and similar offenses—as well as positive laws of marital formation, maintenance, and dissolution; child care, custody, and control; and other aspects of the marital household. "Thou shalt not steal" supported positive laws against theft, burglary, embezzlement, and similar offenses against another's property, as well as waste or noxious or sumptuous use of one's own property. This commandment also supported positive laws of real and personal property and its acquisition, use, maintenance, encumbrance, sale, alienation, and more. On the basis of the commandment "Thou shalt not bear false witness," magistrates were to punish all forms of perjury, dishonesty, fraud, defamation, and other violations of a person's reputation or status in the community. And they were to build the positive laws of oaths, promises, and contracts, of keeping one's word to one's neighbor, as well as the laws of procedure, evidence, and testimony in court proceedings. Finally, on the basis of the commandment "Thou shalt not covet," magistrates were to punish all attempts to perform offensive acts against another's person, property, reputation, or relationships and to establish the basic rules protecting the privacy of one's household from the covetous privations of neighbors.[9]

[9] See detailed sources in Witte, *Law and Protestantism*, 121–176.

Many of these aspects of social intercourse had also been governed by medieval canon law and organized in part under the church's seven sacraments.[10] The sacrament of marriage, for example, supported the positive canon laws of sex, marriage, and family life. The sacrament of penance supported the canon law of crimes against the persons, properties, and reputations of others. The sacraments of baptism and confirmation undergirded the constitutional law of natural rights and duties of Christian believers. The sacrament of holy orders supported the law of the clergy. The sacrament of extreme unction supported the positive laws of burial, inheritance, foundations, and trusts. Lutheran jurists replaced the seven sacraments with the Ten Commandments to organize the various systems of positive law, and they looked to the state, instead of the church, to exercise this jurisdiction.

Equity and Adjudication

Lutheran writers insisted that these new state laws required firm application but also equitable judgment by the judiciary. "The strictest law [can do] the greatest wrong," Luther wrote. Thus, "equity is necessary" in the application of the law. Judges must not "rashly . . . relax laws and discipline." But they must balance firmness and fairness and recognize circumstances that might mitigate against literal application of the rule or that might raise questions that the rule does not and perhaps should not reach. In such instances, "equity will weigh for or against" strict application of the rule, and a wise ruler will know the more just course. "But the weighing must be of such kind that the law is not undermined, for no undermining of natural law and divine law must be allowed."[11]

Lutheran jurist Johann Oldendorp went further in insisting that every application of a legal rule required a judge to apply equity, for every law was, by its nature, general and abstract. No legislator can perfectly anticipate the circumstances in which the rule will be applied. Thus, every application of

[10] See Paul Wilpert, *Lex et Sacramentum in Mittelalter* (W De Gruyter 1969); Harold J Berman, *Law and Revolution: The Formation of the Western Legal Tradition* (Harvard University Press 1983) 165–198; RH Helmholz, *The Spirit of the Classical Canon Law* (repr edn, University of Georgia Press 2010).

[11] WA TR 3, Nos 315, 4178; LW 54:43–44, 325.

every rule has to be governed by equity, lest the rule of law and the justice of the state be compromised.[12]

Oldendorp defined equity as the capacity and responsibility of a judge to make a reasoned and conscientious judgment in each particular case. Equity required the judge to study carefully the rules and the facts of the particular case and to compare them to similar rules and cases. This, he said, was an exercise of "civil reason." Equity also required the judge to consult and apply his conscience, the God-given "law inside people." This was "a judgment of the soul," which required prayer, meditation on the Bible, and sober reflection in search of God's guidance for the case. This pious method was to be used not only for the hard case—whether to execute a felon convicted for a capital crime on slender evidence or to separate a young child dependent on its loving mother in a case of disputed custody—but also in every legal case, since every case required equity. In some cases, this equitable method might yield a strict application of the rule. In other cases, it might compel the judge to suspend a legal rule; to interpret it favorably toward one of the parties; to give special solicitude to parties who were poor, orphaned, widowed, or abused; or to reform and improve the rule to ensure its future equitable application or legislative amendment.[13] As a theory of judicial judgment, Oldendorp's theory of equity was a distinct form of both conscientious practical reasoning and pious judicial activism.

Oldendorp's theory of equity built squarely on Luther's belief in the Christian conscience as the ultimate source of moral decisions. Luther had justified his own defiance of the emperor at the Diet of Worms in 1521 as an act "for God and in my conscience."[14] In his later writings, he also urged every magistrate not only to "have the law as firmly in hand as the sword" but also, Solomon-like, to "cling solely to God, and to be at him constantly, praying for a right understanding beyond that of all the law books and teachers, to rule his subjects."[15] Oldendorp made God-given conscience a constituent element of his theory of legal judgment, and made equitable judgment the vocation of a professional Christian judge. Just as Luther, a learned theologian of the church, could ultimately break the canon law of the church that

[12] See Johann Oldendorp, *Wat byllich und recht ist* (1529) in Erik Wolf (ed), *Quellenbuch zur Geschichte der deutschen Rechtswissenschaft* (Klosterman 1950) 51–68, 59; Johann Oldendorp, *De iure et aequitate forensis disputatio* (Johann I. Köln 1541) 72.

[13] Oldendorp, De iure et aequitate, 13; Johann Oldendorp, *Lexicon Juris* (Egenolph 1553), s.v. "aequitas" and "iudicium"; Johann Oldendorp, *Topicorum Legalium* (np 1545) 194–196.

[14] WA 7:838.

[15] WA 11:272–273.

violated conscience, so the judge, a learned counselor of the state, could ultimately waive the civil law of the state that trespassed these same transcendent norms.

Oldendorp also built on the traditional medieval teaching that the Catholic Church's canon law was the "the mother of exceptions," "the epitome of the law of love," and "the mother of justice."[16] These equitable qualities had traditionally rendered the canon laws applied in church courts an attractive alternative to the civil laws applied in secular courts. Oldendorp's theory sought to render these equitable qualities endemic to all state laws and to all state courts. Law and equity, he believed, were fundamentally conjoined, whatever the source of the law, and whatever the forum for its implementation. It was the duty of the Christian legislator to promulgate civil laws consistent with the moral teachings of divine law and natural law. It was the duty of the Christian judge to interpret these laws with the equitable methods of both civil and spiritual reason.

Before the Protestant Reformation, equity was largely the prerogative of the canon law and ecclesiastical judge. Thus, in medieval Germany, cases that required formal equitable remedies were removed to the church courts for resolution. Likewise in medieval England, equity was administered in the court of the chancellor, staffed by a ranking ecclesiastic trained in canon law. Oldendorp's theory effectively merged law and equity, *ius et aequitas*. This theory helped to support the merger of church courts and state courts; separate courts of equity were no longer required. It helped to support the convergence of canon law and civil law in Lutheran Germany. And it helped to support the growing professionalization of the German judiciary and the requirement that judges be educated both in law and in theology, in civil law and in canon law.[17] Through the writings and work of Luther, Melanchthon, Oldendorp, and many others, Lutheran jurisprudence contributed significantly to the development of modern theories of the state.

[16] Oldendorp, *De iure et aequitate*, 32–33. See Eugen Wohlhaupter, *Aequitas canonica: Eine Studie aus dem kanonischen Recht* (F Schoningh 1931); Harold J Berman, "Medieval English Equity" in Berman (ed), *Faith and Order: The Reconciliation of Law and Religion* (Wm B Eerdmans 1993) 55–82.

[17] See generally Karl H Burmeister, *Das Studium der Rechte im Zeitalter des Humanismus im deutschen Rechtsbereich* (G. Pressler 1974); RH Helmholz (ed), *Canon Law in Protestant Lands* (repr edn, Duncker & Humblot 2013).

Anabaptist Constitutionalism

Early modern Anabaptists expounded a two-kingdoms theory that more fully separated the redeemed realm of religion and the church from the fallen realm of politics and the state.[18] Emerging as a new form of Protestantism in the early 1520s, Anabaptists were scattered into various groups of Amish, Brethren, Hutterites, Mennonites, and later Baptist and Free Church groups on both sides of the Atlantic. But most followed the lead of such theologians as Pilgrim Marpeck (d. 1556), Menno Simons (1496–1561), Dirk Philips (1504–1568), and others who called for a return to the simple teachings of the New Testament and apostolic church.

Separation of Church and State

Emulating the apostolic church, Anabaptist communities ascetically withdrew from civil and political life into small, self-sufficient, and often intensely democratic communities. These communities were governed internally by biblical principles of discipleship, simplicity, charity, and nonresistance. They set their own standards of worship, liturgy, diet, discipline, dress, and education. They handled their own affairs of property, contracts, commerce, marriage, and inheritance—so far as possible by appeal to biblical laws and practices, not those of the state. And they enforced their internal religious laws not by coercion but by persuasion, and not for the sake of retribution but for the redemption of the sinner and restoration of that person to the community. Recalcitrant sinners and community members who grew violent or destructive or persistently betrayed the community's ideals faced shunning and banishment from the community. Moreover, when Anabaptist communities grew too large or too internally divided, they deliberately colonized themselves, eventually spreading from Russia to Ireland to the farthest frontiers of North America.

The state and its law, most Anabaptists believed, was part of the fallen world, to be avoided so far as possible in accordance with biblical injunctions

[18] For illustrative writings, see Walter Klaassen, *Anabaptism in Outline* (Herald Press 1981). For overviews, see William R Estep, *The Anabaptist Story: An Introduction to Sixteenth-Century Anabaptism* (Eerdmans 1996); Robert Friedmann, *The Theology of Anabaptism* (repr edn, Herald Press 1998); Guy F Hershberger (ed), *The Recovery of the Anabaptist Vision* (repr edn, Herald Press 2001); George Huntston Williams, *The Radical Reformation* (3rd rev edn, Truman State University Press 2000).

that Christians should not be "of the world" or "conformed" to it. Once the perfect creation of God, the world was now a fallen, sinful regime that lay beyond "the perfection of Christ" and beyond the daily concern of the Christian believer. God had built a "wall of separation" between the redeemed church and the fallen world, Menno Simons wrote, quoting Ephesians 2:14.[19] God had allowed the world to survive by ordaining magistrates who were empowered through positive laws to use coercion to maintain a modicum of order and peace. Christians should obey the laws of political authorities, so far as the Bible commanded—paying taxes, registering properties, avoiding theft and homicide, keeping promises, and testifying truthfully. But Christians should avoid active participation in and unnecessary interaction with the world and the state—avoiding litigation, oath swearing, state education, banking, large-scale commerce, trade fairs, public festivals, drinking houses, theaters, games, political office, policing, and military service. Most early modern Anabaptists were pacifists, preferring derision, exile, or death to active participation in war or violence. This aversion to common political and civic activities often earned Anabaptists scorn, reprisal, and repression by Catholics and Protestants alike—even violent martyrdom in some instances.[20]

Religious Liberty

While unpopular in its genesis, Anabaptism ultimately proved to be a vital source of Western constitutional arguments for religious liberty. Particularly Baptists and other Free Church groups in England and early America advocated "a wall of separation between the garden of the Church and the wilderness of the world," as Rhode Island founder Roger Williams put it famously in 1643.[21] They also advocated the liberty of conscience of every individual and the freedom of association of every peaceable religious group without state establishments of religion.

"The notion of an [established] Christian commonwealth should be exploded forever," wrote John Leland (1754–1841), the fiery American Baptist preacher in summary of Anabaptist teachings.[22] All religious

[19] Primary texts in Klaasen, *Anabaptism in Outline*, 245–257.
[20] See J Thieleman Van Braght, *Martyr's Mirror* (repr edn, Herald Press 1981).
[21] *The Complete Writings of Roger Williams* (Russell and Russell 1963) 7 vols,, 1:392.
[22] LF Greene (ed), *The Writings of John Leland* (Arno Press 1969) 118.

establishments are "evil," because when "uninspired, fallible men make their own opinions tests of orthodoxy," and then religion is stunted and stilted, "ignorance and superstition prevail, or persecution rages." Establishments inspire hypocrisy because people embrace the religion favored and pampered by law. "Establishments not only wean and alienate the affections of one from another" but also drive nonconformists away from the state, taking their loyalty, work, and taxes with them and leaving dull, anemic religions to propagate themselves or convert others by coercion or bribery. Establishments reduce religion and church into an agent and "trick of the state." And establishments merely cover for the insecurity and doubt of both church leaders, who lack faith in the cogency of their views, and political rulers, who "often fear that if they leave every man to think, speak, and worship as he pleases, that the whole cause [of statecraft] will be wrecked in diversity."[23]

In place of state establishments of religion and Christian commonwealths, Anabaptists advocated religious voluntarism—the freedom of each person to choose, change, or reject religion. God called the adult individual to make a conscientious choice to accept the faith and to signal that acceptance through adult baptism—metaphorically, to scale the wall of separation between the fallen world and the garden of religion to come "within the perfection of Christ." State coercion or control of this choice—either directly through persecution and repression or indirectly through withholding civil rights and benefits from those who made the choice—was an offense both against the individual and against God. A plurality of religions should coexist in the community. It was for God, not the state, to decide which religion should flourish and which should fade.

In place of state patronage of religion, Anabaptists demanded autonomy of church governance. Every religious body, they argued, should be free from state control of its assembly and worship, from state regulations of its property and polity, from state incorporation of its society and clergy, from state interference in its discipline and government, and from state collection of religious tithes and taxes. Some Free Church advocates went further to oppose such traditional state supports of religion as tax exemptions, civil immunities, and property donations. They feared that religious bodies receiving any state benefits would invariably become beholden to the state, dependent on its largess, and distracted from their divine mandates. "If civil Rulers go so far out of their Sphere as to take the Care and Management of religious affairs

[23] Ibid, 179–192.

upon them," reads a 1776 Baptist Declaration, "Farwel[l] to 'the free exercise of Religion.' "[24]

Calvinist Constitutionalism

The Separation and Cooperation of Church and State

Calvinists charted a course between Lutherans, who subordinated the church to the state, and Anabaptists, who withdrew the church from the state and society.[25] Like Anabaptists, Calvinists insisted on a basic separation of the offices and operations of church and state, leaving the church to govern its own doctrine and liturgy, polity, and property, without interference from the state. John Calvin set the foundation for this church-state division in the Ecclesiastical Ordinances of Geneva (1541/1561), which were echoed in many later Calvinist cities.[26] "There is a great difference and unlikeness between the ecclesiastical and civil power" of the church and state, Calvin explained. "A distinction should always be observed between these two clearly distinct areas of responsibility, the civil and the ecclesiastical." The church has no authority to punish crime, to remedy civil wrongs, to collect taxes, to make war, or to meddle in the affairs of the state. The state, in turn, has no authority to preach the Word, to administer the sacraments, to enforce spiritual discipline, to collect tithes, to interfere with church property, to appoint or remove clergy, to obstruct bans or excommunications, or to meddle in the internal affairs of a congregation. To permit any such interference between church and state, said Calvin, would "unwisely mingle these two which have a completely different nature."[27]

[24] "Declaration of the Virginia Association of Baptists (December 25, 1776)" in Julian P. Boyd (ed), *The Papers of Thomas Jefferson* (Princeton University Press 1950) 1:660–661.

[25] For sources, see Emile Rivoire and Victor van Berchem (eds), *Les sources du droit* (Sauerländer 1930). For overviews, see Philip Benedict, *Christ's Church Purely Reformed: A Social History of Calvinism* (Yale University Press 2002); Matthew J Tuininga, *Calvin's Political Theology and the Public Engagement of the Church* (Cambridge University Press 2017); Harro Höpfl, *The Christian Polity of John Calvin* (Cambridge University Press 1982); Robert M Kingdon, *Church and State in Reformation Europe* (Variorum Reprints 1985); Christoph Strohm, *Calvinismus und Recht* (Mohr Siebeck 2008); John Witte Jr, *The Reformation of Rights: Law, Religion, and Human Rights in Early Modern Calvinism* (Cambridge University Press 2007).

[26] In *Ioannis Calvini opera quae supersunt omnia* (G Baum et al ed) (Böhlau 1863–1900) 59 vols, 10/1:15–30 (hereafter CO); the 1541 text is translated in *The Register of the Company of Pastors of Geneva in the Time of Calvin* (Philip E Hughes tr, 1966) 35–52.

[27] John Calvin, *Institutes of the Christian Religion* (John T McNeill ed, Ford Lewis Battles tr, Westminster Press 1960) 3.19.15; 4.11.3–16; 4.20.1–4 (hereafter Institutes [1559]); CO 10/1:215–217, 223–224.

Like Lutherans, on the other hand, Calvinists insisted that each local polity be an overtly Christian commonwealth adhering to the general principles of natural law and translating them into detailed new positive laws of religious worship, Sabbath observance, public morality, marriage and family, crime and tort, contract and business, charity and education. Calvin drafted many of these new laws for Geneva during his tenure there from 1541 to 1564, and many of these piecemeal laws were incorporated into the Civil Edict of Geneva (1568), drafted by Calvinist jurist Germain Colladon (1508–1594).[28] These Genevan laws were also duplicated and expanded in hundreds of Calvinist polities over the next two centuries.

Unlike Lutherans and Anabaptists, however, Calvinists stressed that both church and state officials were to play complementary roles in the creation of the local Christian commonwealth and in the cultivation of the Christian citizen. Calvin did not contemplate a secular society with a plurality of absolutely separated religious and political officials within them. Nor did he contemplate a neutral state that showed no preference among competing concepts of the spiritual and moral good. For Calvin, each community was to be a unitary Christian society, a miniature *corpus Christianum* under God's sovereignty and law. Within this unitary society, the church and the state stood as coordinate powers. Both were ordained by God to help achieve a godly order and discipline in the community and to aid and accommodate each other on a variety of levels.

Calvin rooted this view of church-state cooperation, in part, in the familiar Protestant theory of the "uses of the law"—that is, the purposes or ends of the law in earthly life. Like others, Calvinists stressed the *civil use* of the law: to restrain persons from sinful conduct. "The law is like a halter," Calvin wrote, "to check the raging and otherwise limitlessly ranging lusts of the flesh." Threatened by punishment, persons obeyed the basic commandments of the moral law—to obey authorities, to respect their neighbors' person and property, to remain sexually modest and faithful, to speak truthfully of themselves and their neighbors. The law thus imposed upon everyone "a forced righteousness," an external or "public morality." Although "such public morality does not merit forgiveness of sin," said Calvin, it did allow for a modicum of peace and stability in this sin-ridden world. "Unless there is some restraint, the condition of wild beasts would be better and more desirable than ours."[29]

[28] In Rivoire and Berchem, *Sources du droit*, vol 3, item 1081.
[29] Institutes (1559), 2.7.10, 4.20.3; CO 52:255; CO 39:66.

In a Christian commonwealth, however, law also has an *educational* use of enhancing the spiritual development of believers, of teaching "the works that please God" to those who have already been justified by faith. The law teaches believers not only the "public" or "external" morality common to all persons but also the "private" or "internal" morality that is becoming only of Christians. As a teacher, the law not only coerces them against violence and violation but also cultivates in them charity and love. It not only punishes harmful acts of murder, theft, and fornication but also prohibits evil thoughts of hatred, covetousness, and lust.[30] Through the exercise of this private morality, the saints glorify God, exemplify God's law, and impel other sinners to seek God's grace.

This two-track system of morality corresponded to the proper division of jurisdiction between church and state, as Calvinists saw it. It was the church's responsibility to teach aspirational spiritual norms. It was the state's responsibility to enforce mandatory civil norms. This division of responsibility fit rather neatly into the procedural divisions between the consistory and the council in John Calvin's Geneva. In most cases that did not involve serious crimes; the consistory would first call parties to their higher spiritual duties, backing its recommendations with (threats of) spiritual discipline. If such spiritual counsel failed, the parties were referred to the council to compel them by civil and criminal sanctions to honor at least their basic civil duties.[31]

In sixteenth-century Geneva and other Swiss cities, the consistory was a mixed body of civil and religious officials that served as something of a hearings court and mediation center in most noncriminal cases, as well as an advisory and investigative body for the city council. Among most later Calvinists, the Genevan-style consistory was transformed into an elected body of pastors, elders, deacons, and teachers who governed each local church congregation, but it often played a less structured political and legal role in the broader Christian commonwealth. Yet local clergy still had a strong role in advising magistrates on the positive law of the local community, and local churches and their consistories also generally enjoyed autonomy in administering their own doctrine, liturgy, charity, polity, and property and in administering spiritual discipline over their members without interference from the state courts.

[30] Institutes (1559), 2.7.12; 2.8.6.

[31] See detailed cases and sources in John Witte Jr and Robert M Kingdon, *Sex, Marriage, and Family in John Calvin's Geneva* (Eerdmans 2005, 2019) 2 vols.

Rights, Resistance, and Revolution

Beginning in the 1550s, Calvinists in France, Scotland, the Netherlands, and England faced bitter persecution, repression, and genocide that killed tens of thousands of them over the next century and half. In response, they developed a robust theory of rights, resistance, and revolution against tyranny. This required them, however, to deal with several key biblical texts that called Christians to political obedience. "Let every person be subject to the governing authorities," reads Romans 13:1–5. "For there is no authority except from God, and those that exist have been instituted by God. Therefore, he who resists the authorities resists what God has appointed, and those who resist will come into judgment. For rulers are not a terror to good conduct, but bad. Therefore one must be subject, not only to avoid God's wrath, but for the sake of conscience." 1 Peter 2:13–17 was even more pointed: "Be subject for the Lord's sake to every human institution, whether it be to the emperors as supreme, or to governors as sent by him to punish those who do wrong and to praise those who do right. . . . Live as free men, yet without using your freedom as a pretext for evil." "Honor your father and mother" and other divinely appointed authorities, biblical laws commanded, "so that your days may be long in the land which the Lord your God has given you."[32] All this seemed rather firm and clear biblical teaching that a conscientious Christian must respect and obey the authorities and suffer patiently and prayerfully if they become tyrants.

In defending the Christian right to resist and revolt against tyranny, Calvinists like Theodore Beza (1519–1605), John Knox (ca. 1513–1572), and Philip de Mornay (1549–1623) first flipped these biblical passages onto their heads. Yes, we must honor the authorities "so that our days may be long," they argued. But if our days are being cut short, then we should not honor those authorities who shorten them. Yes, the authorities were "appointed by God to do good." But if they are not doing good, then they could not have been appointed by God. Yes, the magistrate is not "a terror to good conduct but to bad." But if he becomes a terror to good conduct, then he must no longer be a legitimate magistrate. Yes, we must "render to Caesar the things that are Caesar's, and to God the things that are God's." But if Caesar wants or takes what is God's, then we must withhold or retrieve it for God's sake. Yes, "he who resists the authorities resists God." But if the authorities themselves

[32] Exodus 20:12.

resist God, then surely we must avenge God's honor. Yes, "vengeance is mine," God says in the Bible.[33] But we believers, as God's sovereign image bearers and ambassadors, are also God's "instruments of righteousness," and we must execute God's judgment of wrath on earth when needed.[34]

Calvinists also built on the familiar legal doctrine of legitimate self-defense. Defense of oneself and of third parties against attack, using proportionate, even deadly force and violence when necessary, was an ancient legal teaching. The law of resistance to tyranny was simply the law of self-defense writ large, Calvinists argued. When a magistrate exceeds his authority, he forfeits his office and becomes like any other private person. His victims and third parties may resist him passively or actively, just as if he were any other criminal.

Calvinists also drew in the biblical idea of covenant.[35] The political government of each community, they argued, was formed by a three-way covenant among God, the rulers, and the people, modeled in part on ancient biblical covenants. By this covenant, God agreed to protect and bless the rulers and the people in return for their obedience to the laws of God and nature. The rulers agreed to honor these higher laws and protect the people's essential rights, particularly those rights rooted in the Bible. The people agreed to exercise God's political will for the community by electing and petitioning their rulers and by honoring and obeying them so long as the rulers honored God's law and protected the people's rights. If any of the people violated the terms of this political covenant and became criminals, the magistrate could properly prosecute and punish them—and sentence them to death in extreme cases. In turn, however, if any of the magistrates violated the terms of the political covenant and became tyrants, they could be properly resisted and removed from office—and sentenced to death in extreme cases if convicted.

The power to resist and remove tyrants lay not directly with the people, however, for that would produce anarchy. The exercise of this power involved "constitutional judgments" by the lower magistrates, Beza argued. In cases of seeming tyranny, these magistrates were called to judge the tyrant's behavior against the terms of the political covenant—an early statement of the idea of judicial review. If the tyrant was found guilty, he was to be removed from office and could be banished from the community, even executed in extreme

[33] Romans 12:19.

[34] Romans 6:13. See sources in Witte, *Reformation of Rights*, 102–133, 181–202, 219–225.

[35] See Witte, *Reformation of Rights*, 130–139, and chapters 15 and 16 below, by Nicholas Aroney and David VanDrunen respectively.

cases. The remarkable trial and execution of the Stuart king Charles I of England, in 1649, was a textbook example of this stern Calvinist resistance logic in action. But if the tyrant refused to leave or persisted in his tyranny, the lower magistrates were to organize and direct the people in revolt—in all-out revolution if needed to unseat this tyrant.[36] This logic animated Calvinist revolutionary movements in France, the Netherlands, Scotland, England, and eventually America from the later sixteenth to later eighteenth centuries.[37]

Calvinists also built on the idea of fundamental rights, whose chronic and pervasive breach by a tyrant triggered the most basic right to resist and revolt. Early modern Protestants accepted the enumerated lists of rights and liberties set out in classical Roman law and expanded in medieval and early modern laws.[38] But they rearranged, prioritized, and expanded this roll of rights on the basis of the Bible, in part. The most important rights, they reasoned, had to be the religious rights of "liberty of conscience" and "free exercise of religion."[39] After all, persons are created first and foremost as subjects and ambassadors of the Creator God and called to honor God above all else. The Ten Commandments enjoined them to worship God, to observe the Sabbath, and to avoid blasphemy and idolatry. The New Testament ordered the faithful to "obey God rather than men."[40] If the political magistrate—created by this same God and representing God's authority on earth—breaches a person's rights to discharge these religious duties, then nothing can be sacred and secure any longer.

Moreover, protecting religious rights and duties required protecting several other correlative rights that early modern Calvinists came to discover when they were persecuted minorities. The rights of the individual to religious conscience and exercise required attendant rights to assemble, speak, worship, evangelize, educate, parent, travel, and more. The rights of the religious group to worship and govern itself as an ecclesiastical polity required

[36] Théodore de Bèze, *Du Droit des Magistrats* (Robert M Kingdon ed, Droz 1970), translated as Theodore Beza, *Concerning the Rights of Rulers over Their Subjects and the Duties of Subjects toward Their Rulers* (Henri-Louis Gonin tr, Juta 1956, 27, 36–38, 72–74.

[37] See Michael Walzer, *The Revolution of the Saints: A Study in the Origins of Radical Politics* (Harvard University Press 1965); RR Palmer, *The Age of the Democratic Revolution* (Princeton University Press 1959–1964) 2 vols; John W Sap, *Paving the Way for Revolution: Calvinism and the Struggle for a Democratic Constitutional State* (VU Press 2001); David T Ball, *The Historical Origins of Judicial Review, 1536–1803: The Duty to Resist Tyranny* (Edwin Mellen Press 2005).

[38] See chapter 6 above by RH Helmholz and further Allen D Hertzke and Timothy Shah (eds), *Christianity and Freedom* (Cambridge University Press 2016) 2 vols.

[39] Beza, *Rights of Rulers*, 85.

[40] Acts 5:29.

attendant rights to legal personality, corporate property, collective worship, organized charity, parochial education, freedom of press, freedom of contract, freedom of association, and more. And both individuals and groups had to live by many other biblical commandments that set out the rights and duties of life, liberty, property, marriage, family, household, sanctuary, poor relief, charity, education, and more.[41] In the 1560s, Calvinist writers like Christopher Goodman (1520–1603) joined Beza and Knox in calling these rights "unalienable" and "fundamental."[42]

Early modern Protestants enumerated these fundamental rights not only in learned tracts but also in lofty texts forged in the aftermath of revolution against tyranny. In their 1581 Declaration of Independence, for example, Dutch Protestant revolutionaries declared independence from Spain and its tyrannical rules "in accordance with the law of nature and in order to preserve and defend ourselves and our fellow-countrymen, our rights, the privileges and ancient customs and the freedoms of our fatherland," which they then enumerated and expanded at length in national and provincial constitutions.[43] In the 1628 Petition of Right directed against the tyranny of King Charles I, the English Parliament called for protection of such fundamental rights as no taking of "any man's life, liberty," or "property" "but by due process of law"; no taxation without "common consent"; no forced quartering of soldiers or mariners in private homes; no suspension of the writ of habeas corpus; and no criminal prosecution or punishment without a clear statute; among others.[44] Across the Atlantic in 1641, Calvinist jurist and theologian Nathaniel Ward, steeped in Protestant opposition to the tyranny of the English monarchy, set out a twenty-five-page "Body of Liberties" for the new colony in Massachusetts Bay, detailing sundry public, private, procedural, and penal rights.[45] The Toleration Act and Bill of Rights, both passed by Parliament in 1689 in the aftermath of the Glorious Revolution against the tyranny of King James II, added further protections for the freedoms of speech, press, and assembly, an act that governed both the English mother

[41] Beza, *Rights of Rulers*, 28–29, 84–86.

[42] Christopher Goodman, *How Superior Powers Ought to be Obeyd* (1558), (facs edn, Charles H McIlwain ed, Columbia University Press 1931) 160–161. See further Beza, *Rights of Rulers*, 52–53, 74–76, 97–99, 142.

[43] Formally known as the Act of Abjuration (1581), in Herbert H Rowen (ed), *The Low Countries in Early Modern Times: A Documentary History* (Harper & Row 1972) 102.

[44] In Carl Stephenson and Frederick George Marcham, *Sources of English Constitutional History* (rev ed, Harper and Bros 1972) 2 vols, 450–453.

[45] In Edmund S Morgan, *Puritan Political Ideas, 1558–1794* (repr ed, Liberty Fund 2003) 177–203.

country and her many colonies, including in America.[46] These enumerations of rights multiplied in the eighteenth century on both sides of the Atlantic. It is a telling anecdote, however, that already by 1650, almost every right that would appear in the United States Bill of Rights of 1791 had already been defined, defended, and died for by Calvinists.

Written Constitutions

Seventeenth-century Calvinist writers like Johannes Althusius (ca. 1563–1638), John Lilburne (1614–1657), and John Milton (1608–1674) called for the integration of these political covenants and fundamental rights statements into written constitutions. Such constitutions, Althusius argued, provided the commonwealth with "a guiding light of civil life, a scale of justice, a preserver of liberty, a bulwark of public peace and discipline, a refuge for the weak, a bridle for the powerful, a norm and straightener of rulership." For Althusius, a properly governed nation or state needed more than a mythical or ancient founding political covenant or contract. It needed more than just a collection of dusty old charters, like the Magna Carta (1215) and its Continental analogs that once protected the rights of the aristocracy.[47] Rule-of-law commonwealths needed clear and comprehensive written constitutions that bound all rulers and all subjects. Such constitutions should specify in detail the mutual rights and duties, the powers and prerogatives of the rulers and the people, and the principles and procedures for the creation and enforcement of positive laws. "Written constitutions," Althusius wrote, provide the best "fences, walls, guards, or boundaries of our life, guiding us along the appointed way for achieving wisdom, happiness, and peace in human society."[48]

Puritan Calvinists in seventeenth- and eighteenth-century England and New England emphasized strongly that written constitutions needed adequate checks and balances on church and state authorities. While the offices of church and state were ordained by God and represented God's authority

[46] In Stephenson and Marcham, *Sources*, 599–605, 607–608.

[47] See discussion in Robin Griffith-Jones and Mark Hill (eds), *Magna Carta, Religion, and the Rule of Law* (Cambridge University Press 2015).

[48] Johannes Althusius, *Politica Methodice Digesta of Johannes Althusius (Althaus)* (Carl J Friedrich ed, Harvard University Press 1932), partly translated in *Politica Johannes Althusius* (FS Carney ed, tr, Liberty Fund 1995) X.4; XIX.6, 15, 23, 29, 49; XX.18; XXVIII.30–32. For the views of Lilburne, Milton, and other English constitutionalists, see Witte, *Reformation of Rights*, 209–226.

on earth, their individual officers were sinful human beings. Without built-in restraints, even the best officers would slowly convert their offices into instruments of self-gain and self-promotion. Drawing in part on traditional constitutional lore, Puritans thus advocated a number of constitutional safeguards: popular election of ministers and magistrates; limited tenures and rotations of ecclesiastical and political office; separation of church and state; separation of ministerial, disciplinary, and diaconal powers within the church and separation of executive, legislative, and judicial powers within the state; various checks and balances between and among each of these powers; federalist layers of authority with shared and severable sovereignty; open meetings in congregations and towns with rights of petition for the people; clearly enumerated and codified canons and laws for churches and states; and transparent proceedings and records within consistories, courts, and councils.[49]

Conclusions

In *The Hebrew Republic,* Harvard historian Eric Nelson sharply criticizes the "standard narrative" of early modern political and constitutional history. The standard narrative describes the sixteenth and seventeenth century as an era devoted to the separation of religion and politics and to the construction of a secular order built on "pagan classical" learning, Machiavellian politics, and early Enlightenment liberalism. This narrative is largely a myth, Nelson argues, propounded by postmodern secularists. The reality is that the early modern period saw "the full fervor of the Reformation unleashed" and Protestant political and legal teachings integrated into "the mainstream of European intellectual life." It was in this overtly religious milieu that the West built many of its cardinal political and constitutional ideas and institutions. Protestant theological jurisprudence, Catholic neoscholasticism, and Jewish biblical thought, says Nelson, were just as critical to the modern Western political project as the purportedly secular theories of Machiavelli or Hobbes.[50]

This chapter has illustrated briefly "the full fervor of the Reformation unleashed" onto the Western constitutional tradition. The Lutheran,

[49] See sources in Witte, *Reformation of Rights*, 294–320.

[50] Eric Nelson, *The Hebrew Republic: Jewish Sources and the Transformation of European Political Thought* (Harvard University Press 2010) 2–3.

Anabaptist, and Calvinist Reformations produced a wide range of constitutional teachings and reforms for early modern Europe and North America. These teachings reached the theories and laws of churches and states, authorities and liberties, duties and rights, legislation and adjudication, religious establishment and religious freedom, resistance and revolution, written constitutions and rule of law, enumerated powers and bills of rights. Some of these early modern Protestant teachings were highly original and innovative; some were classical, biblical, and medieval teachings recast in new ensembles; still others had analogs in various schools of Catholic neoscholasticism, legal humanism, republicanism, and monarchism that circulated in the day. But the Protestant Reformation proved to be a fertile seedbed for the growth of Western constitutionalism.

8

Modernity

Understanding Law and Constitutionalism in Modernity: The Critical Contribution of English Reformation Public Theology

Joan Lockwood O'Donovan

Christian theological traditions have exercised a constructive and critical influence on the theory and practice of law within and among societies, and on constitutional articulations of the law's controlling ideas, practical principles, and institutional structures. Nevertheless, the extent and value of this influence has been contested among political and legal historians, theorists, and practitioners since the Renaissance. In the last fifty years, conflicting appraisals of secular liberal democracy within and beyond academic circles have invigorated interest in the role of theological traditions in the emergence of contemporary Western polities. Circulating vindications and critiques of secular liberal democracy have variously invoked theological traditions in historically accounting for its worst and its best features.

The "grand" historical narratives of Western political and legal thought, whether primarily critical or supportive of modern developments, have been more successful in alerting recent generations to the continuing effects of theoretical legacies than in providing them with accurate, balanced interpretations of past thinkers and communities. Some formidable critical narratives (e.g., in the writings of Quentin Skinner, Eric Voegelin, and Sheldon Wolin[1]) have indicted Protestant Reformation theology for assaulting Christian Aristotelian ethical and political humanism and presaging modern ethical and political voluntarism, individualism, and statism. My own engagement with English Reformation theology and scholarship, however, has persuaded

[1] Quentin Skinner, *The Foundations of Modern Political Thought*, vol II: *The Age of Reformation* (Cambridge University Press 1978); Eric Voegelin, *The New Science of Politics: An Introduction* (University of Chicago Press 1952); Sheldon S Wolin, *Politics and Vision: Continuity and Innovation in Western Political Thought* (expanded edn, Princeton University Press 2004).

Joan Lockwood O'Donovan, *Modernity: Understanding Law and Constitutionalism in Modernity: The Critical Contribution of English Reformation Public Theology* in *Christianity and Constitutionalism*. Edited by: Nicholas Aroney and Ian Leigh, Oxford University Press. © Oxford University Press 2022. DOI: 10.1093/oso/9780197587256.003.0008

me of the failure of such narratives to appreciate the diagnostic and constructive resources of the Reformation period for addressing distinctively modern political and legal issues.

In what follows, I bring the theological resources of the English Reformation to the task of addressing critically and constructively a prominent—perhaps defining—strand of modern political and legal thought and practice. In so doing I commend to current circles of scholarly political and legal discussion the contemporary relevance of this somewhat neglected Reformation tradition. Readers with an interest in British constitutional law should know that the public theology of the English Reformation is the historical foundation of constitutional law throughout all the royal dominions. However, the contribution of this public theology to the critical understanding of law and constitutionalism within modernity is much less well known.

My account of modern political and legal theory and practice draws on historical narratives in the hope of exhibiting their important heuristic strengths rather than their inevitable weaknesses. The narratives on which I have drawn chart various phases of the liberal contractarian tradition of natural rights, from seventeenth-century figures such as John Selden, Thomas Hobbes, John Locke, and Richard Overton; through Jean-Jacques Rousseau, Immanuel Kant, and the apologists of the American and French Revolutions; to the work of contemporary contractarians such as John Rawls and Robert Nozick. While these narratives are heavily indebted to historical-philosophical studies of individual thinkers and theoretical developments,[2] my own perspective on them has been shaped by the ethical and political insights of English Reformation theology,[3] illuminating certain resemblances between the modern political ethos and ethic[4] and the ethos and ethic to which the English reformers were themselves responding.

Most illuminating are the English reformers' critical responses to four late scholastic and renaissance features of early modern European morality and ethics. These features were its legalism and excessive regulative or prescriptive rigor; its juridical profile and preoccupation with formal and informal

[2] These chiefly come from the writings of Leo Strauss, George Grant, Sheldon Wolin, C. B. Macpherson, and Ian Shapiro. They also intersect at points with the narratives invoked in John Milbank's chapter in this volume. See, e.g., Joan Lockwood O'Donovan, *George Grant and the Twilight of Justice* (University of Toronto Press 1984).

[3] Joan Lockwood O'Donovan, *Theology of Law and Authority in the English Reformation* (Eerdmans 1991).

[4] "Ethos" denotes a particular constellation of moral dispositions, judgments, and actions, and "ethics" denotes reflective theorizing of the moral life.

practices of judging, punishing, and vindicating; its overly individualistic and voluntarist conception of moral agency and action; and its anthropocentric concentration on human rather than divine right, righteousness, judgment, and freedom. The English and continental reformers attacked these features primarily as they appeared within the "spiritual" sphere, in the sacramental, penitential, and ecclesiological thought and practices of the church; but they also (implicitly and explicitly) attacked their manifestations in the rationalist political and economic thought of late scholasticism, increasingly dominated by the theory of natural rights.

The reformers' critical insights may be applied to analogous features of the prevailing ethos, ethics, politics, and law of late modernity in diagnosing their core cause to be the disengagement of human moral agency and action from God's right, righteousness, judgment, and freedom, decisively revealed in the history of Jesus Christ. Of the possible ways to trace historically this theoretical disengagement, I propose that a charting of the liberal contractarian tradition of natural rights most coherently displays interconnections among the more deleterious aspects of the social, political, and legal culture, institutions and practices of liberal, pluralistic, technological democracies.

The public ideological functioning of universal human rights (i.e., of rights ascribable universally to individual human beings and derivatively to groups) came to unrivaled national and international prominence through documents issuing from the United Nations in the two decades following World War II: chiefly, the Universal Declaration of Human Rights of 1948 and the subsequent International Covenants of 1966 on Economic, Social, and Cultural Rights and on Civil and Political Rights. Although these documents did not employ the term "natural rights," they invoked shades of the concept by indicating in their preambles an intrinsic relationship between "the inherent dignity and . . . the equal and inalienable rights of all members of the human family." At the same time, they rendered this relationship ambiguous by failing to give determinate content to the term "inherent human dignity" independent of the universal human possession of rights, despite pronouncing the priority of "dignity" to "rights."[5] It is a historical irony that this failing, apparently necessitated by diverging understandings of human dignity across religious and cultural boundaries, has probably facilitated the

[5] The preamble to the International Covenant on Civil and Political Rights 1966 recognizes that the rights postulated by the Universal Declaration "derive from the inherent dignity of the human person."

global influence of the Western liberal tendency to identify the inherent dignity of human persons with their natural possession of specific rights.

Notwithstanding this failing, the 1970s saw a spate of Christian theological endorsements of the Universal Declaration across the denominational spectrum, regularly explicating human dignity by drawing on the biblical doctrine of the *imago Dei*: the doctrine that mankind was originally created in the image of God, and that fallen humanity, corrupted by sin, has been, is being, and will be restored to God's image in Jesus Christ. It is notable that these theological explications, however differently nuanced, concurred in emphasizing relations of humankind and of individual persons to the triune God, initiated and sustained by God's own action. Equally striking is their apparent consensus about the wholly unproblematic character of moving from a relational theological understanding of human dignity to the concept of inherent, "equal and unalienable" human rights. Rights were merely assumed to express adequately the moral attributes of humanity undergirding political and legal justice; and this assumption was largely made without critical consideration of the powerful liberal contractarian tradition of natural rights. Fortunately, the last fifty years of political and legal scholarship has deprived theologians today of the luxury of taking no cognizance of this tradition.

The Proprietorial Subjectivity of Having Rights

The modern liberal contractarian tradition of natural rights has a long and varied history. However, a conceptual core with broad practical implications for human social and political/legal practice and reflection persists. This core involves an economic and juridical anthropology that understands human beings to be naturally self-owning individuals, proprietors with exclusive powers of disposal over their spiritual and corporeal capacities and acts, effective against the whole world. A remarkably perspicacious account of the proprietary subject of natural rights was articulated by the leading pamphleteer of the English Leveller movement, Richard Overton, in the mid-seventeenth century:[6]

[6] "An Arrow against all Tyrants and Tyranny," October 1646; Liberty Fund online library of liberty: https://oll.libertyfund.org/page/overton-an-arrow-against-all-tyrants-1646.

> To every individual in nature is given an individual property by nature, not to be invaded or usurped by any. For every one, as he is himself, so he hath a self propriety, else could he not be himself; and on this no second may presume to deprive any of without manifest violation and affront to the very principles of nature, and of the rules of equity and justice between man and man. Mine and thine cannot be, except this be. No man hath power over my rights and liberties, and I over no man's.

In Overton's thought, the individual's full property in himself, his capacities and acts, constituting his freedom from other men, underpins all his claims for specific civil, religious, economic, and political rights and freedoms.

The modern tradition portrays free, self-disposing proprietors as driven by passions: most fundamentally, by primary and compelling desires to protect and augment their personal property. Simultaneously, they are conceived as creatures of physical and psychological instincts, on the mechanistic and/or evolutionary models of materialistic science; *and* they are conceived as transcending, controlling subjects who magisterially direct or channel these instincts by autonomous acts of choice. This power of choosing is the subject's original, natural right of freedom, of self-determination, limited only (according to some thinkers) by God's sovereign proprietorial right in his human creatures. Human equality resides fundamentally in the common proprietary freedom of human beings. It resides in the rational wills of individuals conceived as occupying an Archimedean point outside of the causalities of the material universe and outside of, in the sense of prior to, the ordering institutions of society. But equality also resides in common human drives (instincts, emotions) conceived as divorced, partially or completely, from an intelligible order of beings, goods, and ends, given to individuals from beyond themselves.

Crucially, the free pursuit by individuals of self-preservation and self-augmentation undergirds their natural right to appropriate worldly things for their exclusive use (i.e., exclusive of others using these things without their permission). Most influential for the liberal tradition has been Locke's paradigm for relating the natural right of appropriation to the right of private property in external things, and to the juridical securing of the individual's property and its free development. Locke builds on a twofold congruence of natural right and natural obligation that is divinely given and rationally accessible: namely, the individual's natural right to preserve himself in "perfect freedom" derives from the natural obligation of preserving himself; and his right is bounded by the natural obligation "as much as he can, to preserve the rest of mankind" when "his own preservation comes not into competition."[7] From the right of self-preservation, Locke further derives the individual rights of appropriating the earth's bounty for private use, and of prosecuting offenses against the law of nature.

In the economic sphere, Locke's paradigm furnished a moral foundation for indefinite wealth accumulation in a free market money economy. From the individual's ownership of his own labor, Locke argues that private appropriation of the earth's resources through labor is their naturally just, lawful, and efficient use. His well-known theory is that individual labor, by mixing something privately owned (labor) with the naturally common (resources), assimilates the common to the sphere of private (exclusive) use, and simultaneously invests the common with virtually all its utility and value.[8] While recognizing that "the law of nature" limits property acquisition to what the individual can use before it spoils, thus leaving ample resources for others to appropriate through labor,[9] Locke's argument progressively demonstrates that the proscription of waste places virtually no moral obstacles in the way of wealth accumulation through enterprise in an economy where currency accumulates rather than perishable goods, and where higher productivity increases the availability of natural resources to the industrious.[10] Nor does the moral purpose of securing one's self-property place limits on the individual's acquisitive activity, given that the individual's "needs" and "wants" become increasingly indistinguishable with rising productivity, commerce, and international trade.[11] And should grave inequalities of wealth result from inequalities of productive capacity among individuals, the indigent can always voluntarily contract to sell their labor to more prosperous producers.

Thus, Locke's theory of property put in place enduring elements of free market capitalist ideology, including the original or "natural" character of property rights, the validity of unlimited acquisition of property through voluntary exchange, the inseparability of needs and potentially infinite wants in the functioning of (what comes to be called) effective market demand, the equation of the value of goods in exchange with their "usefulness" or "utility,"

[7] *Second Treatise of Government*, 2.6; P Laslett (ed), *Two Treatises of Government* (Cambridge 1988) 271.

[8] *Second Treatise*, 5.25–44; 285–298.

[9] Ibid, 5.31–34; 290–291.

[10] Ibid, 5.36–50; 292–302

[11] Ibid, 5.40–51; 296–302.

and the functioning of alienable labor as an exchangeable commodity in the economic market. Only the elements of scarcity (especially of natural resources) and market competition remained relatively undeveloped.

Intimately connected with natural property right is Locke's investing everyone equally with the natural right to judge infractions of the natural law—whether injuries to themselves (their persons, freedom, or external property) or to others—and to inflict punishment on malefactors proportionate to their transgression. Significantly, he presents these rights as vindicating the rational rules of social conduct divinely given for the "mutual security" of all, and not just the freedom of injured parties.[12] Equally significant is the continuing primacy of these natural rights in civil society. A notable example is that, under the civil contract (compact), injured parties retain to themselves and do not entrust to the magistrate their separate right to demand reparation from the perpetrators of offenses.[13] More importantly, civil society, as the repository of the judicial rights of its compacted members, retains the residual power of public judgment so that, should a civil society entrust the powers of civil judgment to deputies who prove less fitted for the task than its individual members acting independently, that society is entitled to withdraw the powers of public judgment from those agents and invest them in others, either peacefully (by constitutional procedure) or, where necessary, by cooperative revolutionary action (closely resembling coercive judgment in the state of nature).[14]

A century after Locke's *Second Treatise*, the project of reconstructing the civil contract along the lines of a market exchange of rights would occupy a prominent stream of American Revolutionary thought. Addressing the question of which natural rights are alienable in the civil contract and which are inalienable, Thomas Paine proposed that each individual retains those natural rights "in which the power to execute is perfect in the individual as the right itself" and "deposits . . . in the common stock of society" those in which "though the right is perfect in the individual, the power to execute them is defective." To inalienable rights Paine assigns "all the intellectual rights," along with rights of acting for one's own "comfort and happiness . . . not injurious to the natural rights of others"; to alienable rights he paradigmatically

[12] Ibid, 2.8; 272. By contrast, Hobbes's "laws of nature" or stratagems for peace, to curb the unbounded liberty of natural right, prescribed that individuals embroiled in controversy submit their right in all its aspects to the judgment of an impartial arbitrator.

[13] *Second Treatise*, 2.11; 273–274.

[14] Ibid, 2.19; 406–428.

assigns the "right to judge in [one's] own cause," which is imperfect in practice "without the power to redress."[15]

Superficially, Paine's analogy of the joint stock company, in which "every man is a proprietor in society, and draws on the capital as a matter of right,"[16] presents in a most advantageous light the political and legal implications of liberal natural rights. This model of delegated governance apparently exhibits an equitable and stable balance of common and distributive rights (and corresponding obligations), while combining the benefits of administrative expertise with constitutional mechanisms of electing, legislating, and adjudicating that ensure the continuing superiority and equality of the investors' proprietary interests. Such a model seems to offer a framework for fashioning fruitful compromises among opposing political aspirations to elaborate the natural rights tradition in libertarian or welfare capitalist directions,[17] precisely because it safeguards the common conceptual core of acquisitive, calculating, and self-protective individuals seeking to maximize the value of their freedom through the accumulation of external property.

However, contemporary experience and discerning analysis are increasingly undermining confidence in such liberal-egalitarian-rights models by providing evidence that social-moral freedom and its institutional contexts are giving way to technical-scientific, legalistic, and juridical forms of domination: in short, that the social and political project of maximizing equal freedom is turning out to be a project of maximizing equal unfreedom. In other words, the destructive contradictions of the prevailing modern tradition of freedom are proving intractable.

The preponderance in our social and institutional fabric of acquisitive and competitive, commanding and demanding, and judging and punishing practices seems a lamentable confirmation of the continuing primacy of the individual's natural proprietary and judicial rights. Even though governments have become the collective instruments for establishing in law and promoting through policy an expanding catalog of universal rights

[15] *The Rights of Man* (Dolphin edn), with *Reflections on the Revolution in France* (New York: Doubleday & Company, Inc. 1961) 306.

[16] *The Rights of Man*, 306.

[17] Libertarian thought emphasizes the persisting inviolability within civil society of the individual's natural proprietary rights, the minimal protective role of government in market exchange, and the general applicability of market principles to the political arena, whereas the theory of late welfare capitalism limits the natural rights of individuals in scarce external goods by the principle of equality and, from this prepolitical basis, derives some governmental management of market processes of competition, production, and demand, and some equalizing redistribution of property in civil society.

across political, economic, social, and religious terrains, nevertheless, citizens have retained so compelling a concern with securing their rights that all societal institutions, organizations, and activities have become enlisted in the moral-juridical project, as agencies of rights promotion and arbitration, and recipients of proprietary demands and censures.

Interconnected Forms of Freedom and Domination

In advanced liberal-democratic societies, the ideology and practices of politically/legally securing egalitarian rights both drive and are driven by other expressions of the aspiration to maximize individual and collective freedom, in which emancipation of human beings from constraints on their powers of self-creation and self-disposal entails subjecting them to practices of manipulation and control that reduce their capacity for practical judgment and their scope for action. These expressions are legion, and largely derivable from two social sources, broadly defined: from scientific techniques that rationally objectify within predictive systems the natural powers and dynamics of individual and communal life, in order to overcome their perceived deficiencies and limitations through the production of calculated outcomes, and from the popular dissemination of religious and moral relativism, an agonistic social vision and a hermeneutic of suspicion.

Perhaps, the most socially pervasive product of scientific rationality is bureaucratic administration of cooperative work, combining a fixed jurisdictional structure with detailed regulation of defined tasks by explicit rules devised for the achievement of calculable results and regular monitoring of performances for conformity and achievement. Adoption of this universally applicable technique by institutions, organizations, and businesses, under political and economic pressures, has encouraged the purely technical formulation of purposes and practices, and has homogenized and legalized the activity and relationships of workers, to the detriment of their exhibiting practical freedom, imagination, subtlety, and versatility. The outcome across vocational spheres has been widespread frustration, alienation, and flight. Especially in the public services, with their intensive political regulation and surveillance, practitioners are exasperated by their subjection to constantly changing, inappropriate, and counterproductive procedures, rules, and measures of rationality, efficiency, and justice, adopted because only measurable practices and measurable outcomes are transparent enough to stand up under the public scrutiny and litigation fostered by rights legislation. Practitioners are daily aware that such impositions inhibit the maturity of judgment, skills, and wisdom intrinsic to the fruitful pursuit of substantive goods through traditions of common practice.

It is somewhat perplexing, therefore, that professional, academic, and educated discussion has paid insufficient attention to the driving force of proliferating egalitarian rights in the bureaucratic degradation of common activity, and similarly, that institutions and enterprises have made so little progress in mitigating the deleterious effects of excessive bureaucratic control. These failures may reasonably be understood to reflect the tenacious resistance across society to acknowledging any intrinsically illiberal implications of the ideological ethos of rights, so much has it become the warranty of intellectual and moral probity among ordinary people as among the *cognoscenti*. The failures may also reflect widespread blindness to connections between the bureaucratic undermining of social freedom and other technological mechanisms of manipulation that are more frequently discussed as threatening the natural and social conditions of the freedom that they are deployed to maximize and, to an extent, equalize.[18]

The communications media are key educators of both ordinary people and the *cognoscenti*. They have progressively assumed the popular responsibility and authority of social surveillance, inspecting and assessing the orientations and conduct of public and private individuals and enterprises, exposing (among other misdemeanors) failures in their support, provision for, and observance of the equal rights of individuals and groups. This surveillance is intimately connected with the gratuitously inquisitorial role of much public journalism that has noticeably supplanted accurate reporting and informed analyses of events. Whether of a "liberal" or "conservative" stripe, the journalistic media thrives on presenting the supposedly irresolvable combat of opposed positions, on unmasking reasoned argument and debate as self-interested power play, and on magnifying the unmediated diversity of opinion and practice in liberal-democratic society.

[18] In addition to ecologically destructive processes of economic production, distribution, and consumption, there are unknown and imagined evils connected with a broad spectrum of existing and developing technologies—reproductive, genetic, nano, electronic, and nuclear, as well as their controversial present uses. The technological enterprise of harnessing the predictable processes of nature to specified human purposes is bringing into sharper focus for many people the terrifying unpredictability of the natural world.

Implications for Political and Legal Theory and Practice

The interaction of these dynamic forms of the prevailing tradition of freedom has persisting implications for political and legal theory and practice, including the following:

1. Constitutional law articulates the normative rationale of political and legal practice as the protection and realizing of individual and (derivative) collective rights; consequently, an intentionally comprehensive codification of universal rights functions as the encompassing conceptual framework for enacting, implementing, and adjudicating law. These codified and largely justiciable rights make up the controlling language of public justice, of political and legal relationships, to which are subordinated or assimilated the more traditional concepts of public authority, objective right, obligation or duty, divine and natural justice and law, responsible government, rule under law, commonwealth, and public good or benefit.[19]
2. Conceived as universal or natural, these legal rights assimilate to the political, juridical realm, common human goods and right relationships that the longer Western theological tradition has portrayed as belonging to the orders of original creation, redemption, and sanctification, and therefore as prepolitical/juridical and trans-political/juridical. The hegemonic character of universal, natural rights discourse suppresses the foundational and determinative import for human society of social, communicative goods and relationships that are not intrinsically political/juridical and proprietary. These include life itself and the natural necessities sustaining it, marital and family relationships, fellowship in faith and worship of God, collaborative work, language and the communication of knowledge and love, common moral and aesthetic sensibilities, judgments, and practices. Natural law discourse thereby suppresses the dependence of the political/juridical order on, and its ordering to, these goods and relationships that give positive, public substance and form to human freedom.

[19] In their chapters in this volume, Chaplin (chapter 18 below) distinguishes three "irreducible" types of legal relations governed by multiple "modes" of justice in the Christian tradition: namely, rights, duties, and competencies, and Rivers (chapter 13 below) distinguishes four interpretations of the meaning and function of constitutional rights.

3. Political theory and practice tend to adopt the logic and principles of market economics. Contemporary political theorists, enamored of neoclassical economics, conceive the state as a "business run by entrepreneurs," political parties as "firms trying to maximize votes," and "voting preferences as utility functions," while politicians "sell a commodity as entrepreneurs, employ agencies to 'package' their products for advertising, and gear those products to what they believe the market demands."[20] Correspondingly, citizens succumb to consumer consciousness in their dealings with politicians and government, seeking in return for their political support and compliance the best possible protection for and provision of an expanding range of freedoms and entitlements. The formalizing of their (implicitly) contractual relations with the state in bills and charters of rights feeds consumer consciousness by increasing incentives and opportunities to demand legal redress of the failures of governmental and public agencies to furnish the promised goods and services—opportunities further extended by horizontal application of constitutional rights from public to private actors. The overall effect is toward recasting public law as private law, the common good as the aggregation of private goods.
4. The economic modeling of political relationships reinforces two trends in legal theory and practice that accentuate the difference between lawmaking and law adjudicating. One is toward bureaucratizing adjudication: subjecting the adjudicative enterprise to the norm of generating consistent, rationally transparent outcomes through strict compliance with an internal system of determinate rules governing practice, thereby removing it from the uncertainties of lawmaking driven by shifting popular demands. This expresses the liberal aspiration to secure predictably the proprietary rights of autonomous subjects by means of a rational method. The attempt of bureaucratic (formalistic) law to achieve such consistent outcomes in court decisions is inevitably undermined by failure to eradicate the operation of judicial discretion in, for example, construing the "facts" of particular cases and interpreting and applying legal sources, including discordant rules reflecting diverse extralegal orientations and exigencies.[21]

[20] Ian Shapiro, *The Evolution of Rights in Liberal Theory* (Cambridge 1986) 197–198.
[21] This failure is widely canvassed in the jurisprudential schools of natural law, legal realism, postrealism, and deconstructive critical studies.

5. A more dominant trend under a constitutional rights charter is toward asserting the superiority of legal adjudication to lawmaking in providing a more balanced and less partisan public articulation of the value consensus of liberal, democratic, pluralistic polities under the rule of law. As guardian of constitutional justice, the judiciary rivals, even surpasses, the legislature and executive in expanding the legal substance of liberal rights and in establishing their theoretical hegemony. Its exaggerated confidence in the capacity of judicial practice to harmonize rationally the legal field places it in the forefront of contemporary strivings to enlarge the directive, pedagogical, and positive regulative purpose of the political enterprise.
6. Under a constitutional rights charter expressing the values of liberal, democratic pluralism, legal protection of the public right of religious freedom in its communal and institutional dimensions becomes difficult to sustain. The preponderant political pressure is toward either privatizing the authority and practice of religious institutions or intrusive legal regulation of their institutional practices occupying public space. This is because the modern template of legal protection of religious freedom is protection of the maximal equal freedom of religious and moral choice for individuals and not the protection of social traditions of faith, worship, and moral discipline in which the reality of freedom cannot be separated from its concrete relational substance. The difficulties are most acute in the case of historical traditions of public establishment, where the law privileges one or more religious bodies with public authority and responsibilities not accorded to others, for justifications of such unequal treatment of individuals and groups carry little theoretical weight within the contemporary ideology of egalitarian civil rights.[22]

A Public Theological Alternative to Liberal Natural Rights

Once conceding the destructive dynamics of freedom in which the liberal natural rights tradition is deeply implicated, Christian theology understands emancipation as the conversion of individuals from absorption in their own capacities and productive labor; from projects of self-defense,

[22] See the chapter by Rivers in this volume on the recent juridical expansion of the right to equality and the chapter by Leigh on rights of conscience.

self-vindication, and self-aggrandizement; from strivings to create and secure themselves through technical domination of human and nonhuman nature; to the perfections of the triune God revealed in *his* work of creating, sustaining, justifying, and sanctifying. Emancipation is the overcoming of the individual's proprietary self-possession by divine possession, self-love by the love of God, fleshly fear by heavenly fear, justification through works of law by justification through the cross of Christ, humanly contrived certainty by the divinely bestowed certainty of faith, self-fulfillment by the Spirit's sanctifying grace. In short, emancipation of human society from the corrosive dynamics of modern freedom is God's own gracious work, into which he has taken the church's communication of salvation in Jesus Christ.

As servants of this communication, theologians must continue to address the issue of whether the concept of natural rights is soundly and profitably employed within a biblical theological framework. For those critical of (at least some) modern developments, the issue is whether the concept can be rescued. The most impressive example of rescue has been the Roman Catholic magisterial tradition of elaborating human rights, which, since the pontificate of Leo XIII (1878–1903), has tapped into several centuries of premodern and early modern developments in Catholic natural rights thinking, in which different streams of scholastic theology (Scotist, Thomist, Ockamist, and Aristotelian), drawing on canonist legal commentary, cross-fertilized and later intersected with strands of Renaissance ethical and legal humanism.[23]

Selective mining of this legacy has enabled Roman Catholic social teaching to present a more conservative account of natural rights, integrated into the longer canonist and theological tradition of law, predominantly around a Thomist/Aristotelian nexus. Similarly, Protestant thinkers have uncovered in post-Reformation Anglican, Lutheran, and Reformed scholasticism and covenantalism a comparably orthodox Christian framework for integrating universal rights.[24] Among the conceptual relationships in their sources that these contemporary interpretations of rights seek to conserve are the subordination of rights to obligations, of subjective right to objective right, of

[23] For the sources and contributions to natural rights political thought in the late medieval and early modern periods, see Brian Tierney, *The Idea of Natural Rights: Studies on Natural Rights, Natural Law and Church Law* (Eerdmans 1997).

[24] See, e.g., John Witte Jr, *The Reformation of Rights: Religion and Human Rights in Early Modern Calvinism* (Cambridge 2008).

natural rights to revealed divine and natural law, of individual freedom to communal bonds and authority, of human nature to divine grace.

At the same time, the last fifty years of historical scholarship has given us greater appreciation of how heavily dependent the (preponderantly) Protestant framers of modern liberal contractarian rights theory were on pre- and protomodern Catholic developments. Better knowledge of the theoretical and practical trajectories of the earlier rights tradition and of continuities with its modern sequel has provided fresh historical and theological grounds for wondering whether even the most admirable contemporary theological handling of rights can wholly rescue the humanist promise of the natural rights political/legal tradition from the debacle of unbounded freedom, agonistic social relations, institutional legalism, and technological manipulation.

Historically, we have a clearer grasp of the emergence within Catholic theorizing of rights between the thirteenth and early seventeenth centuries of the following ideas: (1) the subjective natural right of individual freedom as unhindered self-determining choice within an arena of divinely permitted—neither required nor prohibited—human action (permissive natural right/law); (2) the invariable interdependence within subjective right (whether natural or positive legal right) of two dimensions of power or control: the subject's proprietary control or power of disposal over his or her actions, and the subject's control by his or her actions over objects of his or her natural/material or social/moral environment (whether things or the actions of others); (3) self-defense as simultaneously an absolute natural right and a natural obligation of individuals and communities under divine and natural law; (4) the primacy of the individual and communal rights of self-defense in the moral foundation of the political contract and the constitution of government; and (5) the alienability of the natural right of individual and communal freedom in binding contracts of service or servitude, especially for the preservation of life.

Mindful of these developments, my task now is to focus theological reservations about the concept of rights in Christian social, political, and legal thought by bringing to bear the evangelical approach of English Reformation public theology to questions of human law and freedom within God's law and freedom revealed in the history of Jesus Christ. This legacy is contained in major theological documents of national church reform produced in the reigns of Edward VI and Elizabeth 1: chiefly, the Book of Common Prayer and Ordinal (1559 edition) and the Thirty-Nine Articles of Religion (1563/

1571), which have a continuing, if attenuated, function as foundational historic standards for Anglican thought and practice, supplemented by the official books of homilies (1547, 1563), which were an indispensable tool of reforming pedagogy and discipline in the two reigns. This theology may accurately be designated "Cranmerian," after Thomas Cranmer, Archbishop of Canterbury from 1533 to 1556, chief designer of the Edwardian prayer books of 1549 and 1552 and Forty-Two Articles of 1553, and author of the pivotal soteriological homilies in the 1547 collection. Cranmerian theology may broadly be described as Augustinian, with Lutheran, Reformed, and Catholic elements, indebted to patristic, late medieval, and contemporary continental theologians.[25]

First, Cranmerian public theology presents law as an aspect of God's Trinitarian perfection, inseparable from all the moments of his free willing and working *ad extra*, so that the concept is a connecting thread running through the ontological, epistemological, soteriological, and ethical spheres.

Second, Cranmerian theology is theocentric, emphasizing the immediate and direct dependence of creaturely being, knowing, and acting on God. Free human action is a reception of what God has already done and given in creation and in history; moreover, it is obedient human response to God's ongoing, manifold communication of his judgments (his law), wherein lies its value and significance. As the divine/human communication mediates all lateral human communication and action, Cranmerian theology resists the hypostasizing of the human will as a faculty of self-determination through choice, and also the liberal concept of permissive natural right/law as a permanent sphere of open-ended choice within broad moral boundaries, both of which have played key roles in natural rights theorizing from early on.

Third, its treatment of law and freedom is Christocentric. Assuming the revelation of Jesus Christ, the eternal Word of the Father, to manifest the unity of God's judgment and action in creation and redemption, Cranmerian theology never presents the moral life of human community apart from Christ's revelation of it conveyed in the New Testament writings. Central to its understanding of the human *imago Dei* is the renewed moral agency and action of redeemed humanity, for which the ground and

[25] Among its continental influences were Luther, Melanchthon, Zwingli, Bullinger, Bucer, Martyr (Martire Vermigli), and Calvin.

possibility is the individual and communal act of faith, in which sinful human beings accept the Father's judgment of condemnation and reconciliation directed toward themselves in the death and resurrection of his Son. The Father's judgment is, simultaneously, his condemnation of the history of sinful human judgment and action put to death with Christ on the cross, his vindication of faithful human judgment and action within a creation raised from the dead and exalted with the resurrected and ascended Christ, and his promise of the fulfillment of all that he has vindicated in the future consummation of Christ's kingdom. Thus, no adequate theological account of human dignity in terms of the *imago Dei* can abstract from the complex act of faith, embracing repentance of past sin, trust in Christ's accomplished work of reconciliation, and hope for a wholly renewed common life in him.

The English and continental reformers present the act of faith as originating not within sinful human subjectivity, but within the divine subjectivity of the Holy Spirit, who, as the spirit of the risen and ascended Christ, incorporates believers into Christ's resurrection life and makes available to them the eschatological freedom promised to his faithful members. This freedom has a threefold relation to God's law: (1) deliverance from sinful blindness and disobedience to the revelation of God's will in the order of created being, good, and objective right; (2) release from the law's condemnation of past sins, and from the oppressiveness of its present demands, encountered as external and alien constraints on human willing and acting; and (3) participation in Christ's lordship over the law, in his perfect obedience to his Father's will that fulfills the law's meaning and purpose.

Fourth, its treatment of law and freedom is ecclesiological. It is through the church's regular practices of communication or "proclamation," the core of which is her common worship, that the Spirit generates, nourishes, strengthens, and purifies faith, hope, and love, renewing human freedom. Worship is, then, faith's first practical obedience: the exemplar or generative form of renewed moral action that imparts its Christological basis and form; its common, unifying character; its outer rule in scripture; and its inner rule by the Holy Spirit.

The Cranmerian liturgies display the subject of every obedient act of worship as, simultaneously, a concrete, visible community of practice and the universal community of Christ's faithful people, to which every worshipping individual and congregation is joined in an active communion. In word and sacrament, the liturgies convey the promise that perfected moral agency in the kingdom of God will be wholly common, communicative, and consensual: that it will be mutual participation in the Spirit's judgments, mutual sharing in the knowledge, love, and freedom of Christ. But they neither identify the faithful in this age of waiting with earthly churches nor affirm that institutional practices of worship are, in themselves, the pure moral action of reconciled community. Rather, they affirm that renewed moral humanity is communicated where the practices of worship exhibit as present reality and promised future the authority of Christ's rule in its social, moral, and epistemic aspects.

Running through Tudor public worship is the rehearsing of the scriptures in speech and song, especially the sequential reading of biblical texts in canonical order, designed to recognize both the primacy of the apostolic recollection of the saving history of Jesus Christ and the indispensable testimony of Israel's history to the creative and saving action of the Father's Word and Spirit. All other liturgical acts—of praise, thanksgiving, confession of sin, preaching, petitionary prayer, and sacramental celebration—are congregational responses to scriptural communication. As a progressive revelation within God's saving purposes of the ground, character, and elements of human "good works," the scriptures give priority to God's explicit commandments as making plain the moral implications of all his recorded judgments, purposes, and actions; and moreover, they show Christ's commandments, interpreted within the whole of his ministry, to be the hermeneutical key to the totality of divine commandments. All revelations of God's law have their historical telos in the revelation of his suffering and triumphant self-giving in his incarnate Son, and so anticipate this final unfolding of moral community.

The church's ethos of proclamation is an ecstatic ethos of belonging to Christ and not to oneself, and of belonging to one another in the fellowship of Christ. Having no proprietary right in, or juridical control over, this belonging, the church's practices of communicating Christ's freedom and law are those of nonproprietary and nonjuridical sharing. Moreover, because judgment over the faithful belongs exclusively to God in Christ, who is both judge and judged, the fundamental and paramount response of the faithful to God's judgment in Christ is not one of public judgment in either the ecclesiastical or civil realms. Correspondingly, the apostolic authority of its ordained ministry is fundamentally evangelical and nonjuridical, including its pastoral dimensions.

Widely repudiating the mediaeval conception of the church as a priestly hierarchy of sacramental and jurisdictional powers unified in the juridical sacrament of penance,[26] the English reformers construe clerical authority as authority to preach and teach God's word, to intercede in prayer and celebrate the sacraments on behalf of the gathered church, to give pastoral counsel, exhortation, admonition, and consolation to those within their care. Likewise, while continuing to affirm the continuity of episcopal with apostolic church government, Cranmerian public theology principally derives episcopal jurisdiction in the church's external polity from the supreme territorial jurisdiction divinely invested in the lay monarch.[27]

Fifth, Cranmerian theology sets the authorities and practices of public proclamation and public judgment in dialectical tension and interdependence. It reasserts the longer theological tradition in which the church's practices were the lens through which created human community was envisaged as constituted by nonproprietary and nonjuridical relationships of mutual service.[28] Accordingly, the patristic/Augustinian mainstream assigned legal property right and coercive jurisdiction to the *saeculum*, the passing age of humanity's continuing subjection to the law of sin and condemnation, conceiving them as institutional restraints on human vice, simultaneously expressive of God's judgment on evildoing and his merciful protection of the goods of human community from the assault of disordered judgments, passions, and affections. In reliance on biblical texts, especially the Pauline locus classicus of Romans 13:1–7, Cranmerian theology presents the practice of public judgment as both an institutional reaction to and anticipation of human wrongdoing, concerned with defining specific deprivations of good, violations of rights, harm and injury to individual and collective subjects, and degrees of culpability.[29]

[26] In sacramental penance, priests heard private confessions by the faithful of their postbaptismal sins, "retained or remitted" the guilt attaching to them according to the sinner's professed contrition, and assessed the seriousness of their sins for the purpose of assigning proportional works of "penance" (punishment) or "satisfaction" to God.

[27] See the Cranmerian liturgies of clerical ordination and episcopal consecration.

[28] This patristic tradition, consolidated by Augustine, held sway through the medieval period until the reception of Aristotle in the West generated greater receptivity to the anchoring of property and government in created nature.

[29] A political sermon typically portrays the "godly order" of the commonweal as requiring that "kings and governors" be the "common revengers" and "correctors" of "all common and private things that be amiss," executing "the right judgment of God's wrath against sin." "A Sermon Concerning the Time of Rebellion" is of composite authorship, but included in JE Cox and Parker Society (eds), *Miscellaneous Writings and Letters of Thomas Cranmer* (Cambridge 1846) 193. Similarly, the prayer

True to its mentors, Cranmerian theology understands the arbitrating judgments of public law to be necessarily ambiguous displays of rationality and justice, underdetermined by God's revealed judgments against human sin. A seminal discussion of the moral ambiguities of political judgments presents their claim on human obedience as depending on a merely demonstrable degree of conformity to (or compatibility with) God's revealed judgments.[30] More importantly, political judgments (unlike the prophetic judgments of preaching) are necessarily incomplete representations of God's reconciling judgment, incapable of communicating the judgment of Christ's suffering love on the cross that justifies the repentant sinner, or the judgment of his triumphant love at God's right hand that regenerates the contrite spirit.

Human law is no more than a remote instrument of the Spirit's saving work, achieving peace as external order, the visible rectification of wrongdoing, the outward reconciliation of antagonistic actors; this peace, nevertheless, may create a social and psychological space for the Holy Spirit's work of inward reconciliation and unification. In the sphere of church polity, public judgment especially curbs damaging social expression of the vices of moral and intellectual pride, causing believers to pit their own judgments against the common judgment respecting church practices neither plainly required nor prohibited by scripture, and so to disrupt the common order and to enter uncharitably into contention with their fellow believers. By compelling individual conceit to defer to outward unity and concord, human laws may prepare the way for the Holy Spirit's action of harmonizing contending judgments in a truly common judgment.[31]

To serve the renewal of created human freedom, then, the practices of political and legal judgment must be undertaken in awareness of their deficiencies and limitations. Failure to resist the temptation to moral perfectionism and to excessive and misdirected public pedagogy assaults the freedom of the divine Spirit of Christ to reveal to repentant believers the fuller meaning and form of the natural obligations of love, within the reconciled human

for the "church militant" in the communion service characteristically beseeches God that all the king's ministers and all "put in authority under him . . . may truly and indifferently minister justice, to the punishment of wickedness and vice, and the maintenance of God's true religion and virtue." JE Booty (ed), *The Book of Common Prayer 1559*, Folger Shakespeare Library (Charlottesville 1976) 382.

[30] Thomas Starkey in *Exhortation to Unity and Obedience* (London ca 1540), drawing on Aquinas, *ST* 1a2ae.95.2.

[31] An argument reiterated throughout Archbishop Whitgift's literary responses to the Presbyterians' broad assault on Elizabethan church practices. J Ayre (ed), *The Works of John Whitgift*, Parker Society (Cambridge 1851–1853) 3 vols.

community inaugurated by God's atoning and vindicating judgment of humankind.[32] At the same time, these practices must recognize in one or another form their divinely ordained scope of protecting from destructive internal and external forces the church's ministries of proclamation, constituting the highest goods of the common life.

When public judgment no longer attests the ordering of jurisdiction to proclamation, it inevitably loses sight of the spiritually peripheral character of its work of protecting human freedom in its manifold social realizations and assumes a false spiritual and social centrality, fostering a legalistic and juridical moral and social ethos that curtails and stifles practical judgment. In the light cast by the evangelical ethic and dialectic of English Reformation public theology, we can more clearly discern the extent to which the prevailing moral-juridical conceptuality of egalitarian natural rights, functioning as the hegemonic rationality of international and national justice and constitutional law, is an ideological crystallization of the destructive self-understanding of sinful human society, elevating its own perverse dynamics over the dynamics of created and restored community.

The conceptuality of egalitarian natural rights displays human moral agency and action not as a "type" of common worship, the core proclamatory practice of faith in Christ—responsive, ecstatic, communicative, conforming to God's trinitarian rule—but rather as a "type" of ownership and governance: self-disposing and self-defensive, isolated in agonistic practices of passing judgment on others, disengaged from God's saving judgment of sinful humankind. At the same time, it converts coercive judgment from a penultimate and limited communal reflection of God's condemning and preserving judgment into a derivative expression of an ultimate, immanent juridical paradigm of human freedom and society. Consequently, it does not serve that evangelical freedom by which the faithful participate in created and renewed human goods, but rather secures sinful human beings in their common bondage and deprivation.

The present hope for late modern societies must be for the overcoming of this misrepresentation and mis-ordering by a chastened service of public justice to the individual and common good of freedom.

[32] Thus, many Elizabethan reforming bishops resisted the Puritan call for corporate sanctification through adoption of the Calvinist church discipline, perceiving the discipline to take an excessively legalistic and juridical approach to good works.

PART II
CHRISTIAN PERSPECTIVES ON CONSTITUTIONALISM

9

Sovereignty

Dual, Plural, and One

Joel Harrison

Jacques Maritain once said, "[T]his concept [sovereignty] is intrinsically wrong and bound to mislead us if we keep on using it."[1] He contended that it can detract from an understanding of the Church's own role in public life, the role of various groups and associations in forming society, and the need for regional and international forms of order. These are significant claims, given that sovereignty has often been treated as foundational both to forming the state and to promulgating law.

In this chapter, I develop Maritain's claim. I begin by discussing the rise of a modern concept of sovereignty as prior to and grounding all law, associated with an unlimited and indivisible power that prioritizes the will of a recognized authority. I then turn to how the Christian tradition contains a consistent thread of challenge. This is reflected in three parts: the parallel authority of priest and king, or church and civil authority; the cultivation of multiple sites of authority, at local, regional, and international levels; and the coordinating, encouraging, and cultivating place role of "monarchical" rule. Rather than sovereign rule, the Christian tradition has emphasized the intertwining of duality, plurality, and the one. Importantly, each of these components is understood as pursuing a shared horizon, a tradition, and a discerning of right. As such, it could be suggested that what is ultimately sovereign is the good itself.

[1] Jacques Maritain, *Man and the State* (University of Chicago Press 1951) 29.

Joel Harrison, *Sovereignty: Dual, Plural, and One* in *Christianity and Constitutionalism.* Edited by: Nicholas Aroney and Ian Leigh, Oxford University Press. © Oxford University Press 2022. DOI: 10.1093/oso/9780197587256.003.0009

Modern Sovereignty

In the late sixteenth century, Jean Bodin identified sovereignty with "the absolute and perpetual power of a commonwealth . . . the highest power of command."[2] For sovereignty to be real and effectual meant that the sovereign must possess a power that was unlimited and indivisible. If the king's power was subject to any obligations or conditions, then he would simply be a delegate, holding power in trust for someone else or some higher power.[3] Sovereignty meant the king's power was only subject to the law of God and of nature, although if he contravened this law he was answerable to God alone; contravention would not provide any alternative authority (the people, the estates) with a legal ground for resistance.[4] Indeed, for Bodin this confirmed the sacrality of sovereignty. The sovereign held God's "scepter and his power," understood as an inalienable right to rule, and so any restraining power would degrade the majesty of exercising what amounted to the divine will.[5]

Being unlimited, this sovereign power must also be indivisible. Bodin argued that any alternative site of authority must be in a relationship of "subjection, service, and obedience."[6] Judgment entails a final determination of obligations, and so to subject the people to the judgment of different or competing sovereigns would be absurd. But the king also bears God's all-powerful image; just as God cannot have an equal without ceasing to be God, so too the king.[7] These claims could justify the use of violence. Sovereignty must be secured externally against any rival authority, such as another nation-state. Much later, Carl Schmitt would characterize war as the ultimate act of politics (meaning state-building) because it determines the existence of a distinct people against an external enemy, revealing that the sovereign's indivisible power rests on the authority to demand a readiness to die in its name.[8] On this view, political authority also means subsuming or eliminating internal rivals in favor of a central power.[9] Thus, the state's emergence entailed

[2] Jean Bodin, *On Sovereignty: Four Chapters from The Six Books of the Commonwealth* (Julian H Franklin tr, Cambridge University Press 1992) 1.

[3] Ibid, 4–5.

[4] Ibid, 31, 115–118.

[5] Ibid, 25–27.

[6] Ibid, 20. See also Martin Loughlin, "Why Sovereignty?" in Richard Rawlings, Peter Leyland, and Alison Young (eds), *Sovereignty and the Law: Domestic, European and International Perspectives* (Oxford University Press, 2013) 34, 38–39 ("Sovereignty expresses a principle of unity: it is an expression of illimitability, perpetuity, and indivisibility").

[7] Bodin, *Sovereignty*, 27, 50.

[8] Carl Schmitt, *The Concept of the Political* (George Schwab tr, University of Chicago Press 2007) 33.

[9] See also Neil Walker, "Sovereignty Frames and Sovereignty Claims" in Richard Rawlings, Peter Leyland, and Alison Young (eds), *Sovereignty and the Law: Domestic, European and International*

expropriating the property and wealth of churches and dissolving ecclesiastical jurisdiction.[10] Bodin was clear in his opposition to any "privilege" the church might hold—to grant clemency, for example.[11] Thomas Hobbes shared this view, claiming that the Leviathan must domesticate any "enthusiasm" or inspiration of the Church.[12] And Schmitt likewise identified the Church as a threat to the state's sovereign authority.[13]

In practice, this subjugation of all alternative authorities extends to entire people groups, especially within colonial countries. Australian law, for example, rests on the fiction that the continent was "settled," meaning that the sovereign colonial authority did not have to treat with any pre-existing Aboriginal and Torres Strait Islander authority.[14] The High Court has rejected the idea of any parallel and enduring Indigenous sovereignty out of perceived necessity—for this would undermine the source of its own authority: a unified imperial, now Australian, sovereignty.[15] Bodin would have agreed. He argued that a unitary locus of total sovereignty was the necessary basis of statehood. His comparable target was a mixed constitution that would divide sovereign power between, for example, monarchic, aristocratic, and democratic roles. A constitution of mixed and plural powers would, he argued, corrupt the state because the sovereign power must have the singular authority to pass law, command obedience, and thus constitute a state.[16] For this reason, Schmitt called sovereignty a "borderline concept." It sits outside of the ordinary legal order as something that can be invoked exceptionally to suspend the law itself (or else to constitute a legal order), but, because of this, sovereignty is still fundamental to the legal order and defined in relation to it. Law, and for Schmitt the political as such, is predicated on sovereignty.[17] To adopt the language of the modern constitutional lawyer, sovereignty sustains

Perspectives (Oxford University Press 2013) 18, 31–32 (noting both the centralizing tendency of sovereignty discourse and its "prize-fighting dimension").

[10] José Casanova, *Public Religions in the Modern World* (University of Chicago Press 1994) 13.

[11] Bodin, *Sovereignty*, 75–77.

[12] Brad S Gregory, *The Unintended Reformation: How a Religious Revolution Secularized Society* (Belknap Press, 2012) 162.

[13] Schmitt, *Concept of the Political*, 37–42.

[14] *Mabo v Queensland (No 2)* (1992) 175 CLR 1.

[15] *Members of the Yorta Yorta Aboriginal Community v Victoria* (2002) 214 CLR 422, 443–444 (Gleeson CJ, Gummow and Hayne JJ).

[16] Bodin, *Sovereignty*, 98–105.

[17] Carl Schmitt, *Political Theology: Four Chapters on the Concept of Sovereignty* (George Schwab tr, University of Chicago Press 2005) 5–7.

the plenary and potentially absolute authority of a particular constitutional actor or actors.[18]

Nonetheless, lawyers today may still fairly ask: does this Bodin-inspired understanding of sovereignty and statecraft continue to have a hold on the legal imagination?

For modern lawyers, discussion of sovereignty has traditionally focused on the formal question of whether a law is duly authorized by the correct body and through the correct procedure: what Ronald Dworkin called law's "pedigree."[19] For those trained in the Westminster system, parliamentary sovereignty is what H. L. A. Hart characterized as the "rule of recognition," the rule according to which lawyers determine whether a law is a valid part of the legal system. Hart argued that such a rule depends for its recognition on the senior officials of the legal system.[20] Sovereignty need not rest in a single person or institution, whose will is law, as Bodin (or John Austin) would have it. Rather, sovereignty may exist institutionally, in the complex system of "secondary rules" that define the conditions of law identifying, law changing, and law interpreting.[21] Nevertheless, this arguably echoes Bodin's focus on a sovereign will divorced from "higher" law. What is relevant is simply whether the law emanates from an institution recognized as having authority to make law. As Jeffrey Goldsworthy argues (positively in his case), sovereignty entails the claim that "morality" cannot constrain law.[22] The sovereign's will constitutes law, leaving any challenge to its status based on natural or divine law as extralegal or moral only.[23]

This continuing emphasis on the potentially unbound will blunts, I suggest, at least one challenge raised against modern sovereignty discourse: internationalism.

Dieter Grimm argues that if sovereignty entails freedom from external control, then no state is sovereign in this sense. International law may no longer depend on state election or acquiescence.[24] Some argue that international bodies may intervene in domestic matters when a state is failing

[18] See Jeffrey Goldsworthy, *The Sovereignty of Parliament: History and Philosophy* (Oxford University Press 2001) 1.

[19] Ronald Dworkin, "Is Law a System of Rules?" in Robert S Summers (ed), *Essays in Legal Philosophy* (Basil Blackwell 1968) 25, 28.

[20] HLA Hart, *The Concept of Law* (3rd edn, Clarendon Press 2012) 94–95.

[21] Ibid, 95–99.

[22] Goldsworthy, *Sovereignty of Parliament*, 17.

[23] Ibid, 232.

[24] See Dieter Grimm, *Sovereignty: The Origin and Future of a Political and Legal Concept* (Columbia University Press 2015) 106–107.

to fulfill fundamental responsibilities toward its citizens.[25] Given such developments, as well as internal devolving of power within states and federal structures, Neil MacCormick has pointed to "post-sovereignty"—an understanding that individuals' lives are anchored in multiple, overlapping institutions.[26] Others have referred to "pooled," "differentiated," "diversified," or "fragmented" sovereignty.[27] *And yet*, some continue to appeal to a stronger claim of sovereignty within this emerging context. For example, Grimm refers to popular sovereignty still enduring, lying dormant: an ultimate, unlimited, constituent power to determine the constitutional order "we, the people," wish to have.[28]

Perhaps a more fruitful challenge to traditional claims of sovereignty lies in constitutionalism itself. Some Commonwealth legal scholars argue that parliamentary sovereignty should be understood as a *principle* (rather than a rule), one that should be generally respected but which is nevertheless a creature of the common law.[29] On this basis, parliamentary sovereignty can be controlled by the common law, which gives paramount importance to the rule of law. And the common law is guarded and developed by the courts.[30] We may say, on this account, that the sovereign state—unlimited and indivisible in Bodin's argument—is constitutionally constrained. Its powers are defined and checked by an independent authority (here, the court), and this is done with reference to certain conventions, legal norms of interpretation, and often rights guarantees. The exercise of authority now depends on complying with such constraints.

Certainly, this challenge is open to qualifications or criticism. For example, Grimm suggests that constitutionalism may concern the exercise of government, leaving untouched claims of ultimate sovereignty vested, perhaps, in the people.[31] Sovereignty always remains as a kind of logical *a priori* lying

[25] See, e.g., Timothy Endicott, "The Logic of Freedom and Power" in Samantha Besson and John Tasioulas (eds), *The Philosophy of International Law* (Oxford University Press 2010) 245, 258.

[26] Neil MacCormick, "Beyond the Sovereign State" (1993) 56 Modern Law Review 1, 17.

[27] See the descriptions in Richard Rawlings, "Introduction: Sovereignty in Question" in Richard Rawlings, Peter Leyland, and Alison Young (eds), *Sovereignty and the Law: Domestic, European and International Perspectives* (Oxford University Press 2013) 1, 6.

[28] See Grimm, *Sovereignty*, 5–9, 109–128. In *R (Miller) v Secretary of State for Exiting the European Union* [2018] AC 61, [60], the Supreme Court emphasized that sovereignty was maintained in the United Kingdom by the continuing power to repeal the application of European Union law.

[29] See, e.g., *R (Jackson) v AG* [2006] 1 AC 262, [126] (HL) (Lord Hope).

[30] See, e.g., TRS Allan, "Parliamentary Sovereignty: Law Politics and Revolution" (1997) 113 Law Quarterly Review 443; TRS Allan, *The Sovereignty of Law: Freedom, Constitution and Common Law* (Oxford University Press 2013) ch 3; and Dame Sian Elias "Sovereignty in the 21st Century: Another Spin on the Merry-Go-Round" (2003) 14 Public Law Review 148.

[31] See Grimm, *Sovereignty*, 106.

behind all law. As to the substance of the claim, some argue that common law constitutionalism, or else judicial review generally, poses a democratic problem; Parliament, not the court, is the deliberative body providing representative voices to decide contentious matters.[32] However, I want to suggest a different possibility: that when we consider the Christian tradition, this characterization of constitutionalism (and its apparent subversion of sovereignty) is too narrow. Goldsworthy, it seems to me, is right. The claim that morality cannot constrain the sovereign power to make law lies at the heart of sovereignty discourse. In other words, asking whether the "law" in question is oriented toward the natural and divine law, whether it pursues the good, is a legal nonstarter. Constitutionalism-as-constraint may map onto this question, asking whether the law complies with certain fundamental norms or guarantees. Some theologians, philosophers, and legal scholars argue that Christian thought points most fundamentally toward a "rights-limited state," emphasizing restraint in favor of individual subjective rights.[33] Christian discourse may indeed point to some form of rights discourse, although as John Milbank's and Julian Rivers's contributions to this volume indicate, what is meant by a right and how this relates to natural law is a contested field.[34] At the very least, I think it is possible to say that the broader sweep of the Christian tradition points to much more than limiting sovereign power in favor of judicial protection of the rule of law and contestable views on individual rights. Rather, Christian constitutionalism is more concerned with facilitating a shared project. That is, it concerns the relative positioning of mutually implicated authorities and groups, each exercising their authority in order to pursue a shared orientation to the good. On this view, sovereignty is not simply constrained by a set of juristic limits—the sovereign will having

[32] See, e.g., Richard Ekins, "Judicial Supremacy and the Rule of Law" (2003) 119 Law Quarterly Review 127.

[33] See, e.g., Nicholas Wolterstorff, *The Mighty and the Almighty: An Essay in Political Theology* (Cambridge University Press 2012) ch 13. In his contribution to this volume, Jonathan Chaplin (chapter 18, below) rightly criticizes Wolterstorff's argument as a narrow account of Christian reflection on political authority. However, the emphasis on restraint as the heart of constitutionalism is seen elsewhere in this volume. It arguably underpins Peter Leithart's discussion of Constantine (chapter 4, above), in which recognizing the Church and religious liberty acts as a proto-separation of powers or checks and balances doctrine, and David McIlroy's reflections on the Trinity (chapter 17, below), in which each person of the Godhead points to limited authority. This strikes me as also too narrow. Participation in the life of the Trinity may, for example, orient us (and the purpose of our constitutional order) toward mutual love and delight; the church's freedom reorients the very purpose of secular law and government. In other words, more than restraint, Christian thought proposes a common project, or so I will argue.

[34] See John Milbank (chapter 20, below) and Julian Rivers (chapter 13, above).

to accommodate the individual's rights. Rather, it is dissolved in the face of a higher goal or purpose. I suggest that this more completely challenges the unlimited and indivisible sovereign.

Duality

Contemporary debates about constitutionalism often juxtapose strong claims for the supremacy of legislatures with equally strong claims for the jurisdiction of the courts. This is the outcome of a secular polity turned entirely inward; one pole of authority is jousting with itself. There is a prior debate to be had, however, one arguably more constitutive of Western constitutional identity. The secular authority, whether a judge, court, or legislative body, was never understood to be the sole authority. Rather, the Christian tradition pointed to the constitutive distinction and relationship between priestly and royal rule. It is through debating the authority of each of these roles that Christian thought and practice radically reoriented the purpose of temporal authority, inaugurating a "secular" space that is nevertheless answerable to a higher end. Within this tradition, talk of sovereignty in the modern sense is misplaced. What is sovereign, if we must speak in such terms, is the continual attempt to enact the tradition, that is, to mediate the rule of God or discern what is true, good, and beautiful through the dual roles of temporal and spiritual authority. Against this, the modern concept of sovereignty arises as a competing theological claim concerning the ultimate authority of one.

This account is important for at least three reasons. First, rather than the unhindered act of sovereignty grounding and authorizing all law, what is "foundational" (but without any real foundational moment) is the attempt to conform to right order, the requirements of natural and divine law, a quest to cultivate and support true human ends. Second, this account points to duality at the heart of a polity—the church and temporal authority. These are separate, but not unrelated; the former's authority is to be respected, requiring its freedom, and the latter is tasked with responding to the claims of the former. Third, the duality then further encourages multiple sites of authority, a plurality. This points to limits on any single sovereign rule, but also a coordinating task for rulers.

Oliver O'Donovan notes that from the late patristics into the medieval period, "[t]he church-state relation comes to be seen in the light of a more ancient, and more functional duality than that of exile: the relation of priest and king."[35] Thus Augustine writes of the Church catholic as the "guardians of truth and followers of right," making "use of the nations as materials for its operations."[36] He exhorts those exercising civil authority to take up "the cause of the church."[37] On this view, civil rulers are "simply caught up [in the] project" of reconciliation and redemption.[38]

In the fifth century, Pope Gelasius I echoed Augustine's thoughts but proposed a distinct role differentiation. He wrote in his *Letter to Emperor Anastasius*, "Two there are, august Emperor, by which this world is ruled: the consecrated authority of priests and the royal power."[39] Here we find what John Milbank calls "mutual subordination": the pope to kings in matters pertaining to this time, kings to the pope in matters of eternity, with kings ultimately exercising rule with direction to matters of eternal concern.[40] For Gelasius, the papacy did not exercise coercive power. For this reason, kingly rule was understood to be somewhat outside the ecclesial domain. In this sense, Christianity proposed a differentiation between law or politics and the Church. But, even here, coercive power was framed as entirely serving a Christian perfectionist end—to ensure stability for the more fundamental exercise of love within the body of Christ.[41] More generally, the priestly role of the Church was higher in dignity and thus exercised suasive authority.[42] This meant that the pope could exercise an "admonitory overruling," or else the sacramental discipline of the Church against temporal rulers when needed.[43]

Authority was thus plural or a matter of overlapping jurisdictions. Christendom was one in its orientation, a "body" directed toward shared

[35] Oliver O'Donovan, *The Desire of Nations: Rediscovering the Roots of Political Theology* (Cambridge University Press 2011) 163.

[36] Augustine, "Of True Religion" in JHS Burleigh (ed and tr), *Augustine: Earlier Writings* (SCM Press 1953) 218, 231.

[37] Augustine, "Letter 134" in EM Atkins and RJ Dodaro (eds), *Augustine: Political Writings* (Cambridge University Press 2001) 63, 64.

[38] Oliver O'Donovan, *The Ways of Judgment* (Eerdmans 2005) 89.

[39] Gelasius I, "Letter to Emperor Anastasius" in Oliver O'Donovan and Joan Lockwood O'Donovan (eds), *From Irenaeus to Grotius: A Sourcebook in Christian Political Thought 100–1625* (Eerdmans 1999) 179.

[40] John Milbank, *Beyond Secular Order: The Representation of Being and the Representation of the People* (Wiley Blackwell 2013) 200–201.

[41] See Milbank, *Beyond Secular Order*, 124, and O'Donovan, *Ways of Judgment*, 134–135 (arguing that the ruler's service responds to a "summons to the perfection of the Kingdom of God" and that "[i]n light of that summons the ruler can appear 'like the angel of God to discern good and evil' (2 Sam. 14:17), the herald of the hidden future to which God summons human society").

[42] See also Jean Bethke Elshtain, *Sovereignty: God, State, and Self* (Basic Books 2008) 12–13.

[43] Milbank, *Beyond Secular Order*, 219.

ends.[44] But as a body it had different parts—groups and offices that undertook different tasks. Yet both the priestly and the kingly roles were found in Christ.[45] Thus Gelasius's dualism—the world ruled by the consecrated authority of priests and royal power—balanced two authorities mediating together the rule of Christ, dealing respectively in sacramental order and public discipline.[46] Between the eleventh and fourteenth centuries, however, rulers within the Roman Church and the Roman Empire invoked Gelasian dualism anachronistically in attempts to combine the two forms of rule into the one person.

We can see the beginnings of this with Pope Gregory VII, whose arguments and reforms were nevertheless in some continuity with prior claims. Responding to the practices of simony (purchasing holy orders or offices), clerical marriage and concubinage, and lay investiture (the granting of ceremonial office by lay patrons), Gregory introduced a number of social and political reforms. Harold Berman described this as amounting to a revolution in the history of the West.[47] Socially, the lower ranks of the church, clerical and lay, were subjected to papal authority and there developed a greater emphasis on personal devotion, ascetic discipline, and coercion. At the same time, the laity was increasingly removed from church functions (e.g., the appointment of clergy).[48] Politically, Gregory construed papal authority as extending to controlling temporal authorities, including the power to act as supreme judge in disputes involving princes. He asserted "constitutional supremacy."[49]

Gregory's reforms can be viewed positively. Their immediate impact was to end corrupt practices between civil and clerical offices and authorities. However, more importantly, they shaped constitutional law and practice. Berman describes the subsequent development of canon law, which then shaped secular law, as a "release of energy and creativity analogous to a

[44] See also Harold J Berman, *Law and Revolution: The Formation of the Western Legal Tradition* (Harvard University Press 1983) 91 (arguing that rather than modern separation, the medieval period was characterized by the ecclesia as the Christian people—*populus christianus*—governed by both priestly and secular rulers).

[45] Christ is both "King of kings" and the "great high priest." See, e.g., 1 Timothy 6:15; Revelation 17:15; Hebrews 4:14.

[46] See O'Donovan, *Desire of the Nations*, 167.

[47] Berman, *Law and Revolution*, Part I, ch 2.

[48] See Charles Taylor, *A Secular Age* (Belknap Press 2007) 265 and Oliver O'Donovan and Joan Lockwood-O'Donovan, "Gregory VII" in Oliver O'Donovan and Joan Lockwood O'Donovan (eds), *From Irenaeus to Grotius: A Sourcebook in Christian Political Thought 100–1625* (Eerdmans 1999) 240.

[49] O'Donovan and Lockwood-O'Donovan, "Gregory VII," 205.

process of nuclear fission."[50] The reforms gave rise to plural legal codes, with overlapping jurisdictions, governing different components of Christendom. And this meant, Berman continues, that the papal revolution crystallized the "principle that royal jurisdiction was not unlimited." Secular authority alone could not determine the boundaries of its power.[51] Indeed, as O'Donovan notes, Gregory introduced the possibility that a ruler's office could be lawfully terminated.[52] But more than simply limiting temporal authority, Gregory's claim was still in continuity with previous patristic and medieval arguments. He wanted temporal authority to be under his tutelage,[53] and he proposed a power to override kingly rule when salvation was at stake. In this way, the higher dignity of spiritual authority and the direction it provides to temporal rule in shaping the community was maintained.[54]

Nevertheless, Gregory's assertion of papal power also set a pattern or shifted the discourse of the Church toward discipline. Charles Taylor points to the Hildebrandine Reforms as the first "attempt to make the mass of the laity, living in the *saeculum*, shape up more fully as Christians."[55] Rather than orienting the community to a life of charity, Gregory asserted a sovereign jurisdiction that would cast the Church as a coercive and disciplinary body; a sovereign body because, as papalists increasingly claimed, the pope exercised an authority unchallenged by any temporal authority.[56] Rather than the higher dignity of spiritual persuasion, the pope exercised a higher power emulating God's *potentia absoluta*.[57] Kings or civil authorities later adopted claims to sovereignty in the same terms.[58] As we see much later with Bodin and later thinkers, this shift came at the expense of plural authorities.

Such political changes were supported philosophically or theologically by an increasing focus on the will. Christian thought had emphasized that what God had ordained—creation—was consistent with His nature.[59]

[50] Berman, *Law and Revolution*, 88.
[51] Ibid, 269.
[52] O'Donovan, *Desire of the Nations*, 238.
[53] Berman, *Law and Revolution*, 111.
[54] In his letter to Bishop Herman, Gregory cites Gelasius as support. See Pope Gregory VII, "Letter 8.21" in Oliver O'Donovan and Joan Lockwood O'Donovan (eds), *From Irenaeus to Grotius: A Sourcebook in Christian Political Thought* (Eerdmans 1999) 243, 246.
[55] Taylor, *A Secular Age*, 265.
[56] See Oliver O'Donovan and Joan Lockwood O'Donovan, "The Struggle Over Empire and the Integration of Aristotle" in Oliver O'Donovan and Joan Lockwood O'Donovan (eds), *From Irenaeus to Grotius: A Sourcebook in Christian Political Thought 100–1625* (Eerdmans 1999) 231.
[57] Milbank, *Beyond Secular Order*, 204.
[58] See also Berman, *Law and Revolution*, 23 (arguing Hildebrand's attempt to concentrate power at the center "almost demanded the invention of the concept of the State").
[59] Bethke Elshtain, *Sovereignty*, 30–34; Gregory, *The Unintended Reformation*, 29–32.

Stating something was "good" was understood to be a nonexhaustive, analogical, reflection on God's own goodness. On this view, determining what nature requires, including persons and their relationships with one another, was thus human reason participating in divine reason. (Here "requires" may, as Milbank argues in this volume, be better understood more as inspiration or a "mode of participated perception."[60]) Such reason was then formulated into law.[61] However, nominalist thinkers increasingly criticized this view. To them, it posed a limit on God's sovereignty.[62] For example, if the good of a person was determined by a nature tending toward a telos (even though this was created), then God's determination of what is good was in some sense bound by nature.[63] What developed instead was an increasing focus on divine will over divine reason, the former understood increasingly as a capacity to exercise an unrestrained sovereign power.[64]

On this argument, "sovereignty" reflects a series of losses. It entails eliminating competing sites of authority or what Rowan Williams calls "graded levels of loyalty."[65] But this is not simply the loss of a check on total power, consistent with constitutionalism-as-constraint. The Christian tradition just described does point to checks and balances; however, it does more than this. The loss of plural authorities also entails removing a teleological referent, an understanding of the end that authority must serve.

Of course, the Christian injection of graded levels of loyalty, plural sites of authority, and orientation toward the good endures. Notably, the Catholic tradition continues to point to the duality of church and civil authority serving a shared end. Most recently, Pope Francis recapitulated the claim, stating, "Civil power finds its limits before the law of God," while "ecclesiastical authority and civil power are called to cooperate for the integral good of the human community."[66] Indeed, for this reason, the Catholic Church advocates for the liberty of the Church—so that it may maintain the authority

[60] Milbank (chapter 20, below).

[61] See Bethke Elshtain, *Sovereignty*, 21–23.

[62] Taylor, *A Secular Age*, 123.

[63] On Protestant Reformers continuing with this concern, see Gregory, *The Unintended Reformation*, 40–43.

[64] See Bethke Elshtain, *Sovereignty*, 40 (discussing William of Ockham) and 80 (arguing Martin Luther continued in similar vein).

[65] Rowan Williams, "Secularism, Faith, and Freedom" in Rowan Williams, *Faith in the Public Square* (Bloomsbury 2012) 23, 29.

[66] Pope Francis, "Message of Holy Father Francis to the President of the Pontifical Council for Promoting Christian Unity on the Occasion of the 13th Inter-Christian Symposium" (The Vatican, 19 August 2013) <http://w2.vatican.va/content/francesco/en/messages/pont-messages/2013/documents/papa-francesco_20130819_xiii-simposio-intercristiano.html>.

to direct the earthly city toward the religious life.[67] Recent religious liberty scholarship has sought to re-emphasize this focus on *libertas ecclesiae*.[68] Unsurprisingly, some liberal scholars have couched their objections to this in terms of sovereignty. On their view, liberty, if it is granted at all, is a matter for determination by the single sovereign authority recognized by the state—itself.[69]

Importantly, in stressing *libertas ecclesia*, "the Church" is not simply a bounded authority structure. Rather, the Christian injection of an alternative body, a source of coherence and meaning that both extends beyond the boundaries of any single civil authority and is found within it, has typically encouraged an emphasis on the importance of associations. Alongside the duality of priest and king, we find a plurality of authority.

Plurality

In the *City of God*, Augustine writes of a "cooperative order," in which all persons are given their "appropriate positions."[70] Within this, he gives emphasis to multiple levels of associations: kingdoms, in the plural, but also homes.[71] Each is oriented toward pursuing the love of God, meaning also the love of one's neighbor as God's beloved.[72] As Nicholas Aroney discusses in his contribution to this volume, Aquinas arguably deepens these reflections. He points to different components of a political and social life exercising independent powers, suggesting forms of corporate representation.[73] More recently, Pope Benedict XVI argued that the Christian life entails establishing "networks of charity." Being loved by God, we must "pour forth God's charity." And this is to be done through "micro-relationships (with friends, with family members or within smaller groups)" and also "macro-relationships (social,

[67] See Pope Paul VI, *Gaudium et Spes: Pastoral Constitution of the Church in the Modern World* (The Vatican, 7 December 1965) [43] and Pope Paul VI, *Dignitatis Humanae: On the Right of the Person and of Communities to Social and Civil Freedom in Matters Religious* (The Vatican, 7 December 1965) [13].

[68] See Richard Garnett, "'The Freedom of the Church': (Towards) an Exposition, Translation, and Defense" (2013) 21 Journal of Contemporary Legal Issues 33.

[69] See Richard Schragger and Micah Schwartzman, "Against Religious Institutionalism" (2013) 99 Virginia Law Review 917, 939–945.

[70] Augustine, *Concerning the City of God Against the Pagans* (Henry Bettenson tr, Penguin 2003) Book 19.13.

[71] Ibid, Book 4.15, 154.

[72] Ibid, Book 15.3, 599.

[73] See Nicholas Aroney (chapter 15, below).

economic and political ones)."[74] In each case, a plurality of sites of community is fundamental.

This follows from an understanding of the Church itself. St. Paul often writes of a *koinōnia*.[75] As O'Donovan explains, the term refers, concretely, to a community and, dynamically, a communion or communication. Combined, then, a *koinōnia* consists in a community formed through the common bestowal of gifts.[76] This has meant that what is "church" has always extended beyond any particular institutional boundary. It can include the enlarged household of the early church, the monastic community, or the guild, town, or village engaged in the mutual exchange of talents.[77] Most people find themselves exercising their gifts and striving to form a community within such sites, and not simply a clearly defined institutional church.[78]

Of course, *ruling* is one form of gift. As Jonathan Chaplin discusses in this volume, some authorities are tasked with the specific goal of securing public and political justice.[79] However, ruling itself is not singular. Within Christendom, rule was also exercised at different levels and locations. The family, the town, the village, and the guild or trade association also operate under forms of law. Customs may exist that, while not emanating from any sovereign source, are nevertheless binding on a group. Luke Bretherton notes that each grouping was considered to be bound to a quest for good order, understood as "participation in right relationships as encountered and empowered through participation in the perichoretic communion of Father, Son, and Holy Spirit."[80] Sovereignty, if we must use the term in this context, could more be understood as distributed among these various groups, each potentially accountable to other groups as they mutually pursue shared ends.

Social pluralist thinkers sought to reinvigorate such ideas for the twentieth century, emphasizing a decentralized participatory or mutualist economy and a more federalist understanding of the state.[81] They argued that plural

[74] Pope Benedict XVI, *Caritas in Veritate: On Integral Human Development in Charity and Truth* (The Vatican, 29 June 2009) [7].

[75] See O'Donovan, *Ways of Judgment*, 242.

[76] Ibid, 242–244.

[77] Ibid, 269–280.

[78] For the personalist development of such ideas, see Joel Harrison, "'A Communion in Good Living': Human Dignity and Religious Liberty beyond the Overlapping Consensus" in Christopher McCrudden (ed), *Understanding Human Dignity* (Oxford University Press 2013) 451.

[79] Chaplin (chapter 18, below).

[80] Luke Bretherton, "Sovereignty" in Nicholas Adams, George Pattison, and Graham Ward (eds), *The Oxford Handbook of Theology and Modern European Thought* (Oxford University Press 2013) 255, 269.

[81] See also ibid, 273. Although different, "sphere sovereignty" is also an attempt to recognize the independence of institutions and groups outside of the state. See further Chaplin (chapter 18, below).

authorities exist in society not as delegates of a single sovereign, but as corporations with a real identity and purpose. This would ensure against a creeping trend: subjecting all such corporations to the will of the sovereign, often reflecting the claimed rights of individuals.[82] John Neville Figgis considered that this trend would undermine the group's "permanent end."[83] He argued that if the group is understood as a vehicle for individual rights, reflected in state law, then it is difficult to conceive of it as appealing to a supernatural life that may transcend individual interests and pose a "standard of morals different from those of the State."[84] This pointed to an arguably Christian claim that the personality of a group exists in its commitment to a right ordering, which is ultimately supernatural. In support of that contention, we can note Otto van Gierke's influence on the pluralists. Discussing authority in the Middle Ages, Gierke pointed to an "organic ordering of parts" that was ultimately directed toward a "supra-individual unity of life."[85]

At stake here is not merely the liberty of a group, resisting claims from the center. First, shared jurisdiction is encouraged. Julian Rivers notes that while this is under increasing pressure, religious organizations have typically operated in "areas of concurrent jurisdiction: rites with civil significance, chaplaincies, schools, social welfare provision and participation in formal public discourse."[86] Second, Gierke's appeal to unity raises an important point. Each of the parts were not subordinated to a central sovereign, but they were nevertheless understood as participating in (and as striving for) a harmonious order. F. W. Maitland thus wrote of a "federalistic structure . . . the body policy as *communitas communitatum*," a point Figgis echoed.[87] On this view, different parts are also given meaning through a commitment to a common purpose; however, this may be expressed in the particular case; the whole and the parts mutually reinforce one another.[88]

[82] See FW Maitland, "Moral Personality and Legal Personality" in HD Hazeltine, G Lapsley, and PH Winefield (eds), *Maitland: Selected Essays* (Cambridge University Press 1936) 223, 232–237 and Paul Q Hirst, "Introduction" in Paul Q Hirst (ed), *The Pluralist Theory of the State: Selected Writings of G.D.H. Cole, J.N. Figgis, and H.J. Laski* (Routledge 1989) 1, 18–19.

[83] John Neville Figgis, "The Great Leviathan" in John Neville Figgis, *Churches in the Modern State* (Longmans, Green and Co 1913) 54, 64.

[84] Ibid, 68.

[85] See George Heiman, *Otto Gierke, Associations and the Law: The Classical and Early Christian Stages* (University of Toronto Press 1977) 7, 9.

[86] Julian Rivers, "The Secularisation of the British Constitution" (2012) 14 Ecclesiastical Law Journal 371, 376–377.

[87] Maitland, "Moral Personality and Legal Personality," 229, and Figgis, "The Great Leviathan," 80.

[88] Bretherton notes that this is like "the Eucharistic body, catholic and distributed simultaneously." Bretherton, "Sovereignty," 259.

For similar reasons of shared jurisdiction, as well as cooperative order, Christian writers have often stressed that federalism, federal-like structures, or else subsidiarity are desirable—as Aroney discusses.[89] As with Gierke's unity, such arguments recognize "lower" or parallel authorities but also the need for an authority reflecting and protecting the unity of the whole. Indeed, the Catholic Church has always argued for the necessity of larger authorities, both regional and a "true world political authority" capable of addressing worldwide problems.[90] Such larger authorities also have the capacity to intervene to ensure the transcendent dignity of the person against an oppressive group.

In theory, this plural layering—from the heights of world order, through regional entities, and further down toward local groupings—echoes an understanding of authority seen in Christendom. Rather than a rival system of jurisdictions, which were then settled by a single sovereign or else a conflict between sovereigns, authority is spread across groups and institutions according to an understanding of how they are best placed to contribute to a shared goal.

The One

In discussing plurality, I have already intimated a necessary connection to something embodying "the one."[91] Plurality is oriented by a unity of purpose. In this final section, I suggest that a person or institution understood as representing the whole may be vital to ensuring the continuity of this purpose and directing the manifold parts of the polity toward it. Still, given how its task is characterized, I argue that we should not understand it as exercising sovereignty—understood still as indivisible and unchallengeable authority. Rather, it exercises service.

Pointing to plural authorities raises a question: who decides in the case of conflict? Goldsworthy expresses this concern when arguing for the legal

[89] Aroney (chapter 15, below).

[90] See, e.g., Pope John XXIII, *Pacim et Terris: On Establishing Universal Peace in Truth, Justice, Charity, and Liberty* (The Vatican, 11 April 1963) [137]; Pope Benedict XVI, *Caritas in Veritate*, [67]; and Pope Francis, *Laudato Si': On Care for Our Common Home* (The Vatican, 24 May 2015) [175].

[91] This contrasts Jacob Levy's and Victor Muniz-Fraticelli's recent pluralist scholarship, which is ultimately much more agonistic. See Jacob T Levy, *Rationalism, Pluralism, and Freedom* (Oxford University Press 2015) 284–295 (emphasizing friction, loss, and disharmony); Victor M Muniz-Fraticelli, *The Structure of Pluralism* (Oxford University Press 2014) 13–28 (emphasizing tragedy and incommensurability).

community's orthodox understanding of parliamentary sovereignty: "What is at stake is the location of ultimate decision-making authority—the right to the 'final word'—in a legal system."[92] Others have expressed similar concerns. For example, Ockham considered that ecclesiastical authority must be subject to the king in order to ensure the unity of government.[93] Schmitt criticized the social pluralists on this basis: they eliminated the sovereign decision maker.[94] And Chaplin in this volume discusses the need for closure, arguing that there cannot be an infinite regress between different decision makers.

This may be the ordinary position—the laws of Parliament are obeyed—and yet it is arguable that constitutional orders sometimes have a remainder of indeterminacy. If the monarch refuses to sign a bill into law, this arguably signals a constitutional crisis with an unknown destiny. Or we may think of debate over "eternity" clauses within constitutions.[95] Here, the constitution itself purports to establish a category of unconstitutional constitutional amendments.[96] This raises significant and contested questions: whether there are fundamental, unamendable norms (in natural law? from within the constitution itself?);[97] whether there remains a constituent power in "the people" outside of the constituted power of a constitution;[98] whether such a constituent power can exist in federal polities; whether such constituent power is outside of law, recognizable at law, revolutionary, simply raw political power, or must always be constituted by legal traditions and constitutional norms.[99]

But the Christian tradition may ask another question that arguably fuels such indeterminacy: can closure be complete if we recognize that the purpose of a "final" authority is to serve something other or higher than itself? Chaplin discusses O'Donovan's contention that the legitimacy of public authority rests on its ability to perform public judgment on the community's behalf. Such a judgment must be binding, but its binding nature is not

[92] Goldsworthy, *The Sovereignty of Parliament*, 3.

[93] See E.F. Jacob, "Ockham as a Political Thinker" in E.F. Jacob (ed.), *Essays in the Conciliar Epoch* (Manchester University Press 1943) 85, 101.

[94] Schmitt, *Political Theology*, 24–25.

[95] See, notably, Article 79 § 3 of the German Basic Law discussed in Ulrich K Preuss, "The Implications of 'Eternity Clauses': The German Experience" (2011) 44 Israel Law Review 429, 440. I am grateful to Julian Rivers for this point.

[96] See Yaniv Roznai, *Unconstitutional Constitutional Amendments* (Oxford University Press 2017).

[97] See Thomas Wischmeyer, "Unconstitutional Constitutional Amendments" (2017) 15 International Journal of Constitutional Law 1242, 1244–1245 (reviewing Roznai).

[98] In the Lisbon Treaty Case, the Federal Constitutional Court of Germany distinguished between the amending authority of a constituted legislature and the "declared will of the German people." BVerfG, June 30, 2009, 2 be 2/08, §§ 216, 228, discussed in Preuss, "Eternity Clauses," 440.

[99] See Preuss, "Eternity Clauses," 445.

grounded in constitutional procedure alone; rather, it is binding because it ultimately serves, on O'Donovan's account, the spheres of communication that constitute community and tradition.[100] As such, I think we can plausibly say that finality is, paradoxically, never a real closure because it is always subject to a form of stewardship and evaluation. Certainly, this poses a question: to whom is appeal made if such service is not rendered or the ordinarily lawful authority acts contrary to its higher purpose? I offer no resolution here. Aquinas considered that the ruler's authority to make law rested on the divine and natural law.[101] Thus, even though there may be no immediate authority to appeal to save the ruler's conscience, the positive law was in fact no law at all, if contrary to divine or natural law.[102] Following this line of thought, even though an appellate authority may be lacking, it still may be right not to think in terms of sovereignty, but rather in terms of service, guardianship, coordination, and leadership.

Precisely where such a role resides in a particular constitutional order can be debated. In Westminster systems, we look to the Parliament. It is a body composed of different parts—democratic in its representative underpinning, (sometimes) "aristocratic" or even socially pluralist in its reflection of wider associations or groupings, and monarchical. These components each embody something necessary or desirable, and brought together in a cooperative unity they are tasked with legislating for the common good. Indeed, this interweaving is reflected in the very notion of kingship or an equivalent "monarchical" role. Here, the single person may come to stand in for the whole—Parliament—but also, symbolically, the entire tradition: a continuous quest for the good in our shared political and civic life.

In the Commonwealth, this is dramatically presented in the coronation oath, in which we can see both anointing and acclamation. Before the altar and in "the presence of all Persons," the Monarch promises in response to the Archbishop of Canterbury to govern according to the laws and customs of her respective territories and to "maintain the Laws of God and the true profession of the Gospel."[103] Similarly, her Governors-General in Australia

[100] O'Donovan, *Ways of Judgment*, 52, 139–147.

[101] See ibid, 188.

[102] Goldsworthy wrongly conflates Aquinas with modern sovereignty discussion on the basis that even Aquinas states that "none is competent to pass sentence on [the ruler] if he acts against the law." See Goldsworthy, *The Sovereignty of Parliament*, 21, discussing Thomas Aquinas, *Summa Theologica*, I-II, q 96. But Aquinas's claim of competence does not affect his central contention, contrary to Goldsworthy's characterization of sovereignty: a "law" is not-law if it conflicts with the natural or divine law. See Aquinas, *Summa Theologica*, I-II, q 95.2.

[103] See *Coronation Oath Act 1688*, I and III.

and New Zealand promise to serve her and to "do right" (Australia) or serve the people (New Zealand) following the laws and usages of those people, with the help of God.[104] Fundamentally, this has Christic overtones. The king or queen is Christ's deputy among the people; Alfred was to "avenge with utmost diligence offenses against Christ."[105] But, like Christ, this king also represents the people. He does so because he arises from the people, *and* because standing in for Christ means adopting Christ's "active and atoning solidarity" for the neighbor.[106] The king, in other words, is for the people.

What this means is that the monarch—as synecdoche for Parliament also—is not simply exercising his or her own will. Rather, his or her rule is "under some overarching oath or covenant with the people," one that is directed toward "architectonic rule" oriented toward the good.[107] That means it is not entirely removed from the people; the representative character of the monarch matters. Christianity has tended to affirm that the people themselves—the entire body—are involved in discerning what goodness requires. The mutual exchange of gifts and, subsequently, cultivating of customs takes place, as discussed, in different local contexts. And this means that the "sovereign" power is often concerned more with coordinating and nurturing such sites, rather than rule from above. Nevertheless, in discerning the good, the monarchical role also entails leading and personal judgment—we place faith in the monarch's wisdom, which in Christian thought is always chastened by the Church's call to charity. Arguably, even Governors-General continue to echo such claims, pointing to their role as acting in service to something truly sovereign—the good.[108]

[104] For Australia, see Commonwealth of Australia, *Gazette*, 1 April 2014, Governor-General's "Oath of Office." For New Zealand, see *Letters Patent Constituting the Office of Governor-General of New Zealand* (SR 1983/225), s 6. See also Nicholas Aroney, "The Rule of Law, Religious Authority, and Oaths of Office" (2018) 6 Journal of Law, Religion and State 195.

[105] See Berman, *Law and Revolution*, 66–67.

[106] Milbank, *Beyond Secular Order*, 249.

[107] John Milbank and Adrian Pabst, *The Politics of Virtue: Post-Liberalism and the Human Future* (Rowman & Littlefield 2016) 196, 206. See also Roger Trigg, "Religion in the Public Forum" (2011) 13 Ecclesiastical Law Journal 274, 279.

[108] See, e.g., His Excellency General the Honourable Sir Peter Cosgrove, "Governor-General Swearing-in Ceremony" (Parliament House, 28 March 2014) https://parlview.aph.gov.au/mediaPlayer.php?videoID=222721#/3 ("There is a role for the Governor-General, in the words of one of my predecessors, to reflect the community to itself").

Conclusion

If we examine sovereignty through a lens informed by Christian thought and historical practice, we see two competing threads. The first points to a relationship between the duality of priest and king, cultivating a plurality of what O'Donovan calls "communications," encouraged and protected by a shared unity expressed in the coordinating and symbolic one. If we must speak of sovereignty within this thread, then it is better perhaps to understand sovereignty as either diffuse and arising through the interactions of these parts or else as the ultimate subordination of these parts to the good. The second thread points to collapsing plural sites of authority in favor of the unity of sovereign rule, whereby right is determined by an act of will emanating from the superior power.

Lawyers may see this discussion as irrelevant to their task. They may claim that their concern lies simply in knowing which institution to follow in what circumstances. They may even argue that what is conventionally discussed as parliamentary sovereignty is capacious enough to cover much of my argument. A single body reflects the diverse elements discussed and can facilitate and respond to the authority of others, including the Church.

However, I have suggested that elements traditionally claimed in Christian thought are lost in modern discussion of sovereignty.

The Christian claim for political authority has traditionally entailed subordination to right, the natural and divine law. "Law" that fails to satisfy this inner justification is considered not-law, albeit one that may still come from a properly constituted authority. Authority on this view consists in the "prior concern and responsibility to care for the over-all common good."[109]

The fundamental duality between priest and king further clarified civil authority's role. It was tasked with defending the polity, and thus the possibility of any social exchange, but this also meant understanding that it is not ultimate. Rather, it exists to further, in its own way, the end of supernatural charity and to exercise its authority in the light of this. This includes recognizing that authority is exercised at different levels or in different locations. It also points beyond constitutionalism-as-constraint to a constitutionalism of higher purpose.

[109] John Finnis, *Natural Law and Natural Rights* (Clarendon Press 1980) 233.

In this way, the post-Bodin notion of an indivisible, unlimited sovereign and the Schmittian focus on sovereign will constituting the political domain are undermined. Rather, sovereignty is dissolved in the diffuse interaction of various parts of the body politic, all understood to be acting in service of, indeed accountable to, something transcendent—the God in whose created order we participate.

10

Rule of Law

The Sacred Roots and Secular Shoots of the Supreme Law

Li-ann Thio

Introduction: Universal Prescription, Contested Concept

While the "rule of law" appears to enjoy favor as a universal prescription for political justice and a key pillar of constitutional government, "higher law" has fallen out of fashion. Contemporary expositions of the rule of law rarely refer to a higher law, favoring instead a laundry list of legal rules and institutions considered necessary to realizing the rule of law.[1] The rule of law is variously conceived as a negative or "thin" ideal, designed to promote limited government, clear rules, and due process, or in more ambitious "thicker" versions, as a concept that embraces the essential moral content and purpose of law. What all conceptions share in common is that they are against autocracy and arbitrariness in the exercise of public power. But if the rule of law is to be an idealized standard against which positive law is evaluated, this begs the question whether it can be thought of and implemented without the concept of a higher law, as the substantive source of principles to which the rule of law must conform.

This was not problematical for Hellenic and biblical streams of Western legal thought, which drew an explicit link between a higher law and the rule of law. Historically, the higher law was rooted in the divine law and natural law traditions.[2] This provided an objective reference point for evaluating

[1] The "anatomical" approach to the rule of law, as opposed to a teleological one: Martin Krygier, "Rule of Law" in Michel Rosenfeld and Andras Sajo (eds), *The Oxford Handbook of Comparative Constitutional Law* (Oxford University Press 2012) 233–249 at 235–240.

[2] Stephen Hall, "The Persistent Spectre: Natural Law, International Order and the Limits of Legal Positivism" (2001) 12(2) EJIL 269–307.

Li-ann Thio, *Rule of Law: The Sacred Roots and Secular Shoots of the Supreme Law* in *Christianity and Constitutionalism*. Edited by: Nicholas Aroney and Ian Leigh, Oxford University Press. © Oxford University Press 2022.
DOI: 10.1093/oso/9780197587256.003.0010

and even voiding inconsistent laws at the lower rung of the legal hierarchy, a higher law over rulers and ruled alike. However, the idea of a higher law has come under siege in an era of legal positivism, legal realism, and postmodernism, which decries "grand theory" and insists that law is not a province autonomous from politics. As such, "law" departs from "the realm of jurisprudence and philosophy" and takes up residence in the "domain of politics"[3] where it becomes a tool to advance particular ideological agendas. As the rule of law is shaped by the conception of law upon which it rests, we find that the thicker its vision, the more controversial it becomes.

The rule of law has attained something of the status of an "international hurrah term,"[4] or what E. P. Thompson described as an "unqualified human good," because it defends citizens from "power's all-intrusive claims."[5] Nonetheless, the idea remains an "essentially contestable concept,"[6] as the many proliferating, completing accounts of rule of law attest. Is it a formal concept or a substantive ideal?[7] Should it be understood in liberal or nonliberal terms?[8] Are its requirements relatively thin or thick? Although it is often possible to identify what the rule of law stands against—anarchy and social disintegration, for example, or an arbitrariness that depersonalizes and imperils individual liberty—consensus about its substantive meaning is lacking, for it is not a term "that admits of a fixed or precise definition."[9] A description of its key elements is therefore an easier path to take. Thus, for example, it has been said that the rule of law involves open, clear, prospective, and stable general laws[10] and their consistent enforcement and adjudication by impartial courts where fair procedures and standards of reasonableness are observed. This reflects the constitutional principle that "the power of the State is vested in the various arms of government and that such power is subject to legal limits,"[11] usually judicially enforced.

[3] Hall, "The Persistent Spectre," 304.

[4] Martin Krygier, "Four Puzzles about the Rule of Law: Why, What, Where? And Who Cares? Sant" Anna Legal Studies STALS Research Paper 4/2015.

[5] EP Thompson, *Whigs and Hunters: The Origins of the Black Act* (Penguin 1977) 266.

[6] E.g., see Michel Rosenfeld, "The Rule of Law and the Legitimacy of Constitutional Democracy" (2001) 74 Southern California Law Review 1307.

[7] Paul Craig, "Formal and Substantive Conceptions of the Rule of Law: An Analytical Framework" [1997] Public Law 467.

[8] See "Varieties of the Rule of Law" in Randall Pereenboom (ed), *Asian Discourses of Rule of Law: Theories and Implementation of Rule of Law in Twelve Asian Countries, France and the US* (Routledge 2004) 1–55.

[9] *Tan Seet Eng v Attorney-General* [2015] SGCA 59 (Singapore Court of Appeal) [1].

[10] On how vagueness of law cannot be avoided and is not necessarily a rule of law deficit, see Timothy Endicott, "The Impossibility of the Rule of Law" (1999) 19(1) OJLS 1–18.

[11] *Tan Seet Eng v Attorney-General* [2015] SGCA 59 (Singapore Court of Appeal) [1].

All substantive conceptions encompass formal conceptions of the rule of law and go further, adding "various content specifications,"[12] thickened by particular political and economic philosophies, all of which have their advocates and detractors. Thus, to some, the rule of law is an "unruly horse" that is "essentially imprecise."[13] Indeed, it often has a paradoxical quality, sometimes siding with the state in the name of public order and the effective implementation of majoritarian will, sometimes limiting state power through the judicial protection of fundamental rights.[14] Some approaches to the rule of law thus focus on the destination to which the rule of law will escort us, or the fate from which it may deliver us.

Most versions of the rule of law are united in opposing the arbitrariness and absolutism that a "government of man"—as distinct from a "government of laws"—may engender. The rule of law is widely understood to be anti-totalitarian, promoting constitutionalism by controlling and channeling public power, requiring governors and the governed to be under the law to prevent law becoming a "sheer tool of domination."[15] In addition, the rule of law requires equality before the law and in the Diceyan conception, "the equal subjection of all classes to the ordinary law of the land administered by the ordinary law courts."[16]

The content and effect of the rule of law are determined by the underlying political ideal upon which it rests, which in turn "invokes a distinctive concept of law, which philosophical reflection can help to elucidate,"[17] as "the link between the rule of law and a 'common good' theory of justice is profound and essential."[18] Whether there is a "higher" law—that is, something beyond the law promulgated by the political state—shapes how we understand the rule of law[19] and the need to refer positive law to "some ideal standard."[20] The rule of law thus begs a theory of law, whether apprehended

[12] Brian Z Tamanaha, *On the Rule of Law: History, Politics, Theory* (Cambridge University Press 2004) 102.

[13] Sir Ivor Jennings, *The Law and the Constitution* (5th edn, University of London Press 1959) 60.

[14] Rosenfeld, "The Rule of Law and the Legitimacy of Constitutional Democracy," 1309.

[15] Gianluigi Palombella, "The Rule of Law as an Institutional Ideal" (2010) 9 Comparative Sociology 6.

[16] Albert Venn Dicey, *An Introduction to the Study of the Law of the Constitution* (10th edn, Macmillan 1959) 202.

[17] TRS Allan, "The Rule of Law" in David Dyzenhaus and Malcolm Thorburn (eds), *Philosophical Foundations of Constitutional Law* (Oxford University Press 2016) 201–220, 201.

[18] Mortimer Sellers, "What Is the Rule of Law and Why Is It So Important" in A Goudappel and E Ballin (eds), *Democracy and the Rule of Law in the European Union* (TMC Asser Press 2016) 3, 11.

[19] Endicott, "The Impossibility of the Rule of Law."

[20] AP d'Entreves, "The Case for Natural Law Re-Examined" (1956) Natural Law Forum 5–52, 6.

formally as *lex* or the more explicitly purposive, justice-oriented *ius*.[21]

To eschew debates over substantive justice, some prefer to focus on formal conceptions of rule of law, for general, transparent, and clear laws have the virtue of providing "effective guidance" to individuals, according them a sphere of independence where they may plan their conduct and avoid acting illegally. This affirms human dignity by treating "humans as persons capable of planning . . . their future"[22] and ordering their affairs within a reliable legal framework. To this, Waldron would add a focus on how the rule of law includes opportunities for argumentation about the law, thus treating ordinary citizens "with respect as active centers of intelligence."[23] Fuller, who viewed law as a purposive enterprise,[24] argued that the eight criteria he identified as aspects of formal legality constituted an internal morality of law. Jurists like Raz have characterized this as an instrumental conception of rule of law that can serve morally good and bad causes, as it does not guarantee the justness of laws.[25]

This minimum content conception may be "compatible with gross violations of human rights"[26] and may point to the "rule of state law" as opposed to the rule of the "law state."[27] No further inquiry into telos is sought. The rule of law is understood to be a necessary but not sufficient component of a just legal and political system, which has to be supplemented by both human rights and democracy, which are related but not integral features of the rule of law. However, this focus on the procedural requirements of the rule of law is not, as Robert George points out, a "morally neutral matter."[28] Indeed, such a focus may occlude an understanding that procedural fairness is part of substantive justice; and this engages the broader question, as

[21] George P Fletcher, "In Honour of Ius et Lex: Some Thoughts on Speaking about Law" ("Ius et Lex" Foundation 2001).

[22] Joseph Raz, "The Rule of Law and Its Virtue," (1977) 93 LQR 195.

[23] Jeremy Waldron, "The Concept and the Rule of Law" (2008), Sibley Lecture, Paper 29, <http://digitalcommons.law.uga.edu/lectures_pre_arch_lectures_sibley/29>.

[24] The criteria are that law must be (1) general, (2) public, (3) nonretroactive, (4) comprehensible, (5) noncontradictory, (6) possible to perform, (7) relatively stable, and (8) administered in ways congruent with the rules as announced. Lon Fuller argued that the various aspects of formal legality, identifying eight criteria, amounted to a moral ideal, but this does not effectively link the rule of law to a higher law: Lon Fuller, 'The Morality that makes law possible' in *The Morality of Law* (rev edn, Yale University Press 1969) 33–94.

[25] Joseph Raz, "The Rule of Law and Its Virtue," 208.

[26] Ibid, 195.

[27] Robert Cooter, "The Rule of State Law Versus the Rule of Law State" in E Buscaglia, W Ratliff, and R Cooter (eds), *The Law and Economics of Development* (JAI Press 1997) 101–148.

[28] Robert George, "Reason, Freedom and the Rule of Law: Their Significance in Western Thought" (2002–2003) 15 Regent University Law Review 187, 188.

Finnis puts it, of "the state of affairs in which a legal system is legally in good shape."[29]

However, the preponderance of modern legal thought that works itself out in secular democracies does not engage with this, on the basis that human law can still be made, used, practiced, and understood, sans reference to higher law.[30] One might argue that it is profitable even within secular legal orders to interrogate the nature and content of higher law and how this impacts the source and nature of the rule of law, the goods it serves, what endangers it, and where its limits lie. This draws us back into the broader conversation about constitutionalism, limited government, human flourishing, and the type of conditions needed for the rule of law to subsist. In this respect, questions about the contested foundational basis for law, whether it needs an external religious or moral basis or whether it is self-standing, cannot be avoided. Those skeptical of higher law justifications disdain it as attracting "all the theological problems which attend any argument from a first cause and which can ultimately only be answered by an act of faith."[31] Higher law is confined to the realm of the mythical, dismissed as a "brooding omnipresence in the sky."[32] Nonetheless, the specter of higher law and its close associations with natural law, which holds that an unjust law is not law, persist.

The idea of higher law can provide a theoretical account of key issues related to normative and conceptual constitutionalism: these include the source and authority of law, the basis for evaluating whether law is just or unjust, and how judges derive meaning when interpreting legal texts, and whether this is legitimate. This may delve into the type of "grand narratives" considered anathema to critical legal studies, but one cannot sidestep the question of legal foundations upon which entire constitutional edifices may be erected. Examining higher law is a key aspect of this inquiry, because it foregrounds the vexed question of the interrelationship of law and morality.

This should be done with the awareness that in espousing a Christian approach to higher law and the rule of law, as with all substantive justice theories, one must subscribe to the authority of that school of thought or historical religion. This involves accepting its implications in the conviction that law by its nature makes moral claims and that moral inquiry may be

[29] John Finnis, *Natural Law and Natural Rights* (Oxford University Press 1980) 9–18.

[30] Steven D Smith, "Higher Law Questions: A Prelude to the Symposium" (2009) 36 Pepperdine Law Review 463–474, 464.

[31] Sir Stephen Sedley, "Human Rights: A Twenty-First Century Agenda" [1995] Public Law 386, 389–390.

[32] Holmes J (dissenting), *Southern Pacific Co. v Jensen* 244 US 205 (1917), 222.

conducted by reference to external, universal principles. In the post-secular West, this is a voice that should not be shut out from the conversation, as it will illuminate the freedoms and values the rule of law alone cannot protect. It may also show how modern humanist conceptions of the rule of law are inadequate.

Rather than perpetually deferring the conversation about legal foundations, we should directly address the implications of a higher law for the rule of law, whether religious foundations are the basis for the rule of law in a secular democratic polity.[33] One may then evaluate the cogency of the proposition that the rule-of-law ideal itself "rests upon the most fundamental beliefs" and a system of presuppositions about authority, human good, civil justice, and the sociality of man, which cumulatively constitutes a "religious system."[34] It is certainly the case that the term "higher law," and the natural law idea of a legal hierarchy of norms it conveys, continues to be central to constitutional discourse, particularly in the proposition that the written constitution prevails over all inconsistent ordinary legislation and executive action by virtue of its supremacy.

This chapter is structured thus. The first part explores the various ways that "higher law" manifests within constitutional discourse and then focuses on the relationship between the higher law, natural law, and its influence on the moral content of positive law. The second part does not propose a fully defined model but offers core ideas of what a Christian vision of higher law and the rule of law might look like, and how man-made law relates to the law and the purposes of God in this present age. Given the drift of modern law away from its theological anchorage, the third part considers whether and how the contemporary version of the rule of law differs significantly from its roots, particularly its Christian sources, and how humanistic constitutions may undermine the rule of law and the liberties and values it seeks to secure. The fourth part offers concluding observations on the contribution of Christianity to the rule-of-law ideal and an apology as to the utility of undertaking this exercise in a postmodern and plural age.

[33] David Novak, "Law: Religious or Secular?" (2000) 86 Virginia Law Review 569, 572.

[34] Craig Stern, "The Common Law and the Religious Foundations of the Rule of Law before Casey" (2004) 38 University of San Francisco Law Review 499, 500.

The Meaning of Higher Law and Its Relation to the Rule of Law

The meaning of higher law has been used to refer to a range of phenomena. In its various usages, it is generally associated with limited government, as higher law is independent of the law promulgated by the political state and paramount to it. Conceptually, the higher law is at the apex of the legal order, against which inconsistent, man-made lower-order norms are evaluated as deficient or considered void. Legal systems may recognize higher law through the political technology of a written constitution with a supremacy clause, which may be considered a positivization of the natural law, and which operates as fundamental law, distinct from ordinary laws. Constitutionalism is thus the "secular legitimation of government"[35] in nontheocratic polities. Constraints on ordinary laws may also be found, however, in the customary law of preliberal political communities representing the "common consciousness"[36] and collective wisdom of the ages, in unwritten fundamental principles relating to fair dealing[37] and rationality,[38] or as manifested through equity, which moderates the law's rigor.[39] Higher law principles may be manifest in unwritten standards or inalienable rights where articulated in the enterprise of constitutional interpretation, requiring the political state to conform with fundamental norms, such as the Indian basic features doctrine.[40] In England, courts now assert the power to define the limits of legislative sovereignty[41] and have declared constitutional rights, such as the right of access to courts,[42] as being inherent to the rule of law, and have recognized that rights are based on "a constitutional or higher legal foundation."[43] Constitutional statutes can also enjoy an immunity from implied repeal,[44] reflecting the twilight of absolutist models of parliamentary supremacy.

[35] Carl J Friedrich, *Limited Government: A Comparison* (Prentice Hall 1974) 110.

[36] Harold J Berman, "Religious Foundations of Western Law" (1975) 28 Catholic University Law Review 490.

[37] Lord Diplock, "Judicial Control of Government" [1979] Malayan Law Journal cxl, cxli.

[38] Sir John Laws, "Wednesbury" in Christopher Forsyth and Ivan Hare (eds), *The Golden Metwand and the Crooked Cord: Essays in Honour of Sir William Wade QC* (Oxford University Press 1998) 185–202.

[39] James M Beck, "The Higher Law" (1918) 4(4) American Bar Association Journal 656–680.

[40] *Kesavananda Bharati v State of Kerala* AIR (1973) SC 1461. The concept has also been adopted elsewhere, such as Malaysia: *Indira Gandhi v Pengarah Jabatan Agama Islam Perak* [2018] 1 MLJ 545.

[41] Lord Hope, *R (Jackson) v Attorney General* [2006] 1 AC 262 [107].

[42] Lord Reed in *R (Unison) v Lord Chancellor* [2017] UKSC 51 noted [66].

[43] Lord Steyn, *Reynolds v Times Newspapers Ltd* [2001] 2 AC 127, 207–208.

[44] Lord Carnwath JSC, *R (Privacy International) v Investigatory Powers Tribunal* [2019] 2 WLR 1219, 1261C.

Higher Law as a Type of Constitutionalism

"Higher law constitutionalism" has been used to describe a certain model of constitutionalism based on the supremacy of the written constitution. This is based on a text[45] that gives juridical expression to the higher law, enacted through "higher" lawmaking procedures that are procedurally more onerous than those for ordinary legislation,[46] and judicially enforceable rights, which limit legislative and executive powers.[47] Such constitutions also codify meta-norms, principles of right and justice that prevail due to their own "intrinsic excellence."[48] The state is to act according to this higher law, is to stay within the constraints of its delegated power, and may be constitutionally required to channel this toward achieving identified objectives in the public interest.

In the influential American scheme, it falls to the courts to interpret the Constitution, to balance rights against competing interests, and to decide how much weight to accord to the "peremptory norms" of the Constitution. Patterson considers that this idea of higher law "came to America from England," where it was elaborated by various political thinkers and jurists. Henri Le Bracton stated in *De Legibus et Consultulinibus Angliae* (1256) that "The King himself ought not to be subject to man, but subject to God and the law, for the law makes the King." As an embedded common law principle, this traveled to former British colonies.[49] According to Sir Edward Coke, the supremacy of fundamental principles of "common right or reason" could control and adjudge as void acts of Parliament, as declared in *Dr. Bonham's* case (1610). As Patterson notes, "common right and reason" was "something permanent and fundamental, and therefore, higher law."[50] In *Marbury and Madison,*[51] Chief Justice Marshall noted that the framers of a written constitution contemplate it as "the fundamental and paramount law of the nation" such that legislative acts repugnant to it are void. As a fundamental law a Constitution "provides the basis upon which law is made and enforced"[52]

[45] A precursor of the more comprehensive written constitution is the Magna Carta, which "gave concrete form to the idea of a higher or fundamental law." See C Perry Patterson, "The Evolution of Constitutionalism" (1948) 32 Minnesota Law Review 427–457, 429, 445.

[46] Marshall CJ in *Marbury v Madison* 5 US 137, 177 (1803).

[47] Alec Stone Sweet, "Constitutionalism, Legal Pluralism and International Regimes" (2009) 16(2) Indiana Journal of Global Studies 621, 630.

[48] Edward S Corwin, *The Higher Law Background of American Constitutional Law* (Cornell University Press 1955).

[49] *Ex parte Sim Soo Koon* [1915] SSLR 2.

[50] Patterson, "The Evolution of Constitutionalism," 429, 435.

[51] 5 U.S. 137, 177 (1803).

[52] KC Wheare, *Modern Constitutions* (OUP 1951) at 91.

and determines who has the power to make laws, execute laws, and adjudicate disputes concerning their meaning and application.

What is the source of the constitution understood in these terms? One view is that it derives its existence from a social contract, based on the idea of popular sovereignty by which "natural law deposits all political authority in the people,"[53] which is in turn associated with the democratic idea of the *pouvoir constituant* (constituent power) as the basis for legitimating basic laws.[54] Another view is that the legitimacy of the Constitution as supreme law flows from the set of interacting principles that it establishes, such as the rule of law, separation of powers and democracy, and its interpretation in light of these principles.[55] These principles jointly constitute a higher law that determines the functions of public institutions and their composition, procedures, and powers.[56]

Even where Parliament is supreme and there is no written constitution, the rule that determines the priority of statute over common law norms, and the doctrine of implied repeal, by which a later statute prevails over one enacted prior in time, both give effect to a pre-existing principle. Professor Wade accordingly observed that Parliament and its powers are "constituted by prior legal rules of constitutional nature."[57] These rules define Parliament, its composition and powers, and the conditions under which it legislates.[58] It is thus a higher law "in the constitutional sense that it organizes the architecture of the legal order as a whole."[59]

It is a "truism" that the rule commanding judicial obedience to statute is a fundamental rule Parliament cannot alter by ordinary legislative procedures because it is necessarily entailed in the very concept of parliamentary sovereignty.[60]

[53] Patterson, "The Evolution of Constitutionalism," 427–457.

[54] Bruce Ackerman, "Higher Lawmaking" in Sanford Levinson (ed), *Responding to Imperfection: The Theory and Practice of Constitutional Amendment* (Princeton University Press 1995) 63.

[55] Pavlos Eleftheriadis, "The Constitution as Higher Law," University of Oxford Faculty of Law Legal Studies Research Paper Series, Working Paper No 04/2008, Jan 2008.

[56] Ibid, 31.

[57] Ibid, 7. This is distinct from views that the composition and process of Parliament are rules of "positive morality" and lie beyond the law, e.g., Richard Ekins, "Acts of Parliament and the Parliament Acts" (2007) 123 LQR 91.

[58] Fundamental rules are not rules about powers, but how power is allocated and how public institutions are recognized in the first place: Eleftheraiadis, "The Constitution as Higher Law."

[59] Ibid, 7.

[60] HWR Wade, "The Basis of Legal Sovereignty" (1955) 13 (2) CLJ 172, 187–188. Wade in his later analysis of the *Factortame (No 1)* case [1990] 2 AC 85 in (1996) 112 LQR 568 considered that a "constitutional revolution" had been effected insofar as the doctrine of implied repeal, which draws from parliamentary sovereignty, was suspended. Laws LJ in *Thoburn v Sunderland City Council* [2002] 3

Higher Law in Normative Terms: Divine and Natural Law

While related to the idea of higher law as a necessary aspect of all constitutional legal orders, higher law can also be viewed in fully normative terms, as the moral foundation of law as a whole. On this view, higher law provides an objective basis for right and wrong that transcends and antecedes state law. However, questions about the nature, origin, and knowledge of such a law immediately arise. Does this conception entail a belief in natural law? And does natural law depend on belief in God? Many higher law theories have ultimate theological roots: the law is ultimately grounded in divine revelation. Others, however, believe that the higher law may be discovered by reason alone.

The higher law concept has a long history in the Western tradition.[61] To Cicero, natural law was rooted in a theory of moral justice, superior to man-made law, and was discoverable by human reason.[62] This reflected the pantheistic tenet of Stoicism, which treats God, nature, and reason interchangeably. To the Jews, however, higher law flowed from a supreme lawgiver in the form of *lex scripta*.[63] To Christians, building on Jewish revelation, the higher moral law was "written on the heart" (Rom. 2:15), impressed upon the human mind as *lex indita*,[64] and testified to by conscience (*lex in hominibus*).[65] This is the basis for both compliance with human authority (Rom. 13:5) and deference

WLR 247 [63]–[64] characterized the European Community Act as a "Constitutional Statute," as recognized by the common law, which may not be impliedly repealed, but may be by unambiguous words in a later statute.

[61] V Bradley Lewis, "Higher Law and the Rule of Law: The Platonic Origin of an Ideal" (2009) 36 Pepperdine Law Review 631, 633; RH Helmholz, "Natural Law and Christianity: A Brief History" in Norman Doe (ed), *Christianity and Natural Law: An Introduction* (Cambridge University Press 2017) 1–16.

[62] Fernando H Llano Alonso, "Cicero and Natural Law" (2012) 98(2) Archives for Philosophy of Law and Social Philosophy 157–159.

[63] Yitzchok Adlerstein, "Theology and the Higher Law," 603, 607; Michael J Broyde, "The Foundations of Law: A Jewish Law View of World Law" (2005) 54 Emory Law Journal 79, 85, discussing Maimonides.

[64] Russell Hittinger, "Natural Law in the Positive Laws: A Legislative or Adjudicative Issue?" (Winter 1993) 55(1) Review of Politics 5–34, 6.

[65] Harold J Berman, "Conscience and Law: The Lutheran Reformation and the Western Legal Tradition" (1987) 5(1) Journal of Law and Religion 177–202, 194. Chief Justice Coke in *Calvin's Case* declared that the law of nature was immutable, prior to judicial or municipal law and part of English. He further said, "The law of nature is that which God at the time of creation of the nature of man infused into his heart, for his preservation and direction; and this is lex aeterna, the moral law, called also the law of nature. And by this law written with the finger of God in the heart of man, were the people of God a long time governed before the law was written by Moses, who was the first reporter or writer of law in the world." 7 Co Rep 1, 77; Eng, Rep 377 (KB 1610).

to God's authority in case of a conflict between human and divine command (Acts 5:29).

For Aquinas and Christopher St. Germain, the law of reason entails the "participation of knowledge of eternal law in a rational creature, revealed to him by the natural light of reason."[66] This involves a sharing of divine reason and an inclination to its proper end, which is to do good and avoid evil.[67] If human or positive law deflects from the law of nature, "it is no longer a law but a perversion of law"[68] and void. Natural law thus both constituted positive law and provided a basis for evaluating the justness of positive law.[69]

William Blackstone considered the obligations of divine and natural law to be of the same intrinsic strength and perpetuity, and he regarded both to be derived from God.[70] Can a concept of higher law as natural law be derived solely from a secularized reason separated from divine revelation? Hans Kelsen considered that "there is no natural law doctrine of any importance which has not a more or less religious character."[71] Arthur Leff went further by arguing that without God there can be no basis for "any coherent . . . ethical or legal system dependent upon finally authoritative extra-systemic premises."[72] On his view, self-deification inevitably follows, because there will always be a need for "a substitute final evaluator."[73] The denial of God is thus "intellectually unsettling"; there is always a counterargument for every argument a human person can make, and there is ultimately "no *a priori* reason to accept one argument over another."[74] Ultimately, "a god" must exist in every legal system as a higher authority that invests the law with legitimacy, authority, and purpose. This will "take the form of a spiritual entity or the state," for if the state does not recognize a standard of right and wrong higher than itself or popular will, then the state, or this popular will, becomes "the ultimate god."[75]

[66] Christopher St German, *Doctor and Student* (T.F.T. Plucknett & J.L. Barton (eds.), Selden Society, 1974).

[67] Patrick McKinley Brenna, "Persons, Participating and 'Higher Law'" (2009) 36 Pepperdine Law Review 475, 488–489.

[68] *Summa Theologica*, I-II, 95.2c.

[69] Friedrich, *Transcendent Justice*, 14.

[70] Sir William Blackstone, *Commentaries on the Laws of England in Four Books* (JB Lippincott Co 1893) vol 1, introduction, Section II.

[71] Quoted in Robert A Panev, "Hans Kelsen and the Role of Religion in Natural Law Doctrine" (2012) 3 Western Australian Jurist 259.

[72] Arthur Allen Leff, "Unspeakable Ethics, Unnatural Law" (1979) 28(6) Duke Law Journal 1229, 1232.

[73] Ibid, 1233.

[74] Yitzchok Adlerstein, "Theology and the Higher Law" (2009) 36 Pepperdine Law Review 603, 608.

[75] Charles E Rice, "The Problem of Unjust Laws" (1981) 26 Catholic Lawyer 278, 279.

Higher law embodies a morality higher than the state, derived from reason and conscience, representing "reason over will and conscience over power."[76] Higher law in the normative sense serves as the moral limit and justification of a legal order, which the rule of law seeks to uphold. But because higher law as natural law depends on the existence of God, it implies an overarching framework of "divine" authority that constitutes and frames the scope of legitimate human authority. For this reason it is not possible to separate the rule of law entirely from a political morality based on theology.[77]

Christianity and the Higher Law/Rule of Law: An Exploration

From the perspective of Christianity, the higher law flows from God, the supreme lawgiver, who promulgated natural law precepts as *lex scripta* in divine text. The Bible is "the Higher Law in fact and in form" and the "beneficent expression of the Divine Character."[78] Man, the creature of God, is subject to the immutable law of Creator God, whose supremacy is "universal and unlimited" and whose law is of unbounded jurisdiction.[79] It is the "very best law for this world, and the only law which ensures justice and happiness to mankind,"[80] preventing oppression, ensuring equality and justice, and providing an "infallible guide to righteousness."[81] As Edward Coke stated, God is "the fountain and founder of all good laws and constitutions."[82] Law is associated with biblical justice and higher law has a supernatural source and pedigree.

Christian theology gives rise to a teleological view of the "law,"[83] where law does not just cater to a "liberalism of fear" but also channels power to accomplish certain objectives or to constitute the identity of a civil polity in service of the divine will. The moral law of God, which reflects his character as a relational, covenant-making God,[84] will inform the content of moral and

[76] Harold J Berman, "Law and Logos" (1994) 44 DePaul Law Review 142, 151.

[77] Mary Liston, Willis, "Theology and the Rule of Law" (2005) 55(3) University of Toronto Law Journal 767–795.

[78] William Hosmer, *The Higher Law in Its Relations to Government with Particular Reference to Slavery and Fugitive Slave Law* (1852) 24, 27.

[79] Ibid, 28.

[80] Ibid, 35.

[81] Ibid, 33.

[82] Sir E. Coke, *Third Reports*, 3, cii.

[83] John Dickinson, "Law behind Law" (1929) Columbia Law Review 113–146.

[84] With the Jews, but with the Abrahamic blessings extended to Gentiles by dint of being grafted into the vine (Israel): see Romans 11, Galatians 3.

legal rights. The functions of law go beyond "command and sanction"; law has symbolic and educative functions in expressing deep values and shaping communal identity. As man is created *imago dei,* and as God is the supreme lawgiver, man in creating constitutions reflects an aspiration *imitatio dei.*[85] Augustine characterized the "three forms of the triune God" as will, reason, and memory.[86] This is reflected in the three corresponding elements one finds in every constitution: power, justice, and culture.[87]

Several key facets of the rule of law shaped by a Christian vision of the higher law can be identified. On this view the essential purpose of positive law is to "make higher law effective in human living,"[88] thus realizing liberty, justice, the common good,[89] and *shalom,* a state of peace and relational well-being. It speaks of legitimate and limited government, established by God to do good for citizens, protecting them against abuses and punishing the wicked (Rom. 13). The rule of law requires the state to prove its powers and stay within its limits. Part of the common good is securing public order and guarding against despotism, as the biblical understanding of man is that he is sinful and susceptible to corruption and abuses of power. Men are not angels, and modern constitutionalism has devised checks and balances based on principles with widespread currency, such as the rule of law, separation of powers, and subsidiarity to allocate, diffuse, and regulate power. The rule of law as a form of accountability addresses the fear of the unbounded discretion of regulators and prosecutors.

The first facet of the rule of law shaped by a Christian vision is that all human government should be below and not above the law,[90] that is, *Lex Rex*, rather than *Rex Lex.*[91] Henri De Bracton, the father of the common law, stated that the king was subject to God "for he is not truly king, where will and pleasure rules, and not the law."[92] All authority is from God, and those he delegates it to must serve his purposes.[93] Owing to man's sinful nature,

[85] Harold J Berman, "Law and Logos" (1994) 44(1) DePaul Law Review 143, 150.
[86] St Augustine, *Confessions*, (EB Pusey Translation 1907) 317–318.
[87] Donald Lutz, "Thinking about Constitutionalism at the Start of the Twenty-First Century" (2000) 30(4) Publius 115–135.
[88] Patrick McKinley Brennan, "An Essay on Christian Constitutionalism: Building in the Divine Style, for the Common Good(s)," (2015) 16 Rutgers Journal of Law and Religion 478–540, 504.
[89] God establishes human authority for "your good" and invests governors with "the sword" to punish wrongdoers (Rom. 13:1–5). Thomas Aquinas, *Summa Theologica* Q.90, art 2.
[90] Deuteronomy 17:18–19.
[91] Samuel Rutherford, *Lex Rex (1644)* (Portage Publications 2000).
[92] Quoted in Blackstone's Commentaries on the Laws of England, Book 1, ch 6, "Of the King's Duties," 226.
[93] John 19:11 (NKJV): Jesus said to Pilate: "You could have no power at all against Me unless it had been given you from above."

no one should wield unlimited authority and governors should be subject to external restraints. Civil authorities are to respect the supremacy of God's higher law over state law, as positive law that is unjust is a "corruption of law."[94] Ockham considered that "any civil law which is repugnant to divine law or manifest reason is not law,"[95] as the *lex divina/lex dei* "overrules contrary human law no matter by whom promulgated."[96]

Second, it follows that the state should not be "totalizing"; there are spheres of human life into which it may not intrude.[97] Caesar should receive his due, no more, no less. This has given rise to the structural division of social life into the "sacred" and the "secular," which effectively operates as a limit on government power, by a separation of powers.[98] A related idea is that of subsidiarity, which implies limits on the scope of public authority: individuals and lesser communities within society are responsible for their own appropriate functions, while larger institutions such as the state must not interfere with or absorb the lesser, but only intervene to "encourage, stimulate, regulate supplement and complement" them, that is, to render them *subsiduum* or aid.[99]

This might, for example, be reflected in the recognition that religious education belongs at home rather than in public schools, or that parents may decide the kind of education their children receive, such as when they have religious objections to sex education classes.[100]

Third, those who adjudicate should not be partial, but judge fairly between rich and poor alike (Lev. 19:15). This principle supports the constitutional prescription of an independent judiciary and judicial review as an engine of the rule of law under which public officials are subject to judicial control in the exercise of their official discretion.[101] Furthermore, they should observe rules of natural justice, as God did in Eden with humanity, giving a fair hearing and a reasoned opinion for his judgment (Gen. 3:9–13).

This principle of impartiality has significant ramifications for human equality. As men and women are theologically coequal image bearers of

94 Thomas Aquinas, *Summa Theologica* Q.95, art 2.
95 William of Ockham, Dialogus, Part I, Bk 6, ch 100, 629.
96 Ockham, Dialogus, Part III, Tractatus 11, Liber II, ch 4, 904.
97 Matthew 22:21.
98 Richard Mohr, "The Christian Origins of Secularism and the Rule of Law" in N Hosen and R Mohr (eds), *Law and Religion in Public Life: The Contemporary Debate* (Routledge 2011) 34.
99 Kent A Van Til, "Subsidiarity and Sphere-Sovereignty: A Match Made in . . . ?" (2008) 69 Theological Studies 610, 611. See chapter by Iain Benson in this volume.
100 Article 26(3), Universal Declaration of Human Rights (1948).
101 Laws LJ in *R (Cart) v Upper Tribunal* [2010] 1 All ER 908 (CA) [34].

God, they are morally and relationally equal, and complementary. Meister Eckhart stated that women were to have the same essential rights as men, as "God . . . made woman from man's side, so that she ought to be equal to him." Neither does God draw distinctions on grounds of ethnicity or economic status.[102] This provides a normative basis for the principle of equality under the law, which is integral to the rule of law. Thus, the obligations of the law should be imposed without unreasonable discrimination, a precursor to the equal protection of the law.

Fourth, the function of the state is to safeguard the fundamental rights of members of its community and to render decent treatment to aliens.[103] Friedrich identifies the "Christian doctrine of personality" as a root of the idea of restraints in constitutional thinking, based on "the transcendental importance of each man's soul."[104] In particular, individuals, created *imago dei* and with free moral choices, ought to enjoy the right to liberty of conscience as an aspect of religious freedom, which is closely allied to free speech, intellectual freedom, and viewpoint diversity.[105] This rests on the idea that faith is not to be coerced, which supports a voluntarist conception of religious freedom encompassing the right to have, not have, or change a religious belief.[106]

Lastly, the higher law embodying the will of God determines what sorts of conduct the law proscribes and permits. For Theodore Beza, common law principles of nature still linger after the Fall. It was therefore possible to glean from the ancient histories of Greece, Rome, and the Germanic tribes the kinds of conduct that violate the natural law. Beza gave as examples "infanticide, incest, sodomy, concubinage, prostitution, and the improper marriages of children, of eunuchs, or of the mentally handicapped." Positive laws could not "countenance such open violations of the laws of nature and the laws of God"[107] as this is considered deleterious to human flourishing, which for Finnis entails securing basic goods that can be identified by "practical reasonableness."[108]

[102] Galatians 3:28.

[103] Exodus 22:21; Deuteronomy 24:14, 17–22.

[104] Carl J Friedrich, *Limited Government: A Comparison* (Prentice-Hall 1974) 12–13.

[105] John T Noonan Jr, "Principled or Pragmatic Foundations for the Freedom of Conscience?" (1987) 5(1) Journal of Law and Religion 203–212, 204–205.

[106] 2 Peter 3:9.

[107] John Witte Jr, "Rights, Resistance and Revolution in the Western Tradition: Early Protestant Foundations" (2008) 26(3) Law and History Review 545–570, 547.

[108] John Finnis, *Natural Law & Natural Rights* (2nd edn, OUP 2011).

The Shoot Diverges from the Root: The Higher Law and Humanist Constitutions

If the foundations be destroyed, what can the righteous do?

—Proverbs 11:3

As a conceptual necessity, all evaluative standards require a source of normative authority or higher law from which to draw its content. Two major jurisprudential shifts caused the religious connection[109] between the higher law and rule of law to be replaced by a normative rival, a humanist ideology that can assume individualist and collectivist forms.[110] These may borrow from the intellectual foundations of a biblically shaped higher law, but they have sharply diverged from these foundations and may actually undermine rule-of-law values.

First, the natural law tradition shifted from the perennial to the school of Enlightenment jurisprudence, driven by a humanism that denied "any power or moral value superior to that of humanity."[111] The perennial variety of natural law identified objective principles that served a vision of human flourishing from whence objective natural rights and basic goods were derived through practical reasoning. Enlightenment naturalism severed Law's root in religion by adopting a secularized variant of the higher law derived from human reason, detached from its theocentric moorings.

However, reason is a capacious idea into which a range of ideologies may be poured. The higher law or natural law became a tool of political strategy, capable of subjugating individual interests to the collective whole, or else valorizing individual interests to the exclusion of other legitimate concerns. "Natural law" became an empty container for political ideologies.

The second shift was the ascendancy of legal positivism and its rejection of metaphysical abstractions. This established a conceptual apartheid between law and morality, in pursuit of "legal science," a field autonomous from politics and ideology. Jurists like John Austin excluded higher law from the province of his command theory of law, consigning this to the realm of morality

[109] For a discussion on religion as part of the history of the rule of law and how the rule of law is not just a state-building project but "a project with its own internally coherent theology or system of beliefs," see Mark Fathi Massoud, "Theology of the Rule of Law" (2019) 11 Hague Journal on the Rule of Law 485–419.

[110] Stephen Hall, "The Persistent Spectre: Natural Law, International Order and the Limits of Legal Positivism" (2001) 12(2) EJIL 269–307, 42.

[111] Collins Concise English Dictionary.

or ethics.[112] Legal positivism oriented law toward formalism and a focus on issues of legal validity rather than an evaluation of their content, assessed against a vision of law as embodying substantive justice.

The way in which law unhinged from objective principles can undermine the rule of law is illustrated by two contemporary examples: the collectivist setting of the Chinese Communist Party (CCP) and the individualist setting epitomized by American hyperliberal individualism. In 1982, the Chinese constitution was amended to include article 4, which declared that the People's Republic of China (PRC) was "a socialist country under the rule of law" or a *fazhi* (法制). However, this rule of law with Chinese characteristics[113] is an instrumental conception that does not limit the central government but is deployed as a tool of effective governance by the National People's Congress (NPC), the highest body of the CCP, the leading force of state and society reflecting the "people's democratic dictatorship."[114] Its inclusion was part of a broader modernizing project of legal reform, motivated by a shift toward a market economy. The rule of law seeks to promote commercial transactions through clear and consistent rules. However, there is no robust judicial independence in China, as the highest judicial organ, the Supreme People's Court (SPC), is responsible to the NPC,[115] and the NPC Standing Committee is the final interpreter of the constitution.[116] Judicial review does not apply to the CCP, which enjoys supreme power. The Chinese constitution also contains a list of civil-political and socioeconomic rights;[117] however, after the SPC in 2001 recognized a constitutional right to education, the NPC Standing Committee in 2008 reversed this decision, issuing a declaration that rights in the constitution are nonjusticiable.[118] Thus, the rule of law functioned as a tool to advance the agenda of the CCP and its primacy and

[112] John Austin, *Lecture V, The Province of Jurisprudence Determined (1832)* (1995) 106–163.

[113] Ignazio Castellucci, "Rule of Law with Chinese Characteristics" (2007) 13(1) Annual Survey of International & Comparative Law 35–58. See Lucas Brang, "Carl Schmitt and the Evolution of Chinese Constitutional Theory: Conceptual Transfer and the Unexpected Paths of legal Globalisation" (2020) 9(1) Global Constitutionalism 117–154.

[114] Arts 2, 58, Constitution of the People's Republic of China (1982) ("PRC Constitution").

[115] Art 128, PRC Constitution.

[116] Art 67, PRC Constitution.

[117] Arts 38–50, PRC Constitution.

[118] Supreme People's Court, Decision on Abolishing the Relevant Judicial Interpretations (the Seventh Batch) Promulgated before the End of 2007, 18 December 2008 (最高人民法院关于废止 2007 年底以前发布的有关司法解释(第七批)的决定). Thomas E Kellogg, "The Death of Constitutional Litigation in China" (2009) 9(7) China Brief. There have been instances of citizens invoking the constitution in making petitions to political leaders: Elizabeth J Perry, "Chinese Conception of 'Rights': From Mencius to Mao - and Now" (March 2008) 6(1) Perspectives on Politics 37–50.

to promote socialist legality while preserving a Mao-like cult of personality, currently in the form of "Xi Jinping Thought," which was constitutionally enshrined in 2018.[119]

In contrast, in liberal settings that have a rights-oriented, court-centric brand of constitutionalism, the rule of law may also be undermined through expansive readings of constitutional rights clauses in rights adjudication, driven by the subjective political preferences of activist judges in the name of "living tree" interpretive approaches. The basic liberal commitment is to normative individualism, which views the individual as atomistic and vulnerable against the state, rather than situated within a community. Free-standing autonomy as an ultimate value is promoted through the vehicle of rights, which are justiciable entitlements judicially enforced against somebody. Ronald Dworkin, for example, advocated a "rights based" rather than "rule book" conception of the rule of law designed to "capture and enforce moral rights."[120] To avoid metaphysics, Dworkin identified the source of these rights in how a community understands moral rights pursuant to achieving what he terms "equal respect and concern." This is itself a substantive theory not free from controversy. While Dworkin's faith is in the ability of judges to accurately ascertain what community standards are, it is by no means clear why a judge, as opposed to a legislator, should make determinations on morally controversial questions, such as euthanasia, abortion, and who may enter civil marriage. Dworkin's faith is misplaced in not seriously taking the depth and intractability of competing moral viewpoints on intractable social controversies.[121]

Judges engage in social engineering when they take sides on polarized controversies in declaring ex cathedra unwritten rights derived from "penumbras" or broad readings of open-ended texts. The American courts have read existing rights broadly to find new rights in positive law, servicing a "hypertrophic personal autonomy."[122] Exemplary of this "living tree" interpretative approach is the construction of the US Fourteenth Amendment, which provides: "No state shall . . . deprive any person of life, liberty or property, without due process of law." From this, an extratextual privacy right was derived and judicially pronounced to include a right to an abortion in the

[119] "China to Enshrine Xi's Thought into State Constitution amid National 'Fervor,'" Reuters, 19 January 2018.

[120] Ronald Dworkin, *A Matter of Principle* (Harvard University Press 1985) 11.

[121] E.g., Brian Tamanaha, *On the Rule of Law: History, Politics, Theory* (Cambridge University Press 2004) 103–104.

[122] Stephen J Hall, "The Persistent Spectre" (2001) 12 EJIL 269–307, 304.

controversial case of *Roe v. Wade.*[123] In developing reproductive autonomy rights, Judge Kennedy in *Casey v. Planned Parenthood*[124] stated that central to the Fourteenth Amendment were "choices central to personal dignity and autonomy"; he further made the solipsistic pronouncement: "At the heart of liberty is the right to define one's own concept of existence, of meaning, of the universe, and of the mystery of human life." This radical metavision of autonomy smacks of a brand of juristocracy[125] or "rule by judges" that undermines the rule of law, as it speaks of partial judges, of the Supreme Court becoming the source of "higher law." Depending on one's political preferences, a countermajoritarian court "can appear either as hero or villain."[126] From a Christian perspective, reproductive autonomy constitutes a radically unjust violation of the right to life of the vulnerable category of the unborn person[127] and a failure of a deficient rule of law to protect basic rights.

Commentators have thus fairly noted that in the American setting, "higher law" has frequently been reduced to judicial discretion.[128] In this, judges have adopted a faux "natural law" approach only in the limited sense of applying unwritten constitutional standards they discover, discern, or declare. Consequently, they are "too bold in exalting matters of opinion to the pedestal of Natural Law and even in erecting their prejudices into immutable principles."[129] The idea of the rule of law as an objective reference point is thus incoherent apart from religious presuppositions that can provide a transcendental anchor for the law in relation to which the government is under as opposed to an absolutist state. In relation to "thick," rights-based conceptions of the rule of law, the gateway for proliferating autonomy-maximizing rights claims has been opened. Friedrich has identified this as

[123] *Roe v Wade* 410 US 113 (1973).

[124] 505 US 833 (1992).

[125] James Grant, "The Rise of Juristocracy" (Spring 2010) 34(2) Wilson Quarterly 16–22.

[126] Michael J Klarman, "What's So Great about Constitutionalism?" (1998–1999) 93(1) Northwestern University Law Review 145–194, 162. This valorization of autonomy was later used to expand upon erotic liberties, e.g., *Lawrence v Texas* 539 US 558 (2003).

[127] Psalm 139:13–16 grounds the view that life starts from conception. This is recognized in various basic laws, including article 4, American Convention on Human Rights, UNTS No. 17955; Art II (Freedom and Responsibility), Hungarian Constitution (2011); Art II Section 12, Constitution of the Republic of the Philippines (1987).

[128] Gary L McDowell, "Coke, Corwin and the Constitution: The 'Higher Law Background' Reconsidered" (1993) 55(3) Review of Politics 393–420, 407.

[129] John Wu, "The Natural Law and our Common Law" (1954) 23(1) Fordham Law Review 13, 42.

a key part of the "humanist core of constitutionalism" in an age "where the religious foundations of constitutionalism have almost vanished."[130]

Interpretation is of course not a purely mechanical exercise, but judicial courage must be accompanied by judicial modesty as judges "are not the ultimate repositories of human wisdom in answering the kinds of social, economic and political questions with which parliament and administrators have to deal."[131] Alternative approaches more respectful of the separation of powers do exist, in jurisdictions where nontextual approaches to constitutional interpretation are deprecated as a repudiation of constitutional supremacy.[132] For example, Singapore courts in interpreting the article 9 "life and personal liberty" clause of the constitution have focused on historical materials drawing from constitutional drafting and the common law, including the Magna Carta, to find certain rights beyond freedom from bodily restraint and unlawful detention, so as to prohibit unlawful use of force against a person through amputations, mutilations, assaults, beatings, wounding, etc.[133] However, time and again, Singapore courts have refused to legislate new rights into the constitution "under the guise of interpreting existing constitutional principles."[134] For example, invitations to read a right of privacy into article 9 in a constitutional challenge to an antisodomy penal law were rejected.[135] In upholding the rule of law and the separation of coequal branches, Singapore courts strive to treat law as representing "the voice of objectivity,"[136] above subjective politics as far as possible, by nurturing a disciplining culture of reason giving, in seeking to balance majoritarian will and countermajoritarian checks.

Within the natural law tradition, inalienable rights are God given. This means that a religious higher law[137] will determine the scope and parameters of constitutional rights and how to interpret them. Wu pointed out that if this was remembered, there would be "no danger of abusing the concept of

[130] Carl J Friedrich, *Transcendent Justice: The Religious Dimension of Constitutionalism* (Duke University Press 1964) 115–116.

[131] Lord Diplock, "Judicial Control of Government" [1979] Malayan Law Journal cxli, cxlvii.

[132] Attorney-General VK Rajah, "Interpreting the Constitution," *Straits Times* (Singapore) 30 May 2015.

[133] *Yong Vui Kong v PP* [2015] 2 SLR 1120 [13]–[23].

[134] *Yong Vui Kong v PP* [2010] 3 SLR 489 [122].

[135] This was expressed as "a right of personal autonomy allowing a person to enjoy and express affection and love towards another human being." *Lim Meng Suang v AG* [2015] 1 SLR 26 [30], [43].

[136] *Lim Meng Suang v AG* [2015] 1 SLR 26 [5].

[137] For an Islamic perspective, see Tengku Ahmad Hazri, "The Rule of Law in Islam: Between Formalism and Substantivism" (2016) 7(1) Islamic and Civilisational Renewal 65–80, https://www.academia.edu/29814557/The_Rule_of_Law_in_Islam_Between_Formalism_and_Substantivism.

natural law for justifying a materialistic individualism; because we know that God who gave us liberty gave us also reason and a supernatural destiny," that the natural rights we have come with natural duties, including love of God and love of our neighbor, which would be part of the common good.[138] In a postsecular world in which the deep secularization of Western Europe is now understood to be exceptional, religious traditions are re-emerging "as alternative sources of political and moral meaning."[139] In this context, Christianity has a legitimate role to play in conversations about the foundations of the rule of law and its relation to higher law, given the loss of momentum of the "progress of disenchantment."[140]

Concluding Observations

Revisiting the contributions of Christianity to understanding the higher law/rule of law is a worthwhile endeavor for various reasons.

First, it challenges the hegemony of the dominant conception of the rule of law, which conflates the rule of law with liberalism. This hampers imaginative space when it comes to thinking of alternatives where the rule of law can exist independently of liberalism.[141] We live in a postmodern age in which grand narratives are treated with impatience. However, it is in the context of that postmodern plurality that we see the re-emergence within constitutional scholarship of an interaction of law and religion in which religion resists being absorbed by law's empire.[142] In the face of a resurgent theocratic constitutionalism,[143] revisiting the religious foundations of the rule of law is timely. This makes it important to excavate the cultural biases of dominant conceptions of higher law and the rule of law, evaluating their strengths and deficiencies. We need to grapple with foundational and unsettled questions

[138] John Wu, "The Natural Law and our Common Law" (1954) 23(1) Fordham Law Review 13, 40–41.

[139] Zachary Calo, "Religion, Human Rights and Post-Secular Legal Theory" (2011) 85 St John's Law Review 415–519, 507.

[140] Charles Taylor, *Modern Social Imaginaries* (Duke University Press 2003) 49.

[141] See "Varieties of the Rule of Law" in Randall Pereenboom (ed), *Asian Discourses of Rule of Law: Theories and Implementation of Rule of Law in Twelve Asian Countries, France and the US* (Routledge 2004) 1–55.

[142] Ran Hirschl and Ayelet Shachar, "'The New Wall of Separation': Permitting Diversity, Restricting Competition" (2009) 30 Cardozo Law Review 2535–2560, 2537.

[143] Ran Hirschl, *Constitutional Theocracy* (Harvard University Press 2010); Moamen Gouda, "Islamic Constitutionalism and Rule of Law: A Constitutional Economics Perspective" (2013) 24(1) Constitutional Political Economy 57–85.

about the source, authority, and content of law particularly as these bear on the nature of the rule of law, the role of courts, etc. It is possible to then ask whether religious foundations of law are a necessary pillar of higher law and the rule of law, especially if law is to be autonomous from politics.

Second, the Christian tradition offers an "origin story" for higher law and the rule of law. The rediscovery of the Christian origins of many modern constitutional ideas, particularly of the Anglo-American variety,[144] is important in establishing a baseline from which to understand how the contemporary conception of rule of law developed after the point of rupture when law was severed from its religious roots and to appreciate its contours in an age where positivism dominates. It is also important to assess whether humanistic justifications for the rule of law suffice to secure freedom, or whether secular intolerance undermines this. If the rule of law posits a vision of human flourishing, Christian theology and understanding of God as a God of righteousness and justice may present a competing, counterhegemonic alternative to liberal ideology.

A multiplicity of views can inform and reform discourse to better reflect the lived realities of a plural, postmodern world. In the postsecular landscape of the liberal West an array of questions remain: Is "law" secular or religious in nature?[145] Does a defense of the rule of law require affirming something like natural law? What is the role of religion in shaping moral worldviews that in turn form the basis for legal order? These questions raise a host of issues concerning God, human nature, and the basis for social life—questions to which there are no universally accepted answers.

Christian natural law is revisited, not with the intent of rearticulating a grand theory imbued with universalist ambitions. The intent is dialogue and viewpoint diversity, in the conviction that religious faith is a normative resource and source of deep political meaning in legal discourse. A particularist account is offered as an appropriate contribution in a pluralist age where there are many voices crying in the wilderness. What is needed is an honest and constructive dialogue about the rule of law and the visions of human flourishing associated with it. For some, this may provide a hopeful normative resource, a way to recover a morally compelling message with directive

144 Augusto Zimmerman, "God, Locke and Montesquieu: Some Thoughts Concerning the Religious Foundations of Modern Constitutionalism" (2010) 1 Western Australian Jurist 1. Robert Lowery Clinton, *God and Man in the Law: The Foundations of Anglo-American Constitutionalism* (University Press of Kansas 1997).

145 David Novak, "Law: Religious or Secular" (2000) 86 Va L Rev 569.

force. Recovered insights may help advance reformation in the search for a just society, no matter how imperfectly realized in a fallen world.

While some may ask whether there is a higher law/rule of law beyond the "metaphysical abstraction of generous idealists,"[146] the rule of law is a lived reality in constitutional and political practice. The rule of law presumes the objectivity of law, but claims of objectivity and determinacy are skeptically received by legal realists. Nonetheless, there are judges who treat law as an objective reality above the fray of subjective politics.[147] There is also a continuing public perception that "judges are bound by a body of fixed overriding law, that they apply that law impersonally as well as impartially, that they exercise no individual choice and have no program of their own to advance."[148] This vision of law as a body of stable, accessible rules reflects a formal conception of rule of law, where judges are able to find and declare pre-existing law. It is a vision that continues to wield strong public appeal in some settings. Nonetheless, none of us believe in fairy tales now;[149] some degree of judicial lawmaking takes place, and the question is, what degree is legitimate?[150] A Christian conception of higher law/rule of law may shed insight into these and other important constitutional issues, in the space between metaphysics and mundane rule following, the cynical despair of "law as politics," the aridity of legal formalism, and the naivete of "law as utopia."

[146] James M Beck, "The Higher Law" (1918) 4(4) American Bar Association Journal 656–680.

[147] See, for example, *Lim Meng Suang v AG* [2014] SGCA 53 [7].

[148] Paul J Mishkin, "Foreword: The High Court, the Great Writ and the Due Process of Time and Law" (1965) 79 Harv L Rev 56, 61.

[149] Quoting Lord Reid, "The Judge as Law Maker" (1972–1973) 12 JSPTL (NS) 22, in *Lim Meng Suang v AG* [2015] 1 SLR 53 [78].

[150] *Lim Meng Suang v AG* (2015) 1 SLR 26 [77].

11

Democracy

Self-Government and the Kingdom of Heaven

Richard Ekins

Introduction

It is good for a people to rule itself and a good constitution is a framework for reasoned self-government, making it possible for the people jointly to reason and act to secure their common good. These propositions find powerful support within the Christian tradition of political thought and practice, a tradition on which this chapter draws to explore and elaborate the constitutional significance of self-government. It begins, in the next section, by noting the tradition's grasp of what it is to rule and to be ruled, central to which is the idea of kingship. The third section considers the foundations of legitimate authority and the conditions under which God raises up and casts down authorities, arguing that the consent of the governed is not the foundation of justified authority but that the social fact of who the people are willing to support is relevant to the location of authority. In the fourth section, the discussion turns to the reasons rulers have to share authority and to create representative assemblies, which in due course may become the central focus of public deliberation and choice. The promise of such representative institutions—to enable joint action despite disagreement—is only likely to be realized, the fifth section argues, in circumstances where a people recognizes itself as sharing a common good to which elites and masses alike are jointly committed. Self-government does not entail that a people may do as it pleases: like any other ruler, a free people is subject to God and reason. However, self-governing peoples are well placed to decide for themselves what should be done, and the sixth section considers and contests the ways in which human rights law and supranational institutions undercut this freedom. Thus, the chapter aims to explain how and why, and to what extent,

Richard Ekins, *Democracy: Self-Government and the Kingdom of Heaven* in *Christianity and Constitutionalism*.
Edited by: Nicholas Aroney and Ian Leigh, Oxford University Press. © Oxford University Press 2022.
DOI: 10.1093/oso/9780197587256.003.0011

self-government should be sought by those who seek first the kingdom of heaven.

Rulership in the Kingdom of Heaven

"Repent, for the kingdom of heaven is at hand."[1] How should one think about the authority of rulers in this light? St. Paul's famous passage in Romans 13 is part of the answer, of course, which I discuss further below. But Christian thought about government has also been informed by how Israel was ruled and, in particular, by the model of kingship made out in the scriptures, a model that helps articulate the objects of government and suggests grounds for sharing participation in government.

The Jews were the chosen people of God, called to be a light to the nations and to prepare the way for Christ. In the early period, there was no king save God, who ruled by way of judges He raised up.[2] Moses and his successors ruled, but not alone, for God heard Moses's plea that his burdens were too great for one man to discharge and shared the responsibility to rule with the elders. Their sharing in authority, Aquinas reasons, introduced an aristocratic *and* a democratic element to what otherwise simply had the form of a kingdom (rule by one man), for the seventy-two elders ruled, under Moses, and were chosen from the people.[3] The scriptures also disclose a model of divine kingship, with God caring for His people, making a covenant with them, which He honors, and appointing others to rule subject to His law. Reciprocity of king and people and subjection to law are thus central to divine kingship and by extension to human rule.

In the time of Samuel,[4] the judges are replaced by a king, God having allowed the people's request, while also warning them that rule by a king may mean abuse of the people. Still, God goes on to specify how the king is to be chosen, that he must not be an alien, must not raise an army of horsemen, must not wed many wives or amass great treasures, must study God's law, must avoid prideful disdain of others, and must keep God's commandments

[1] Matthew 3:2, 4:17.

[2] Burnside, in this volume; see also E Nelson, *The Hebrew Republic* (HUP 2010).

[3] Aquinas, *Summa Theologiae* (ST) I-II q 105 a 1; N Aroney, "Subsidiarity, Federalism and the Best Constitution: Thomas Aquinas on City, Province and Empire" (2007) 26 Law and Philosophy 161, 210–212, 217.

[4] M Halbertal and S Holmes, *The Beginning of Politics: Power in the Biblical Book of Samuel* (PUP 2017).

if his rule is to endure.[5] The people of Israel are a nation set apart, whose exclusivity the king is to preserve—in his person (not being an alien), his marriage, and his study of the law. The king represents the people and is pivotal to their fulfillment of their covenant with God. In this way, in loyalty to the king, the people of God may jointly follow His commandments, with Israel ruling itself rather than being ruled by a foreign power. The subjection of Israel to foreign rule is a punishment, the consequence of departing from the covenant, with exile in a foreign land frustrating Israel's capacity to live as it should. The rule of the kings exposes the people to many abuses, as foretold, and prophets are raised up to preach repentance, on the part of both the king and the people.[6] The scriptures thus make out a model of kingship, in the person of God and in His judges and kings, a model in which the ruler represents the people, is responsible for their good, is subject to God's law, but may often fall short.

Christ is the new king but He did not come to restore Jewish self-government. Instead, He confounds the Messianic expectations of a military ruler; humbles Himself; preaches repentance, forgiveness of sins, and salvation of all who turn to Him; dies and is resurrected; and proclaims that His kingdom is not of this world. He sends His disciples to make followers of every nation. Early Christians were all subjects of the Roman Empire, exposed to foreign rule. The temptation for early Christians, understandably enough, was to think that following Christ set them free from obligation to temporal authority. It is this position that St. Paul sets right in Romans 13,[7] teaching that followers of Christ should submit to the governing authorities, for conscience's sake rather than simply to avoid punishment, and should pay taxes to support those who govern. The Apostle states that the authorities that exist have been established by God, such that rebellion against rulers is rebellion against God. He says further that the authorities are God's servants for the good of those who are ruled, agents of His wrath, who will punish wrongdoers.

I turn in the next section to the question of *how* God establishes authorities. For now, I note that St. Paul's specification of the responsibility of rulers implies important limits on their capacity to bind the ruled in conscience. They act for the good of those they rule; they are God's servants; their jurisdiction is to punish wrongdoers. There is no inconsistency between this

[5] Deuteronomy 17:14–20.
[6] G Maddox, *Religion and the Rise of Democracy* (Routledge 1995).
[7] See further Bertschmann, in this volume.

passage and defiance of imperial power by martyrs and saints when that power requires apostasy or immorality.[8]

Romans 13 is not a paean to the virtues of self-government. It is written first and foremost to the ruled to explain why they should do as the ruler directs. This object of address is itself significant, for St. Paul invites his readers to recognize that they are called by God to obey freely, for conscience's sake, to support government with obedience, taxes, and respect. It is not far from this account to Aquinas's prescription of law as an ordinance for the common good in the mind of the ruler, which the ruled adopts as if it were his own.[9] True, rule on St. Paul's account might very well be foreign and in a sense external, something done to one rather than by one. Nonetheless, St. Paul here gives those who are ruled the dignity, which rulers also ought to recognize, of reasoning agents, capable of responding to the ruler's character as God's servant for their good, stressing that rule is *for* them and that they have an active part to play in helping rulers do God's work. In other words, rule is no longer something simply done to you, but an opportunity to share in a common project.

Ruled and ruler alike are subject to God, and one should not read Romans 13 without recalling the radical, fundamental equality that the Gospels proclaim and the Epistles elaborate.[10] The incarnation transforms the standing of human beings, confirming that we are all made in the image of God and that what we do to the least amongst us we do to Christ. The universal call to repent and follow Him entails that each person is capable of repentance and of discipleship and is to be recognized to be a creature fundamentally similar to oneself.[11] St. Paul's remarks in Galatians that in Christ there is no slave or free, no male or female, no Jew or Gentile are radical, and rightly so, but follow straightforwardly from the Gospels themselves.[12] The initial question for Christians was how the equality of believers should bear on the structure of the Church and on how believers treated one another. But it was also relevant, plainly enough, to how rulers should act, and perhaps also to who should rule. St. Paul in Romans 13 addresses the ruled rather than the ruler, although he implies some of the responsibilities of rulers too. The need

[8] Acts 5:29; Nicholas Wolterstorff, *Mighty and the Almighty: An Essay in Political Theology* (CUP 2012) 13–14.

[9] Aquinas, ST, I-II q 91 a 1, q 92 a 1c, 2c; see also J Finnis, *Aquinas* (OUP 1999) 255–256.

[10] See also Genesis 1:27 ("So God created mankind in his own image").

[11] J Locke, *Two Treatises on Government*, II, para 6; see also J Waldron, *God Locke and Equality* (CUP 2002) 79–80.

[12] Galatians 3:28.

for further specification of the latter becomes acute when rulers converted to Christianity and when the authority of Rome faltered.[13] Still, it is striking that until Aquinas's time, Christians had relatively little to say about the classical question of which regime is best.[14]

For early Christians, imperial Rome was a mortal threat.[15] But as Christianity spread, and especially when emperors converted, it must have seemed that it was providential that the Gospels were proclaimed within the Roman Empire and thus that imperial rule, with a Christian emperor, was ideal, not least since it chimed with the universal message of the Gospels.[16] Still, this assumption was and is problematic, jarring with the recognition that there are many nations and failing to engage with the inadequacies of empire, which may secure common defense and provide some public goods, including prosperity, but is not a form of government well placed to perceive or to advance the common good of a complete political community. The thinness of the community that is an empire, the distance between the ruler and the ruled, and the consequent shallowness of the ruler's capacity to rule well all militate against empire as a stable, ideal political form. After the fall of Rome, the political experience of Christendom was one of authority painstakingly being built up in many kingdoms, each of which participated in a universal Church, with kings and other temporal rulers being subject, at least in principle, to spiritual discipline for failings of justice and morality.[17] Christ's recognition of temporal authority,[18] echoed in Romans 13, entails that Christians are members of the Church and of some political community. This division is fundamental to Christian political thought and humbles temporal authority, which is limited in reach and answers to a higher power. The Christian ruler has to think about how to exercise his authority in light of the truths of the Christian faith; and ordinary Christians often have to decide which putative authority to recognize or to decide precisely what we owe to one another, to recall Romans 13:7.

[13] Augustine, *City of God*, Book 5.24; R Williams, "Politics and the Soul: Reading the *City of God*" in Rowan Williams, *On Augustine* (Bloomsbury 2016) 107, 123.

[14] O O'Donovan, *The Ways of Judgment* (Eerdmans 2005) 165.

[15] Bertschmann and Leithart, in this volume.

[16] See Eusebius, "From a Speech on the Dedication of the Holy Sepulchre Church" in O O'Donovan and JL O'Donovan (eds), *From Irenaeus to Grotius: A Sourcebook in Christian Political Thought 100–1625* (Eerdmans 1999) 58.

[17] Gelasius I, "Letter to Emperor Anastasius" in O'Donovan and O'Donovan (eds), *From Irenaeus to Grotius*, 179. See further Harrison, in this volume.

[18] Matthew 22:21.

In short, the early Christian tradition recognizes the importance of government and assumes kingship to be ideal. This is kingship characterized by the exemplars of God's rule over Israel, the servant-kingship of Christ, and the duties of Israel's kings to the people of God and to God himself. Old Testament kingship is a representative office, instituted for the good of the people and requiring discipline and humility to exercise well. Likewise, in a very different political context and alongside the radical equality of the Gospels, St. Paul articulates the duty of the ruler to act for the good of the ruled and the reciprocal duty of the ruled to obey for conscience's sake,[19] to pay one's taxes and honor one's rulers. While many early Christians assume the imperial form is an ideal, Christendom comes to be formed by many kingdoms, with kings and peoples joined in one Church.

How Authorities Are Raised Up

St. Paul's passage in Romans is not first and foremost about *who* should rule. It takes for granted that there are authorities—and that they are God's servants for our good—but adds that there is no authority except that which God has established. How does God establish authority? The classical natural law tradition answers that "authority (and thus the *responsibility* of governing) in a community is to be exercised by those who can in fact effectively settle co-ordination problems."[20] What this means is that if some person or body has the capacity to direct how others will act—if what they say will in fact be followed and complied with—then that person or body has a duty to govern and others have a presumptive duty to be governed.[21] This capacity will arise in different ways in different times and places—it may be grounded in charisma, tradition, fear of force, or respect for age or wisdom. When a person or body who has this capacity exercises it for the common good, those they direct are subject to authority and have a duty to conform. Thus, God raises up authorities by permitting some person or body in fact to have the capacity to direct others, which constitutes authority when he, she, or it takes up the responsibility to govern.[22] The misuse of one's capacity is not an exercise of authority: no person or body is an authority if his, her, or their actions are not

[19] Cf. O'Donovan, *Ways of Judgment*, 127–128.
[20] J Finnis, *Natural Law and Natural Rights* (2nd edn, OUP 2011) 246 (hereafter "NLNR").
[21] L Green, "The Duty to Govern" (2007) 13 Legal Theory 165.
[22] O'Donovan, *Ways of Judgment*, 135.

a means to the good of those for whom they are responsible, in which case they are not God's servant for our good. Likewise, God overthrows authorities when He permits the erosion or collapse of the person or body's capacity to direct others, whether by way of military defeat or demise of prestige or respect, and raises up some other person or body in their place.

This account of the origins of authority puts self-government in its place. The foundation of legitimate authority is the capacity to secure the common good. It is not the consent of the governed or the transmission by the people of some inherent power we have to rule ourselves. There is no such inherent power, and its transfer or exercise is not what constitutes justified authority.[23] The mistaken view that the consent of the governed is fundamental to the authority of rulers is a misconceived response to important truths that the Christian tradition has articulated over time—viz. no one has a natural right to rule, persons are made in the image of God, and government should be ordered by law and not usurped. In aiming to ascertain who, here and now, is entitled to rule, we rightly look to law, to authoritative determination of this very question, if such is to be found. The moral importance of legal title has tempted many people to think that one may always trace justified authority back to some lawful act, which, when taken together with the equality of all persons and the absence of other lawful alternatives, is transmuted into authorization by (a majority of) the governed.[24] The mistake is to think that because it is good for the location of authority to be settled by law, authority must always begin with a lawful exercise, or transfer, of power. In a time of troubles where no one rules, authority emerges (God raises it up) when the capacity to direct others is conjoined with the disposition to govern others for the common good. It would be unreasonable to wait on authorization from those one can govern when authorization would not be forthcoming and when waiting for it would neglect the common good.

The stress on consent turns on the false idea that without some voluntary act of will on our part no obligation to obey another arises. Voluntary acts (promises, agreements) often create obligations, but we are all subject to duties that we do not choose, which we should observe. The call to repent is intelligible because we have breached such duties. The voluntarist mistake is grounded in changing ideas about the character of God, which bear on the extent to which He is radically free to will as He pleases, such that His

[23] Cf. Marsilius of Padua, "Defensor Pacis (1324)" in O'Donovan and O'Donovan (eds), *From Irenaeus to Grotius*, 427, 432.
[24] Finnis, NLNR, 247–248.

sovereignty consists in unbounded freedom, or whether He is instead bound by His nature, acting on reasons that constitute His character.[25] The rise of the former view informs early modern political theory, marking out a dubious idea of what it is to be a free person and a sovereign polity.[26] God is not a capricious ruler; He is unchanging and good. The ruler, like the ruled, is subject to God and to the law written on his and their hearts, which is to say to the moral principles right reason uncovers. It would be wrong to resist the authority of another who has the capacity to rule well, and is exercising that capacity for the common good, simply because one has not consented. Rather, one should ask whether one *should* consent, which would turn precisely on whether the other person is willing and able to govern.

Self-government is an answer to the question of who should govern. But the answer takes for granted the need for government and does not obscure the truth that whoever can govern should govern. Still, often there will be more than one person or body that asserts a capacity to govern, and those who are to be ruled have a responsibility to reason about which of them should govern. More to the point, the willingness by ordinary persons to support some putative ruler may constitute (or buttress) his or its capacity to rule. Thus, in many cases, the ruled have a share in determining the location of authority, even in the time of troubles, by virtue of the significance of who they are willing to support. Like the responsibility to govern, this is a responsibility that the ruled must exercise, giving (or withholding) their support in ways that make it possible for the community to be ruled for the good of all. Again, there can be and is justified authority that does not rest on the consent of the governed. But in a well-ordered community, the governed *will* consent and this (limited but real) unity of ruler and ruled makes possible government that is less coercive and more capable than would otherwise be the case. The responsible ruler will secure the common good and will cultivate the consent of the governed, inviting them to recognize his authority and wielding that authority in ways that keep the peace. Any good king should aspire to rule over a free people, whose good he protects and whose laws he keeps.

It is good for the question of who rules to be settled by authority, ruling out unbounded contestation over which person or group is capable of governing, contestation that risks peace. Amongst the first duties of a new

[25] JB Elshtain, *Sovereignty: God, State and Self* (Basic Books 2008); Harrison, in this volume.
[26] R Ekins, "How to Be a Free People" (2013) American Journal of Jurisprudence 163, 180.

ruler—the one who in the time of troubles is raised up with the capacity to direct others—is to enact laws that settle authoritatively who is to exercise authority in the kingdom on his demise and/or who in the kingdom is to have a share in authority during his reign, viz. who are his ministers or servants and on what terms they act. The Christian king, conscious of his duty to God and his people, should aim to choose laws of succession and public office that will make intelligent provision for peaceful, stable government over time. This will require the king, with the advice of others, to judge the capacities of others in his kingdom to participate effectively in government, to imagine future possibilities, good and bad, and to choose a framework for government that will be robust and reasonable. The Christian king should take a sober *and* charitable view of those he rules, who, like him, are made in the image of God, fallen sinners for whom Christ died, who are capable of repentance and self-direction, and are called to live as saints and, if need be, martyrs. Those he rules are thus moral agents and in the final sense his equals. Whether and how far to share government with them may turn on particular judgments about their capacities, here and now or in the near future, to govern well, considerations also relevant to who should govern when authority is absent. Recognizing that those he rules are his brothers and sisters in Christ need not entail abdication of government in their favor, for this might be a betrayal of his responsibility for their good. However, this insight should be a constant spur to avoid pride or tyranny and a standing reason to encourage others to live well, to take responsibility for their lives and for one another, in subsidiary groups and, to the extent possible consistent with the common good, in government.

The Christian tradition grounds authority on capacity to secure the common good rather than on consent of the governed.[27] Whether ordinary people are in fact willing to support a putative ruler may settle whether the ruler has, or continues to have, authority. If at all possible, the location of authority should be settled by law, law which the lawmaker should frame in light of the nature of persons and the prospects for stable, good government over time. While kings may be lawfully resisted and even deposed, they may also truly exercise authority. The nature of kingship and the way in which justified royal rule may lead to self-government are my next subject.

[27] See for Catholic Encyclicals: Pope John XXIII, *Pacem et Terris: On Establishing Universal Peace in Truth, Justice, Charity, and Liberty* (The Vatican, 11 April 1963) [54] and Pope Paul VI, *Gaudium et Spes: Pastoral Constitution on the Church in the Modern World* (The Vatican, 7 December 1965) [74].

From Royal Authority to Representative Democracy

Kingship has always loomed large in the Christian political imagination. This has been reflected at times in the internal organization of the Church, with the Papacy developing into a sovereign office. There are good reasons for kingship, and in many times and places it has been reasonable for Christians and others to build up royal authority, to serve the king loyally, and to oppose rebellion. The reasons are not mysterious: the common good calls for robust and decisive agency to defend the realm, to give justice, to choose and uphold good laws. The unity and coherence that one person—a single agent—may provide is in principle an apt means to this end. The classical preference for monarchy, for rule by one person, is intelligible.[28] However, there are also very good reasons for authority to be shared widely, for mixed government in which the advantages of monarchy are leavened with the advantages of aristocracy and democracy. This section traces the reasons for sharing authority and the historical development of fully representative institutions.

The responsibility of the king is to secure the common good. This requires the king to maintain and to develop the capacity effectively to coordinate others, which will turn in part on whether his subjects—especially his mighty subjects—continue to recognize his authority. The king may secure, or shore up, this recognition partly by giving the ruled assurances as to how his authority will be exercised, by concluding charters (like the covenant between God and His people) that extend certain rights and protections against the king or his servants. The unity of the kingdom consists in the people's shared willingness to live together and to recognize common authority in general and of the king in particular. The king represents the kingdom, personifying and leading it in common action, with loyal subjects jointly committed to his rule. Rule by a king who is one's own, who represents the kingdom, has sworn and accepted oaths of fealty,[29] and recognizes his responsibility for the common good—this is not foreign or tyrannical rule, and to the extent that it is willingly accepted this is a way in which we rule ourselves. Nonetheless, this is self-government only in an attenuated sense, for, to the extent that the king is free to reason and choose alone, he rules over the people rather than providing a way for his subjects to share in government.[30]

[28] Finnis, *Aquinas*, 261–262.
[29] N Aroney, "The Rule of Law, Religious Authority, and Oaths of Office" (2018) 6 Journal of Law, Religion and State 195.
[30] O'Donovan, *Ways of Judgment*, 158, and Ekins "How to Be a Free People," 172, 174.

The point of building up royal authority is to enable the common good to be secured, in part by enabling the laws of the community to be made and changed directly in response to reasons. When kings make laws that conform to the rule of law, they address their subjects as persons capable of responding to reason. Their subjects have a modest share in lawmaking insofar as they adopt the lawmaking decision of the king as if it were their own. They share in lawmaking more robustly where kingship is "political" rather than "regal," to use Aquinas's distinction,[31] which means that royal authority is exercised subject to laws that the king alone cannot change without the agreement of the people. The king who acts in violation of such laws may rightly be resisted, for he does not thereby exercise authority. The same is true even when the king has plenary lawmaking power if or when he acts (or his servants act) in ways that his own law forbids. The king's freedom to change the law does not license lawless rule, which his loyal subjects may rightly resist.[32]

There are good reasons to prefer political to regal kingship and to establish or make royal authority subject to laws that kings cannot change alone. Fortescue, writing in the midst of the political turmoil of the fourteenth century, defended political kingship partly on the grounds that the freedom of a king to act lawlessly or to despoil his people was not a freedom worth having.[33] Any good king will aim to rule with the willing cooperation of his subjects, both to keep the peace and to make it possible for him more effectively to coordinate their action and to be God's servant for their good. This follows from the more general principle Aquinas articulates in saying that the first point "to be observed concerning the right ordering of rulers in a state or nation . . . is that all should take some share in the government: for this form of constitution ensures peace among the people, commends itself to all, and is most enduring."[34] This is a foundational principle for thinking about how authority should be located within a political community. A constitution that gives all persons some share in government "ensures peace" and "is most enduring" because it joins us together as willing participants in the common project of government for our common good. This makes it less likely that government will be undertaken for the private good, or without attention to the complexity of the common good of those for whom it should

[31] Finnis, *Aquinas*, 258–259.
[32] Ibid, 259–260; Witte, in this volume.
[33] J Fortescue, *In Praise of the Laws of England* (CUP 1997).
[34] Aquinas, ST, I-II q 105, a 1.

be exercised. Sharing authority with all recognizes the equality of all persons and their capacity to repent, to take responsibility for their lives, and to participate intelligently in public life. Such a constitution "commends itself to all" because it is fair and because sharing government amongst many hands is likely to make the conditions and concerns of the ruled salient to those who rule, which may prevent injustice and encourage government that is attentive to—solicitous of—the good of the people.

It follows that kings should be disposed to share authority with their subjects, provided that this will not undermine the prospects of the kingdom being ruled justly and effectively. Kings had good reason to summon a council of great men with whom they act in relation to high policy and a parliament consisting of leading men of the realm and humbler men chosen by or drawn from the many places and groups that make up the realm. The point of calling a parliament was to secure the realm's willing cooperation in consent to taxation and to other far-reaching decisions, especially to change the law. The technique worked by extending to those summoned (and those whom they represented and thus made present in the assembly) a share in the decision about what is to be done, honoring them as persons capable of reasonable choice, of taking up responsibility for a shared good. A kingdom of willing subjects, secure from lawless rule and free to participate in reasoning and decision-making about matters that touch on all, was and is a strong kingdom, capable of acting decisively in common defense and of living peacefully in harmony together.

There is more than one just constitution, and Aquinas's general principle does not settle the extent to which the people should share in government. This will often be a question of fine judgment. However, it is worth noting Aquinas's prescription for mixed government.[35] Aquinas stresses the importance of the overarching rule of a single person but recognizes also the importance of many others exercising authority. The many have a share in government insofar as all are eligible to govern, the rules are chosen by all, and rulers are chosen from and by the people. Such a scheme provides the unified, coherent agency that is necessary for government, recognizes the complexity of government and the need for multiple offices, and affirms the importance of entitlement to hold office being open to and controlled by all. It is a scheme for capable government disciplined by its internal constitution and by the active roles that it envisages for the people.

[35] Aquinas, ST, I-II, q 105 a 1c.

One sees a scheme of this kind developing over the centuries in England—representative institutions arise by virtue of the exercise of royal authority but in the end become the institutions which exercise that authority. The resulting constitution provides for mixed government: the executive is unified and capable, providing leadership in, but at the same time radically dependent on, an assembly that represents the whole community. The political authorities are structured to enable good government in a way that shares authority with all citizens. The scheme is not a second-best form of direct democracy—the point is not to transmit antecedent popular political preferences into policy. Rather, the scheme makes provision for public deliberation and decision to settle who rules, by way of election and parliamentary dynamics, and to frame how they rule, by making government dependent on Parliament and Parliament on the people. Thus, the people govern themselves by way of their representative institutions, exercising authority directly as voters and represented in the deliberations of the assembly and the actions of government. This complex joint action, in which the people participate and are represented, is self-government.

Royal authority casts a long shadow over our governing arrangements. Constitutionalism begins with the idea of the good king, so important in Jewish and Christian thinking, and strives to make institutional provision for his government. The king's subjection to God, his equality with his subjects, and the exemplars of kingship in the scriptures all support political kingship and the sharing of government with the governed when possible. The rise of representative institutions, especially an assembly, helps make for self-government, which is better government, more attentive to the good of those who are governed, less prone to descent into tyranny, and more stable.

"A Kingdom Divided Against Itself Cannot Stand"

Self-government is complex group action. It involves citizens jointly intending to be governed by way of their representative institutions, participating in public deliberation and decision-making and accepting that those institutions have authority to act on their behalf. The promise of representative institutions is that they fairly and intelligently resolve questions about how we should be governed, making it possible for us to participate in our government, without sacrificing the coherent, effective action that government requires. This promise is only likely to be realized in political communities in which citizens share a stable joint intention to be governed by one another.

Many scholars stress the relationship between democracy and uncertainty. For Adam Przeworski, democracy "institutionalizes uncertainty" over policy outcomes.[36] For Robert Dahl, "the democratic process is a gamble on the possibilities that a people, in acting autonomously, will learn how to act rightly."[37] Relatedly, Jeremy Waldron emphasizes the centrality of disagreement to politics, with the point of an elected assembly being to provide a fair means to settle those disagreements.[38] There is much truth in this analysis. Representative democracies are open to radical policy changes; elections and parliamentary votes matter; disagreement is important and widespread. But the analysis is incomplete without adding that in well-ordered political communities disagreement and uncertainty are nested within a framework of trust and sympathy between citizens who jointly intend their common good but disagree about how best to pursue it. In other words, it is a fundamental precondition of self-government over time that citizens are confident that other citizens, and their representatives, share a common good with them. Otherwise, the peaceful succession of rulers will not be one moment in a continuous process of self-government, where we are free in the future to contest our present defeat, but a mortal threat. In the latter frame, political opponents would not be fellow citizens with whom one disagrees but enemies, in which case commitment to the discipline of self-government will break down.

For self-government to endure, or even to be a gamble worth taking, there must be "an underlying mutuality of trust that all concerned have the same particular commonwealth in mind."[39] This requires all those with a share in government, all citizens, to recognize that they share a common good and to intend to act jointly to secure it.[40] Citizens must trust one another, not unconditionally for of course vigilance is warranted, but sufficiently to make it rational to share public life together. For self-government to work, citizens must love one another, recognizing others as neighbors with whom they

[36] *Democracy and the Market* (CUP 1991) 10–14.

[37] *Democracy and Its Critics* (Yale University Press 1989) 192.

[38] *Law and Disagreement* (OUP 1999).

[39] J Finnis, "Reflections and Responses" in R George and J Keown (eds), *Reason, Morality and Law* (OUP 2013) 459, 563.

[40] Ekins, "How to Be a Free People," 170; see also O'Donovan, *Ways of Judgment*, 150; compare Augustine, *City of God*, Book 19.24 ("a people is an assemblage of reasonable beings bound together by a common agreement as to the objects of their love").

share a predicament and an opportunity. They must recognize one another as members of a particular community, with a distinct common good for which they alone are responsible. The point is not that outsiders are to be disdained, let alone injured or exploited, but that particular obligations are owed to those with whom one lives and with whom one shares much. The same analysis holds for the Church, for we are called to love one another as Christ loves us, to share much with our brothers and sisters, in a way that illustrates our calling to follow Him. Love of country, sharing of language, history, and custom, is often a condition for good government.

Notwithstanding our equality in Christ, there is a diversity of callings and positions within the Church.[41] The same holds for the body politic: the distinction between rulers and ruled is important even if self-government is in part the exercise of sharing government with all who are ruled. Political elites lead political life, which is unavoidable and unobjectionable provided they are drawn from and engage constantly with the masses and provided anyone is eligible to run for office. For elite leadership to enable self-government, rather than to render it hollow, the masses must be able to trust, and/or to ensure, that elites are concerned for the same commonwealth. The sharp divergence in material interest between elites, say landed aristocracy or industrial magnates, and masses, say peasants or workers, has of course often been a source of conflict. Part of the promise of self-government is that it forces the powerful to attend to those who are otherwise weak, to listen to the condition of those they would otherwise ignore, to give an account for decisions that concern them, and to abandon unjust privileges. Helping the poor and the lowly share in government will often be part of how Christians respond to Christ's challenge concerning how we treat the least amongst us.

The project of self-government is consistent with fierce disagreement but not with certain kinds of social division. The engine of democratic politics is competition between political parties united around particular principles,[42] often anchored in the material interest of particular classes but with an agenda to govern in the interests of the country at large. The political party that secures a majority in the democratic assembly should attempt to govern, but other political parties present in the assembly have a duty and a liberty to oppose the majority.[43] It is possible for elites to ossify into a distinct governing

[41] 1 Corinthians 12:12–31.

[42] E Burke, *Thoughts on the Cause of the Present Discontents* (1770).

[43] G Webber, "Loyal Opposition and the Political Constitution" (2017) 37 Oxford Journal of Legal Studies 357.

class, with little interest in or sympathy for those they govern. Here, power is exercised over the masses whose involvement in politics is theatrical rather than real, with little attempt to involve them in joint action by way of party or parliamentary initiative. A governing class that viewed its primary political allegiance as located elsewhere, beyond the country in question, would be particularly dangerous. This might arise from a disinterested utilitarianism, in which the division between citizen and noncitizen is taken to be arbitrary. Or it might involve a commitment to institutions of supranational rule rather than of national government.

If the foundation for self-government is, as I suggest, mutuality of trust, then the distinction between citizen and noncitizen is critical. The primary object of state action is the common good of its citizens. This is not to say that states should pursue this at any costs or by any means, still less that they should be indifferent to the consequences their actions have for noncitizens. But unless citizens stand to government in a special relationship, as bearers of common duties, entitled to common benefits, sympathy, fellow feeling, and trust between citizens will dry up.[44] The universal reach of the Gospels has sometimes encouraged Christians to assume a corresponding political cosmopolitanism, which condemns differential treatment of citizen and noncitizen, especially when the latter is desperate or impoverished, a vulnerable migrant or asylum seeker. This is a mistake. Of course citizen and noncitizen alike are made in the image of God, and all should be citizens of some political community that protects them. But just as Christians have special responsibilities to their brothers and sisters in Christ, and children to their parents, and parents to their children, so too there is reason to preserve and deepen the connections between citizens.[45] The nation (people) is a natural society, as is the family, and warrants support.[46] The unity of the people is the precondition for effective government, for self-government, and for justice between peoples.

[44] R Ekins, "The State's Right to Exclude Asylum-Seekers and (Some) Refugees" in D Miller et al (eds) *The Philosophy of Refuge* (CUP 2019, 39).

[45] N Biggar, *Between Kin and Cosmopolis* (James Clarke 2014).

[46] Pope John Paul II, *Memory & Identity* (Weidenfeld & Nicolson 2005) 77–78.

Binding the Demos

The rise of fully representative institutions in Christian states is no accident, but rather a working out of the conjunction of Judeo-Christian ideas of kingship and equality, elaborated by Aquinas and others in conversation with the classical Greek focus on mixed government. However, one might think, and some do, that self-government is not something to treasure.[47] Rather, it is a temptation to resist, not only because the Christian is to reject the self, but because a people convinced of its right to rule would be a terrible ruler—powerful, unchecked, capricious, and arbitrary. It would unleash "the sovereignty of the mob," to adopt Tracey Rowland's resonant phrase.[48] The sin of pride means that any agent, collective or individual, that prioritizes self is doomed to fall. I agree that it is true and important that one can give political power too much honor, to mistake it for an object of eternal significance, and to overlook the limits that rightly govern it.[49] Self-government might introduce the particular risk that we effectively worship ourselves, which might manifest itself in stark assertions about our freedom as a people to do as we please simply because this is our will. That is, a free people might assert absolute sovereignty.[50] This would be wrong for, like any other ruler, the people may misuse its authority and, like every person, democratic citizens (and the citizenry at large) are subject to the will of God and to the principles of morality. However, the assertion of a people's right to rule itself need not, and very often does not, involve rejection of right and wrong. Rather, the assertion is freedom from foreign rule or from rule by kings or oligarchs or even well-meaning civil servants. Instead, under God, we alone are jointly responsible for deliberating about how we should live. The assertion may be too simple if it ignores the importance of representative institutions, but those institutions stake their moral claim in their capacity to unite the governed in reason and choice—they are the vanguard of a free people.

It is true that a self-governing people should act justly. It does not follow that justice requires legal, justiciable restraints on the lawmaking authority of its representative institutions.[51] The virtue of bills of rights and

[47] Oliver O'Donovan states baldly that "Augustine thought that no community could have an interest in whether it was self-governed or ruled by others," *Ways of Judgment*, 212, quoting *City of God*, Book 5.17.

[48] Rowland, in this volume.

[49] Farrow, in this volume.

[50] Harrison, in this volume.

[51] Julian Rivers notes the contingency of such restraints in his chapter in this volume.

international rights conventions is that they recognize that there are indeed limits on public authority. However, these legal measures are fraught with danger. If human rights laws are chosen by a free people by way of their political institutions, and are clearly and correctly specified in this authoritative choice, then they may help secure justice and courts may uphold them against subsequent political action consistently with self-government.[52] But this is not how modern human rights law works. Rather, what is affirmed in positive law is an underspecified proposition or propositions, which courts are invited and required to develop by way of further lawmaking choices. This mode of constitution making involves an open-ended transfer of power to the judges, who may or may not specify rights in morally upright ways. How rights should be understood, where the limits on authority truly lie, is a matter of political controversy, the answer to which cannot be assumed to be obvious to courts and the resolution of which ought to fall to those representative institutions that are structured to choose intelligently and openly on citizens' behalf.

The legislative assembly of a free people should not assume that it may do as it pleases. That the law confers on the assembly plenary authority, as in the United Kingdom, does not entail or incline towards prideful self-assertion. Legislators may not recognize the natural law as such but, like other citizens, they reason directly about justice, decency, and the requirements of the common good. Natural law requires positive law, not least to uphold and specify human rights; it does not require judicial review or human rights law. The decisive question, for a particular community in its particular circumstances, is whether affirming a bill of rights and authorizing a court to superintend the political authorities will tend to secure justice or whether it will distort politics and frustrate reasoned self-government. In the conditions of many modern Western states, human rights adjudication will often tend to compromise justice, to prevent a people from ruling itself well. For, modern human rights law is unmoored from natural law foundations in absolute human rights: it is a body of law that commonly invites skepticism about the good, privileges autonomy, and invites judges to choose freely in each successive case.[53] The willingness of lawyers and scholars at times to talk about human rights law as a substitute (secular) religion is revealing.

[52] Ekins, "How to Be a Free People" 174, 176.

[53] R Ekins, "Human Rights and the Separation of Powers" (2015) 34 University of Queensland Law Journal 217.

Notwithstanding its historical connection to the truth that justice limits authority, human rights law is not an escape from the need for responsible human choice, not a guarantee of justice, but rather another institutional scheme, one that trades on a failure of charity towards other citizens and licenses a relatively lawless, incompetent mode of authority, exercised by a narrow caste. This flouts the disciplines of responsible lawmaking painstakingly built up over centuries.

Fear of self-government fuels enthusiasm for human rights law. It also explains much enthusiasm for supranational institutions. The two come together of course in such regimes as the European Convention on Human Rights, which commits member states to secure a set of rights and establishes a court to adjudicate disputes about their application. But the phenomenon stretches more broadly, with many Western states increasingly entangled in supranational institutions, which exercise authority over states. European integration is the most obvious and important example. This is quite different to international law more generally. It is true and important that self-governing states are governed by law in their interactions, whether by treaty or custom. The origins of international law lie in Christian thinkers—Grotius, Vitoria, Vattel, and others—thinking through the principles that should govern fellowship amongst equal political communities. On the contrary, supranational rule subjects these communities to institutions that they jointly found but which then have an agenda and a capacity of their own, the point of which is to exercise rule in some way detached from the reasoning and choice of those communities. This distance from the demos is part of the appeal. The institutions are not wholly severed from states, of course, but the incapacity of any state to hold them to account is fundamental: they are intended to hold states to account. This arrangement is sometimes defended, in the European context, either as sui generis or as the seeds of federation. What it is, alas, is simply a partial state, a set of institutions with the capacity to take some action, and especially to frustrate other states from acting, but lacking full capacity to rule effectively and lacking especially any relationship to a people they might represent.

That Christians are often enthusiasts for supranational institutions is in one way unsurprising.[54] It seems to chime with the early cosmopolitanism of the Church and with the universalism of the Gospels. But love for neighbor and the salvation of the world requires or justifies neither indifference to

[54] J Maritain, *Man and the State* (Catholic University of America Press 1951) 50–51.

peoples nor premature assertion of political forms that appear to resonate with the truth that Christ is king of all and yet which cannot rule well. The rise of supranational institutions bears more than a passing resemblance to restoration of empire, to imposition of external restraint on peoples who are judged unable to rule themselves. This may not always be wrong, but it is scarcely ideal and is certainly wrong to the extent that it compromises government for the common good. The subjection of otherwise free peoples to supranational institutions, such as those of the European Union (EU), has this very effect precisely because government that is detached from those it governs is less likely to be competent, to be accepted by those it rules, and to be subject to processes that discipline it.[55] The citizens of particular EU member states have little reason to be confident that EU institutions have their common good in view.[56] They lack freedom effectively to participate fully in their own government, which undercuts the common feeling and mutual sympathy on which the project of government is grounded. It will not end well. States should often found and participate in international institutions but should not surrender their capacity to rule to bodies that are incapable of discharging the responsibility to rule, responsibility which this chapter has argued generally requires uniting a people in deliberation and action, that is, in self-government.

Conclusion

The Christian tradition's understanding of self-government begins with a model of kingship according to law, in which the king represents the people and is subject to God and reason. The model is extended by recognizing the importance of sharing authority with the ruled, which helps ground good government and recognizes our fundamental equality as children of God, fallen but called to repent. There is no natural right to rule, but nothing fundamental about consent of the governed either. Who can rule should rule—God raises them up and makes them responsible for the common good. In settling the location of authority, one should aim for mixed government in which the people share in government, most notably by way of representative assemblies. The move from political kingship to parliamentary (or

[55] Cf. Milbank, in this volume.
[56] I Kraztev, *After Europe* (UPenn Press 2017).

presidential) government is a rational move, which minimizes tyranny, improves competence, and is fair. It honors the standing of the governed, elevating their importance and making their interests count. It is what we owe to the least amongst us, all of whom are also made in the image of God. We cannot govern ourselves, or be governed well, without forming a people, and our political institutions should enable us to govern ourselves peacefully despite disagreement. Every form of government may do injustice, and self-government is not a good to pursue at all costs. The people are not free to do as they please, and each of us has rights against others. Still, the importance of self-government does provide reasons for a free people to be slow to introduce or subject itself to positive legal limitations on its power to rule itself, whether those limitations arise from human rights law or supranational institutions.

12

Separation of Powers

The Biblical Foundations of the Separation of Powers and the Catalytic Judicial Role

Carlos Bernal[1]

Introduction

This chapter argues that the Bible provides a justification for the separation of powers and, in particular, for a conception according to which, judges should be empowered with a catalytic role. It claims that, following the scriptures, prophets play a catalytic role in incentivizing political authorities to behave in a virtuous manner in protecting the rights and interests of the people. An appropriate conception of the separation of powers in a constitutional democracy requires reigniting that role. Judges are in the best position to play it. The judiciary should prompt the other branches to act according to their mission but not to supplant them.

This claim has theoretical and practical significance. From the theoretical perspective, it contributes to reflections on best strategies of institutional design and political practices of separation of powers, political accountability, and guarantee of rights in constitutional democracies. From the practical perspective, it encourages judges to find a middle ground between extreme deference to political authorities and judicial supremacy. This middle ground is a role of catalyzing law and policymaking activity.

To accomplish the outlined goal, this chapter will proceed as follows. The second section will account for the concept of separation of powers and spell out some significant conceptions. In particular, it will contrast three conceptions: a strict conception, a conception based on judicial supremacy, and a conception in which judges both ensure that political authorities

[1] Professor at the University of Dayton School of Law. I thank Nicholas Aroney and Maria Viana for inspiring me with valuable ideas in the process of drafting this chapter.

Carlos Bernal, *Separation of Powers: The Biblical Foundations of the Separation of Powers and the Catalytic Judicial Role* in *Christianity and Constitutionalism*. Edited by: Nicholas Aroney and Ian Leigh, Oxford University Press. © Oxford University Press 2022. DOI: 10.1093/oso/9780197587256.003.0012

exercise power within their constitutional limits and play a catalytic role. The third and fourth sections will show how the biblical account on prophets provides grounds for the latter conception of the separation of powers. The fifth and sixth sections will highlight the practical and theoretical relevance of that conception, in particular, concerning two aspects of contemporary comparative constitutionalism debate: the adjudication of economic and social rights, and the limitations on the exercise of the power to amend the constitution. These illustrations could be transplanted, mutatis mutandis, to other fields, such as the limitations to the rise of the executive action. The last section will state the conclusions.

The Separation of Powers: Concept and Conceptions

The separation of powers is an essential element of constitutionalism. Constitutionalism is a doctrine at whose core there are two claims: one conceptual and one normative. They relate to the idea of limiting the exercise of political power through law with the aim of protecting rights and achieving the common good.[2] The conceptual claim outlines a form of government created, structured, and limited by a set of legal norms entrenched or grounded in a constitution. The normative claim states that the exercise of political power should be limited by those legal norms, and that government should comply with those limitations.[3]

The separation of powers is a necessary strategy for enforcing legal limitations on the exercise of political power. This necessity is practical. There cannot be an institutional entrenchment of constitutionalism without a separation of powers. The separation of powers enables the capacity of parliament to hold the government politically to account, and the capacity of the judiciary to render the political authorities legally responsible for overstepping the boundaries of their constitutional powers or for not fulfilling their duties. This is why, according to Article 16 of the French Declaration of the Rights of Man and of the Citizen, a society in which there is no separation of

[2] This is a negative conception of constitutionalism. There are alternative (positive) views according to which, the separation of powers implies that each branch of government should contribute, in its distinctive way, to the common good. On a positive view, see Nick Barber, *The Principles of Constitutionalism* (Oxford University Press 2018). Chapter 3 introduces an interpretation of the separation of powers from Barber's positive account of constitutionalism.

[3] Wil Waluchow, "Constitutionalism" in Edward N Zalta (ed), *The Stanford Encyclopedia of Philosophy* (Spring 2018 edn).

powers has no constitution at all.[4] A system that institutionalizes the rule of law and the protection of rights but not the separation of powers is an ethical but not a constitutional order.

In recent years there has been theoretical and comparative debate about which conception of the separation of power best suits democratic constitutionalism. An essential element of the separation of powers is a triple division of competences within the state: functional, institutional, and personal. The functional division amounts to the individuation and distinction of the competences to make, execute, and adjudicate law.[5] The institutional division involves the empowerment of three different institutions with these competences: parliament, the government, and the judiciary. Finally, the personal division requires that different individuals hold office in each of those state institutions.

There are various conceptions of the separation of powers. A strict conception would insist that each branch of government should be restricted to an independent exercise of its characteristic function: only the parliament can make law, only the government can execute law, and only the judiciary can adjudicate law.[6] There are less stringent conceptions, however. In a recent study, David Bilchitz and David Landau observe that some constitutions "tend to . . . give relatively flexible instructions to political institutions,"[7] and that throughout the world there has been "an increase in the executive power"[8] and "a decrease in legislative legitimacy and importance."[9] In this context, they point out, courts are playing a more "aggressive role,"[10] "styling themselves as a check on the executive power and a valid option for filling democratic deficits."[11] This perspective would overcome the failure of the strict conception of the separation of powers in repairing those deficits and the lack of sufficient guarantee of rights.

It is possible to connect some weaker conceptions of the separation of powers to a tendency toward judicial supremacy in constitutional

[4] See Article 16 of the French Declaration of the Rights of Man and of the Citizen: a "society in which the observance of the law is not assured, nor the separation of powers defined, has no constitution at all."

[5] See Aristotle, *Politics*, Book IV, ch 14.

[6] See Montesquieu, *The Spirit of the Laws*, Book XI.

[7] See David Bilchitz and David Landau, "Introduction: The Evolution of the Separation of Powers in the Global South and Global North" in David Bilchitz and David Landau (eds), *The Evolution of the Separation of Powers between the Global North and the Global South* (Elgar 2018) 3.

[8] Ibid, 4.

[9] Ibid.

[10] Ibid.

[11] Ibid.

law.[12] Judicial supremacy involves the view that judges can and should have constitutional power to override the decisions made by the other branches of government.[13] This conception allocates a function to the judges that goes far beyond the task of ensuring that political authorities abide by their constitutional limits. Overriding could even imply that judges substitute the legislature's or executive's decision on what should be done.

Nevertheless, the conception of the separation of powers, which encompasses judicial supremacy, has elicited strong objections. For instance, according to Jeremy Waldron, judicial supremacy "disenfranchises ordinary citizens and brushes aside cherished principles of representation and political equality in the final resolution of issues about rights."[14] Moreover, Mark Tushnet has argued that judicial supremacy implies "a substantial restriction on the power of the people to govern themselves."[15] This is the case, in particular, in constitutional interpretation and implementation. When there are various competing and reasonable interpretations as to the meaning of constitutional provisions, "why should the Court's reasonable interpretation prevail over the legislature's (also) reasonable one?"[16] The courts have been considered to be, on this view, an unjustly empowered elite and their supremacy an undesired aristocratic element in the democratic system.[17] If the constitution is made by the people, then the people, through their elected representatives, and not the judges should have supremacy in interpreting the constitution and implementing it. The interpretations and decisions of the people and their representatives should be ultimate and be capable of trumping all other interpretations of the constitutional text.

John Locke's conception of the separation of powers resonates in these arguments, particularly his claim that the legislative power is supreme. According to that claim, the legislature should have ultimate authority over "how the force of the commonwealth shall be employed."[18] Moreover, Locke

[12] See Nuno Garoupa, "Comparing Judicial Activism—Can We Say that the US Supreme Court Is More Activist Than the German Constitutional Court" (2016) 72(4) Revista Portuguesa de Filosofia 1089–1105; James P Wenzel, Shaun Bowler, and David J Lanoue, "Legislating from the State Bench: A Comparative Analysis of Judicial Activism" (1997) 25(3) American Politics Research 363–379.

[13] See Phyllis M Schlafty, *The Supremacist: The Tyranny of Judges and How to Stop It* (Spence 2004).

[14] See Jeremy Waldron, "The Core of the Case against Judicial Review" (2006) 115 Yale Law Journal 1353.

[15] Mark Tushnet, *Weak Courts Strong Rights: Judicial Review and Social Welfare Rights in Comparative Constitutional Law* (Princeton University Press 2009) x–xi.

[16] Ibid, 21.

[17] Larry Kramer, *The People Themselves: Popular Constitutionalism and Judicial Review* (Oxford University Press 2004) 7.

[18] John Locke, *Two Treatises of Government* (P Laslett ed, Cambridge University Press 1988) 2.143.

insisted on the supremacy of the legislative over the executive power with the argument that "what can give laws to another, must needs be superior to him."[19] In this respect, Locke did not theorize the role of a judiciary but conceived it to be an aspect of the executive power to interpret the laws and apply them to specific cases, supported by the use of force where necessary.[20]

Despite objections such as these, several factors have generated the increase in judicial supremacy worldwide. Among them is the fact that constitutions have become more detailed in their specifications and more far reaching in their requirements, entrenching generous and expansive catalogs of constitutional rights directly enforceable via judicial review.[21] In these circumstances the courts are enforcing precise constitutional directives and determining constitutional provisions by means of abstract and concrete procedures of constitutional review.

Furthermore, relevant scholars have defended judicial supremacy for these reasons. For instance, according to Schauer, a constitution is "a series of rules that impose second-order constraints on the first-order policy preferences of the people and of their elective representative and executive officials."[22] These second-order constraints serve the long-term and deeper values of the people. Within this framework, judicial supremacy is a justified external enforcement of second-order constraints whereby it aims to protect the long-term interests of the people from their own short-term desires.[23] The judicial interpretation of the second-order constraints should prevail over the interpretation by the people's representatives in parliament, for these are cases of a conflict between long-term values and short-term desires. The people, in such situations, are experiencing a conflict of interest. They do not have enough "mental separation" to be able to consider the issues before them with fairness and impartiality while having regard to their long-term principled commitments.[24]

19 Ibid, 2.2150.

20 Ibid, 2.88–89.

21 Mila Versteeg and Emily Zackin, "Constitutions Unentrenched: Towards an Alternative Theory of Constitutional Design" (2016) 110 American Political Science Review 657.

22 Frederick Schauer, "Judicial Review and the Modest Constitution" (2004) (92)4 California Law Review 1045.

23 Ibid, 1057.

24 Ibid.

The Establishment of an Independent Judiciary in the Bible

Within the framework of this debate on the separation of powers, there are two relevant questions concerning the project of singling out the links between Christianity and constitutionalism. The first is whether the Bible provides a normative grounding for the principle of the separation of powers. The second is whether the Bible supports a particular conception of it and, if so, whether it supports a strict view, a conception encompassing judicial supremacy, or a third way. As a third way I will consider here a perspective that allocates to judges both the role of ensuring compliance with constitutional limitations and a catalytic role.

Regarding the first question, the Bible grounds the principle of separation of powers as an essential element of the state. In Deuteronomy, God commanded Moses to establish an independent judiciary, just as the people of Israel were about to take possession of the promised land. Establishing an independent judiciary was a solution to the practical problem of deciding disputes among a vastly increased number of persons.[25] Moses therefore appointed "wise and respected men"[26] and empowered them with the function to hear the disputes between the people and to judge their cases with fairness and impartiality.[27] Moses reserved for himself the competence to decide hard cases.[28]

Exodus 18, in recounting the same phenomenon, offers a reason for the solution. Jethro, Moses's father-in-law, saw Moses serving as judge for the people "from morning till evening."[29] Considered this work to be too heavy for Moses,[30] he recommended that Moses

> select capable men from all the people—men who fear God, trustworthy men who hate dishonest gain—and appoint them as officials over thousands, hundreds, fifties and tens. Have them serve as judges for the people at all times but have them bring every difficult case to you; the simple cases they can decide themselves. That will make your load lighter, because

[25] See Deuteronomy 1:9–13.
[26] See Deuteronomy 1:15.
[27] See Deuteronomy 1:16–17.
[28] Ibid.
[29] See Exodus 18:13.
[30] See Exodus 18:17–18.

> they will share it with you. If you do this and God so commands, you will be able to stand the strain, and all these people will go home satisfied.[31]

According to the scriptures, Moses did everything Jethro said.[32] The establishment of an independent judiciary took place long before the institutionalization of the king. This might be interpreted as a sign of the pre-eminence of the former over the latter.[33]

In addition, the Old Testament outlines the limitation of political authority and the separation of powers as essential elements of government.[34] Deuteronomy 17 describes a separation between God, who is the lawgiver;[35] the courts, which were empowered with the function of adjudicating cases in accordance with the divine law;[36] and the king, selected according to God's criteria,[37] and whose rule was also limited by the law.[38]

Other scriptures reiterate and enhance the principle according to which the power of the king is limited in a normative and empirical way. On the one hand, Psalm 72 says that the king should exercise his power to secure justice.[39] In 1 Chronicles 28:8 David admonishes his successor, Solomon, to "be careful to follow all the commands of the Lord your God."[40] Furthermore, according to Deuteronomy, the king should not acquire "many horses for himself." This speaks of a limited power to use force, particularly for warfare. The New Testament reiterates the limited character of government, in particular, by describing authorities as servants of the community and the common good.[41] The authorities were also conceived as established by God to punish evil and praise the good.[42]

Concerning the separation of powers, Jonathan Burnside argues that Deuteronomy 16:18–18:22 sets out a system of separation of powers and checks and balances between four kinds of authorities: judges, the king, priests, and prophets.[43] He highlights that this was a way in which the people

[31] See Exodus 18:22–23.
[32] See Exodus 18:25–26.
[33] See Jonathan Burnside, "Torah and Constitutionalism," in this volume.
[34] See Li-ann Thio, "Higher Law/Rule of Law," in this volume.
[35] See Deuteronomy 17:3.
[36] See Deuteronomy 17:8.
[37] See Deuteronomy, 17:15.
[38] See Deuteronomy, 17:18–20.
[39] See Psalm 72:1–2.
[40] See 1 Chronicles 28:8.
[41] Richard Ekins, "Self-Government and the Kingdom of Heaven," in this volume.
[42] See Romans 13:1.
[43] Jonathan Burnside, "Torah and Constitutionalism," in this volume.

of Israel could distance themselves from the form of government they had endured in Egypt. In contrast to the authoritarian pharaoh, the Israelites established a system in which a single human authority could never concentrate all political power.[44] Moreover, as Ekins points out, the limitation of the power of the king is aligned with God's warning that "rule by a king may mean abuse of the people."[45]

The Function of Ensuring Compliance with Constitutional Limitations and the Catalytic Role of Prophets in the Bible

Concerning the second question, namely, what conception of the separation of powers does the Bible support, in addition to the judicial function, the Old Testament outlines how prophets played the role of ensuring compliance of political authorities with divine law limitations,[46] and a catalytic role. The prophets called the other branches back to their mission when they deviated. Analogically, nowadays the judiciary should prompt the other branches to act according to their mission but not to supplant them.

The prophets played an institutional role established by divine law for the governance of the people.[47] They played a catalytic role in admonishing the people of Israel, and especially their kings and judges, to behave in virtuous ways;[48] to respect God's commands; and to govern with justice. According to Maddox, prophets maintained "the government under surveillance, exposing corruptions and inefficiencies."[49] They opposed the misuse of political power.[50] Moreover, they "announce to kings and rulers that their course of action is the wrong one, and that they should pursue a different line."[51] They catalyzed political authorities to carry out "alternative policies."[52] The

[44] Ibid.

[45] Richard Ekins, "Self-Government and the Kingdom of Heaven," in this volume. In the scriptures, see 1 Samuel, 8:8–18.

[46] Algernon Sidney, *Discourses Concerning Government* (Booksellers of London and Westminster 1689) 1.

[47] See Dorothea H. Bertschmann, "'But Our Constitution Is in Heaven': New Testament Sketches on the People of God between Divine Law and Earthly Rulers," in this volume.

[48] On the relevance of virtue in Christian legal thought, see Nicholas Aroney, "Subsidiarity, Federalism and the Best Constitution: Thomas Aquinas on City, Province and Empire" (2007) 26 Law and Philosophy 161.

[49] Graham Maddox, "Hebrew Prophecy and the Foundations of Political Opposition" (2008) 21(1) Australian Religious Studies Review 71.

[50] Ibid, 72.

[51] Ibid, 75.

[52] Ibid.

prophets exercised independent power: they neither ruled nor aspired to become rulers[53] and relied only upon God's authority.[54]

The Bible provides interesting examples of the way prophets performed their role. Instances of that performance are how Samuel rendered Saul accountable for violating God's commands,[55] and how Nathan rendered David accountable for breaking God's laws.[56] Even more relevant is the way in which Nathan's judgment catalyzed David's repentance and God's forgiveness.[57]

Other examples also show how the Bible allocated to prophets to role to ensure compliance of the king to God's laws. God commanded Saul to "attack the Amalekites and totally destroy all that belongs to them." He added: "Do not spare them; put to death men and women, children and infants, cattle and sheep, camels and donkeys."[58] Nevertheless, Saul and the army "spared Agag and the best of the sheep and cattle, the fat calves and lambs—everything that was good."[59] When Samuel held Saul accountable, the king interpreted his actions to be compliant to God's command. He argued as follows: "The soldiers brought them from the Amalekites; they spared the best of the sheep and cattle to sacrifice to the Lord your God, but we totally destroyed the rest."[60] Despite that, Samuel accused Saul of disobeying God's command.[61] Saul replied as follows: "But I did obey the Lord," Saul said. "I went on the mission the Lord assigned me. I completely destroyed the Amalekites and brought back Agag their king. The soldiers took sheep and cattle from the plunder, the best of what was devoted to God, in order to sacrifice them to the Lord your God at Gilgal."[62] Notwithstanding, Samuel judged Saul for failing to comply with God's command. Samuel said: "Does the Lord delight

[53] Ibid, 76–77.

[54] Ibid, 75.

[55] See 1 Samuel 15:22–23. "But Samuel replied: 'Does the Lord delight in burnt offerings and sacrifices as much as in obeying the Lord? To obey is better than sacrifice, and to heed is better than the fat of rams. For rebellion is like the sin of divination, and arrogance like the evil of idolatry. Because you have rejected the word of the Lord, he has rejected you as king.' "

[56] See 2 Samuel 12:7–10. "Then Nathan said to David, "You are the man! This is what the Lord, the God of Israel, says: 'I anointed you king over Israel, and I delivered you from the hand of Saul. I gave your master's house to you, and your master's wives into your arms. I gave you all Israel and Judah. And if all this had been too little, I would have given you even more. Why did you despise the word of the Lord by doing what is evil in his eyes? You struck down Uriah the Hittite with the sword and took his wife to be your own. You killed him with the sword of the Ammonites. Now, therefore, the sword will never depart from your house, because you despised me and took the wife of Uriah the Hittite to be your own."

[57] See 2 Samuel 12:13. "Then David said to Nathan, 'I have sinned against the Lord.' "

[58] See 1 Samuel 15:1–3.

[59] 1 Samuel 15:9.

[60] 1 Samuel 15:15.

[61] See 1 Samuel 15:19. Samuel says to Saul: "Why did you not obey the Lord?"

[62] 1 Samuel 15:20–21.

in burnt offerings and sacrifices as much as in obeying the Lord? To obey is better than sacrifice, and to heed is better than the fat of rams. For rebellion is like the sin of divination, and arrogance like the evil of idolatry. Because you have rejected the word of the Lord, he has rejected you as king."[63] Saul then accepted Samuel's admonition.[64] God also backed Samuel by giving the throne of Israel to David.[65]

Other examples illustrate the catalytic role of prophets. In 1 Kings 13, a prophet admonished Jeroboam after the king had induced the people to worship golden calves at the Bethel altar. The prophet cried out that the altar would break. Then, the king stretched his hand and ordered to seize the prophet. However, at that time, the king's hand shriveled up, so that he could not pull it back. For this reason, the king requested the prophet to pray for the restoration of the hand. After the prayer, God backed the prophet: the hand was restored.

Furthermore, in 1 Kings 21, enticed by Jezebel, Ahab induced the people to stone Naboth. Ahab also illegitimately took Naboth's vineyard. Then, Elijah admonished Ahab and warned him about God's punishment. This catalyzed Ahab's repentance, and God's mercy.[66] Also, in 1 Kings 18:41–46, Elijah admonished Ahab before the end of the drought. God backed Elijah by sending heavy rain. Moreover, in 1 Kings 20, after Ben-Hadad, king of Aram, had attacked Samaria and had threated Israel, a prophet catalyzed Ahab to begin the battle against Ben-Hadad, in spite of the power of Aram's army. Ahab obeyed and won the battle.

Finally, the prophets admonished political authorities to use their power in favor of the poor. For instance, Jeremiah 22:16 exhorted the king to defend "the cause of the poor and the needy,"[67] and Isaiah defended the poor, the fatherless, and the widows against unfair rulers.[68]

An interesting question is whether, and if so how, the principle of separation of powers should encompass the function of ensuring compliance with constitutional limitations and the catalytic role of prophets. There are various possibilities at stake. Should only the church perform those roles? Should

[63] 1 Samuel 15:22–23.

[64] See 1 Samuel 15:24. "Then Saul said to Samuel, 'I have sinned. I violated the Lord's command and your instructions.'"

[65] See 1 Samuel 16:1.

[66] See 1 Kings 18:29. "Have you noticed how Ahab has humbled himself before me? Because he has humbled himself, I will not bring this disaster in his day, but I will bring it on his house in the days of his son."

[67] See Jeremiah 22:16.

[68] See Isaiah 1:23, 10:1–2.

judges play the function of controlling compliance with the constitution, while the church should reclaim the catalytic role?

I would like to argue that within the framework of democratic constitutionalism, judges should control compliance with constitutional limitations and play the catalytic role concerning the implementation of the constitution. The structure of democratic representation, grounded in free elections after expensive campaigns funded by all kinds of sources, could lead political authorities to act for protecting interests other than the ones corresponding to the common good and the realization of individual rights. There can also be blind spots and bureaucratic hurdles creating difficulties to achieve those aims. In those scenarios, judges should catalyze political authorities to seek the common good and protect individual rights.[69] Judges should also give legal and political visibility to hidden social problems and create incentives for the elimination of bureaucratic hurdles.

Hence, contrary to a strict conception of the separation of powers, according to which the role of the judges should be "invisible"[70] and secondary, the Bible could ground a conception of a judiciary, empowered with a catalytic role. It is possible to characterize the catalytic role with three properties, which, for example, are to be found in the exchange between Nathan and David. First, there is dialogue and cooperation between the judge and the political authority. Second, this dialogue generates a virtuous change of direction in the political authority. And third, the dialogue implies that the intervention of the judge in the power of the political authority is rather weak. This is also different from a conception of separation of powers encompassing judicial supremacy.

The exercise by judges of the catalytic role is crucial concerning relevant contemporary issues in comparative constitutional law. Some examples are limiting the rise of the executive power, the power of political authorities to amend the constitution, and the realization of economic and social rights. At least in these three areas judges should cooperate with and incentivize political authorities to act in a virtuous way for designing and implementing policies leading, respectively, to the achievement of the common good and the respect of freedoms,[71] the preservation of constitutional democracy in

[69] On a defense of rights, see Julian Rivers, "Christian Constitutional Rights?," in this volume.

[70] In the Spirit of Laws, Montesquieu outlines the role of judges as follows: The judges must be "no more than the mouth that pronounces the words of the law, mere passive beings, incapable of moderating either its force or rigour," <https://oll.libertyfund.org/titles/montesquieu-complete-works-vol-1-the-spirit-of-laws> accessed 21 February 2019.

[71] Oliver O'Donovan historically links the concentration of power in the executive to the shift from the hegemony of natural law, discovered by judges, to the rise of the acceptance of positive law, made

constitutional amendment, and the reduction of inequality by means of the protection of economic and social rights. In what follows, I will only address the last two issues.

The Catalytic Role of Judges and the Adjudication of Economic and Social Rights

Judges should catalyze political authorities to design and implement policies leading to the satisfaction of basic needs of all citizens and the reduction of inequality. The constitutional entrenchment of economic and social rights is a strategy, adopted worldwide and, in particular, in the so-called Global South, to achieve those goals.

There are various ways in which constitutions protect economic and social rights. Constitutions belonging to the first category of liberal constitutionalism included provisions entrenching what Mark Tushnet calls "nonjusticiable" or "merely declaratory rights," that is, rights that courts would not enforce.[72] Several current constitutions still institute economic and social rights in that way.[73] Nevertheless, the majority of today's constitutions entrench justiciable economic and social rights.[74]

The core debate concerning the adjudication of those rights revolves around the role of judges. Apex courts around the world have conceived their role in different ways. For instance, the first jurisprudence developed by the South African Constitutional Court about the adjudication of cases under sections 26.2 and 27.2 of the 1996 South African Constitution mirrors a conception in which judges undertake a weak review of the reasonableness of the measures taken by political authorities to realize economic and social

by political authorities. See "Government as Judgment," (1999) First Things <https://www.firstthings.com/article/1999/04/004-government-as-judgment> accessed 1 March 2019. Within this context, judges performing a catalytic function could counterbalance the power of the executive.

[72] Mark Tushnet, *Weak Courts, Strong Rights: Judicial Review and Social Welfare Rights in Comparative Constitutional Law* (Princeton University Press 2008) 238.

[73] For instance, Article 53.3 of the 1978 Spanish Constitution states that economic and social rights constitutional provisions "shall guide legislation, judicial practice and actions by the public authorities." These provisions belong to Part I, chapter 3 of the Spanish Constitution, which is entitled: "Principles Governing Economic and Social Policy." Provisions belonging to this chapter guarantee economic and social rights of the family, children, and mothers (Article 39); workers (Articles 40, 41, and 42); disabled individuals (Article 49); and the elderly (Article 50), and the rights to health (Article 43) and housing (Article 47) as well.

[74] See, Courtney Jung, Ran Hirschl, and Evan Rosevear, "Economic and Social Rights in National Constitutions" (2014) 62(4) American Journal of Comparative Law 1043–1094.

rights. A strict conception of the principle of separation of powers underpins this sort of judicial review that is highly deferential to political authorities.[75] Scholars have contended that this conception of the judicial role does not suffice for an adequate protection of economic and social rights.[76]

On the other extreme, Latin American courts conceive themselves as central institutions for the realization of economic and social rights. Arguing that, due to the incapacity or lack of interest of political authorities, those rights have not been implemented by means of public policies, Latin American judges have overstepped the boundaries of the separation of powers and have enacted strong remedies that sometimes amount to social programs. Some of those remedies seek to protect the minimum core of economic and social rights, which judges identify with a bundle of specific claims and benefits that should be satisfied under any circumstance. However, in particular in the so-called structural cases, some other remedies amount to commands directed to political authorities to implement appropriate legal, financial, and administrative programs to ensure that the state meets the demands imposed by those rights. This is clearly an instance of a conception of the separation of powers based on judicial supremacy.

The case law of the Colombian Constitutional Court offers a variety of examples in which judges have issued strong remedies directed at the protection of the minimum core of economic and social rights. For instance, the court has adopted a doctrine of a vital minimum, under which each citizen has a constitutional right to enjoy the necessary means for a basic level of subsistence.[77] In this respect, the standard of the minimum core is different from reasonableness. The former justifies courts to determine the minimum amount and quality of goods and services that political authorities should deliver to the individuals; the latter acknowledges that only the legislature and the executive are empowered to determine what the minimum amount should be. The jurisprudence of the Colombian Constitutional Court also

[75] See, for example, *Minister of Health v Treatment Action Campaign* (No. 2) 2002 5 SA 721 (CC), paras 30–39. See also Sandra Liebenberg, *Socio-Economic Rights: Adjudication under a Transformative Constitution* (Juta 2010) 132.

[76] See, among others, David Bilchitz, *Poverty and Fundamental Rights: The Justification and Enforcement of Socio-Economic Rights* (Oxford University Press 2007) 187; Anashri Pillay, "Economic and Social Rights Adjudication: Developing Principles of Judicial Restraint in South African and the United Kingdom" (2013) 3 Public Law 599–617; and Carol Steinberg, "Can Reasonableness Protect the Poor? A Review of South Africa's Socio-Economic Rights Jurisprudence" (2006) 123 South African Law Journal 264–284.

[77] See, among others, the judgments of the Colombian Constitutional Court SU-559/1997, T-068/1998, T-153/1998, SU-090/2000, T-068/2010, T-025/2004, and T-760/2008

provides examples of judicial design of social policies for structural issues. The three more significant cases concern policies regarding the rights of inmates,[78] the rights of internally displaced people,[79] and the health system.[80]

This judicial practice has given rise to strong objections. They relate to some problems of judicial supremacy. The criticisms comprehend institutional concerns related to the capacity of courts to adjudicate economic and social rights claims.[81] They also encompass reservations about the compatibility between this judicial practice, on the one hand, and the principles of the rule of law and separation of powers along with the foundations of representative democracy, on the other.[82] There has also been discussion of the effectiveness of this activist judicial practice for achieving the aforementioned aims linked to the satisfaction of basic needs and elimination of inequality. Surprising evidence points to the fact that, at least in some Latin American countries, the constitutional enforcement of economic and social rights has not benefited the poor. They have improved financial circumstances of middle-class citizens that are somehow able to meet their basic needs by means of ordinary market possibilities.[83]

A fruitful third way designed on the basis of the biblical catalytic role of judges could lead constitutional courts to a more effective protection of economic and social rights. This strategy could also be less intrusive upon the principle of the separation of powers. As Nathan approached David and catalyzed a reaction leading him to repent, courts should engage in dialogue and cooperation with other branches of government with the aim of generating a change of behavior (repentance precisely means change of behavior) for achieving effective protection of those rights. That cooperation should encompass dialogue on the levels and modes of satisfaction of those rights that are available at a particular time, given the limitation of financial resources. It can also comprehend joint analysis of data and empirical information useful

[78] See, among others, the Judgments T-153/98, T-388/2013, T-282/2014, T-762/2015, and T-197/17.

[79] See the Judgment T-25/2004.

[80] See, among others, the Judgment T-760/2008.

[81] See Katharine Young, *Constituting Economic and Social Rights* (Oxford University Press 2012).

[82] See Aoife Nolan, "Ireland: The Separation of Powers Doctrine vs. Socio-Economic Rights" in Malcolm Langford (ed), *Social Rights Jurisprudence: Emerging Trends in International and Comparative Law* (Cambridge University Press 2009).

[83] See David Landau, "The Reality of Social Rights Enforcement" (2012) 53(1) Harvard International Law Journal: 190–246; and Octavio Ferraz, "Health Inequalities, Rights and Courts: The Social Impact of the 'Judicialization of Health' in Brazil" in Alicia E Yamin and Siri Gloppen (eds), *Litigating Health Rights: Can Courts Bring More Justice to Health?* (Harvard University Press 2011) ch 4.

to diagnose the situation of the right-holders and, from time to time, the effectiveness of the remedies jointly implemented.[84]

The Judgment T-91/2018 of the Colombian Constitutional Court offers an example in which judges can play this catalytic role. Ten middle school students requested the education authorities to open a high school within a poor small town in a region devastated by the Colombian internal armed conflict. Due to financial restrictions, a government decree provides that only if there is a minimum of twenty-two students can a high school class be opened. Relying on this provision, the education agency denied the request. The students filed a constitutional complaint requesting the protection of their right to education.

The Colombian Constitutional Court considered the case. It had at least three alternatives before it. First, it could have followed the trend of the early South African constitutional jurisprudence. This would have led the court to defer to the judgment of the political authorities. Second, it could have issued a strong remedy and commanded the authorities to open the high school. While the former would not have efficiently protected the right, the latter would have resulted in a strong interference with education policies and budget distributions. Instead, the court followed a catalytic strategy. During the proceedings, the court began a dialogue with the education authorities. The court asked what possibilities were available for offering the students places in high school classes in neighboring towns. The education agency identified two high schools twenty kilometers away where the students could continue their education. In the judgment, the court ordered the authorities to initiate a meaningful dialogue with the claimants and to agree upon two matters: in which high school the students would continue their education, and how the education authorities would fund the transportation. The engagement between the claimants and the authorities was very fruitful. After few days, they achieved an agreement. The students are now enrolled in a high school and the municipal government is funding the transportation.

[84] Within the scope of the adjudication of economic and social rights, Katharine Young speaks about the catalytic role of a court in a broader sense. In her conception, this role encompasses different strategies of judicial review: "deferential, conversational, experimentalist, managerial, and peremptory." According to Young, those strategies "open a scene of action, beyond that of the courts and the elected branches, to situate the Court within a web of relations involving litigants, beneficiaries of rights who are similarly situated to the litigants, other parties who will be harmed or helped by the judicial action, and the wider public." See "A Typology of Economic and Social Rights Adjudication: Exploring the Catalytic Function of Judicial Review" (2010) 8(3) International Journal of Constitutional Law 391.

The Catalytic Role of Judges and the Limits of Amending the Constitution

Judges should also catalyze political authorities to preserve the principle of constitutional democracy when constitutional amendments are considered. A constitutional amendment is a kind of formal constitutional change. A constitutional change is a modification in the set of valid constitutional norms. Constitutional changes can be formal or informal. The difference between constitutional provisions and constitutional norms facilitates the understanding of these modalities.[85] Constitutional provisions are the statements of a written constitution. In the case of written constitutions, the set of meanings expressed by the constitutional provisions are constitutional norms.[86] Those meanings can be articulated in prescriptive propositions, which state that something is constitutionally commanded, prohibited, or permitted, or that a constitutional power or immunity is granted to a particular person, office, or institution.

Formal constitutional changes involve an alteration in one or more constitutional provisions whose effect is a modification in the set of valid constitutional norms. In contrast, an informal constitutional change is a modification in the set of valid constitutional norms that takes place without a modification in the set of constitutional provisions. Constitutional mutation by interpretation,[87] infra-constitutional mutation,[88] and constitutional desuetude[89] are types of informal constitutional change.

[85] On the distinction between provision and norm in constitutional law, see Vezio Crisafulli, "Disposizione (e norma)" *XIII Enciclopedia del Diritto* (1964) 165 and 203. Also, within the field of constitutional rights, see Robert Alexy, *A Theory of Constitutional Rights* (Oxford University Press 2002) 32.

[86] Being the meaning expressed by a constitutional provision is a sufficient but not a necessary condition of constitutional norms. There are also constitutional norms that express the meaning of (unwritten) constitutional conventions, principles, rules, and practices or of judicial constitutional principles or rules.

[87] This concept refers to the case in which judges attribute a new meaning to an old constitutional provision. Concerning a non-state-related context, Julian Arato has shown how informal constitutional change can take place in any legislative and political practice of constitutional interpretation, in addition to the practice of interpretation by the judges. See Julian Arato, "Treaty Interpretation and Constitutional Transformation: Informal Change in International Organizations" (2013) 38 Yale Journal of International Law 304.

[88] This concept refers to change that occurs by the enactment of ordinary legislation, ratification of international treaties, the undertaking of executive action, or the mise en scène of political practices that, despite being inconsistent with the constitution, is neither challenged in the courts nor judicially declared unconstitutional. On this concept, see Carlos Bernal, "Informal Constitutional Change" (2014) 62 American Journal of Comparative Law 495.

[89] On constitutional desuetude, see Richard Albert, "Constitutional Amendment by Constitutional Desuetude" (2014) 62 American Journal of Comparative Law 641.

There are three basic kinds of formal constitutional change: enactment, amendment, and derogation of a constitution. Constitutional texts usually regulate procedures for constitutional amendment. This is an institutional strategy for balancing two aims intrinsic to the enactment of a constitution that are sometimes in tension: on the one hand, seeking political and legal stability by entrenching some principles, rules, and rights and the structure of the state; on the other, enabling constituted authorities to respond to new social demands by means of changing the provisions of the constitution.[90]

The concept of constitutional amendment is ambiguous. "Constitutional amendment" refers to any formal constitutional change that is enacted by successfully following the constitutional rules for constitutional amendment. Constitutional amendments can have different degrees of intensity, scope, and purpose. Intense and broad constitutional amendments can unmake a constitution and even destruct the entrenchment of democratic constitutionalism. For this reason, the literature and jurisprudence from various jurisdictions have used the concepts of constitutional "revision,"[91] "dismemberment,"[92] "substitution," and "replacement" for designating constitutional amendments that imply deeper alterations of essential constitutional elements, the identity of the constitution, or its basic structure. Furthermore, autocrats have employed and can use constitutional amendments to destruct democratic constitutionalism by perpetuating themselves in power or diminishing checks and balances and mechanisms for political and legal accountability. This is what David Landau calls "abusive constitutionalism,"[93] a practice that creates the risk of destruction of democratic constitutionalism window-dressed as an amendment to the constitution.[94]

[90] In The Federalist No. 43, Madison argued that Article V of the American Constitution achieved a balance between those goals: it "guards equally against that extreme facility which would render the Constitution too mutable; and that extreme difficulty which might perpetuate its discovered faults." See James Madison, "The Federalist No. XLIII" in Alexander Hamilton, John Jay, and James Madison, *Federalist, on the New Constitution* (B Warner 1817) 239.

[91] For an illuminating discussion on the differences between constitutional revision and constitutional amendment, see Richard Albert, "Amendment and Revision in the Unmaking of Constitutions" in David Landau and Hanna Lerner (eds), *Handbook on Comparative Constitution-Making* (Edward Elgar, 2019) 117 <https://papers.ssrn.com/sol3/papers2.cfm?abstract_id=2841110> accessed 30 December 2018. Also, see Donald S Lutz, "Toward a Theory of Constitutional Amendment" (1994) 88(2) American Political Science Review 356.

[92] Richard Albert, "Constitutional Amendment and Dismemberment" (2018) 43 Yale Journal of International Law 2–82.

[93] See, on the concept of abusive constitutionalism, David Landau, "Abusive Constitutionalism" (2013) 47 University of California Davis Law Review 189–200, 195, and Rosalind Dixon and David Landau, "Constraining Constitutional Change" (2015) 50 Wake Forest Law Review 859–890, 862.

[94] See, on the window-dressing argument, David Landau, "The Importance of Constitution-Making" (2011–2012) 89 (3) Denver University Law Review 611–633.

As a matter of institutional design, constitution makers can adopt two extreme strategies. On the one hand, if they want to seek political and legal stability or create a strong mechanism for preventing abusive constitutionalism, they can adopt rigid and very demanding amending procedures. On the other hand, if constitution makers want to enable constituted authorities to respond to new social demands by means of changing the constitutional provisions, they can foresee flexible procedures to amend the constitution.

Both strategies create undeniable risks. If the constitution foresees only one procedure for constitutional amendment, and it is too democratically demanding, such as the procedures foreseen by the US and Australian Constitutions, the risk that constitutional amendments destroy democratic constitutionalism or unmake the constitution is low. However, political authorities will struggle to adapt the constitution to new realities or to correct mistakes. They will have to rely on informal constitutional changes. This might lead to a democratic evasion for updating the constitution. If, as it happens in countries such as the United States, constitutional interpretation and mutation is the usual way the constitution is updated, then the people themselves and their representatives are deprived of the opportunity to deliberate about possible modifications of the constitution and undertake them.

Nevertheless, if amendment procedures are too easy and accessible, then political authorities will not face problems in updating the constitution but rather will be too easily able to destroy democratic constitutionalism or unmake the constitution by means of a constitutional amendment.

A strategy enjoying increasing worldwide popularity is judicial use of the doctrine of unconstitutional constitutional amendments.[95] The basis of this doctrine is the recognition that there are explicit and implicit limits to the constitutional amendment power. While unamendability provisions entrench explicit limits, courts have recognized implicit limitations. A way to make those limits enforceable is the constitutional review of constitutional amendments. This strategy empowers judges to strike down constitutional amendments on substantive grounds when they alter the basic structure of the constitution, its identity, or essential elements in such a way that the constitution can be considered replaced or substituted by another. Instances of this kind of constitutional review are the Indian jurisprudence on the basic

[95] See Yaniv Roznai, *Unconstitutional Constitutional Amendments. The Limits of Amendment* Powers (Oxford University Press 2017).

structure of the constitution[96] and the constitutional replacement doctrine of the Colombian Constitutional Court.[97]

As Roznai reports,[98] judges are spreading the use of these doctrines around the world. However, how should judges undertake this review?

Again, there are various possibilities. First, judges could be fully deferential to political authorities undertaking constitutional amendments, regardless of the way in which the amendments are achieved by political authorities and their impact to constitutional democracy. Second, judges may exercise intense judicial review aimed at preventing abusive constitutionalism and preserving democracy. This latter strategy would imply a far-reaching interference of judges with the principle of separation of powers. Judges would end up limiting the role of parliaments and other constituted powers to use the constitutional amendment rules for updating the constitution.

A third way is catalytic. Over the time, in a practice of constitutional review of constitutional amendments, courts could catalyze political authorities to create fair and inclusive deliberation for amending the constitution and, in particular, the provisions entrenching the essential elements of democratic constitutionalism. In this way, judges could institute two balancing rules:

(1) The more a constitutional amendment changes the entrenchment of essential elements of democratic constitutionalism or the identity of the constitution, the more deliberative should be the procedure for approving it.

[96] Since *Kesavananda Bharati v. State of Kerala*, AIR 1973 SC 1461, the Indian Supreme Court has held that the parliament's amending power does not encompass the authorization to change the basic structure of the constitution. In *Minerva Mills Ltd. v. Union of India*, AIR 1980 SC 1789, that court linked the concept of basic structure to the identity of the constitution. A disputed question is still: What elements do belong to the basic structure? See Sudhir Krishnaswamy, *Democracy and Constitutionalism in India: A Study of the Basic Structure Doctrine* (Oxford University Press 2011) 71f. Also, Madhav Khosla, "Constitutional Amendment" in Sujit Choudhry, Madhav Khosla, and Pratap Bhanu Mehta (eds), *The Oxford Handbook of the Indian Constitution* (Oxford University Press 2016) 232–250, 235f. On the doctrine of the basic structure in comparative perspective, see Aharon Barak, "Unconstitutional Constitutional Amendments" (2011) 44 Israeli Law Review 321–341.

[97] See Judgments C-970/2004, C-971/2004, C-1040/2005, C-588/2009, C-141/2010, C-397/2010, C-574/2011, C-170/2012, C-249/2012, C-288/12, C-317/2012, C-1056/2012, C-010/2013, C-579/2013, C-577/2014, and C-332/2017. For a critical explanation of this doctrine, see Carlos Bernal, "Unconstitutional Constitutional Amendments in the Case Study of Colombia: An Analysis of the Justification and Meaning of the Constitutional Replacement Doctrine" (2013) 11 (2) International Journal of Constitutional Law 339–357.

[98] See Roznai, *Unconstitutional Constitutional Amendments*.

(2) The less a constitutional amendment is the result of a fair and inclusive deliberative procedure, the more intensive should be the judicial review of the constitutional amendment.

These rules institutionalize the features of the catalytic judicial function, namely, a dialogue between judges and political authorities on how the latter can amend the constitution without eroding democratic constitutionalism and increasing the deliberative quality of their outcomes.

The Judgment C-332/17 of the Colombian Constitutional Court provides an example of the way a court can exercise its catalytic function by applying those rules. In that judgment, the court reviewed a constitutional amendment that institutionalized a special fast-track procedure for implementing the Peace Agreement signed in 2016 by the Colombian government and the Revolutionary Armed Forces of Colombia (FARC). Essential features of that procedure included a government monopoly over the power to introduce bills for constitutional amendments and laws; halving the number of debates required for approval of constitutional amendments (four instead of eight debates) and of laws (two instead of four debates); requiring that changes to bills introduced by Congress are not valid without governmental approval; and a requirement for bills to be voted on in their entirety, thereby prohibiting the practice of voting on isolated provisions.

Members of the main opposition party challenged the constitutionality of the last two features. Appealing to the doctrine of unconstitutional constitutional amendments, they contested provisions of Constitutional Amendment 1/2016, arguing that those features partially replaced an essential constitutional principle, namely, the separation of powers. The government approval of modifications and voting as a whole excessively empowered the executive branch, to the detriment of congressional competences.

In its judgment, the court applied its constitutional replacement doctrine and declared these two features of the fast-track procedure unconstitutional. Certainly, the court acknowledged that the constitutionality of transitional justice instruments ought to be analyzed using more flexible standards. However, it also held that, even from this viewpoint, government approval and voting as a whole were disproportionate limitations to the separation of powers and deliberative democracy. A full-fledged legislative deliberation, one that guarantees political pluralism and the political rights of minorities, was infeasible under those conditions. Moreover, it was particularly significant for the court that the Congress had approved the amendment without deliberation. The opposition party, which had won a plebiscite rejecting the peace agreement, had refused to vote on that constitutional amendment. Thus, the court struck down the amendment for the sake of catalyzing deliberative democracy in procedures for amending the constitution.

Conclusion

In this chapter I have claimed that the Bible sets out a system of separation of powers and checks and balances between different authorities: God, the king, the judges, the priests, and the prophets. I also emphasized the relevance of the catalytic function prophets performed. This function consisted in a dialogue with the king with the aim of triggering a change of direction, influencing the king to behave in a virtuous manner and to seek the common good and the protection of the interests of the people.

I also contended that this function is the basis for a model of separation of powers within the framework of democratic constitutionalism. In this model, judges should play a catalytic function. By performing this function, judges should act in a nonintensive manner. Judges should give legal and political visibility to hidden social problems and create incentives for the elimination of bureaucratic hurdles. By means of a dialogue, they should incentivize political authorities to seek the common good and protect individual rights. Some examples show how a catalytic judicial function of this sort respects the powers of parliament and government while at the same time achieving its ultimate goals.

13

Rights and Freedoms

Christian Constitutional Rights?

Julian Rivers[1]

The Global Rule of Constitutional Rights

The history of constitutional rights is both older and newer than that of its close cousin, international human rights. It is older in the sense that the natural rights theories that emerged in the seventeenth and eighteenth centuries came to have political and legal salience within nation-states long before international legal protection was systematically developed after the Second World War. However, the history of constitutional rights is also newer than, or at least roughly contemporaneous with, international human rights protection, in the sense that judicial review for the protection of abstract fundamental rights, and in particular judicial review at the behest of individual right-holders, is a constitutional development that in many countries has only followed in the wake of international legal protection.

That this is a growing phenomenon of the second half of the twentieth century is true even in the case of the United States. While there are a few older examples,[2] constitutional review only started in earnest with *Brown v. Board of Education* in 1954.[3] Likewise, in Germany, although the Basic Law of 1949 commenced with a clear and robust statement of basic rights, as well as processes for institutional enforcement, the procedural right to bring an individual complaint to vindicate those rights was treated with caution and only raised to constitutional status two decades later.[4] France and the United

[1] University of Bristol Law School. I am grateful to conference participants Patrick Capps, Nicholas Aroney, and Ian Leigh for their comments on earlier drafts.

[2] Notoriously so, in cases such as *Dred Scott v Sandford* 60 US 393 (1857) and *Lochner v New York* 198 US 45 (1905).

[3] 347 US 483.

[4] Julian Rivers, "Stemming the Flood of Constitutional Complaints in Germany" [1994] Public Law 553.

Julian Rivers, *Rights and Freedoms: Christian Constitutional Rights?* in *Christianity and Constitutionalism*.
Edited by: Nicholas Aroney and Ian Leigh, Oxford University Press. © Oxford University Press 2022.
DOI: 10.1093/oso/9780197587256.003.0013

Kingdom joined the development of constitutional rights later still, and in both cases individual constitutional protection only developed long after individual citizens had been given the right to have recourse to the European Court of Human Rights.[5]

In their study of the global diffusion of constitutional rights, Benedikt Goderis and Mila Versteeg trace the presence of 108 different constitutional rights in formal constitutional documents from 1946 to 2006.[6] That large number gives a slightly false impression, since it is inflated by the care they take to track textual variations. The right to equality, for example, covers twenty rights, only one of which is the general right to equality. Equality is one of seven groups of rights, the others being "political, democratic and accountability rights," "life, liberty, physical integrity and privacy," "fair trial rights," "socio-economic rights," "women, children and family rights," and a final category of "minority rights, environmental rights and other 'new rights.'" Over the sixty-year period covered by the Goderis/Versteeg study, the number of constitutions tripled from 63 to 188, and in almost every case the proportion of constitutions identifying any given right also increased.[7] The overwhelming message is that for the last seventy years the constitutional rights catalogs of the world have been expanding fairly steadily.

As a general trend, more and more countries also have judicial regimes of constitutional review.[8] However, not all rights are justiciable, with the most notable area of controversy being the legal enforceability of socioeconomic rights.[9] There is also a considerable variation in the content of the economic and social rights protected. The right to education is undoubtedly the oldest, found already in some eighteenth-century instruments, and now practically universal. By contrast, for example, very few constitutions yet protect the right to food and water. But only about a third of constitutions make all their economic and social rights justiciable. In another third they are purely aspirational, and a further third distinguish between rights in this respect. As a

[5] For France, see Myriam Hunter-Henin, "Constitutional Developments and Human Rights in France" (2011) 60 International and Comparative Law Quarterly 167. The United Kingdom gave citizens the right of access to the ECHR in 1966, but only brought the Human Rights Act into force in 2000.

[6] Benedikt Goderis and Mila Versteeg, "The Diffusion of Constitutional Rights" (2014) 39 International Review of Law and Economics 1–19. There are, of course, outliers, such as Australia, which only has scattered references to rights in its constitution of 1901.

[7] The two genuine losses are the right to bear arms and the right to petition.

[8] By 2011, 83%. See Tom Ginsburg and Mila Versteeg, "Why Do Countries Adopt Constitutional Review?" (2014) 30 Journal of Law, Economics and Organization 587.

[9] Courtney Jung, Ran Hirschl, and Evan Rosevear, "Economic and Social Rights in National Constitutions" (2014) 62 American Journal of Comparative Law 1043.

rule, common-law countries tend to avoid juridifying economic and social rights, while civilian countries tend to embrace it. There is no obvious correlation between this institutional decision and the actual state of economic and social development in a country; some very prosperous and egalitarian countries reject the judicial enforcement of such rights at the constitutional level. The Scandinavian states spring to mind.

Ran Hirschl observes that constitutional courts "borrow" from foreign jurisdictions for a wide range of reasons.[10] However, some patterns in that borrowing are clearly apparent. Certain courts occupy a dominant position: the Canadian Supreme Court, the German Federal Constitutional Court, and the European Court of Human Rights have now overtaken the US Supreme Court and British courts in global influence. Borrowing is much more likely to take place in contested matters of rights interpretation and application than in structural questions of jurisdiction and powers. Judges in the highest courts are more likely to belong to a global intellectual elite who favor the advance of universalist liberal democratic tendencies in their own countries over particularist, often religious, visions. Hirschl provides an extended analysis of the politics of the Israeli Supreme Court, not least under the presidency of Aharon Barak, within this framing.

The United States presents a model of clearly bounded rights (in rhetoric, if not in practice), integrated into all areas of law, upheld by a strong judicial branch in the face of all other branches of government. But this historically influential model is no longer dominant. As constitutional rights protection has spread across the globe, so also a greater measure of diversity has been absorbed into their structure. Constitutional rights are flexible in multiple dimensions. Most courts are willing to embrace some version or other of "living tree" doctrine, allowing for the evolution of substantive rights, in terms of both the type of right protected (negative, positive, procedural, etc.) and the scope of protection. Evolution has not resulted in contraction, but nor has it needed to, since the scope of countervailing constitutional goods is also open to development. The expansion on both sides of the balance of rights and their limits offers ever-increasing scope for judicial discretion.[11] The "global model" of constitutional rights is one in which the doctrine of proportionality structures a process of judicial reasoning in balancing a

[10] Ran Hirschl, *Comparative Matters: The Renaissance of Comparative Constitutional Law* (Oxford University Press 2014) ch 1.

[11] Robert Alexy calls this a "wide theory" of the scope of rights. Robert Alexy, *A Theory of Constitutional Rights* (Oxford University Press 2002) 200–217.

wide range of constitutional goods.[12] David Beatty even calls this feature of modern constitutionalism "the ultimate rule of law."[13]

On top of this layer of flexibility there are superimposed several doctrines that determine the relationship of the judiciary to other branches of government. Rights can be protected in more or less robust and intrusive form, and can be subject to greater or lesser shaping by other institutions, not least by legislatures.[14] Some commentators have talked about the emergence of a "commonwealth" model of constitutional rights protection to reflect this feature of balanced institutionalization.[15] In the weakest form of judicial protection still compatible with the designation "constitutional," rights are secured within the common law and merely function as interpretative matrices for the construction of primary legislation.[16] Moreover, as the German and French examples show, it should not be assumed that constitutional rights are only judicially cognizable at the behest of individual, or private corporate, claimants. Political institutions such as parliamentary groups and local government bodies may also be entitled to bring claims. And finally, the judiciary is required to position its national (and subnational) legal orders in relation to globalizing pressures, adopting supranational conformity or national distinctiveness at will. As Alexander Somek has recently argued, constitutional debate has now moved beyond questions of both the distribution of power among institutions of state and the pursuit of dignity and rights to a third level of global responsiveness and integration.[17]

All this means that from a theoretical point of view, a constitutional right is merely a legal power to have a judge check the content of any law by reference to a set of privileged abstract values, as mediated by the interactions of the various branches of government in an increasingly interconnected global legal environment.[18] From this perspective, the US protection of

[12] Kai Möller, *The Global Model of Constitutional Rights* (Oxford University Press 2012); Aharon Barak, *Proportionality: Constitutional Rights and Their Limitations* (Cambridge University Press 2012).

[13] David Beatty, *The Ultimate Rule of Law* (Oxford University Press 2004).

[14] Julian Rivers, "Proportionality and Variable Intensity of Review" (2006) 65 Cambridge Law Journal 174–207.

[15] Stephen Gardbaum, *The New Commonwealth Model of Constitutionalism: Theory and Practice* (Cambridge University Press 2013).

[16] The limits of this common law model of constitutional rights have been explored extensively by T. R. S. Allan. See his *Law, Liberty and Justice* (Clarendon Press 1993) ch 6, and subsequent works.

[17] Alexander Somek, *The Cosmopolitan Constitution* (Oxford University Press 2014).

[18] Proposals for a "baseline" intensity of review overstate the rigidity of constitutional rights doctrine. See Cora Chan, "Proportionality and Invariable Baseline Intensity of Review" (2013) 33 Legal Studies 1–21.

constitutional rights is simply one (now rather insular and rigid) point on a spectrum of possibilities subject to internal constitutional manipulation. The global rise, textual convergence, and judicial malleability of constitutional rights has made debates about the concept and content of constitutional rights less and less significant and focused attention on their correct construction and application instead.

Critique of the Concept of Constitutional Rights

Constitutional rights need to be set within the broader political tradition out of which they emerged if we are to get critical purchase on them from a Christian, or indeed any other comprehensive philosophical, perspective. Yet there is a problem in knowing just how broadly to frame the object of our critique. Ancient precursors such as the Magna Carta or the English Bill of Rights 1689 undoubtedly contained precepts that have some substantive continuity with modern rights. But for the most part instruments such as these were catalogs of grievances, not systematic statements of political right. There is a danger that we elide the question of constitutional rights with that of constitutional government more generally. And if we follow Harold Berman on that question, we will need to start with *Dictatus Papae* (1075) and the Gregorian Reforms of the Church.[19] Behind that stands an even longer, and still relevant, Christian tradition of political theory.[20]

A more immediately relevant starting point is the seventeenth-century transition from natural law theory to natural rights theory. This bore fruit in the eighteenth century in a wide range of competing conceptions of constitutional right. As Dan Edelstein has recently shown, natural rights theorists differed markedly on the question of what happened to those rights as one entered political society.[21] Those advocating "abridgement" argued that rights had to be surrendered to political authority as a condition for security and peace. Thomas Hobbes provides the most obvious example. "Transfer" theorists, such as John Locke, argued instead that natural rights were handed over to government to uphold on our behalf. "Preservationists" argued that

[19] Harold J Berman, *Law and Revolution: The Formation of the Western Legal Tradition* (Harvard University Press 1983).

[20] Oliver O'Donovan and Joan Lockwood O'Donovan (eds), *From Irenaeus to Grotius: A Sourcebook in Christian Political Thought* (Eerdmans 1999); Oliver O'Donovan and Joan Lockwood O'Donovan (eds), *Bonds of Imperfection: Christian Politics, Past and Present* (Eerdmans 2004).

[21] Dan Edelstein, *On the Spirit of Rights* (University of Chicago Press 2019).

natural rights survived the transition to the civil condition and could still be relied on by individuals against tyrannical governments.

Each of the three groups tended to emphasize a different institution within government. Abridgement theorists emphasized the role of the executive power, transfer theorists the legislature, and preservationists the judiciary. As the eighteenth century proceeded, so the preservationists came to predominate and shape new constitutional settlements. In practice, however, the three basic approaches manifested themselves in hybrid forms. The French Declaration of the Rights of Man is fundamentally preservationist but allows, and indeed only permits, the limitation of rights by legislative authority.[22] English common law reached the same conclusion in the famous case of *Entick v. Carrington*.[23] Immanuel Kant's doctrine of "innate right" functions in the same way as a presumption against law allowing for legislative rebuttal.[24] Even abridgement theory has had a long survival in the exemption of prerogative powers from legislative or judicial oversight.

Up to the late eighteenth century, the debate would seem to be neutral from a Christian perspective—one can find more- or less-orthodox Christians in each of Edelstein's three groupings.[25] It took on the mantel of religious controversy in 1791 when Pope Pius VI denounced the French Revolution in his papal encyclicals *Quod Aliquantum* and *Adeo nota*.[26] The counterrevolutionary Louis de Bonald famously responded to new claims of the "rights of man" by insisting that we should speak rather of the "rights of God." This cemented a relationship between Catholicism and counterrevolutionary thought lasting for more than a century. Even here, Christian opposition was not monolithic. Benjamin Constant tried hard to associate liberal political principles with liberal Protestantism, as they had been in the United States.[27]

The complexity of the relationship between Christianity and the nascent articulation of constitutional rights is well illustrated in the thought of William Blackstone and Edmund Burke. Blackstone's *Commentaries on the Laws of England* (1765–1769) were the first systematic statement of English common law in several centuries, and they were thoroughly preservationist

[22] Article 4. Edelstein overlooks the role of *loi* in shaping the enjoyment of *droits* in ibid, ch 7.

[23] (1765) 19 St Tr 1030, 95 ER 807.

[24] See Patrick Capps and Julian Rivers, "Kant's Concept of Law" (2018) 63 American Journal of Jurisprudence 259–294, 277–282.

[25] As Jeremy Waldron has emphasized, John Locke made considerable efforts to defend his theory from a Christian perspective. Jeremy Waldron, *God, Locke and Equality: Christian Foundations in Locke's Political Thought* (Cambridge University Press 2002).

[26] Edelstein, On the Spirit of Rights, 196–201.

[27] Helena Rosenblatt, *The Lost History of Liberalism* (Princeton University Press 2018) ch 2.

in structure. Without wanting to attribute to Blackstone a proto-Dworkinian theory of law, he offered a constructive interpretation of English law according to a Lockean scheme of absolute and subsidiary rights. As he explains at the beginning of his great work:

> By the absolute rights of individuals we mean those which are so in their primary and strictest sense; such as would belong to their persons merely in a state of nature, and which every man is entitled to enjoy whether out of society or in it. . . . [T]he first and primary end of human laws is to maintain and regulate these absolute rights of individuals.[28]

There are three absolute rights for Blackstone: the right to personal security, the right to personal liberty, and the right to property. By the right to security, he means the right to be secure in life, limbs, body, health, and reputation. By liberty, he means the power to go where one will without imprisonment or restraint except by due process of law. Not surprisingly, his defense of property is robust, although even he allows that property can be taken for public purposes if authorized by law and in return for fair compensation. To ensure that these absolute rights are guaranteed in practice, Blackstone identifies five subordinate, auxiliary, or political rights provided by the constitution to secure the actual enjoyment of rights: representation in Parliament, the control of the prerogative by the courts, the right of access to the courts, the right to petition for redress of grievance, and (as a final safeguard) the right to bear arms to defend oneself.

Blackstone argued that this thoroughly rights-inflected account of English law was consonant with his own fairly conservative protestant Christianity. His opening definitions of law and rights are predominantly deist, depending substantially upon "laws of nature" impressed by a benevolent Creator on the hearts of man. However, he still recognizes the superiority of divine revelation, and by the time he comes to discuss "offences against God and religion" (Book IV, ch. 4), his tolerant, indeed rather complacent, Anglicanism is on full view.[29]

Edmund Burke was also convinced that religion is the basis of civil society, and that religious, political, and legal culture are organically related.[30]

[28] William Blackstone, *Commentaries on the Laws of England* (1765–1769), Bk 1, ch 1.

[29] For Blackstone's high Anglican churchmanship more generally, see Wilfrid Prest, *William Blackstone: Law and Letters in the Eighteenth Century* (Oxford University Press 2008).

[30] Edmund Burke, *Reflections on the Revolution in France* (Penguin Classics 2004) 186–187.

He thought that Christianity (preferably Protestant) was "one great source of civilisation" and that the French revolutionaries were mad to jettison it.[31] At times, he seems to share in the blanket condemnation of the "rights of man" offered by Catholic counterrevolutionaries:

> As soon as this system [the rights of man] arrived among them, Pandora's box, replete with every mortal evil, seemed to fly open, hell itself to yawn, and every daemon of mischief to overspread the face of the earth.[32]

However, that is not the whole story. It may be a stretch to call Burke a "liberal pluralist," but he was certainly a Whig with a lively concern for the oppressed peoples of Ireland, America, and India. He was no mere reactionary.[33] In the 1767 Annual Register, Burke had eulogized Blackstone's new *Commentaries on the Laws of England*.[34] Presumably Burke was happy to read past its relatively brief Lockean philosophical foundations, affirming instead the substance of Blackstone's account as an expression of "the uniform policy of our constitution to claim and assert our liberties as an entailed inheritance derived to us from our forefathers, and to be transmitted to our posterity."[35] He was sympathetic to the argument of the American revolutionaries that these "antient and indubitable rights and liberties" were not, in practice, respected in Britain's handling of her colonies—a point that remained pertinent to the very end of Britain's empire. Many of the colonial constitutions of 1776, and in due course the "Bill of Rights" of the federal Constitution, contained a systematic restatement of Blackstonian fundamental rights in order more effectually to secure their protection in practice. Burke had no problem with that.

However, Burke and his fellow critics saw in Jeffersonian deism and still more the atheism of the Jacobins a sinful attempt to establish the authority of human reason in the rejection of the rule of God. Locating the origin of political authority in "man" and building a powerful unitary state superior to

[31] Ibid, 188.

[32] Edmund Burke, "On the Quebec Government Bill," 6 May 1791, printed in the *Parliamentary Register*, vol 19, 321.

[33] There is a fascinating exchange between Conor Cruise O'Brien and Isaiah Berlin on the question of Burke's possible "liberal pluralism" in the appendix to Conor Cruise O'Brien, *The Great Melody: A Thematic Biography of Edmund Burke* (Sinclair-Stevenson 1992) 605–618. Isaiah Berlin concedes that to call Burke a reactionary was a mistake.

[34] Or, at least, the first two books. See *Annual Register, or a View of the History, Politics and Literature for the Year 1767*, 286–307. It is only fair to note that Burke's authorship of the review is not without doubt. But he refers to Blackstone elsewhere in complimentary terms, e.g., *Reflections on the Revolution in France* (Penguin Classics 2004) 117.

[35] Edmund Burke, *Reflections on the Revolution in France* (Penguin Classics 2004) 119.

all other forms of human association on the grounds of that secular starting point, even to the point of creating a new civil religion with its own goddess, rituals, and holy days, understandably provoked charges of the anti-Christian nature of constitutional rights. It was the radical assault on the property and independence of the French church and its clergy, not human rights as such, that produced the pope's horrified reaction. The foolishness of such outright spiritual rebellion was made increasingly manifest to its critics in the horrendous violence that accompanied the overthrow of established legal orders, including those of Church and civil society, in the name of these new secular values. Constitutional rights could be a vehicle for that atheist revolution.

Burke's preference for constitutional rights in their Blackstonian, legally immanent, form was conservative as well as Christian.[36] For the conservative, abstract statements of rights unsettle the moral compromises that are the hallmark of political decision taking and legal practice. The character of a people is expressed in these compromises. These are not fixed for all time; as new constellations of power arise, so political commitments and arrangements mutate, but they do so in response to the real interests of individuals and groups. Abstract statements of constitutional rights convey a spurious aura of justice, universality, and finality while perpetually unsettling good working compromises in the name of a merely abstract ideal.

> The pretended rights of these theorists are all extremes; and in proportion as they are metaphysically true, they are morally and politically false. The rights of men are in a sort of middle, incapable of definition, but not impossible to be discerned.[37]

Part of the historic critique of constitutional rights has involved playing the "radical" French and the "conservative" English versions against each other. A. V. Dicey's defense of the British absence of a constitutional code of rights is classically Blackstonian—much more so than Dicey was prepared to admit.[38] One still sees this caution about the false promise of political ideals and the

[36] It is much less clear that Burke's conservatism was more Christian than Locke's (or Blackstone's) liberalism, as argued by Samuel Burgess, *Edmund Burke's Battle with Liberalism: His Christian Philosophy and Why It Matters Today* (Wilberforce Publications 2017). Is that not simply a prejudice in favor of historical over philosophical legitimation?

[37] Edmund Burke, *Reflections on the Revolution in France* (Penguin Classics 2004) 153. It is hard not to be reminded at this point of the doctrine of proportionality.

[38] A. V. Dicey, *Introduction to the Study of the Constitution* (10th edn, Macmillan 1959). Dicey's rather sniffy account of Blackstone's *Commentaries* in his 1909 inaugural lecture can be found in (1932) 4 Cambridge Law Journal 286.

real pragmatic value of embedded legal remedies in the British engagement with the early international human rights movement after the Second World War.[39] But one of the most notable effects of the modern development of justiciable rights is that to become practically workable they have to become much more nuanced and relativized in the light of a wide range of other constitutional goods. Real rights inevitably lose their ideal simplicity. Modern-day human and constitutional rights thus represent a combined legacy of both Burke's immanent historically derived legality and the transcendent politics of the French Revolution.

Any sense that the acceptance of constitutional rights aligns with denominational differences within Christianity is also undermined by quite different twentieth-century divisions. In a reversal of late eighteenth- and nineteenth-century tendencies, the most notable defenders of natural law and natural rights have been Catholic new natural law theorists.[40] The most radical rejection of this entire tradition is associated with the Protestant theologian Karl Barth.[41] Starting from a Reformed notion of the deeply alienating effects of sin, Barth argued that there can be no reasonable grasp of human goods apart from that given by faith in Jesus Christ. A more prominent line of modern critique associated with "radical orthodoxy" focuses more narrowly on natural rights.[42] The argument here is, typically, that medieval political thought took a wrong turn when it brought into too close association the concepts of property and justice, thus generating the idea of an individual right. Ever since their illegitimate conception, rights both express the idea of human alienation from each other (there is a part of justice that belongs to me and not to you) and prove vulnerable to the adoption of false conceptions of justice (there is material property that belongs to me and not to you, liberty that I have and you do not, etc.). The language of rights must therefore be rejected in favor of some different account of the structure of justice, such as one in terms of "right order," not "rights." It is easy, but incautious, to suppose that

[39] A. W. Brian Simpson, *Human Rights and the End of Empire: Britain and the Genesis of the European Convention* (Oxford University Press 2001).

[40] John Finnis, *Natural Law and Natural Rights* (Clarendon Press 1980); Robert P George, *In Defense of Natural Law* (Clarendon Press 1998). Finnis himself would seem to be an abridgement theorist.

[41] Stephen J Grabill, *Rediscovering the Natural Law in Reformed Theological Ethics* (Wm B Eerdmans 2006), esp ch 1.

[42] Joan Lockwood O'Donovan, "The Concept of Rights in Christian Moral Discourse" in Michael Cromartie (ed), *A Preserving Grace: Protestants, Catholics and Natural Law* (Wm B Eerdmans 1997); John Milbank, "Against Human Rights: Liberty in the Western Tradition" (2012) 1 Oxford Journal of Law and Religion 203.

such a position is authentically Burkean. The Marxist overtones are at least as pronounced.

Some of the confusion lies in the fact that—as a matter of constitutional practice—the language of rights is misleading. The substantive element of a constitutional right lies in an abstract interest or constitutional good, capable of grounding a number of more precise legal positions (rights) through processes of legal reasoning.[43] Rights only become absolute once argument and reasoning are complete. The status of a "right" only differs from other public goods in the procedural advantages associated with it: one can legally defend one's specific interest in one's own liberty, but not one's undifferentiated interest in national security. Liberty as such and security as such are formally identical; they need reconciling with each other, whether through social, political, or legal processes.[44] So the question is not what one makes of the language of rights. Rather, it is an institutional and structural question: what role should individuals, relatively stable legal texts (constitutions), and judiciaries have in securing some political interests and goods as opposed to others?

The long and diverse history of Christian political thought suggests three central concerns that emerge repeatedly and in different forms: respect for the value and moral accountability of the individual;[45] the defense of a specific social domain of "church" that, while still being subject to law, is not subject to "secular" governmental authority; and the articulation of conditions for a common political good,[46] based on the premise of a universal human nature. Human and constitutional rights are based on the moral priority of the individual human person and the value of making certain limits on, and mandates for, state action relatively secure in the face of political and social pressures. This was the mid-twentieth-century lesson that Jacques Maritain and other Catholic and non-Catholic human rights advocates learned from fascism and communism.[47] They also secure the protection of a domain of civil liberty that in its freedoms of thought, expression, association, and assembly is church shaped. Rights of political participation, as well as other social, economic, and cultural rights, identify basic elements of a common

[43] Robert Alexy, *A Theory of Constitutional Rights* (J Rivers tr, Oxford University Press 2000) ch 4.

[44] I follow Alexy, and not Ronald Dworkin, in denying any relevant distinction between principles and policies.

[45] Larry Siedentop, *Inventing the Individual: The Origins of Western Liberalism* (Allen Lane 2014).

[46] See Jonathan Chaplin's contribution to this volume.

[47] Jacques Maritain, *The Rights of Man and Natural Law* (Geoffrey Bles 1944).

good. Whether grounded in human dignity as the image bearers of God,[48] in the value we have consequent on being loved by God,[49] or in the entire spiritual narrative of "creation, life, faith, sin, penitence and redemption,"[50] Christian theological anthropology finds plausible expression in a political order based on fundamental constitutional rights as opposed to any alternative such as a purely procedural majoritarian democracy, a confessional state, or an authoritarian executive form of government. These are the practical options from which we must choose—not between abstract theological, moral, or political theories.[51]

Critique of the Content of Constitutional Rights

The second question concerns the extent to which Christian political thought engages with the content of constitutional rights. Here, it is helpful to draw a distinction between the enumeration and textual formulation of rights on one hand and their interpretation and application on the other. The former is authoritative, and in some sense "higher" law; it will be considered in this section. The latter is a matter of judicial, scholarly, and popular contestation; it will be considered in the next. At the same time, the two aspects are related in that those negotiating constitutional (and international) rights instruments will inevitably seek to create textual "pegs" for their preferred interpretations. The best-known example of this concerns the freedom to change one's religion or belief in Article 18 of the Universal Declaration of Human Rights 1948 (UDHR).[52] When it came to be given legal force in international covenants, several Muslim-majority countries objected to this phrase.[53] The objection led to a more neutral formulation in Article 18 of

48 Kieran Cronin, *Rights and Christian Ethics* (Cambridge University Press 1994); Roger Ruston, *Human Rights and the Image of God* (SCM Press 2004); Claudia Welz, *Humanity in God's Image: An Interdisciplinary Exploration* (Oxford University Press 2016).

49 Nicholas Wolterstorff, *Justice: Rights and Wrong* (Princeton University Press 2008).

50 Jeremy Waldron, *One Another's Equals: The Basis of Human Equality* (Belknap Press 2017) 205.

51 Gustav Radbruch is equally clear-sighted in his recognition that we have to choose between political forms that are directed toward individual, collective, or transpersonal goods. See Gustav Radbruch, *Philosophy of Law* (1932) § 7, in *The Legal Philosophies of Lask, Radbruch and Dabin* (Kurt Wilk tr, Harvard University Press 1950). One must leave for another time the argument whether a "relational" starting point must make this choice.

52 The same formulation is used in the European Convention on Human Rights 1950 (ECHR), Art. 9.

53 The debate can be followed in Paul M Taylor, *Freedom of Religion: UN and European Human Rights Law and Practice* (Cambridge University Press 2005) 27–42.

the International Covenant on Civil and Political Rights 1966 (ICCPR). The international consensus is that "to have or to adopt a religion" (ICCPR) still includes the "freedom to change" (UDHR/European Convention on Human Rights 1950 [ECHR]), but this is clearly now a matter of interpretation. A more recent example would be the textual shift from the right of "men and women" to marry (UDHR/ECHR/ICCPR) to the neutral "right to marry" in Article 9 of the EU Charter of Fundamental Rights 2000. In short, ideological disagreement tends to get textually suppressed for the sake of immediate political consensus and thus deferred to later interpretative disagreement and resolution.

In spite of this pragmatic pressure toward textual consensus, in recent work Samuel Moyn claims to detect a regressive Christian influence on the content of international human rights instruments.[54] On his account, Christianity has generally been hostile to human rights. However, in the aftermath of the Second World War, Christians, led by Pope Pius XII, experienced a thorough conversion. A new commitment to human rights was grounded in human dignity as understood by the ethics of personalism. This appropriation had a decidedly religious inflection. Human rights, now grounded in human dignity, were captured for the morally conservative political agenda of European Christian democracy, thus denying their original secular emancipatory purpose.

Moyn's thesis is highly problematic in several respects. The UDHR represented the first tentative steps in the post-Westphalian reordering of international law. If Christians were doing a new thing in 1948, so was everyone else. Many of the key architects of the postwar human rights regime were not Christian, or at least not obviously thinking Christianly about what they were doing. The Lebanese participant in the drafting of the UDHR, Charles Malik, is the notable exception, but one only needs to look at the ground-breaking preliminary work of Hersch Lauterpacht, work carried out at the request of the American Jewish Committee, not to speak of the other participants in the drafting committee, to find clear counterexamples.[55]

However, this is not to deny all forms of continuity. The architects of the UDHR were explicitly drawing on two centuries of national constitutional experience with bills of rights. We have already noted in the previous section

[54] Samuel Moyn, *Christian Human Rights* (University of Pennsylvania Press 2015).

[55] Sir Hersch Lauterpacht, *An International Bill of the Rights of Man* (1945; Oxford University Press 2013). On Lauterpacht's seminal involvement, see AW Brian Simpson, "Hersch Lauterpacht and the Genesis of the Age of Human Rights" (2004) 120 Law Quarterly Review 49–80.

historic defenders of constitutional rights from within the Christian tradition. Thomas Pink and John Finnis have also argued for a much higher degree of continuity than Moyn accepts between mid-twentieth-century (Catholic) Christian democracy and the earlier tradition of Catholic political thought.[56] Moyn suggests that the supposedly late conversion of Catholic Christians to the cause of human rights can be seen in their dignity-inflected content. But there was a much greater degree of "borrowing" from previous constitutional texts than Moyn allows.[57] Human rights and constitutional rights have had a mutually reinforcing role. As has already been pointed out, the general trajectory has been to both expand the rights protected and abstract away from any emerging ideological disagreements. The contrast between an original secular, liberal, progressive, and emancipatory code of rights and some new socially and morally conservative restatement of human rights in the mid-twentieth century is simply not visible in the resulting texts.

It would require considerable work in reconstructing the historic lines of influence from one constitutional text to another to demonstrate this basic continuity thesis conclusively. Here there is only space to note some of the most obvious counterexamples to Moyn's argument.

First of all, there is a patently high degree of continuity between the constitutional rights defended by eighteenth-century writers and instruments such as the ECHR 1950 or the ICCPR 1966. The content of almost all these rights can be found in Blackstone's *Commentaries*. In many cases, they are already identified as general "rights." In some cases, such as the right to respect for private and family life, home, and correspondence and the right to marry and found a family according to national laws, the content is broadly similar without being enumerated as rights. Freedom of expression, assembly, and association feature in his account more by way of implication in discussing their limits. As to the right to vote, of course, Blackstone's view of the franchise was not as extensive as ours, but in essence he thought of political participation as a matter of right as well. The most obvious difference is in freedom of thought, conscience, and religion and the associated right of parents to secure the religious upbringing of their children. Here he defends the still rather restrictive laws of mid-eighteenth-century England by reference to

[56] Thomas Pink, "Samuel Moyn – *Christian Human Rights*" (2017) 28 King's Law Journal 6; John Finnis, "On Moyn's *Christian Human Rights* (2015)" (2017) 28 King's Law Journal 12. Dan Edelstein supports this analysis.

[57] Philip Alston has also criticized Moyn's "myopia" in this regard. See Philp Alston, "Book Review. Does the Past matter? On the Origin of Human Rights" (2013) 126 Harvard Law Review 2043, 2066–2070.

securing the position of the established church and the defense of the state from foreign political influence. But his sympathies clearly lay with freedom of conscience if only it were safe to give it free rein. This cautious attitude toward freedom of religion, or—what comes to much the same thing—this unwillingness to let go of historic features of the Christian confessional state, is a feature of many constitutions at the time, including those of most of the American states, with their new bills of rights. The otherwise rather "liberal" Spanish Constitution of 1812 was rigidly and exclusively Roman Catholic at just this point. The separation of religious and civil power that now informs our understanding of freedom of religion is a mid-nineteenth-century development, as seen both by developments in the United Kingdom and, for example, in the progressive Belgian Constitution of 1831.[58] This point applies even in the United States.[59]

Any idea that the UDHR is "conservative" or "Christian" in content can easily be rebutted by looking at a second example: the substantial constitutional rights section of the Weimar Imperial Constitution of 1919 (WRV).[60] For all its ill fate, that constitution was a serious attempt to thrash out a detailed and workable compromise between conservatives, nationalists, liberals, and Marxists. Chapter II contains the "fundamental rights and duties of Germans" set out in fifty-seven articles. The overlap with the UDHR is very close. The main differences are that the Weimar Constitution contains a specific right of diplomatic protection, it explicitly abolishes censorship (with some exceptions), it still contains the old "right of petition," it explicitly states that there should be no compulsion to reveal one's religion or participate in religious rites, and it contains an express right to freedom of contract. One could argue that these are mostly implicit in more broadly phrased human rights. Unsurprisingly, it goes into rather more detail on the legal status of civil servants, the education system, and employer-worker relationships, but the basic principles behind these provisions are those of the UDHR, that is, equal access to public service, universal education with a particular role for parents, and the right to form trade unions to defend one's

[58] Julian Rivers, *The Law of Organized Religions* (Oxford University Press 2010) ch 1; Edwige Lefebvre, "The Belgian Constitution on 1831: The Citizen Burgher" *Zentrum für Europäische Rechtspolitik*, Diskussionspapier 4/97.

[59] See Steven K Green, *The Second Disestablishment: Church and State in Nineteenth-Century America* (Oxford University Press 2010). We should not be misled by the First Amendment's limitation of *federal* power—which did not apply to individual state establishments.

[60] English version translated by Howard Lee McBain and Lindsay Rogers, <https://en.wikisource.org/wiki/Weimar_constitution> accessed 18 April 2018.

economic interests. The Weimar Constitution abolishes any state church but proceeds to create a special regime for the public status of religious organizations that applies to this day.[61] The UDHR says nothing about the highly diverse relationships between the state and religion across the world's constitutions—so long as basic rights of religious liberty and nondiscrimination are protected. German pluralism, French secularism, and British symbolic establishment are all options. Given the practical need to achieve a wide consensus, what is remarkable about the UDHR is not any supposedly conservative inflection but how much of the inherited acquisition of constitutional rights in developed political systems managed to find a place. Everything in the UDHR was already there in Weimar, and the vast majority of Weimar found its way into the UDHR.

If Moyn's thesis that the UDHR is distinctively Christian fails to persuade, one might think his argument would at least have more success in respect of the Irish Constitution of 1937. It is here that he claims the new Catholic Christian inflection of rights had its first success. It is undoubtedly true that the preamble of the Irish Constitution locates the constitution clearly within a narrative of Christian national identity, a point reinforced by the theistic inflection of oaths of public office,[62] by the idea that public power is exercised by the people "under God,"[63] and by the explicit recognition that "public worship is due to Almighty God."[64] But beyond that, when it comes to individual rights, the constitution secures freedom of religion and conscience, nonendowment of religion (except for the support of schools), nondiscrimination, and internal autonomy.[65] There is no religious establishment. It went as far as recognizing the "special position" of the Roman Catholic Church on account of its majority position but immediately proceeded to "recognize" other religious denominations as well, including Jewish congregations.[66] This was clearly not a constitution for atheists, but at the same time it contained no legal privileges for the Roman Catholic Church.

Article 41 secures the rights of the family as the "natural primary and fundamental unit group of Society." It proceeds to commit the state to ensuring that mothers are "not obliged by economic necessity to engage in labour to the neglect of their duties in the home," and it raises the prohibition of

[61] Basic Law 1949, Art. 140 preserves WRV 1919, Arts. 136–139 and 141.
[62] Arts. 12, 31, 34.
[63] Art. 6.
[64] Art. 44.1.1.
[65] Art. 44.2
[66] Art. 44.1.2 and 3. Removed by the Fifth Amendment on 5 January 1973.

divorce and abortion (still widespread across Europe at the time) to constitutional status.[67] Here is the clearest expression of Catholic social thought. But it is important to set it in context. The Weimar Imperial Constitution of 1919 also states that marriage and the family are under the specific protection of the constitution, that it is the job of the state to support families, and that motherhood gives rise to a special claim to protection and support.[68] It might not say that the family enjoys "inalienable and imprescriptible rights," but it does say that the upbringing of children is the "highest duty and natural right of parents."[69] For sure, the language is not *quite* as insistent as that of the Irish Constitution, but the underlying assumptions are very close. The clearest difference of emphasis is that the Weimar Constitution reinforces the equal rights of both sexes in marriage (although not in parenthood), whereas the Irish Constitution is silent at this point.

In introducing "Directives of Social Policy," which are largely concerned with the duty to manage the economy for the good of all, the Irish Constitution of 1937 took a step unfamiliar to the common-law world.[70] In this sense, the constitution was progressive, although in avoiding the language of "rights" it remained rooted in the common-law tradition. It is here that the concept of dignity finds its historic place. Once again, the Weimar Imperial Constitution had already led the way. The basic principle that stands at the head of Weimar's section on economic life runs as follows:

> In compliance with the principles of justice, the ordering of economic life has the goal of guaranteeing a dignified existence (lit. *menschenwürdigen Dasein*, a "worthy-of-human existence") for all. Within these limits, economic liberty for the individual is to be secured.[71]

It is thus not obvious that when the preamble to the Irish Constitution also mentioned the goal of ensuring the "dignity of the individual" it meant anything more than the duty to secure the socioeconomic basis of human well-being. Dignity is clearly not presented as the foundation of all rights. But then nor does the UDHR treat it as such either. What the UDHR actually says is that "inherent dignity and the equal and inalienable rights of all

[67] Prohibition on divorce removed by Fifteenth Amendment of 17 June 1996. Abortion has been (and is still) subject to several amendments.
[68] WRV 1919, Art. 119.
[69] Art. 120.
[70] Art. 45.
[71] WRV 1919, Art. 151 (author's translation).

members of the human family are the foundation of freedom, justice and peace in the world." Dignity might be a master concept in some theoretical accounts of human rights, including some Christian conceptions of human rights, but that is not what the UDHR, the Irish Constitution, or the Weimar Constitution says.[72]

Morsink shows that at key points in the discussions leading up to the UDHR, the majority rejected attempts to inject a more Catholic, or even theistic, inflection into the textual formulation.[73] For example, the text effectively followed Weimar and not the Irish Constitution in omitting any suggestion that the family had "inalienable and imprescriptible rights."[74] And this example can stand for the question of the content of constitutional rights in general. Christian thinkers may have had slightly different emphases—among themselves and with non-Christians—and they understandably have sought (and as often as not failed) to anchor such nuances in the text, but it is hard to identify any clear difference of basic content. The most that can be said for Moyn's thesis that mid-twentieth-century Christian democracy influenced the content of human rights is that human dignity gradually moved from being a socialist value informing rights designed to secure the material conditions for a tolerable human existence to being the master value of the entire catalog of rights. This is seen most clearly in the German Basic Law of 1949, which makes human dignity the inviolable *über*-principle of the whole catalog of constitutional rights. But even here, the impact of this rationalizing adjustment has been felt only in the gradual reinterpretation of existing rights over a much longer period of time, rather than in any novel content.[75] And, of course, dignity itself need not be construed in any particularly religious or secular way.[76]

[72] There is a comprehensive discussion of "dignity" in Christopher McCrudden (ed), *Understanding Human Dignity* (Oxford University Press/British Academy 2013).

[73] Johannes Morsink, *The Universal Declaration of Human Rights: Origins, Drafting and Intent* (University of Pennsylvania Press 1999), esp ch 8.

[74] Ibid, 254–256.

[75] See Donald Kommers and Russell A Miller, *The Constitutional Jurisprudence of the Federal Republic of Germany* (3rd edn, Duke University Press 2012) ch 7.

[76] See Michael Rosen, *Dignity: Its History and Meaning* (Harvard University Press 2012). On the ambiguous legal impact of "dignity," see Aurora Plomer and Dimitrios Tsarapatsanis, "The Symmetry of Human Dignity as a Constitutional Value and Fundamental Human Right in Europe" (2012) 1 Yearbook of International Law and Jurisprudence 113.

Critique of the Construction of Constitutional Rights

Given the widespread dominance of constitutional rights discourse, the emergence over the last hundred years of a more or less universal core content, and the flexibility of interpretation and enforcement, most debates about constitutional rights are no longer about the concept as a whole, or even their content. Rather, they are about the correct interpretation and balancing of rights with other important public goods in the context of specific cases. It is in this area that a set of particularly Christian concerns can be identified.

In his helpful review of the interactions between Roman Catholic and secular human rights discourses, Christopher McCrudden sets out both a number of commonalities and some important divergences.[77] Rather than any straightforward conflict, we should think in terms of differing conceptions of rights that only partially overlap. According to McCrudden, Roman Catholic teaching tends to align itself with state-empowering, or positive, conceptions of rights, with a particular emphasis on socioeconomic rights, rather than the state-limiting, or negative, conception of older constitutional traditions. It grounds these rights in a dignitarian conception of human value and thus produces a deontological, noninstrumental understanding of rights. It emphasizes the role of nonstate actors in securing the practical enjoyment of rights, and it also tends toward proportionality-based reasoning and the balancing of rights with duties to secure the common good.

In all these respects, Roman Catholic conceptions of constitutional rights can be aligned with significant strands within the secular literature and state practice. However, McCrudden also observes a number of divergences in which the official teaching of the Church sets out a more distinctive position. These can be rearranged into those which affect the status and those which affect the content of rights. In terms of status, McCrudden notes the theological grounding of dignity, which tends to emerge as a strong natural law position invalidating incompatible state law. Rights are also situated within a communitarian context; the autonomous individual is not supreme. And there is ultimately a subordination of freedom and dialogical ways of knowing rights to a commitment to truth about the nature and value of human existence. In terms of interpretation, the key elements are the extension of right-holder

[77] Christopher McCrudden, "Legal and Roman Catholic Conceptions of Human Rights: Convergence, Divergence and Dialogue?" (2012) 1 Oxford Journal of Law and Religion 185.

status to the unborn and severely disabled (particularly in relation to the right to life), the foundational nature of freedom of religion, and differing views of the requirements of equality, particularly in relation to women and sexual minorities.

Protestant Christian engagement with fundamental rights tends to have a slightly different emphasis. Individual liberty, particularly in the guise of freedom of conscience, ranks more highly in the implicit order of values, and concern for social justice rather less so. It is possible that this difference of emphasis reflects deep-rooted cultural differences. Protestant Christianity has historically been more closely aligned with common-law jurisdictions, whereas Roman Catholicism has been present in civilian ones. There is thus a loose correlation between Protestantism and political tendencies toward small government along with a judicially protected sphere of civil liberty. What holds both elements in common is a suspicion of concentrations of power, whether ecclesiastical or civil. There is a corresponding caution about entrenching rights such as socioeconomic rights that feature primarily as political mandates for state action. Roman Catholicism, by contrast, aligns more closely with positive views of both church and state as instruments for the care of the whole person. Thus, the relatively libertarian cast of the common law still has a certain theological resonance.[78]

However, differences between Protestant and Catholic emphases in interpreting constitutional rights are becoming less significant as they lose their cultural dominance in the face of various secular ideologies. Moyn is to that extent correct; the ethical context within which human rights were interpreted and applied in the mid-twentieth century seems, from the perspective of the early twenty-first century, more recognizably Christian. But even here there is no straightforward trajectory. The influences are complex and intertwined, as can be seen from the example of freedom of religion.[79]

Freedom-of-religion cases only really took off in the European Court of Human Rights from *Kokkinakis* onward.[80] While it is possible to read the court's ultimate failure to protect Lautsi's right to be educated free from the presence of a crucifix, or the failure to protect Sahin, Dahlab, and Dogru's rights to be free to wear the Islamic veil in public, as remnants of Christian

[78] The classic treatment of this point is, of course, Max Weber, *The Protestant ethic and the spirit of capitalism* (Talcott Parsons tr, 2nd edn, Allen and Unwin 1976).

[79] A full discussion of the tensions between Christian and secular conceptions of religious liberty can be found in Rex Ahdar and Ian Leigh, *Religious Liberty in the Liberal State* (2nd edn., Oxford University Press 2013).

[80] *Kokkinakis v Greece* (A-260/A), (1994) 7 EHRR 397.

bias,[81] it is actually much more plausible to see both Lautsi and the Islamic veil cases as the unwillingness of the court to undermine its own legitimacy by too radical a challenge to the inherited majority cultures of the states in question, whether Catholic or secular. Freedom of conscience has always been a Cinderella right precisely because it expresses the most direct rejection of majority culture and its law. Seen against the background of early attempts to limit freedom of conscience to the *forum internum*, and restrictions of freedom of religion in cases of contractual agreement, one should be noticing the success of *Eweida* rather than the failure of *Ladele*, *McFarlane*, or *Chaplin*.[82]

Another important line of cases concerns the Article 9 rights of churches and other religious organizations. To start with, the Commission and Court tended to interpret Article 9 in highly individualistic terms, and only from about 2000 did the case law take a decided turn toward a more collectivist interpretation of freedom of religion.[83] It is probable that this is a delayed response to the fall of communism in the central and Eastern European states, and the need to construct "liberal" church-state regimes in those countries now toying with the re-establishment of orthodox Christianity. But the expansion of freedom of religion from a merely individual and personal faith to the collective administrative autonomy of a religious organization in its internal affairs is one that fits well with basic Christian assumptions about the proper relationship between church and state.[84] Overall, the narrative here is one of clarifying and strengthening freedom of religion, even if the court is not always as ambitious as one might wish.

Similar accounts of other specific constitutional rights could also be constructed. One suspects, for example, that the right to equality is beginning to lose its mooring as an essentially liberal (and, I would argue, Christian) principle requiring us to overlook, or ignore, our differences in public contexts and becoming instead a positive requirement to affirm each other's self-constructed identities, even when those identities reflect

[81] This is Moyn's argument in *Christian Human Rights*, ch 4. If he were correct, it would be a counterexample to his own thesis of late twentieth-century secularization in human rights case law.

[82] *Eweida et al v United Kingdom* (48420/10), 57 EHRR 8.

[83] The key case is *Hasan & Chaush v Bulgaria* (30985/96), (2002) 34 EHRR 55. See discussion in Julian Rivers, *The Law of Organized Religions*, 50–71.

[84] The main area of legal dispute is currently over the extent of "ministerial exceptions" to employment law. For a comparative discussion, see articles by Pamela Slotte, Helge Årsheim, Marie Ashe, Emma Svensson, Peter W. Edge, Carmen Garcimartin and Lisbet Christoffersen in (2015) 4(2) Oxford Journal of Law and Religion.

ideologies we think are mistaken and not conducive to human flourishing.[85] But once again, the reconstruction of the equality case law and its interaction with Christian political thought will be complex and unlikely to present a narrative either of triumphant amelioration or apocalyptic doom. Privacy and family rights represent further areas of contestation between more or less (and internally contested) Christian accounts.

Conclusion

One can see how it would be possible to sketch a dystopian vision of an ebullient global constitutional rights ideology rooted in a commitment to radical human autonomy, upheld by an elite network of "liberal" judges convinced of the morality of their cause and immune to all local correction. Yet as the literature on constitutional convergence never ceases to point out, there are always new local pressures and new resolutions. The idea that the global protection of constitutional rights will stabilize around a single preferred ideology is implausible. The main contribution of Christians will be to make the case for particular solutions to concrete problems of freedom, equality, community, security, order, and well-being on the grounds that these best secure human flourishing in the context of unresolved disputes about human identity and ultimate purpose. And that, one hopes, is the desire of all well-intentioned people. In that sense, the constitutional rights project is neither distinctively Christian nor anti-Christian. It has potential either way. The challenge will be whether Christians engaging in this area can move beyond merely pragmatic advocacy for particular preferred solutions to maintain a coherent and compelling theory of constitutional rights for the good of all.

[85] This problem is exposed when one starts to consider what it means for a public body to "promote" religious equality. See Julian Rivers, "Promoting Religious Equality" (2012) 1 Oxford Journal of Law and Religion 386.

14

Religious Freedom

Freedom of Conscience: Assessing the Christian Contribution

Ian Leigh

Introduction

Modern thought tends to differentiate between freedom of conscience and freedom of religion. Freedom of conscience is seen to be centered on an individual's ability to live consistently with their fundamental beliefs, whether those beliefs are religious or not. The emphasis is on being able to live with moral integrity or authenticity. For example, Jocelyn Maclure and Charles Taylor refer to conscience as the "core beliefs that allow individuals to structure their moral identity," which aid them in giving direction to life and in exercising a faculty for judgment when faced with conflicts of values, and which cannot be transgressed without violating their sense of moral integrity.[1] This is a narrower concept than freedom of religion, which protects not only personal belief but also communal or institutional aspects, as well as practice, worship, and the performance of ritual, teaching, proselytism, and charity.[2]

Until recently, freedom of conscience was most closely associated with questions such as religious oaths and conscientious objection to military service. Recent controversial conscience-based claims in the realms of health care and business by providers of goods and services and by public officials have, however, refocused attention on the right and ignited a debate about its limits, because of their (contested) impact on abortion, contraception,

[1] J Maclure and C Taylor, *Secularism and Freedom of Conscience* (Harvard UP 2011) 89–90 and chs 8 and 10 more generally. Cf. Joseph Raz's account of conscientious objection: J Raz, *The Authority of Law* (Oxford 1979) 264.

[2] On the differences see further R Ahdar, "Is Freedom of Conscience Superior to Freedom of Religion?" (2018) 7 Oxford Journal of Law and Religion 124–142 and N Chapman, "Disentangling Conscience and Religion" (2013) University of Illinois Law LR 1457.

Ian Leigh, *Religious Freedom: Freedom of Conscience: Assessing the Christian Contribution* in *Christianity and Constitutionalism*. Edited by: Nicholas Aroney and Ian Leigh, Oxford University Press. © Oxford University Press 2022.
DOI: 10.1093/oso/9780197587256.003.0014

and LGBT rights.[3] This therefore is an appropriate time for a re-evaluation of its Christian roots. In this chapter I aim to assess the contribution of Christian thought about freedom of conscience to liberal constitutionalism. Specifically, what did Christian beliefs contribute and what was their impact on constitutional development, and where do Christian rationales diverge from modern constitutional approaches?

By way of initial clarification, we need first to briefly trace the history of the terminology. From the sixteenth to nineteenth centuries, what is now called freedom of religion and belief, so far as it existed at all, went under the name of freedom of conscience. John Rawls goes so far as to claim that equal liberty of conscience was the forerunner to civil liberty.[4] Some contemporary commentators continue to follow this historical usage—notably Martha Nussbaum in her *Liberty of Conscience*.[5] This more general right is not my focus here; rather, my concern is to explicate the Christian contribution to the narrower field now associated with freedom of conscience per se. As liberty of conscience received recognition in constitutional texts, the difference in terminology—at first nearly accidental—became more significant. In the modern era the field has been dominated by constitutional texts following the US pattern by referring to the free exercise of religion and by adopting much of the accompanying jurisprudence. Conscience has until recently been largely overlooked—a Cinderella right, overshadowed, in this instance, by its more precocious younger sister.

Freedom of conscience re-emerged as a general legal right in modern human rights law post-1945.[6] The preamble to the Universal Declaration on Human Rights 1948 (UDHR) refers to human beings "endowed with conscience" (Art. 1) and the UDHR drew on domestic constitutions explicitly protecting freedom of conscience alongside religion as the basis for Article 18, protecting freedom of thought, conscience, and religion.[7] This is mirrored in Article 18 of the International Covenant on Civil and Political

[3] See especially S Mancini and M Rosenfeld (eds), *The Conscience Wars: Rethinking the Balance between Religion, Identity and Equality* (Cambridge University Press 2018); J Adenitire (ed), *Religious Beliefs and Conscientious Exemptions in a Liberal State* (Hart Publishing 2019).

[4] J Rawls, *Political Liberalism* (Columbia University Press 1993) xxiv ff.

[5] M Nussbaum, *Liberty of Conscience: In Defense of America's Tradition of Religious Equality* (Basic Books 2008).

[6] The fullest (though now dated) account is L Hammer, *The International Human Right to Freedom of Conscience: Some Suggestions for Its Development and Application* (Ashgate Pub Limited 2001). For more recent accounts focusing on conscientious objection: H Bielefeldt, N Ghanea, and M Wiener, *Freedom of Religion of Belief: An International Law Commentary* (Oxford 2016) 258–305; G Puppinck, *Conscientious Objection and Human Rights: A Systematic Analysis* (Brill 2017).

[7] Hammer, *The International Human Right to Freedom of Conscience*, 32.

Rights (ICCPR) and Article 9 of the European Convention on Human Rights (ECHR): both treaties protect the qualified freedom to manifest one's *religion or belief* but do not refer explicitly in this context to manifestation of *conscience*. This drafting appears to make the distinction between religion and conscience potentially decisive in cases where the question is whether particular conscientious acts or objections are protected. Freedom of conscience under human rights law is associated with conscientious refusals by individuals of various kinds, mainly, of course, conscientious objection to military service.

It is helpful at the outset to explicate what is meant by conscience and how this relates to freedom of conscience.

As C. S. Lewis points out, the idea of conscience as an inner voice or lawgiver is one of a number of competing and overlapping usages that emerged from the earlier sense of *conscientia* (Latin) or *suneidis* (Greek), which denoted sharing knowledge (with another or oneself).[8] Alberto Giubilini differentiates four basic meanings of conscience, which can overlap: self-knowledge and self-assessment; a faculty for, or body of, moral knowledge or beliefs; a motivation to act morally; and self-identifying moral commitments.[9] Of these, it is the final category (which implies both moral subjectivity and that an individual is in some sense defined by their chosen commitments) that is most closely associated with contemporary freedom of conscience.

Plainly, recognition of conscience in the sense of an inner capacity to discern right and wrong and to apply that understanding to one's conduct (whether actual or contemplated) does not begin or end with Christian thought. Indeed, recent scholarship, notably Richard Sorabji's *Moral Conscience through the Ages*,[10] presents a narrative emphasizing the secular nature of conscience, beginning from classical roots.[11] Equally, it would be naïve to suggest that there is a single, consistent, Christian approach to conscience, spanning both the millennia and different traditions.[12] What can be said, however, is that writers in the Christian tradition, beginning with

[8] CS Lewis, *Studies in Words* (2nd edn, Cambridge 2013) ch 8. For a recent full study see R Sorabji, *Moral Conscience through the Ages: Fifth Century BC to the Present* (Oxford 2014).

[9] *Stanford Encyclopedia of Philosophy*, entry "Conscience" (first published 14 March 2016) <https://plato.stanford.edu/entries/conscience/>.

[10] R Sorabji, *Moral Conscience through the Ages*.

[11] See also Nussbaum, *Liberty of Conscience*.

[12] On the approach of different Christian traditions to freedom of religion and of conscience: T Shah and A Hertzke (eds), *Christianity and Freedom*, vol 1; *Historical Perspectives* (Cambridge University Press 2016).

biblical authors, present a series of varied perspectives on conscience that challenge the contemporary understanding that conscience protects an individual's autonomy by allowing them to live consistently with their core beliefs, subjectively understood.

Christian Approaches

Biblical Foundations of Freedom of Conscience

The use of biblical passages in relation to freedom of conscience falls into four distinct categories: discerning the nature of moral conscience, explicating the teaching and attitude of Jesus toward religious disagreement, providing accounts of heroes of faith who obeyed God's direct instructions or what they discerned to be God's will to defy the authorities, and giving instruction about conduct that implicates the believer's or a fellow believer's conscience. Clearly, the second and third of these overlap with more general constitutional questions addressing the relationship of religion with the state.[13] The second is of particular interest in relation to religious freedom but less so in relation to freedom of conscience as a distinct category and is not discussed here.[14] The third category addresses what is effectively a subquestion—what we would now call conscientious objection[15]—which, although important, is not the primary focus here. For this reason, more attention will be devoted to the fourth question—instructions about conduct implicating conscience.

Questions of conscience arose in the early church principally in relation to apparent tensions between the old law-based dispensation of Jewish believers and the new dispensation based on faith.[16] Romans 14 and 1 Corinthians 8:4–9 are key New Testament passages addressing disagreements over dietary requirements, consumption of food offered to idols, and days of worship in the early Church. Several important principles emerge: those with a mature understanding that allow them to eat all types of food should not look down on others who have more tender consciences and only eat vegetables,

[13] For broader discussions of biblical attitudes toward the state see chapters 2 and 3 above, by Burnside and Bertschmann respectively.

[14] In debates about religious persecution and for religious liberty by writers from the early Church fathers through to the seventeenth century, conflicting interpretations of the parables of the Great Banquet (Luke 14:16–24) and of the Tares (or Weeds) (Matt. 13:24–30) were pivotal.

[15] 295 below.

[16] See also Chapman, "Disentangling Religion and Conscience," 1481–1482.

while the vegetarians should not judge the omnivores. Judgment of whether believers have correctly understood and fulfilled their religious obligations on these questions is for God rather than for fellow Christians. The fact that God has accepted their faith and commitment is all the more reason not to make such judgments (Rom. 14:3). In the case of these matters of conscience, those who believe they are free to eat all foods may freely do so (Rom. 14:22) unless by so doing they cause a fellow believer to stumble (Rom. 14:20–21 and 1 Cor. 8:9–13); the strong must act considerately toward the weak (Rom. 15:1). On the other hand, the person with the more tender conscience should not go against their convictions since it would be sinful for them to do what they believe to be wrong (Rom. 14:23).

These guidelines are given in relation to everyday questions of conduct within the church and do not address a believer's civic obligations or conduct toward people with entirely different beliefs or moral standards. Nonetheless, there are some general pointers here about how to approach questions of conscience in a Christian framework. There is an obvious emphasis on personal responsibility before God for one's beliefs or actions, and as we shall see, later writers based their defense of religious freedom upon this. The New Testament passages cannot, however, mean that *all* judgments on matters of belief or behavior must be avoided so that all such questions are covered by personal conscience. Paul's letters contain many examples to the contrary where he leaves no doubt that specific immoral behavior by individuals is to be condemned. Moreover, without a substantial measure of agreement on key doctrine, the church would have no common belief, and again Paul's letters repeatedly point to some beliefs as erroneous and others as orthodox. His approach suggests instead that a distinction needs to be made between matters left to individual conscience and those covered by universal prescription. This is the origin of an influential concept—*adiaphora* or *things indifferent*—which was invoked for centuries by later thinkers.[17] By arguing that on such nonessential questions it would nonetheless be wrong for the believer with the tenderer or weaker conscience to go against it, Paul seems on the face of it to be advocating that on nonessential questions other people's interests should be put first. On closer examination, however, this is not a blueprint for always conceding to other people's rights and freedoms in matters of conscience. It is noticeable that his concern is with the believer

[17] For contrasting approaches to *adiaphora* by Erasmus, Hooker, and Locke with regard to conscience see Forst, *Toleration in Conflict*, 104–105, 174, and 213–215, respectively.

whose conscience is more robust not exercising the full extent of their *liberty*, rather than acting against their own conscience. Nonetheless, clearly Paul regards those with an immature or tender conscience over not eating meat as *mistaken*.[18] In that sense his approach to religious disagreement to some extent foreshadows what (sixteen centuries later) would come to be called "toleration."

Two Christian Traditions

This section argues that there are two significant strands to Christian thinking about conscience. The first—and in terms of its influence on liberal constitutionalism, dominant—strand associates conscience with individual belief. It tends to see freedom of religion in Protestant terms (i.e., belief centered and genuinely personally held in order to be of any value) so that the right of freedom of conscience has a high degree of convergence with it. I term this first strand *conscience as moral belief*. Although this approach has its origins in early Christian thought,[19] for the purpose of the discussion here it is the impact of Christian writers and thinkers in the seventeenth century, famously John Locke and Roger Williams, but also some of their less known predecessors, on the foundations of liberal constitutionalism that are of interest. The second, associated with Thomism and natural law thinking and reflected in modern Catholic law thought, stresses that conscience is a form of moral knowledge—of oneself and one's actions and (indirectly) of the divine law. This strand draws on the biblical understanding that an individual's conscience stands in need of development or formation, and that it can be mistaken. This opens the possibility of questioning or debating claims of conscience. In view of its emphasis on reflection and deliberation I term this second strand *conscience as moral judgement*.

[18] Later Christian writers grappled with the perplexing problem of how to approach someone who conscientiously acts based on an erroneous belief. This has some contemporary relevance, e.g., in cases of conscientious objection to the "morning after" pill by pharmacists and others because of the (scientifically doubtful) argument that it acts as an abortifacient.

[19] Notably in the writings of Tertullian (160–220) and Lactantius (ca. 250–325): Sorabji, *Moral Conscience through the Ages*, 48; and Elizabeth DaPalma Digeser, "Lactantius on Religious Liberty and His Influence on Constantine" in Shah and Hertzke (eds), *Christianity and Freedom*. 90–102.

Conscience as Moral Belief

Although earlier writers had argued against religious persecution,[20] the English Baptist Thomas Helwys (1550–1616) appears to have been the first writer to refer to a right to freedom of conscience, in his pamphlet, published in 1612, *A Short Declaration on the Mystery of Iniquity*.[21] From his reading of Luke chapters 8 and 9, recording Christ's action in simply passing by towns and villages where the inhabitants would not welcome him, Helwys concluded that there was a duty of "spiritual obedience" only and that coercion in religious questions was impermissible since men would be personally answerable to God for their choice of religion and coercion would not be an excuse.[22] Moreover, he argued that freedom of conscience should apply to everyone:

> Men's religion to God is between God and themselves. The king shall not answer for it. Neither may the king be judge between God and man. Let them be heretics, Turks, Jews, or whatsoever, it appertains not to the earthly power to punish them in the least measure.[23]

The immediate consequence of those words (written by way of an inscription to James I when Helwys sent him the *Short Declaration*) was that Helwys was sent to Newgate Prison on the king's instructions (he died there in 1616). His arguments anticipated the much better-known *Letter Concerning Toleration* by Locke some seventy years later.

From the reformation onward, the claim for freedom of conscience was often termed "toleration"[24]—a term that gives a faithful impression of its

[20] Notably Sebastian Castellio (1515–1563): P Zagorin, *How the Idea of Religious Toleration Came to the West* (Princeton University Press 2003) ch 4.

[21] Thomas Helwys, *A Short Declaration on the Mystery of Iniquity* (R Groves ed, Mercer University Press 1998). I am grateful to Mark Hill and Paul Weller for drawing Helwys to my attention. See also W van de Voll, "English Protestants and the Emergence of Human Rights" (2017) 18 Theological Reflections; Euro-Asian Journal of Theology 71–89; Walter B Shurden, "Thomas Helwys, *A Short Declaration on the Mystery of Iniquity*" <http://centerforbaptiststudies.org/resources/iniquity.htm> accessed 29 July 2019. In 1614 another early English Baptist, John Murton, published a treatise, "A Most Humble Supplication of Many of the King's Most Loyal Subjects ready to testify all civil obedience by the Oath of Allegiance or otherwise and that od Conscience who are persecuted (only for differing in region) contrary to Divine and Human Testimonies"; see Robert Louis Wilken, "The Christian Roots of Religious Liberty" in Shah and Hertzke (eds), *Christianity and Freedom*, 62, 75–76.

[22] Helwys, *A Short Declaration on the Mystery of Iniquity*, 37.

[23] Ibid, 53.

[24] H Kamen, *The Rise of Toleration* (Wiedenfeld and Nicholson 1967); Zagorin, *How the Idea of Religious Toleration Came to the West*; R Forst, *Toleration in Conflict: Past and Present* (Cambridge University Press 2013).

impetus and limits. Toleration was predominantly a question about how Christian majorities or rulers should treat other Christians whose beliefs or practices they regarded as erroneous.[25] Various arguments, backed by scriptural interpretation, were presented against persecution and discrimination of minority Christian groups, and these slowly gained the ascendancy over theological justifications for persecution. Many of the arguments were in a sense pragmatic, rather than based on a principled case for freedom of conscience, namely that this was a way to end religious conflict and that in any event persecution was ineffective since it could not bring about genuine belief, which was only effective if voluntary. Other writers drew on the distinction between temporal and spiritual authority to emphasize the lack of jurisdiction or competence for the magistrate over questions of religious truth.[26]

The influence of the writings of John Locke is undisputed, but although his *Letter Concerning Toleration* is rightly celebrated as a significant milestone in thinking about religious liberty, Locke's thought is more complex than many accounts give credit for. He only arrived at the position in the *Letter* at the end of a considerable process of reflection:[27] his earlier writing on the subject is more authoritarian and accords a significantly narrower field to freedom of conscience. Moreover, the *Letter* contains a thin account of the nature of conscience—a topic that he addressed more substantially in his *Essay Concerning Human Understanding.*[28]

Locke argues for toleration of people whose beliefs he regards as *wrong.* Toleration, however, did not disable even the ruler from attempting to persuade (but not to coerce) others of truth in matters of belief.[29] This position is different to that of his contemporary Pierre Bayle, who advanced an argument for conscience based in part on the uncertainty principle.[30] Rather, Locke argues from the doctrine of the Priesthood of All Believers against the assumption by any human authority—whether within the church or

[25] Although as a side argument some writers addressed the implications for other religions (notably Jews and Muslims), this was a minor preoccupation compared to the more pressing concern of inter-Christian conflict.

[26] E.g., Castellio: Zagorin, *How Religious Toleration Came to the West,* 115. On the two swords and the two kingdoms: see Witte, ch. 7 in this volume.

[27] Sorabji, *Moral Conscience through the Ages,* 147ff.

[28] Chapman, "Disentangling Conscience and Religion," 1489.

[29] J Horton and S Mendus (eds), *John Locke: A Letter Concerning Toleration in Focus* (London Routledge 1991) 18–19.

[30] On Bayle see P King, *Toleration* (Frank Cass 1998) 90–99; Sorabji, *Moral Conscience through the Ages,* 154–157; Forst, *Toleration in Conflict,* 238, 262–265, and 481–483.

state—of the power to determine with finality matters of religious controversy.[31] Locke's primary argument is that religious persecution is *ineffective*.[32] Since a Church is a voluntary society, it is beyond the power of civil authorities to coerce individuals in matters of belief: faith was only effective if freely arrived at and genuinely held. The means available to the state only concern outward compulsion of the person, and this can never produce genuine belief. He does not provide (or aim to provide) a general case for toleration in a liberal state. Locke is, after all, one Christian writing for other Christians (including rulers) in the context of a society that is outwardly at least predominantly Christian,[33] giving reasons why religious persecution on religious grounds is indefensible.

The central importance that Locke accords to personal belief in his defense of toleration means that he gives lesser prominence to protection to manifestations of religious belief. Moreover, in his early writings Locke argued that compulsion in "things indifferent" (including forms of worship) was permissible.[34] This turns the Pauline approach to conscience[35] on its head by treating the "indifferent" category as liable to compulsion, rather than an occasion for freedom. Later, however, Locke revised his view and argued that the state could not compel concerning worship, since this was not in the category of *adiaphora* and was inseparable from matters of faith.[36] Nevertheless, he would allow restrictions on religious practice to be imposed for nonreligious reasons (e.g., public health reasons in the case of animal sacrifice) and he provides no guidance on the weight to be given to the two considerations.

In Locke's discussion of whether conscience can be bound in matters indifferent we find a foretaste of the modern debate about whether freedom of conscience only concerns the internal forum or whether it also encompasses (like freedom of religion and belief) a qualified right to manifest one's

[31] For example, Horton and Mendus, *John Locke: A Letter Concerning Toleration in Focus,* 18 and 50–51.

[32] Some have therefore criticized Locke for failing to provide a moral argument against religious persecution. For general accounts of the limitations of Locke's argument see M Cranston, "John Locke and the Case for Toleration" and J Waldron, "Locke: Toleration and the Rationality of Persecution" in Horton and Mendus (eds), *John Locke: A Letter Concerning Toleration in Focus.*

[33] See further Rivers, ch. 13 above.

[34] Sorabji, *Moral Conscience through the Ages,* 146–148. See also https://www.researchgate.net/publication/288006141_Things_indifferent_in_locke's_writings_on_toleration.

[35] See 284 above.

[36] Forst, *Toleration in Conflict,* 215, referring to the "Essay on Toleration" (1667).

beliefs.[37] It is worth bearing in mind, however, that the regulatory competence in indifferent civil matters that Locke recognized in his later writing is hardly comparable to the extensive reach of the modern state (his examples in the *Essay* concern the education of children and the use of property).[38] Moreover, he recognized the risk of anarchy if individual beliefs are allowed free rein to trump legal obligations. In his *First Tract on Government* (written between 1660 and 1662) Locke anticipated the possibility that if conscience was understood to limit the jurisdiction of the magistrate over "things indifferent," people would be tempted to exploit this immunity by devising strategic arguments: "conscience and religion shall presently mingle itself with all their actions and be spread over their whole lives to protect them from the reach of the magistrate."[39]

Overall, the imprint of *conscience as moral belief* can be seen in the modern understanding of conscience as the core or ultimate beliefs that an individual holds.[40] This individualistic, belief-centered, Protestant view of conscience gives rise to a paradox—when stripped of its religious anchor it collapses too easily into an individualistic claim to a right to "be true to oneself," perhaps exemplified in Thoreau's *On the Duty of Civil Disobedience* (1854).[41] But, as Thomas Paine had astutely noted sixty years earlier, "man worships not himself, but his Maker; and the liberty of conscience which he claims, is not for the service of *himself*, but of his God."[42] Moreover, the tradition tends to treat beliefs as static and leaves little or no room for questioning them. This reluctance gives rise, in the legal sphere, to controversy over whether all statements that an individual's conscience would be compromised by certain actions have to be presumptively accepted by the courts.[43]

[37] See I Leigh, "The Legal Recognition of Freedom of Conscience as Conscientious Objection: Familiar Problems and New Lessons" in R Ahdar (ed), *Research Handbook on Law and Religion* (Edward Elgar 2018) 378–396.

[38] Forst, *Toleration in Conflict*, 216.

[39] Quoted in ibid, 212.

[40] Cf. 280 above.

[41] Henry David Thoreau, *Walden and On the Duty to Civil Disobedience* (orig pub 1854, Scribner 1962).

[42] Paine, *Rights of Man*, 49.

[43] Under most modern constitutional provisions protecting freedom of conscience, religion, or belief, the putative right can be limited or balanced with reference to other societal interests, so that a generous initial approach does not predetermine the outcome. The US First Amendment is anomalous in not permitting formal limitations to the right so that the question assumes greater significance. See further R Ahdar and I Leigh, *Religious Freedom in the Liberal State* (2nd edn, Oxford 2013) ch 6.

Conscience as Moral Judgment

In contrast, a second strand of Christian thought, associated with Thomism and natural law thinking, sees conscience as a human faculty that is not innately fully fledged but rather that is fallible and has to be "schooled" or "formed" to attain proper moral judgment. Rather than being intuitive, judgments of conscience are arrived at through a reflective and considered process.

John Henry Newman in his *Letter to Duke of Norfolk* (1875) referred to the emergence of a "counterfeit" version of conscience derived from "self-will," rather than genuine conscience—the interpretation of moral duties owed to the Creator (the apprehension of the divine law).[44] Newman used a variety of terms, describing true conscience as a "Moral Governor," "a Lawgiver and a Judge," a "stern monitor," "a divine voice, speaking within us," "the voice of God," and "the internal witness of both the existence and law of God." He contrasted this with what he took to be the dominant contemporary view, which he called "a fancy or an opinion":

> When men advocate the rights of conscience, they in no sense mean the rights of the Creator, nor the duty to Him, in thought and deed, of the creature; but the right of thinking, speaking, writing, and acting, according to their judgment or their humour, without any thought of God at all. They do not even pretend to go by any moral rule, but they demand . . . for each to be his own master in all things, and to profess what he pleases, asking no one's leave, and accounting priest or preacher, speaker or writer, unutterably impertinent, who dares to say a word against his going to perdition, if he like it, in his own way. Conscience has rights because it has duties; but in this age, with a large portion of the public, it is the very right and freedom of conscience to dispense with conscience, to ignore a Lawgiver and Judge, to be independent of unseen obligations. It becomes a licence to take up any or no religion, to take up this or that and let it go again . . . to boast of being above all religions and to be an impartial critic of each of them. Conscience is a stern monitor, but in this century it has been superseded by a counterfeit. . . . It is the right of self-will.

[44] http://www.newmanreader.org/works/anglicans/volume2/gladstone/section5.html> accessed 11 September 2019.

Robert George follows Newman in arguing that conscience is not an outworking of autonomy, feeling, or emotion (what he calls "conscience as self-will"), but rather "is one's last best judgment specifying the bearing of moral principles one grasps, yet in no way makes up for oneself, on concrete proposals for action."[45] Older Christian writers in the first camp, such as Locke or Williams, would certainly agree that to follow one's conscience meant to fulfill one's duty to worship God according to one's religious beliefs. This much is common ground; the difference in emphasis comes in relation to the question of the need for the formation of conscience—a doctrine now especially associated with Catholic thought.[46]

The New Testament foundations for this approach are that *suneidēsis* is fallible: one can have a "good or clean conscience,"[47] but one can also have a corrupt or warped "conscience."[48] Even Paul does not trust his own judgment of himself.[49] A Christian believer can have a weak or immature conscience.[50] Overall, as Sorabji concludes,[51] the New Testament does not use *suneidēsis* to refer to an innate awareness of moral truths; nor does it present conscience as "God's voice" or as something infallible. This reflects the underlying worry about the capacity of human beings in a fallen world for self-deceit or ignorance.[52] Conscience can be underdeveloped, mistaken, or dulled.

Not surprisingly, then, a long strand in Christian teaching regards conscience as a faculty that needs to be formed, trained, or developed rather than to be taken as found.[53] The *Catechism of the Catholic Church* summarizes this approach, stating:

> Conscience must be informed and moral judgment enlightened. A well-formed conscience is upright and truthful. It formulates its judgments according to reason, in conformity with the true good willed by the wisdom of the Creator. The education of conscience is indispensable for human beings

[45] R George, *Conscience and Its Enemies: Confronting the Dogmas of Liberal Secularism* (ISI Books 2013) 112.

[46] C Curran, "Conscience in the Light of Catholic Moral Tradition" in C Curran (ed), *Conscience: Readings in Moral Theology no. 14* (Paulist Press 2004).

[47] I Tim. 1:5, 19; 3:9.

[48] I Tim. 4:2; Titus 1:15.

[49] I Cor. 4:4 (using the verb *sunoida*).

[50] See discussion of Romans 14 and 1 Corinthians 8:4–9 above.

[51] Sorabji, *Moral Conscience Through the Ages*, 32–33.

[52] Bishop Joseph Butler (1692–1752) warned of the risk of self-deceit in matters of conscience: *Fifteen Sermons Preached at the Rolls Chapel* (1726) sermons Vii and X <http://www.ccel.org/ccel/butler/sermons.pdf> accessed 29 October 2019.

[53] And in the Old Testament, see Ps. 119:33, 125, 133, 135.

who are subjected to negative influences and tempted by sin to prefer their own judgment and to reject authoritative teachings.[54]

This process of education of the conscience is a lifelong task[55] in which the Word of God must be assimilated "in faith and prayer and put it into practice, conscience must be examined 'before the Lord's Cross . . . assisted by the gifts of the Holy Spirit, aided by the witness or advice of others and guided by the authoritative teaching of the Church.'"[56]

The *conscience as moral judgment* strand of Christian thinking has negative historical associations with the notorious dictum that "error has no rights," used by the Roman Catholic church to justify persecution until its change of heart with the Second Vatican Council. However, in a climate more receptive to conscience claims it offers a possible counterweight to the unbridled individualism and subjectivity of belief-centered conscience claims.

Freedom of Conscience and the Growth of Constitutionalism

In England the growth of religious toleration that began in 1689[57] was to be a slow process drawn out over the next two centuries. The main target was legal penalties imposed from the 1550s onward: compulsion to attend the Church of England and prescribing the use of the Book of Common Prayer, forbidding nonconforming congregations or requiring their registration, together with discriminatory laws that imposed disabilities on minority religious groups (such as the Test Acts, which prevented them from being elected to Parliament or occupying other public positions).[58] Requirements to swear religious oaths were relaxed incrementally beginning with the introduction under the Toleration Act 1689 of an alternative "declaration of fidelity" for

[54] *Catechism of the Catholic Church*, 1783.

[55] Ibid, 1784.

[56] Ibid, 1785.

[57] Magna Carta (1215) addressed some specific grievances about ecclesiastical appointments and property in Article 1 ("the English Church shall be free"), but this was a limited recognition of Church autonomy, rather than of free exercise or freedom of conscience. For a recent assessment: R Griffith-Jones and M Hill (eds), *Magna Carta, Religion and the Rule of Law* (Cambridge University Press 2015).

[58] On the legal landmarks in the development of religious toleration see St John Robilliard, *Religion and the Law* (Manchester 1984) appendix; J Dingemans, C Yeginsu, T Cross, and H Masood, *The Protections for Religious Rights: Law and Practice* (Oxford 2013) 3–10.

certain dissenters in place of the oaths of allegiance and of supremacy.[59] Even with the final lifting of most disabilities faced by religious minorities in the nineteenth century, protection for nonreligious conscience was still lacking until the campaigns of the atheist member of Parliament Charles Bradlaugh in the 1880s led to the introduction of affirmations for those unable or unwilling to take a religious oath.[60] In the United States there was a very different trajectory, leading to rejection of the limited concept of toleration in favor of constitutional protection for freedom of conscience. As Thomas Paine was later to argue: "Toleration is not the opposite of intolerance, but it is the counterfeit of it. Both are despotisms. The one assumes to itself the right of withholding liberty of conscience, and the other of granting it."[61] More than 150 years earlier Roger Williams, a controversial Baptist minister, was forced to flee from Puritan Massachusetts in 1636 to avoid imminent arrest and to found a settlement at Providence that would become the new colony of Rhode Island. Williams wrote in defense of liberty of conscience in *The Bloudy Tenet* (1647)[62]—a riposte to the defense of religious persecution by the Boston Congregationalist clergyman Rev. Joseph Cotton. The charter obtained by Williams from Charles II in 1663 for the new settlement was the first legal text to refer to liberty of conscience, rather than toleration, that is, to "freely and fully have and enjoy his and their own judgments and consciences, in matters of religious concernments . . . they behaving themselves peaceably and quietly, and not using this liberty to licentiousness and profaneness, nor to the civil injury or outward disturbance of others."[63] The influence of Roger Williams and of the Rhode Island Charter was relatively minor in comparison to Williams's more famous successors,[64] but Martha Nussbaum nonetheless argues that the charter was significant in pioneering the idea of religious accommodation.[65]

[59] Braithwaite, *Conscientious Objection to Compulsions under Law*, 22ff.

[60] Oaths Act 1888 (see now Oaths Act 1978, s 5).

[61] Thomas Paine, *Rights of Man* (Wordsworths Classics of World Literature 1996) 49. For painstaking historical analysis see Michael W McConnell, "The Origins and Historical Understanding of Free Exercise of Religion" (1990) 103 Harv Law Rev 1409.

[62] Roger Williams, *The Bloudy Tenet Washed and Made White in the Blood of the Lambe: Being Discussed and Discharged of Blood-Guiltinesse by Just Defence* (1647).

[63] Rhode Island Royal Charter (1663) <https://en.wikipedia.org/wiki/Rhode_Island_Royal_Charter#Provisions> accessed 14 October 2019.

[64] Williams's writings were neglected until rediscovered in the late eighteenth century by Isaac Backus: McConnell, "The Origins and Historical Understanding of Free Exercise of Religion," 1426.

[65] Nussbaum, *Liberty of Conscience*, 50

Foremost among those successors was John Locke, who assisted in drafting the Fundamental Constitutions of Carolina (1669).[66] The text acknowledged that it was not "reasonable" to abuse "the natives of that place" who were strangers to Christianity for their usages and customs, that in a community of diverse opinions religious persecution was offensive to Almighty God, and that Jews should be treated with gentleness and respect.[67] Without referring to freedom of conscience as such, it also provided for recognition of religious diversity in accepting sworn legal testimony.[68] Locke's later *Letter Concerning Toleration* undoubtedly influenced the founding fathers, notably Jefferson and Madison, first in drafting the Virginia constitution and then the Bill of Rights.[69] Prior to the adoption of the religion clause in the US First Amendment several of the state constitutions referred to the right of freedom to worship according to the dictates of conscience,[70] and "liberty of conscience" was generally understood in this way "among almost all Americans"[71] at that time. Indeed, the text of that most celebrated of constitutional protections of religious liberty might easily have turned out differently. James Madison's original proposal was for a protection for "the full and equal rights of conscience."[72] It seems clear that he was seeking to protect the freedom of different Christian denominations to follow their own forms of worship and teaching. As the various drafts were debated, little discussion seems to have turned, however, on the difference between freedom of conscience and freedom of religion. Madison's proposal was replaced in later drafts by "the equal rights of conscience" and "the rights of conscience." There is no clear record of why the conference settled on the final wording ("Congress shall make no law respecting an establishment of religion, or prohibiting the free exercise thereof"), but it does not appear to be because conscience was clearly understood to be something distinct.

Michael McConnell has convincingly demonstrated that early American constitutional history showed clear recognition of the perennial questions raised by freedom of conscience and its relationship to religion, in particular how to approach nonreligious conscience, the limits of conscience claims,

[66] <https://avalon.law.yale.edu/17th_century/nc05.asp> accessed 15 October 2019.

[67] Fundamental Constitutions of Carolina (1669), Art 97.

[68] Ibid, Art 100.III.

[69] McConnell, *Origins*, 1428–1431.

[70] North Carolina CONST art XIX (Dec 18, 1776); New Jersey CONST art XVIII (July 2, 1776); Pennsylvania CONST art II (Sep 28, 1776); Vermont CONST ch I, § III (July 8, 1777).

[71] Chapman, "Disentangling Conscience and Religion," 1466.

[72] In addition, he unsuccessfully proposed under the Second Amendment to exempt from military service any person "religiously scrupulous of bearing arms": ibid, 1468.

and whether freedom of conscience gave exemption from other general legal duties.[73] The practice of equating conscience with freedom of religion meant that there was no general acceptance of toleration of nonreligious conscience. Indeed, Locke's writing argues against this and the proviso for "licentiousness" in some early state constitutions was intended to exclude any such possibility.[74] Roger Williams was an outlier in espousing freedom of conscience for Native Americans and atheists, although these distinguishing features also explain his appeal for contemporary writers.[75] The second question that the writers and drafters grappled with was whether legal protection for conscience was solely a matter of freedom of belief or whether it extended to actions. As noted earlier, Locke's writing became slightly more flexible on this question.[76] Roger Williams advocated religious accommodation to protect freedom of belief, worship, and practice, subject to limitations to prevent violating the rights of others and breaches of public order and morality.[77] In a *Letter to the Town of Providence* (1655), responding to Baptists who objected to joining the town militia, he argued laws concerning "common Peace and Preservation" could override conscience objections. Limitations on conscience were explicitly addressed in some texts. As we have seen, the Charter of Rhode Island anticipated the question of the impact of the exercise of individual conscience on third parties. Interestingly, New York added the qualification: "*Provided*, That the liberty of conscience, hereby granted, shall not be so construed as to excuse acts of licentiousness, or justify practices inconsistent with the peace or safety of this State."[78]

The question of conscientious objection merits a brief separate discussion. Conscientious objection to military service is often held up by modern commentators as the paradigmatic case of freedom of conscience.[79] It is a practice that until recent decades has been largely shaped by the advocacy and resistance of Christian groups. The earliest Christians refused to serve in the Roman army, but this was not merely because of pacifism: legionnaires

[73] McConnell, "Origins and Historical Understanding of the Free Exercise of Religion."

[74] Ibid, 1429.

[75] See especially Nussbaum, *Liberty of Conscience*, 41ff, arguing that Williams's thought anticipated Locke's *Letter Concerning Toleration* "in every major point" and was superior to it.

[76] See nn. 36–38 above.

[77] Nussbaum, *Liberty of Conscience*, 49.

[78] New York CONST art XXXVIII (Apr 20, 1777).

[79] The first legal use of the phrase "conscientious objection" was, however, in a different context. The UK Vaccination Act 1898, s. 2 provided a procedure for parents to certify their conscientious belief that vaccination would be prejudicial to their child's health. The certificate acted as a defense to prosecution of the parent. See further Constance Braithwaite, *Conscientious Objections to Compulsions under the Law* (William Sessions 1995) 81.

were required to swear an oath treating the emperor as divine. Moreover, Christians felt no obligation to enter into service of a non-Christian state.[80] Later the adoption of Christianity as the religion of the Roman Empire produced a change in outlook so that, as Field observes, "from the time of Constantine to the Reformation uncompromising Pacifism practically disappears from Christian thought."[81] Nonetheless, in the pre-Reformation period several small Christian groups that were opposed to participation in warfare emerged (notably the Waldensians, the Lollards, and the Bohemian Brethren).[82] Following the Reformation others such as early Baptists, Mennonites, and Quakers adopted total pacifism. The fruit of these centuries of resistance and activism by dissenting Christian minority groups has been the widespread recognition of a constitutional right of conscientious objection. In particular, Quakers have had considerable success in advocacy for the recognition of conscientious objection through their engagement with international organizations, and the Jehovah's Witnesses have also been instrumental in bringing claims of conscientious objection in many countries since their formation in the 1870s.

Objection to liability to service in militia on grounds of conscience by dissenting religious groups had been intermittently recognized in legislation from the seventeenth century onward. The earliest legislation was in 1665 in Massachusetts, followed by Rhode Island in 1673, and then each of the original thirteen colonies, with the exception of Georgia.[83] In the United Kingdom the first recognition was under the Militia Act 1757.[84] For the most part these exemptions applied to members of named pacifist Christian denominations, such as Quakers and Mennonites. Following the introduction of mass conscription in the two world wars of 1914–1918 and 1939–1945, however, conscientious objection to military service came to be recognized more widely.[85]

[80] At the end of the second century Tertullian (160–230) objected to the practice of even peacetime service in the Roman army: L May, *Contingent Pacifism* (Cambridge 2015) 26–29.

[81] GC Field, *Pacifism and Conscientious Objection* (Cambridge 1945) 2.

[82] Margaret E Hirst, *The Quakers in Peace and War* (Swarthmore Press 1923) 24–28.

[83] John Whiteclay Chambers II, "Conscientious Objectors and the American State from Colonial Times to the Present" in Charles C Moskos and John Whiteclay Chambers (eds), *The New Conscientious Objection: From Sacred to Secular Resistance* (Oxford University Press 1993) 26.

[84] Braithwaite, *Conscientious Objection from Compulsions under the Law*, 114.

[85] In the United Kingdom: Military Service Act 1916, s. 2 (allowing for exemption for "conscientious objection to the undertaking of combatant service" on the decision of a Military Service Tribunal). In World War II the provisions of the Military Training Act 1939 and the National Service (Armed Forces) Act 1939 were wider in recognizing objections also to registration in the military service register and to performing military service: Braithwaite, *Conscientious Objection to Compulsions under the Law*, 181.

A right of this kind (or a right of alternative service) now appears in the modern constitutions of nearly sixty countries.[86] The recognition of this as a constitutional right is a post–World War II phenomenon: the earliest instance was Article 4(3) of the 1949 Grundgesetz of the Federal Republic of Germany.[87] The European Union drew on national constitutions and legislation in recognizing a general right of conscientious objection in its Charter of Fundamental Rights in 2000.[88] Recognition in international human rights jurisprudence of the United Nations and the Council of Europe is equally recent.[89] Alongside its juridification, conscientious objection is also undergoing a process of secularization.[90] While a significant number of existing legal texts and decisions recognizing the right refer to religious objections only, it is nonetheless clear that to deny nonreligious objectors equivalent protection would violate constitutional and human rights nondiscrimination norms, and equal protection is the trajectory.[91]

Freedom of Conscience and Contemporary Liberal Constitutionalism

Although classical Christian writers paid relatively little attention to freedom of conscience for nonbelievers, the question of the nonreligious conscience presents a series of challenges to modern liberal democracies, both theoretical and practical. The close historical association of conscience and freedom of religion gives rise to a number of tensions between the two in

[86] The Constitute website lists the constitutions of some fifty-eight countries providing for a right of conscientious objection to military service. <https://www.constituteproject.org/> accessed 4 November 2019. In a few instances the right is a more general one not limited to military service.

[87] See also Article 12a2 governing alternative service. Earlier references to freedom of conscience appear in the (unimplemented) 1849 Constitution, in the Weimar Constitution of 1919, in the Swiss Constitution of 1874, and in the Portuguese Constitution of 1911 but do not provide for manifestation of inner belief: Jose de Sousa e Brito, "Conscientious Objection" in T Lindholm, W Cole Durham Jr, and B Tahzib-Lie, *Facilitating Freedom of Religion or Belief: A Deskbook* (Brill | Nijhoff 2004) 273, 276.

[88] "The right to conscientious objection is recognised, in accordance with the national laws governing the exercise of this right" (Art. 10.2 of the Charter of Fundamental Rights of the European Union). See *Official Journal* 2007 C303/02.

[89] See *Yeo-Bum Yoon and Myung-Jin Choi v Republic of Korea*, CCPR/C/88/D/1321-1322/2004, UN Human Rights Committee, 23 January 2007, and *Bayatyan v Armenia*, App No 23459/03 (ECHR, 7 July 2011).

[90] Moskos and Chambers, *The New Conscientious Objection*.

[91] See, e.g., *United States v Seeger*, 380 US 163 (1965) (interpreting the Selective Services conscientious objector exemption to exempt a draftee with objections based on nonreligious moral considerations) and *Welsh v United States*, 398 US 333 (1970).

contemporary constitutional discourse. These tensions are central to current debates about the general justification for freedom of conscience—which to be acceptable under liberal theory has to be nonreligious and even-handed as between "comprehensive doctrines." They apply equally to the distributive question of who is entitled to enjoy the right (corporations? public officials?) and the practical questions of whether such claims are conclusory or nonjusticiable.

First, there is the difficulty of finding a theoretical basis for protection of freedom of conscience that is nonsectarian. Famously, John Rawls argued that freedom of conscience was the first of civil liberties and used the emergence of religious toleration as the model for his contractarian approach. He argued that persons in the original position would agree upon equal liberty of conscience in order to protect their religious and moral freedom from persecution, since they would be ignorant of their religious and moral views or whether they are part of a majority or minority in society.[92] But Rawls's view of conscience as such is ambiguous and underdeveloped,[93] and his assumption that religion is fundamentally a matter of individual conviction and belief has been criticized as privileging a Protestant approach,[94] rather than approaches to religion based on practice of ritual or on culture, and consequently of failing to offer a neutral, egalitarian, constitutional foundation.

By contrast, in her recent book *Liberalism's Religion* political philosopher Cécile Laborde advances a liberal egalitarian approach to religion that, she contends, is grounded on liberal values such as moral individualism.[95] Building on Andrew Koppelman's deconstructive approach,[96] Laborde argues in favor of "disaggregating" the concept of religious freedom. Religion, she contends, is multidimensional and its various discrete features ("conscience, truth claims, culture, projects and preferences, modes of association, political ideology, community, way of life") can also be found in nonreligious conceptions and connect to different liberal values.[97] One such value

[92] J Rawls, *A Theory of Justice*, 206–207.

[93] Chapman, "Disentangling Conscience and Religion," 1471–1480, arguing that Rawls fails to adequately distinguish conscience and religion.

[94] Cécile Laborde describes this as the "Protestant critique": C Laborde, *Liberalism's Religion* (Harvard University Press 2017) ch 1.

[95] Ibid. Laborde's contribution is a wide-ranging, rich, and important one that cannot be fully assessed here. Her treatment of conscience is found in ch. 6 of *Liberalism's Religion* ("Disaggregating Religion in Freedom of Religion: Individual Exemptions and Liberal Justice").

[96] Koppelman points out that law uses "religion" as a proxy for different related goods: A Koppelman, "Conscience, Volitional Necessity, and Religious Exemptions" (2009) 15 Legal Theory 215.

[97] Laborde, *Liberalism's Religion*, 240.

pertinent to freedom of conscience is integrity, which, Laborde argues, is grounded in values of identity, autonomy, moral agency, and self-respect and can be valued by both religious and nonreligious citizens.[98] Integrity attaches even if individuals acting in accordance with their conscience are mistaken about their moral duties. Ethical and moral commitments are candidates for legal exemption because (unlike mere preferences) they "cannot be sacrificed without feelings of remorse, shame or guilt."[99]

A second consequence of the uneasy relationship of conscience and religion is that it gives rise to calls for definitional reform. A number of scholars have argued that freedom of conscience could in effect render freedom of religion redundant or that the existing coverage can be replicated under rights to freedom of expression, association, privacy, and conscience.[100] In his posthumously published Einstein lectures Ronald Dworkin argued that a right to ethical independence (i.e., forbidding governments from restricting freedom because it assumes that one way for people to live their lives is better than another) could replace the right to religious freedom.[101] In part, these various arguments are a response to the longstanding controversy in the United States in particular to "religious exemptions"[102]—used to refer not only to statutory provisions but also to any claim that the free exercise of religion can give protection against the application of neutral and general legal rules. For others this is anathema—a project intended to undermine the distinctiveness of freedom of religion, to deny its historical salience, and to constrain religious liberty within an impoverished liberal straitjacket.[103]

Although the literature purports to be of general application, in fact much of it is premised on particular features of US constitutional law that cannot be assumed to apply elsewhere, notably the "specialness" of religion under the First Amendment and the treatment of free exercise claims under the Religious Freedom Restoration Act (RFRA). By singling out religion for protection, the First Amendment in effect encourages conscience claims to be equated with religious beliefs in order to attract constitutional protection.[104]

[98] Ibid, 203–204.

[99] Ibid. 204.

[100] E.g., Christopher Eisgruber and Lawrence Sager, *Religious Freedom and the Constitution* (Harvard UP 2007). See also B Leiter, *Why Tolerate Religion?* (Princeton UP 2013), arguing that religious obligations should not be treated preferentially, and John Adenitire, *A General Right to Conscientious Objection: Beyond Religious Privilege* (Cambridge University Press 2020).

[101] R Dworkin, *Religion without God* (Harvard University Press 2013) ch 3.

[102] K Vallier and M Weber (eds), *Religious Exemptions* (Oxford 2018).

[103] Kathleen Brady, *The Distinctiveness of Religion in American Law: Rethinking Religion Clause Jurisprudence* (CUP 2015).

[104] Cf. *United States v Seeger*, 380 US 163 (1965).

This in turn presents the dilemma that the protection from the courts questioning theological beliefs that applies by virtue of the establishment clause and under RFRA will apply to successful conscience claims—even those that appear to be nonreligious and where there is no underlying rationale related to religious autonomy. The inevitable consequence is to create pressure to find other means by which such claims can be limited. In contrast, constitutions that protect freedom of conscience explicitly alongside religion and which deal in terms with how such claims can be limited do not face the same problems that the wording of the First Amendment throws up.

Claims to freedom of conscience are often regarded critically as special pleading—a claim to exemption from neutral general laws.[105] Moreover, conscience claims are interpreted by proponents and critics as nonjusticiable albeit for different reasons. For critics they are inherently subjective, whereas many proponents equate nonjusticiability with defense of religious autonomy. In the background controversy has been stirred following the US Supreme Court decision in *Hobby Lobby*[106] over whether commercial bodies (particularly closely held companies) are entitled to the benefit of freedom of conscience. In a widely cited article from 2015 NeJaime and Siegel focus on a rise in indirect, secondary, or "complicity" conscience claims, especially related to sexual ethics, which they contend differ from long-established conscience claims in both nature and scope.[107] Several writers follow NeJaime and Siegel in treating such claims in the United States as essentially a type of political action, which they contend is a bad-faith rear-guard action by religious conservative opponents of LGBT and health care reform.[108] Some commentators recognize the genuineness of complicity-based conscience claims but argue that they should not prevail where the rights or interests

[105] B Barry, *Culture and Equality: An Egalitarian Critique of Multiculturalism* (Harvard UP 2001).

[106] *Burwell v Hobby Lobby Stores, Inc*, 537 US 354 (2014), confirming the applicability of the Religious Freedom Restoration Act to a claim by a private company that, because of the religious concerns of its owners, refused to provide certain kinds of birth control in their employee insurance plans, as required by the Federal Affordable Care Act 2010.

[107] Douglas NeJaime and Reva Siegel, "Conscience Wars: Complicity-Based Conscience Claims in Religion and Politics" (2015) 124 Yale Law Journal 2516. For a compelling refutation see Douglas Laycock, "Religious Liberty for Politically Active Minority Groups: A Response to NeJaime and Siegel" (2016) 125 Yale LJ Forum 369 (arguing that claimants do not forfeit the constitutional right to conscientious objection because of their exercise of the right of political speech on the same topic).

[108] Robert Post, "The Politics of Religion Democracy and the Conscience Wars" in S Mancini and M Rosenfeld (eds), *The Conscience Wars: Rethinking the Balance between Religion, Identity and Equality* (Cambridge University Press 2018); Timothy McCarthy, "Insisting on Complicity" (2018) 18 Contemporary Political Theory 1–21.

of other people are affected.[109] Others contend that such claims should not be recognized if made by corporations,[110] by public officials,[111] or by certain professional groups, especially medical professionals if to do so would clash with the rights or interests of patients or service users.[112]

Conclusion

Freedom of conscience is an expression at once familiar and puzzling. Familiarly, it stands as a synonym for freedom of religion—a form of legal protection for religious belief and practice. The puzzling part is what this has to do with either *conscience as moral belief* or *conscience as moral judgement*. The two usages appear disconnected. The reason this *seems* odd is because of modern patterns of thought that emphasize religion as chosen beliefs leading to individual fulfillment—and not, as older writers did, as a question of conviction and duty. In modern times we have lost sight of this perspective, although at the reformation and through the age of toleration it was a commonplace understanding. This historical amnesia helps to explain why some contemporary conscience claims are quite so controversial.

As noted earlier, it is difficult if not impossible to identify a single unified or dominant Christian view of conscience. Nonetheless, the *conscience-as-moral-belief strand of Christian thought* has had a decisive influence in grounding both constitutional protection for conscience in general and the right of conscientious objection to military service in particular.

What could a recovered Christian conception of freedom of conscience contribute to current debates about conscience claims by public officials, companies, or medical practitioners? It might help to educate against two

[109] Amy Sepinwall, "Conscience and Complicity: Assessing Pleas for Religious Exemptions after Hobby Lobby" (2015) 82 U Chicago L Rev 1897 (arguing that religious exemptions impose a substantial burden on third parties).

[110] Claims that businesses cannot have consciences are, however, inconsistent with widely applauded forms of ethical business behavior or corporate social responsibility (e.g., investing in the community, subsidizing environmental protection, paying living wage, etc.):B Scharffs, "Our Fractured Attitude towards Corporate Conscience" in D Robinson and R Williams (eds), *Religious Liberty: Essays on First Amendment Law* (Cambridge University Press 2016).

[111] It is sometimes claimed that officials should not be permitted the luxury of recognition of claims moral complicity: R Moon, "Conscientious Objections by Civil Servants: The Case of Marriage Commissioners and Same Sex Civil Marriages" in B Berger and R Moon, *Religion and the Exercise of Public Authority* (Hart 2016).

[112] For discussion see M Wicclair, *Conscientious Objection in Health Care: An Ethical Analysis* (Cambridge University Press 2011) ch 2.

prevailing tendencies—that of regarding beliefs as a type of preference to which little weight attaches when other interests are at stake and the treatment of conscience as necessarily subjective. Contrary to stereotypical representations in much of the contemporary literature, three points emerge from an examination of Christian approaches. First, Christian writers are agreed that conscience is a matter of duty, not preference. This stands in contrast to the attempt of contemporary liberal theorists like Laborde to ground freedom of conscience on "integrity-protecting commitments" based on autonomy. Second, many Christian writers, from Paul onward, have recognized that claims of conscience have limits, to take account of the interests of third parties. Third, there is a clear strand of Christian thought, now most closely associated with Catholicism, that sees conscience not as an intuitive moral reflex-action but treats conscience as a faculty for moral decision-making that can be trained or formed—what I have called *conscience as moral judgement*. This is consistent with an expectation that those claiming freedom of conscience will be able to explain how certain actions implicate their core beliefs and why those beliefs are important to them. That assumption runs contrary to the prevailing legal orthodoxy that claims of conscience are inherently subjective and cannot be questioned: it opens the possibility of questioning decisions based on errors in conscience or interrogating whether they are mistaken. As renewed attention is now focused on freedom of conscience in constitutional adjudication, they have much to teach us about resolving seemingly intractable controversies.

15

Federalism

A Legal, Political, and Religious Archaeology

Nicholas Aroney

Introduction

Federal forms of government have a lineage reaching deep into the Middle Ages and classical antiquity. Federalism also has an important historical relationship with Christianity, especially Reformed Christianity. The story of the development of federalism runs in three intermingling streams. The first of these streams is legal and is particularly concerned with the institution of the international treaty. The second stream is political and particularly concerns the institution of the confederation. The third stream is religious and particularly concerns the institution of the covenant. This chapter offers an archaeology of federalism based on an investigation of each of these three streams. However, as will be seen, the three streams intermingle so much that they often become virtually indistinguishable, for federalism is simultaneously a profoundly legal, political, and religious phenomenon.

Law: International Treaty

The term "federal" is derived from a Latin root, *foedus*, which in Roman law referred to a treaty formed between Rome and one or more allied states.[1] Such treaties (*foedera*) established a condition of *societas* or *amicitia* between Rome and its allies (the latter being called *foederati*, *socii*, or *amici*). These treaties of alliance were either formally equal (*foedus aequum*) or unequal

[1] Wolfgang Kunkel, *An Introduction to Roman Legal and Constitutional History* (2nd edn, JM Kelly tr, Clarendon Press, 1973) 38; Adolf Berger, *Encyclopedic Dictionary of Roman Law* (American Philosophical Society 1953 [1991]) 474.

Nicholas Aroney, *Federalism: A Legal, Political, and Religious Archaeology* in *Christianity and Constitutionalism*.
Edited by: Nicholas Aroney and Ian Leigh, Oxford University Press. © Oxford University Press 2022.
DOI: 10.1093/oso/9780197587256.003.0015

(*foedus iniquum*) in the terms they imposed: the former prescribed a duty of assistance in the case of attack by third parties, while the latter obligated the *foederati* to acknowledge Rome's supremacy and greatness (*māiestās*), usually following capitulation by the defeated state. Treaties were therefore often negotiated by Roman military commanders but were ratified at Rome by a vote of the *comitia centuriata*.

For these reasons, the term *foedus* is frequently translated as "treaty" or "alliance." However, the modern, specifically legal connotations of these words do not quite capture the very rich set of social, political, and religious qualities that the *foedus* instantiated in Roman law and culture. The *foedera* were properly established through religious ceremonies in which oaths were exchanged and sacrifices made under the supervision of the *fetiales*, a special class of priests who administered the *ius fetiale*, the sacred law regulating juridical relations between peoples.[2]

In this connection it is intriguing to note that the term *foedus* appears to have even older roots in a reconstructed Indo-European term **bhoidh-* (o-grade), which some linguists have suggested carried the meaning of binding and being bound, both literally and metaphorically, such as by an oath, pledge, or covenant.[3] **Bhidh-* (zero-grade) also appears to be the linguistic ancestor of the Latin *fides* and the Greek *pistis*, both of which are associated with the ideas of faith, trust, and loyalty but understood in a variety of contexts: moral, philosophical, political, and religious.[4] While rules of linguistic derivation suggest that the terms are distinct, there is also a remarkable similarity between these terms and the Hindi *bandh* (band, bond) and the German *bund* (covenant, association, federation),[5] all of which are thought to be derived from the Indo-European **bhendh-*, a term that may also have carried the sense of binding and being bound.[6]

[2] JW Rich, "The Fetiales and Roman International Relations" in James H Richardson and Frederico Santangelo (eds), *Priests and State in the Roman World* (Stuttgart 2011) 187.

[3] Oxford English Dictionary (1989), sv "federal"; Julius Porkorny, *Indogermanishes Etymologisches Wörterbuch* (Francke Verlag 1951) 117; A Ernout and A Meillet, *Dictionnaire Étymologique de la Langue Latine Histoire des Mots* (M. Niemeyer 1967) 243–234; TG Tucker, *A Concise Etymological Dictionary of Latin* (1931) vi–viii, xiii, 99; SE Mann, *An Indo-European Comparative Dictionary* (H. Buske 1984) 70–71, 88, 90.

[4] Emile Benveniste, *Indo-European Language and Society* (Faber and Faber 1973) 95–98; Bill Gladhill, *Rethinking Roman Alliance: A Study in Poetics and Society* (Cambridge University Press 2016) 20–22.

[5] The German *bund* is the root of several important politico-legal terms, such as *Bundesstat* (federal state), *Staatenbund* (confederation of states), and, more recently, *Staatenverbund* (association of sovereign states) used to designate the European Union.

[6] WM Lindsay, *The Latin Language: An Historical Account of Latin Sounds, Stems, and Flexions* (Clarendon Press 1894) 290; Mann, *An Indo-European Comparative Dictionary*, 71.

This deeper etymology offers some corroboration of the observation that the institution of the Roman *foedus* was part of a wider practice—broadly characteristic of the many civilizations of the Mediterranean basin, including Babylon, Egypt, Assyria, and Greece—in which alliances were formed among nations through oath-sanctioned treaties sworn before their respective gods.[7] As with the Roman *foedera*, many of these treaty-covenants were not agreements among equals but were the imposed terms of a hegemonic relationship between suzerain and vassal. Although the specific terms and rituals differed from one culture to another, the structural similarities point to a common origin and a shared set of understandings about the role of oaths in binding kings and nations to their obligations.[8] To have this binding effect under conditions of polytheism, all the gods of the relevant nations were invoked as witnesses to the treaties. It is in this context that the distinctive covenant (*b'rit*) between Yahweh and Israel recorded in the Bible must be understood,[9] as well as the strong monotheistic prohibitions on the entry by Israel into alliances with Canaanite nations.[10]

The practice of confirming treaties with an oath continued after the Christianization of Rome, particularly in the practices of the Byzantine Empire and the Germanic successor kingdoms, but now on the basis of a shared trinitarian monotheism.[11] In the Latin West, oath-taking ceremonies were held in churches and princes often expressly submitted themselves to ecclesiastical jurisdiction in such matters. The enforcement of treaties accordingly fell within the jurisdiction of the courts of the Church, for the breaking of a promise, especially an oath, was a grave sin and a serious breach of canon law. Much of the old Roman practice was forgotten, but fragments

[7] See Gábor Sulyok, "Treaties, Origin" in Rüdiger Wolfrum (ed), *Max Planck Encyclopedia of Public International Law* (Oxford University Press 2015) .

[8] Paul Karavites, *Promise-Giving and Treaty-Making: Homer and the Near East* (Brill 1992); Moshe Weinfeld, "Covenant Terminology in the Ancient Near East and Its Influence on the West" (1973) 93 Journal of the American Oriental Society 190. See also Alan H Sommerstein and Isabelle C Torrance, *Oaths and Swearing in Ancient Greece* (De Gruyter 2014).

[9] George E Mendenhall, *Law and Covenant in Israel and the Ancient Near East* (Biblical Colloquium 1955); Dennis J McCarthy, *Treaty and Covenant: A Study in Form in the Ancient Oriental Documents and in the Old Testament* (Pontifical Biblical Institute 1963); Delbert R Hillers, *Covenant: The History of a Biblical Idea* (John Hopkins 1973).

[10] Exodus 23:32–33; 34:12–16; Deuteronomy 7:2; Judges 2:1–3. The Bible nonetheless records numerous treaties and alliances involving the surrounding tribes and nations: e.g., Genesis 14:13; 21:22–34; 26:26–34; 31:44–54; Numbers 25:1–3; Joshua 1:10–16; 9:1–27; I Samuel 27:2–12; II Samuel 3:17–21; 5:1–3; 9:10; I Kings 5:12–18; 9:11–14; 9:16; 15:18–20; 20:31–34; II Kings 16:6–9; 20:12–18; 23:29; I Maccabees 8; 12:1–2; 14:20; 15:17.

[11] I here rely on Randall Lesaffer, "Peace Treaties and the Formation of International Law" in Bardo Fassbender and Anne Peters (eds), *Oxford Handbook of the History of International Law* (Oxford University Press 2012) 71, 73–77, 83.

in Justinian's *Digest* touched on the matter. The *Pax Constantiae* of 1183, a treaty between Frederick I Barbarosa and the Lombard League that was included in the medieval collection of the *Coprus Juris Civilis*, was commented on by Baldus de Ulbaldus (1327–1400) and others.[12] Isidore of Seville's (ca. 560–636) definition of the *ius gentium* as including *foedera pacis* was also reproduced in Gratian's *Decretum* (ca. 1140) and gave rise to further commentary. During the Middle Ages treaties were understood to be a particular, albeit significant, kind of contract, to which principles of private law and Christian conscience were applicable. The canon law principle of *pacta sunt servanda* thus played a key role in supporting the duties owed by the parties to the medieval *foedera*, alongside the binding oath taken by the ruler in the act of ratification of the treaty negotiated by his diplomats.

The Reformation saw the end of the widespread reliance on ecclesiastical jurisdiction to enforce international treaties, with the result that the oath and *pacta sunt servanda* had to bear most of the load. Also of profound significance was the emergence of the modern nation-state and its claim to sovereignty, a claim that involved a refusal to acknowledge any superior authority (*superiorem non recognoscentes*) and an assertion of absolute authority over all within its territorial jurisdiction, as classically articulated by Jean Bodin (1530–1596) and Thomas Hobbes (1588–1679).[13] It was not until after the Enlightenment had its full influence, however, that the practice of grounding international treaties on an explicit oath also came to an end. As Allen Hertz has pointed out, thereafter the binding force of international treaties had to depend upon a natural law obligation to keep one's promises, or else the geo-political self-interest of states and the threat of military intervention.[14] And even here, the natural law basis of international law underwent change. While Francisco de Vitoria (1483–1546) continued to hold that natural law is the first and highest source of international law, with rules based on mutual consent providing a secondary and supplementary role, Francisco Suárez (1548–1617) reversed this order, proposing that international law is in essence a kind of positive human law, albeit one that is founded on and derives its stability from natural law. Alberico Gentili (1552–1608) and Hugo Grotius

[12] Randall Lesaffer, "Roman Law and the Intellectual History of International Law" in Anne Orford and Florian Hoffmann (eds), *Oxford Handbook of the Theory of International Law* (Oxford University Press 2016) 38, 49.

[13] For more detail, see Nicholas Aroney, "Christianity, Sovereignty and Global Law" in Rafael Domingo and John Witte Jr (eds), *Christianity and Global Law* (Routledge 2020).

[14] Allen Hertz, "Medieval Treaty Obligation" (1991) 6 Connecticut Journal of International Law 425, 431.

(1583–1645) took this further by eliminating the specifically religious content of the natural law foundation of international law. International law increasingly came under a secularizing influence in the hands of Samuel Pufendorf (1632–1694) and especially Emer de Vattel (1714–1767), who grounded international law solely on natural and positive law without any reference to its religious foundations.[15]

In early modern international law the power to enter international treaties accordingly became a mark of statehood. The significance of the power can be seen in the fact that John Locke considered the "federative" power of the commonwealth—the "power of war and peace, leagues and alliances, and all the transactions, with all persons and communities without the commonwealth"—to be one of three basic powers of a state, alongside the executive and the legislative power.[16] The significance of the federative power is also seen in the fact that following the Peace of Westphalia in 1648, one of the key rights obtained by the German principalities within the Holy Roman Empire was the *ius foederationis*, the power to enter treaties.[17] Today it is one of the most significant measures of the autonomy of the constituent states of a federation whether they retain this capacity or it is transferred, as is more common, to the federation as a whole.

Politics: The Confederation

A related Latin term, *confoederatio*, was often used to designate the league or association brought into being through the institution of the *foedera*, such as the *Confoederatio Helvetica* established by the Alpine communities of Uri, Schwyz, and Unterwalden in the late thirteenth century, the original core cantons of the modern federation of Switzerland.[18] While grounded in an agreement between distinct communities of people, a confederation of this

[15] Antje Von Ungern-Sternberg, "Religion and Religious Intervention" in Bardo Fassbender and Anne Peters (eds), *Oxford Handbook of the History of International Law* (Oxford University Press 2012) 294, 297–299.

[16] John Locke, *Two Treatises of Government* (Cambridge University Press 1960[1689]) §146; see also Hugo Grotius, *De Iure Belli Ac Pacis Libris Tres* (Carnegie Institution 1913[1646]) 263 [ii.vi.i].

[17] Helmut Steinberger, "Historic Influences of American Constitutionalism upon German Constitutional Development: Federalism and Judicial Review" (1997) 36 Columbia Journal of Transnational Law 189, 197.

[18] Murray Forsyth, *Unions of States: The Theory and Practice of Confederation* (Leicester University Press 1981) ch 2; Frederick K Lister, *The Later Security Confederations: The American, "New" Swiss, and German Unions* (Greenwood Press 2001) ch 4.

kind could give rise to close relationships among the parties, described as a kind of oath-bound fellowship. This is echoed in the fact that even today the official name of the Swiss federation in German is the *Schweizerische Eidgenossenschaft*. The German word refers to the founding oath (*Eid*) of the federalized community, a supreme form of commitment sworn before God by covenanted companions (*Genossen*) who are equal in rights and commit themselves for a limited period or in perpetuity, thus giving rise to a "fellowship of the oath."

The earliest extant document of the Swiss confederation, nominally dated 1291, records the solemn oath (*iuramento*) by which the cantons of Uri, Schwyz, and Unterwalden committed themselves to mutual defense, common arbitration of disputes, and cooperation in the adjudication and punishment of crimes.[19] The arrangement was essentially a military alliance, but it appealed to the common good (*communi utilitate*) of the confederates (*conspirati*) and aspired to permanency (*in perpetuum duraturis*). It also referred to the confederates as having met in common council (*communi etiam consilio*) and having unanimously consented (*favore unanimi*) to the terms of the agreement.

After a decisive victory over Habsburg forces in 1315, it appears that Uri, Schwyz, and Unterwalden (the latter incorporating Nidwalden and Obwalden) renewed and extended the terms of the compact, each agreeing not to enter treaties or engage in negotiations without the consent of the confederation.[20] Through the course of the fourteenth century, several other nearby self-governing communities—the cities of Lucerne (1333), Zurich (1351), and Bern (1353) and the rural districts of Glarus (1352) and Zug (1352)—also joined the confederation. The confederating treaties often contained peculiar features negotiated by the particular parties.[21] Although these variations complicated the arrangements between the cantons, they underscored the essentially consensual, treaty-based nature of the system. The confederation expanded again over the next two centuries, Fribourg and Solothurn joining in 1481, Basel and Schaffhausen in 1501, and Appenzell in 1513. During this period several other neighboring cities and their subject territories also formed alliances with the confederation, but these, together with several subject territories of the confederation itself, would not become full members until the early nineteenth century.

19 Alliance between Uri, Schwyz, and Unterwalden (1291).
20 Pact of Brunnen (*Morgartenbrief*) (1315).
21 David Lasserre, *Alliances Confederales 1291–1815* (Eugene Rentsch, 1941).

Although originally part of the Duchy of Swabia and formally within the territorial jurisdiction of the Holy Roman Empire, the Swiss cantons exercised significant autonomy. Indeed, it had been in the context of the collapse of the Hohenstaufen dynasty in Swabia that Uri, Schwyz, and Unterwalden first formed the confederation in the late thirteenth century. By the fifteenth century, most of the cantons had secured the privilege of "imperial immediacy" (*Reichsfreiheit*) either as rural communities (Uri and Schwyz) or as "free" or "imperial cities" of the empire (*Freie Städte* or *Freie Reichsstädte*).[22] This status meant that rather than being subject to intermediate territorial princes or lords, they were under the direct authority of the emperor, which enabled them to assert and exercise independent powers of local self-government in combination with the other confederate cantons. In the case of Basel, as a "free city" originally under the rule of a prince-bishop, this also meant immunity from imperial taxation. The autonomy of each canton was jealously guarded, but this was combined with a commitment to joint action, particularly in the defense of each member of the confederation and the peaceful resolution of internal disputes. This led to several confrontations with the empire, especially after the Golden Bull issued by the Imperial Diet in 1356 outlawed all "conjurationes, confederationes, and conspirationes," a ruling directed against the many city alliances (*Städtebund*) beginning to emerge and thrive throughout Europe.[23] The Swiss confederation successfully resisted imperial Habsburg and Burgundian forces on several occasions, culminating in a decisive victory in the Swabian War of 1499. In the terms of peace set out in the Treaty of Basel (1499), Emperor Maximilian was forced to abandon his claims over the territories of the confederation, according it de facto independence, a status formally recognized in the Peace of Westphalia in 1648, giving the confederation the same standing as the most powerful princely states and kingdoms of Europe.

Switzerland enjoyed uninterrupted territorial independence until the late eighteenth century when it was overrun by the Napoleonic forces of republican France. The French instituted a unitary system based on the ideas of the revolution: Switzerland was renamed *La République helvétique* and

[22] Joachim Whaley, *Germany and the Holy Roman Empire, Volume I: Maximilian I to the Peace of Westphalia, 1493–1648* (Oxford University Press 2012) 26.

[23] These included the long-lived Hanseatic League (1159–1862), a commercial confederation of merchant guilds and market towns comprising several of the main ports of northern Europe. See Frederick K Lister, *The Early Security Confederations: From the Ancient Greeks to the United Colonies of New England* (Greenwood Press 1999) ch 3.

proclaimed to be "one and indivisible."[24] The cantons were reduced to administrative districts and some were merged, weakening their collective representation in the newly created national assembly. These measures were deeply unpopular, however, especially in the inner cantons, and the imposed government collapsed following the withdrawal of French troops. Napoleon personally responded in his famous *l'Acte de Médiation* of 1803, restoring the confederal system, but with the addition of six new cantons: two formerly associated states, St. Gallen and Grisons, and four formerly subject territories, Argau, Thurgau, Ticino, and Vaud. This system, premised on the sovereignty of the constituent cantons but with expanded powers for the government of the confederation, continued until the fall of Napoleon in 1813. Three new cantons (Valais, Neuchatel, and Geneva) were thereafter admitted to the confederation and, following the Congress of Vienna, the Swiss cantons and Diet adopted a new Federal Pact in 1815, which continued in operation until 1848.

The confederal relationship between the cantons allowed each to determine its own religious faith and identity. During the Reformation, Switzerland became split between cantons that became Protestant (particularly the powerful city cantons of Zurich, Berne, and Basel) and those that remained Roman Catholic (including the alpine cantons of Uri, Schwyz, Unterwalden, Lucerne, and Zug). This contributed to political tensions, the formation of intercantonal alliances, and civil wars in 1531, 1656, 1712, and 1847. The first of these was resolved by the second Peace of Kappel (1531), in which the signatory cantons generally agreed to respect the particular religious faith practiced in other cantons, anticipating the *Cuius regio, eius religio* principle adopted by the Peace of Augsburg (1555). Disputes over common territories and the treatment of religious minorities continued for the next three centuries, resolved sometimes by open war and at other times by mediation, particularly through formal peace treaties (*Landfrieden*) agreed to in 1529, 1531, 1656, and 1712.

The confederal relationship also allowed each canton to determine its own internal form of government. The rural cantons of Uri, Schwyz, Unterwalden, Glarus, and Appenzell, as well as the city canton of Zug, were governed by general assemblies (*Landsgemeinde*) at which a limited class of citizens participated in debate and voted directly on issues. Most of the city cantons, however, were practically oligarchic: from the seventeenth century,

[24] Echoing the French Constitution of 1795, Art 1. See Mark H Lerner, "The Helvetic Republic: An Ambivalent Reception of French Revolutionary Liberty" (2004) 18(1) French History 50, 68.

Berne, Fribourg, Lucerne, and Solothurn were ruled, in practice, by a small hereditary aristocracy, and Zurich and Basel by leading merchant families elected by the powerful guilds. In the eighteenth century, liberal and radical movements spread particularly in the Protestant cities and demands were made for the establishment of democratic constitutions. The short-lived Helvetic constitution imposed by the French embodied many of the objectives of the radicals, including universal male citizenship, but was eclipsed by a return to the ancien régime through the Federal Pact (*Bundesvertrag*) of 1815. Over the next decades, many of the Protestant cantons, constituting a majority of both the cantons and the population, adopted liberal democratic constitutions, while several of the Catholic cantons remained politically conservative and formed themselves into a defensive alliance called the *Sonderbund*. Tensions escalated in the 1830s, and there was a brief civil war in 1847 in which the forces of the confederation under the control of the liberals prevailed. In the next year the liberal majority in the Diet adopted a new constitution, which marked the transition of Switzerland from a relatively decentralized confederation to a more centralized federation.

Although the Constitution of 1848 was submitted to all twenty-five cantons for ratification, contrary to the requirement of unanimity under the Federal Pact of 1815, the new constitution was imposed by a majority of cantons on a minority that were not prepared to ratify it.[25] The new constitution thus appealed to the authority of both the cantons and the people, expressed by majority vote. In addition, the new constitution provided that it could be amended by a referendum at which a majority of voters in a majority of cantons as well as a majority of voters in the federation as a whole approved of the proposed change. Pursuant to this procedure, the Swiss Constitution has been altered numerous times, including major revisions in 1874 and 1999.[26]

Religion: Covenant and Oath

The prominence of terms such as *foedus* and *confoederatio* in medieval law and politics suggests that our contemporary understandings and institutions

[25] Swiss Constitution (1848), Transitionary Provisions, Art 2; Preamble and Resolution of the Federal Diet, 12 September 1848.

[26] Andreas Würgler, "Confédération" in *Dictionnaire Historique De La Suisse* (2002) <http://www.hls-dhs-dss.ch/textes/f/F26413.php>.

of federalism may have an overlapping legal, political, and religious provenance. Of their influence, Davis has observed that

> in the idea of covenant, and the synonymous ideas of promise, commitment, undertaking, or obligating, vowing, and plighting one's word to a course of conduct in relation to others, we come upon a vital bonding device of civilization.[27]

However, most political philosophy and constitutional theory has tended to overlook the significance of these ideas and the tradition they represent, in favor of other ways of understanding the nature and grounds of law, politics, and constitutionalism. Indeed, federalism is a neglected theme in most accounts of Western constitutionalism.[28] Why is this so? Two reasons suggest themselves. The first concerns the influence of Greek and especially Aristotelian political philosophy; the second concerns the nature of contemporary state theory. Between these two developments a political philosophy of federalism and a corresponding theology of the covenant did flourish for a time and had a lasting influence on fundamental features of many contemporary constitutions. To explain the rise and decline of this federal-covenantal theory, it is therefore necessary to begin with Aristotle and Ancient Greece, and then turn to modern theories of the state.

Although political scholarship has long been fascinated by the often fiercely independent democratic city-states (*poleis*) of Ancient Greece, it is now recognized that "almost half of all city-states in mainland Greece and the Peloponnese were integrated in one federal state or another."[29] Aristotle seems to have been fully aware of these political arrangements; he may even have described the governing institutions of the Lycian League.[30]

[27] Solomon Rufus Davis, *The Federal Principle: A Journey through Time in Quest of a Meaning* (University of California Press 1978) 3.

[28] Thomas O Hueglin, *Early Modern Concepts for a Late Modern World: Althusius on Community and Federalism* (Wilfrid Laurier University Press 1999); Donald Livingston, "The Founding and the Enlightenment: Two Theories of Sovereignty" in Gary Gregg (ed), *Vital Remnants: America's Founding and the Western Tradition* (ISI Books 1998).

[29] Hans Beck and Peter Funke, "An Introduction to Federalism in Greek Antiquity" in Hans Beck and Peter Funke (eds), *Federalism in Greek Antiquity* (Cambridge University Press 2015) 1, 3. See also Edward E Freeman, *History of Federal Government in Greece and Italy* (2nd edn, Macmillan 1893); V Ehrenberg, *The Greek State* (2nd edn, London: Methuen 1969) 103–131; JAO Larsen, *Greek Federal States: Their Institutions and History* (Oxford 1968) 202–207.

[30] Larsen, *Greek Federal States*, xi; JAO Larsen, "Representation and Democracy in Hellenistic Federalism" (1945) 40 Classical Philology 55, 78; Newman, *Politics of Aristotle*, vol II, 232. For the texts, see K Müller, *Fragmenta historicum graecorum: Apollodori Bibliotheca cum fragmentis*, 5 vols (Paris, 1848–1874), vol II, 102–177, esp fragments 91 and 145.

However, unlike Xenophon, Polybius, Plutarch, and others,[31] he appears to have given little attention to them. In the two passages of the *Politics* in which he approached the matter directly,[32] he drew a sharp and critical distinction between the *polis* itself and the various kinds of treaty-relationship that might be formed between a plurality of poleis.[33] Such treaties, Aristotle asserted, are merely "agreements (*sunthekai*) about imports, engagements (*sumbola*) to do no wrong against one another, and written articles of alliance (*summarchias*)."[34] Such agreements are therefore formed to secure only limited goals, such as commercial intercourse and mutual defense, and the contracting parties are not concerned about the moral welfare or internal virtues and vices of each other. Moreover, in a mere alliance there is no magistracy common to the contracting parties and there can be no real government (*politeuma*) common to city-states united merely by a treaty.[35] The *polis*, by contrast, is a union of men formed to pursue the good life, which is man's highest end.[36] Political justice can only be secured among those who share life together within the context of a city-state,[37] for "man" (*anthropos*) is by nature a "political animal" (*politikon zôion*), an animal whose nature is fulfilled only in the *polis*.[38] Aristotle thus considered that an alliance or league between two or more states cannot constitute a truly political community, for the nature of the two is fundamentally different.[39]

These features of Aristotle's thought contributed to the relative neglect of federalism in later political philosophy. However, there were elements in his thought that could be developed in that direction. Prime among these was his account of the origin of the *polis* as a composition of households (*oikiôn*) and villages (*kômôn*),[40] or as he later put it, as a community (*koinônia*) of households and clans (*genesi*), or of clans and villages.[41] Although Aristotle considered the *polis* to be of much greater importance than the smaller

[31] See Cinzia Bearzot, "Federalism in Greek Antiquity" in Hans Beck and Peter Funke (eds), *Ancient Theoretical Reflections on Federalism* (Cambridge University Press 2015) 503, 505–511.

[32] See also *Politics*, 1326b, discussing *ethnoi*, a term that could embrace federations: see ibid, 504.

[33] *Politics*, II.2, III.9. See Newman, *Politics of Aristotle*, III, 203–206.

[34] *Politics*, III.9.

[35] *Politics*, III.9, 1280a40–1280b2.

[36] *Politics*, II.2, III.9.

[37] *Nicomachean Ethics*, 1134a24-30.

[38] *Politics*, I.2, 1253a2–3, III.6, 1278b19–20. On the complexity of Aristotle's conception of the city-state, see WH Ambler, "Aristotle's Understanding of the Naturalness of the City" (1985) 47 Review of Politics 163–185.

[39] *Politics*, II.2, 1261a25–33.

[40] *Politics*, I.1–2, 1252a18–22, 1252b10–18, 28–31.

[41] *Politics*, III.9, 1280b34–35, 1280b40.

communities of which it is composed, he denied that it should simply replace or supplant them. Distinguishing his position from that of Plato,[42] Aristotle opposed an "extreme unification" of the city-state and rejected the proposition that "the highest unity of a state is its highest good."[43] Rather, a plurality or multitude of persons (*plêthos*) is of the very nature of a state and a "lesser degree of unity is preferable to the greater."[44] The *polis* should not, therefore, altogether displace smaller associations, such as the household.[45] For the city-state, the village and the household are all species of community (*koinônia*) and should be respected as such.[46]

Aristotle did not develop these elements into anything resembling a theory of federalism because, although families, clans, and villages may be historically prior to the *polis*, he considered the *polis* to be prior to them in nature or essence, just as the whole is prior to the part.[47] On his view, all these other smaller or less significant kinds of association—clans, tribes, religious guilds, and social clubs—are formed for limited and partial goods—in contrast to the *polis*, which is constituted for the common good.[48] It was the primacy of the *polis* and its goals that prevented Aristotle from developing a political theory of federalism. Such a theory could only arise when that primacy was challenged as a matter of principle. That effective challenge occurred with the advent of Christianity and, in particular, the institution of the church and the growth of a complex web of associations, corporations, villages, towns, and cities that characterized medieval Christendom and which John Milbank has called "complex space."[49] In this new theological and institutional context, the constituent elements of Aristotle's theory of the *polis* provided material for the later development of a more federalistic theory of political association.[50]

[42] *Republic*, V, 449a–466d.

[43] *Politics*, II.2, 1261b6–15.

[44] *Politics*, II.2, 1260b36–1261b15.

[45] *Republic*, III, 416d; V, 449a–466d. See, generally, D Dobbs, "Aristotle's Anticommunism" (1985) 29(1) American Journal of Political Science 29–46.

[46] WJ Booth, "Politics and the Household: A Commentary on Aristotle's *Politics* Book One" (1981) 2 History of Political Thought 203–226.

[47] *Politics*, I.2, 1253a18–29. See also *Metaphysics*, VII.10–11 and Newman, *Politics of Aristotle*, vol II, 125–127.

[48] *Nicomachean Ethics*, VIII.9, 1160a9–30; *Politics*, III.9, 1280b36–39. Even among classical political writers who gave more attention to the question—such as Xenophon, Polybius, and Plutarch—only a relatively thin theory emerged: Bearzot, "Federalism in Greek Antiquity," 505–511.

[49] John Milbank, "On Complex Space," *The Word Made Strange: Theology, Language, Culture* (Blackwell 1997) 268.

[50] As recent scholarship has shown, federations at the smaller scale of households, hamlets, and villages also occurred: Denis Rousset, "Microfederalism in Central Greece" in Hans Beck and Peter Funke (eds), *Federalism in Greek Antiquity* (Cambridge University Press 2015).

It is well known that, writing in this medieval context, Thomas Aquinas sought to synthesize the philosophy of Aristotle with Christian theology.[51] What is less widely appreciated is Aquinas's seminal reworking of Aristotle's political theory, in which his account of the construction of the city-state out of its constituent households and villages was expanded to take into account the much larger and more complicated political and ecclesiastical context of Aquinas's time, a context in which towns, cities, principalities, kingdoms, and imperial provinces were intermingled with a complex array of spiritual confraternities, monastic orders, local parishes, and provincial dioceses, all within the context of the overarching institutions of the Holy Roman Empire and the Roman Catholic Church as a whole.

Adapting Aristotle to this context, in his commentary on the *Nicomachean Ethics*, Aquinas decisively qualified Aristotle's assertion that human beings are political animals that find their fulfillment in the *polis*. He did not directly contradict the claim, but rather insisted that it must be understood only in relation to "human affairs" and with respect to the order of "nature"—as distinct from the "ultimate things" addressed in sacred theology and in which human beings find their ultimate and eternal fulfilment.[52] Similarly, Aquinas made clear that while Aristotle's *polis* might be a "whole" of which its component households and villages are a "part," the *polis* does not constitute an "absolute unity" but rather a "unity of order" in which the smaller component units have genuinely independent powers of operation.[53] As Aquinas elsewhere explained, a single congregation or community may include many other corresponding communities (*una congregatio vel communitas includit aliam*).[54] For Aquinas, groups of human beings naturally form themselves into systems of graded orders (*gradibus unionis*), whether in the church, the state, or other forms of human association.

These qualifications of Aristotle's political philosophy extended to Aquinas's account of human nature. Rather than follow Aristotle by always defining human beings simply as a "political animals," Aquinas preferred to refer to them as "political and social" or simply "social" animals, and added in one place that human beings are also by nature "domestic."[55] Similarly,

[51] See, e.g., *Summa contra Gentiles* (1259–1265) 1.9.1; 1.3.2, 4; 1.7.3.
[52] *Eth*, I.9.10–11 [112–113].
[53] *Eth*, I.1.5 [5].
[54] *Sent*, IV.24.3.2.3.
[55] *Summa Theologiae* (1265–1268, 1271–1273) I, 96.4; I-II, 61.5, 72.4, 95.4; *De Regno ad regem Cypri* (ca 1267) I.1.3 [4], I.13.2 [94]; *ScG*, III.85.11; *Eth*, I.1.4 [4], VII.6.7 [1391], VIII.12.18 (1719–1720); *Sententia libri Politicorum* (1269–1272), I.1.29 [37].

although he followed Aristotle in regarding self-sufficiency to be the essential characteristic of the *polis* or *civitas* that distinguishes it from a mere household or neighborhood,[56] Aquinas treated self-sufficiency in relative terms: households and neighborhoods can also possess a kind self-sufficiency in themselves, and wider political units such as provinces, kingdoms, and nations may possess degrees of self-sufficiency and completeness that surpass that of an individual city.[57]

Aquinas's basic principle was that "a government is the more perfect according as it is more universal, extends to more matters, and attains a more ultimate end."[58] The Christian doctrine of the church as an institution that is catholic or universal, as well as the corresponding existence of an empire consisting of self-governing kingdoms and principalities, suggested that Aristotle's fixation on political communities on the scale of individual cities could not stand. Aquinas therefore routinely used alternative terms to express this diversity of political forms and scales. Sometimes he used generic terms, such as "civic community" or "political society"; other times he referred alternatively to the concrete institutions of city, kingdom, or province (*civitas*, *regnum*, *provincia*).

Aquinas also developed a typology of different kinds of association that distinguished public societies (cities, kingdoms, and provinces) from private societies (households, business partnerships, craft guilds, and religious associations), but which nonetheless classified them all as particular kinds of "society."[59] He understood these various forms of society to possess both a degree of separateness and independence from each other and a degree of integration and interdependence. An individual might be a member of a particular private society that, to a certain extent, governs itself, while at the same time by virtue of that membership he may be a member of a wider public society of which the smaller society is a part; indeed, an individual might even be a citizen of more than one city.[60]

This idea of a vast plurality of political, ecclesiastical, social, and economic communities, themselves composed of smaller constituent communities,

[56] *Pol*, I.1.3 [11], I.1.7–9 [15–17], I.1.23–25 [31–33], I.1.30–32 [38–40]; *ST*, I-II, 90.3 ad 3, II-II, 47.11, 50.1.

[57] *De Regno*, I.2.4 [14]; I.14.5 [100]; *Quaestiones Disputatae de Veritate* (1256–1259), 5.3 co; *ST*, I-II, 91.1, 21.4, 100.5; *ScG*, I.42, 70–71, 78, 85–86, 93, 102, II.39, 42, III.64, 98.

[58] *ST*, II-II, 50.1.

[59] *Contra impugnantes Dei cultum et Religionem* (1256) II.2, co; see also *Impugn*, II.3, ad 6; *Pol*, I.1.23 [31].

[60] *Impugn*, II.2, ad 2 and ad 3.

suggested that the smaller constituent communities ought to be corporately represented in the governing institutions of the larger. Aquinas supported this idea from texts of the Old and New Testaments in which the construction of the nation of Israel out of a plurality of tribes, clans, and families[61] was understood to parallel the construction of the universal church out of a plurality of self-governing dioceses and parishes, integrated through a hierarchy of courts of appeal that themselves were constituted by representatives of the constituent communities.[62] Even the pope was understood to be a limited monarch, constrained by the fundamental beliefs, standards, and institutions of the Christian faith.[63] Accordingly, while Aquinas clearly favored monarchical rule,[64] he also wished to guard against tyranny, and he suggested several ways in which the authority of kings ought to be tempered, including through compacts (*pacta*) that place constitutional limits on their powers, procedures by which tyrannical kings can be deposed, and systems of "mixed government" that enable all to have a share in ruling.[65] Notably, Aquinas also said that it is one of the hallmarks of a tyrant that he deliberately undermines all forms of social solidarity among his subjects, preventing them from joining in various associations (*confederationes*) even though these are the primary means through which friendship, familiarity, and trust are generated.[66]

Only a glimmer of these constitutional ideas appears in Aristotle's writings. This was in part due to the fact that classical antiquity had no conception of church and state as separate and distinct institutions. However, the seeds of the distinction were in Christianity from the very beginning.[67] Combined with the Roman law concept of *jurisdictio*, medieval jurists developed the idea that church and state, and many other particular institutions besides, each possessed discrete and limited jurisdiction over particular matters.[68] Aquinas followed this lead by drawing a definite distinction between spiritual and temporal authority. In those matters that affect the salvation of the

[61] *ST*, I-II, 105.1 res., citing Exodus 18:21 and Deuteronomy 1:13, 15.

[62] *Impugn*, II.3; *Expositio in Lucam*, commenting on Luke 10:1.

[63] *Impugn*, II.3.

[64] *ScG*, IV.76.4; *De Regno*, I.3.1–4 [15–19].

[65] *Pol.*, II.7.4 [245]; *De Regno*, I.7.1–12 [41–52]; *ST*, I-II, 95.4 and 105.1. For more detail, see Nicholas Aroney, "Subsidiarity, Federalism and the Best Constitution: Thomas Aquinas on City, Province and Empire" (2007) 26 Law and Philosophy 161, 198–220.

[66] *De Regno*, I.4.7 [27].

[67] Mark 12:17; Acts 5:29.

[68] Harold J Berman, *Law and Revolution: The Formation of the Western Legal Tradition* (Harvard University Press 1983) 205–215.

soul, spiritual power is to be followed, whereas in those matters that concern the civil welfare, the temporal should be obeyed.[69] While church and state are different in nature and purpose, they are both "public associations" and "perfect communities."[70]

The Calvinist political philosopher and jurist Johannes Althusius (1557–1638),[71] building on both Aristotle and Aquinas, took for granted the same vast plurality of political and other forms of human community—hamlets, villages, neighborhoods, cities, kingdoms, and provinces—when constructing the first recognizably "modern" theory of federalism, developed principally on the basis of the politico-theological concept of the covenant.[72] The starting point of Althusius's theory was the proposition that

> politics is the art of associating men for the purpose of establishing, cultivating, and conserving social life among them. Whence it is called "symbiotics." The subject matter of politics is therefore association (*consociatio*), in which the symbiotes (*symbiotici*) pledge themselves each to the other, by explicit or tacit agreement, to mutual communication of whatever is useful and necessary for the harmonious exercise of social life.[73]

For Althusius, this proposition applies to all kinds of consociation, including the family, the collegium, the city, the province, and the commonwealth or "universal association." Each of these larger associations is formed by "the bond of an associating and uniting agreement" among the smaller associations of which each larger consociation is composed. Thus, the most simple private associations (families and colleges) are initiated by "a special covenant" (*pactum*) among individuals,[74] while larger public associations (towns, cities, provinces, and the commonwealth) are derived from the primary

[69] *Scriptum super Sententiis magistri Petri Lombardi* (1256) II.44 exposito textus. But see also *De Regno*, I.16.2 [115].

[70] *Impugn*, II.2, ad 9; *ST*, II-II, 31.3 ad 3; 43.8.

[71] For background, see John Witte Jr, "Natural Rights, Popular Sovereignty, and Covenant Politics: Johannes Althusius and the Dutch Revolt and Republic" (2010) 87(4) University of Detroit Mercy Law Review 565.

[72] Johannes Althusius, *Politica methodice digesta atque exemplis sacris & profanes illustrata* (3rd edn, Herborn 1614). For a translation, see Frederick Carney (tr), *Politica: An Abridged Translation* (Liberty Fund 1995). See Carl J Friedrich, *Trends of Federalism in Theory and Practice* (Praeger 1968) 12.

[73] *Politica* I:1–2, 17.

[74] *Politica*, II:2–5; see also IV:1–5, 8, 12, 17, 22. Despite its grounding in nature and necessity, even the family is initiated by covenant; the collegium, a "spontaneous and merely voluntary society," is emphatically formed by covenanted agreement (*pacta conventum*) and common consent.

associations, for "without this primary association others are able neither to arise nor to endure."[75] Moreover, the various collegia are customarily distributed into the three estates (clergy, nobility, and people),[76] and it is through the three estates that "the people of a provincial city, realm, or polity" consent to and ultimately control its affairs.

Accordingly, a local community (village, town, or city) is a kind of public association "composed of many families and collegia living in the same place."[77] Likewise, the province consists of its orders and estates, or the larger collegia,[78] and the universal association arises when "many cities and provinces obligate themselves to hold, organize, use, and defend . . . the right of the realm."[79] Finally, the universal association is "an imperium, realm, commonwealth, and people united in one body by the agreement of many symbiotic associations and particular bodies, and brought together under one right."[80] All this follows, Althusius argued, because "families, cities and provinces existed by nature prior to realms, and gave birth to them."[81] The members of the commonwealth are not "individuals, families and collegia," but rather "cities, provinces and regions agreeing among themselves on a single body constituted by mutual union and communication."[82] The true bond of the commonwealth is the consensus and trust established through a "tacit or expressed promise" among its corporate members.[83]

Central to Althusius's theory was the idea of covenant. The universal commonwealth is created by a covenant or federal pact entered into by the constituent communities, and the supreme magistrate is likewise instituted "by covenant or constitution."[84] Althusius therefore used the terms "constitution" and "covenant" interchangeably, for the *lex fundamentalis* "is nothing other than certain covenants by which many cities and provinces come together and agree to establish . . . one and the same commonwealth."[85] For him, federal covenantalism *is* federal constitutionalism, and vice versa. Althusius did

[75] *Politica*, II:2. The city is thus grounded in "the common consent and covenant of each and all": *Politica*, VI:7.
[76] *Politica*, IV:30.
[77] *Politica*, V:8, 10.
[78] *Politica*, VIII:2, 40.
[79] *Politica*, IX:1.
[80] *Politica*, IX:3.
[81] *Politica*, IX:3.
[82] *Politica*, IX:5.
[83] *Politica*, IX:7.
[84] *Politica*, XIX:23
[85] *Politica*, XIX:49.

not discard the concept of *maiestas* or sovereignty altogether.[86] But unlike Bodin and Hobbes, he ascribed it to "the total people associated in one symbiotic body from many smaller associations," the "entire associated body of the realm," in the "consent and concord of the associated bodies."[87] The constitutive status of the provinces and cities and their reserved sphere of rights thus presented "an insuperable barrier" of fundamental law to the exercise of any authority within the commonwealth.[88]

Modern federalism is often traced to the innovations in statecraft pioneered by the founders of the American Constitution. While there is little evidence to suggest that Althusius was read directly by the Americans, as John Witte has shown, much the same covenantal idea permeated American colonial political thought and political activity.[89] Famously, the Mayflower Compact of 1620, subscribed by the first inhabitants of the colony established at Plymouth in what is now the American state of Massachusetts, recited the formation of the colony on the basis of a solemn and mutual "covenant."[90] Similar language was employed by the *Fundamental Orders of Connecticut* of 1639, the original constitution of the state, but this time to give effect to a federating covenant between the people of the three constituent towns of the colony. Much the same language was used in the "consociation" formed by the Articles of Confederation of the United Colonies of New England in 1643, the Articles of Confederation of the United States of America drafted in 1776, and eventually the Constitution of the United States drafted in 1787 and ratified in 1788–1789. Since that time, federations have proliferated throughout the world.

[86] *Politica* IX:20–21.

[87] *Politica*, 1614 Preface, IX:18–19.

[88] *Politica*, IX:3–4, 7, 13, 15–24; XVIII:69, 85, 105; XIX:7–8, 49; XXXVIII:7, 53, 71–73, 76, 110–114. See, further, Nicholas Aroney and Simon Kennedy, "Johannes Althusius's Cosmopolitan Defense of Local Politics" in Lee Ward (ed), *Cosmopolitanism and Its Discontents: Rethinking Politics in the Age of Brexit and Trump* (Rowman & Littlefield 2020).

[89] John Witte, "Blest Be the Ties That Bind: Covenant and Community in Puritan Thought" (1987) 36 Emory Law Journal 579; John Witte Jr, "How to Govern a City on a Hill: The Early Puritan Contribution to American Constitutionalism" (1990) 39 Emory Law Journal 41.

[90] This compact and numerous others are collected in Donald Lutz, *Colonial Origins of the American Constitution: A Documentary History* (Liberty Fund 1998). See also Stephen L Schechter, Richard B Bernstein, and Donald S. Lutz (eds), *Roots of the Republic: American Founding Documents Interpreted* (Madison House 1990).

Epilogue

While Althusius's writings offered a fully developed theory of federalism, they were neglected until rediscovered by Otto von Gierke in 1880.[91] Why the neglect of such an important author, and why the neglect of federal theory generally? The work of Olivier Beaud offers a final explanation.[92] Beaud maintains that federations are a special type of constitutional arrangement that cannot be understood or explained using the tools of conventional state theory. State theory rests on the concept of a unitary locus of constituent power from which the constituted powers of the state derive their authority. A viable theory of federations must rest, he argues, on the idea of a plurality of political entities that agree to form a larger political community of which they are the constituent states. As James Bryce put it, the result is "a Commonwealth of commonwealths, a Republic of republics, a State which, while one, is nevertheless composed of other States even more essential to its existence than it is to theirs."[93] However, the emergence of the state as a dominating form of political governance, and the development of a body of state theory around it, has led to federations being regarded as secondary and derivative.

According to mainstream state theory, the most important question in jurisprudence is to identify the location of the unitary source of sovereign power on which the whole political system rests.[94] On this view, the ordinary condition of the state is to be a unitary political community, predicated on a single locus of sovereignty, exercised internally over all persons and groups falling within its jurisdiction, and employed externally as a claim of autonomy and independence as against any foreign power. When applied to the theorization of federal systems, two consequences follow. The first is that the federation is understood as a particular type of state or a particular type of relation between states, rather than as a political form that is distinct from and stands alongside the concept of the state. The second is that the main preoccupation of the theory is to identify a single locus of sovereignty. The consequence is that a sharp distinction is generated between two types of federal system. The first type, conventionally called a "confederation" or

[91] Otto von Gierke, *Johannes Althusius und die Entwicklung der naturrechtlichen Staatstheorien* (Breslau 1880).
[92] Olivier Beaud, *Théorie De La Fédération* (Presses Universitaires de France 2009).
[93] James Bryce, *The American Commonwealth* (2nd edn, Macmillan 1889) I, 12–15, 332.
[94] See the chapter by Joel Harrison in this volume.

Staatenbund, is an association of states in which each individual state retains its sovereignty. The second type, called a "federal-state" or *Bundesstaat*, is a single state in which governing powers are divided between levels of government, but in which sovereignty remains concentrated in a unitary locus of constituent power.[95]

This distinction between *Staatenbund* and *Bundesstaat* rests more on the application of an *a priori* theory of the nature of the state than a careful investigation of the empirical features and practical working of federations. There are undoubtedly important differences between several of the older "confederations" (Dutch Republic 1581, United States of America 1781, Switzerland 1815, German Empire 1871, Australia 1888) and the newer "federations" (United States of America 1789, Mexico 1821, Switzerland 1948, Argentina 1853, Canada 1865, Brazil 1889, Australia 1901, India 1947, Germany 1949, Malaysia 1963). But the key empirical difference lies in the direct juridical relationship between the federal institutions of government and individual citizens, not the location of sovereignty. When the formative processes by which both kinds of system have come into being are closely examined, it becomes clear that the consent of the constituent states was required in each case in which the federation or the confederation was formed by aggregation of pre-existing states.[96]

In mainstream state theory, sovereignty has a tendency to absoluteness: it asserts an authority that supervenes on any competing loyalty or allegiance and it claims, in its extreme form, the right to reconstruct the entire ensemble of human relationships.[97] The assertion of this kind of sovereignty is incompatible with federalism, because federalism involves a plurality of overlapping political authorities, neither of which has an ultimate constitutional ascendency. Sometimes it is argued that the idea of sovereignty can be preserved within a federation through its ascription to "the people" of the federation as a whole.[98] However, every such attempt encounters the problem that

[95] See, e.g., Georg Jellinek, *Die Lehre Von Den Staatenverbindungen* (Alfred Holder 1882) and John W Burgess, *Political Science and Comparative Constitutional Law* (Ginn and Co 1890). For a discussion, see Nicholas Aroney, "The Influence of German and Swiss State-Theory on Late Nineteenth Century British, American and Australian Conceptions of Federalism" (2010) 59 International and Comparative Law Quarterly 669.

[96] The situation is different, and more complex, in cases of devolution within a formerly unitary state, such as Spain since 1978, Belgium in 1993, Italy since the 1990s, and the United Kingdom in 1998.

[97] For the theological antecedents of political and legal conceptions of sovereignty, see also Aroney, "Christianity, Sovereignty and Global Law."

[98] E.g., Samuel H Beer, *To Make a Nation: The Rediscovery of American Federalism* (Belknap Press 1993).

modern federations do not appeal simply to "We, the people," but more precisely to "We, the peoples."[99] In other words, federations routinely recognize multiple political identities not only in their distributions of power between "federal" and "state" institutions of government but also in the composition and construction of those institutions so that they represent the people of the federation and the peoples of the states, as well as in the very formation of the federation in the first place—through an agreement, compact, or covenant between constituent states.[100] For this reason, as Carl Schmitt acknowledged, in a federation, the question of sovereignty "always remains open."[101]

Federations are the institutional expression of legal, political, and religious ideas and practices that pre-date the modern sovereign state. As the etymological origin of the term "federal" suggests, federations owe much to the Roman *foedus*, a legally binding treaty vouchsafed by religious oaths and dependent for its implementation on the bona fides of the contracting parties. The oldest extant federation, Switzerland, founded on a kind of *foedus*, established an oath-bound fellowship (*Eidgenossenschaft*) in which the parties committed themselves to mutual defense, common arbitration of disputes, and cooperation in the adjudication and punishment of crimes. Although the federations of the contemporary world display a great deal of range and variety, as Davis pointed out, the one concept that unifies them all is the idea of the covenant (*b'rit, foedus, bund*). Aristotle was aware of the many leagues that had been formed among the Greek city-states of his time, but he underplayed their significance because he believed that ultimate human fulfillment can only be secured in the *polis*. It was the new theological, philosophical, and institutional contexts of medieval and reformation Christianity, building on the Greek and Roman inheritance, that made possible the phenomenon of federalism as we know it today. This involved far-reaching changes in the institutional architecture of society, premised on the founding duality of church and empire and supplemented, over time, by

[99] Henry Paul Monaghan, "We the People[s], Original Understanding, and Constitutional Amendment" (1996) 96(1) Columbia Law Review 121; Kalypso Nicolaïdis, "We, the Peoples of Europe . . . " (2004) 83(6) Foreign Affairs 97; Stephen Tierney, "'We the Peoples': Constituent Power and Constitutionalism in Plurinational States" in Martin Loughlin and Neil Walker (eds), *The Paradox of Constitutionalism* (Oxford University Press 2008) 229.

[100] Nicholas Aroney, "Formation, Representation and Amendment in Federal Constitutions" (2006) 54(1) American Journal of Comparative Law 277.

[101] Carl Schmitt, *Constitutional Theory* (Jeffrey Seitzer tr, Duke University Press 2008) § 29.III.1, 390.

the development of a multiplicity of authority structures and jurisdictions that were not only ecclesiastical and civil but also mercantile, scholarly, charitable, and religious. Thomas Aquinas adapted Aristotelian political philosophy to this new context, but it was Johannes Althusius who gave it recognizably federal—which is to say, covenantal—form.

PART III

CHRISTIAN THEOLOGY AND CONSTITUTIONALISM

16

Revelation

Scripture and Covenant

David VanDrunen

Christianity claims that there is a living and Triune God and that this God reveals himself to human beings. In giving this revelation, God has entrusted his people with a holy book, the Bible, that regulates their belief and action. But to serve this purpose, the Bible needs to be interpreted.

These three interrelated subjects—revelation, scripture, and hermeneutics—have crucial implications for constitutionalism and are the focus of this chapter. I first consider the significance of the claim that divine revelation exists, especially for constitutional issues regarding sovereignty and moral truth. Second, I reflect on the idea that God has revealed himself through human beings, by making them in his image, and I describe the ramifications of this doctrine for political community and political authority. The rest of the chapter then focuses on the biblical covenants. These covenants not only are means by which God reveals himself but also provide a hermeneutical framework for interpreting scripture. Through this study, I argue for the foundational importance of the Noahic covenant and explore several ways that it should shape a Christian account of constitutionalism. The chapter concludes by considering the constitutional implications of the Abrahamic, Mosaic, and new covenants that follow in the scriptures.

Divine Revelation: Preliminary Considerations

If a transcendent God exists, that fact alone suggests the need for constitutions that constrain the pretensions of finite creatures who claim dominion.[1] But

[1] I understand constitutionalism to represent the ideal of *limited* government, bound by a fundamental law that constrains civil officials. See Charles Howard McIlwain, *Constitutionalism Ancient and Modern* (rev edn, Cornell University Press 1947) 21.

David VanDrunen, *Revelation: Scripture and Covenant* in *Christianity and Constitutionalism*. Edited by: Nicholas Aroney and Ian Leigh, Oxford University Press. © Oxford University Press 2022. DOI: 10.1093/oso/9780197587256.003.0016

if this God were merely transcendent and thus distant and uninterested in the world, rulers might plausibly dismiss his existence as irrelevant for political community. The Christian doctrine of revelation provides a powerful response. The transcendent God is intimately involved in creation. He does not remain distant but makes himself known. In doing so, God places his claims on human beings and holds them accountable before his judgment. As our subsequent discussion of covenant will show, he does this not as a detached despot, but as a loving God in relationship to his creatures.

The distinction between *natural* and *special* revelation is helpful.[2] Natural revelation refers to God's manifestation through the created order, in a way evident to all people. Psalm 19:1 captures this succinctly: "The heavens declare the glory of God, and the sky above proclaims his handiwork."[3] Paul addresses the issue in more detail: "What can be known about God is plain to them [human beings], because God has shown it to them. For his invisible attributes, namely, his eternal power and divine nature, have been clearly perceived, ever since the creation of the world, in the things that have been made" (Rom 1:19–20). Paul explains that all people are thus accountable to God, for they actually know him through this revelation, although they fail to honor him (Rom 1:20–21). If natural revelation brings *accountability*, it must make known humanity's moral responsibilities before God, and not simply abstract information about him. This implies that natural law is one aspect of natural revelation, as considered later.[4]

Special revelation refers to God's extraordinary words and deeds that clarify and supplement natural revelation. God's deeds themselves are revelatory: "You are the God who works wonders; you have made known your might among the peoples" (Ps. 77:14). But God also speaks through prophetic messengers. The true prophet stands "in the council of the Lord to see and to hear his word" (Jer. 23:18) and then speaks that word faithfully to the people (Jer. 23:28). According to classical Christian theology, scripture *is*

[2] This distinction is common in my own Reformed theological tradition, as well as in other Protestant circles. For a classic discussion from the Reformed perspective, see Herman Bavinck, *Reformed Dogmatics*, vol 1, *Prolegomena* (John Bolt ed, John Vriend tr, Baker Academic 2003) 301–385.

[3] Scripture quotations are from The Holy Bible, English Standard Version (ESV), copyright © 2001 by Crossway Bibles, a publishing ministry of Good News Publishers. Used by permission. All rights reserved.

[4] Most Christian theologians have believed that Paul explicitly addresses natural law shortly thereafter, in Romans 2:14–15. This is a contested issue among contemporary New Testament scholars; for a defense of a natural law interpretation and consideration of counterarguments, see David VanDrunen, *Divine Covenants and Moral Order: A Biblical Theology of Natural Law* (Eerdmans 2014) 233–251.

special revelation, not just a human record of it. This is what the Bible claims about itself. Scripture is "thus says the Lord" (Jer. 31:2, etc.). It is "breathed out by God" (2 Tim. 3:16), written as the prophets "were carried along by the Holy Spirit" (2 Pet. 1:21).

This brief discussion of revelation already points to an important implication for constitutionalism: it implies that no human being is truly *sovereign*.[5] The notion of sovereignty has shaped much modern political and legal theory. Does each political community need to have one person or group of people that has the final say as to what is law? Some scholars claim that the whole point of constitutions is to provide an alternative to sovereignty.[6] Others defend the idea of sovereignty and seek to show how a constitution can function effectively within such a system.[7] The present study cannot delve deeply into this debate, but Christian teaching that there is a self-revealing God to whom all are accountable calls the whole notion of *human* sovereignty into question. The most powerful human ruler must answer to God, but there is no one greater to whom God must answer. God is the only true sovereign. How best to distribute authority in a political community is a difficult question with no single obvious answer. But a Christian theology of revelation provides initial reason to think that constitutions serve a very useful role when they constrain the power of rulers and hence discourage the notion of political sovereignty.[8]

A further implication follows: the Christian doctrine of revelation suggests that constitutionalism should be concerned with both institutional and moral constraints. Scott Gordon argues for constitutionalism as an alternative to political sovereignty but associates constitutionalism only with institutional checks and balances, or "countervailance." He recognizes that many constitutionalists also seek to constrain rulers through declaration of moral rights or appeal to natural law but claims that, without countervailing institutional structures, political authorities will simply interpret such moral principles in their own way or ignore them altogether.[9] This point is well taken.

[5] See chapter 9 above, by Harrison.

[6] E.g., Scott Gordon, *Controlling the State: Constitutionalism from Ancient Athens to Today* (Harvard University Press 1999).

[7] E.g., AV Dicey, *Introduction to the Study of the Law of the Constitution* (10th edn, St Martin's 1960), in which British parliamentary sovereignty is a major theme. Gordon (n. 5 above) argues that Parliament is actually *not* sovereign in Great Britain; see *Controlling the State*, ch 9.

[8] Here and elsewhere I assume that constitutions are normative and not merely descriptive, unlike the view of JAG Griffith, for example, in "The Political Constitution" (1979) 42(1) Modern Law Review 19.

[9] E.g., Gordon, *Controlling the State*, 256, 319. See also chapter 12 above, by Bernal.

But the notion of divine self-revelation implies that constitutions are properly concerned about more than institutional constraints. Concern about restraining power begs the question why we wish to restrain power in the first place. Surely it is because such restraint promotes good and suppresses evil. Gordon himself believes that constitutionalism-as-countervailance protects *liberty*—a morally loaded term, albeit vague. From a Christian perspective, God's unique sovereignty entails that all people, even rulers, are morally accountable to him. In the present postmodern context, many people dismiss any claim to moral truth as a veiled assertion of power or expression of personal preference.[10] While alert to the fact that moral claims *can* be little but that, Christians cannot become moral relativists or skeptics and dare not pretend that constitutionalism is amoral or morally neutral.[11] Christians profess that God is truth, and thus believe his revelation is true. Constraining rulers institutionally is worthwhile only if there is something worth preserving and promoting.

Revelation and the Image of God

The Christian scriptures begin with a magnificent account of God as creator and ruler of all things. Genesis 1–2 communicates what I claimed earlier: God alone is the true sovereign. God calls all things into existence, puts them in right order, prescribes their proper functions, and holds them accountable for their actions. But God's formation of humans in his own image and likeness is the climax of creation (1:26–27). This both enriches our doctrine of revelation and, though Genesis 1–2 is first and foremost about *God's* sovereign rule, identifies the responsibilities and limits of *human* rule.

First, it is worth noting that human beings, as the image of God, are *themselves* divine revelation. In describing humans as God's likeness, scripture indicates that they reflect God, and thus display something important about him. The Bible, of course, is full of polemics against idolatry. Idolatry is perverse not only because there is only one true God but also because that God has already made an image of himself: the human race. Ironically, humans

[10] One of the most influential studies of American constitutionalism in recent decades embraces this perspective; see Sanford Levinson, *Constitutional Faith* (Princeton University Press 1988) 171–172.

[11] Accordingly, H. Jefferson Powell persuasively argues that American constitutionalism has been a moral tradition; see *The Moral Tradition of American Constitutionalism: A Theological Interpretation* (Duke University Press 1993).

end up becoming like the idols they make rather than faithfully imaging the God who made them (see Ps. 115:8; Rom. 1:23).

A second consideration follows. Since bearing the image of God is divine revelation, human beings understand something about the image from natural revelation as well as special revelation. Simply by knowing themselves, they know the God who created them. God made them in the image and according to the likeness (Gen. 1:26), and thus the image is constitutive of human existence, not something added on to a human nature that is independently intelligible. Therefore, the things scripture says about the image—to which we turn momentarily—are not foreign to human beings but natural. They are not obscure but familiar. In other words, the reality of the image has *universal* implications, not simply for Christians or others who know the scriptures.

This brings us to our third consideration, what the image of God actually is. Many Christian theologians have understood the image to reside in certain capabilities of human nature, such as rationality or volitionality. More recently, biblical scholars have come to a broad consensus that to be the image, according to Genesis 1, is to be God's royal representative on earth. This view has much to commend it.[12] Any reader can see on the face of the text that when God creates humans in his image he immediately calls them to a royal task, that is, ruling the rest of creation (Gen. 1:26). In fact, the Hebrew grammatical construction likely indicates the presence of a purpose clause, which would suggest the following translation: "Let us make man in our image, after our likeness, *and so let him* rule."[13] This makes sense in context. Genesis 1 portrays God as a great king who exercises supreme rule over the world, and thus those who bear his likeness appropriately exercise rule as well, albeit subordinate rule.[14] To put it briefly, the image is thoroughly moral. To bear God's image is to have a royal commission.

The fourth consideration draws these issues into the orbit of constitutionalism. One striking feature of Genesis 1 is that God appoints human beings to rule the rest of the world but does not appoint some human beings to rule over other human beings. As commentators note, many ancient Near Eastern

[12] For a description of this consensus, see Gunnlaugur A Jónsson, *The Image of God: Genesis 1:26–28 in a Century of Old Testament Research* (Almqvist & Wiksell 1988). For an exegetical defense of this view, see VanDrunen, *Divine Covenants*, 42–68.

[13] See Paul Joüon, SJ, *Grammar of Biblical Hebrew* (T. Muraoka tr and rev, Editrice Pontificio Instituto Biblico 1991) 2:381.

[14] Throughout this chapter, I assume that since human rule in this world is to image God's rule, human rule must be benevolent, not exploitative.

texts speak of gods creating humans in their image, but ordinarily it is only the special few—the kings—who enjoy this privilege.[15] It is remarkable, therefore, that Genesis ascribes the image of God to all human beings promiscuously. God simply creates generic "man," "male and female," in his image (Gen. 1:26–27). Thus, the very first chapter of scripture makes all human beings fundamentally equal, explicitly rejecting the ancient Near Eastern royal propaganda that ascribed unique divine privilege to the potentate. *All* human beings bear God's image and thus have a rightful share in the commission to benevolent rule of the world. This does not prohibit the future division of labor within the human community in which some people exercise political authority over others—indeed, scripture elsewhere assents to such arrangements (e.g., Rom. 13:1–7; 1 Pet. 2:13–17). But it does indicate that political authorities ought to treat members of the community as fellow divine image bearers, as those of equal worth and dignity to themselves. Magistrates and ordinary citizens enjoy a common call to rule the world at large. Political authority must serve this end, not the selfish interests of civil officials.

These things reinforce the preliminary conclusions about constitutionalism in the previous section. On the one hand, the universal character of divine image bearing confirms my initial skepticism about sovereignty and suggests that constitutional countervailance is fitting. Even if only some hold civil office, to organize civil authority in a hierarchical scheme in which one person or group stands alone at the top runs against the grain of the common human rule envisioned in Genesis 1. On the other hand, the biblical portrayal of the image indicates that constitutionalism cannot simply be a matter of countervailing institutions. Institutional safeguards require a moral purpose. Claims to political power need to be checked because all human beings have an innate dignity worthy of protection and a divine calling to participate in benevolent rule of the world. Limitations upon government ought to exist not for their own sake but to promote humanity's universal moral commission.

This is the ideal, but there is also a dark side. Immediately after the grand account of creation, Genesis narrates the fall into sin. The human race failed to live according to God's natural and special revelation, and thus God cursed it (Gen. 3). After a brief account of primeval history (Gen. 4–5), Genesis describes the corruption of the world and how God judged it through a great

[15] E.g., see Richard Middleton, *The Liberating Image: The* Imago Dei *in Genesis 1* (Brazos 2005) chs 3–4.

flood (Gen. 6–7). The chief problem, scripture tells us, was that the world was "filled with violence" (Gen. 6:11). The chief perpetrators were kings who took any women they wanted for their harems (Gen. 6:2)[16] and mighty warriors who roamed the earth (Gen. 6:4). Powerful men claimed political dominion over others, so it appears, unhindered by the rule of law or accountability to any but themselves. It seems little stretch to say that lack of constitutional constraints—moral or institutional—provoked the judgment of the flood. Curbing the abuse of power stemming from human sin (whether called by that name or not) is an omnipresent concern of constitutionalism, and rightly so.

Covenant and Revelation

Following the account of the great flood and the re-creation scene that follows (Gen. 8:1–20), Genesis records a covenant that God made with Noah and the whole creation (Gen. 8:21–9:17).[17] This brings us to a major focus of the chapter, the series of divine-human covenants in the unfolding biblical story.[18] In this brief section, I describe the general significance of covenant for the present study. In the following sections, I discuss the Noahic covenant specifically and explore its pivotal role for a Christian analysis of constitutionalism, followed by reflection on what the subsequent biblical covenants contribute to this analysis.

Covenant is undeniably an important theme in the Bible and is intimately related to the main themes of this chapter: revelation, scripture, and hermeneutics. At major turning points in biblical history, God makes covenants to define his relationship with people, to make promises, and to demand obedience. The establishment of a covenant is a revelational event. The Noahic, Abrahamic, Mosaic, Davidic, and new covenants were all accompanied by special revelation that described what God was doing and specified the proper response to it. In the case of the Mosaic and new covenants, God appointed prophetic servants to record this special revelation for future generations,

[16] See David Novak, *Natural Law in Judaism* (Cambridge University Press 1997) 36–37.

[17] Although the word "covenant" does not appear until Genesis 9:9, there is compelling reason to believe that the description of the covenant begins in 8:21. See Stephen D Mason, "Another Flood? Genesis 9 and Isaiah's Broken Eternal Covenant" (2007) 32(2) Journal for the Study of the Old Testament 184–186.

[18] There is good evidence that Genesis 1–2 also describes a covenant enactment, despite lack of the word "covenant," but I do not believe one's view of that issue is decisive for my argument here.

what we now know as the Torah and New Testament. The covenants are hermeneutically important because they provide interpretive clues for understanding both the big picture of the biblical message and its finer details. The covenants provide a framework for understanding how God relates to his people at a particular period in biblical history. Subsequent parts of scripture often appeal back to earlier covenants, recalling promises to Abraham or David, for example, or reminding of commands or threats given through Moses. And as the biblical canon advances from the Abrahamic to Mosaic to Davidic to new covenants, readers can see the progress of the story as a whole and chart the fulfillment of God's purposes. It is also worth noting that these covenants are simultaneously relational and legal. God does not deal with this world as an anonymous stranger, but rather enters into bonds of various degrees of intimacy with his creatures. And these relationships have a legal dimension. Although there is no single model for what constitutes a biblical covenant, God typically seals them with oaths, gives commands (even in overt legal form), demands obedience, and sometimes threatens judgment for rebellion. In fact, covenants play a sort of constitutional role in the relationships between God and human beings, insofar as they provide a fundamental framework defining the obligations of both parties to one another.

It is worth noting that scripture speaks of intrahuman covenants as well as divine-human covenants. If God enters relationships with creatures through covenant, and if human beings bear God's image, it seems fitting that human beings would relate to each other in a covenantal manner. Perhaps we can understand humanity's social nature and inclination to form mutually beneficial associations as a reflection of the covenantal character of their primal relationship with God. Scripture envisions marriage as a covenant bond (e.g., Mal. 2:14) and describes civil compacts as covenants (e.g., Gen. 21:31–32; 26:28–31). Some Christians today continue to speak of marriage in covenantal terms, and a number of Christian and Jewish political thinkers have described civil associations as forms of covenant.[19] The solemn, enduring, and legal-relational character of covenant makes it an attractive candidate for Christians seeking a paradigm for understanding political constitutions. The fact that formal enactment does not seem necessary for a political

[19] From a Christian perspective, see Johannes Althusius, *Politica* (Frederick S Carney tr, Liberty Fund 1995). From a Jewish perspective, see David Novak, *The Jewish Social Contract: An Essay in Political Theology* (Princeton University Press 2005), esp ch 2. See also the chapters of Nicholas Aroney and John Witte in this volume.

constitution, however, presents a conceptual challenge for those wishing to press this paradigm rigidly.

The Noahic Covenant

I now turn specifically to the Noahic covenant. I focus first on its most obvious point of relevance for constitutionalism, namely, its call to the human community to pursue justice in the face of violence, in light of the image of God (Gen. 9:6). Then I contemplate the universal relevance of the Noahic covenant and unpack some of its implications for constitutionalism.

Moral Foundations and Dispersion of Power

I argued earlier that God's creation of human beings in his image, with a moral commission to rule this world, has important ramifications for constitutionalism. The account of the Noahic covenant raises similar issues, and they reinforce some of my preliminary conclusions about sovereignty and moral truth.

The Noahic covenant's moral commission has both continuity and discontinuity with the creation mandate of Genesis 1:26–28. One obvious point of continuity is the repetition of the decree to be fruitful, multiply, and fill the earth (Gen. 9:1, 7; see 1:28). An obvious point of discontinuity is the absence of a command to rule or subdue other creatures (as in Gen. 1:26, 28). In fact, the Noahic covenant indicates that God himself will do much of the subduing he delegated to humanity at creation (see Gen. 9:2). Yet the idea of human rule is far from absent in the Noahic covenant. Genesis 9:5–6 addresses a dimension of human rule not present in Genesis 1: securing intrahuman justice. God declares that he is the ultimate judge, who will demand a reckoning from every creature that sheds human blood (Gen. 9:5). But he also delegates authority to human beings to administer justice for themselves: "Whoever sheds the blood of man, by man shall his blood be shed, for God made man in his own image" (Gen. 9:6). This shift in focus from Genesis 1 to Genesis 9 makes sense. In a fallen world, which the Noahic covenant addresses, the prospects for successful dominion have dimmed, and thus this covenant lacks the grand commission to rule and subdue other creatures. What takes center stage in a sinful context is something unnecessary in the original creation: redressing violence. But the fact that the Noahic covenant commissions the pursuit of intrahuman justice as a consequence of divine image bearing indicates that this postlapsarian human rule is organically related to the rule God commissioned at creation.[20]

These initial observations about the Noahic covenant confirm some of the important implications for constitutionalism suggested previously. First, Genesis 9:6 adds further reason to challenge claims to political sovereignty and to support jurisdictional checks on power. The text's appeal to the image of God recalls prior biblical teaching that God created all people universally in his image and thus that everyone has a share in the general responsibility to rule. The Noahic covenant reinforces this. For one thing, Genesis 9:6 does not address civil authorities specifically or set apart particular people to carry out justice, but rather addresses the human community broadly. That is, doing justice is a *human* responsibility, not just the responsibility of particular humans. Another aspect of this text exhibits the fundamental equality of all human beings. For Genesis 9:6, *whoever* sheds the blood of *any* other human being deserves to have his or her own blood shed in response. The point of this call to justice, it bears emphasis, is not capital punishment per se but the principle of *proportionality*. As with the *lex talionis* formula familiar in the Torah (Exod. 21:23–25; Lev. 24:18–21; Deut. 19:21), justice does not hinge on physical mutilation but on whether the punishment fits the crime.[21] In Genesis 9:6, the blood of any murderer, whether prince or pauper, is a just price for the blood of any victim, whether prince or pauper. One person's blood is of equal value to any other person's. Again, none of these considerations makes division of labor inappropriate; the community may grant special judicial responsibilities to some of its members. But such authority figures have no intrinsically greater worth than anybody else, and the authority they wield is on behalf of the community as a whole. Especially in light of the pervasiveness of sin, which the Noahic covenant describes (Gen. 8:21), entrusting one person or group of people with unchecked power seems both inappropriate and dangerous.

[20] The appeal to the image of God in Genesis 9:6 is ambiguous. It could explain why murder deserves such a serious penalty (i.e., because the victim was a divine image bearer) or why God grants such a weighty responsibility to humans (i.e., they can avenge murder because they bear the image). Although most readers of Genesis seem to assume the former reading, I believe the latter has a stronger case. In Genesis 1:26, the image of God entailed a commission to rule, and thus it makes sense that Genesis 9:6 would appeal to the image to justify the exercise of judicial authority. See VanDrunen, *Divine Covenants*, 116–117.

[21] See William Ian Miller, *Eye for an Eye* (Cambridge University Press 2006).

Beyond these institutional concerns, second, Genesis 9:6 also raises moral considerations for constitutionalism. This text, long before scripture says anything specific about legitimate civil office, highlights the need for *justice*. As noted earlier, Genesis blames violence for provoking the great flood, and especially violence by kings and military warriors—those who likely cloaked assertions of power in the garb of civil authority (Gen. 6:2, 4, 11–13). The Noahic covenant seems designed to address precisely this problem. It justifies use of violence, but only for the sake of redressing another person's violence. That is to say, the Noahic covenant legitimates coercion of another human being only to the extent it promotes justice. The larger narrative of Genesis 6–9, therefore, confirms our constitutional inclination to restrain the actions of government officials, but with moral concerns about justice in the forefront.

Along similar lines, Genesis 9:6 lends support to the goal of many constitutions to protect basic human rights and not merely to establish institutional checks and balances. The Noahic covenant does not provide much detail as to what human law or political authority ought to look like, but the little it says is presumably foundational. And its focus is avenging *any* human being who has suffered violence. Whatever else a legal and political system can or ought to do, the Noahic covenant indicates that it must aim to protect all people from unjust coercion. From this perspective, it is difficult to imagine how a constitution purporting to be a community's fundamental law could be inattentive to human rights (whether or not it uses that terminology).

Universal Relevance

The Noahic covenant's emphasis on just human rule makes it of interest for constitutionalism. The *universality* of this covenant adds considerably to this interest. In this subsection, I first discuss the evidence for its universality and then reflect on the binding character of the Noahic covenant for political constitutions today.

The universal nature of the Noahic covenant is clear on the face of the text. While some later biblical covenants have universal features, the Noahic covenant is universal in ways that none of the rest are. God entered the covenant with both Noah and his offspring after him (Gen. 9:8), which in context means *all* human beings from that time forward. God also established the covenant with "every living creature" (Gen. 9:10, 12, 15–16), indeed, with "all flesh" (Gen. 9:17). For humans and animals alike, the covenant is "for all future generations" (Gen. 9:12). God covenants not only with living creatures but also with "the earth" (Gen. 9:13). The covenant extends even to the cosmic forces of nature, for God promises that "seedtime and harvest, cold and heat, summer and winter, day and night, shall not cease" (Gen. 8:22). The inevitable conclusion is that this is a universal covenant without qualification. It encompasses the entire world that we know. The text indicates that the covenant is universal with respect to time as well, for its promises stand good "while the earth remains" (Gen. 8:22). From the New Testament standpoint, God put it into effect until Christ's second coming and the day of judgment.

These considerations indicate that the Noahic covenant is not just generally relevant for questions of constitutionalism but actually binding upon all political communities today, and thus that their constitutions ought to reflect its terms. At the headwaters of human history after the cataclysmic flood, God established the Noahic covenant with the entire human race and took special care to stipulate that justice be served in the face of violence. Therefore, when human communities establish courts, governments, and other mechanisms to secure peace and justice, they do so authorized by divine covenant and under obligation to its terms. If accurate, this conclusion has profound consequences. No political community is autonomous. Every government is in relationship to God, whether acknowledged or not. And this relationship to God comes specifically through the *Noahic* covenant, not one of the later biblical covenants. As considered later, God entered the Abrahamic covenant with Abraham's household, the Mosaic covenant with ancient Israel, and the new covenant with the church. While these covenants provide insights into contemporary constitutional issues, no political community today is in relationship to God through one of these covenants. But every political community is in relationship to God through the Noahic covenant.

This claim has powerful explanatory value, as I unpack further later, but it also raises some difficult questions. One of them is how political communities are supposed to know they are in relationship to God through the Noahic covenant, and hence how they should conduct themselves according to its terms. The Old Testament describes the terms of the Noahic covenant, but the Old Testament was *Israel's* covenant book, not that of any other political community. Likewise, the Old and New Testaments are the *church's* covenant book. The people of a great many political communities through history, furthermore, have not even been aware of the Bible's existence, let alone professed faith in its teaching. So how do political communities know about the Noahic covenant and its requirements? The answer, I believe, is that the requirements of this covenant are not cryptic decrees of God's arbitrary will but are instead demands that accord with human nature and the world around. That is to say, the terms of the Noahic covenant are not obscure but familiar. Its call to pursue justice, for example, is rooted in human identity as divine image bearer. To be made in the image of God is to be a creature designed to do justice. The covenant's call to be fruitful, multiply, and fill the earth, likewise, reflects the original creational design that image bearers should reflect God's creativity in their stewardship of the world. Another way to put it is that the moral order communicated by the Noahic covenant is not so much positive law as a summary of the natural law. While Genesis 8:21–9:17 provides helpful clarification and context, human beings do not need to read Genesis in order to understand their basic responsibilities before God under the Noahic covenant.[22]

This conclusion raises all the usual philosophical questions about natural law theory. To keep within the scope of this chapter, I simply add that scripture provides corroborating evidence for my claim. In the early biblical narratives, for example, we read of the judgment of Sodom and Gomorrah (Gen. 19). These cities were not in relationship to God through the Abrahamic covenant (Gen. 15, 17) and God did not judge them according to its terms, yet he held them accountable for their gross abuse of justice. They evidently knew enough of the moral substance of the Noahic covenant to be obligated to obey it. Later in the canon, many Old Testament prophets proclaim oracles against the Gentile nations surrounding Israel. These nations did not stand with Israel at the foot of Mount Sinai (Exod. 19) and were not under the requirements of Torah, but God held them accountable for their hubris and injustice. In one vivid example, Amos begins his prophecy by denouncing six Gentile communities for blatant injustices such as slave trading, treaty breaking, and ripping open pregnant women (Amos 1:3-2:3), but he only accuses *Judah* of rejecting "the [Mosaic] law of the Lord" and not keeping "his statutes" (Amos 2:4). Like Sodom, these Gentiles nations without the scriptures apparently knew enough of their Noahic covenantal requirements that God could justly judge their atrocities. In the New Testament, Romans 13:1–7 says that God has appointed the (pagan) magistrates of Rome to

[22] For a fuller defense of this claim, see VanDrunen, *Divine Covenants*, ch 2.

approve the good and to punish the wrongdoer. Christ did not enter the new covenant with the Roman government, and the New Testament never judges it by that covenant's standards. Nor did most Roman magistrates have any knowledge of Genesis. Yet God expected Roman civil officials to "bear the sword" with justice—the fundamental requirement of the Noahic covenant. In short, throughout the scriptures, God treats political communities as accountable to the Noahic covenant and thus as cognizant of its basic demands.[23] Thus, the constitutional implications of the Noahic covenant identified previously are of universal relevance.

The Question of Liberalism

Many people associate constitutionalism with liberalism. While it is clear that constitutional concerns and arrangements long preceded the emergence of anything we know as liberalism, this conviction is understandable. The main point of constitutions, to many minds, is to protect the rights and liberties considered distinctively liberal, such as freedoms of speech, press, association, and religion. This raises another large issue, but perhaps an unavoidable one. Does the foundational importance of the Noahic covenant indicate that constitutions ought to be liberal, in one way or another? Much depends on how one defines "liberalism," but I believe the answer is a qualified yes.[24]

On the one hand, the Noahic covenant indicates that constitutions should *not* be liberal, if liberalism is understood as a worldview or ideology. For many scholars, liberalism represents a commitment to individual autonomy and neutrality with respect to competing political goods.[25] But if political communities are in relationship to God through the Noahic covenant and are obligated to pursue justice according to its terms, then no community is autonomous and none can claim to be neutral with respect to moral commitments.

On the other hand, a more modest sort of liberalism requires a different assessment. Liberalism can be understood not as a worldview but as a polity.

[23] See further VanDrunen, *Divine Covenants*, chs 3–5.

[24] For a more detailed argument in support of this claim, see David VanDrunen, *Politics after Christendom: Political Theology in a Fractured World* (Zondervan Academic 2020) 357–383.

[25] From a proponent of liberalism, see, e.g., Bruce A Ackerman, *Social Justice in the Liberal State* (Yale University Press 1980) 10–11, 54. From a critic, see, e.g., Patrick J Deneen, *Conserving America? Essays on Present Discontents* (St Augustine's Press 2016) 2–3.

A liberal polity acknowledges that members of political communities will be diverse in the ways they look and the ways they think about important issues. It does not impose uniformity upon them but seeks to secure a peaceful and just order among those who remain different. A liberal polity therefore promotes a broad measure of tolerance among its members and seeks to protect the liberty of people to look, think, act, and worship in different ways, if they do so peacefully. This sort of liberalism does not require its adherents to embrace a myth of autonomy or neutrality, but simply to refrain from using the state to impose racial, theological, and many other kinds of uniformity upon the political community.

This modest liberalism provokes difficult questions of its own, and even a basic idea such as freedom of religion raises a host of theoretical and practical challenges. Nevertheless, I believe the foundational role of the Noahic covenant suggests that constitutions ought to be liberal in this broad, modest sense—although some may understandably prefer another term to "liberalism." For one thing, I suggest that the universal character of the Noahic covenant, considered earlier, supports a modestly liberal constitution. The Noahic covenant commissions the human community as a whole to seek justice and calls for protection of the whole human community from violence. In other words, it reserves neither civil office nor the benefits of civil justice for those of a particular race or creed (to name two frequent sources of political advantage or disadvantage). The Noahic covenant provides no detailed public policy, but it presents a vision for a legal order that is common and pluralistic rather than exclusive and exclusionary. Insofar as liberal polities have sought to recognize constitutional safeguards against state discrimination on the basis of things such as race and creed, they promote this Noahic vision.

Another characteristic of the Noahic covenant bolsters the case for a modestly liberal constitution. The Noahic covenant is not only universal in nature but also *preservative* rather than *redemptive*. In it, God promises never again to destroy the world with a flood, re-establishes the regular cycles of the natural order, puts boundaries between humans and other animals, and authorizes judicial action against violence. But what the covenant does *not* promise is also striking. It does not promise familiar biblical blessings of a coming Messiah, forgiveness of sins, or a new creation. The covenant's blessings are all geared toward preservation of this world, not its redemption, toward the mitigation of evil, not its final destruction. It points to a political community with limited ends, not one aiming to be a holy commonwealth or to realize the eschatological kingdom. Its focus, we might say, is upon penultimate things rather than ultimate.

The relevance for liberalism seems clear. Liberalism, in its classical forms, has resisted attempts to portray government or the broader political community in redemptive or sacred categories. It does not entail rejection of the holy or of a promised redemption, but rather prohibits usurping the state for these purposes. It assigns jurisdiction to the state in penultimate matters only. Insofar as liberal constitutions have sought to realize these goals through broad freedom of religion and corresponding liberties, and through moving away from religious establishments that privilege those who make the right confession, I believe they capture important concerns of the Noahic covenant, even if unwittingly.

As I conclude this discussion of the Noahic covenant, I offer a final observation. Seeing the Noahic covenant as the foundation for political community and as the bond of relationship between such communities and God helps Christians avoid a false dilemma in which constitutions either must do everything or may do nothing. The Noahic covenant, as I have argued, calls for a morally substantive justice to underlie the legal order *and* it holds out a vision of political community with modest ambitions and penultimate aims. Constitutional government can promote very important ends—the relative peace and order of this present age—without seeking what Christians regard as the most important end, Christ's eschatological kingdom. Christians may rightly challenge the pretentious claims of a constitutional order without rejecting it as a *false* peace.[26] It may simply represent a *provisional* peace.

Subsequent Biblical Covenants

In the final section of this chapter I turn to the three major biblical covenants that follow, whose establishments mark decisive turning points in the biblical

[26] I think here of Powell's statement that "the peace of constitutionalism is a false 'peace.'" See *The Moral Tradition*, 264. In larger context, Powell utilizes the work of John Howard Yoder and Stanley Hauerwas to evaluate American constitutionalism from an "anti-Constantinian" perspective. I appreciate many of Powell's concerns and think many aspects of the Constantinian legacy are at odds with my own perspective. But I believe a weakness of a Yoderian-Hauerwasian approach is its failure to defend the legitimacy of political authority insofar as it seeks penultimate ends, even if not the ends of Christ's peaceful kingdom. For a positive account of the contributions of Constantine and Constantinianism to constitutionalism, see the essay by Peter Leithart in this volume.

story: the Abrahamic, Mosaic, and new covenants.[27] My contention is that none of these covenants has the *direct* relevance for constitutionalism that the Noahic covenant has, for the simple reason that contemporary political communities are grounded in the Noahic covenant and not in any of the others. Nevertheless, these covenants are indirectly relevant in various ways, and considering them fills out a Christian approach to constitutionalism from a broader biblical perspective.

The Abrahamic Covenant

The Abrahamic covenant, I believe, has relatively little to contribute to our study of constitutionalism. Through it, God set apart Abraham and his household, promised him numerous offspring, and swore that all nations of the world would be blessed through him (Gen. 15, 17). It makes occasional references with political flavor—kings will come from Abraham's line (Gen. 17:6) and Abraham is to teach his household to do righteousness and justice (Gen. 18:19)—but is largely indifferent to civil law and institutions. Whatever its political ramifications, they relate to a distant future. Though this covenant sets Abraham apart from his surrounding culture in terms of religious devotion, it leaves him to sojourn in neighboring political communities. Among some, he finds justice and is able to enter covenants of peace (e.g., Gen. 20; 21:22–34). Others he evidently distrusts and seeks to keep at a distance (Gen. 14:21–24).

The Mosaic Covenant

Matters change drastically for the offspring of Abraham when God brings them to Mount Sinai after the exodus from Egypt. Here God gave Israel his law by the hand of Moses, supplemented later by additional teaching (Deuteronomy) on the plains of Moab. God established the Abrahamic covenant with an extended household; he established the Mosaic covenant with a great nation. The Abrahamic covenant left Abraham's household to sojourn

[27] Due to space restraints, I do not consider the Davidic covenant separately, although many of its implications for constitutionalism arise in my discussions of the Mosaic and new covenants.

in other people's lands; the Mosaic covenant directed Israel how to live in a promised land of their own.

The Torah was clearly a constitution of sorts. While it is longer and more detailed than we ordinarily expect of constitutions, the Torah was Israel's fundamental law. God prohibited the people from changing it or even adding to it (e.g., Deut. 4:2). Kings were to keep a copy on hand and abide by it (Deut. 17:18–20). Yet it was a *fundamental* law rather than the entirety of it. Despite the Torah's detail on some points, it was far from comprehensive, remaining silent on many important areas of life. Israelites would have to develop additional laws and customs to organize their life together.[28] Yet the Torah set the boundaries. Israel was a constitutional commonwealth, and the Torah was its constitution.

What significance does ancient Israel's constitution have for political communities today? One important point, as indicated previously, is that the Torah *is not* and *cannot be* the constitution of any contemporary political community. This exemplifies the value of interpreting scripture through the framework of the biblical covenants. The Torah is a covenantal document (see especially Exod. 24). It established a constitution for a particular nation, the people of Israel, to define their unique way of life in their land of promise and thereby to accomplish God's special purposes in history. As Paul puts it, God gave the law to Israel as a "guardian until Christ" (Gal. 3:24). No political community today can claim the covenantal promises that accompanied Torah. Nor can any contemporary community claim the status Israel enjoyed. God made Israel a holy commonwealth (Exod. 19:6). This entailed forcibly clearing the promised land of Gentile peoples and executing idolaters, blasphemers, and Sabbath breakers. Needless to say, the Torah was not a liberal constitution, even in the modest and penultimate sense the Noahic covenant encourages. To say that Christians should see the Noahic covenant, not the Mosaic covenant, as foundational for contemporary constitutions is a conclusion with profound implications for some of the most basic constitutional questions.

Yet Christians also believe that "*all* Scripture is . . . profitable for teaching, for reproof, for correction, and for training in righteousness" (2 Tim. 3:16). Other contributors to this volume explore the many positive insights the Torah provides for contemporary constitutionalism,[29] and thus I offer only

[28] For helpful discussion of this point, see Jonathan Burnside, *God, Justice, and Society: Aspects of Law and Legality in the Bible* (Oxford University Press 2011), and Bernard S Jackson, *Wisdom-Laws: A Study of the Mishpatim of Exodus 21:1–22:16* (Oxford University Press 2006).

[29] See especially the chapter by Jonathan Burnside in this volume.

a brief observation: if *even Israel* needed constitutional constraints on power, the political communities who lack their spiritual advantages surely need them all the more. Israel experienced God's mighty works of redemption, received his prophetic revelation, were made his "treasured possession" (Exod. 19:5), and had God's holy presence in their midst through their tabernacle and temple. Yet their king—even of the royal Davidic line—was to be under the law, his heart thereby kept from being "lifted up above his brothers" (Deut. 16:18–20). And the Torah did not simply leave it to the king's good will whether he would observe the constraints of the law. It also dispersed power among several offices, including judge, priest, Levite, and prophet (see Deut. 17:8–18:22)—a system of checks and balances. Torah granted sovereignty to no one.

The New Covenant

The climactic establishment of the new covenant in Christ, and the corresponding New Testament documents, add little directly to our study of constitutionalism. Only a couple of New Testament texts provide explicit instruction about civil government, and they describe it in terms readily predictable from the Noahic covenant, without reference to Christ or his death and resurrection (Rom. 13:1–7; 1 Pet. 2:13–17). Other chapters in this volume explore New Testament themes relevant for constitutionalism,[30] so I offer only a few thoughts, some explaining and some qualifying this initial observation.

By way of explanation: the New Testament has little direct teaching about civil government because it is so focused upon a different polity: the church here and now and the everlasting city/kingdom to come. God established the new covenant in Christ's blood (Luke 22:20), and Christ shed his blood for the church (Eph. 5:25–27). The church, in turn, manifests the eschatological kingdom of God (Matt. 16:18–19) achieved through this covenant (see Luke 22:29–30). The New Testament never associates an ordinary political community with this kingdom. Paul makes use of his Roman citizenship to gain certain temporal advantages (Acts 16:37; 22:25; 25:11), but he emphasizes that Christians' true citizenship is in heaven (Phil. 3:20). Christians "here . . . have no lasting city" but "seek the city that is to come" (Heb. 13:14).

[30] See especially chapter 3 above by D. H. Bertschmann.

The "Jerusalem above" is their mother (Gal. 5:26). The church is a thoroughly *political* entity, but it points to a heavenly *polis* rather than an earthly one.

Yet this leads to an important qualification: although New Testament texts add little directly to our study of constitutionalism, its teaching about Christ, the church, the kingdom, and heavenly citizenship resoundingly confirm why contemporary governments need constitutional constraints. The exalted Christ has all authority on heaven and earth (Matt. 28:18), and thus every claim of political sovereignty is pretentious. Christ has built his church (Matt. 16:18), and thus the state cannot have jurisdiction over the spiritual lives of its citizens. Political authorities are *servants* of God for the good (Rom. 13:4); when they elevate themselves above God, Christians rightly "obey God rather than men" (Acts 5:29). Perhaps we could say that the New Testament's relative indifference to civil government is its own way of communicating that constitutional constraints—both moral and institutional—remain thoroughly fitting in these last days.

Conclusion

Christianity holds that the living God reveals himself, both in nature and by special prophetic word, especially through scripture. A central theme of scripture is covenant, which provides a matrix for biblical interpretation. Through the Noahic covenant, God preserves the present world and commissions human communities to pursue justice for all. And while this preservative covenant continues its work, God has also established the Abrahamic, Mosaic, and new covenants to accomplish his grand redemptive purposes that culminate in the new creation.

I have argued that the Noahic covenant is the most important of these covenants for considering constitutionalism from the Christian perspective. Through this covenant, God has entered into a relationship with all contemporary political communities and thus holds their civil authorities accountable for securing justice. Government officials and institutions may be legitimate, but none of them is truly sovereign. The later biblical covenants confirm this great concern of constitutionalism, especially by pointing believers to a political community that endures, a "heavenly" kingdom that "cannot be shaken" (Heb. 12:22, 28).

17

Trinity

Against Leviathan: The Implications of Trinitarian Theology for Constitutionalism

David McIlroy

> In the name of the Most Holy Trinity, from Whom is all authority and to Whom, as our final end, all actions both of men and States must be referred, We, the people of Éire, Humbly acknowledging all our obligations to our Divine Lord, Jesus Christ, . . . Do hereby adopt, enact and give to ourselves this Constitution.
>
> —Constitution of Ireland, 1 July 1937[1]

Introduction: How Not to Use the Trinity in Political Theology

Both Karl Barth in the first half of the twentieth century and Colin Gunton toward its end insisted on the centrality of the Trinity for Christian understandings of doctrine and ethics.[2] However, enthusiasm for the doctrine of the Trinity can lead to overconfidence about our understanding of the inner life of the Godhead, a lack of attention to the shape of salvation history, and shallow analogies in which the Trinity functions as a justification for ethical preferences chosen on other grounds. We cannot proceed too hastily or overconfidently, for doing so decides the sort of vision of God we want, and then projects that into the Godhead. The trinitarian God is created in our image and then functions as a symbol validating human desires.

[1] I am grateful to Oran Doyle for drawing this to my attention.

[2] Karl Barth, *Church Dogmatics* (GW Bromiley and TF Torrance tr, T&T Clark 1956–1977); CE Gunton, *The Promise of Trinitarian Theology* (T&T Clark 1991).

David McIlroy, *Trinity: Against Leviathan: The Implications of Trinitarian Theology for Constitutionalism* in *Christianity and Constitutionalism*. Edited by: Nicholas Aroney and Ian Leigh, Oxford University Press.
DOI: 10.1093/oso/9780197587256.003.0017

Montesquieu's doctrine of the separation of powers is frequently described as establishing a trinity of legislative, executive, and judicial powers.[3] It might appear tempting to identify those powers with the persons of the Trinity as follows: legislative (God the Father), executive (God the Son), judicial (God the Holy Spirit). Such a temptation has to be resisted because it is obvious that the consequence is to create a procrustean bed. While the Father as the source of the Trinity's action can be readily identified with the legislature in the British constitutional system where Parliament is sovereign, this would not follow in other constitutional arrangements. The Son not only carries out the will of the Father but also has been entrusted with the function of judgment. God the Holy Spirit is closely identified with wisdom in the Eastern tradition, and there is therefore justification in linking the Spirit to the function of interpreting what God requires of us. There is also warrant for this in relation to the Old Testament law.[4] The Spirit's role expressed in John 16:8–11 as convicting the world of its sin, revealing the standards of God's righteousness, and demonstrating Christ's judgment could be regarded as judicial. However, the Spirit mediates and demonstrates not the Spirit's own judgment, but the judgment of Christ. Furthermore, although God the Son in his incarnation and passion executed the key moment of divine action on earth,[5] God acted before and since. The Holy Spirit is not just judicial; the Spirit is also, perhaps even primarily, executive, carrying out God's plan of salvation in, through, and beyond the Church.

Forcing the Trinity to fit our preconceptions about a balanced constitution will not do. We have to proceed more circumspectly. There are no shortcuts to paying careful attention to what the Bible reveals about the actions of the triune God in salvation history. Christian theology affirms two things about the Trinity: on the one hand, all three persons of the Trinity are involved in every action of God in the world (as Augustine put it, *acta trinitatis ad extra indivisa sunt*); on the other hand, it is fitting to regard different persons of the Trinity as central to different actions of God. Thus, God's works can properly be regarded as characteristic of (the theological expression is "appropriated to") the different persons, while always affirming that all the Godhead

[3] Matthew P Bergman, "Montesquieu's Theory of Government and the Framing of the American Constitution" (1990) 18 Pepperdine Law Review 1, 17; Bruce Cutting and Alexander Kouzmin, *Refounding Political Governance: The Metaphysics of Public Administration* (Bentham eBooks 2011) 69–70.

[4] Jonathan Burnside, "Inspired Justice" (2002) 1 Justice Reflections JR-1; David McIlroy, *A Biblical View of Law and Justice* (Paternoster 2004) 143–147.

[5] Tom Smail, *Like Father, Like Son: The Trinity Imaged in Our Humanity* (Paternoster 2005) 70.

is involved in the creation of the world, the incarnation of the Son, and the activities of the Spirit.

The implications of the Trinity for constitutionalism are therefore to be discerned from the acts of the triune God in salvation history: through the work of creation appropriated to the Father, through the redemption wrought by the incarnation of the Son, and through the pattern of the Spirit's witness to the work of the Father and of the Son.

The salvation historical approach employed in this chapter will therefore look at the implications of the work of God the Father for the rule of law, of the work of Jesus on the idea of ruling as service and protecting dignity, and of the work of the Holy Spirit as the agent of freedom and perfection. These reflections establish that rulers are to be held accountable, that power should be dispersed between different organs of government, and that the authority of other communities and institutions should be recognized by those who hold political power.

A Salvation Historical Approach to the Implication of the Trinity for Constitutionalism

The Christian doctrine of the Trinity has to be approached from the perspective of salvation history. Apart from that history, the Trinity could only be a speculation, and probably an unnecessary one at that. The Trinity cannot be understood apart from salvation history, but by the same token it is not possible to arrive at an authentically Christian view of salvation history without constantly understanding it in terms of the actions of the trinitarian God.

A trinitarian theology of law must pay close attention to three narratives. First is the nature of God's disclosure of Godself and of God's acts in scripture. The God of the Old Testament is shown to be the living God, exercising sovereignty over all the nations and acting in covenant faithfulness to God's people.[6] Jesus Christ reveals that living God to be Father and to have acted in person to reconcile the world to Godself. That revelation culminates in the trinitarian events of the crucifixion, resurrection, ascension, and Pentecost in which the God-man offers himself as the acceptable sacrifice of obedience to God, is raised to new life, ascends into the presence of the Father, and releases the Spirit upon his Church, that is to say his body.

[6] McIlroy, *A Biblical View of Law and Justice*, 65–67, 105–112.

The second narrative is the history of God's work among the nations. Wherever the Spirit is at work, the Spirit bears testimony to the kingship of Christ and the Fatherhood of God. The Spirit reveals too the inescapable call and commands of God, which no human being can safely ignore.

The third narrative to be attended to is God's work in reconciling people to Godself, by the Son, through the Spirit. This third narrative is the story of men and women wooed by the Spirit of God, reconciled to the Father through the Son of God, brought into the fellowship of the Church, and transformed by the Spirit of the Father into the likeness of the Son.

Human law must respond to these narratives. As we shall see, it must recognize the created order, address the claims and concerns of Jesus Christ, and accept its limitations in the face of work of the Spirit for which the Church is the proper instrument. A constitutional order for a well-governed but limited State will, as it responds to these narratives, bear indirect witness to the law given in creation and pointing, through its own incompleteness, to the need for transformation that good legislation, policing, and judgment alone are wholly insufficient to achieve.

God the Father and the Rule of Law

Only God Is a Law unto Godself

One of the major assertions of the Hebrew scriptures is that there is only one God and this God is the creator of the universe. YHWH is not a creation of the universe, like the gods of the Egyptians and the Babylonians. YHWH is not a being who can be represented by a created object (Deut. 4:15–20). YHWH is wholly other. God is the ground of being rather than the greatest being in a chain of beings (Acts 17:27–28). God's essence is something very unlike human beings (2 Sam. 7:22). To this claim about the nature of God, the New Testament adds the revelation that the Father, Son, and Holy Spirit, and their interrelationships, constitute the very being of God. It is for this reason that Christians approach God the Father through the Son and by the Spirit.

The triune God is a law unto Godself. God is bound by nothing other than by God's own nature. Because in God there is no difference between act and potential, God cannot be any way other than God is. God has no need of an external standard to guide God's actions because God's nature is God's own rule.

In this life at least, human beings are wholly unlike God in this respect.[7] We are not who we ought to be. We do not do the things we ought to do and we do the things we ought not to do. This difference between God and us is a reason all human power should be subject to checks and balances. As Thio says in her chapter in this volume: "Owing to man's sinful nature, no one should wield unlimited authority and governors should be subject to external restraints."

Speculation about what God *could*, theoretically, do has proved unhelpful in many areas of theology, and especially in political theology, as it led first to the idea of absolute sovereignty and then, in reaction against absolutism to the assertion of autonomy, property and rights conceived in terms of the unencumbered, uncommitted, sovereign individual.[8] Joan Lockwood O'Donovan explores in her chapter in this volume how liberalism polices these individuals through bureaucracy and subjects them to market discipline.

The aseity of God means that God never acts in a way that is incongruent with God's nature. Nonetheless, although God has no need to bind Godself in order to be able to keep to a steady course of action, the Hebrew scriptures reveal God to be a God who enters into covenants, who makes commitments to Adam (Gen. 1:26–29), to Noah (Gen. 9:1–7), to Abraham (Gen. 15:18, 17:1–8), to the Israelites under Moses (Exod. 19:3–6, 24:1–8), and to David (2 Sam. 7:5–16), to act in particular ways. It is God's fidelity rather than God's omnipotence that is to be the lodestar for rulers. As Aroney and VanDrunen explore in their chapters in this volume, the idea of covenant provided a clear and durable category for underscoring international treaties, federations, and the mutual obligations of rulers and their subjects.

The biblical covenants, echoing as they do the forms of a political treaty and the vows made at a marriage, are therefore an appropriate model for a constitution, a means by which rulers should commit themselves to keep faith with the people.[9] Just as God has bound Godself to God's people through the covenant, so human rulers are called to do likewise through a constitution.

[7] In David McIlroy, *A Trinitarian Theology of Law* (Paternoster 2009) ch 5, I argue for an account of theosis in which the indwelling of the Holy Spirit in the *eschaton* renders breaches of divine law and unloving actions unthinkable.

[8] Dale K Van Kley, *The Religious Origins of the French Revolution: From Calvin to the Civil Constitutions 1560–1791* (Yale University Press 1996) 2.

[9] Jürgen Moltmann "Covenant or Leviathan? Political Theology for Modern Times" (1994) 47 Scottish Journal of Theology 19–41.

A constitution acts as a symbolic means of transforming power relationships from relationships of mere domination and subjugation into relationships of reciprocity.[10]

A striking feature of the vision of kingship in the Hebrew scriptures is that rulers are regarded as subject to law. As Burnside's chapter explores, Deuteronomy operates both as a sort of Israelite constitution and as a commentary on the Israelites' experience over slavery under pharaonic rule. Unlike the sacral pharaohs of Egypt or the other rulers of the ancient Near East, who were regarded either as gods or as mouthpieces for the gods, the kings of Israel and Judah were not to consider themselves better than their fellow Israelites (Deut. 17:20). They were always accountable before the people for upholding God's law.

The First Temple refrain *Yhwh malak* ("the LORD is King"), which might be regarded as the leitmotiv of Oliver O'Donovan's political theology, constantly emphasized that YHWH was the people's overlord. The Israelite king's role was to safeguard the relationship between the people and YHWH through protection of the land and enforcement of the law, but he was not free to redefine that relationship. The kings were always answerable to God's law.[11] This is made explicit in Deuteronomy 17:18, which envisages the newly enthroned king writing for himself on a scroll a copy of the Mosaic Law from which he will read all the days of his life.

Natural Law as the Law Binding Authority

The triune God has ordered creation in, for, and to Godself. The created world has been planned by the Father, is ordered to the Son, and is accomplished by the Spirit. In Christian theology, creation is not seen as a static mass but rather as a living organized realm that finds its origin in the will of the Father, its cohesion in Christ, and its direction in the Spirit. In the same way, the triune God wills that, within that creation, human political communities be ordered in ways that establish peace and even harmony.

Creation is ordered not just according to scientific laws but also according to moral laws. While rulers may judge it necessary to permit deviations from those moral laws, they may not oblige their subjects to act contrary to those

[10] Jürgen Moltmann, *The Way of Jesus Christ: Christology in Messianic Dimensions* (SCM 1990) 246

[11] Oliver O'Donovan, *The Desire of the Nations: Rediscovering the Roots of Political Theology* (Cambridge University Press 1996) 62.

moral laws. God alone creates ex nihilo. Human rulers must respond to the created order and their judgments must be informed by the natural law that is inherent within creation.

Christian natural law theory takes the existence of nature as created within time and subject to the realities of geography and history. No serious Christian theologian has ever suggested that a ruler ought simply to impose an ahistorical natural law regardless of the local conditions.[12] On the contrary, as Oliver O'Donovan has reminded us, from the earliest days of Western patristic political thought, "the ruler's authoritative acts interpreted not only divine law (in an admittedly imperfect and incomplete way) but also human law, customary and statute, that embodied the common judgment of the whole community."[13] Rulers ought to operate within the tradition of collective judgment of the communities they govern. This approach means that Justinian, revered in the Middle Ages as the "model for the Christian lawmaker,"[14] was not lauded as an innovator but as a codifier of the moral and legal judgments of classical Roman civilization, as tempered and informed by its adoption of Christianity.

While a trinitarian account of law does not rest content with the natural law as God's last word on the subject of human behavior and human authority, one reason natural law is important is as a reminder that the foundation for stable political rule is the common grace of God that defines what counts as human flourishing and provides the conditions for human life to flourish on earth. Whatever its date, the book of Daniel spells out an understanding of Nebuchadnezzar's power as held from the Lord (Dan. 2:31–35) and subject to a duty to do what is right and to be kind to the oppressed (Dan. 4:27).[15] In the same way, the prophets' oracles against the nations emphasize how all rulers are accountable for breaches of the natural law.[16]

[12] Aquinas, *Summa Theologiae* I-II.96.2; 97.1. Calvin, *Institutes of Christian Religion*, Book 4, ch 20, para 16.

[13] Oliver O'Donovan and Joan Lockwood O'Donovan, *Bonds of Imperfection: Christian Politics, Past and Present* (Eerdmans 2004) 227.

[14] O'Donovan, *Bonds of Imperfection*, 211.

[15] Dewi Hughes, *God of the Poor: A Biblical Vision of God's Present Rule* (OM Publishing 1998) 27–28.

[16] McIlroy, *A Biblical View of Law and Justice*, ch 5.

The Work of Jesus

Jesus and the Protection of Dignity

The shape of the Incarnation is striking. Jesus was born without power or status, became a refugee, lived as a sojourner, and died a criminal's death. He was not afraid to associate with prostitutes and tax collectors (Matt. 9:9–10, 11:19, 21:31–32; Mark 2:14–16; Luke 5:27–30, 7:34; 15:1, 19:1–2) or to meet with Samaritans (Luke 9:51–55, 10:25–33, 17:16; John 4:1–40), Greeks (Mark 7:24–30, John 12:20–36), or Romans (Matt. 8:5–13). The willingness of God's Son to identify himself with these people demonstrates that all human beings are to be treated with dignity.

This is not just a matter of treating people well as individuals but also of recognizing the importance of the social institutions that give people a sense of belonging, fellowship, support, and purpose. While Jesus claimed the ultimate allegiance of his followers (Luke 14:26), Christianity does not eliminate but instead validates communal identities (Acts 6:1–6, 10:1–48; 1 Cor. 1:24), families (Mark 7:10–13; 1 Tim. 5:4), and social institutions (1 Tim. 5:3).

What Jesus demonstrated through his life and death is the value of all human beings, who are to be treated with dignity and respect. Rivers explores in his chapter the importance of dignity to Christian reflection on constitutional and other rights. Constitutional documents can make important statements about the need for dignity and respect and how that dignity and respect are to be given effect within a particular context and history.

Jesus and the Limits of Human Authority

Throughout each of the Gospels, the question of authority underlies Jesus's interactions with the religious and political leaders. The question comes to a head in Jesus's exchanges with Pilate. The events leading up to the crucifixion demonstrate, with a bittersweet irony, that whether they like it or not, political authorities are only mandated by Christ, who gives them their justification to fulfill the tasks that he has ordained (John 18:28–39).[17] Jesus's

[17] Oliver O'Donovan, *The Desire of the Nations*, 140–141.

encounters with Herod and Pilate desacralize political rule. The claims to divinity made within the Roman Empire are unmasked as overreaching.[18]

Jesus's life, death, and resurrection relativized the importance of the political rulers of the Roman Empire. The cross stands over human legal orders and emphasizes that they cannot, and are not called to, reconcile us to God. The resurrection announces that Jesus Christ is king, and therefore all human rulers are answerable to him.[19] It points, through the ascension, to the Last Judgment and the *eschaton*. The Second Coming announces the reality of a final judgment and so renders all human rule provisional. Rulers rule for over a limited territory, for a limited time, and with limited objects in view (relative peace and relative justice). In this way too, their rule is framed and bounded.

Christians were martyred because their proclamation of Jesus as Lord and their refusal to offer sacrifices to the divine emperors were a direct defiance of the inflated claims the Roman emperors made for their jurisdiction. Because Jesus Christ is Lord, Caesar is not. Rulers are answerable to God; they are not to act as mortal gods. The king or emperor is not the vicar of Christ, is not clothed with the authority of the ascended Christ, and is not answerable to God alone rather than to their people. The public and prior nature of the natural law, of the divine law revealed in scripture, and of the Church provide the basis for tyranny to be opposed and for rulers to be held to account in this age. Constitutionalism addresses the perennial temptation of tyranny by reminding rulers that they are subject to a prior framework of law.

Jesus combines universal kingship, ultimate power, and perfect identification with an expression of his people's longings. He will be the final judge, but the time for his judgment has not yet come. Therefore, as Oliver O'Donovan has argued, government is to be minimally representative and minimally coercive, because the ultimate locus for human representation and human judgment is to be found elsewhere: in Christ. The second person of the Trinity is the only human being to whom we owe total obedience. A constitution reflects this truth by specifying that political rulers are dependent on prior and continuing authorization for the power they wield.[20]

Karl Barth understood the first implication of the kingship of Jesus for politics. He knew that it meant the dethroning of all human pretensions to

[18] Jürgen Moltmann, *The Church in the Power of the Spirit: A Contribution to Messianic Ecclesiology* (2nd edn, SCM 1992) 178.

[19] McIlroy, *A Biblical View of Law and Justice*, ch 6 and 180–182.

[20] Oliver O'Donovan, *The Ways of Judgment* (Eerdmans 2005) 165–166, 184.

absolute power or absolute authority. If Jesus is king, then no one else is. This led Barth to frame the Barmen Declaration[21] as a rallying point for Christian opposition to Adolf Hitler.

Christian theologians offer differing assessments about whether government is a necessary evil or to be regarded more positively than that. From the warnings given in Deuteronomy 17:14–20 onward, there has been a concern not only about the evil rulers can restrain but also about the evil rulers can perpetrate. Because of original sin, evil and violence must be restrained. However, also because of original sin, political authorities mandated to restrain evil lay claims to omnipotence and to divine honors. As Oliver O'Donovan puts it, "the best Christian political thought . . . emphasises the need to set up restraints in both directions, against evil and against the evil implicit in the restraint of evil," by seeking to constrain the use of force "to the service of the common good."[22] Thus, Stephen Langton, archbishop of Canterbury, drafted the Magna Carta, which placed the authority of the king of England (King John) under the rule of law, requiring the king to uphold justice and preventing English citizens from being imprisoned, outlawed, or dispossessed without trial.[23]

The Holy Spirit and Freedom

The shape of the work of the Holy Spirit provides further reasons for constitutional limits on the power of government. The Holy Spirit is the Spirit of freedom (Isa. 61:1; 2 Cor. 3:17). The Spirit is the agent through whom human beings freely turn to God the Father and the agent who transforms human beings into the likeness of God the Son. Belief in the Spirit gives Christianity a distinctive account of worship: worship is not mere performance of a ritual; it is a sacrifice that must be freely offered. By contrast, government's power is limited because governments cannot perform the change of heart required for true conversion, true worship, or true sanctification.

[21] <http://www.ucc.org/beliefs_barmen-declaration>

[22] Oliver O'Donovan, *Peace and Certainty: A Theological Essay on Deterrence* (Clarendon 1989) 26–27.

[23] These provisions, clauses 39 and 40 in the 1215 charter, clause 29 in the 1297 statute, remain in force in English law to the present day.

Freedom of Religion as a Limit to the Power of Government

Whatever sense is to be made of the book of Revelation, the vision of history that is given in that book is one in which the primary role of the Church is that of faithful witness to Jesus Christ, who is "the firstborn from the dead, and the ruler of the kings of the earth" (Rev. 1:4).[24] Jesus's kingdom is "not of this world" (John 18:36), which is to say that it does not advance through military power and physical coercion. In Zechariah's vision, the Lord declares that the *missio Dei* will be accomplished "not by might, nor by power, but by my Spirit, says the Lord of hosts" (Zech. 4:6).

A trinitarian theology of law therefore sees the Church as the means through which the Spirit makes God's appeal to humanity to be reconciled to God, and understands that appeal to be made without violence.

Human governments not only do not have authority to require faith in a non-Christian religion or a heresy but also do not have jurisdiction to command people to belong to the Church or to have faith in Christ (if the two can be divided). Human beings are called by God to worship God, not commanded by political authority to do so. Force of arms is not a fitting means of bringing about faith. It was because Lactantius and Tertullian[25] had confidence in the work of the Spirit that they argued against attempts to secure faith through political coercion.[26] As John Locke would note many centuries later, secular government ought not to compel religious observance because to do so is for rulers to presume to arrogate to themselves a work that is reserved to the Holy Spirit.[27] Where a secular account of freedom of religion appeals solely to free will, a Christian account sees free will as responding to a prior movement of the Holy Spirit that is beyond the control of any government.[28]

Therefore, the corollary of the doctrine of the Spirit is that governments lack competence to require religious conformity from their citizens. This is

[24] Richard Bauckham, *The Theology of the Book of Revelation* (CUP 1993) 110.

[25] Lactantius, *The Divine Institutes*, Book V, chs XIX to XXI, in *Institutes* in AC Coxe (ed), *The Ante-Nicene Fathers*, vol VII: *Fathers of the Third and Fourth Centuries* (Christian Lit Publ Co 1887). Lactantius's argument for freedom of conscience is discussed further in Leithart's chapter in this volume.

[26] Luke Bretherton, *Hospitality as Holiness* (Routledge 2010) 123–126; McIlroy, *A Trinitarian Theology of Law*, ch 5.

[27] Locke appeals in *An Essay Concerning Toleration* to the fact that men are to be brought to God not by any human compulsion but by "the inward constraints of [God's] own spirit on their minds":*Political Writings* (Penguin Classics 1993) 189.

[28] Bretherton, *Hospitality as Holiness*, 123–126.

an important symbolic marker that there are limits to the powers of government and that religious institutions have their own integrity and authority. These limits may be appropriately reflected in constitutional documents guaranteeing freedom of religion.

Perfection as beyond the Competence of the State

The category of law plays a different role in Christianity from Islam and Judaism. The religious law of the Pentateuch has, at least since the days of Ezra the priest, been the dominant category for understanding the individual's relationship to G-d in many forms of Judaism. The Shari'a has been central to many approaches to Islam from the time of Mohammed.[29] By contrast, Christianity regards it as impossible for fallen human beings to please God by obedience to law alone.

In the Christian reading of the Hebrew scriptures, the failure of ancient Israel to live up to the standards set out in the Mosaic Law is a demonstration that laws, however good, are not capable of perfecting the lives of their subjects.[30] The history of the kingdoms of Israel-Judah is that despite having God-given laws and despite having the priesthood and the prophets, neither the kings nor the people were capable of keeping God's laws and of living just and holy lives. In the end, the depressing conclusion of the first half of the book of Jeremiah is that "The heart is deceitful above all things and beyond cure" (Jer. 17:9).

As Paul presents the argument in Romans chapters 7 and 8, the problem is not that the Mosaic Law was misguided in its intentions; it was that it could not overcome the evil within human nature. As N. T. Wright puts it: "the 'problem of Romans 7' . . . is emphatically *not* that of 'man under the law' . . . but of 'the law under man.' "[31] The lessons Christianity draws from the history of the Old Testament is that a society cannot be perfected through law alone. A trinitarian theology of law therefore rejects a perfectionist

[29] Patricia Crone, *God's Rule: Government and Islam* (Columbia University Press 2004) 8–9 claims that "Living in accordance with God's law was the essence of religion. . . . [T]he law . . . remained the heart of Islam in all its forms.' See also Joseph Schacht, *An Introduction to Islamic Law* (OUP 1964) 1; Rex Ahdar and Nicholas Aroney, "The Topography of Shari'a in the Western Political Landscape" in Ahdar and Aroney (eds), *Shari'a in the West* (OUP 2010) 2–6

[30] McIlroy, *A Biblical View of Law and Justice*, ch 7.

[31] NT Wright, *The Climax of the Covenant: Christ and the Law in Pauline Theology* (T&. Clark 1991) 209.

account of law in which human rulers are competent to ensure the virtue of the communities they govern.[32]

Without a change of heart, people's behavior and attitudes will not *really* change. Both Jeremiah (Jer. 31:33–34) and his contemporary, Ezekiel (Ezek. 36:26), were given visions of a new covenant, in which God would cleanse God's people and give them a new heart and a new spirit. Under this new covenant, God promised to "*put my Spirit in you and move you to follow my decrees and to be careful to keep my laws*" (Ezek. 36:27, 11:19–20).

If the Old Testament is read as demonstrating the fallenness and inadequacies of human legal systems, even if their laws *are* God given, then the prophecies about the Holy Spirit in Jeremiah and Ezekiel promise a change of heart through the giving of the Spirit, which will make justice, righteousness, holiness, and social virtue possible.

The appropriation of sanctification to the Holy Spirit limits the jurisdiction of human rulers. Christian political thought recognizes only one, all-wise, all-powerful, sovereign King Jesus.[33] Whereas Plato could suggest that the philosopher-kings ought to work toward perfecting the *polis* and all within it, Christian theology insists that human rulers do not have the power or the authority to perfect their subjects.

This rebuttal of perfectionism goes beyond questions of religion. As Karl Barth saw so clearly, the Christian Church must reject any form of rule that seeks to dominate and dictate the lives of its subjects. A ruler or government that erects itself as the ultimate arbiter of right and wrong or as ultimate claim on the loyalty of its subjects is Antichrist.[34]

Because the Spirit is the agent of sanctification and law is an instrument that is not capable of producing just people, the task of law is necessarily more limited, seeking to maintain a measure of peace, justice, and freedom so that true virtue may flourish alongside other less worthy patterns of life. The role of the ruler is to enable their people to pursue their proper ends, rather than subordinating them to a single, grand project of society. Because the Spirit's work of sanctification will not be complete until the *eschaton*, as Farrow argues in his chapter in this volume, human law is tasked with restraining lawlessness but without pretending to achieve perfection. When that perfection is realized, human beings will experience incorporation into the life

[32] John Finnis, *Aquinas: Moral, Political, and Legal Theory* (OUP 1999) 222–252.

[33] Oliver O'Donovan, *On the Thirty Nine Articles: A Conversation with Tudor Christianity* (Paternoster 1986) 98.

[34] Oliver O'Donovan, *The Desire of the Nations*, 274.

of the triune God, sharing, through God the Son and by the indwelling of the fullness of God the Holy Spirit, a fully realized relationship with God the Father.

Thus, the doctrine of the Holy Spirit provides a Christian defense not just of freedom of religion against the totalitarian state but also of a pluralist vision of society where an overambitious government does not impose strict conformity to an all-encompassing social vision. In this pluralist vision, "*Such peace as can be kept and such justice as is defended in keeping it define and limit each other.*"[35]

The Trinity and the Constitution

On the basis of these insights, we can make some more general comments about constitutionalism. Within the trinitarian account of salvation history, human rule is given by the providence of God for the avoidance of the complete collapse of human society. Human politics therefore harks back to the original good order of creation and looks forward to the shalom of the eternal city. Both are out of its reach. It therefore stands like a signpost pointing at them.

It is the trinitarian logic of Christian political thought that underlay theological arguments for political liberalism and pluralism[36] and gives the "Christian constitutionalism"[37] of Oliver O'Donovan its richness. The key purpose of a constitution is to make rulers serve their subjects.

Rulers Are to Be Held Accountable

Human law is made under and administered and accountable to the divine law, both natural and revealed. That law reveals the basic orientations for human flourishing and the dignity of each human being. Rulers are responsible for preserving the peace so that human beings may flourish and for

[35] Oliver O'Donovan, *Peace and Certainty,* 116, emphasis mine.

[36] Oliver O'Donovan, *On the Thirty Nine Articles*, 76, 99.

[37] Jonathan Chaplin, "Political Eschatology and Responsible Government: Oliver O'Donovan's 'Christian Liberalism'" in Bartholomew et al (eds) *A Royal Priesthood?* (Paternoster 2002) 265–230, 269, 283 n 74.

restraining injustices that violate human dignity and cause other intolerable wrongs.

Attention to the doctrine of the Trinity and to salvation history means that there is no place within Christian theology for Hobbes's Leviathan or Hegel's vision of the state as "the march of God on Earth." The state, whether understood as government or as nation, is not a mortal god, to be obeyed uncritically and sacrificed to. Though the references to the Trinity and to "our Divine Lord, Jesus Christ" seem to be doing little work in the 1937 Irish Constitution, they are affirming that the Irish state is subject to a higher authority.

A constitution ought to be a written record that no individual or organ of government should have unfettered power. Oliver O'Donovan defines judgment as "an act of moral discrimination that pronounces upon a preceding act or existing state of affairs to establish a new public context."[38] A constitution is a judgment about the nature of the unity of a people and the basic contours within which they will be governed. A constitution should reflect a widespread agreement within a political community about how it understands the law to which its rulers are answerable.[39] Constitutions make rule legitimate by subjecting political representation to law.[40] Constitutions set a framework "of common practices in which the exercise of political authority has a regular position."[41] Constitutions regularize political rule, both by authorizing it and by stating the limits of its authority.

Power Should Be Dispersed between Different Organs of Government

Although the Trinity does not dictate the precise shape of human government, there are some conceptions of rule that it excludes. Moltmann is right that the doctrine of the Trinity problematizes the equation: "one God – one Logos – one Nomos – one emperor – one church – one empire."[42]

Political absolutism is like a perennial weed. It is attractive to those who have reached the summit of political power, it is seductive to those who

[38] Oliver O'Donovan, *The Ways of Judgment*, 7.
[39] Oliver O'Donovan, *Bonds of Imperfection*, 294.
[40] Oliver O'Donovan, *The Ways of Judgment*, 165.
[41] Ibid, 135.
[42] Jürgen Moltmann, *The Crucified God* (2nd edn, SCM 1974, 2001) 339.

face circumstances in which security appears to be the paramount imperative, and it appears inevitable where there is insufficient commitment to the common good of the polity to sustain other more consultative and representative forms of government.

The overblown claims and counterclaims to universal jurisdiction made by Holy Roman emperors and medieval popes are greater proof of the power of that temptation than they are evidence of the ineffectiveness of the doctrine of the Trinity to shape a Christian understanding of constitutional government.[43] Joan Lockwood O'Donovan and Oliver O'Donovan have done this generation of theologians a great service in showing just how committed medieval and early modern Christian theologians were to defending "the right of political society to protect itself against the lawlessness of rulers (against their insupportable violations of divine, natural, and positive laws)."[44]

The incarnation of the Son and the giving of the Spirit reveal a differentiation of function within the Godhead. The different roles of the persons of the Trinity do not compromise the unity of the Godhead. The Trinity is not a dilution of the unity of monotheism but rather a redefinition of what "oneness" means, making possible conceptions of unity in plurality, mutual respect, and service that are richer and more fruitful than solitary absolutism.[45] If a differentiation of function exists within the Godhead, how much more does human rule need to be shared and dispersed,[46] albeit within a unitary structure so as to remain coherent? Christians have both positive and negative reasons to support this. Positively, the triune nature of Godself, the original goodness of the ordering of creation in all its diversity, and the destiny of human beings to be incorporated within the life of the triune God are all reasons to affirm that rule can be shared by different persons and between different organs of government without inevitable or inexorable conflict. Negatively, because human beings are both fallible and finite, and therefore it is impossible for human beings to control and to foresee everything, human rule has to be divided up. A constitution provides a framework for this division.

[43] It is beyond the scope of this chapter to consider how absolute Caesaro-papism was in the Byzantine Empire, or the extent to which the subjugation of the Russian Orthodox Church under Peter the Great was a result of the Byzantine legacy or of Peter the Great's admiration of the absolutist rulers in the West.

[44] Oliver O'Donovan, *Bonds of Imperfection*, 165.

[45] John Milbank, "The Archbishop of Canterbury: The Man and the Theology Behind the Shari'a Lecture" in Ahdar and Aroney (eds), *Shari'a in the West*, 56.

[46] John Milbank, "The Gift of Ruling: Secularization and Political Authority" (2004) 85 New Blackfriars 212–238, 224–225.

The Authority of Other Communities and Institutions Should Be Recognized

A trinitarian approach to constitutional law insists that there are limits on political authority. Robert Markus overstated his case that the existence of a secular society was the internal logic of Augustine's thought.[47] Nonetheless, Oliver O'Donovan has convincingly demonstrated that intrinsic to Christian thought down the years is the idea of (1) a government with its own integrity from religious institutions and (2) that government having only limited powers or competence or sphere of authority.

The limits on political authority are twofold. First, there is a limit on political power. No one within the *polis* is given absolute power. Second, there is a limit on the *polis*. The *polis* is not understood to be the only society, the all-sufficient society, or the most important society. Instead, the Church stands over against the *polis* as an independent institution affirming that citizenship of heaven is ultimately more important than citizenship of the United Kingdom or the United States.

The Church, as an institution, witnesses Jesus's authority as the king of kings. As Leithart's chapter demonstrates, the Church is a visible symbol that government is not the sole or the ultimate authority in all matters. For example, the natural law gives parents authority over their children. Abraham Kuyper argued that the common grace of the Holy Spirit endows social institutions with their own authority in pursuit of distinct goods. In Kuyper's conception of *Souvereiniteit in eigen kring* (sphere sovereignty),[48] each type of social institution pursuing a specific good enjoys the right to regulate itself. The right to regulate itself arises both because there are distinct goods to be pursued and because there are different reasonable conceptions of the means by which such goods should be pursued. So, for example, education is a distinct good that all schools pursue, but there are different reasonable conceptions of whether education should be delivered in a Catholic school, a Protestant school, a Muslim school, a liberal school, a private school, a state school, a single-sex school, a coeducational school, etc. Therefore, beyond the separation of powers within the sphere of government and the protection of Church and State against one another, a trinitarian approach

[47] Robert Markus, *Saeculum: History and Society in the Theology of St. Augustine* (CUP 1970).

[48] Kuyper, *Anti-Revolutionnaire Staatkunde*, I, 265ff.

to constitutionalism would recognize the proper scope of authorities and institutions other than government.[49]

Precisely by being a witness to the kingship of Jesus, the Church calls the attention of rulers to other communities and institutions that must be given their proper place if the polity is to be ruled justly. Linguistic communities, Indigenous peoples, and traditional ways of life need to be respected and valued in a just constitutional settlement.

The Purpose and Limits of Government Should Be Stated

The purpose of government is judgment, that discernment of the institutional forms and rules that must be put in place to do the justice that must be done. A constitution must declare that the polity is committed to justice; to claim otherwise would be nonsense.[50]

Political power is not the agent of salvation or sanctification; it is not the deliverer from all evil, but only its most insupportable manifestations. The purpose of government is to work toward the welfare of all but not to minister to salvation. The evil of which government itself is capable must be guarded against. Thus, a trinitarian understanding of human rule is that the authority of rulers is responsive to the prior law revealed in nature, in Christ, and in the traditions of the community that is to be governed. The authority of rulers is therefore provisional and limited in terms of the ends it may properly pursue. Constitutional arrangements should subordinate the ability of rulers to use violence and the capacity of rulers to represent the polity to the task of judging justly.

As we have seen, the acts of the Trinity in salvation history support the idea of a constitution as a document that recognizes the claims of individuals and groups arising out of nature and out of the geography, history, and traditions of the polity in question. A constitution should therefore shape rule within a polity so that, in however distorted and imperfect a fashion, wrongs are addressed and genuine human goods are preserved and promoted for the benefit of all within that polity. Such a framework for constitutional

[49] Nicholas Wolterstorff, *The Mighty and the Almighty: An Essay in Political Authority* (CUP 2012) ch 14.

[50] Robert Alexy, *The Argument from Injustice: A Reply to Legal Positivism* (OUP 2002) 36.

government provides a *saeculum*, a time, for people to choose to pursue the heavenly good of the knowledge and love of God.[51]

A trinitarian perspective on constitutionalism realizes that a constitution can express and constitute a collective political identity but it cannot sustain that identity in isolation. The 1936 Soviet Constitution is a stark and chilling reminder that no matter how exemplary a constitution may appear on paper, it will not protect human dignity and promote human flourishing if there is no commitment on the part of rulers to honor it.

The Constitution Should Be Respected but Not Worshipped

A trinitarian approach to constitutionalism reminds us that all human rule is provisional. A trinitarian account of constitutionalism is not an exercise in seeking to uncover a self-sustaining basis upon which the millennial social order is to be constructed. There are very few polities that have stable identities stretching back over hundreds of years and even fewer whose constitutions have not been revised at regular intervals. It is, however, worth reminding those of us who live on the peculiar island of Britain (and have not paid sufficient attention to the last century of history on the island of Ireland) that a constitution may properly be amended or replaced when it no longer represents a just settlement that reflects the collective judgments of the community that are subject to it. As Oliver O'Donovan reminds us: "political structures are historically fluid, not, as some other structures are, given in nature."[52] The *need* for political authority is a constant in this fallen world; its *form* is not. Constitutions have an important role in stabilizing and regularizing political rule for a time but they are not, any more than any other symbol of the nation, to become a totem. To refuse to amend or replace a constitution that is no longer regarded as a defensible attempt at a just settlement is to attempt to hold back the ocean. When a constitution becomes a vehicle for the deification of the state or an object of worship in its own right, there is idolatry.

A trinitarian approach to law affirms the importance of constitutions but does not prescribe a particular form. A political order is a provision of God's

[51] David McIlroy, "Idols and Grace: Re-envisioning Political Liberalism as Political Limitism" (2010) 11 Political Theology 205–225.

[52] Oliver O'Donovan, *The Desire of the Nations*, 14.

common grace, ultimately dependent for its stability on the movement of the Spirit of God. No constitutional arrangement can therefore be, in principle, beyond the scope of reform or revision if it no longer serves the purposes of justice. What a constitution ought to be is a means of specifying and crystallizing a community's understanding of liberties and of the balance of interests that must not be revised without serious deliberation. There is, in the end, only one king whose rule is eternal.

Conclusion

Christian theology understands governments as ruling within a given context. That context includes the divine act of creation, appropriated to God the Father; the divine act of redemption, appropriated to God the Son; and the divine act of sanctification, appropriated to God the Holy Spirit. Each of those three acts in salvation history sets limits on the freedom of action of rulers.

A biblically faithful doctrine of the Trinity leads to the conclusions that political and lawmaking authority should be used to preserve the good gifts given by God the Father in creation; should be concerned to promote dignity, justice, and mercy to all which are key concerns of God; and should leave space for the work of his Holy Spirit to transform people's lives in the light of the good news of the death and resurrection of God the Son.

Constitutions are an important means by which rulers are to be held to account, power is to be appropriately dispersed among different organs of government, the authority of other communities and institutions within the polity is to be recognized, and the purpose and limits of government are to be laid out. A trinitarian account of constitutions stresses their practical necessity in a fallen world without pretending that a particular constitution is a permanent or perfect form.

18

Justice

Constitutional Design and the Purpose of the Political Community[1]

Jonathan Chaplin

> The true nature of a constitution and of constitutionalism, its *differentia specifica* by which it contrasts with all non-constitutional regimes, is discovered by asking: What is the political function of a constitution?
>
> —Carl J. Friedrich[2]

In this chapter I argue that the nature of a political constitution can only adequately be specified with reference to an account of the characteristic "political function," or purpose, of the political community.[3] Drawing on sources from twentieth- and twenty-first-century Reformed Protestant thought,[4] I propose that the purpose of the political community be construed in terms of a capacious and complex account of "justice," and that from such an account broad principles of normative constitutional design emerge. The chapter sketches a preliminary outline of such an approach.

[1] I am grateful to the editors for very helpful comments on an earlier draft. The usual disclaimer applies.

[2] Carl J Friedrich, *Transcendent Justice: The Religious Dimension of Constitutionalism* (Duke University Press 1964) 16.

[3] By "the political community" I mean any territorial political order, at any level, not only "the state."

[4] On earlier periods, see the chapters by Witte and Lockwood O'Donovan.

Jonathan Chaplin, *Justice: Constitutional Design and the Purpose of the Political Community* in *Christianity and Constitutionalism*. Edited by: Nicholas Aroney and Ian Leigh, Oxford University Press. © Oxford University Press 2022.
DOI: 10.1093/oso/9780197587256.003.0018

Mapping "Complex Justice"

I propose that well-formed law advances a specific normative purpose, namely to realize "justice" in human social relationships. Such relationships can be as diverse as a contract of sale and purchase, the minimum penalty for homicide, the process required to claim a welfare entitlement, or the terms of an international peace treaty. The assumption that law serves a normative purpose such as justice is, of course, controversial in legal philosophy but has been well defended elsewhere in this volume.[5] Law may be thought to pursue other purposes as well, such as the promotion of order or certainty in social relationships.[6] Yet these important objectives could be achieved by means of highly discriminatory or oppressive laws (such as China's former "one child" law). Nor is it enough to suggest that law exists merely to realize a generic ethical goal such as "fairness," although that will sometimes be the operative legal norm in particular cases (such as contracts or due process). In most cases, an appeal to mere fairness will lack the specificity sufficient to indicate what justice requires, such as in determining, say, the nature of parental rights over, and duties to, children or the content of children's rights. To determine these, much of the Christian tradition has thought it necessary to spell out something like a moral ontology of the family, which law does not create but to which it defers even as it regulates aspects of the family. The same applies to most other areas of social relationship, including the economy. Goals such as order, certainty, or fairness cannot capture the distinctive societal telos of law but should be seen as subordinate implications (or by-products—justice itself creates "order") of a wider norm of justice governing the realm of law as a whole.[7]

As a starting point, the classical (Ulpinian) definition of justice will suffice, namely justice as "rendition"—"rendering to each their due." Of course, everything then depends on what specific content we put into the term "due." On that the Christian tradition has had distinctive proposals to make, going beyond and sometimes departing radically from pagan Greco-Roman

[5] E.g., the chapters by Witte, McIlroy, Thio, and Milbank. For an extended defense of this claim see David McIlroy, *The End of Law: How Law's Claims Relate to Law's Aims* (Edward Elgar 2019).

[6] The Thomistic proposal that a key purpose of law is promoting "virtue" is given an insightful contemporary rendition in Cathleen Kaveny, *Law's Virtues: Fostering Autonomy and Solidarity in American Society* (Georgetown University Press 2012).

[7] This is one specification of Robert Alexy's claim that law contains a claim to "moral correctness." See David McIlroy, "When Is a Regime Not a Legal System? Alexy on Moral Correctness and Social Efficacy" (2013) 26 Ratio Juris 65–84.

notions, and variously converging with or contending against the dominant conceptions of what is due to various agents that have emerged from secularizing Enlightenment sources.

To map some features of the complex territory of justice as they pertain to law, I note three important differentiations within the broader concept of justice, each recognized in various strands of Christian thought.[8] To adapt Michael Walzer's language, justice is not "simple"—sourced by a single generative principle, whether harmony, liberty, rights, equality, or some other—but "complex," embracing numerous interacting and diverse principles, interests, and goals, each also attending to and given shape by changing historical circumstance.[9] It is true that Thomas defines justice (*justitia*) as "right" (*ius*).[10] But that is not posited as a simple principle in this sense, for he then proceeds to elaborate the substantive content of right by attending to the particularity of (inter alia) variously differentiated created goods or relations. The weight of the Christian political and legal tradition witnesses powerfully to the complexity, as well as to the ultimate (if never fully graspable) unity, of justice, even if it has sometimes egregiously misconstrued its contents.[11]

The first distinction refers to what I shall term the *modes* in which justice manifests itself in law. Here Protestant theologian Paul Tillich's notion of "tributive justice," what might be termed "tribution" (or "rendition"), is helpful.

> Tributive or proportional justice . . . appears as distributive, attributive, retributive [corrective] justice, giving everything proportionally to what it deserves, positively or negatively. It [measures] the power of being of all things in terms of what shall be given to them or what shall be withheld from them. I have called this form of justice tributive because it decides about the tribute a thing or person ought to receive according to his special powers of being. . . . Attributive justice attributes to beings what they are

[8] I shall not employ the familiar Aristotelian-Thomist distinction between "general" and "particular" justice. What I treat later as "constitutional justice" and "public justice" touch upon both. See Jean Porter, *Justice as a Virtue: A Thomistic Perspective* (Eerdmans 2016).

[9] Michael Walzer, *Spheres of Justice: A Defence of Pluralism and Equality* (Blackwell 1983), which presents an account of "complex equality." My terms also parallel Milbank's distinction between "complex" and "simple" space. See "On Complex Space," in John Milbank, *The Word Made Strange: Theology, Language and Culture* (Blackwell 1997) 268–292.

[10] *ST*, 2a2ae.57.1.

[11] For example, by construing the family in patriarchal ways, or radically unequal market outcomes as determined by providence.

> and can claim to be. Distributive justice gives to any being the proportion of goods which is due to him; retributive justice does the same, but in negative terms, in terms of deprivation of goods or active punishment. . . . In the realm of law and law-enforcement the tributive form of justice is the norm.[12]

I offer five comments on this proposal. First, we can construe what Tillich calls "special powers of being" as referring to the identity and purpose of a thing as given in created orderings (to which I return shortly). Second, on Tillich's reading, attributive justice is the most fundamental, since it is essentially a recognition of, and deference to, such orderings. Attributive justice in this sense is a necessary presupposition of other modes of justice—indeed, on my argument, of all manifestations. Third, to the modes Tillich lists, one might add "contributive" justice, referring to what different beings ought to give to others—from which various specific duties and obligations might arise. Fourth, while Tillich does not include "commutative" justice in this list, it could be construed as a special kind of distribution (the rightful distribution of entitlements and obligations in exchange relationships between two equals). Fifth, we can add "restorative" justice as a distinct mode, witnessing to a redemptive moment in the doing of justice (on which more below).

The second differentiation refers to the *type of legal relation* in view, governed by justice. A threefold distinction utilized by Dutch Neo-Calvinist legal philosopher Herman Dooyeweerd is helpful here. He identifies a universal realm of law (the "juridical aspect" of created reality) governed by "intrinsic normative legal principles,"[13] displaying three irreducible categories of legal phenomena: rights, duties, and competences (a list that is not exhaustive).[14] All are types of legal relation because they are intrinsically social phenomena. This point is especially important with regard to individual

[12] Paul Tillich, *Love, Power, and Justice: Ontological Analyses and Ethical Applications* (Oxford University Press 1954) 63–66.

[13] This would be Dooyeweerd's preferred language to what Thio in her chapter terms a "higher law" above human law. See Jonathan Chaplin, *Herman Dooyeweerd: Christian Philosopher of State and Civil Society* (University of Notre Dame Press 2011) 187–193. His "principles" would be much "thicker" than are implied in Lon Fuller's "inner morality of law" (*The Morality of Law* [rev edn, Yale University Press 1964]).

[14] See Chaplin, *Herman Dooyeweerd*, 194–195; John Witte, "The Development of Herman Dooyeweerd's Concept of Rights" in Jonathan Chaplin and Paul Marshall (eds), *Political Theory and Christian Vision: Essays in Memory of Bernard Zylstra* (University Press of America 1994) 27–55. Compare Wesley Hohfeld's famous typology of "jural relations": "right," "liberty," "power," "immunity," set out in David Campbell and Philip Thomas, (eds.), *Fundamental Legal Conceptions as Applied in Judicial Reasoning* (Routledge 2016).

rights, misconstrued in much modern liberal political theory as the primordial source of justice. Such rights are inherently relational.[15] It is not only that the hypothetical, wholly solitary individual would never have occasion to claim his or her rights but also that the very concept of a right is unimaginable apart from a pre-existing realm of sociality—what Anglican theologian Oliver O'Donovan terms the sphere of "social communication."[16] Attempts to reduce all legal relations to rights (plural) founder on the uneven landscape of legal reality itself, in which it proves impossible to derive all duties from rights (a parent's duty to care for a child is misconceived if it is seen as a mere derivation from a child's right to care) or rights from duties (the rights of citizens are not mere derivations of the duty of states to do justice), or to redescribe all competences as rights (American states' rights are better construed as states' competences).[17] Whether or not we agree with Protestant philosopher Nicholas Wolterstorff that justice, construed as a *moral* principle, can be adequately specified in the language of "rights," it seems clear that, construed as a *legal* principle, it cannot. I discuss Wolterstorff's conception later.

The third type of differentiation gets us closest to the empirical reality of human social life and refers to the concrete *content* or subject matter of justice—the type of human relationship involved—such as the examples I cited earlier: the justice of contracts, of punishments, of welfare entitlements, of peace treaties, and so forth. Among human relationships we may also include a multiplicity of social forms such as friendships, partnerships, associations, institutions, communities, networks (such as markets), and so forth. All give rise to complex issues of justice.

The four examples just cited are also, incidentally, instances of commutative, corrective, distributive, and restorative justice, respectively. In fact, many types of human relationship—a contract, a marriage, an educational relationship, a trade union, a constitutional procedure—could be the occasion of any of the modes of justice and any of the three types of legal reality.[18]

The foregoing suggests the need for an account of justice capacious enough to afford a place for all the complex instances of differentiated justice noted

[15] A point noted by Nicholas Wolterstorff in his *Justice: Rights and Wrongs* (Princeton University Press 2008) 4.

[16] Oliver O'Donovan, *The Ways of Judgment* (Eerdmans 2005) ch 14.

[17] Some such phenomena could be classed as "immunities."

[18] The standard branches of modern law—contract, tort, property, commercial, family, public, administrative, constitutional, international, etc.—do not correspond exactly to these various types of human relationship.

previously (there are obviously more), yet specific enough to avoid collapsing into an all-embracing generic goal such as "whatever is conducive to a flourishing human social life," or, as the Christian tradition has typically named that comprehensive aspiration, "the common good." The common good has always been seen as embracing more than the mere satisfaction of justice (I say more about this later). The account, then, must respect the irreducibility of justice as a unique imperative within the moral order. Justice, I am proposing, is that dimension of such order embracing the many mandates of "tribution."

In Christian moral theology, of course, justice is only one of many such imperatives (and the moral order contains much more than imperatives). For example, justice is typically distinguished from love but is not in essential tension with it. On this relation, Wolterstorff invokes both Moses and Jesus to propose an understanding of the relation "such that the imperative to act justly is not in conflict with the law of love, not a restriction thereon, not even a supplement, but such that doing justice is an *example* of love."[19]

What, then, is this moral order of which justice is one irreducible dimension? I understand it as the entire fabric of moral meaning given in the comprehensive orders of creation, providence, and redemption.[20] Creation is a divine ordering of reality in which multiple kinds of normative differentiations manifest themselves. As Reformed theologian Emil Brunner puts it, justice is grounded in an "underived, primal order of things established by no human law-giver" and "stands above all human apportioning and must be the standard for all human apportioning if is to be 'just.'"[21] Justice is rooted in the "order of creation" and creation is "primal allocation."[22]

> What corresponds to the Creator's ordinance is just—to that ordinance which bestows on every creature, with its being, the law of its being and its relationship to other creatures. The "primal order" to which everyone refers in using the words "just" or "unjust," the due which is rendered to each man, is the order of creation, which is the will of the Creator made manifest. . . . The rights of man are rights which, so to speak, God gives men at their birth. The rights of communities are rights which go back to a

[19] Nicholas Wolterstorff, *Justice in Love* (Eerdmans 2011) 84.

[20] McIlroy's "trinitarian" reading of justice and law and Burnside's reading in terms of the Torah offer complementary theological framings.

[21] Emil Brunner, *Justice and the Social Order* (Lutterworth 1945) 24.

[22] Ibid, 49.

> definite relationship between men based on the order of creation—for instance, that of man and woman in marriage. In the last resort all justice means these constants of creation as a basis on which every human being receives his due.[23]

This rather starkly primordialist formulation needs to be enriched and complicated, first, by a providentialist recognition of the historical unfolding of created order, which Dooyeweerd captures in the pregnant phrase the "process of disclosure" (*ontsluitingsproces*). This alludes to the dynamic and highly variegated development of particular human relationships and social forms (and their distinctive modes of justice and types of legal relation) over time. The developmental dynamic is inherent to created order and is not a mere artifice of subjective human will; creation was always pregnant with myriad evolving potentialities. Such a notion helps preempt any countenancing of the static, unjust "natural orders" defended by German nationalist theologians in the 1930s and 1940s, against which Reformed theologians Karl Barth and Dietrich Bonhoeffer so compellingly protested.[24]

Second, Brunner's formulation needs to be further rounded out by an eschatological account of how redemption impacts upon creational justice. Redemption is not a repristination of original creation order but rather a restorative transformation of that primal order *as it has unfolded in time*—"in this age" (the *saeculum*)—a process including a consummative gathering up of all that has been good in that unfolding. We need not construe redemption as introducing ontologically unprecedented dimensions of justice but rather as variously illumining, purifying, deepening, and liberating justice (in all its modes) and law (in all its types) in a way fitting for the new creation that is the destiny of history. In that age to come (the *eschaton*) human relationships—and the noncoercive law that, I submit, will still be needed to order and guide them—will fully reflect just attributions.[25]

[23] Ibid, 83–84. Brunner asserts, problematically, that justice, in the sense of "mine and thine," is "incidental to the gospel" (ibid, 18) and stands in a "dialectical" relationship to love (ibid, 23; cf. ch 15).

[24] Dietrich Bonhoeffer, *Ethics* (Dietrich Bonhoeffer Works, vol 6, Fortress Press 2009) 388ff.

[25] On the wider significance of eschatology for law, see Farrow's chapter.

Specifying Constitutional Justice

So much for law in general as oriented to (complex) justice. What about constitutional law? If law exists to advance justice, constitutional law exists to realize constitutional justice, namely the establishing of relations of justice among the various members (citizens), other residents (permanent or temporary), and component parts (offices, organs, institutions[26]) of a political community. Constitutional law is the constituting and ordering law of the polity itself, specifying, inter alia, the extensive array of legal rights enjoyed by, the duties falling upon, and the competences wielded by those various agents and parts of the polity.[27] These include matters such as specifying the voting age (an individual right), protecting the powers of associations (institutional competences), identifying the obligations of public officeholders (a public duty), and determining the scope of judicial review (a public competence). One could also detail here instances, within the polity, of distributive justice (who holds what offices), contributive justice (taxation, jury and military service), and retributive justice (judicial corrections of breaches of constitutional law). Constitutional justice, then, embraces a great deal more than a code of human rights, the promotion of which is but one of several constitutional goods that a just constitution needs to balance.[28] Justice, I propose, is the overarching constitutional good.

Determining the content of constitutional justice presupposes just attributions that pertain specifically to the distinctive nature of and internal relations within the polity. What Dooyeweerd terms the "sphere of justice" of the polity—the entire ensemble of tributions characteristic of the political community—is unique to that type of community, even though there are obviously analogies with those of others. Thus, for instance, the rights and duties of citizens (members of the polity) cannot be equated with those pertaining to membership in a trade union. For example, grounds for expulsion from the former are rightly much more tightly drawn than those for the latter because the polity is a comprehensive, inclusive protective association, whereas a trade union has a much narrower protective remit. Thus, it is impermissible for a state to render one of its own citizens stateless.

[26] Or constituent parts of a federation, although some might construe these as "members."

[27] Aspects of international law (such as judgments of the European Court of Human Rights) recognized within domestic jurisdictions should also be included.

[28] I agree with Rivers that constitutional rights are better seen as "an immanent legal value" than as a "transcendent political ideal."

This seemingly technical point draws our attention to the wider importance of maintaining a clear distinction between the legal sphere of the polity itself—the law codifying its *internal* sphere of justice (i.e., what I am calling "constitutional justice")—and *external* relations of justice between the polity and that which is outside it, such as persons in nonpolitical roles and many nonstate associations. To refer to this "external justice" I will use a term of art coined by Dooyeweerd, "public justice."[29] The polity as a whole is responsible for securing public justice across a whole society, and it does so through a wide range of legal and policy instruments and in all areas of public policy (economic, health, education, transport, etc.). Public justice will also reflect the various *modes of justice*: retributive justice will be expressed via the processes of criminal and civil law, or tort; distributive and contributive justice via, for example, legislation guiding fiscal and social policy; commutative justice via contract and commercial law; and so forth. It will also encounter every *type of legal relation* and find itself addressing many *types of human relationship*.

As the polity promotes public justice, it must adhere to all the norms of justice proper to its own internal order—that is, it must act according to those procedural and substantive norms that secure constitutional justice.[30] The rule of law is the most fundamental of these, the heart of which is that the state itself must always act according to law and may be held accountable by judicial bodies for breaches of it. A justly ordered society requires a justly ordered constitution: public justice presupposes constitutional justice.[31]

If constitutional law (and theory) is focused primarily on constitutional justice, political theory is focused primarily on public justice. Political theorists typically have in mind the justice of public, societal relations as a whole, and they come up with widely varying conceptions of (and names for) what I am calling public justice. Sometimes they have some account of distributive or social justice in view (distribution according to needs, desert, entitlement, merit, equality, etc.), although they should not and often do not confine themselves to this. For the same reasons as lawyers, they should avoid lapsing into reliance on any simple notion of public justice. Socialists who define public justice reductively as equality quickly (or belatedly) discover

[29] See Chaplin, *Herman Dooyeweerd*, chs 9, 10.

[30] F. A. Hayek understood this point well. The "constitution of liberty"—what he saw as the central purpose of the state—had major implications for constitutional design. See *The Constitution of Liberty* (Routledge Kegan Paul 1960).

[31] I do not address here the complex question of whether a manifestly unjust law (even an "unjust constitution") might yet be "valid."

that this term, vital as it is in certain areas, does far too little work to specify what the purpose of the state is and how it might, via a suite of laws and policies, address problems of social and economic deprivation or the excessive concentrations of economic power sustaining them. It is hard to squeeze an anti-monopoly law merely out of the notion of equality. Liberals meet a similar problem. Egalitarian liberal John Rawls's problematic attempt to found a polity on "justice as fairness" illustrates the limitations of a simple notion of public justice.

The task for political theorists, then, is to elaborate a capacious enough account of complex public justice that captures the larger purpose of the political community as a whole. I now outline such an account.

Elaborating Public Justice

A Protestant account typically proceeds from scripture. Paul's account of "the authorities" in Romans 13 has long been a locus classicus (albeit a contested one) for this tradition. Wolterstorff's restatement of a Pauline view in *The Mighty and the Almighty* serves as a useful platform for the articulation of my own position.[32] Wolterstorff proposes that the purpose of political authority is to protect the rights of citizens—in other words, as he argues elsewhere, to do them justice.[33] Political authorities possess what he terms "performance-authority," a right or permission one has to perform some action,[34] which must be distinguished from their "positional authority," the authority to issue directives that fall within the jurisdiction attaching to an institutional position.[35] One form of performance authority is the "authority to govern," governance being a necessary requirement of cooperative action toward some end. To have authority to govern someone is to have "the *potestas* [the rightful power] to issue directives to him that bind him—directives that generate in him the obligation to act as directed."[36] The state's authority to govern is unique in two senses: it is public governance (i.e., it extends across the

[32] Nicholas Wolterstorff, *The Mighty and the Almighty: An Essay in Political Theology* (Cambridge University Press 2012).
[33] Wolterstorff, *Justice: Rights and Wrongs*.
[34] Wolterstorff, *The Mighty and the Almighty*, 48.
[35] Ibid, 79.
[36] Ibid, 78.

entire public), and it is ultimate, in the sense that there is no higher authority to which appeal can be made against its rulings (on which more later).[37]

Reading Romans 13 in the light of these concepts, Wolterstorff proposes that, for Paul, "the God-assigned task of government is to exercise governance over the public for the purpose of *curbing wrongdoing*," or "protecting the rights of the public."[38] We are morally obligated to submit to government because it has been appointed by God to protect rights/curb injustice. "Paul is . . . saying that whoever finds himself in [a position of governmental authority], however that came about, has a commission from God, an assignment, to serve God by exercising governance over the public for the purpose of executing anger on wrongdoers."[39] This includes deterring wrongdoing and protecting the public from its effects.[40] This divinely authorized purpose of the office of government then specifies the limits of its authority. According to Paul, "Not only does God's authorization not extend to authorizing the state itself to become a wrongdoer; God does not *permit* the government to issue directives . . . that constitute wrongdoing."[41] A further implication is that the task of a rights-limited state is not to "pressure citizens into becoming virtuous and pious," but only to "pressure [them] into not perpetrating injustice."[42] This implies a protectionist rather than a perfectionist view of political authority.[43]

Wolterstorff elaborates this conception via a Pauline account of the separation between the authorities of state and church, one that has proved influential in the "Dissenting" wing of Protestantism as distinct to its "Establishment" wing.[44] The traditional "two rules" doctrine prevalent in Christendom erroneously construed church and polity as coterminous and thus often justified the use of state law either to enforce true religion or to disadvantage those who dissented from it. Wolterstorff outlines what he takes (as I do) to be a more reliable New Testament view in which the church is a transnational, socially inclusive global fellowship, no longer tied to any

[37] Arguably this may not be true of federations. See Aroney's chapter.
[38] Wolterstorff, *The Mighty and the Almighty*, 90.
[39] Ibid, 95.
[40] Ibid, 89–90.
[41] Ibid, 92. This does not yet resolve whether citizens are permitted to resist the directives of an unjust ruler. Wolterstorff notes that early modern Calvinists looked to a specific class of public officials ("lower magistrates") to act in the case of tyranny (ibid, 75).
[42] Ibid, 98–99.
[43] Wolterstorff's reading of Romans 13 is compatible with Bertschmann's more modest one, while going beyond it.
[44] On the "Tudor" variant of the latter, see Lockwood O'Donovan's chapter.

territorial political order as was ancient Israel, and answerable to the transcendent authority of Jesus Christ, an authority that will be denied or ignored by most. As a result of the consequent division of loyalties created by the presence of the church, it "cannot express the shared religious identity of [a whole] people, since there is no such identity," for "[w]henever the church enters a society, it destroys whatever religio-ethical unity that society may have possessed. Now there is only religious pluralism."[45] From such an ecclesiology follows a commitment to the defense of the associational rights and competences of the church, and equally that of other religious bodies, and, by implication, of many other types of association, vis-à-vis the state, and to the protection of individual religious freedom for all.[46] Together these amount to a weighty mandate for the state and impose substantial external limits on its authority. Wolterstorff asserts, rather ambitiously, that this Pauline conception of the rights-limited state is substantially embodied in our modern liberal democracies. We can retain the more modest conclusion that it at least provides a plausible theological preference today for a state embodying what I am calling constitutional justice and public justice.

Wolterstorff's account requires correction on one point and elaboration on two others. The correction is this. If my earlier account of justice is plausible, his assumption that the content of justice can be fully specified in terms of rights turns out to be too confining. Even the capacious definition of rights he defends (in *Justice: Rights and Wrongs*) is not complex enough to embrace many of the pluriform features of the constitutionally limited state he rightly favors. For example, it lacks an account of the multiple competences that need to be specified in a constitution, such as the highly differentiated powers of many diverse public bodies or the duties incumbent on many citizens (e.g., paying taxes). These cannot be derived entirely from a set of either individual or associational rights.

The first point inviting elaboration concerns the very purpose of the state. Wolterstorff's view reduces the fundamental duty of the state to the protection of citizens' rights. Yet he himself poses the question whether state authority could after all extend beyond mere rights protection—could it, for example, include "promoting the common good"? His response is that there is nothing in his protectionist view that would *prevent* the state from going beyond what justice requires and performing other acts pursuant to the common good,[47]

[45] Wolterstorff, *The Mighty and the Almighty*, 123.
[46] Ibid, 124–125.
[47] Ibid, 114.

but that if it did so it would require a different account of obligation.[48] I do not see why it does. What it requires is a more capacious conception of public justice as *embracing* certain elements of what is often termed the common good. A tacit assumption in Wolterstorff's account suggests a way forward, however. Departing at this point from many Protestant thinkers, Wolterstorff seems to reject the "providentialist" patristic view that political authority is essentially remedial, instituted by God as a merciful, but necessarily coercive, response to the disorder occasioned by sin.[49] Instead, he appears to favor (as I do) a version of the "naturalist" conception, associated with Thomism, according to which political authority arises out of the inherent inclinations of created social human nature; as he puts it, public governance is a necessary requirement of cooperative action toward some end. I suggest, then, that we can construe the mandate of public justice as one instance (there are others) of this need for a coordination of many particular acts toward a common end, a need arising even in the absence of sin. Of the various modes of public justice I noted earlier, only retributive and restorative justice are occasioned by sin. The fundamental mode, attributive or primal justice (as Tillich and Brunner term it), and its applications in distributive, commutative, and contributive justice arise out of the created imperatives of human social nature.

Now Wolterstorff himself employs a parallel concept of primary (prelapsarian) justice,[50] but because he interprets it through the narrowing lens of rights, he cannot find conceptual space for those elements of the common good that are matters of justice but are more than rights. One example might be a state-provided immunization program: this is more than the state's satisfaction of the collected "rights to health" of multiple individuals. Another might be the justice of a transportation infrastructure, which, while it does indeed respond to the rights of geographically isolated human settlements to adequate means of communication and exchange with other, more favorably located ones, goes well beyond what an aggregation of such rights could demand.[51] I propose these examples be understood as common (or public) goods that fall within the state's remit for promoting public justice.

[48] Nicholas Wolterstorff, "Accounting for the Political Authority of the State" in Nicholas Wolterstorff, *Understanding Liberal Democracy: Essays in Political Philosophy* (Oxford University Press 2012) 245–274.

[49] Wolterstorff, *The Mighty and the Almighty*, 59–60.

[50] Wolterstorff, *Justice: Rights and Wrongs*.

[51] What counts as "adequacy" is partly affected by what is physically and economically possible, which are prudential matters (though these need not be construed in terms of a "utilitarian" calculus).

"The public" itself has a just claim to them. They are elements of what is often termed the common good, but they stand out as also being both matters of justice (not all elements of the common good are, e.g., the quality of a people's cultural artifacts) and public in scope (not all elements of the common good are public, e.g., the virtue-generating capacities of particular families).

The second matter on which Wolterstorff's account of political authority invites elaboration is the question of democracy. He presents his account of political authority in *The Mighty and the Almighty* as one "from above," while adding that it is compatible with an account "from below," one he develops elsewhere[52] and which is constructed out of everyone's natural right to an institutional arrangement that protects us from wrongdoing.[53] In this account, authority to govern flows upward from those possessing such a natural right rather than downward from God's authorizing of governors to protect those rights.[54]

Accounts from above and below are indeed compatible, but they also need to be *theoretically integrated*, and they can be if we locate both in relation to a larger conception of the purpose of the polity. Justifications of an account from below have been framed in various ways in Reformed thought. Perhaps the most historically influential has been the appeal to the politically empowering consequences of the doctrine of the priesthood of all believers and its corollary, the equality of all human vocations (on which, see Witte's chapter). As Dahl observes, it was concluded from the experience of Puritan congregations that "all men were equal not only in the eyes of God but equally qualified to understand the word of God, to participate in church government, and by extension to govern the commonwealth."[55] This, buttressed by other arguments,[56] yields what can be termed a "divine right of citizenship," deriving from God's directly conferring upon citizens a vocation to act as responsible discerners of and active participants in the concrete struggle for public justice. Thus, both political institutions and citizens share

[52] Wolterstorff, "Accounting."

[53] This is a "natural duty of justice" theory of political obligation. For a more extensive one also indebted to Reformed thought, see Philip Shadd, *Understanding Legitimacy: Political Theory and Neo-Calvinist Social Thought* (Lexington Press 2017).

[54] The proposal for an "account from below" is not new in the Christian tradition. Aroney's chapter alludes to the role of such a collective right of "the people" in the emergence of federalism.

[55] Robert Dahl, *Democracy and Its Critics* (Yale University Press 1989) 32. See also Robert D Woodberry and Timothy S Shah. "Christianity and Democracy: The Pioneering Protestants" (2004) 15 Journal of Democracy 47–61.

[56] E.g., Reinhold Niebuhr, *The Children of Light and the Children of Darkness: A Vindication of Democracy and a Critique of Its Traditional Defenders* (University of Chicago Press 1944).

a common vocation to pursue public justice, and it is from their complementary contributions to such a vocation that their various constitutional duties, rights, and competences arise.

From the foregoing, three broad implications follow that serve as a bridge to a treatment of contemporary constitutional matters in the fourth section. First, the polity is but one type of human relationship with its own distinctive sphere of justice. Uniquely, the polity is the institution charged with overseeing justice, through law, across the entire public space of a territorially delimited community. Many institutions may be said to have a public remit: media outlets; trade unions; and, in Christian theology, the church.[57] In fulfilling that public remit, they contribute in distinctive ways to the common good. But only the political community is empowered to impose legally binding justice across a whole territory. That is *its* distinctive contribution to the common good. It is what a just constitution must enable.

Second, the political community's duty of promoting public justice includes the protection of the justice interests of any and every agent operating in public space within a territory, irrespective of any other memberships, identities, or affiliations they may enjoy. "Public" in this sense means territorial inclusivity and is closely associated with the principle of political equality among citizens, which grounds an extensive suite of personal rights and freedoms (including both civil and political rights and, I would argue, certain socioeconomic and cultural rights).[58] The public space of which the state is the custodian also includes many types of human association, each with their various rights, duties, and competences. The political community is neither ontologically nor morally prior to those other types of association, and it is legally prior only within its own sphere of justice. In keeping with the neo-Calvinist principle of sphere sovereignty,[59] it is bound to respect these plural sources of original social authority. The mandate of political authority is restricted to those aspects of personal, associational, and societal life in which issues of justice arise, and which have a public significance. Justice issues lacking a public dimension are, prima facie, left to interpersonal resolution

[57] It is properly deemed public in three senses: "the gospel is public truth"; the church is bound to "speak truth to power" (as Lockwood O'Donovan's and Farrow's chapters suggest); and (as Leithart's chapter shows) the very arrival of the church itself opened up new "public space" by reining in the imperial pretensions of the Roman state.

[58] I leave aside the question of how many such rights are suitable for inclusion in a constitution. See Rivers's chapter.

[59] See Chaplin, *Herman Dooyeweerd*, 139–147. The principle is akin to the Catholic principle of "subsidiarity" (see Hittinger's chapter).

or addressed internally by the relevant associations (ecclesiastical or university courts, etc.). Pursuant to the latter, a just polity must therefore promote a robust civil society of independent, self-governing associations.

Third, where those two criteria are met—justice and publicness—the political community may engage in a wide range of lawful actions to address (negatively) the relevant public injustice or to promote (positively) necessary conditions conducive to just relationships. Earlier I cited the provision of public transport infrastructure or health programs as examples. Another would be the pursuit of a family policy supporting public conditions conducive to stable family life (marriage laws, entitlements to parental leave, child benefits, etc.). It also includes securing the fundamental public rights of children, if necessary against their parents, since families—indeed, any human association—are not islands of immunity from public justice. Public justice involves a dynamic process of just adjudication among all the legitimate claims and interests thrown up by persons, associations, and wider societal networks (such as markets or media). It can take numerous forms and require numerous kinds of action and must be realized through law that is procedurally and substantively just and legitimated via democratic process.[60]

Tracing Contemporary Constitutional Implications

If the previous account of public justice is plausible, the following conclusions suggest themselves regarding the normative design of a "public justice–friendly" constitution. They are not straightforward inferences from the foregoing, nor are they remotely comprehensive, but are offered as illustrative examples of principles and practices that, in the contemporary world, seem likely to enhance a polity's capacity to discharge its core duty.

First, and fundamentally, constitutions exist not only to order a political community but also to facilitate the realization of its overriding normative purpose of pursuing public justice in wider society.[61] This raises the question whether it is advisable for a constitution to commit itself explicitly to such a goal. Many constitutions do in fact contain "substantive purpose" clauses

[60] Although note that legal and democratic processes aren't in themselves sufficient to guarantee that the political community respects the limits of its proper authority. In a fallen world there are no such guarantees.

[61] I leave open the question of whether a constitution is better suited to promote public justice if it is codified ("written").

indicating the larger goals to be pursued by the political community.[62] As Rivers notes, the 1919 Weimar Constitution and the 1937 Irish Constitution contained specific provisions naming marriage and family life as worthy of state support and imposing on the state a duty to secure certain social and economic rights. Weimar's statement that "the ordering of economic life must comply with the principles of justice with the goal of securing a dignified existence for all" is, I think, a good example of a purpose clause congenial to my account.

Such explicit substantive purpose clauses are not, however, essential to a state's actual pursuit of public justice. What matters is that the substantive contents and political effects of the constitution are, all things considered, in fact conducive to its pursuit. Whether purpose clauses help in this regard depends on a range of considerations. They can, for example, help delegitimate political standpoints that a political community has concluded are fundamentally aberrant, such as racist, ethnic nationalist, extreme libertarian, theocratic, or totalitarian socialist conceptions. They can also include provisions deemed essential to a state's self-definition. These can be weak or strong. At the weaker end, the Basic Law of Germany names Germany as a "democratic and social federal state" (Art 20.1), without detailed elaboration. At the stronger end, the Indian Constitution in 1976 declared India a "socialist" state committed to social and economic justice and including very specific Directive Principles of State Policy to that end. The Bhutan Constitution stipulates, pursuant to its Buddhist vision of ecological justice, that 60 percent of the country's land mass must remain forested (Art 5.3) and imposes a "fundamental duty" on every citizen "to contribute to the protection of the natural environment" (Art 5.1).[63] Western constitutional theorists may dismiss these latter two as examples of an "illiberal" Asian mindset, but on my account of public justice there is no reason in principle why purpose clauses like these should be excluded.

I note, however, the danger that the more broadly such purposes are drawn, the more aspirational, the less enforceable, the more ideologically manipulable, and eventually the less credible they become. Indeed, because the meaning of public justice is properly subject to continual democratic contestation, a constitution should not fix too many specific substantive

[62] These are much broader than "substantive due process" clauses.

[63] See also the preamble to the Philippines Constitution. I am grateful to Li-ann Thio for these examples.

objectives but must leave most to ordinary processes of legislation and policy. Otherwise every democratic disagreement, whether over financial regulation, marriage law, or welfare reform, risks escalating into a constitutional contest. A suitably just constitutional framework can permit the election of governments pursuing highly divergent conceptions of public justice. Yet a constitutional framework will inevitably be more conducive to certain such conceptions and obstructive of others. Arguably, then, the German Federal Constitutional Court's 1954 ruling that the Basic Law was neutral with regard to economic systems, and thus could not explicitly favor a social market economy, was too restrictive.[64]

Second, the constitution of a political community must help create institutions actually capable of exercising public justice: they must be organizationally coherent (able to engage in "joined-up policymaking"), administratively capable (able to implement policy), coercively resourced (able to enforce the law), behaviorally transparent (so as to curb corruption and limit the undue influence of special interests), and so forth. While it takes much more than constitutional provisions to realize such ends (a minimum level of economic resources, a culture of trust and integrity, etc.), it takes no less.

Third, a just constitution should seek to limit and disperse sovereignty. As Harrison shows in his chapter, the notion of sovereignty—which in medieval Christian jurisprudence typically meant only the highest power within a plural order of mutually limiting jurisdictions—has been profoundly misconstrued in modern political and legal thought under the influence of monistic conceptions of the state and legal positivism. Neo-Calvinist theologian and statesman Abraham Kuyper thus repudiated the notions of both state sovereignty and popular sovereignty in favor of sphere sovereignty, implying a wide distribution of social and legal authority among the state and numerous independent nonstate associations.[65] Perhaps the one defensible sense of legal sovereignty refers to the fact that the polity has to provide some prospect of legal closure in case of seemingly intractable disputes, so that decisions on them are not endlessly mired in a labyrinth of constitutional processes.[66] There may often be a single institutional custodian of such

[64] Carl-Christoph Schweitzer et al (eds), *Politics and Government in the Federal Republic of Germany: Basic Documents* (Berg 1984) 263.

[65] Abraham Kuyper, *Lectures on Calvinism* (Eerdmans 1934) ch III.

[66] Yet most polities in fact contain unresolved jurisdictional ambiguities, a fact that can help prevent undue concentrations of power and sustain long-term stability. I'm grateful to Nicholas Aroney for this observation.

sovereignty, perhaps a highest constitutional court[67] (but it would be equally unhelpful to speak of judicial sovereignty or the sovereignty of the constitution). That the UK Constitution is premised on the problematic doctrine of parliamentary sovereignty is a blemish, not a virtue.[68] To privilege one organ of state—or even the people—as the repository of the sovereignty of the whole political community is to render both constitutional and public justice fragile.

Fourth, political authorities must be capable of being held to account for their pursuit of public justice. For it to be effective, accountability implies the possibility not only of a theological or moral assessment of the actions of political authorities by members of that political community (churches or other agents in civil society, as they "speak truth to power") but also of legal enforcement of sanctions against such authorities when they violate justice, and of a corrective remedy. The enforcement capacity must itself be part of the constitution.[69]

In addition to legal accountability capacities, a constitution must also provide political accountability capacities. Two sources of such a capacity are well established in the strongest modern constitutional democracies: the accountability of the executive to representative legislatures (a modern "lower magistrate") (my fifth point)[70] and the accountability of both legislatures and executives to citizens (my sixth point).

Fifth, then, there must be robust arrangements for the accountability of executives to representative legislatures. In parliamentary systems these include the very legitimation of the executive (in the United Kingdom, in a "confidence" vote) since the latter is created by the former, whereas in presidential systems executive legitimation occurs through direct election. Whatever the model, the goal should be to hold executives effectively accountable to the demands of both public and constitutional justice. That demanding aspiration could require many things, but two can serve as examples. One is specialist committees with sufficient power to interrogate and expose unjust executive acts and mandate a change in government

[67] In his chapter, Harrison wonders whether even this is essential.

[68] The specific historical origins of the doctrine are well understood. Today the UK Parliament faces the different problem of its subordination to "executive dictatorship."

[69] For example, it must be possible to force a review of unjust legislation, dismiss a demonstrably unjust executive, void an unjust election, etc., without recourse to extralegal methods.

[70] This and an independent judiciary are elements in the doctrine of the "separation of powers" (on which see Endicott's chapter). On the issue of the vertical distribution of governmental powers in federalism or strong local government, see the chapters by Aroney and Milbank.

policy.[71] Another is forms of bicameralism in which upper chambers serve as an independent source of executive scrutiny and a national platform for societal voices that lower chambers may not adequately allow, such as occupational, professional, local/regional, or convictional ones, or voices that are politically disempowered, economically poor, or culturally marginalized.

Sixth, the accountability of legislatures and executives to citizens covers a broad terrain (and is partly already realized through representative assemblies). It raises the wider democratic question of the role of the people (i.e., the citizenry) within a political community. Developing the idea of a "divine right of citizens," I propose this role be understood as the vocation (albeit not a legal duty) to engage in the continuous and demanding task of forming considered convictions about public justice and deliberating and acting on them, together with fellow citizens. The term "popular sovereignty" is a distraction from the task of clarifying this vocation. Nevertheless, such a vocation does imply, first, the periodic popular election of leaders. The right to vote, held by all suitably eligible persons, is an indispensable right of citizens, even if only one component of the complex justice of a well-formed political community. It also implies, second, the continuing availability of effective channels of political influence and the political rights required to enable their use (of speech, expression, conscience, association, protest, civil disobedience, office holding). What is required, then, is both a representative democracy and a participatory one in which citizens are alert to their responsibilities for discerning and promoting public justice and free, motivated, and resourced to discharge them. Constitutions cannot themselves generate such a participatory outcome, but they can facilitate it by supplying the necessary legal conditions for its emergence.

Evidently, the outputs of the citizens' democratic activities today rarely lead to any unanimous voice but are incorrigibly pluralistic and, at best, often fragmented or contradictory. As a highly diverse body of citizens advances its competing convictions about public justice via multiple channels of democratic influence, this is hardly surprising. So it is not helpful to construe democratic processes as "channelling the popular will" since such a will is only (if ever) clearly identifiable on very rare occasions (the United Kingdom's

[71] This might suggest a model somewhere between US congressional committees, which can be both overmighty and vulnerable to extracongressional special interests, and UK parliamentary select committees, which are too weak.

2016 EU referendum was certainly not one of them). Here we need to allude to the distinctive responsibility of political parties in orchestrating citizens' convictions into coherent programs based on shared convictions about public justice, mobilizing wide popular support behind them, and then steering a policy program if the party enters government. Wide membership, vigorous political education, and representative internal democratic procedures are necessary to these ends.

Seventh, one specific constitutional procedure turns out to comport particularly well with the "conviction politics" I am here commending. Electors will bring a variety of affiliations, interests, and prejudices to the electoral process, but by far the most important thing they should bring is convictions about public justice. This is why political parties should be constituted as associations of political conviction rather than as coalitions of interests or mere electoral machines. The most reliable way to enhance the representation of voters' and parties' convictions, especially minority ones that constituency-based plurality systems consistently underrepresent, is some form of proportional representation.[72]

Eighth, while I have presented public justice as a notion with a distinctively Christian provenance, I do not suggest that this provenance be explicitly mentioned in a constitution. On the contrary, public justice mandates the formal religious impartiality of the state. This is inconsistent with the official constitutional privileging of any particular religious or secular faith. It is far preferable that the deepest justifications (Christian or otherwise) for a conception of public justice be advanced "from below"—from the open spaces of a free, plural, and boisterous civil society—than that they be enshrined "from above" in a constitution with which all must be able to identify as "their own."

[72] Some systems of proportional representation (e.g., single transferable vote and alternative member systems) can accommodate the retention of geographical constituencies, where this is thought valuable for the representation of "place."

19

Christology

Christology and Constitutionalism

Tracey Rowland

Christology and constitutionalism are not commonly juxtaposed. Christology is generally understood to be a particular, somewhat technical topic of systematic theology, and constitutionalism to be a particular, albeit fundamental, aspect of contemporary systems of law. The two therefore on first glance appear to inhabit very different domains. However, to assume so is to misunderstand both. The disciplines of law and theology so often run into each other that it does become necessary to consider the connections between the two. The connections exist, not only in premodern theocratic states, but also even in modern democracies. Abraham Kuyper, who was the prime minister of the Netherlands from 1901 to 1905, famously remarked that "no single piece of our mental world is to be hermetically sealed off from the rest, and [further] there is not a square inch in the whole domain of our human existence over which Christ, who is Sovereign over *all*, does not cry: 'Mine!' "[1] Later in the twentieth century the Polish poet and philosopher Karol Wojtyła began the first encyclical of his pontificate with the words "The Redeemer of man, Jesus Christ, is the center of the universe and of history."[2] This was his direct shot at Marxist sociology according to which the dynamic of history is class conflict. Following the demise of European Communism in 1990, Wojtyła's Jewish compatriot Adam Michnik reflected that "we are the children of our Judeo-Christian culture, and we know that this culture, which recommends loyalty to the state, commands us to bend our knees only before God. We know therefore, that we should put faithfulness to truth above participation in power. We know, by reaching for our roots, that the

[1] Abraham Kuyper, "Sphere Sovereignty" in James D Bratt (ed), *Abraham Kuyper, A Centennial Reader* (Eerdmans 1998) 488.

[2] John Paul II, *The Encyclicals of John Paul II* Michael J Miller ed and tr, (Our Sunday Visitor 1996) 48.

Tracey Rowland, *Christology: Christology and Constitutionalism* in *Christianity and Constitutionalism*.
Edited by: Nicholas Aroney and Ian Leigh, Oxford University Press.
DOI: 10.1093/oso/9780197587256.003.0019

truth of politics resides, in the end, in the politics of truth. . . . We reject belief in political utopia."[3] Consistent with the stance of the opponents of Marxism, Dietrich Bonhoeffer, one of the Christian martyrs under Fascism, declared:

> He [Jesus Christ] stands between us and God, and for that very reason he stands between us and all other men and things. *He is the Mediator*, not only between God and man, but between man and man, between man and reality. Since the whole world was created through him and unto him (John 1.3; I Cor. 8.6; Heb. 1.2), he is the sole Mediator in the world. . . . Of course, there are plenty of gods who offer men direct access, and the world naturally uses every means in its power to retain its direct hold on men, but that is the very reason why it is so bitterly opposed to Christ, the Mediator.[4]

In a reflection on Acts 4:12, which carries the statement that there is no other name under heaven by which men might be saved other than that of Jesus Christ, Cardinal Angelo Scola concluded:

> No other answer, no other foundation will be given to man than the one that has already been laid; but nevertheless man's freedom can fail to ratify the answer that has come to him or her by grace. This framework constitutes the scenario within which history unfolds and to the degree that human freedom withdraws itself from this encounter, the encounter takes on the characteristics of a clash. Man's historical life occurs thus in the sign of the dialectic between the claim of Christ and the claim of the world. . . . The claim of Christ is total and it admits no exceptions.[5]

Any scholar who takes seriously the kinds of claims made previously by this sample of outstanding twentieth- to twenty-first-century intellectuals is forced to confront the issue of the relationship between Christology and constitutional law. Since human life is inherently social, Christology and constitutionalism have found themselves in a relationship, and the process of sorting out the protocols of this relationship is a major issue for both theology and constitutional law.

[3] Adam Michnik, "After the Revolution: The New Dangers to the New Democracies" *New Republic* (2 July 1990) 28–29.

[4] Dietrich Bonhoeffer, *The Cost of Discipleship* (Touchstone 1995) 95.

[5] Angelo Scola, "Claim of Christ, Claim of the World: On the Trinitarian Encyclicals of John Paul II" (Fall 1991) 18 Communio: International Catholic Review 322–331.

This chapter will proceed in four parts: first, an outline of the basic principles of Christology as they were framed at the Council of Chalcedon in 451; second, an account of contemporary theological critiques of liberalism, especially of what the twentieth-century political theorist John Rawls called "political liberalism"; third, a section on the theological meaning of the kingship of Christ, including the Pauline concept of "restoring all things in Christ," which is the most common intersection for reflections on constitutional law and Christology; and finally, the 2016 event of the enthronement of Christ as king of Poland as a case study of postsecular engagements of Christology with constitutional theory.

Christology and Chalcedonian Adverbs

The study of Christology usually begins with the declarations of the early Church Councils of Nicaea (325), Constantinople (381, 553, and 680), and Chalcedon (451). Scholars speak of the "Chalcedonian adverbs" referring to the four most basic Christological principles about how the human and divine natures of Christ are related—without confusion, change, division, or separation. These principles were formulated as a response to Arianism, a teaching that denied the divinity of Christ; Apollinarism, a teaching that denied the humanity of Christ; Nestorianism, which denied the unity of the two natures of Christ; and Eutychianism, which denied the distinction between the divine and human natures. The four adverbs of the Chalcedonian settlement—without confusion, change, division, or separation—are not limited in their application to describing the relationship between the divinity and humanity of Christ. They are frequently employed by theologians to describe and analyze other relationships that represent *distinct* but not completely *separate* human and social realities. These include such critical couplets as the concepts of "nature and grace," "faith and reason," and, most important for constitutional law, the "church and state" relationship.

In his *Foundations of Social Order: Studies in the Creeds and Councils of the Early Church*, Rousas John Rushdoony explained the link between the Chalcedonian adverbs and political philosophy in the following terms:

> If the two natures of Christ were confused, it meant that the door was opened to the divinizing of human nature; man and the state were then potentially divine. If the human nature of Christ were reduced or denied,

> His role as man's incarnate saviour was reduced or denied, and man's saviour again became the state. If Christ's deity were reduced, then His saving power was nullified. If His humanity and deity were not in true union the incarnation was then not real, and the distance between God and man remained as great as ever.[6]

The major significance of Chalcedonian Christology for constitutional law was thus the de-divinization of the state.[7] This process was charted by the historian Charles Norris Cochrane in his *Christianity and Classical Culture*. Cochrane wrote of the Christians' "radical revision" of the first principles of political theory such that it was no longer possible "to attain a goal of permanent security, peace and freedom through political action, especially through submission to the 'virtue and fortune' of a political leader."[8] This rejection of the state as the highest horizon in human life was especially strong in the works of St. Augustine, hence the phrase "from Augustus to Augustine."[9]

Although the four Gospels offer little or no advice on matters of civil government, the legitimacy of the state is affirmed in St. Paul's Letter to the Romans 13:1: "Let every person be in subjection to the governing authorities. For there is no authority except from God and those which exist are established by God." Christ's famous statement recorded in Matthew 22:21—"Render to Caesar the things that are Caesar's; and to God the things that are God's"—is also construed by some scholars as an affirmation of the legitimacy of civil government, although other exegetes, prominent among them Oliver O'Donovan, suggest that this reading makes too much of an off-the-cuff statement made in response to an entrapment question.[10] In any event, when St. Augustine composed *The City of God*, he accepted the fact of civil authority and wrote:

> This heavenly city, then, while it sojourns on earth, calls citizens out of all nations, and gathers together a society of pilgrims of all languages, not scrupling about diversities in the manners, laws, and institutions whereby earthly peace is secured and maintained, but recognizing that, however

[6] RJ Rushdoony, *Foundations of Social Order: Studies in the Creeds and Councils of the Early Church* (Presbyterian and Reformed Publishing Company 1972).
[7] See Leithart, chapter 4 above.
[8] Charles Norris Cochrane, *Christianity and Classical Culture* (Oxford University Press 1940) vi.
[9] St. Augustine died in 430; the Council of Chalcedon was held in 451.
[10] Oliver O'Donovan, *The Desire of the Nations: Rediscovering the Roots of Political Theology* (Cambridge University Press 1996) 82–93. See also the Bertschmann chapter in this volume.

> various these are, they all tend to one and the same end of earthly peace. It therefore is so far from rescinding and abolishing these diversities, that it even preserves and adopts them, so long only as no hindrance to the worship of the one supreme and true God is thus introduced.[11]

In Augustinian and later Christian political theory in the tradition of St. Thomas Aquinas (1225–1274), the role of the state is to enable communities of people to achieve things relating to their common good they would otherwise be unable to achieve were it not for the logistical support provided by some form of civil government. In the contemporary context one thinks, for example, of a national public transport service; a national health service; an air force, navy, and army; a foreign office; medical and other scientific research; and so on. As Robert P. Kraynak has explained: "The distinction of the two cities [in the thought of Augustine] means that the spiritual and the political realms are instituted by God and accountable to God: but they are guided by different kinds of law and serve different ends."[12]

The theme of the different kinds of law is treated by St. Thomas Aquinas in his *Summa theologica* where he distinguished between laws that are (1) eternal, (2) natural, (3) human, and (4) divine. Eternal law is the order of the universe pre-existing in the mind of God (*Logos*), the natural law is the human person's participation in the eternal law, human law is a reference to the "more particular determinations of certain matters devised by human reason," and divine law refers to the will of God as revealed in the Old and New Testaments. It is typical for political theorists in the Thomist tradition and for magisterial documents of the Catholic Church to speak of the need for political judgments to be guided by the principles of the natural law.[13]

It is not possible in this chapter to outline all the different versions of natural law theory, but suffice to say that the general idea among theistic scholars is that there is such a thing as a human ecology or principles for human flourishing that are related to the eternal law because the human person has been

[11] St Augustine, *The City of God*, Book XIX, ch 17.

[12] Robert P Kraynak, *Christian Faith and Modern Democracy: God and Politics in a Fallen World* (University of Notre Dame Press 2001) 184.

[13] There is an analog for this in Jewish thought with the Noahide Law. See Rabbi Shimon Cowan, *The Theory and Practice of Universal Ethics: The Noahide Laws* (Kehot Publication Society 2015). See also David Novak, *Natural Law in Judaism* (Cambridge University Press 2008) and Hava Tirosh-Samuelson and Aaron W Hughes (eds), *David Novak: Natural Law and Revealed Torah* (Brill Academic 2013). The works of Ulrich Kühn and Per-Erik Persson are also evidence of an interest in natural law (rooted in trinitarian anthropology) from within the Lutheran tradition. See also Burnside's chapter in this volume.

made in the image of God. Since all persons of every nation share in the same humanity and require the same kinds of temporal goods for their welfare, it follows that decisions of political leaders should be made by reference to the principles that will foster such welfare. Because prudential judgment will often be required to work out the most effective way(s) to foster the common good, people may legitimately differ among themselves about the best policies and procedures. What should be held in common, at least according to Thomist political theories, is the baseline principle of regard for the natural law. There are, however, many nonteleological accounts of natural law in modern political theory for which Christology and indeed theism in general are completely irrelevant. Matthew Levering has offered a summary of these in his *Biblical Natural Law: A Theocentric and Teleological Approach*. Levering observes that once the idea of a divine creation with an associated telos is dismissed, new versions of a law of nature are presented.[14] If, however, there is no God and no universal human nature as Nietzsche and his disciples have argued, then there can be no teleological account of natural law, and natural law so understood is useless as a guide for government policy and legislation.

In contrast to Augustinian and Thomistic understandings of the relationship between Church and state mediated by the idea of a human ecology and divinely implanted natural law, the totalitarian regimes of the twentieth century attempted to reverse the process of the de-divinization of the state. They substituted materialist ideologies of human development for the natural law, theistically understood, and sought to impose these ideologies through the machinery of the state. This led to state-imposed atheism (under Communism) with its concept of a new "Soviet man" and the promotion of neopagan ideologies that deified the nation, or *Volk*, and its political ruler (in a hard form under German Fascism, in a softer form under various military dictatorships where a cult was built up around the personality of the leader and all alternative political voices were silenced).

Clerical theocracy is also an approach to government that fails to recognize the distinction between the spiritual and temporal realms. Theocratic rule tries to unite the two realms under the governance of clerical leaders, thereby absorbing the state into the spiritual order. Just as the ancient Monophysites failed to duly acknowledge the distinction between the divinity and humanity

14 Matthew Levering, *Biblical Natural Law: A Theocentric and Teleological Approach* (Oxford University Press 2008) 138–139.

of Christ and fused the two in such a manner that the divine subsumed the human, so too governments can take a Monophysite form by subsuming the temporal into the spiritual. Today this is a problem in some Islamic countries where no public expression of non-Islamic religious belief is allowed and all forms of non-Islamic proselytism are forbidden. In the past similar problems arose in Elizabethan and Cromwellian England and in Spain and Portugal during the operation of the Inquisition.

While the "Monophysite state" has traditionally been associated with theocratic forms of government, it has become commonplace to find scholars arguing that the contemporary liberal state is itself moving in a Monophysite direction. This is an element of the meta-crisis of contemporary liberalism. In the name of liberty, the modern liberal state is destroying the freedoms of religious people. The liberal constitutional theory used to defend the subservience of the spiritual to the political is known as the moral neutrality of the state. The concept was promoted by John Rawls (1921–2002) in his *A Theory of Justice* (1971) and *Political Liberalism* (1993), works that were taken up by a whole generation of political theorists.[15] According to this doctrine, governments are not merely required to tolerate a diverse range of religious practices, which is one understanding of religious freedom, but to remain neutral in a broad range of social policy conflicts that rest upon competing moral claims of different religious and philosophical traditions. According to some versions of state neutrality theory, the concepts of neutrality and equality are linked or blurred so that citizens/subjects are not merely recognized to be equal before the law, but there must also be a public recognition of the *moral equality* of their different lifestyle choices. According to this understanding of neutrality, morality itself must be democratized. Rawls explained the principle when he said that if a person wants to spend his life counting blades of grass, then that is the good life for him, and no other member of the public has any standing to judge otherwise.[16]

Theological Criticisms of the Liberal Tradition

A chorus of theological scholars have argued that the liberal tradition is intrinsically (but negatively) related to the Judeo-Greek-Christian synthesis

[15] Other notable neutrality theorists include Bruce Ackerman, Charles Larmore, and Ronald Dworkin.

[16] John Rawls, *A Theory of Justice* (Harvard University Press 1971) 432.

that begins to unravel in the late thirteenth century with the undermining of the *analogia entis,* which destroys the Augustinian-Thomist understanding of natural law. This moment in the intellectual history is then succeeded by too sharp a separation between nature and grace in the sixteenth century, followed by too sharp a separation of faith and reason in the eighteenth century, and further, from the time of Thomas Hobbes (1588–1679) at least, these sharp separations are confounded by the additional factor of a new neopagan soteriology. These genealogies map the long stage 1 of liberalism. Liberalism continues to gain momentum until the moment of the cultural crisis of the 1960s when stage 2 liberalism starts to develop. Whereas (using the metaphors of the Chalcedonian adverbs outlined in the first Christological section of this chapter) stage 1 liberalism is criticized for making Nestorian mistakes (sharply dividing things that are different but intrinsically related), stage 2 liberalism is criticized for making the Monophysite mistake of failing to acknowledge important distinctions. Stage 2 tries to subsume the spiritual into the political, and liberalism itself becomes an ersatz religion with the liberal state taking upon itself the mantel of humanity's savior. Some of the seminal works in this field are the following:

Liberalism as the Severance of the Synthesis of Greco-Roman Philosophy with Judeo-Christian Revelation

Many criticisms of the liberal tradition begin with the thesis put forward by Alasdair MacIntyre in his trilogy *After Virtue* (1981), *Whose Justice? Which Morality?* (1988), and *Three Rival Versions of Moral Enquiry* (1990). MacIntyre's argument is that liberalism is the result of the severance of the synthesis of Greco-Roman philosophy with Judeo-Christian revelation. According to MacIntyre, the synthesis began to unravel with the rise of Franciscan nominalism in the fourteenth century, resulting in today's three-fronted culture war between theists who believe in integrating faith and reason, liberals who believe in keeping faith and reason strictly separated, and postmoderns who believe that reason is never free from theological presuppositions but nonetheless argue that the human intellect is powerless to judge the superiority of one theological proposition over another. MacIntyre further argues that the liberal tradition has developed a whole range of idioms or conceptual devices to paper over contested first principles in public debates so that the philosophical differences between the actors in the culture wars can never be brought into public discourse and subjected to intellectual scrutiny. Foremost among these conceptual devices are the notions of "rights" and "neutrality." In short, for MacIntyre the liberal political tradition is a kind of tapestry made from fragments of the synthesis that become detached from their earlier positions and reset in a new framework that remains parasitic on the old but is nonetheless different, and in significant ways hostile, to any project that seeks to reconnect reason with revelation.

Liberalism as a Sophistic Rhetoric of Consensus

Catherine Pickstock is in general agreement with this reading, but she adds to MacIntyre's narrative the judgment that the synthesis was not merely *severed*, but that critical strands in the intellectual "DNA" were *mutated*. Not only were key couplets like faith and reason and nature and grace severed from each other in a Nestorian-style heresy, but also the very meaning of the concepts "reason" and "nature" came to be understood in a new, decidedly modern, way. This notion of a mutation in the meaning of the critical concepts can also be found in the intellectual histories of Louis Dupré and Charles Taylor.[17] While agreeing with MacIntyre that the rot set in, so to speak, with the rise of Franciscan nominalism, Pickstock narrows her focus to the specific contribution of Duns Scotus, whose treatment of the Thomistic *analogia entis* fostered a collapse of the teleological account of natural law.[18] Exit the *analogia entis* and theories of government end up based on contractual (rather than ontological) relations between the governors and the governed. These merely contractual relationships were undergirded by nothing stronger than a rhetoric of consensus that Pickstock reads as a modern deployment of sophistry.

[17] Louis Dupré, *Passage to Modernity: An Essay in the Hermeneutics of Nature and Culture* (Yale University Press 1993) and *The Enlightenment and the Intellectual Foundations of Modern Culture* (Yale University Press 2005); Charles Taylor, *Sources of the Self: Making of the Modern Identity* (Harvard University Press 1989) and *A Secular Age* (Belknap Press of Harvard University Press 2007).

[18] Catherine Pickstock, "Duns Scotus: His Historical and Contemporary Significance" (October 2005) 21(4) *Modern Theology* 543–574; "Liturgy, Art and Politics" (2000) 16(2) *Modern Theology* 159–180; "Liturgy and Modernity" (1998) 113 *Telos: Critical Theory of the Contemporary* 19–40; "The Univocalist Mode of Production" in C Davis et al (eds), *Theology and the Political: The New Debate* (Duke UP 2005) 281–325.

Liberalism as a Negative Form of Liberty Only

John Milbank concurs with Pickstock.[19] In a recent coauthored work, *The Politics of Virtue: Post-Liberalism and the Human Future*, Milbank and Adrian Pabst argue that the social-cultural liberalism of the left and the economic-political liberalism of the right share the same starting position of a merely negative conception of liberty. Once the ontological foundations of social relations and in particular of natural law have been eroded, one is left with these merely negative conceptions. In the absence of any shared ontological understanding they rest on two pillars: "a procedural, formalistic conception of justice and an instrumental notion of reason."[20] The combined result is that "individuals are proclaimed 'autonomous' when all the while they are subjected to the instrumental logic of bureaucratic control and commercial exchange."[21] Milbank and Pabst affirm the judgment of the Slovenian philosopher Slavoj Žižek that negative liberty has led to "an explosion of legal and moral rules, an endless procession of legalization and moralization, presented as the fight against all forms of discrimination."[22] The paradox is that in the name of liberty, liberties are destroyed by layers and layers of red tape and bureaucratic protocols and anti-discrimination laws. In his work *The Tyranny of Liberalism* James Kalb makes an almost identical observation to Žižek.[23] Kalb argues that since liberal governments want to protect people from oppression, they try to eradicate all nonliberal values and standards from more and more areas of social life, until in the end, the only permissible public value is liberalism itself.[24]

In their most recent work, Milbank and Pabst conclude that the history of the century (1914–2014) suggests that "if the state does not acknowledge the need to be guided by higher principles than power or wealth, then one of two consequences will ensure: either the state invests politics and the economy with quasi-sacred significance, like Fascism, Communism and

[19] John Milbank, *Being Reconciled: Ontology and Pardon* (Routledge 2003) 121; *The Future of Love: Essays in Political Theology* (SCM Press 2009); and *Beyond Secular Order: The Representation of Being and the Representation of the People* (Wiley Blackwell 2013).

[20] John Milbank and Adrian Pabst, *The Politics of Virtue: Post-Liberalism and the Human Future* (Rowman and Littlefield 2016) 18.

[21] Ibid, 19.

[22] Slavoj Žižek, "Liberalism and Its Discontents" (October 2012) ABC Religion and Ethics 26, quoted by Milbank and Pabst, *The Politics of Virtue*, 20.

[23] James Kalb, *The Tyranny of Liberalism, Understanding and Overcoming Administered Freedom, Inquisitorial Tolerance, and Equality by Command* (ISI Books 2009).

[24] James Kalb, "Interview with Annamarie Adkins on *The Tyranny of Liberalism*" Zenit News Service (27 March 2009).

Neo-liberalism, or else the state ends up adopting a political religion with theocratic tendencies."[25] This danger was often acknowledged in the more political speeches of Joseph Ratzinger/Benedict XVI. He argued that the state itself is not the source of truth and morality; it must receive from outside itself "the essential measure of knowledge and truth with regard to that which is good,"[26] and further, "from the beginning, Christianity has understood itself as the religion of the 'Logos,' as the religious according to reason."[27]

Liberalism as the Idolatry of the State and Parody of Christian Soteriology

Four authors who are particularly helpful for examining the theocratic tendencies of contemporary liberalism are William T. Cavanaugh, Paul Edward Gottfried, Benjamin Wiker, and Ryszard Legutko.[28] In his essay "The Myth of the State as Saviour," Cavanaugh explains how liberal political theory seeks to offer an alternative soteriology to that of Christianity in which the role of Christ as savior is usurped by the state. In this alternative soteriology the original peace of the Garden of Eden is replaced by the Hobbesian war of all against all in the state of nature. The coercive powers of the state, not the grace of the Incarnation, becomes the instrument of social peace. In *After Liberalism*, Gottfried observed that contrary to the spirit of nineteenth-century liberalism (often called aristocratic liberalism) with its Romantic-movement emphasis on individuality, the contemporary liberal state is more interested in the promotion of cultural uniformity. This task has provided employment within the state bureaucracy for social psychologists and even people with the job description "behavioral economist" whose moral and political judgments are taken as "expert" opinions. Gottfried calls them "psychiatric theologians" since they are a modern secular analog for a priesthood. In

[25] Milbank and Pabst, *The Politics of Virtue*, 234.

[26] Joseph Ratzinger, *Values in a Time of Upheaval* (Ignatius 2007) 67–68.

[27] Joseph Ratzinger, Address delivered at the Convent of St. Scholastica, Subiaco, 1 April 2005. Published in numerous places including Tracey Rowland, *Ratzinger's Faith* (Oxford University Press 2010) 156–165, 163.

[28] William T Cavanaugh, *Theopolitical Imagination* (T&T Clark 2002); Paul Edward Gottfried, *After Liberalism: Mass Democracy in the Managerial State* (Princeton University Press 2001); Benjamin Wiker, *Worshipping the State: How Liberalism Became Our State Religion* (Regnery 2013) and Ryszard Legutko, *The Demon in Democracy: Totalitarian Temptations in Free Societies* (Encounter Books 2016). Legutko served as the minister of education, secretary of state, and deputy speaker of the Polish Senate. He is currently a member of the European Parliament and a professor of philosophy at Poland's Jagiellonian University.

tacit agreement with MacIntyre, Gottfried argues that much of the rhetoric of modern political life is designed to conceal both the power of these psychiatric theologians and the questionable legitimacy of their supposed expert status.[29] In *The Demon in Democracy*, Legutko argues that both Communism and liberalism share the same hostility to Christianity and a propensity for totalitarian behavior. As Legutko expresses the principle: "for the ideologues of liberal democracy it is necessary to intervene deeply into the social substance—where the roots of status and recognition reside—either through direct political action or indirectly by changing the laws, making appropriate judicial decisions, and adjusting morality and social mores drastically to guarantee equality."[30] The Marxists did the same. All these authors agree that contemporary liberalism has a totalitarian propensity because of the desire of its proponents to harness the power of the state for social engineering projects, even if that means restricting freedom and interfering in family life and other private institutions.

Liberalism as the Bifurcation of the Self and the Form of the Machine

The liberal attempt to completely separate the political from the transcendent has also led to the idea that it is normal, indeed almost a social virtue, for a human person to have two completely separate selves—a public self and a private self. It is precisely for this reason that Roberto Unger has suggested that it is "schizophrenia" or the "bifurcation of the individual self that brings to life the hidden truth of the moral condition liberal psychology prescribes."[31] A similar observation was made by Vaclav Havel (1936–2011), the first post-Communist president of the Czech Republic. He noted that in countries where liberalism is the prevailing political philosophy people behave as though they are playing for a number of different teams at once, each with different uniforms, and as though they do not know to which of the teams they ultimately belong.[32] Within contemporary liberal societies

[29] For more extensive articles developing this topic see Tracey Rowland, "The Authority of '*Experts*' and the Ethos of Modern Institutions" (2001) 28(4) Communio International Catholic Review 746–765 and "The Bureaucratic Usurpation of Grace" 2014 4(1) Solidarity: The Journal of Catholic Social Thought and Secular Ethics 1–16.

[30] Legutko, *The Demon in Democracy*, 62.

[31] Roberto Unger, *Knowledge and Politics* (Free Press 1975) 58.

[32] Vaclav Havel, *Open Letters: Selected Prose 1965–1990* (Faber & Faber 1991) 95.

the habit of wearing different "masks" in different social contexts becomes a social survival mechanism. David L. Schindler has described this kind of liberal culture as having the form of a machine. Since liberalism eschews the possibility of there being any overarching principle of social integration, the human person is forced to compartmentalize his or her life in a mechanistic way.[33]

Liberalism as the Dictatorship of Relativism

Jürgen Habermas, one of Europe's leading political theorists, has called for an openness of liberal society to religious thought. However, he continues to maintain that a liberal democracy does not require any metaphysical or religious foundation. Analogous arguments are made by liberal theorists about human rights. They are said to be fully functional as free-standing principles without any metaphysical or religious foundations. These presumptions were challenged by Joseph Ratzinger in his famous debate with Habermas.[34] As noted earlier, Ratzinger has consistently argued that unless the laws of the state can be said to have a foundation in truth, then there is nothing to protect individual citizens from the sovereignty of the mob. The state, he insists, "must learn that there is a continued existence of truth which is not subject to consensus but which precedes it and makes it possible."[35] This principle was the subject of a doctrinal note from the Congregation of the Doctrine of the Faith, which Ratzinger directed in 2002. The document stated:

> Political freedom cannot be based upon the relativistic idea that all conceptions of the human person's good have the same value and truth, but rather, on the fact that political life is concerned with very concrete realisations of the true human and social good in given historical, geographic, economic, technological and cultural contexts.[36]

[33] David L Schindler, "Christological Aesthetics and *Evangelium Vitae*: Towards a Definition of Liberalism" (1995) 22 Communio: International Catholic Review 193–224, 201.

[34] Joseph Ratzinger and Jürgen Habermas, *The Dialectics of Secularisation: On Reason and Religion* (Ignatius Press 2007).

[35] Joseph Ratzinger, *Church, Ecumenism and Politics: New Essays in Ecclesiology* (Robert Nowell tr, Crossroad 1988) 219.

[36] Congregation for the Doctrine of the Faith, Doctrinal Note on Some Questions Regarding the Participation of Catholics in Political Life, 24 November 2002.

The phrase "the dictatorship of relativism" was used by Ratzinger in his homily to the College of Cardinals on April 18, 2005, to describe a culture that does not "recognise anything as definitive and whose ultimate goal consists solely of one's own ego and desires."[37] Ratzinger's "dictatorship of relativism" would seem to be the tyranny of political liberalism, or what was earlier described as stage 2 liberalism, by another name.

Here it should be acknowledged that several Christian scholars have over the past century attempted a rapprochement between Christianity and the liberal tradition and that this project gained a lot of traction after the Second World War when the liberal democracies were held in high moral regard for their contribution to the defeat of German fascism. Foremost among these rapprochement scholars are Jacques Maritain (1882–1973), John Courtney Murray, SJ (1904–1967), and John Finnis.[38] Common to each of these authors was the presumption that it was possible to build a social theory, upon which all could agree, regardless of their theological convictions, on the basis of some common agreement about the goods of human flourishing. Contemporary political liberalism, however, eschews the possibility of any such agreement since it rejects baseline concepts like a universal human nature, a natural law, and a common good.

If one rejects the liberal tradition as deeply flawed and inclined toward totalitarian forms of government, the question immediately arises as to alternatives. Liberals will refer to the totalitarian moments in Christian civilization such as the period of the Spanish and Portuguese Inquisitions or the imposition of puritanical theology in Cromwellian England as nondesirable alternatives. Contemporary theologians readily agree that these periods in Christian history are shameful and should never be repeated. They highlight the dangers of failing to distinguish the authority of the state from the authority of the Church, and in particular, they highlight the danger of harnessing the power of the state to promote the perceived temporal interests of the Church. At the Second Vatican Council the bishops attempted to deal with the shameful elements in Catholic social history in the document *Dignitatis Humanae,* otherwise known as the *Decree on Religious Freedom.*

[37] Joseph Ratzinger, Homily to the College of Cardinals, Vatican City, Monday 18 April 2005.

[38] See, e.g., Jacques Maritain, *Man and the State* (Catholic University of America Press 1998); Jacques Maritain, *Christianity and Democracy: The Rights of Man and Natural Law* (Ignatius Press 2012); John Courtney Murray, *We Hold These Truths: Catholic Reflections on the American Proposition* (Sheed & Ward 1960); John Finnis, *Natural Law and Natural Rights* (Clarendon 1980); and John Finnis, *Aquinas* (Oxford University Press 1998).

The very first paragraph of the *Decree* expresses the principle that "the truth cannot impose itself except by virtue of its own truth."[39]

What many theologians argue is that it is possible to have a juridical separation of the powers of the church and the state without subscribing to some version of liberal political theory.[40] In a European context such a position is often described as a form of Christian democracy. Under a Christian democracy the powers of legislators are circumscribed by the natural law. In *The Politics of Virtue*, Milbank and Pabst argue that liberals cannot pretend to have invented values such as freedom, equality, toleration, individual rights, constitutionalism, mixed and balanced government, the rule of law, limits on both state and market power, fair detention, fair trial, right to defense, habeas corpus, good treatment of the convicted, trial by peers, need of proof for guilt, and requirements for restitution, reparation, and rehabilitation of offenders.[41] These ideas, they emphasize, are all of Greco-Roman, Germanic, or Christian provenance. They suggest that one can have all of these constitutional and political elements without the reliance on liberal ideology. For example, unlike the natural right doctrines that consider the rights of individuals qua individuals, the preliberal common law understanding of rights and responsibilities began with an individual who was already socially situated, that is, already existing within a network of social relationships.[42] The task, as many theologians see it, is to disentangle these many positive elements of Western constitutional systems from their attachment to liberal political theory, and in particular, to demonstrate that various forms of state neutrality are decidedly nonneutral in effect and, indeed, often lead to a totalitarian imposition of anti-Christian social engineering policies.

[39] For an extensive analysis of this document and its relationship to the liberal tradition see David L Schindler, "Religious Freedom, Truth and American Liberalism: Another Look at John Courtney Murray" (1994) 21(4) Communio: International Catholic Review 696–741. and David L Schindler and Nicholas J Healy Jr, *Freedom, Truth and Human Dignity: The Second Vatican Council's Declaration on Religious Freedom* (Eerdmans 2015).

[40] See the chapter by Witte in this volume.

[41] Milbank and Pabst, *The Politics of Virtue*, 29.

[42] For accounts of the Christian foundations of the common-law system see Alan Harding, *Medieval Law and the Foundations of the State* (Oxford University Press 2001); Harold J Berman, "Religious Foundations of Law in the West: An Historical Perspective" (Summer 1983) 1 Journal of Law and Religion 3–43; Augusto Zimmermann, *Christian Foundations of the Common Law,* vol 1: *England,* vol 2: *The United States,* and vol 3: *Australia* (Connor Court 2018).

Understanding the Kingship of Christ

In St. Paul's Letter to the Ephesians 1:9 one finds a reference to the recapitulation of all things in heaven and on earth in Christ. This theme was taken up by St. Irenaeus of Lyons in his *Adversus Haereses*, III, 21, 9, where he refers to Christ as the "eternal king" who will recapitulate all things in himself.[43] An extensive scriptural analysis of the kingship of Christ theme can also be found in Oscar Cullmann's *The Early Church*.[44]

In 1903 Pope Pius X addressed the subject of the restoration of all things in Christ in his encyclical *E supremi*, and in 1925 Pius XI developed the theme in his *Quas Primas* while establishing the Feast of Christ the King. This feast is not exclusive to the Catholic Church. Anglican, Lutheran, and many other Protestant churches have adopted it and often celebrate Christ the King Sunday. In the following paragraph Stanley Hauerwas (from the Anabaptist tradition) and Michael Baxter (a Catholic) together endorse the political theology behind this feast:

> We have quoted so profusely from *Quas Primas* because Pius XI resists the temptation to conceive of politics as a procedural arrangement which precludes any strong account of the good. Put differently, Pius XI resists the urge to conceive of politics in anything less than soteriological terms. Separating politics from soteriology has become the norm among theologians today, but as we see it, this only lays the theoretical groundwork for religious indifferentism, for assuming that we can discern the political apart from the Christ. And this, in turn, paves the way for what we Christians must regard as a truly frightening national agenda—domesticating religious passion, submerging people's energy in the self-interested pursuit of material comfort, constructing an arrangement in which religion is subordinated to the political order.[45]

What Hauerwas and Baxter call "separating soteriology from politics" has been a strong inclination in some strands of Protestantism, especially those evolving from the ideas of Martin Luther for whom there were distinctly "two kingdoms," one over which Christ reigned and one that lay outside

[43] John Paul II, "All Creation Will Be 'Recapitulated' in Christ" General Audience 14 February 2001.
[44] Oscar Cullmann, *The Early Church* (AJB Higgins ed, SCM Press 1955).
[45] Stanley Hauerwas and Michael Baxter, "The Kingship of Christ: Why Freedom of 'Belief' Is Not Enough" (1992–1993) 42 De Paul Law Review 107–127, 124.

the effects of the Incarnation. David VanDrunen is a contemporary theologian associated with a resurgence in "two kingdoms" thinking.[46] Timothy P. Palmer, however, has been critical of any strong account of the two kingdoms that would leave some "secular" sphere impervious to the grace of the Incarnation.[47] Oliver O'Donovan presents the mainstream contemporary Protestant position in the following statement:

> As in speaking of the Incarnation itself we cannot affirm the hypostatic union without the two natures, so with the Kingdom of God we cannot conceive the *henosis* of political and spiritual without the duality of the two terms held together in it. That is why those who have asserted that a conception of Two Kingdoms is fundamental to Christian political thought have spoken truly, though at great risk of distorting the truth if they simply leave it at that. The unity of the kingdoms, we may say, is the heart of the Gospel, their duality is the pericardium. Proclaiming the unity of God's rule in Christ is the task of Christian witness; understanding that duality is the chief assistance rendered by Christian reflection.[48]

Speaking in a different theological dialect but nonetheless reaching the same conclusion, Ernest Fortin, in his St. Augustine Lecture of 1971, wrote: "The Church is not an entity distinct from the world but the world reconciled until itself and unto God: *mundus reconciliatus ecclesia*."[49]

Abraham Kuyper's account of the kingship of Christ is closer to Fortin and O'Donovan than to VanDrunen. Kuyper thought that the world, so to speak, could be carved up into different social spheres such as family life and professional life but that in each of these spheres there are particular ways of respecting the sovereignty of Christ, particular precepts to be followed. The basic idea of this "sphere sovereignty" is that each sphere has its own character and each is directly under divine rule. This approach sits well with Catholic social theory and in particular with elements of that theory located

[46] See, e.g., David VanDrunen, *Natural Law and the Two Kingdoms: A Study in the Development of Reformed Social Thought* (Eerdmans 2010) and *Living in God's Two Kingdoms: A Biblical Vision for Christianity and Culture* (Crossway 2010). See also VanDrunen, chapter 16 above.

[47] David VanDrunen, "The Two Kingdoms: A Reassessment of the Transformationist Calvin" (November 2005) 40 Calvin Theological Journal 248–266 and Timothy P Palmer, "Calvin the Transformationist and the Kingship of Christ" (2007) 35(3) Pro Rege 32–39.

[48] Oliver O'Donovan, *The Desire of the Nations: Rediscovering the Roots of Political Theology* (Cambridge University Press 1996) 82.

[49] Ernest Fortin, *Political Realism and Christianity in the Thought of St. Augustine* (Villanova University Press 1972) 25.

within the Thomist tradition that emphasize the idea of subsidiarity and the notion that God created all things with their own stability, truth, goodness, and proper laws and order.[50]

Perhaps the starkest example, however, of the nexus between the kingship of Christ as a theme in theology and the kingship of Christ as an element of constitutional law is the 2016 declaration of the Polish government that Christ is the king of Poland. This will be the subject of the final section of this chapter.

The Case of Poland

In November 2016 the "enthronement" or recognition of Christ as king of Poland was declared during a ceremony held in Krakow in the official presence of the president of Poland, Andrzej Duda. This act did not change any of the constitutional arrangements of the Polish government formally speaking. No amendment to this effect was made to any of the Polish legal instruments. However, this public ritual acknowledging the sovereignty of Christ did imply that there is something higher than the mere will of the people.[51]

The movement in favor of the enthronement was begun by Rozalia Celakówna (1901–1944), a nurse working in Krakow who had mystical experiences.[52] The poet Juliusz Słowacki had earlier made reference to the concept in 1846. Marcin Majewski argues that enthronement requires the state to recognize that while the Church and state are distinct entities, they are both subordinate to divine ethics (a principle the fathers of the Second Vatican Council embedded in paragraphs 20 and 41 of *Gaudium et spes*, the Pastoral Constitution on the Church in the Modern World). According to

[50] For a more developed account of this topic see Tracey Rowland, "The Humanism of the Incarnation: Catholic, Barthian and Dutch Reformed" (2015) 13(1) Nova et Vetera 125–54.

[51] It could be argued that the 1937 preamble to the Constitution of Éire with its reference to the Holy Trinity did something similar. Cf. McIlroy chapter 17, above. It is beyond the scope of this chapter to compare the preamble to the Constitution of Éire and the Polish act of "enthronement" to analogous elements in Anglican theology and British constitutional law. However, for those who would like to investigate this matter further, the works of the scholars Paul Avis and Ian Bradley would be helpful entry points. See, e.g., Paul Avis, *The Anglican Understanding of the Church: An Introduction* (SPCK 2000) and *The Church in the Theology of the Reformers* (Wipf and Stock 2002), and Ian Bradley, *God Save the Queen: The Spiritual Dimensions of Monarchy* (Continuum 2012). Both of these authors examine the theological and constitutional significance of the queen's coronation oath.

[52] The author is indebted to the translation assistance of Helenka Pasztetnik for material in this section.

Majewski, enthronement is an *anamnesis* of the biblical truth that God, and not the human person, is the source of moral law and authority.[53]

Another Polish scholar, Pawel Rojek, has argued that the foundation for the enthronement concept may be found in the Christocentric anthropology also set out in *Gaudium et spes* (para. 22).[54] Since humanity is said to have been made in the image and likeness of God (Gen. 1:27), Christology, and indeed the whole of trinitarian theology, is directly linked to anthropology, and anthropology in turn is linked to soteriology and eschatology, and these in turn are linked to political theory and ultimately constitutional law. As Brock Bingaman explained in his work *All Things New: The Trinitarian Nature of the Human Calling in Maximus the Confessor*, "the synthesis of Christ's person becomes the paradigm for the restoration of the cosmos and the pattern for the Christian life."[55]

A third Polish author, Piotr Popiołek, reads Poland's enthronement of Christ as king as an exercise in postsecular constitutionalism.[56] For Popiołek, postsecular theology, such as that offered by the British radical orthodoxy circle of scholars (predominately John Milbank, Adrian Pabst, and Catherine Pickstock), has demonstrated that in its negation of Christianity, secular modernity is simply neopagan and the liberal state in its guise as humanity's alternative savior to Christ is simply an idol. Popiołek therefore sees enthronement as a dramatic way of making the point that the legislation of the Polish state is or ought to be subordinate to a higher law. A synthesis could be made of the arguments of all three of the Polish scholars (Majewski, Rojek, and Popiołek) by combining radically orthodox critiques of liberal theory with the theological anthropology undergirding *Gaudium et spes* as found developed in the works of David L. Schindler.[57]

In a different context, the debate over whether or not to mention God in documents of the European Union, Martin Mosebach argued that the

[53] Marcin Majewski, *Intronizacja Jezusa Króla* (Wydawnictwo, 2016).

[54] Pawel Rojek, "Ludowy Postsekularyzm" (2014) 36 Pressje 8–23. Rojek is a philosopher and sociologist, lecturer at the Pontifical University of John Paul II, and head of the editorial board of the quarterly *Pressje*.

[55] B Bingaman, *All Things New: The Trinitarian Nature of the Human Calling in Maximus the Confessor and Jürgen Habermas*, (Pickwick Publications 2014) 38. See also n 26 on p 38 where he draws attention to Hans Urs von Balthasar's endorsement of the significance of the synthesis of Maximus.

[56] Piotr Popiołek, "Radykalna intronizacja: Chrystus Krol Polski I Teologia Postsekularna" (2014) 36 Pressje 95–108. Note: This author is a scholar based in Krakow, not the fashion designer who shares the same name.

[57] See, e.g., David L Schindler, *Heart of the World: Centre of the Church* (Eerdmans 1996) and *Ordering Love: Liberal Societies and the Memory of God* (Eerdmans 2011).

mention of God implies that the state possesses legitimacy so long as it guards the law that was not created by it. The rule of law, he says, is something before which not only the individual citizen but also the state itself must bow, and no one bows to something that one has made oneself. The mention of God is a reminder to the state that it is not perfect or complete in itself and that there is something higher than it. The state is not humanity's savior.[58] Although Mosebach made these observations in the context of the European Union, it could be argued that Poland's enthronement civic ritual was designed to serve the same purpose that Mosebach hoped the mention of God might serve in the founding documents of the European Union. Its effect was to declare that for Poland the civil law ought to be subordinate to a higher law. This in turn means that for Polish constitutional law the citizens of the state are seen to have strong metaphysical foundations for the "rights" and social freedoms they enjoy.

Recent Polish constitutional law has been in a state of turmoil, though the controversies have not centered around theological issues, but around separation of powers issues that followed the attempt of the Civic Platform Party (*Platforma Obywatelska*) to stack the Constitutional Tribunal with its own preferred judges before losing office in 2015, and the actions of the Law and Justice Party (*Prawo i Sprawiedliwość*) to deny recognition to the judges appointed by their predecessors and to appoint their own preferred candidates. The literature in this field is filled with claims and counterclaims about the political motivations lying behind support for either one of the parties. Whatever one makes of this extensive body of argumentation, the issues pertain to the respective powers of the judicial, executive, and legislative branches of government, not to questions pertaining to the relationship between theology, political philosophy, and constitutional law.

Conclusion

It has been said of Central Europe that it is not a region, the frontiers of which can be traced on a map, like, for example, the countries of Central America. It is rather a kingdom of the mind.[59] Georgy Konrad, author of the *Intellectuals on the Road to Class Power* and *Anti-Politics*, described the essential quality

[58] Martin Mosebach, *Das Subversive am Christentum* (Sankt Ulrich Verlag 2012).
[59] Timothy Garton Ash, "L'Europe centrale existe-t-elle?" 1986 (10) Lettre Internationale 5–6.

of Central European thought as a "challenge to the ruling system of clichés."[60] At the time of writing this chapter there has been much talk about the significance of the "Visegrád" or "V4 Alliance"—comprising Poland, Hungary, Czechia (formerly the Czech Republic), and Slovakia, with the possible future inclusion of Austria. These nations have found themselves at odds with many directives and political theories driving the European Union. As a generalization the political leaders of this group are not opposed to a high degree of European economic integration, but they are opposed to a loss of state sovereignty in matters pertaining to social policy and immigration. They are resistant to the social engineering policies emanating from Brussels. In Konrad's words, they are offering a challenge to the "ruling system of clichés," which are the standard bearers of what is now called "political liberalism"—the label promoted by John Rawls to highlight the idea that versions of liberalism resting on the notion of the morally neutral state are, or ought to be, "political, not metaphysical." The fact that such a challenge is coming from countries formerly within the Soviet sphere can be explained, at least in part, by the fact that the intellectual leaders of these countries are more acutely aware of the similarities between Marxism and contemporary political liberalism than their counterparts in countries that were fortunate to fall on the other side of the Iron Curtain. In the twentieth century, countries of the former Hapsburg Empire (i.e., most of Central Europe) were "laboratories" for grand social engineering experiments that failed, so it is not so surprising that it is within these societies today that one finds the strongest support for what Piotr Popiołek calls "postsecular constitutionalism."

One way to consider the whole notion of "postsecular constitutionalism" is to think of it as affirming concepts such as human freedom, equality before the law, mixed and balanced government, the rule of law, limits on state power, and other elements commonly found within contemporary democratic constitutions but underpinning them with a Judeo-Christian theological foundation. This is an alternative to the jurisprudence of political liberalism with its rejection of appeals to concepts like truth and goodness, universal human nature, and a common good existing beyond the notion of the absolute autonomy of the individual. According to this reading the contemporary Central European interest in postsecular constitutional theory is a response to political liberalism's "Monophysite" tendencies to subsume and subordinate the spiritual within the political. As Oliver O'Donovan has

[60] Georgy Konrad, "Mein Traum von Europea" (September 1985) 81 Kursbuch 175–193.

remarked: "A 'pure' political theory which can make it a matter of intellectual conscience to disinterest itself in the transcendent is not one that any humane thinker need feel guilt about rejecting."[61]

One final important observation is that in Christian accounts of the state it is always assumed that no perfect society will ever exist this side of the renewal of the cosmos. All human attempts to improve social conditions will be limited by the human condition itself and there will always be the danger of moving too far in either Nestorian or Monophysite directions, to use the language of Chalcedonian Christology.[62]

[61] Oliver O'Donovan, *The Desire of the Nations*, 122.

[62] At the time of writing this chapter the author was a member of the International Theological Commission's (ITC) subcommittee on religious freedom. If material in this section bears a resemblance to material that finally appears in the ITC document it is because the author contributed to the drafting of the ITC document, *not* that the author has lifted material from the ITC document without attribution.

20

Natural Law

Natural Law and Natural Right Revisited

John Milbank

Introduction

Discussions of natural law and natural right inevitably include discussions of their historical genesis, and where they do not, then often a fictive genesis is assumed, in a way that vitiates the substantive claims for law and right that are being made. This is most evidently the case for modern natural right, since this manifestly has an origin—it has been asserted always in particular circumstances and within a particular conceptuality that helps to determine the sense of the concept. But it is also the case for natural law, because any attempt to ignore its origins in the classical and medieval past and especially its links to theology and metaphysics inevitably denature it and produce a novel, modern doctrine that is often much more reducible to a modern natural rights doctrine than its proponents imagine.[1]

I will attempt, in this chapter, to sketch briefly the historical development of natural right in relation to the older notion of natural law. My contention will be that the latter notion has, until recently, always been more dominant than the former, and that for a long time natural right was usually thought of in the context of natural law. Even where notions of subjective right started to become more important in the Middle Ages, early modernity, and the Enlightenment, they were often not subjectively founded in the will or capacity of the individual, but still within conceptions of an objective cosmic right order, however etiolated. And even where they were so subjectively founded, starting in the Middle Ages with several Franciscan theorists, natural right necessarily presented itself as a revised notion of natural law or

[1] This is true of the "new natural law" doctrine of John Finnis and Germain Grisez. For a critique see Russell Hittinger, *Critique of the New Natural Law Theory* (Notre Dame UP 1989).

John Milbank, *Natural Law: Natural Law and Natural Right Revisited* in *Christianity and Constitutionalism.* Edited by: Nicholas Aroney and Ian Leigh, Oxford University Press. © Oxford University Press 2022.
DOI: 10.1093/oso/9780197587256.003.0020

of cosmic order, now perversely construed as a pure regime of power and willing. In this way, the link of *ius*, whether viewed as objective right (or law) or as subjective right, with conceptions of *divine government* did not immediately disappear.

Notions of divine government imply not just the normative but also the descriptive: not just how we *should* govern human society under divine norms but also how this society is *in fact* governed by God, either with or despite our human intentions. Once natural law had become natural right according to a revised notion of divine rule, this providential aspect of his governance could not simply be ignored but was rather transmuted in a bifurcated way: either as the divine or natural distilling of order out of the chaos of individual choices, according to the "cunning of reason," or else, in Rousseau's model, as the human governmental mediation of the divine "general will" through the harmonization of perspectivally different human liberties, insofar as these can be made to agree in a "live and let live" coordination of negative freedoms.[2] Thereby the "general will" of the human state results. Its risk, as we shall see, is state terror, whereas the risk of supposed natural coordination is anarchy and habitual criminality.

But in either case, a certain mutated theology still hovers. By contrast, once a full secularization of rights theory is attempted, it becomes wholly unclear just why rights can be added to facts, what is the ground of their legitimation, and in precisely what they should consist. In consequence, the ready assumption that one can oppose secular natural rights to sacral or metaphysical natural law starts to look questionable. Rather, even today, one is talking about alternative theologies or metaphysics. And what is more, as I shall argue, when correctly understood, natural law can appear to be the less dogmatic, more open, and more intuitively correct metaphysical perspective: able, indeed, to incorporate whatever is (often ambivalently) valid in the modern development of natural or human right, while securing this gain more surely on an objective rather than subjective foundation, which is all too liable to overturn right in the name of right. At the same time, natural law is able, as natural right is not, to consider also the equity of *relational* human situations and not leave these at the mercy of legal positivism and political utility.

[2] For the dependence of Rousseau here respectively on Leibnizian and Malebranchian metaphysics, see Alexis Philonenko, *Jean-Jacques Rousseau et al Pensée du Malheur* (Vrin 1984) 3 vols, plus, for a summary, Luc Rerry and Alain Renaut, *Political Philosophy 3:From the Rights of Man to the Republican Idea* (Franklin Philip tr, Chicago UP 1992) 52–55 and Patrick Riley, *The General Will Before Rousseau: The Transformation of the Divine into the Civic* (Princeton UP 1986).

By the same token, such a theology does not hand history over either to an impersonal or a statist coordination, but rather returns it to a cooperative human work that seeks, by a kind of ecological faith, one might say, to search continuously for "the right way" for human beings to be among themselves and within the wider natural order. Again, I want to submit that something that sounds shockingly theological is in fact more in tune with habitual human behavior (as it remains, even today) than the dominant official secular theories that only hold back from the brink of a nihilism (without either law or right) by the incoherent virtue of a lingering attachment to theories that logically require a theological grounding, however perversely voluntaristic.

Histories of Natural Law

In terms of historical approaches to natural right, one can approximately distinguish three main tendencies: the first is a "whiggish" or progressivist tendency to see a gradual development of notions of subjective rights all the way from ancient Rome (and even, quite erroneously, the Bible)[3] until the present day. This tendency confuses the many examples of subjective natural *ius* with a grounding of these same rights in pure individual identity or self-assertion.[4] Equally, it tends to ignore the correlation of subjective right with conceptions of the enforceability of such right by sovereign political powers, by projecting backward a very recent notion of pure "human rights." These are somehow conceived as no longer suspended within the aporetic space between the naturally given and the legally enactable.

In a very commendable, detailed, and learned reaction against this tendency, Samuel Moyn has adopted a second "archaeological" approach to rights history (he sometimes himself says "antiquarian") that seeks to disinter different layers of legal time without imagining that he is uncovering

[3] See Nicholas Wolterstorff, *Justice; Rights and Wrongs* (Princeton UP 2008) 65–131. It is by contrast obvious that the main perspective of the Hebrew Bible/Old Testament upon justice is as distributivist as that of Aristotle: see, e.g., Exod. 23:10–12; Deut. 14:20, 15:1–18, 23:20–21; Lev. 19:10–11, 23:25–28, 25:29–55; Numb. 35–36; Josh. 13–19, concerning the regulations of land usage. Moreover, God's primary concern with the flourishing of his people as linked with their righteousness suggests eudaemonism more than deontology or utility. There is not much need to labor these points. Wolterstorff's view cannot be historically plausible, as he attempts to force the Bible into the matrix of Lockean voluntarism and a distorted covenantalism becomes artificial conventionalism.

[4] See John Milbank, "Against Human Rights: Liberty in the Western Tradition" (April 2012) 1(1) Oxford Journal of Law and Religion 203–234.

the organic roots of what came later.[5] Rather, for his historiography, other conceptions and practices were dumped on top of the older levels, reusing their vocabulary misleadingly to different ends. Thus, to begin with in Hobbes and Locke, "rights" were primarily about protecting property from arbitrary power, albeit at the price of establishing unqualified state sovereignty. In the revolutionary era, by contrast, rights were linked to the establishment of a state power that aimed to emancipate individuals from customary or social hierarchical control and to engender equality of opportunity. Immediately before and after 1945 rights were radically reconstrued in Christian, natural law–based personalist, dignitarian, and communitarian terms.[6] In the 1970s they reverted, with a further secularizing twist, to a nation-state context, in association with natural liberation struggles. Today, in further contrast, rights have become globalized and depoliticized as primarily confined to preventing inhuman horrors (such as torture) or securing minimal individual access to justice and to voting (etc.) rather than achieving more widespread social and political liberation.

In this way one could see Moyn's approach as anti-genealogical. But a third, genealogical approach, that I would want to stress at least equally, need not at all be blind to the instances of rupture and discontinuity. While eschewing any notion of a straightforward progressive development, it nevertheless rightly takes note of the ways in which later conceptions of rights would be impossible without the intellectual moves involved in earlier ones and their persistence over a *longue durée*. Thus, the contemporary "thin" notion of right as limiting the worst damage is clearly a long-term derivative of the Hobbesian founding of politics upon a negatively distilled order that begins with human fear as the prime fact, besides early modern nonteleological and minimalist conceptions of ethics that have focused on "sympathy" with our shared human physical condition rather than on controverted claims for ultimate human purpose—as indeed Moyn himself has helped to show.[7]

Equally, it is somewhat wrong to suppose that the revolutionary account of rights, whether in the 1790s or the 1970s, is a simple reversal of the

[5] Samuel Moyn, *The Last Utopia: Human Rights in History* (Harvard UP 2010) and *Human Rights and the Uses of History* (Verso 2014).

[6] Samuel Moyn, "Personalism, Community and the Origins of Human Rights" in Stefan-Ludwig Hoffmann (ed), *Human Rights in the Twentieth Century* (CUP 2010) 85–106.

[7] Samuel Moyn, "Empathy in History, Empathising with Humanity" (October 2006) 45(3) History and Theory397–415.

property-based account of right, as Costas Douzinas tends to argue.[8] Rather, it is the case that property and revolution are twins. Just because the new prime duty of the state is to protect life and property, Hobbes, never mind Locke, claimed that the legitimacy of government lapses if it fails to do so.[9] This implies a new individual or mass right to rebellion that is quite different from traditional medieval "rights to resist" which empowered lesser constitutional bodies to overturn higher ones if they had grossly lapsed in their exercise of responsibility.[10] Certainly, what one can anachronistically call the "liberalism" of Hobbes and Locke was concerned first with the freedom of inequitable property ownership secured by the state's monopoly on violence. But once such a state has started to remove the various particular liberties and customary privileges that had existed at a lower level, then inevitably "counter-rights" start to be asserted against the original rights—rights to extend the franchise in order that the state be not merely on the side of big property, rights to equality of entry into social and economic competition. Thus, the revolutionary traditions have continued to be fixated on ownership, while demanding a more egalitarian access to it.

While, indeed, the nonstatist traditions of socialism refused the language of rights in the name of distributive justice and social reciprocity,[11] welfarist social democracy has been largely concerned with rights as entitlements. Even Marxism remains focussed on the rights-property-revolution triangle insofar as it thinks of a general will as controlling a collective property and suggests that equity means the "right" of the individual to receive all he needs, matched with the equal collective right of the general will to demand from each such individual the full measure of his means. Although Marxism recognizes the liberal revolutionary suppression of the social, it tends to reduce the social to an "immediate" Leibnizian coincidence of the individual with the species, downplaying the primacy of reciprocal bonds of agreement as to social value.[12] In both cases, it would seem that the *content* of rights must be technologically determined according to supposedly objective

[8] Costas Douzinas, "Philosophy and the Right to Resistance" in Costas Douzinas and Conor Gearty (eds). *The Meaning of Rights: The Philosophy and Social Theory of Human Rights* (CUP 2014) 85–105.

[9] Thomas Hobbes, *Leviathan,* Part 2, ch 21, 114.

[10] On this point see Christopher A Ferrara, *Liberty: The God That Failed: Policing the Sacred and Constructing the Secular State from Locke to Obama* (Angelico 2012) 74–79.

[11] For the nonliberalism and therefore also the nonleftism of nineteenth-century socialism, see Jean-Claude Michéa, *Les Mystères de la Gauche* (Flammarion 2014).

[12] Karl Marx, "On the Jewish Question," in *Early Writings* (Penguin 1975) 229–234.

criteria and that the operator of an ensuing social machine must be an evermore bureaucratic government.

As to the legitimacy of such a government, the natural rights perspective here enters into an aporia, as Costas Douzinas has well explained.[13] On the one hand, since modern right is at bottom power, legitimacy is grounded in de facto control; on the other hand, once this control is recognized, then no other force may legitimately be used against it. This contradiction appears most glaringly to view in the opinions of both Kant and Hegel that, while revolution can never be justified,[14] once it has been successful, legitimation is accorded retrospectively. In this view, which is prefigured by Hobbes, can be seen the force of revolution as both the reinsertion of founding nature into operationalizing polity and its theorization as a new covert theology of divine government.

The above kind of truly critical perspective upon the liberal legacy, going beyond the usual leftist "immanent critique," demonstrates the ways in which modern conservatism and modern liberal-leftism are locked in to exactly the same rights-based paradigm.

Theologies of Natural Law

Ultimately, one can only attain to such a perspective by invoking both the contrast and the continuity of natural right with natural law. The latter is much misunderstood. It has a double historical origin. First, it can be located in the works of Philo Judaeus as a coming together of Hebrew notions of the cosmos as subject to an omnipotent personal rule, with a Greek metaphysical discourse concerning the structures of being. This strand of natural law is thoroughly biblical in origin. Indeed, Philo thinks of the revealed law of the Hebrew Bible as alone fully proclaiming the natural law, even if the world constitutes a kind of *megalopolis* with one law and one constitution, to which the constitutions of cities are dubious "additions." The Decalogue is a saving deliverance from this addition: thus it was proclaimed far from cities in the "deep desert" and unlike human law is offered as pure redemptive counsel, unaccompanied by any (extrinsic) punitive sanctions.[15]

[13] Douzimas, "Philosophy and the Right to Resistance."

[14] Because it is a revolt against the positive sovereign guarantee of the very possibility of order, which is ultimately for both—despite Hegel's qualifications—the securing of private dominium.

[15] Philo, *The Decalogue*, I, 2; XXIII, 176–177.

By contrast, for the Greeks nomos and physis were generally set in opposition to each other.[16] To be sure, they had strong concepts of "natural justice," but that could betoken a link to an ontological order that was ultimately impersonal and perhaps indifferently reserved behind and beyond human affairs. The personalization of ultimate being after Philo, as sustained by the Christian Church fathers, implied a yet greater exaltation of equity, in terms of the divine rule by "economic" adaptation to our circumstances and equally an assumption of historical providence or of divine government of all human history, in continuity with his government of nature.[17] Thus, for Tertullian, the natural law was inherently known to Adam and Eve, who failed to keep it, while the patriarchs prior to Moses again adhered to this unwritten law. For Gregory of Nyssa also, natural law was originally engraved within human nature and he also says that it was restored to nature by the Incarnation, with Moses's giving of the written law being only a foretype of this event. In consequence, the Church alone fully follows and enacts on earth the natural law through her "economy," in such a way as to compensate for the constitutively protean malleability and "absence of a nature" that uniquely defines the human animal.[18] It is therefore far from being the case that natural law was conceived in opposition to temporality or in contrast with the law of revelation. Indeed, the first council of Arles described the natural law as being "the first grace of God."[19]

The second historical origin, whose relation to the first is somewhat obscure, lies in Stoicism. Here the coincidence of physis with nomos is attained, not by the raising of personally enacted law from a middling divine to a fully transcendent height, but rather by the bringing down of divine will to full coincidence with immanent nature and with fate.[20] If Philo's *megalopolis* denotes a "politicisation of nature," since the ontological is now coincident with divine governance, the Stoic *cosmopolis* denotes inversely a "naturalisation of politics." This coincides with its internationalization, initially to some degree convergent with the literal extent of the Roman Empire, though also exceeding it as an ideal order. A mark of this ambiguity is Cicero's identification of the natural law with Roman rule and order itself.[21]

[16] Philo, *On Joseph*, VI, 28; VII, 32.

[17] On all this see (despite several debatable claims) the highly acute and original work of Giorgio Agamben, *The Kingdom and the Glory* (Lorenzo Chiesa tr, Stanford UP 2013).

[18] See Russell Hittinger, "Natural Law and Modern Catholic Theology" in Michael Cromartie (ed), *A Preserving Grace: Protestants, Catholics and Natural Law* (Eerdmans 1997) 1–30.

[19] See Hittinger, "Natural Law and Modern Catholic Theology," 5.

[20] See Malcolm Schofield, *The Stoic Idea of the City* (Chicago UP 1999).

[21] See Hittinger, "Natural Law and Modern Catholic Theology."

It is for this reason that there ensues from Stoicism, by way of Cicero and much Roman thought, a certain prefiguration of the transition from natural law to natural right, which is newly important in the Renaissance and the eighteenth century and central to the arguably first "liberal" theory of Hugo Grotius, which is not accidentally first focussed on the *ius gentium*.[22] To overemphasize, as Moyn does, the cobelonging of private natural right with absolute state sovereignty is to overlook the aporetic authorization of rights by prepolitical nature and yet the operative enactment of this authorization only by the state.

Stoic morality was bifurcated between the *bios* and the *polis*. On the one hand it advocated a resigned identification of the individual with the fate of the natural *cosmopolis*, on the other a dutiful fulfilling of civic *officium* within a specific polity that, in default of any teleological order of just flourishing within a fated and cyclically doomed universe, begins to be defined in terms of both individual and collective utility. At the same time and for the same reasons, the now nonteleological main purpose of the civic empire is for Cicero already the protection of individual life and private property.[23]

Thomist Natural Law

Aspects of the Stoic view were variously integrated into a more fundamentally Philonian view within the Christian era. In the most famous Christian statement of natural law by Thomas Aquinas, these two elements are reinforced by the perspectives of mainly Aristotle, but also Augustine. As for Philo, Aquinas's statement includes, crucially, the affirmation that God is the governor of the world he has created. Law is first of all eternal law, coincident with the *Logos*, the second person of the Trinity, and all other law, natural, revealed, and positive, is only true law insofar as it *participates* in this eternal law.[24] Yet this participation also happens necessarily: in the case of suborganic and most organic nature indeed automatically, insofar as each thing seeks to conserve its own nature and being; in the case of animals additionally by instinct insofar as they feed and reproduce themselves; in the case of rational spirits with the further addition of conscious collaboration or, if

[22] Benjamin Straumann, *Roman Law in the State of Nature: The Classical Foundations of Hugo Grotius' Natural Law* (CUP 2015).
[23] Cicero, *On Duties*, II, xxi, 73, xxii, 78.
[24] ST I.II q 93 a1.

this collaboration be refused, by inevitable negative and corrective impact.[25] If human beings do not participate in eternal justice, then they simply do not flourish.

As to the imperative content of this conscious participation in divine government, it is in one sense both vague and minimal. In no way does Aquinas think, unlike later theorists like Suarez, that divine commands can be "read off" nature and then applied to culture.[26] For Aquinas, the "naturalness" of the law refers as much to its mode of participated perception of the eternal by creatures as to its enforcement through them. But its perception by human beings is confined to its inspiring and rudimentary *seminalia* and does not extend to details. Some canonists were already trying to turn the natural law into a decisionistic instrument. Aquinas, however, generally does not, except in his discussion of polygamy in the *Sentence Commentary*, and there he concludes that the verdict of the natural law is uncertain: polygamy is rather ruled out by typological analogy—as Christ has only one bride, the Church, so men should not take plural wives.[27]

For Aquinas, because the natural law yields so little positive law directly, it must be supplemented by the weight of human tradition, example, and teaching. However, there is no cleavage in Aquinas between nature and positivity, as there is none between intellect and will. The variety and circumstantiality of positive law for him only betokens a prudential and economic attention to equity that the character of natural law itself enjoins. Thus, in effect, for fallen man the discernment of natural law is a work of time and culture and its supplementation by human addition is just what natural law, in its very naturalness, for us most of all requires.

Thus, insofar as we are both created "things" and "created animals" subject to divine government, we must *necessarily* follow the natural law of both self-preservation and self-perpetuation. Beyond that point, as rational animals we are naturally inclined both to live in society and to seek to contemplate the truth, which, for Aquinas, means being ultimately bound to seek unity with God in the beatific vision. Since this vision only comes by grace, and since for Aquinas all of nature is grace-given,[28] it is clear that he does not see the level of "natural law" as totally autonomous with respect to the revealed

[25] ST I.II q 94 a2.
[26] See John Finnis, *Natural Law and Natural Rights* (OUP 2011) 45.
[27] ST "Supplement" and see Russell Hittinger, "Natural Law and Modern Catholic Theology."
[28] ST II.II q 2 a9 ad 1.

law, which gives a deeper degree of participation in the eternal law of God.[29] Indeed, in his *Romans Commentary* he makes it clear that to imagine that one could fulfill the natural law without the aid of grace would be to fall into the heresy of the Pelagians.[30] And while he thinks that we discern the natural law through the natural architectonic virtue of prudence, he also declares that prudence can only be perfected by the "counsel" that is the gift of the Holy Spirit.[31] Again, there is a link to the divine government of history here: the divine prudence, or providence, is infinitely more perfect than ours, on account of divine omniscience. But thanks to the Incarnation, something of this historical as well as ethical sense has now been imparted to us.

Indeed, for Aquinas the proper exercise of the natural law is dependent upon the Incarnation. As Russell Hittinger has stressed, Aquinas did not share the view of most modern Thomists that the Fall left the ethical sense of the human mind in some essential region unimpaired. Nor, a fortiori, did he share the post-Kantian perspective of John Finnis and Germain Grisez that the natural law takes its origins from cognitive rather than ontological structures, or deploys more *a priori* reasoning than it does *a posteriori* observation.[32] To the contrary, just because the Fall involves an insane refusal of divine government, the entire ontological order is wrecked, including the operation of the natural law among human beings. Some glimmerings of it remained *post lapsum*, since total depravity would be impossible short of ontological nullity (because participation in the good is germane to any existence). Nevertheless, the natural law was essentially in this epoch "destroyed" (as Aquinas explicitly says, in a late writing), since the divine government now operates negatively, to human chastisement.[33] It could only be restored through grace: first by the giving of the written law and finally through the incarnation of the *Logos* who is also *Nomos* itself. There was, therefore, as Hittinger underlines, no positive "time of the natural law," having recourse to an ahistorical norm for Aquinas, unlike the majority of modern Thomists.

[29] See Eugene F Rogers Jr, *Aquinas and the Supreme Court: Race, Gender and the Failure of Natural Law in Thomas's Biblical Commentaries* (Wiley-Blackwell 2013).

[30] Aquinas, *In Romans* 2:14 (§ 216).

[31] ST II.II q 52.

[32] Hittinger, "Natural Law."

[33] Hittinger, "Natural Law," 7.

Natural Law and Postsecularity

This account of Aquinas runs counter to most modern Catholic attempts to make his natural law theory "universally relevant" to those of all beliefs and none. Does it therefore render natural law completely irrelevant to people in the world today? To the contrary, it is the most seemingly alien features that, when properly considered, can also be seen as now most congenial in a postmodern and perhaps postsecular era.

First, the opening of law and justice to divinely given grace has a pre-echo in Aristotle's suggestion that justice is contained within friendship rather than the other way around and is only fulfilled, paradoxically beyond justice, as friendship, which expresses the gratuitous eternal spiral of the dance of the three graces.[34] Somehow, then, the free exchange of gifts is more than necessary for Aristotle and yet the most necessary thing of all. Love exceeds justice, yet if justice is for harmony and community, it can only be completed by the interplay of love. And this of course implies that any legitimate human state must be concerned with promoting good relationships—certainly with fair transactions, but even beyond that with the fostering of meaningful fraternity and sorority. Clearly, again, this lies in excess of the more limited concern of natural rights with equal given individual status, leaving the state "agnostic" as to any concern with what goes on "between us," despite the fact that all of actual, content-filled life is always to do with this interval.

How, though, can the political state be concerned with "grace," with ritual belief, style, and practice in a pluralist society? Here again, the real Aquinas can be of help. For him, although there is ultimately no clear dividing line between natural and revealed law, there is nonetheless a distinction. Consequently, there may be alternative and even coexisting religious "completions" of a more widely accepted shared order, and also they can contribute to and intermingle in that generally shared sense of order, just because this distinction implies no firmly locatable boundary. Although, of course, Aquinas made no such pluralist suggestion of this kind, it becomes all the more conceivable insofar as for him the natural law of political practice and philosophical contemplation is to be discerned by the judging faculty of *synderesis* in terms of (rather vague and ineffable) "principles," and by the circumstantially attuned faculty of *prudentia* in the case of "application." This is unlike some early modern scholastic conceptions, which discern natural

[34] Aristotle, *Eudemian Ethics*, VII, x, 5–20; *Nicomachean Ethics*, VIII–IX.

law by rational assumptions from which conclusions are deduced according to an abstract theoretical logic.[35] Hence, one could read him as saying that the affirmation of law is the regulative assertion for practical knowledge (though with ontological bearing) that there *exists* objective good, not made up by us. It is possible, in consequence, for us to make an individual effort to discern and to engage in a continued collective debate (as for Socrates, Plato, Aristotle, etc.) about this goodness that we can only share in by living a properly human life. It is then also possible, with various degrees of assent, to allow that religious intuition and tradition contribute to or complete this process of debate and discernment.

Arguably, Aquinas's outlook runs more with current nonreflexive instinctual common sense than do natural rights perspectives. On the whole, people imagine that their interactions with others are amenable to equitable assessment; that prices should not be extortionate and salaries impossibly bloated (despite "the market"); that the relative needs of women, men, and children in relationships can be ethically and then legally mediated; and that sentencing and judgments in courts should be proportionate rather than determined solely by precedent and deterrent effect. Likewise, they still often suppose that there should be some sort of approximate match between human ability, achievement, and needs on the one hand and rewards and resources on the other.[36] Currently, we see an inchoate global rebellion against economic inequity and yet it is clear that neither economic liberalism nor the welfarist liberalism of entitlement can do much about this in default of a *cultural* shift that would see the lack of such equity as both dishonorable and dishonoring.

Aquinas's linking of natural law to a certain supernaturalized account of history seems, of course, yet more alien and unhelpful in a secular era—yet natural rights accounts have been unable to dispense with theologies of history. And one problem with these theologies is that they tend to involve a sharp rupture between the natural and the cultural, according to a "biopolitical" cleavage that renders modern thought problematically divided between the thesis that humanity belongs to a factually given nature on the one hand, and the equally strong view that it is an artificial construct on the other. In the case of early modern scholasticism, this cleavage encourages the view that the natural law is now *theoretically* "based upon" given factual

[35] See Rogers, *Aquinas and the Supreme Court*, 23–146.
[36] See John Milbank, "Dignity Rather than Right" (2014) 5(7) Open Insight 77–124.

features that then dictate deductively the norms of practical construction. This perspective facilitates a Stoicizing drift toward the primacy of self and social preservation, besides a greater stress on the biologically given natural units that are human individuals, rather than upon cultural relationships that now tend to be seen as more "artificial" or, especially in the case of Francisco Suarez, as the vehicles for a willed confirmation that the naturally suggested does indeed possess legal force.[37] For Suarez, in keeping with Stoicism rather than Aquinas, the natural law derives from the structures of our reasoning in detachment from social and cultural insertion. This reasoning is exercised by theoretical observation of rationally graspable consistencies in nature—a stress that tends to downplay the teleological. But the actual force of law added to nature comes from will alone—human or divine—and for this reason Suarez already articulates the scission and yet problematic co-dependence between *bios* and *polis* that is so fundamental to the perspective of Thomas Hobbes.[38]

In consequence, this shift encourages a further swerve away from an objective to a subjective foundation of now already more subjectivized right. Powers and capacities become not so much signs of dutiful responsibilities as themselves the subjective source of naturalized subjective rights, even if these remain underwritten by the divine absolute power, itself seen as the source of God's overriding legitimacy.[39]

By contrast, Aquinas's perspective assumes that, while culture "adds to" nature and does not simply copy or "represent" it, it can indeed do so "naturally," just because what we take to be valuable human habits can be seen as completing, in a somehow intended way, that which naturally precedes us.[40] The alternative is to suppose with Hobbes that "what is really going on" is just prehuman material forces working through humanity, while all our proud cultural artifices are so many fairy tales. But again, one could submit that this is not how humans regularly and almost automatically think, if they are not corrupted by modern liberal pseudo-reflexivity. People imagine spontaneously that in the best aspects of their lives they are in multiple ways

[37] See Michel Villey, *La formation,* 347–368. See also on late scholasticism and the transition to Grotius, Heinrich Rommen, *Natural Law: A Study in Legal and Social History and Philosophy* (Thomas R Hanley tr, Liberty Fund 2014 [1936]).

[38] Villey, *La formation,* 360–362.

[39] Hobbes, *Leviathan,* Part 3, ch XXXII.

[40] Natural law is not itself for Aquinas a habit, but consistently following it can become so. For a brilliant argument concerning the nonarbitrariness and yet nonmimicry of linguistic and cultural "addition," see Rowan Williams, *The Edge of Words: God and the Habits of Language* (Bloomsbury 2014). See also Félix Ravaisson, *On Habit* (Clare Carlisle and Mark Sinclair tr, Continuum 2008).

"beautifying" the world and that this cannot be a fantasy, else beauty would be an illusion and not worth the effort. Here it is important to note that it is not Aquinas who is guilty of misconstruing facts as values, and so of seeing merely given nature as an unproblematic guide to life, but rather the early modern revision of natural law and its evolution into foundational natural rights.

The point here is that Hobbes, in an exemplary fashion, *at once* claims simply to read-off from nature and yet *at the same time* sees values as entirely a construct, since their content is arbitrary and their real "substance" is now merely formal and materially constrained. Aquinas, to the contrary, just because he is innocent of any cleavage between fact/value, as of any nature/culture duality, takes it to be the case that nature is already a process that generates newly different and meaningful "forms," including psychic forms, and that human culture continues this process in an intensified way, such that "added value" is also a further emergence of the naturally factual. It is clearly teleology that provides the linkage between these two.[41] Thus, Thomas is able to think both that we are freely participating in the eternal law as natural creatures through our exercise of judgment and that thereby we are in conformity with nature and mediate the divine government. It is for this reason that, far from thinking of the natural law as an unalterable code, he declares that it may imply different courses of action in different circumstances.[42] Thereby, he recognizes the dynamism of nature as such—the unalterable lies for him with eternity, and not with finitude or time, whose consistent measures arrive only insofar as they bend toward the eternal.

The History of Natural Right

Given this revisionary account of natural law in Western history, how does it relate to the story of natural rights? In the case of Aquinas, as with many other medieval theologians, and the canon law itself, the Christian exaltation of individual uniqueness and liberty led to a greater recognition of subjective rights in the sense of both claim and exercise rights. However, the claims generally remained claims upon others to exercise primary duties, while

[41] I consider that there are very good arguments for natural and biological teleology that are indispensable for a natural law outlook, but these cannot be developed here.

[42] ST I.II q 94 aa4–5.

exercise rights were attached to social roles whose duties were derived from justice as distribution.[43] Later, in the sixteenth century, in the case of both Catholic and Calvinist thought, there was a greater development of the idea of "rights" as attaching to human beings as such, especially with respect to life, freedom, and ownership. These universal claim-rights of humans upon all other humans were now indeed overemphasized, in relative neglect of equity (upon which see further later).[44] They were not as yet usually based on a subjective foundation, sundered from notions of right cosmic order. But the concept of order was now regarded too theoretically and "factually," rather than prudentially, encouraging a false "non-negotiability" of fundamental right and obligation. Thus, rights to feed and clothe and protect oneself followed in Catholic teaching from one's duty to do so as God's creature, as revealed by the factual circumstances of one's given nature, while Protestant defenses of the liberty of religious conscience similarly derived from the view that without this right one could not do one's sincere, unconstrained duty toward God.[45]

Here one can note that today it is becoming clear that, without any sense of religion as necessarily an intrinsic good, the rights of religious freedom are liable to lapse, even though so many of our other liberties are in historical reality derived from them.

By contrast, the substitution of a general right of conscience for religious liberty is likely in practice to inhibit all religious and group freedoms, because it tends always to favor the plea of the individual against any form of perceived "pressure"—as, for example, the wearing of religious symbols at work, or the demands of a nonpolitical corporate body that its members adhere to its regulations. Since most of our capacities are achieved through collaboration and association, the real effect of this is eventually to reduce even individual freedoms.

Indeed, the historical development of religious freedom in terms of the right to associate and to form rule-bound subcommunities has been crucial to the history of Western liberty. This right was much developed, in the wake of medieval corporate jurisprudence, by Calvinist thinkers like Althusius in the Netherlands. But here again it was considered subordinate to our *duty* to

[43] See Milbank, "Against Human Rights."

[44] See Annabel S Brett, *Liberty, Right and Nature: Individual Rights in Later Scholastic Thought* (CUP 2003).

[45] See John Witte Jr, *The Reformation of Rights: Law, Religion and Human Rights in Early Modern Calvinism* (CUP 2007). Even if "human rights" is here something of an anachronistic misnomer, the book makes an important addition to the history of rights theory.

enter into neighborly formations. Sometimes, indeed, the grounding of this natural law lay ultimately in the divine will rather than the divine reason, but that did not *necessarily* mean that the primacy of self-determination was echoed at the human level.[46] All the same, one can also note here, with Michel Villey, that Althusius, unlike Aquinas, derives the right of associations themselves finally from the individual right to associate, rather than from the embodiment of relational justice that an association has entered into. So here, as in other instances, an overweighting toward a subjective content of rights does start to slide toward their subjective foundation, though without explicitly getting there.[47]

Later developments of the Protestant legacy, shading off into enlightenment, tended to cast off the voluntarist residue in any case, though generally also to lose the "covenanting" impulse in favor of more individualist Stoic notions of *officium,* combined with "sentimental" and at times egoistically projected notions of fellow-feeling. It seems to have been exactly the unnatural hybrid of contract theory with the ethics of sympathy that led to the eventual replacement of natural rights with the rights of man, thereby somewhat obscuring the biopolitical aporia as to the relative naturalness or civility of all human *ius.*[48]

It then follows that, as several scholars have now shown, most natural rights thinking up till, and even including, the American Revolution still remained inserted in a natural law, cosmic order context, even if the increasing focus upon subjective property rights implicitly tended to unsettle this adherence.[49] Rights, however to the fore, remained, if one looks closely, even for someone like Thomas Jefferson, ultimately subordinate to duties to others and to God. Nevertheless, from early modernity onward there is an imbalance, as compared with Aquinas. It is considerably forgotten, as Annabel Brett rightly stresses, that justice is mainly *ad alterum,* even if one properly claims the assertion of universal natural rights (as correlated with duty and "generally" rather than "universally" holding) to religious liberty, security of life and property, free speech, etc., as legitimate advances, compatible (given the limiting protocols just indicated) with the spirit of genuine Thomism.[50]

46 John Witte Jr, *The Reformation of Rights,* 143–207.

47 Villey, *La formation,* 513–527.

48 See Knud Haakonssen, *Natural Law and Moral Philosophy: From Grotius to the Scottish Enlightenment* (CUP 1996) 310–341; Moyn, *Human Rights and the Uses of History,* 1–18.

49 Haakonssen, *Natural Law and Moral Philosophy,* passim.

50 Annabel S Brett, *Liberty, Right and Nature: Individual Rights in Later Scholastic Thought* (CUP 2010) passim.

But what happens *between people* in terms of economic interaction and social behavior tended to get relatively (if as yet by no means completely) amoralized and so handed over to power and convention or the spectacle of mere fashion and customs of untrustworthy *politesse.* Just by reason of this neglect of the relational, the explicit stress tended to fall upon rights rather than duties, even though the latter remained precariously foundational, since the main anxiety of the age was to ensure that people could exercise their perceived responsibility without interference.

Modern Theologies of Rights

After the seventeenth century, pure self-founded natural rights emerge roughly in two versions, which can be associated respectively with the American and the French Revolutions. And it is important to take careful note of this linkage, which effectively wrenches natural right away from natural law in the double name of the absolutely sovereign state and the originally isolated individual—arguably in defiance of all more fundamental social realities, before the revolutions and since.

In the "American" case, one can note three circumstances, which all have to do with the fact that natural rights cannot really be sufficient to provide a political foundation.

First, the individuals who enter into a contract with mere self-interest on either side are bound to find, as George Grant and Jean-Claude Michéa have variously argued, that the contract comes to rule them, rather than the other way round.[51] A contract is an impersonal formal procedure and therefore is in automatic alliance with technology and bureaucracy. Thus, in a liberal society on the American model, the space of free choice will be more and more constrained, though more and more closely guarded, while the public sphere will be handed over to impenetrable process, beyond the reach of reciprocal and consensual alteration.

As Werner Hammacher has argued, the possessive individualist construal of rights can never really suppress the anarchic agonism of its starting presupposition, whereby everyone is potentially an enemy to everyone else, with no positive construal of human collective or social identity, as affirmed by

[51] George Parkin Grant, *English-Speaking Justice* (Notre Dame UP 1985); Jean-Claude Michéa, *The Realm of Lesser Evil* (David Fernbach tr, Polity 2009).

Marx's idea of man as "species being."[52] The notion that one should exercise one's own liberty only insofar as it does not intrude upon the freedom of others is not, in isolation, actionable as a moral imperative. It is obvious that this boundary is always in some degree breached and also that the very erection of a boundary depends on the contingent establishing of arbitrary property boundaries, without which the reach and range of what is strictly "one's own" has to remain elusive. The Hobbes-Locke model of possessive individualism (whereby selfhood is defined in terms of self-ownership)[53] tacitly acknowledges this state of affairs by regarding the nontransgressable boundary of noninterference between people as not intuitively *a priori*, but rather as only establishable by agreed-upon, fictionally "initial," contractual convention.

But what is more, this contract is only enforceable by an all-powerful sovereign "state" whose novel "statehood" is itself defined by artificially achieved stasis, rather than by any claim to participation in divine equity. Since, after the official commencement, it is the state (even if, as for Locke, subject to some representational checks) that must continuously define and redefine the actual content of contractual boundaries, this means that established natural rights only have civic existence when, in reality, the originally violent natural liberty of some is civilly licensed to be enacted over others. In consequence their supposedly "absolute" right (both natural and civil) is in reality inhibited as a paradoxical precondition of the very possibility of asserting "absolute" rights at all.

Secondly, since rights are natural and yet only exist through contractual agreement under the state, they necessarily enter an aporia. This further illustrates Hammacher's crucial point that the artificial contractual suppression of original natural anarchy *depends* on the continued constrained channeling of this very anarchy. As Hannah Arendt pointed out, one only needs natural rights when one cannot have them since, as in the case of the refugee, one falls outside the scope of the state.[54] In that case, it becomes undecidable whether or not outcasts have rights. It is pointless to say here with Jacques Rancière that a zero-rights position is never actually reached, because this only means that all humans, even refugees, enter into some

[52] Werner Hammacher, "The Right Not to Use Rights" in Hent de Vries and Lawrence E. Sullivan (eds), *Political Theologies: Public Religions in a Post-Secular World* (Fordham UP 2006) 671–690.

[53] Locke, *Two Treatises*, Second Treatise, ch V, 27; Hobbes, *Leviathan*, Part I, ch XIV, 64.

[54] Hannah Arendt, *The Origins of Totalitarianism* (Harcourt 1968) 290–302.

sort of minimal polity.[55] The point is the asymptotic tendency toward what Giorgio Agamben calls *homo sacer,* rather than its impossible actual attainment.[56] If their rights are undecidable as between "already there" and "not as yet enacted," then, inevitably, states will decide to activate some natural not-as-yet rights and to ignore others, or even to suppress already existent political rights according to international law in the name of the protection of rights in general. This last possibility connects to a further aporetic dimension regarding natural rights that has already been invoked—the fact that they belong absolutely to the individual but do so in the contractual interests of all as guaranteed by the state. Just as the individual may well decide in revolutionary fashion that his or her rights are after all not respected by the state (and there are no real *criteria* for this, so the anti-federal militiamen in the US outback are perfectly respectable Lockeans), so likewise the state may decide that certain legitimate freedoms or protections must be suspended in the interests of state security that alone renders natural rights operable. One does not need to spell out how all these things have been exemplified in recent American history.

In the third place, the cult of a foundational possessive individualism of itself clearly courts social, economic, and even political disorder. To compensate for this, American and initially Anglo-Saxon, and before that French Jansenist proto- liberalism had to have recourse to a theory of history whereby God or nature governs fallen men despite or through their amoral passions or even deranged instincts.[57] But once more, the reality of the heterogenesis of ends is the dominance of impersonal, technological processes, which in reality are manipulated or tacitly encouraged by several visible, human hands, whether of egoistic individuals, monopolies, or the entrepreneurial state. At the same time there has, at least till recently, always remained by contrast a more cooperative and intentional aspect to the market economy, driven by a teleological love of things and people (as, for example, with the history of Quaker- or Methodist-led manufacturing) than the theory of pure "capitalism" would allow. And finally, the more this theory of history has been enacted, the more we see that the ends of amoral or malign actions are a mass

[55] Jacques Rancière, "Who Is the Subject of the Rights of Man?" (2004) 103(2/3) South Atlantic Quarterly 297–310.

[56] Giorgio Agamben, *Homo Sacer: Sovereign Power and Bare Life* (Daniel Heller-Roazen tr, Stanford UP 1998)and *State of Exception* (Kevin Attell tr, Chicago UP 2005).

[57] See Simone Meysonnier, *La Balance et l'Horloge: La genèse de la pensée libérale en France au XVIIIe siècle* (Les Éditions de la Passion 1989) 35–51; Serge Latouche, *L'invention de l'économie* (Albin Michel 2005) 154–160.

criminal compounding of the nature of the original isolated intentions. Here a false theology still governs us to our continued peril.

In the second, "French" version of natural right, the theory of possessive individualism is apparently abandoned, by first Rousseau and then Kant, in the name of a purer presence to self of a freedom that one cannot possess. But arguably this is to simply occupy the other, anti-legal, possession-free half of the Franciscan cleavage between person and property, and it is no accident that Rousseau shares with the Franciscan spirituals the conception of an isolated and pure, originally quasi-animal human existence. Thus, not right as possession is here emphasized, but the right simply to have right, or the freedom simply to be free as one is given to be (beyond and before any self-creation) and even to dispense with possession, and thereby right itself as dominium and consent to any dominium if one so chooses.[58] For this theory, then, in the case of Rousseau, the collective right of the people, founded ultimately in their individual natural rights, can never be alienated to any representatives, as it lies beyond the scope of a possession that can be sold or transferred.

Given this endemic insecurity of pure freedom in the face of alien possession, the French way has tried to supplement pure freedom with collective vigilance and state organization, just as the American way has tried to supplement possessive individualism with the cunning of reason. But if the latter risks criminality and anarchy, gun crime and mob rule, the former from the outset has risked terror, as famously analyzed by Hegel, in terms of an endless search to root out any exercise of assertive positive freedom or of teleological virtue that might inhibit the pure, supposedly "virtuous" options of negative liberty.[59] And all this has also from the outset been strongly sauced with a sense of sympathy and pity for inhibited "victims," as again Hannah Arendt once argued.[60] Obvious terror may have speedily passed, but Fichte's advocacy of the French way as pure atemporal practice (in contrast to Hegel's "Anglo-Saxon" advocacy of historical heterogenesis) is allied in his thinking, as Hegel also noticed, to a continuous intensification of police regulation, of the kind that has grown exponentially in our own day—restricting all our substantive freedoms in the name of liberty itself.

[58] See Hammacher, "The Right Not to Use Rights." But Hammacher in the end also goes in the impossible Rousseauist direction of wanting *yet more* unmediated rights attached to supposedly pure Levinasian "alterities."

[59] See John Milbank, *Theology and Social Theory* (2nd edn, Blackwell 2006) 147–176.

[60] Hannah Arendt, *On Revolution* (Penguin 2009) 89; Moyn, *Human Rights and the Uses of History*, 8–10.

In the end, for the Rousseauian-Kantian trajectory, the essence of right, even ethical right as moral law, lies not in its release or exercise, but always in its inhibition with regard to the acknowledging of the freedom of others. This inhibition is not, as for classical or medieval tradition, a matter of my own inherent flourishing, of suppressing false desires in favor of truer ones, but always the suppression of desire tout court in recognition of an after all heteronomous social obligation, impinging extrinsically.

Absolute rights to life, liberty, and property are never in practice absolute, because only the state defines their legitimate bounds and must constantly protect its right to define these bounds, else the absoluteness of rights itself will be a dead letter.

And of course one can deconstruct this scenario, As Hegel saw, the truth of the matter is that the supposedly noumenal is also political: for it is only if liberty and truth are defined in literally formal and so disguisedly human legal terms that one could imagine that any imperative is both categorical and imperative, because then alone the boundaries between the free and the unfree, the true and the untrue are uncontroversial, in a spurious independence of all circumstance. The truth of this maneuver is that, by subordinating even the ethical to the law, as with Kant, one will in reality and in the long term (as we see today) define the publicly ethical in terms of the legal, this being in reality the only imperative that is categorically operative. As Michel Villey insisted, the assumption of natural law and of the older European juridical tradition is just the opposite: the subordination of *lex* to *ius* as objective right, and so of legislation to a goodness existing independently of the human.

Conclusions

In all the ways that I have indicated in this chapter, one can readily argue that liberalism, even Kantian liberalism, is not, after all, metaphysically agnostic. To the contrary, the other aspect to its ethical minimalism is clearly a materializing and reductive ontology. This observation therefore challenges the liberal assumption that liberal societies are really neutral as to belief or metaphysical assertion. Perhaps such neutrality is impossible, in which case one could argue that the public and established bias ought to run toward nobler, more "ideally realist" beliefs and affirmations, likely to be more romantically aspiring.

This all implies, I think, that justice is a wider context than rights, and that rights should be adjudicated in the context of justice. Rights without justice prove exponentially expandable and then unmediable. How are we to coordinate, for example, the right of an immigrant to nondeportation with the right of citizens to security from terrorism—to allude to some recent instances? On the other hand, justice without regard to rights, properly understood, can sink into positivism and utilitarianism. We need to consider both the initiatory and claim rights of individuals (as founded in the natural order) and the equity of relations, and to link these together in terms of the always mutual belonging of rights and duties. One can say that each individual has a claim right—rather than outright "entitlement"—to expect that other human beings, and the public at large, including its state aspect, will help them to find work, accommodation, health, education, and security, combined with the enabling of creative work, beautiful housing, preventive health, ethically formative education, and true adventure besides security. However if this is seen primarily and foundationally as a right and not as a collective duty, then all we are doing is building at once both a further bed of resources for unfettered capitalism and a further licence to state control and instrumentalization of our lives.

21

Subsidiarity

Origins and Contemporary Aspects

Iain T. Benson[1]

Introduction

This chapter discusses the nature and ongoing relevance of the principle of subsidiarity in constitutional law. Subsidiarity is, in brief, an organizing principle. The Latin term subsidium (literally: help or aid) underlies the concept, which states that as much as possible matters should be organized in ways so that the larger aspects of a society (nation, state, etc.) assist the local, the smaller, and the more personal aspects (persons, families, associations, etc.) to undertake their proper functions. As a consequence, subsidiarity furthers diversity rather than homogeneity and the local rather than the distant. The justification for this ordering is so that the smaller aspects are enabled to realize those ends that are proper to their true natures rather than being submerged or interfered with unduly by the larger powers surrounding them. The principle is found in Aristotle but was developed principally in Roman Catholic social philosophy. The idea is derived not from anthropology but from the nature of human society. Aristotle noted that the city is naturally composed of certain natural groupings—families, tribes, associations, neighborhoods, villages—and that these groupings are sufficient for some tasks but not for others.[2] The city may assist the smaller by giving them what they need to survive and achieve their goals. The social doctrine of the Catholic Church has given increasing attention to subsidiarity, and

[1] The author acknowledges Nicholas Aroney and Ian Leigh, and Russell Hittinger, Mary Ann Glendon, Bradley Miller, Peter Lauwers, Shaun de Freitas, Shann Turnbull, Jamie Hardigg, Steven Lovell-Jones, and Peter Williams. He also acknowledges, with thanks, the Small Circle Philosopher's Group and, in particular, Christo Lombaard (Pretoria) and Kristof Vanhoutte (Paris Institute for Critical Thinking).

[2] *Politics*, 1252 b 10–29.

Iain T. Benson, *Subsidiarity: Origins and Contemporary Aspects* in *Christianity and Constitutionalism.*
Edited by: Nicholas Aroney and Ian Leigh, Oxford University Press. © Oxford University Press 2022.
DOI: 10.1093/oso/9780197587256.003.0021

analogous ideas have been developed within Protestant thought, as will be discussed in this chapter.[3]

Recent work shows that subsidiarity principles are relevant across diverse areas of contemporary culture. A partial list would include federalism,[4] globalization, environment sustainability, elder care,[5] corporate governance,[6] localism,[7] economic and monetary reform,[8] and greater civil society involvement in constitutional development.[9] Subsidiarity, grasped in its fullness, is more than de-centralization since it is concerned particularly with matters at their proper level, not simply their "smaller" level (as is sometimes stated erroneously).

This chapter consists of five substantial parts. The first part reviews important definitions and conceptual frames in contemporary culture relevant to our thinking about subsidiarity. The second part deals with some of the background and origins of subsidiarity in classical and other historical and theological contexts. The third part discusses civil society and related notions as a specific nexus for subsidiarity. The fourth part turns to key related concepts and several questionable distinctions that pose challenges to applying subsidiarity today. The fifth part discusses, by way of conclusion, conceptions of subsidiarity as furthering either diversity or homogeneity and why moves toward statism increasingly have a "religious" character.

[3] Roland Minnerath, "The Fundamental Principles of Social Doctrine. The Issue of Their Interpretation" in Margaret S Archer and Pierpaolo Donati (eds), *Pursuing the Common Good: How Solidarity and Subsidiarity Can Work Together*, Acta 14, Proceedings of the 14th Plenary Session of the Pontifical Academy of Social Sciences (Pontificia Academia Scientiarum 2008) 45–56, 51–54.

[4] Jacob Deem, Robyn Hollander, and AJ Brown, "Subsidiarity in the Australian Public Sector: Finding Pragmatism in the Principle" (2015) 74(4) Australian Journal of Public Administration 419–434, 432. See also Nicholas Aroney's chapter on "Federalism" in this volume (chapter 15, above).

[5] Lucia A Silecchia, "The When and Where of Love: Subsidiarity as a Framework for Care of the Elderly" in Robert F Cochran Jr and Zachary R Calo (eds), *Agape, Justice and Law: How Might Christian Love Shape Law?* (Cambridge University Press 2017) 209–277.

[6] E.g., Shann Turnbull, "Stakeholder Governance: A Cybernetic and Property Rights Analysis" in RI Tricker (ed), *The History of Management Thought: Corporate Governance* (Ashgate 2000) 401–403.

[7] See *Policy Studies*: Mark Evans, David Marsh, and Gerry Stoker, "Understanding Localism" (2013) 34(4) Policy Studies 401–407.

[8] Elinor Ostrom, "Beyond Markets and States: Polycentric Governance of Complex Economic Systems" <https://www.nobelprize.org/prizes/economic-sciences/2009/ostrom/lecture/> accessed 5 June 2020.

[9] See the section later in this chapter discussing the South African Charter of Religious Rights and Freedoms.

The Nature of Subsidiarity

While the principle of subsidiarity is nondenominational, its conceptual development has occurred mainly within the social thought of the Roman Catholic Church. Put succinctly, subsidiarity provides the framework or organizing principles of a culture, while its sister concept, solidarity, is the moral or ethical principle that operates within that frame. The result of the proper relationship between these two principles—organization and moral content—is then worked out as justice and the common good. Subsidiarity proceeds from an understanding of human beings as persons in relation—in contrast to the "autonomous individuals" of contemporary liberal theory. According to the *Compendium of the Social Doctrine of the Church*, "a community of a higher order should not interfere in the internal life of a community of a lower order, depriving the latter of its functions, but rather should support it in case of need and help to co-ordinate its activity with the activities of the rest of society, always with a view to the common good."[10]

Subsidiarity relates to local forms including municipalities, school boards, education, guilds and trade unions, socio-professional groups, associations of a wide variety, and, importantly, the family. It connects directly with wider "civil society" notions as well as to the region, the state, and beyond. The principle has both positive and negative aspects. Positively, it means that all communities should encourage and enable individuals to exercise self-responsibility, with larger communities assisting the smaller. Negatively, communities must not deprive smaller communities or individuals of the opportunity to exercise their own functions. Minnerath notes the importance of "participation," which is defined as the expression of "the equal dignity of each person and of his or her common vocation to deal with the issues concerning him or her."[11] Whereas the common good and solidarity derive from the nature of the person, subsidiarity "arises from the need for good governance" and is a movement that begins from the bottom up, not the top down.[12] As Minnerath notes, the principle "demands the real practice of a democracy of proximity."[13]

[10] *The Compendium of the Social Doctrine of the Church* (Editrice Vaticana 2009) para. 433, 187ff.; see also Pope Pius XI, *Quadragesimo Anno* (15 May 1931) para 79; Pope John XIII, *Pacem in Terris* (11 April 1963) para 140–141 (the universal authority securing the proper function of local public authorities); J Messner, *Social Ethics: Natural Law in the Modern World* (JJ Doherty tr, B. Herder Book Co. 1949) 196ff. Subsidiarity overlaps with notions of sovereignty and federalism: see chapters 9 and 15 by Harrison and Aroney, respectively, in this volume.

[11] *Politics*, 1252 b 51.

[12] Ibid, 56.

[13] Ibid, 53.

Subsidiarity is a *check* on command and control hierarchies, not a *block*: the state still has its proper function.[14] The larger and smaller dimensions of a culture have their proper roles, which may include horizontal and vertical relations. Statist approaches that favor the highest level of control are antithetical to the spirit of subsidiarity but consistent with Marxist-Leninism and socialism.[15] Chiliastic socialist societies throughout history have subverted private property, religion, and the family to centralize power.[16] Hittinger calls subsidiarity "the deepest and most searching element in modern Catholic social thought."[17]

Protestant and classical thinkers have developed similar notions to the Roman Catholic doctrine of subsidiarity, and contemporary scholarship shows an increasing interest in the relevance of the concept.[18] The varied and different ways in which Roman Catholic and Protestant theology embrace or reject philosophy, while important to consideration or rejection of subsidiarity, are beyond the scope of this chapter.[19]

Protestant writer Johannes Althusius (1557–1638) understood that all social union is both federal and covenantal, creating a single pluralistic order of intersecting covenantal associations including "simple" or "private"

[14] See *Compendium of the Social Doctrine of the Church*, para 188. State intervention to "create conditions of greater, equality, justice and peace," as long as necessary and only in relation to the situation's *exceptional* nature, may be advisable.

[15] Igor Shafarevich, *The Socialist Phenomenon* (Harper & Row 1980) 269. On communist strategy with respect to associations see Sheila Fitzpatrick, *The Commissariat of the Enlightenment: Soviet Organization of Education and the Arts under Lunarcharsky* (Cambridge University Press 1970) 227ff.

[16] Karl Marx criticized individualism under capitalism. See Shlomo Avineri, *The Social and Political Thought of Karl Marx* (Cambridge University Press 1968) 33, 84–95. Pope Leo XIII in his influential encyclical *Rerum Novarum* (On the Condition of the Working Classes) (1891) noted the problems of scale in relation to both socialism and capitalism, and the importance of the protection of family life and the property of private societies and associations (paras 9, 38–40).

[17] Russell Hittinger, "Social Pluralism and Subsidiarity in Catholic Social Doctrine" (2002) 16 *Annales Theologici* 385, 407; *Catechism*, para 1884.

[18] Jonathan Chaplin, "Subsidiarity as a Political Norm" in Jonathan Chaplin and Paul Marshall (eds), *Political Theory and Christian Vision* (University Press of America 1994); Jonathan Chaplin, "Subsidiarity and Social Pluralism" in M Evans and A Zimmerman (eds), *Global Perspectives on Subsidiarity, Ius Gentium: Comparative Perspectives on Law and Justice* (Springer 2014) 65–83; D McIlroy, "Subsidiarity and Sphere Sovereignty: Christian Reflections on the Size, Shape and Scope of Government" (2003) 45 Journal of Church and State 739; Rex Ahdar and Ian Leigh, *Religious Freedom on the Liberal State* (2nd edn, OUP 2013) 110ff.; Norman Doe, *Christian Law: Contemporary Principles* (CUP 2013) 346ff.

[19] From a Catholic perspective: Thomas Gilby, *Between Community and Society: A Philosophy and Theology of the State* (Longmans 1953); from a Protestant perspective: Emil Brunner, *Justice and the Social Order* (Mary Hottinger tr, Lutterworth Press 1945); and from an Eastern Orthodox perspective: Cyril Hovorun, *Political Orthodoxies: The Unorthodoxies of the Church Coerced* (Fortress Press 2018).

associations (family and collegium) and "mixed" or "public" associations (city, province, and commonwealth).[20] Scholars have also addressed Neo-Calvinism and Catholicism in relation to the Protestant concept of sphere sovereignty and the relation between Church and state post–Vatican II within the Roman Catholic context.[21]

James W. Skillen and Rockne M. McCarthy expressed concerns about the Catholic approach to the incorporation of Greek thought, particularly teleology, and the relationship between grace and nature and what they saw as a tendency toward individualism.[22] These concerns have been addressed by Catholic scholar Russell Hittinger, who notes that the theme of *munera* in Catholic thought is similar to "sphere sovereignty."[23] Hittinger explains the difference between Catholic and "liberal discourse" in which the Catholic was suspicious of the market model of social pluralism and focused on the intrinsic importance of social forms (family, private school, churches, labor unions), whereas the liberal saw society principally in instrumental ways (power checking power).[24]

Subsidiarity, says Hittinger, does not tell us who has which function or *munus*. One has to look elsewhere, that is, to natural positive or divine law.[25] He then makes four important observations: first, the principle does not require action at the "lowest possible level" but, rather, at the "proper level"; second, no deficiency in the person or office is implied by receipt of the subsidium; third, sometimes real deficiencies (such as a family breakdown) require another power to assist; and fourth, the principle does not of itself constitute a social ontology—rather, the *esse proprium* of each office or institution is presupposed and should not be usurped.

[20] Thomas O Hueglin, *Early Modern Concepts for a Late Modern World: Althusius on Community and Federalism* (Wilfred Laurier University Press 1999) 152–168. On dignity in Althusius's writings and its tie with subsidiarity, see Nicholas Aroney, "The Social Ontology of Human Dignity" in Angus JL Menuge and Barry W Bussey (eds), *The Inherence of Human Dignity: Foundations of Human Dignity* (Anthem 2021) vol 1, 165–183, 175–178.

[21] David T Koyzis "Persuaded, Not Commanded: Neo-Calvinism, *Dignitatus Humanae*, and Religious Freedom" in Kenneth L Grasso and Robert P Hunt (eds), *Religious Freedom: Contemporary Reflections on Vatican II's Declaration on Religious Liberty* (Rowman & Littlefield 2006) 115–133.

[22] James W Skillen and Rockne M McCarthy (eds), "In Critique of Subsidiarity and Autonomy" in *Political Order and the Plural Structure of Society* (Scholar's Press 1991) 382ff.

[23] Russell Hittinger, "Social Pluralism and Subsidiarity in Catholic Social Doctrine" (2002) 16 Annales Theologici 385, 397.

[24] Ibid, 388. Hittinger states that "the idea of *munus* hold[s] together the Aristotelean notion of an *ergon* or characteristic function . . .with the more biblical concept of vocation or mission" (392). See also, Joel Harrison's discussion of plurality in chapter 9 above on "Sovereignty."

[25] Ibid, 395.

These *munera* include the prior rights of family, children, the Church, its seminaries, schools, and charitable organizations, and these provide "the teleological and social framework for the juridical conception of rights."[26] Many of the problematic characteristics of the modern state that have emerged over the last four centuries emerge precisely because powers have been abstracted from the inner nature of the *munera*.

Hittinger notes that *regalitas* (the quality or property of ruling) "is embedded within the structure of human personality"[27] and, quoting *Christofidelis Laici* (1988), notes: "the lay faithful participate . . . in the threefold *munus* of Christ as Priest, Prophet and King."[28]

Historical Origins of Subsidiarity

Subsidiarity has its roots in a particular holistic understanding of nature in which parts are necessarily related to the whole. Along with the related concept of solidarity, both emerge from an understanding of the cosmos as a governed order, the purpose of which can be identified by natural reason observing nature. The concept of subsidiarity must thus be understood as a form and dimension of "natural law" thinking. All human persons as well as human culture and society share a common nature and inherent purposes. To recognize what is good for a person or society, one has to understand how good is assessed. Determining whether a thing (law, concept, institution, practice, etc.) is "fit for purpose" requires relating techné (skills or art—the questions of "how") to telos (the end or purpose of the thing—the question of "why"). Law and politics have the purpose of furthering what is ultimately justice for people and this, within Catholic social thought, relates the organizing principle of subsidiarity with the anthropological and moral understanding of solidarity, which, working together, produce justice and the common good.

At the center of the Catholic social doctrine is the conception of the dignity of the human person and the necessary sociality of human beings. Minnerath tells us this doctrine is inspired by biblical anthropology and the theology of

[26] Ibid, 396–397.
[27] Ibid, 399
[28] *Christifidelis Laici,* Apost Exhort (30 December 1988) para 14; AAs/81 (1989), 410, Enchiridion Vaticanum vol 11, 1050, Hittinger, "Social Pluralism and Subsidiarity in Catholic Social Doctrine" 405.

creation and certain categories drawn from Graeco-Roman thought. Legal positivism and individualism have led to a drifting in interpretations of dignity, common good, solidarity, and subsidiarity that, because the four social virtues of "freedom, truth, justice and solidarity" are not met, lead in the direction of oppression and anarchy.[29]

For Aristotle, man was a *zoon politikon*,[30] a social and political animal endowed with reason. Nicholas Aroney notes that Aristotle's city-state (*polis*) is a composition of two smaller categories of community: the household (*oikia*) and the village (*kome*).[31] Life within the *polis* requires a common perception of the good—or what Aristotle called *sunaisthesis*.[32] Differing from the centralized vision of Plato,[33] Aristotle opposed an extreme unification of the *polis*.

Aquinas developed the idea of differing communities and set out a wider range of private and public forms of human associations and government. He distinguished "public societies" such as cities, provinces, and kingdoms from "private societies" such as households, business partnerships, craft guilds, and religious associations[34] and noted that the tyrant deliberately undermines all forms of social solidarity among subjects and prevents them from joining or enjoying the fruits of various compacts and associations (*confederationes*) from which social friendship, familiarity, and trust are generated.[35]

Aroney observes that the common good has distinctively political dimensions that both John Finnis and Aquinas refer to as the "public good." An encompassing common good is not the same thing as the "public good" and must be limited, and the state should not attempt to enact the wider

[29] Minnerath, "The Fundamental Principles of Social Doctrine," 49.

[30] *Nichomachean Ethics*, 1097b. See also Kung Chuan Hsiao, *Political Pluralism* (Harcourt, Brace & Co. 1927), which reviews Aristotle's notion of sociality and then calls for "a revival of the ethical-teleological viewpoint" (247).

[31] *Politics*, I.1–2. See also Nicholas Aroney, "Subsidiarity in the Writings of Aristotle and Aquinas" in M Evans and A Zimmermann (eds), *Global Perspectives on Subsidiarity* (Springer Dordrecht 2014). Aroney notes that a "household" was broader and had "an emphasis very different from the close marital, parental and filial bonds with which we associate the family today" (13).

[32] John von Heyking, *The Form of Politics: Aristotle and Plato on Friendship* (McGill-Queens University Press 2016) xiii.

[33] *Republic*, V, 449a–466d.

[34] *De Regno*, I 4.7.27; *Republic*, V, 449a–466d. Aroney gives the biblical background for Aquinas's categorizations and notes the nation of Israel was formed out of a plurality of tribes, clans, and families (ST, I-II, 105.1 res, citing Exodus 18:21 and Deuteronomy 1:13, 15). See further Aroney's chapter on "Federalism" in this volume (chapter 15 above).

[35] Nicholas Aroney, "Subsidiarity in the Writings of Aristotle and Aquinas" in M. Evans and A. Zimmermann (eds.), *Global Perspectives on Subsidiarity* (Springer Netherlands, 2014) 9–27, 22.

notion. The external conditions should allow individuals, families, and associations to contribute but should not subject them to an unlimited public authority.[36] While the framework is hierarchical, it includes a wide diversity of jurisdictions that should be properly understood not merely in terms of subordinacy, but as coordinate in relation to specific capacities, each of which have their own jurisdictions that should be respected. Aroney notes, "None of this appears in any of Aristotle's extant writings."[37]

Civil Society, Guilds, Associations, and Local and Informal Rule

Ordering is involved in all human systems (law and politics) whether or not it is acknowledged. The hierarchical aspect means that wherever sovereignty is recognized, the scope and nature of its powers will be present and regulated by law or custom, expressly or implicitly. The term "recognized" here is important because law often recognizes what it does not create and various matters are properly understood as "prior to law" such as liberty itself, the family, friendship, and in most cases religion.

The ideas of civil society, associations, and what we might term "local governance" are important related background notions in any discussion of subsidiarity. Each category may be understood as forms either of homogeneity or of diversity. If we conceive of human beings as parts of a whole merely, without associational or mediating aspects, then we will miss the importance of diversity. On the other hand, if we view human beings as merely individuals, then the question of what binds them together becomes pressing. Both civil society and local governance raise questions of how human beings relate and whether life is viewed as organic or as technological, quantitative, and mechanistic. Civil society and devolved local governance emerge out of conceptions of society that give a preference to the organic and diverse rather than the mechanistic and homogenous.

[36] Ibid, 24, citing John Finnis, *Aquinas: Moral, Political and Legal Theory* (Oxford University Press 1998) 236–237 and n80.

[37] Aroney, "Subsidiarity in the Writings of Aristotle and Aquinas," 22.

Local Governance

The nature and scope of local governance is a live issue today and takes us back to first principles spanning millennia.[38] Elliot and Bailey argue that local government can only occur (or reoccur) properly if "the relevant actors come to see interference in local affairs as improper" and that "the autonomy of local government [needs to be] substantially augmented."[39]

Recent legislation in Scotland, passed unanimously, and which is intended to import the European Charter of Local Self-Government into Scots Law,[40] shows that the issue of local government is very much alive in Britain at the moment. The charter is an international treaty of the Council of Europe signed by the United Kingdom in 1997. It is designed to advance local authorities' governance and finances to the local level as much as possible according to law. The term "subsidiarity" does not appear in the charter's preamble or substantive provisions, but the principle's spirit is there and its adoption by the Council of Europe suggests it has both popularity and continuing relevance alongside the disaffection occasioned by lack of local accountability that has developed over time.

Civil Society, Guilds, and Towns

For Charles Taylor, civil society is "a web of autonomous associations, independent of the state, which [bind] citizens together in matters of common concern, and by their mere existence or action [can] have an effect on public policy."[41] The nexus of families, groups, neighborhoods, and associations that make up civil society was neither foreseen nor planned by anyone; the social is prior to but intimately and organically related to organizing structures that

[38] See Ian Leigh, "The Changing Nature of the Local State" in J Jowell, D Oliver, and C O'Cinneide (eds), *The Changing Constitution* (8th edn, Oxford University Press 2015).

[39] M Elliot and S Bailey, "Taking Local Government Seriously" (2009) 68 Cambridge LJ 436–472, 472.

[40] European Charter of Local Self-Government (Incorporation) (Scotland) Bill (SP Bill 70) introduced into the Scottish Parliament 5 May 2020. The charter says that public responsibilities "shall generally be exercised, in preference, by those authorities which are closest to the citizen" Council of Europe, Article 4(3) of the European Charter of Local Self-Government, Strasbourg, 15. X. 1985, European Treaty Series No 122. <https://archive2021.parliament.scot/parliamentarybusiness/currentcommittees/115604.aspx> accessed 10 May 2021.

[41] Charles Taylor, "Invoking Civil Society" in *Philosophical Arguments* (Harvard University Press 1995) 204–224, 204.

order relationships with or without law.[42] A recognition of "the autonomy of spheres" makes for a greater sharing of social goods than any other conceivable arrangement and its absence would constitute, in fact, the missing dimension of sociality.

All these views contradict theorists who view social institutions as "constructions" furthering a mechanistic and abstract rather than organic and actual conception of culture.[43] Families are shaped by public law, but that does not mean that they are "socially constructed.[44] Theologically, this might be further understood by saying that one cannot love "humanity, only one's family, friends, neighbors, or persons with whom one has contact. Put this way, the interaction between principles of religion, associations, and theories of ordering (including constitutions themselves) becomes apparent. While these dimensions are prior to the state, the law necessarily meets and intersects with them. Where secularism, understood as an anti-religious ideology, is dominant, then religion and civil society in relation to religion will tend to be disregarded. On the other hand, where religion matters and is understood to be important, the place of religious tradition and associations will call for an approach to constitutional law that is more respectful of that importance.

Historically the powers of local rulers were not always, or even primarily, thought of as legislative: many rules pertaining to work or charity emanated from what we would now refer to as "nongovernmental" bodies. What is at issue is what counts as "law," and it is important to recall that law was not historically and is not even now only or always what emanates from judges and formal legislative chambers. Both historically and in contemporary constitutionalism there is scope for laws or rules to develop, in a sense, extralegislatively. In both England and the United States towns and other groupings, such as guilds, had considerable rule and lawmaking ability at different points in history. This can only be discussed here in broad-brush

[42] James Q Wilson, *The Moral Sense* (Free Press 1993) 246; Michael Walzer, *Spheres of Justice* (Basil Blackwell 1983) 321; and Mary Ann Glendon, *Rights Talk: The Impoverishment of Political Discourse* (Free Press 1991) 109–144.

[43] See John Ehrenberg, *Civil Society: The Critical History of an Idea* (New York University Press 1999) 109ff and Augustus Pulszky, *The Theory of Law and Civil Society* (T Fisher Unwin 1888) 232–235, tracing the "organic" versus "mechanistic" visions of society back to the Greeks.

[44] William Galston, "Religion and Limits" in Douglas Farrow (ed), *Recognizing Religion in a Secular Society* (McGill-Queens 2004) 41, 47, See, on the problems of assuming "construction" rather than inherency, Iain T Benson, "Getting Religion and Belief Wrong by Definition: A Response to Sullivan and Hurd" in Iain T Benson, Michael Quinlan, and A Keith Thompson (eds), *Religious Freedom in Australia: A New Terra Nullius*? (Shepherd Street Press/Connor Court 2019) 332–358.

fashion, but both commerce and charities were, for centuries, governed not by the sovereign or larger legislative bodies but by towns, guilds, or charters crafted by civil society groups.[45] Whereas the state in the Middle Ages had concerned itself with military protection and the administration of the law, leaving trade regulation and charities such as hospitals largely to religion and the guilds, following the reign of Henry VIII the state "made itself responsible for the religious life of the people [and] now began to concern itself with the promotion of industry and commerce."[46]

The relationship between the sovereign and the people as it involved the election of aldermen (before the earliest election of members of Parliament) is described in detail as an aspect of "the complete independence of administration" exercised by, for example, the weaver's guild in relation to rights they exercised in "holding courts, trying offenders, enforcing their sentences and assuming as they did, complete independence of administration."[47] Law as we understand it now was not the rule.

In a survey of the charters of towns, cities, and states in colonial and post-revolutionary America, Amasa Eaton described an "overlooked history" that contradicts the received view that the towns and cities were "the creatures of the legislature and subject to their will," noting that scope existed to make laws distinct from the constitution of the states within which they were situated.[48]

The South African Charter of Religious Rights and Freedoms: A Civil Society Charter

That contemporary law has the capacity to return to an alternative way of imaging law is evidenced in an interesting provision of the South African Constitution. Given the essentially one-party character of the South African state (the ruling African National Congress Party having an apparently unassailable majority position in national elections since the end of Apartheid

[45] The medieval guild "established a complete system of industrial control . . . in pursuit of a common calling and . . . enveloped the life of the Medieval craftsman in a network of restrictions which bound him hand and foot." See AJ Penty, *A Guildsman's Interpretation of History* (George Allen & Unwin 1920) 38.

[46] Ibid, 228.

[47] William Stubbs, *The Constitutional History of England* (Clarendon Press 1880) vol III, 619.

[48] Amasa M Eaton, "The Right to Local Self-Government" (February 1900) XIII(6) Harvard Law Review 58, 138.

in the 1990s), the Constitution of the Republic of South Africa of 1996 introduced an innovative provision, Section 234.[49] This provision allows for the creation of "additional Charters of Rights" that emerge from civil society rather than through the usual mechanisms of courts and Parliament. It was long imagined that the first use of this provision might be, and so it turned out, the creation of a South African Charter of Religious Rights and Freedoms. The charter was eventually signed by representatives of all the major religions and many nongovernmental organizations at a public meeting in Johannesburg, South Africa, in October 2010 attended by the deputy chief justice of the constitutional court, a university chancellor, and with greetings brought from the Canadian Senate. One might ask: what exactly is the charter in terms of traditional contemporary legal thinking?

Despite the fact that it has yet to be adopted formally, the charter is being used by legal counsel in cases touching upon the panoply of rights it describes and by religious bodies themselves to teach how religions understand the provisions touching on state-religion relations in South Africa. Its provisions on matters such as parental rights in education, the relationship between the state and the religions, respect for conscience and religion in health care, access to traditional lands, fair access to the media by minority groups, etc., were framed *from the perspective* of the signatory religions and nongovernmental institutions.[50] This acknowledgment that civil society institutions might play an important role in the articulation of fundamental constitutional principles represents a new way (or, perhaps, a return to old ways) of thinking about the traditional difference between the "ascending" and "descending" theories of sovereign power (and therefore law).[51] To date, the charter represents the only use of Section 234 and its ultimate influence

[49] Section 234 of the Constitution of the Republic of South Africa 1996 reads: "234. Charters of Rights: In order to deepen the culture of democracy established by the Constitution, Parliament may adopt Charters of Rights consistent with the provisions of the Constitution."

[50] The South African Charter of Religious Rights and Freedoms may be found here: <https://www.strasbourgconsortium.org/content/blurb/files/South%20African%20Charter.pdf>. For the process and background to the charter see Iain T Benson, "The South African Charter of Religious Rights and Freedoms" (2011) 4 (1) International Journal of Religious Freedom 125–134. The writer was one of the principal drafters of the charter. See also Pieter Coertzen, "Constitution, Charter and Religions in South Africa" (2014) 1 AHRLJ 8 and Rassie Malherbe, "The Background and Context of the Proposed South African Charter of Religious Rights and Freedoms" (2011) BYU L Rev 612–636. The original intention of the framers was to take the charter to the government for passage, but on later consideration it was decided that to do so would endanger its status and integrity as a "civil society" document, so that course was abandoned as ill-advised. Section 234 speaks, after all, of "adoption," not passage by law in the usual sense.

[51] See Patrick Parkinson, *Tradition and Change in Australian Law* (5th edn, Thomson Reuters 2013) 98–99.

remains to be seen. There is no reason that such "citizen charters" could not be developed in other countries as a means of developing new kinds of "law beyond law" to address emergent issues.[52]

Contemporary Concepts or Movements that Further or Inhibit Subsidiarity within Constitutionalism

The concepts discussed previously are undercut by many contemporary currents and various conceptual shifts that have changed how we think about persons, communities, and the state. Subsidiarity's focus on the dignity of the person implies a criticism of any concept of a citizen understood as an isolated individual who is not socially integrated or that is swallowed up on a homogeneous agglomeration. Related to this is whether organizing principles, such as respect for freedoms of religion and association, tend toward centralization or de-centralization, to community or individualistic atomism. Charles Taylor confirms that Aristotle's subsidiarity is consistent with personalism and inconsistent with individualism.[53] In a similar manner, what sort of structuring model for society is imagined then instantiated in law is critical to whether there is scope for subsidiarity to emerge practically or whether our conceptions of law and the state will interfere with more organic and holistic conceptions.

As mentioned earlier, Charles Taylor described two main structuring models: civil society or some variant of "Marxist-Leninist vanguard-party"

[52] A competing view of the use of the constitution embraces "transformational constitutionalism." This, without due attention to subsidiarity principles, would lead to the hypertrophy of law discussed later in this chapter. Propounding this approach to the constitution is Karl Klare, "Legal Culture and Transformational Constitutionalism" (1998) 14 SAJHR 155. Responding with a concern about "legal authoritarianism," see Theunis Roux "How, When and Why Does Faith in Law's Autonomy From Politics Decline? A Comparative Constitutional-Cultural Analysis" [2017] UNSWLRS 16.

[53] Charles Taylor, *Philosophy and the Human Sciences, Philosophical Papers, 2* (Cambridge University Press 1985) 187–210, asks why "we even begin to find it reasonable to start political theory with an assertion of individual rights and give these primacy?" (189). On liberalism's wrestle with individualism see Will Kymlicka, *Contemporary Political Philosophy* (Clarendon Press 1990) 216ff and Tracey Rowland's chapter in this volume (chapter 19). See, in relation to Calvin's thought, L Dumont, "Christian Beginnings of Modern Individualism" in Michael Carrithers, Steven Collins, and Steven Lukes (eds), *The Category of the Person: Anthropology, Philosophy, History* (Cambridge University Press 1985) 93–122, and, generally, John MacMurray, *The Self as Agent* (Faber and Faber 1957) and *Persons in Relation* (Faber and Faber 1958), Charles Taylor, *Sources of the Self* (Harvard University Press 2002) and Thomas Langan, *Human Being: A Philosophical Anthropology* (Missouri University Press 2009) 11–12. For sexuality and the "person" see Roger Scruton, *Sexual Desire* (Free Press 1986) 36ff; JB Coates, *The Crisis of the Person: Some Personalist Interpretations* (Longmans, Green and Co. 1949) 235–248; O Carter Snead, "An Anthropological Solution" in *What It Means to Be Human: The Case for the Body in Public Bioethics* (Harvard Univ Press 2020) 65–105.

organization.[54] Emerging in general terms from the latter, contemporary cultural Marxism, now understood as "identity politics," with its rejection of universal human reason and nature, subordinates all aspects of associational life to the interests of the party or the splinter identity group. These reductionist theories show that preoccupation with power relations based on race, sex, sexual orientation, "gender," or abstract "inclusion" leads to what Graham Good has described as a "new sectarianism" that forms a "carceral vision" leading to the betrayal of humanism itself.[55]

Ideas such as a "global civil society" raise questions for the local dimensions of lived communities upon which subsidiarity focuses.[56] William Galston refers to a part's wish to dominate the whole as "civic totalism" and traces three distinct forms in Aristotle, Hobbes, and Rousseau.[57] John Gray discusses pseudo-liberalism that seeks convergence and forces "agreement" rather than a genuine liberalism embodying ongoing toleration, accommodation, and modus vivendi.[58] Civic totalists and convergence advocates oppose genuine diversity as their approaches tend to be homogenizing, statist, or globalist in intent—universal government is framed from the top down. The deployment of terms such as "diversity," "equality/deep equality," "liberalism," or "inclusion" to further convergence or totalism often usurp the accommodation, toleration, and modus vivendi essential to subsidiarity and, as that theory sets out, freedom and liberty themselves.

Nicolas Berdayev notes the state's tendency to reach into autonomous spheres and become totalitarian.[59] In contrast to the Middle Ages, whose conception of common culture was characterized by the idea of organic unity in which every part presupposed the unity of the whole, many contemporary

54 Taylor, "Invoking Civil Society," 204–205.

55 Graham Good, *Humanism Betrayed* (McGill-Queens 2001).

56 For concepts of civil society not favorable to diversity see Ralf Dahrendorf, "Citizenship and Social Class" in Martin Bulmer and Anthony M Rees (eds), *Citizenship Today: The Contemporary Relevance of T. H. Marshall* (Routledge 1996) 25–48. Here, civil society and citizenship are coextensive, ignoring any ongoing modus vivendi and subsidiarity.

57 William A Galston, "Religion and the Limits of Liberal Democracy" in D Farrow (ed), *Recognizing Religion in a Secular Society* (McGill-Queens 2004) 41–50, 43–44, 49; John Gray, *Two Faces of Liberalism* (New Press 2000) 20–21. See also Peter Lauwers, "Liberal Pluralism and the Challenge of Religious Diversity" in Iain T Benson and Barry W Bussey (eds), *Religion, Liberty and the Jurisdictional Limits of Law* (LexisNexis 2017) 29–63.

58 Maurice Cowling, *Mill and Liberalism* (Cambridge University Press 1963) xii–xiii notes what Cowling refers to as John Stuart Mill's anti-Christian purpose.

59 Nicholas Berdayev, *The Realm of Spirit and the Realm of Caesar* (Donald A Lowrie tr, Green Press 1953) 72, 76–77. On communist opposition/hatred of Christianity and its fundamental problem as "the relation between man and society" see Nicholas Berdayev, *The Origin of Russian Communism* (RM French tr, Bles 1937) 191–229, 221ff.

theorists, including some who seem genuinely sympathetic to the place of religions within culture, tend toward a homogeneous conception of the state, expanding its role expressly or impliedly to those dimensions that should be protected from homogenization. This "bleaching out" may sometimes be done under the guise of "neutrality," but when the moves are examined, "such [so-called] state neutrality in respect of religious minorities is only superficial, masking an underlying current which flows in the opposite direction."[60] On this reading, areas of law once considered private are made increasingly subject to state regulation.[61]

Where religion is no longer the background and frame of the culture, the state is compelled to perform the functions of a church (for which by its nature it is radically unfitted) and the distinction between public and private spheres is blurred, resulting in "the crisis of the personal."[62] The persons who wield political power should not have untrammeled authority over the life of religious communities or other associations and their members in part because the private/public distinction is important to protect human rights from challenges emerging from what Jean Bethke Elshtain well described as a "politics of displacement,"[63] which tended to blur conceptual boundaries and eliminate the public/private distinction that, in fact, makes politics possible.[64] William Galston points out that "pluralist politics is a politics of recognition rather than construction. It respects the diverse spheres of human activity; it does not understand itself as creating or constituting those activities."[65]

Certain scholars, for example, in recent works, support common but erroneous or rather sharp divisions between "religion" and "the secular," "constitutionalism and religion," "law and religion," or blended notions such as "constitutional theocracy." In all these cases, a fuller understanding of relationships between law, religion, and society, incorporating the concepts

[60] See Julian Rivers, *The Law of Organized Religions: Between Establishment and Secularism* (Oxford University Press 2010) 340–343, and with respect to "neutrality" at 343. See also David L Schindler, *Heart of the World, Centre of the Church* (T&T Clark 1996) 159ff. on liberalism, Catholicism, and neutrality.

[61] Ibid.

[62] This "crisis of the personal" according to John Macmurray, *The Self as Agent* (Faber & Faber 1957) 30–31 "is the crisis of liberalism which was an effort, however ambiguous, to subordinate the functional organization of society to the personal life of its members. . . . The declared intention [of Communism] was to achieve a form of society in which the government of men would give place to the administration of things."

[63] Jean Bethke Elshtain, *Democracy on Trial* (Basic Books 1995) 39–40.

[64] Ibid, 40.

[65] William A Galston, "Religion and the Limits of Liberal Democracy" in D Farrow (ed), *Recognizing Religion in a Secular Society* (McGill-Queens 2004) 41–50, 43–44, 49.

we have seen in subsidiarity, are absent.[66] "Secular," for example, once meant the order of time in contradistinction to eternity, or the time between the departure of Christ and his return; it was not a nonreligious or nonsacred conception—as is evidenced in the Catholic tradition with its references to "secular clergy" and "secular institutes." That it now means for some "non-religious" or "excluding religion" ought to give pause to those who analyze the proper relations between the public sphere and religious associations. Subsidiarity, with its careful marshaling of concepts, understood historically offers greater clarity around such terms as "belief/unbeliever," "faith," "secular," "secularism," "law," "constitution/constitutionalism," and the "public/private" divide to name but a few.

First, it is important to note that religion, agnosticism, and atheism are differing *belief* systems, all of which are entitled to play an active role within the public sphere and to form properly "public" programs for their followers. Second, religion itself is an *equality* right, and thus a proper analysis of conflicts should be undertaken with respect to the *context* in which they occur and not on the basis of an elevation of one principle (equality or law) over another (religion).[67] It is, however, important not to overlook the importance of religious law and ordering to religious communities as well as three important differences between law and religion as they will coexist in contemporary open societies: (1) religions are voluntarily joined, whereas being subject to the law is not an option; (2) religions bind by affection, whereas law binds by coercion; and (3) religions are genuine communities, whereas law is not and cannot form communities in itself.[68] Such bifurcations between law

[66] A variety of ways of characterising the relationship exhibit the shades of meanings and confusions as well as illuminations that abound in this area, see: Joel Harrison, *Post-Religious Liberty* (Cambridge University Press 2020) 181, "religion and the secular"; Benjamin Berger, "Liberal Constitutionalism and the Unsettling of the Secular" in Rex Adhar (ed), *Research Handbook on Law and Religion* (Edward Elgar 2018) 198–220; see also Ran Hirschl, *Constitutional Theocracy* (Harvard University Press 2010) 79, 239, where "constitutionalism" and "religion" are imagined as opposites; see also Lorenzo Zucca, "Law v. Religion" in Lorenzo Zucca and Camil Ungereanu (eds), *Law, State and Religion in the New Europe: Debates and Dilemmas* (Cambridge University Press 2012) 137–159, 138, which bifurcates "law" and "religion" in similar fashion.

[67] Iain T Benson, "The Necessity for a Contextual Analysis for Equality and Nondiscrimination" in Jane F Adolph, Robert L Fastiggi, and Michael A Vacca (eds), *Equality and Non-discrimination: Catholic Roots, Current Challenges* (Pickwick 2019) 63–75. For a discussion of the terms "secular" and "faith" see Iain T Benson, "The Goal of Excluding Religion from the Idea of Public Benefit: Some Aspects of Neo-Secularist Strategies" in Barry W Bussey (ed), *The Status of Religion and The Public Benefit in Charity Law* (Anthem, 2020) 225–240, 231–233, and relation to the work of Berger and others: Iain T Benson, "The Case for Religious Inclusivism and the Judicial Recognition of Religious Associational Rights: A Response to Lenta" (2008) 1 Constitutional Court Review 297–312.

[68] *International Covenant of Civil and Political Rights* (ICCPR) UN General Assembly resolution 2200A (XXI) 16 December 1966 entry into force 23 March 1976 reads: "Everyone shall have the right to freedom of thought, conscience and religion. This right shall include freedom to have or to adopt

and religion—on occasion by scholars who hold a favorable disposition to the role of religion in culture—are, in fact, consistent with the exclusionary ideology of secularism, a term first coined by George Jacob Holyoake in 1851 for an ideology that falsely claimed neutrality.[69]

A good example of the error of homogeneity and failure to deal seriously with diversity is the Supreme Court of Canada's decision in *Trinity Western University* (2018 SCC)[70] denying an Evangelical Protestant university the accreditation of a law school because its "community covenant" spoke to a traditionalist conception of marriage and sexual relations. The British Columbia Court of Appeal judgment, which would have allowed accreditation of the law school, focused on the necessity allowing differences of belief within a democracy.[71] The unanimous decision of five judges of the British Columbia Court of Appeal was overturned by a majority of judges of the Supreme Court of Canada. John Gray's description of illiberal convergence and William Galston's description of "civic totalism" apply well to the Supreme Court of Canada's majority decision.

Secularism, properly understood, and contrary to the claims that it can exist in "open" or "pluralistic" or "public" forms, when understood historically offers no positive resources for constitutionalism. An open public sphere does not start off with the anti-religious squint evidenced by secularism. The "institutional" or "group" dimensions of religious freedom have

a religion or belief of his choice, and freedom, *either individually or in community* with others *and in public or private*, to manifest his religion or belief in worship, observance, practice and teaching" (emphasis added).

[69] Holyoake's secularist strategy is discussed in Owen Chadwick, *The Secularization of the European Mind in the Nineteenth Century* (Cambridge UP 1975) 88ff and Iain T Benson, "Considering Secularism" in Douglas Farrow (ed), *Recognizing Religion in a Secular Society* (McGill-Queens UP 2004) 83–98. Against this background the neologisms "open secularism" or "pluralistic secularism" are non sequiturs that amount to the equivalent of "healthy botulism." The neologism of "open-secularism" is taken out of its historical context and suggested as a possible reality in Jocelyn Maclure and Charles Taylor, *Secularism and Freedom of Conscience* (Harvard University Press 2011) 58–60; with respect, it simply adds confusion to what is being discussed.

[70] The two judgments are *Law Society of British Columbia v Trinity Western University and Brayden Volkenant* (2018) 2 SCR 293 and *Trinity Western University and Brayden Volkenant v. Law Society of Upper Canada* (2018) 2 SCR 453. See, for criticisms of the decision, Greg Walsh, "Trinity Western University and the Future of Conservative Religious Education" in Barry W Bussey and Angus JL Menuge (eds), *The Inherence of Human Dignity: Law and Religious Liberty* (Anthem 2021) vol 2, 185–202; Barry W Bussey, "Making Registered Charitable Status of Religious Organizations Subject to *Charter* Values" in Barry W Bussey (ed), *The Status of Religion and the Public Benefit of Charity Law* (Anthem Press 2020) 159–203; see also John von Heyking, "The Challenge and Promise of Religious Associations to Liberal Democratic Order" in Iain T Benson and Barry W Bussey (eds), *Religion, Liberty and the Jurisdictional Limits of Law* (LexisNexis 2017) 89–114, which discusses Tocqueville's critique of "the political logic of equality."

[71] *Trinity Western Law School and the Law Society of British Columbia* (BCCA 2016).

great importance to all of society and should not be subordinated to the driving paradigm of one viewpoint and group over others, as in the *Trinity Western University* decision where subsidiarity rights were accorded no weight in what was purported to be "balancing." Individualism and what sociologist Robert Nisbet refers to as "the centralization of authority" leads to the state's "penetration of traditional social authorities" in ways contrary to the maintenance of the social elements of the political order.[72] Recent criticisms suggest that the court has developed an unworkable standard and application with respect to proportionality, minimal impairment, and balancing of the interests in such cases.[73]

Systems and Life-worlds

Finally, it is useful to consider Jürgen Habermas's useful distinction between "life-worlds" and "systems."[74] The distinction is one that fits very well within the foregoing discussion of the importance of attention to associational life in relation to the role of law and the state in view of the goods attributed to functioning according to subsidiarity (as diversity) and not against it.

According to Habermas, "life-worlds" are the sets of shared meanings that constitute the many and varied voluntary associations to be found in free societies. "Systems," by contrast, are nonvoluntary and parasitic upon the life-worlds they colonize. Law and politics are "systems" in this schema, and most voluntary associations including religions are life-worlds.[75] Robert N. Bellah criticizes Habermas's schema as insufficiently aware of the role religions might play in "transforming the distortions of modernity that Habermas has so acutely analyzed."[76] Bellah notes Habermas's "incomplete

[72] Robert A Nisbet, *The Social Bond* (Alfred A Knopf 1970) 385. The primordial, group, and social goods of religion are well articulated in a South African Constitutional Court decision: see *Minister of Home Affairs and another v Fourie et al* 2006 (1) SA 524 (CC) at para 36 per Sachs J. Generally, on the nature of associational liberty and the problems of convergence, see Iain T Benson, *An Associational Framework for the Reconciliation of Competing Rights Claims Involving the Freedom of Religion* (PhD dissertation, University of the Witwatersrand 2013).

[73] Carmelle Dielemann, "Accommodating Rights in Administrative Law: A Critique of the Doré / Loyola Framework" (2021) 34 Cdn Jour of Admin Law & Practice 197–218.

[74] U. Steinhoff, *The Philosophy of Jürgen Habermas: A Critical Introduction* (Oxford UP, 2009) 210ff.

[75] Jürgen Habermas, *The Structural Transformation of the Public Sphere,* (tr) T. Burger and F. Lawrence (Harvard University Press, 1989). See Iain T Benson, "Pluralism, Lifeworlds, Civic Virtues and Civil Charters" in M Christian Green and Pieter Coertzen (eds), *Religious Pluralism in Africa—Prospects and Limitations* (SUN Press 2016) 287–306.

[76] See Robert N Bellah, "How to Understand the Church in an Individualistic Society" in Rodney L Petersen (ed), *Christianity and Civil Society* (Orbis Books 1995) 1–14, 5, and "Stories as Arrows: The

focus on autonomy" and failure to embrace "community" and points to subsidiarity as possessing a "rich set of implications" that revivify the life-worlds that Habermas seeks but cannot reach. For that task, Bellah urges the need for myth and tradition—in short, for religions.[77]

Conclusion: The Future of Subsidiarity in Constitutionalism?

The holistic application of the doctrine of subsidiarity requires a robust anthropology and incorporates local diversities while respecting the priority of associations. Philosophical reductions, including those reviewed previously, nullify the benefits of the doctrine. Whether or not a society may be deemed "open" or "closed" relates to the presence or absence of personal choice and decisions. A closed society restricts these freedoms. A focus on litigating rights disputes results in "winners and losers," reducing the scope for consensus and preventing modus vivendi.[78] What is also needed is a degree of consensus particularly in relation to living together with disagreement and difference, especially in multicultural and plural societies.

Lord Acton understood that the maintenance of liberty and freedom in legal regimes depends on respect for "multiple associations . . . [and] the limitation of the public authority."[79] For Acton, "the tendencies of centralization, of corruption, and of absolutism" can only be effectively opposed by "the influence of a divided patriotism"[80] and a recognition of the importance of multiple associations. Law and politics need to be understood as having their own important *but limited* jurisdictions.

Michael Polanyi has noted the importance of maintaining beliefs and traditions in relation to freedom and control:

Religious Response to Modernity" in Arvind Sharma (ed), *Religion in a Secular City: Essays in Honour of Harvey Cox* (Trinity Press International 2001) 91–104.

[77] Bellah, "Stories as Arrows," 101–103.

[78] Karl Popper, *The Open Society and its Enemies: Plato* (Princeton University Press 1971) 172–173. In relation to litigation and its limits, see Charles Taylor, *The Malaise of Modernity* (Anansi 2001) 116, 120.

[79] Baron Acton, *The History of Freedom and Other Essays* (Macmillan and Co, Ltd, 1907) 288–289.

[80] Ibid.

> If the citizens are dedicated to certain transcendent obligations and particularly to such general ideals as truth, justice, charity and these are embodied in the tradition of the community to which allegiance is maintained, a great many issues between citizens . . . can be left . . .—and are necessarily left—for the individual consciences to decide. The moment, however, a community ceases to be dedicated through its members to transcendent ideals, it can continue to exist undisrupted only by submission to a single centre of unlimited secular power.[81]

Polanyi implies that the most important and primary locations for the maintenance of "traditions" are associations, particularly religious associations.

T. S. Eliot recognized that a Christian society may use a structure like the parochial system that is in direct contact with the smallest units of the community and individual members and that the maintenance of a culture and society depended in part on the relationship between the part and the whole.[82]

The foregoing brings us to a fundamental question: how can politicians and those involved in law (legislators, judges, and lawyers) appreciate their own proper limits if law itself becomes not merely authoritative but, in a quasi-religious manner, *dogmatic*? How can they respect religions if in addition to losing a deep understanding of philosophy, religion, and tradition, the law itself has become *sectarian*, administering, in fact, "constitutional *theocracies*"? As Voegelin noted, this form of neo-gnosticism is itself an "ersatz *religion*" jealously defending its own formulations while deriding or subordinating with increasing disrespect the beliefs of others. He notes that "re-divinization [of modern political mass movements] has its origins in Christianity itself, deriving from components that were suppressed as heretical by the universal church"[83] For him, "Gnostic movements were not satisfied with filling the vacuum of civil theology; they tended to abolish Christianity."[84] For Voegelin, Gnosticism is nothing less than a civil religion, and in a memorable formulation he terms this movement an "immanentization of the eschaton"

[81] Michael Polanyi, *Science, Faith and Society* (University of Chicago Press 1946, 2nd imp 1966) 78–79; TS Eliot, *The Idea of a Christian Society* (Faber & Faber 1939) 47 and *Notes Towards the Definition of Culture* (Faber & Faber 1948). In the latter, Eliot notes: "the culture of Europe could not survive the complete disappearance of the Christian Faith . . . if Christianity goes, the whole of our culture goes" (122).

[82] Eliot, *The Idea of a Christian Society*, 47.

[83] Eric Voegelin, *The New Science of Politics: An Introduction* (Chicago Univ Press 1952) 107, 179.

[84] Ibid, 163.

that amounts to an "ersatz religion."[85] Canadian philosopher George Grant discussed a situation in which technique is victorious as in a "new relation to tradition" that is "hostile to the moral teachings of the past"—a condition in fact that amounts to a "theology of technique," which he says goes by the name of "liberalism," and by which he meant "the belief that man's essence is his freedom."[86]

Contemporary Italian philosopher Giorgio Agamben holds that nothing that becomes hypertrophic is properly healthy and that "with the eclipse of the messianic experience of the culmination of the law and of time comes an unprecedented hypertrophy of law—one that, under the guise of legislating everything, betrays its legitimacy through legalistic excess."[87]

Russian writer Nicholas Berdayev writes of the extreme *étatism* of Russian communism that takes the form of "the terrible hypertrophy of the state in Russian history."[88] Man's "power over nature" now threatened by "servitude to old cosmic and new technical forces" can only be accomplished, he believes, by "a rejuvenated Christianity" that is "true to its prophetic spirit" and "which turned towards the Kingdom of God."[89]

Writing about the same time as Berdayev, Spanish philosopher José Ortega y Gasset commented that the result of excessive state intervention on society would be fatal: "spontaneous social action will be broken up over and over again by State intervention; no new seed will be able to fructify. Society will have to live *for* the State, man *for* the governmental machine."[90] This warning is neither exaggerated nor untimely as evidenced by current developments.

Fears about undue state intervention in the life-worlds of associations have been given a new urgency due to the development of evermore efficient means of surveillance before and particularly under the state of exception relating to health concerns. In a recent article by a Chinese and two Italian authors, the new technologies of state surveillance used by the Chinese Communist regime are welcomed as a new normative model for the West. Far from decrying the movement away from the rule of law to the rule by technology, the article regards the advent of widespread global surveillance as inevitable and essential and announces the superiority of the Chinese approach *for global adoption*. The authors write: "we can predict that the

[85] Eric Voegelin, *Science, Politics and Gnosticism* (Henry Regnery and Company 1968) 83–114.
[86] George Grant, *Philosophy in the Mass Age* (Copp Clark 1959, 1966) iv.
[87] Gorgio Agamben, *The Church and the Kingdom* (Leland De La Durantaye tr, Seagull 2012) 40–41.
[88] Berdayev, *The Origin of Russian Communism*, 227.
[89] Ibid, 229.
[90] José Ortega y Gasset, *Revolt of the Masses* (Norton 1930, 1957) 121, emphasis in original.

Chinese advantage in emergency law and the development of a new global patten of law, *the rule of technology,* might point to the emergence of an unexpected Chinese legal leadership, determined by the final collapse of liberal constitutionalism provoked by Covid 19 [and the rise of populism]."[91]

Against this future vision of the rule of law captive to and assisted by a technological domination of life-worlds, which many would see as dystopic and despotic, what alternatives exist? Some have called for a different sort of revolution—one consistent with the long tradition adumbrated in this chapter but that centrally involves the turning of mind and heart based on the traditional teachings of Christianity.[92]

Paradoxically, at the very time that de-centralization and localization are starting to be viewed as essential to so many diverse areas, various theories evidence a loss of conviction in the principles of universality and integrated diversity necessary to maintain a holistic approach that respects the traditions that protect diversity within the whole. There is a deep paradox here and it is appropriate to ask: how can a *theocratic* constitutionalism achieve justice and the common good without incorporating the ordering principles uniquely marshaled within subsidiarity and traditions that developed and alone can nurture it?

The practice of subsidiarity is best lived and maintained within associations committed to the visions of an ordered cosmos that embrace and support it. Homogeneous approaches, including some of those described in this chapter, seem unlikely to sustain, much less perpetuate, the essential concepts of universal reason, human nature, the person, and the larger relations beyond the neighborhood and community that are the essence of lived and diverse subsidiarity and that are anathema to totalitarianisms.[93]

The commons, properly understood, is that realm of existence in which different moral traditions and languages of meaning, not always understood or accepted by those outside the group, can coexist rather than be unnecessarily interfered with by laws and "systems" that tend toward coercion. We are at the end of a history that believed liberalism was sufficient even if aspects

[91] See Ugo Mattei, Liu Guanghua, and Emanuele Ariano, "The Chinese Advantage in Emergency Law" (2021) 21(1) Global Jurist 1–58, 58.

[92] Philip Allot, "International Society and the Idea of Justice" in Mary Ann Glendon, Juan José Llach, Marcelo Sánchez Sorondo (eds), *Charity and Justice in the Relations amongst Peoples and Nations*, Acta 13, Proceedings of the Pontifical Academy of Social Sciences (Pontificia Academia Scientarium Socialium 2007) 41–48, 48. On the necessity of a "new constitutional organization of the human family" that involves a bottom-up conception of globalization that serves both pluralism and participation, see Kenneth R Himes, *Christianity and the Political Order* (Orbis Books 2013) 211ff.

[93] Hannah Arendt, *The Origins of Totalitarianism* (Harcourt Brace Jovanovich 1973, new edn) 438.

of it are still deemed necessary. Homogeneity is not the home of freedom. It has been well said that liberal social ontologies "impose a secularising model of the relationship between the individual, the group and the state that is not neutral among religions and cultures."[94] Such models, whether of "liberal" or postliberal *illiberal* varieties, are not and by their own presuppositions *cannot* be respectful of differing but differentially legitimate alternative accounts of meaning. Subsidiarity acts as a check and balance against overweening homogeneity in all its forms and its embrace and development by constitutionalism is exigent.

[94] See Nicholas Aroney, "Freedom of Religion as an Associational Right" (2014) 33(1) University of Queensland Law Journal 153–186 and Nicholas Aroney and Patrick Parkinson, "Associational Freedom, Anti-Discrimination and the New Multiculturalism" (2019) 44 Australian Journal of Legal Philosophy 1, 27.

22

Eschatology

The Greater Operation of Liberty

Douglas Farrow

The most important things to notice about Christian eschatology, in the context of constitutional law, are these: first, its capacity to orient law to liberty; second, its capacity to order liberty within a divine economy of law and liberty; third, its capacity to restrain both lawlessness and the overreach of law, that is, to cultivate in law a proper sense of modesty without undermining its authority; and fourth, its capacity to direct concerns with human justice (both as a virtue of the soul and as an achievement in society) to their proper ground in God. Christian eschatology makes clear that doing justice to man begins with doing justice to God and that doing justice to God begins in a grateful acknowledgment of the sovereign goodness of God.

Of course, it has these capacities, or rather it fulfills them, only where it is believed. Even Kant, who did not believe, allowed that positing some of Christian eschatology's most basic elements (viz., God, freedom, and immortality) could reinforce respect for law and liberty. What Kant and his heirs did not realize, however, is that these elements cannot stand alone or without appeal to other equally basic elements, especially the resurrection, ascension, and Parousia of Jesus. It is precisely these latter elements—these narrative elements that defy any attempt to turn them into empty abstractions—that make possible the correlation of law with liberty, of authority with modesty, of theonomy with autonomy. It is these latter elements that supply the surest ground for higher law and so for constitutional liberties; that secure rights without loss of right; that silence the siren song of perfectibility dogmas and curb our most dangerous utopian dreams.[1] It is they that make room

[1] "The touchstone of constitutionalism is the concept of limited government under a higher law" (David Fellman, "Constitutionalism" in Philip Wiener [ed], *Dictionary of the History of Ideas: Studies of Selected Pivotal Ideas* vol 1 [1973] 485). But whence arises this higher law? Much rests on the answer to that.

Douglas Farrow, *Eschatology: The Greater Operation of Liberty* in *Christianity and Constitutionalism*.
Edited by: Nicholas Aroney and Ian Leigh, Oxford University Press.
DOI: 10.1093/oso/9780197587256.003.0022

for democracy while refusing to make of democracy an idol, and for judicial review without permitting judges to fancy themselves gods. It is they that also underwrite the separation of powers and the principle of subsidiarity. Without these narrative elements there would never have arisen in Europe the kind of constitutionalism to which it gave birth—the kind that today is very much in jeopardy due to their neglect or disavowal.[2]

Now obviously this is a very large and, for many, counterintuitive claim, on which it is not possible fully to make good here. Thankfully, however, it is not without prior exposition. Moreover, its primary exposition is not theoretical but institutional; whatever of this kind of thinking is embodied in particular constitutions and political structures, it is all present, at least incipiently, in the Church. All I want to attempt, then, is the elucidation of a few basic principles that rest, ultimately, on Christian eschatology, and a quick sketch of how the loss of purchase on those principles undermines a healthy constitutionalism.[3] Their application or reapplication to the specific tasks of constitutional law is for others (some of whom have written in the present volume) who are more familiar with those tasks.

Law and Liberty

Law of some sort is a distinguishing feature of every people, and especially of every civilization that merits the label. The idea of law as ordered liberty, however, though not without analogs elsewhere, is a Judeo-Christian heritage. It has its roots in Exodus 19–20, wherein the giving of the Torah is prefaced by a recapitulation of the divine act of deliverance from Egypt. Israel's new liberty is derived from the covenant between God and Abraham, and it is effected for the sake of that covenant, which is now to have constitutional and legal features that will maintain the people in liberty and on the path to a

[2] The authors of *The Paris Statement: A Europe We Can Believe In* (2017) rightly insist that "the European ideal is one of solidarity based on assent to a body of law that applies to all, but is limited in its demands" (§5). They are equally right that this ideal is quickly eroding and that the work of renewal must begin "with theological self-knowledge" (§24). What can that mean but relearning the biblical narrative? See, e.g., Oliver O'Donovan, *The Desire of the Nations: Rediscovering the Roots of Political Theology* (Cambridge University Press 1996).

[3] I am using "constitutionalism" in what I take to be the standard sense, referring to the legally entrenched limitation of a state or government's powers by means of principles, rules, rights, distribution of power, etc., apart from which its decrees or actions lack legitimacy and are unlawful. By "Christian eschatology" I mean Church teaching not only on the last things but also on whatever has to do with the passage from the old creation to the new.

still greater liberty, a liberty that God in due course will bring about for them, and for the whole world, in fulfillment of his promises.

This understanding was taken up in the Christian permutation of first-century Judaism, with its talk of a new or renewed covenant ratified in the blood of the Messiah. It was taken up in the very idea of the Church, as the people of the new exodus accomplished by Jesus in his death and resurrection and ascension. The Church is a covenantal reality, with power from heaven to bind and to set free. That power is exercised by the Messiah's delegates, the apostles, who together with their successors, the bishops, govern the faithful. Jesus indicates that it will extend at his coming to judgment of the tribes of Israel, and Paul to the judgment of the angels.[4] This binding and loosing concerns sins, first of all, and not matters of territorial sovereignty and the like. And yet it reflects the fact that lordship has been given to the Messiah, not only over the people of God, but also over all peoples; not only over the promised land, but also over all lands. His delegates, together with all the faithful, are like ambassadors. They are sent to announce his sovereignty and to cultivate expectation of his Parousia, his arrival in glory to claim what is his, and in claiming it to liberate it once and for all.[5]

Here was a very strange sort of sovereignty, then, not in heaven—though the idea of a sovereign *man* in heaven, not the mere genius or apotheosis of a man, was certainly peculiar—but rather on earth in the form of the Church, which just because it had been promised possession of all things needed to defend none, except by spiritual means.[6] This was a sovereignty of word and sacrament, not of secular laws and coercive powers. It was territorial, all right; that is, it was soon organized by dioceses, around episcopal *cathedrae*. And it was intensely interested also in the secular or temporal welfare of the people with whose eternal welfare it was chiefly charged. It gradually developed its own laws and legal system, which became entwined with their secular counterparts, such as Justinian's *Corpus Iuris Civilis*.[7] In the West, as the Roman Empire collapsed, it had to set about reinventing secular

[4] "Do you not know that we are to judge angels? How much more, matters pertaining to this life!" (1 Cor. 6:3). Cf. Deut. 4:8–10; Wis. 3:4–7; Matt. 19:28; Rev. 20:4.

[5] Some constitutional scholars take a sectarian view of the churches as little more than voluntary societies, hence as more or less harmless when composed of law-abiding people, but this Lockean approach doesn't do Christianity justice. From the very outset (see, e.g., 1 Thess. 1:6–10, with Acts 17:7) its leaders saw themselves as bearing an official announcement about the one whom God had exalted to "his right hand as Founder and Saviour" (ἀρχηγὸν καὶ σωτῆρα, Acts 5:31). Everyone, including Caesar, knew this to have political and legal implications.

[6] Augustine, *De civitate dei* 22.6.

[7] See ch 6 above, by Helmholz.

counterparts. But the sovereignty of the Church was and is a distinct kind of sovereignty, exercised in expectation of a reality still hidden, a reality properly manifested in the *saeculum* only eucharistically.

Now, it is just here, in its eucharistic connection, that law gets oriented to liberty in a profoundly new fashion. The pioneer (following St. Paul) was Irenaeus of Lyons, who made it his business to address Marcionite and Gnostic repudiations of Israel, of the Torah, and of the God of Israel—that is, to show that Christianity was not in any way a religion that rejected either the present creation or the laws that govern it, whether divine, natural, or civil. He did this by demonstrating that Jesus had not abolished the law of Moses but in fulfilling it had deepened and widened its scope and power by imbuing the covenant people with a new spirit of liberty based on affection and gratitude.[8] Lest it be thought that this was somehow a matter of religion only, he added that those precepts that were natural to all were likewise prised open and ennobled by a more generous recognition of the goods they serve[9]—which indeed he said prophetically, projecting outward from Christ and the Church and forward into history, for he and his community lived still in a hostile pagan environment that produced many martyrs.

Those who have received in their souls the power of liberty, says Irenaeus, love and follow God *sine vinculis*.[10] The return of the Son to the Father and the adoption of fellow humans into his filial relation with the Father mean that the spirit of the law, and not the letter only, is operative within them. And this is the spirit of gratitude, the spirit of the Eucharist. The Eucharist resituates law itself within a free economy of gift and gratitude. It witnesses to the fact that God, the ground of all law, needs nothing whatever from man, not even his sacrifices, but always, out of his bounty, gives freely to man what is good for him. Law, like everything else that tends or should tend to human

[8] "All these teachings, indeed, [he supplied not] as one dissolving the law, but by way of fulfilling and extending and expanding it among us; as if one were to say that, the greater the operation of liberty, the more ingrained in us has become subjection and affection toward our liberator" (*Adversus haereses* 4.13.3, translation mine). An antinomian streak in the Reformation obscured this point by denying the authority of tradition, as indeed did its contrary, viz., the legalistic moralism to be found in both Catholic and Protestant manualism. Their modern equivalents are to be found, respectively, in a denial of epistemic access to any putative laws or commands of God other than those dictated by reason and, conversely, in the suffocating layers of positive law, detached from both natural and divine law, that are currently being spun out in the name of a greater operation of liberty.

[9] "Those laws that are natural, and liberal, and common to all, he has enlarged and expanded, generously and ungrudgingly granting to men, through adoption, to know God [as] Father, and to love him whole-heartedly, and to follow his word unswervingly, abstaining not only from evil deeds but even from the desire of them" (*Haer.* 4.16.5, translation mine).

[10] 4.13.2; cf. 4.16.5.

flourishing, is thus drawn into an economy not of necessity but of freedom—an economy not of mere reciprocity, of distributive and retributive justice, but of generosity and love in the Holy Spirit.[11] Justice is not at all lacking to this economy, as Irenaeus is careful to point out; but justice alone does not do it justice.[12] This is the liberal economy par excellence, and it is marked by voluntary liberality: "In the Church, sympathy, and compassion, and steadfastness, and truth, for the aid and encouragement of mankind, are not only displayed without fee or reward, but we ourselves lay out for the benefit of others our own means; and inasmuch as those who are cured very frequently do not possess the things which they require, they receive them from us."[13]

Secular law cannot fully emulate this, of course, because it cannot assume the filial option for man that the Church, through baptism, does assume. But it can acknowledge (unless its idea of secularity is atheistic, or theistic in some anti-Christian sense) that law ultimately is a function of love and a servant of liberty, and that gratitude to God is a sine qua non for any form of law, even civil law, that intends this servitude. Conversely, it can acknowledge with Irenaeus that law is the form that freedom takes, and that law is not dissolved by the good news that God has acted in Jesus Christ to set free those who wish to be free.

The idea of freedom is not a Christian invention, any more than is the idea of justice and equity. But just as Judeo-Christian thinking about justice and equity has had an enormous impact on Western law, so also has Christian thinking about freedom. The desire for freedom is not merely the chafing of a people or of an individual against the bonds of servitude to some oppressor—whether a real oppressor, such as a tyrant, or one of the imaginary oppressors that decadent liberalism, to keep itself in business, is now inventing willy-nilly. It is that, but to focus on that is to underestimate freedom. The desire for freedom is a desire of God, who is freedom itself. Freedom, then, is not a negative concept: the absence of some or all restraint. Freedom is not the polar opposite of necessity, to be held in some eternal dialectical tension. How could it be, when in God there is no such necessity, nor any possibility

[11] God himself "stands in need of nothing" (2.2.4) and, just so, freely creates and disposes everything else, each with its own suitable nature, in a lawful and harmonious arrangement. The human creature God invites on toward himself, however, so as to receive a divine capacity, viz., eternal life and the liberty to order its own affairs in a godly fashion (4.38.3; cf. 2.15.3, 2.28.1).

[12] See 3.25. Cf. Aquinas, ST 1.21.4: "Whatever is done by Him in created things, is done according to proper order and proportion, wherein consists the idea of justice. . . . Now the work of divine justice always presupposes the work of mercy, and is founded thereupon." Hence nothing is due to creatures, from other creatures, but what is a fitting response to God's prior goodness.

[13] *Haer.* 2.31.3; cf. Augustine, *De moribus ecclesiae* 53.

of external restraint? Nor is freedom a matter of indifference, the capacity to sin or not sin, for God has no such capacity and is not in the least indifferent. Freedom (as Anselm explains to those who posit such things) is at first, for the human agent, the capacity to preserve justice in the soul, to preserve, for its own sake, the divine gift of rectitude of will.[14] More than that, freedom is learning to share in the liberality of God, who gives to all without stinting. Freedom is finally a share in God himself, and in the happiness of God. For a people, then, or for a *polis*, freedom is whatever serves and does not inhibit the advance of its members toward God. That is why the most fundamental affirmation of freedom in any society is its respect for the *libertas ecclesiae*—something for which the Church had constantly to struggle even in Christendom, not to speak of modernity.[15]

On this approach, law does not merely restrain, nor does it function primarily to liberate from restraints. Rather, in restraining, it helps to perfect those who are subject to it. Natural law points the way to human flourishing, the divine Torah to human happiness. Both are pedagogical and, as such, not only entirely compatible with but also essential to human freedom. There is neither justice in the soul nor any possibility of preserving justice where there is no such law. There is no field, either, for the exercise of liberality or for progress in love, progress toward God. And what does all that mean for civil or positive law, and particularly for constitutional law? It means that, in its restrictions and in its permissions, it ought always to be open to man's eschatological end of union with God, which end all law is intended to serve. It means that it cannot forbid any activity that tends to that end and that it cannot protect any activity that makes it impossible, particularly, of course, killing. That some parliaments and courts are now finding in our constitutions rights to kill is a sure and certain sign that they have lost or deliberately abandoned these bearings—that they no longer understand either freedom or law Christianly.

Liberty and Progress

We shall have to come back to that in discussing the relation between theonomy and autonomy, and the challenge in positive law of respecting both.

[14] See *De libertate* and *De concordia*.

[15] See further my *Desiring a Better Country* (McGill-Queen's University Press 2015) chs 4–5.

But this is already the place to contrast the Christian approach we are outlining with its modern secularist counterpart, which is busy revising constitutions and laws according to its own rather different eschatology. That eschatology is really no more than the myth of progress, or of human perfectibility in the present world, so ably traced by John Passmore.[16] Lessing thrust it into the limelight, by tinkering with Joachim of Fiore in *On the Education of the Human Race*.[17] Hegel gave it a new form in his lectures on the Philosophy of History and on the Philosophy of Right, where (even in defending civil society as a distinct sphere of human endeavor) he dubbed the advance of the state "the march of God in history."[18] In our own time, Harold Berman took up the neo-Joachimite vision from Rosenstock-Hüssy, suggesting that globalism and the advance of international law are a fresh work of the Holy Spirit—an idea not without Catholic credentials, despite the fact that Joachim's ideas were repudiated already in the thirteenth century.[19] Berman quotes Rosenstock approvingly: "The story of salvation on earth is the advance of the singular against the plural. Salvation came into a world of many gods, many lands, many peoples. Over against these, it set up a singular—one God, one world, one humankind."[20]

This flattened-out eschatology, with its universal Church of Man governed by a political singularity, has in common with Christianity's medieval competitor, Islam, that it can tolerate no reversals. It drives the regnant progressive liberalism of our era, which, as Adrian Vermeule has observed, has an analogous intolerance and hostility to the Church of Jesus Christ.[21] The key figure here, in the Anglosphere, is not so much John Locke or James Madison, say, as J. S. Mill. Mill, who asserted confidently that "no one whose opinion deserves a moment's consideration can doubt that most of the great positive evils of the world are in themselves removable, and will, if human

[16] John Passmore, *The Perfectibility of Man* (Charles Scribner's Sons 1970). This myth can find no justification in its own nominalist milieu, for the idea of "mankind" or "the race" can find no justification.

[17] "It was an evil day for Christian thought when prophecy became the fashionable category for political reflection in place of practical reasonableness" (Oliver O'Donovan, *The Ways of Judgment* [Eerdmans 2005] xv). Lessing, who proposed to render reasonable the prophecy of Joachim, only repeated the mistake; see *Education* §82ff.

[18] VPR §248.

[19] See Farrow, "Baking Bricks for Babel?" (2010) 8(4) Nova et Vetera745–762.

[20] "The Holy Spirit: The God of History" (April–June 2004), Living Pulpit 33, 1–2.

[21] In review of Ryszard Legutko's *The Demon in Democracy* ("Liturgy of Liberalism" [January 2017] First Things 57–60), Vermeule agrees that "the Revolution's descendants not only possess a theology and eschatology, but a central sacrament and an accompanying liturgy," as well as a fervent conviction "that the clock of Progress should never be turned back." (Vermeule's own political theology, however, is also problematic on my view.)

affairs continue to improve, be in the end reduced within narrow limits,"[22] is well known for thinking that adherents of what he liked to call Calvinism were among those whose opinions did not deserve a moment's consideration and that Christianity itself qualified as a positive evil. Mill did know, naturally, that man ought to love his neighbor. Why otherwise would one take up the burden of ridding the world of evils? Mill did not think, however, that one ought to love God, which is to say, he had no time for the first great commandment but thought perhaps something could be made of the second. Absent the ordering principle contained in the first, he deduced that one loved one's neighbor primarily by doing him no harm, viz., by putting no obstacle to freedom or happiness in his path.

This produced a sea change in thinking about law. But, again, what is freedom? What is happiness? What indeed is harm, where there is no consensus about the good, about happiness, about what freedom is for? Mill's harm principle is an injunction against interference, but no society of men can be made to rest on that, for a society is a society by reason of its common convictions, which must and will find formal expression both in law and in custom. Mill's ideas, translated into law and custom by his many disciples, have turned his harm principle into something other than what it purports to be. In recent decades it has become increasingly clear that the injunction against interference is, primarily, an injunction against the Christianity Mill hated.[23] In that Christianity, just because of the first commandment, it makes much more sense to say with Augustine that we should "harm no one and do good to whomever we can."[24] Here the relation to the neighbor is defined positively as well as negatively. If the first commandment is to pursue "our own good in our own way," the second may very well be put negatively: "Do not attempt to deprive others of theirs, or impede their efforts to obtain it." But if the first is to love God, to honor and seek the goodness that is God, then the second will be to love the neighbor as oneself, which means seeking his or her welfare both in body and in soul, "making the health of the soul the standard in treating the body."[25] That makes for a different idea of freedom on the political level. It makes for a different idea of law. A free society will be

[22] *Utilitarianism*, ch 2.

[23] See Maurice Cowling, *Mill and Liberalism* (2nd edn, Cambridge University Press 1990).

[24] *Civ.* 19.14.

[25] *Mor.* 56. Cf. Mill, *On Liberty*, ch 3: "The only freedom which deserves the name is that of pursuing our own good in our own way, so long as we do not attempt to deprive others of theirs, or impede their efforts to obtain it." Because there is no God principle here, there is no true neighbor principle either.

a society free for God, not from God, and just so, a society for and with the fellow man, not a society of individuals.

The society Mill sought does not simply isolate the neighbor; it is sure to impose on him a new and different and more draconian set of restrictions.[26] In Augustine's society it will be said, for example, that if you wish to marry you will have to meet certain requirements, for marriage is integral to the common good. In Mill's society it will be said, if you make such stipulations you impede my private good, by withholding from me the public approbation I desire. So marriage ceases to be a public good and becomes a private one, with two consequences: marriage can no longer serve as an instrument of public good, and those who maintain that it is a public good cannot do so without public abuse. Should they seek relief in a claim to religious freedom, they will find that relief short-lived. Why? Because religious freedom itself is predicated on God as the source of goods, whether public or private. More specifically, religious freedom is predicated on the God who is free and who cannot be known or loved except in freedom.

This warrants a word of elaboration, religious freedom being as fundamental to a free society as marriage. (The one establishes the fact that the first duty of every citizen is to God, not the state; the other establishes, through recognition of the prepolitical bond between a man and a woman and their children, that people are not simply citizens, but first of all families.) Within a couple of decades of Irenaeus's exposition of freedom, we find Tertullian arguing that the persecution of Christians is wrong because religion, being a matter of faith, is a matter of freedom and therefore cannot be coerced.[27] This was a revolution, theologically and politically, though religious freedom

[26] Cf. Bruce Frohnen, "Is Constitutionalism Liberal?" (2011) 33(3) Campbell Law Review 529–558: "I maintain that there is a prejudice among lawyers in particular that constitutions must be liberal in order to be worthy of the name. To be fully legitimate, likely to last, and worthy of support, on this view, a constitution must embody certain principles, namely rule by consent, the rule of law, mechanisms limiting governmental power, and individual rights. Yet none of these putatively liberal goods are in fact liberal. Indeed, all that is liberal in 'liberal' constitutionalism is an insistence that only individual rights be recognized, and that these rights be read so as to maximize individual autonomy and equality. The result is a concentration of power in the state that undermines the essential virtues of and necessary for constitutionalism."

[27] "We are worshippers of one God, of whose existence and character Nature teaches all men. You think that others, too, are gods, whom we know to be devils. However, it is a fundamental human right, a privilege of nature, that every man should worship according to his own convictions: one man's religion neither harms nor helps another man. It is assuredly no part of religion to compel religion—to which the free-will and not force should lead us—the sacrificial victims even being required of a willing mind. You will render no real service to your gods by compelling us to sacrifice. For they can have no desire of offerings from the unwilling, unless they are animated by a spirit of contention, which is altogether undivine" (*Ad Scapulam* 2). This novel line was followed by Lactantius (*Institutiones divinae* 49) and Augustine (*In Ioannis evangelium tractatus* 26.2) and has

only came about in actuality because Christians refused to be coerced. But the revolution is reversed when it is determined that God, if there is a God, is of no public relevance and that the fundamental public good is that no one should be impeded in his or her pursuit of private goods. On such a premise religious freedom, like marriage, can appear as no more than a strictly private construct, which will have to be balanced at law against the private constructs of others. It is perfectly obvious where all this leads. It leads back to the persecution of Christians and of others like them, who fancy that there is a God, and because of God a common good. It does not lead forward to greater freedom, but back to unfreedom.

Authority and Modesty

The society built along Irenaean/Augustinian lines was built, notably, on two eschatological facts and two eschatological principles. The first fact: In the resurrection and ascension of Jesus Christ, a completely just man had acceded, by divine will and design, to universal power. The first principle, which Augustine made explicit: Therefore, in human affairs, justice should always precede power. Certainly, genuine authority rests on justice. *Potentia quippe adiuncta iustitiae, vel iustitia accedente potentiae, iudiciariam potestatem facit.*[28] This principle had a variety of effects, among them rendering all exercise of authority, whether political or juridical, responsible to natural and divine law and of doubtful validity the further it strayed therefrom. But the fact was first and the principle second. A generous Lord and righteous judge sat enthroned in heavenly session. Real power and real authority belonged to him. Earthly rulers would have to reckon with that (as Tertullian explained to Scapulus and Ambrose to Valentinian). Their powers were already curtailed; they were up against new limits. This paved the way for a new kind of constitutionalism, distinct both from what went before it and from what came after it: from what came before it, because law, even the highest and most sacred law of a people, had now to be measured by something higher yet; from what

more than a little to do with the advance of the idea of consent also in the political sphere. See further Robert Louis Wilken, *Liberty in the Things of God: The Christian Origins of Religious Freedom* (Yale 2019).

[28] "For power joined to justice, or justice acceding to power, constitutes judicial authority" (*Trin.* 4.17).

came after it, because what came after it (even in Locke) attempted to attain to the principle without resting on the person, and soon began to fall from that lofty height into legal positivism. With the loss of the person went a loss of tradition, both politically and juridically.[29] Law has even begun to think of itself, quite incoherently, as both culturally transcendent—"ascending above the realm of the particular, rising above culture"[30]—and strictly beholden to culture, aloft in whatever winds of change are blowing through a culture.

The second fact is that only this completely just man is fit to combine priestly with kingly representation, and so to rule both righteously and mercifully. The second principle follows: In human affairs during the *saeculum*, prior to the Parousia, there should be a division of powers, in the nations at large as formerly in Israel. Bishops are not kings, nor kings bishops. "Two there are," in the famous Gelasian phrase, who rule a society that wishes to be Christian.[31] Moreover, there must be modesty, the humility of an eschatological reserve, in the exercise of the power proper to each office, both because it is proper to but one of the two and because the holder of the office is not a completely just man, but rather a man who will be judged by the Just Man. From this second principle came the legal distinction between Church and state, and the long struggle for the *libertas ecclesiae*[32] that today is going poorly for the Church, as it has many times before, with this difference: according to the state, there are no longer two, but one only; hence the *libertas ecclesiae* is a concept with little purchase.

There is a third eschatological fact that we must not overlook, however, one Irenaeus knew well and Augustine came round to. It is a fact completely at odds with the thesis that has prevailed since Lessing about history as progress. History is indeed progress, but it is progress in evil as well as in good. In the present age, the age of the proclamation of messianic justice and authority, history is as much the march of evil as of good, for evil is parasitic

[29] "Political authority arises where power, the execution of right, and the perpetuation of tradition are assured together in one coordinated agency" (O'Donovan, *Ways of Judgment*, 142). O'Donovan insists that each element of this theorem is indispensable and that it is a mistake to fixate on constitutions, which upsets the balance between them (159ff). Tradition begins to disappear. Even legal precedent suffers, as we now know. Moreover, the representative function of authority, viewed as an act of collective judgment—which had come to light in Christ and helped to create new constitutional possibilities—becomes distorted, raising questions about legitimacy that constitutionalism, on its own, cannot resolve.

[30] Benjamin Berger, *Law's Religion* (University of Toronto Press 2015) 12.

[31] *Famuli vestrae pietatis* (494). That a bishop simultaneously holds secular authority, as a bishop palatine or prince-archbishop or even a pontiff, is a transgression of this principle.

[32] See the chapter by Leithart in this volume.

upon good.[33] In Augustine's terms, history is the stage of a contest between the city of God and the city of man, a contest that will be resolved only by the appearance of the Son of Man. From this a further principle follows: No great modesty is to be expected from the state where it refuses to acknowledge the Son of Man. The state that purports to be neutral is not in fact neutral, for it cannot evade the implications of the proclamation of messianic justice and authority. It must act as if they were true or as if they were not. *Tertium non datur*.

Now, I have criticized within Catholicism those who have tried, lately, to reimagine the Church as essentially apolitical and the state as essentially areligious. I have also criticized those who fancy a constitutionally Catholic state as a *de iure* realization of the reign of Jesus Christ. Both of these approaches operate with a serious eschatological deficit. The one forgets that the Church is a *polis* within the *polis* and that the state, in being desacralized by the reign of Christ, is also made responsible to that reign. The other forgets that the *saeculum* is an age of proclamation and decision, that it is not yet the age of the kingdom of God on earth. Both, in other words, overlook the true import of the ascension of Christ, and this oversight falsifies their respective political programs. One vainly imagines a state fulfilling its function without reference to divine law; the other expects the state to be what it cannot be, namely, a vehicle for the enforcement of divine law. One deprives the gospel of its legal and political import; the other deprives law and politics of their present responsibility to respect the proclamation of the gospel by respecting the character of the age, as an age of decision about the gospel. One forgets that the Church can propose, the other that the Church must not impose.[34]

A good example of the proper relationship of Church to state in matters of the common good—of its dual role as proposer of sound policy and as protector of citizens and families from policy overreach or underreach—can be found in Leo XIII's encyclical, *Rerum novarum* (1891), which seeks a third way between regimented socialism and unbridled capitalism, both of which interfere in human flourishing by undermining the neighbor love that ought to characterize civil society. *Evangelium vitae* (1995) and *Dignitas personae* (2008) supply more recent examples, relevant to the formation of laws governing medicine and basic matters of life and death, such as abortion and euthanasia.

[33] See further my *Ascension Theology* (T&T Clark 2011) ch 6.
[34] See further *Desiring a Better Country*, 92ff.

In all such interventions of the Church there is at work a fourth eschatological fact: the resurrection of Jesus in the flesh. The resurrection reaffirms Jewish faith in the goodness of the body, and in the integrity of the person as a body/soul unity. It establishes a fourth principle, the principle that the person cannot be regarded for the purposes of the state as divisible, in the fashion of Rousseau, for example, who in his work on the social contract was insistent that the realm of the body belongs to the state even where the realm of the soul is thought to belong to God. For this reason, he determined Christianity to be incompatible with the new republic he sought. Catholicism in particular should have no place. Legal means for removing Catholicism and Christianity generally are still being devised today, not under Rousseau's rubric of civil religion but under the rubrics of civic pluralism, state neutrality, and individual autonomy, for the sake of which constitutional change is effected or demanded. The Church, of course, resists this, believing that the dignity of the person precedes and exceeds any determination of the state and that the Church is now the proper locus of the person—that the Church itself exceeds the state and must be left free to assist persons as only the Church can.[35] All of this requires that the state exercise its authority over the person, even as regards the body, with due modesty and restraint, not only in the matter of capital punishment, say, but in liberty of movement, right of privacy, freedom to marry and reproduce and educate offspring, or even to practice conscientious objection without unjust reprisals. It also requires the principle of subsidiarity, for it is the very embodiedness of human existence that makes remote and abstract government impractical and oppressive.

Theonomy and Autonomy

Just here we may turn to the problem of theonomy and autonomy, for a growing inability to think about the person as essentially embodied is now producing curious results, from so-called reproductive rights to same-sex marriage and transgender rights, to assisted suicide and euthanasia: all

[35] "Established on a solid metaphysics of the person/hypostasis, the Church's doctrine regarding Christ Jesus was led to place the will and freedom of action at the heart of the understanding of human nature—a determination that had the greatest importance for the development of the notion of person in Christian culture" (Gilles Emery, "The Dignity of Being a Substance: Person, Subsistence, and Nature" [2011] 9[4] Nova et Vetera 991–1001). Emery reminds us that "the human person is not a 'rational individual,' but a subsisting being of a rational nature," lest we lose sight of the relational dimensions of the person.

presented as forms of respect for human dignity and autonomy, hence as constitutionally mandated, yet all in defiance of genuine personhood and of the divine and natural laws governing persons, hence signs of the crisis into which the very idea of higher law is descending.

The dislocation of the idea of personhood from its trinitarian and sacramental setting into its modern nominalist context has deprived it of its richest meanings and reduced it to a highly abstract notion of autonomous agency. Autonomy itself has come to mean what it never could have meant in the prenominalist era.[36] Indeed, it has come to mean the very thing that Anselm thought characteristic of the devil, viz., an inordinate grasping after likeness to God, through the attempt to will with a will subject to no one, not even God.[37] Autonomous willing of just this sort is what the myth of autonomy is all about. It is what the modern notion of liberty is about. Recall the notorious passage from *Planned Parenthood v. Casey*: "At the heart of liberty is the right to define one's own concept of existence, of meaning, of the universe, and of the mystery of human life."[38]

The occasion of that claim is no accident. One cannot defend the destruction of a human being in the womb without indulging in such absurdities. Only if we are "free" to determine for ourselves the nature and meaning of our own existence and to posit a universe of our own making can we justify this taking of innocent life. But once we start down this path, there is no stopping. To make good on our liberty so conceived, we must continually reinvent reality. It is not sufficient to approve a right of disposal over our own offspring. We must assert an absolute right over our own bodies and the structures that contain them. Having invented a right to contracept, we invent a right to abort. Having invented a right to contracept and abort, we invent a right to "marry" a person of the same sex. And having invented a right to marry a person of the same sex, we invent a right to change our sex. Or rather, we invent "gender"—a way of being sexual without being sexual. All of this, and now the right to dispose of ourselves by state-assisted suicide, we present as proof of our autonomy and dignity. The body of the aborted

[36] On the history of the idea, see my "Autonomy: *Sic transit anima ad infernum*," *Theological Negotiations*, ch 7 (Baker Academic 2018) 171–208. See also the chapter by Milbank in this volume.

[37] There is everything right in seeking likeness to God, but there is nothing right in "inordinate" seeking—in making oneself equal to God by positing an autonomous will that owes God nothing. The devil is condemned *quia præsumpsit habere propriam voluntatem* and to will as if subject to no one. "It is for God alone thus to will something by his own will, such that he follows no higher will" (*De casu diaboli* 4).

[38] 505 US 833 (1992).

fetus thus carries within itself the whole body of law.[39] We advance from legal fiction to legal fiction in our pursuit of an autonomy we cannot have, an autonomy in which there is no heteronomy and, above all, no theonomy. And so we come to a place where the habeas corpus principle stands on its head. The body must *not* show itself: not on a birth certificate, not on a passport, not on the door to the loo. I am who I say I am, and you must recognize me as such, my body notwithstanding.

In this attempt to overcome the body, to prevent it from bearing witness to the truth, Judeo-Christian eschatology is supplanted by an eschatology basically Gnostic in character, an eschatology that threatens to make the law incoherent because of its inability to reckon with hard evidence. Increasingly, the only evidence required for a court's or any public institution's attribution "of existence, of meaning, of the universe, and of the mystery of human life" is sheer assertion. This *non habeas* holds no hope of actual liberty. It is rather an exercise in trying to cheat reality, and the God who establishes reality, by a false claim to God-likeness. It is not the dignity of one who has justice or is at least called to justice,[40] but rather the revolt of power against justice. It is not the autonomy of one whose body obeys his soul because his soul loves and obeys God, thus ruling all things well.[41] It is rather the autonomy of one who, in order to have it, must cede to an always corrupt or being corrupted state authority, to the rule of the unjust over the unjust, the power to authenticate as real that which is not real. Thus does our autonomy doctrine mask the immodest beast that covets unlimited power over its subjects. What it denies to God, that most provident ruler who seeks for his subjects a true share in his own happiness and freedom, it willingly grants to Leviathan. And with delicious irony it grants it constitutionally, in defense of "dignity"—the very thing the state can never supply and its subjects can never create.[42]

The matter of dignity is just where constitutional law most needs religion's help. Unfortunately, law today will not let religion help—not even Christianity, which together with Judaism is the *fons et origo* of the idea and of the respect that follows from it—because law renders religion itself as a mere species of autonomy. It refuses to allow that religion has any purchase on reality, except as the instantiation of autonomous choice. Law's rendering

[39] Cf. Daniel Moody, *The Flesh Made Word* (Createspace Independent Publishing Platform, 2016).

[40] "To be under obligation with respect to justice manifests a natural dignity" (Anselm, *De casu* 16).

[41] Cf. Augustine, *Mor.* 25, *CD* 22.21ff.

[42] Still the most potent response to Mill is Leo XIII's *Libertas praestantissimum* (1888), in which it is insisted that theonomy is the guarantor of freedom and dignity and that civil law must be compatible with natural and divine law in order to bind the conscience.

of religion, as Benjamin Berger has ably argued, posits something essentially private and deserving of public scrutiny only where it begins to encroach on public policy or decision-making. Religion does not ground autonomy and thus deserve respect and protection—quite the reverse. "Religion has force in the eyes of the law to the extent that it is aligned with autonomy and choice."[43] What this means in practice is that law tolerates religion only within the boundaries established by its own approach to autonomy.

Thus does law raise itself up as a kind of philosopher-queen, though it is no such thing. And thus does the state take its revenge on Tertullian: by turning his principle that religion cannot be either privately or publicly coerced, because it is grounded in faith, into an assertion that religion does not matter publicly because it is grounded in faith, or rather, that it matters only where it attempts to stake any public claim, and there it may very well be coerced and forced into line. Religion, after all, as faith, is pure individual preference and competing preferences must be managed by the state, the benignly secular or "neutral" state.[44]

The Greater Operation of Liberty?

If the making of constitutions is an attempt to project and protect an ordered liberty, by subjecting lower law to a higher, this making presupposes order in the universe.[45] It presupposes a hierarchy of jurisdiction and an ultimate source of what is right and just. It also presupposes certain common ends, which determine its principles. It presupposes happiness as that which all seek, as well as those lesser ends that are common to a particular people in their own context. It comprehends, or tries to comprehend, the difference between the universal and the local, between restraints that liberate and "liberties" that restrain, between law that guides toward the goal and law that

[43] *Law's Religion*, 90f. "We protect autonomy because we privilege the individual; equally, the individual is valued because that individual is the source of choice, which is understood as the expression of freedom and autonomy. From these intimately interrelated aspects of law's rendering of religion, the jurisprudence leads us naturally to the third aspect of law's understanding of religion—that religion is a private matter. . . . Once so situated, religion is bound not by reason, but by preferences. It is therefore a matter of choice and, as such, an expression of the autonomous individual. This is the triptych of religion painted by the brush of modern Canadian constitutionalism" (99).

[44] I agree with Berger that "the pacific image of a rights-based tolerance and accommodation deployed by a basically autonomous legal order sitting above the realm of culture" is untenable (ibid, 16), that law is every bit as much embedded in culture as religion and that its own judgments about religion are precarious and often evangelical if not coercive (cf. 130).

[45] See ch 10 above, by Thio.

deflects from it. Constitutions are a demanding business, as is their interpretation and application. They require, and embody, a teleology, and hence also a distinction between liberty and licence.[46]

But a teleology is one thing and an eschatology another. The one tells us what we are for and what we are aiming at, and the other tells us how and when and in what fashion we hope to achieve it or see it achieved. We cannot do without a teleology, but is it strictly necessary, constitutionally speaking, to have an eschatology? May we not respect the right to life, liberty, and the pursuit of happiness without dabbling in eschatology? Are not our shared ends (if we are talking not about the Church, which has a covenant and constitution of a higher order, but about an ordinary people or nation) temporal only? Is eschatology not a dangerous thing for a mundane constitution to take on board, perhaps even a basic category mistake? Does it not represent an effort to ground lower law in a law too high or remote? To ground it in what is believed by some but not all, in what divides rather than unites? That there is a connection between teleology and liberty may be granted. But is there any real connection between eschatology and liberty?

Historically, the answer to that last question is yes. Christendom, which was nothing if not an eschatological construct, produced constitutions that protect liberty, even those that came in the twilight of Christendom or were devised so as to confirm its collapse. But what of it? Is today's burgeoning field of constitutional law, belonging to a secularist culture obsessed with liberty, not evidence that eschatology is not required? Au contraire, it is evidence that one eschatology is being substituted for another. Ryszard Legutko is right that in the prevailing liberalism—he would say in its very roots, insofar as those roots are found in the illiberalism of the French Revolution—there is an eschatology and even a liturgy. Nor should we suppose that in the Anglosphere, with its gentler Lockean plantings, its constitutional cultivars that owe rather more to Christianity, things are much different. If they were, we would not be witnessing the present religious fervor to demolish the remains of Christendom morally, culturally, and legally.[47] In the final analysis,

[46] Locke agrees: "But though this be a state of liberty, yet it is not a state of licence. . . . The state of Nature has a law of Nature to govern it, which obliges everyone, and reason, which is that law, teaches all mankind who will but consult it, that being all equal and independent, no one ought to harm another in his life, health, liberty or possessions; for men being all the workmanship of one omnipotent and infinitely wise Maker . . . are His property . . . made to last during His, not one another's pleasure" (*Second Treatise of Civil Government*, 2.6).

[47] We would not have to ask, e.g., why "the triumph of same-sex marriage [was] followed so rapidly by the opening of a new regulatory and juridical frontier, the recognition of transgender identity" (see again n 26). Legutko and Vermeule, though they underestimate the force of the logic as regards

the idea of liberty remains eschatological, even if the eschatology in question is ersatz in the sense that it lacks any possible dénouement and must instead be endlessly transgressive.[48]

It seems, in fact, that eschatology is that which cannot now not be thought. Arguably, eschatology always was necessary, though it might (as among the Stoics and Platonists) be a circular and history-suspicious or even history-denying eschatology. A history-affirming eschatology became necessary when Moses led Israel out of Egypt, which is to say, when the covenant with Abraham took constitutional form.[49] Nothing has changed in that respect. Whether Jewish or Christian or Islamic, or indebted to Locke or Lessing (in whom the ancient circularity reappeared) or Rousseau or Hegel or Mill or even Marx, our constitutional thinking is integrally tied to visions of history and the goal of history, to visions of the happiness of man. As such it is both teleological and eschatological and cannot be analyzed properly where that is ignored. Moreover, a change in eschatology requires a change in teleology and vice versa. What could be plainer than that?

That teleology is not enough was made clear by Augustine. Starting with the most fundamental and universal concern of teleology, the happiness that all men want, he undertook to show that happiness is inconceivable without immortality, something the Platonists had already begun to grasp. But he also undertook to show that it was inconceivable without the very eschatology that the Platonists (like most everyone else, apart from some Jews) found impossibly foreign, viz., that which spoke of the resurrection of the body. Working backward from there, he pointed out that if happiness is not attainable, then teleology itself is lost, and with it the virtues we cultivate for happiness's sake. The next casualty is reason, of which we are sure to despair, for there can be no rational ordering of our lives and loves if they are not held together by the expectation of happiness.[50]

the body, suggest that the answer here requires us to recognize that liberalism has its own "sacramental character" and "feels an inner compulsion to manifest its pious loyalty" to progress.

[48] Augusto Del Noce, *The Crisis of Modernity* (McGill-Queens 2014) 241 pointed out that, with Giovanni Gentile, authority was "brought inside the spirit itself." In Gentile's own formula, "the will is 'free as it makes itself free; it is subjected to the law that it unceasingly keeps creating.'" This has its analogy in religious modernism, "as a critique of authority in the name of conscience, or in the name of a historical process thought to be providential and irreversible because willed by God, a process which eliminates every 'fixism'" (237). Del Noce also points out that the true outcome of this process is "the complete dependence of man" on the state (245).

[49] On the Torah as Israel's constitution, see the chapter by Burnside in this volume, and Novak, *The Jewish Social Contract* (Princeton 2005) 81, 148f.

[50] See *De trinitate* 13.6ff.

How far the discourse of modern constitutionalism is indebted to political theorists who are trying to ward off despair by positing man as the project-creating animal, without ever asking either whether man himself is a project of God or whether his own projects can make sense without God and without the promise of happiness, others may judge. But one thing I notice from the periphery of this discourse is that both political and legal theory seem ever more inclined to posit principles and to undertake projects that interfere with liberty, even while they claim to enhance it. Liberties once ordinary, desired and demanded by all, disappear and are replaced by liberties extraordinary, desired and demanded by the few. Law still tutors the people, of course, but it directs them to ends they do not desire or demand—the abolition of sex, for example, and with sex freedom of religion, and with freedom of religion freedom of speech and association and even of thought. Law has begun to make itself the enemy rather than the friend of civil society. In its teaching there is indeed a "fulfilling and extending and expanding" of the law among us, but not the greater operation of liberty.[51] I dare say, with Irenaeus, that the greater operation of liberty among us requires a renewed, and ever greater, "subjection and affection toward our Liberator." That is right and just, and the hope not only of our salvation but also of the salvation of law, which seems to me, as it expands, to be dissolving before our very eyes, or at all events dissolving the nexus of authority and freedom that constitutionalism ought to serve.

[51] "A thoroughly atheistic society," says Novak (*Jewish Social Contract*, 216), "is one in which public recognition of the moral sovereignty of the creator God is outlawed, and where the religious beliefs and practices of the citizens are relegated to an ever narrower private sphere. Moreover, inevitably, the elimination of the creator God in public makes room for the establishment of some other god, one subject to greater human control. Society, like nature, abhors a vacuum."

Index

This index does not include references to the topics generally addressed by entire chapters in this volume, such as 'democracy', 'federalism' and 'justice'.

For the benefit of digital users, indexed terms that span two pages (e.g., 52–53) may, on occasion, appear on only one of those pages.

Biblical References

The manufacturer's authorised representative in the EU for product safety is Oxford University Press España S.A. of El Parque Empresarial San Fernando de Henares, Avenida de Castilla, 2 - 28830 Madrid (www.oup.es/en or product.safety@oup.com). OUP España S.A. also acts as importer into Spain of products made by the manufacturer.
Printed and bound by CPI Group (UK) Ltd, Croydon, CR0 4YY
14/09/2026
02216288-0010